Depth A fairly strong impression of spatial depth can be obtained even from a flat picture. By assigning a different size to different distances, the painter makes us see one chair as close by, another far away at the back wall. The overlapping of shapes locates the pool table in front of the waiter, who in turn appears before the empty table in the corner. Viewed as a whole, the floor and the side walls of the room converge toward a vanishing point at the eyelevel of the observer. (Van Gogh)

Vincent Van Gogh, The Night Café, *Yale University Art Gallery, Bequest of Stephen Carlton Clark*

Experience In every act of vision, the shapes and colors directly seen interact with a store of memory images that accumulated during a lifetime. This enables us to recognize even in a severely reduced pattern the figure of a woman making an early telephone call. The outlines of face, hair, and morning robe are characteristic enough to stand for the missing varieties of texture, the shading of roundness, and the details of particular features. (Avery)

Milton Avery, Morning Call, 1946, *Hirshhorn Museum and Sculpture Garden, Smithsonian Institution*

The Psychology of Being Human

The Psychology of Being Human

Second Edition

ELTON B. McNEIL
University of Michigan

ZICK RUBIN
Brandeis University

Canfield Press San Francisco
A Department of Harper & Row Publishers, Inc.
New York Hagerstown London

Editor: Ted Ricks
Production Editor: Jon Baker
Designer: Michael Rogondino
Manufacturing Manager: Laura Argento
Artist: Billie Yeaman
Photographic Researchers: Tonna Gibert
Kay James Audry Ross
Compositor: Typothetae

Library of Congress Cataloging in Publication Data

McNeil, Elton Burbank, 1924–1974.
The psychology of being human.

Bibliography: p.
Includes index.
1. Psychology I. Rubin, Zick, joint author.
II. Title.
BF121.M296 1977 150 76-51225
ISBN 0-06-385434-1

77 78 79 10 9 8 7 6 5 4 3 2 1

NOTE FROM THE PUBLISHER

In 1973, Dr. Elton B. McNeil set out to write a comprehensive introduction to the science of psychology that also explored the personal and social implications of the field. Before *The Psychology of Being Human* few introductory textbook in psychology went as far in applying contemporary psychology to everyday life or in presenting psychology in such a warm and personal way. The enthusiastic response which the book has received in the United States and Canada indicates that he struck a responsive chord.

The death of Elton B. McNeil, a week before the publication of the first edition, was an unfortunate loss to the field of psychology. In seeking a person to revise *The Psychology of Being Human,* we were faced with the challenge of finding someone who was knowledgeable of the current psychological theory and research, able to write in as engaging a manner as Dr. McNeil, and as committed to his distinctive approach to psychology. We feel especially fortunate, therefore, that we were able to persuade Dr. Zick Rubin to undertake this task.

Zick Rubin, a leading researcher in the field of social psychology and has brought to this edition his own personal approach to psychology.

We hope you enjoy this exciting edition as much as we have.

Theodore C. Ricks

ABOUT THE AUTHORS

Elton B. McNeil was someone for whom psychology was a pleasure and his vitality easily translated into a zest for his many roles as clinician, writer, consultant, and especially as teacher. He was the chief psychologist and director of the clinical training center for emotionally disturbed and delinquent boys at the University of Michigan Fresh Air Camp, and he served in the Peace Corps as a field selection officer. He was also widely known in the Detroit area for his television programs produced at the University of Michigan, especially *The Quiet Furies.*

Dr. McNeil began his interest in psychology at Harvard University where he received his B.A. in experimental psychology and continued it at the University of Michigan where he received his doctorate in clinical psychology. He remained at the University of Michigan for 22 years teaching undergraduate and graduate courses in clinical child psychology, clinical psychology, psychotherapy, and introductory psychology. His professional career included serving on the editorial boards of *Child Development* and the *Journal of Conflict Resolution.*

Dr. McNeil also wrote and edited many books throughout his career. Among the books now in print are: *The Quiet Furies, The Nature of Human Conflict, Human Socialization, The Psychoses, Neurosis and Personality Disorders,* and *Being Human,* a collection of essays which led directly to the development of *The Psychology of Being Human.*

Zick Rubin received his B.A. in 1965 from Yale University, where he was a psychology major and the managing editor of the *Yale Daily News.* He received his Ph.D. from the University of Michigan in 1969, and then taught at Harvard University for seven years before assuming his present position as Professor of Social Psychology at Brandeis University. Dr. Rubin's research has centered on social interaction and relationships, and he received the Socio-Psychological Prize of the American Association of the Advancement of Science for his research on the social psychology of romantic love. In 1977-78 he will be a visiting fellow at the Institute of Human Development at the University of California, Berkeley, to conduct research on children's social development. Dr. Rubin has taught courses on writing in the behaviorial sciences, and his own writing has appeared in popular as well as professional publications. He is the author of *Liking and Loving: An Invitation to Social Psychology* (1973), and editor of *Doing Unto Others: Joining, Molding, Conforming, Helping, Loving* (1974). He is also a member of the Council of the Society for the Psychological Study of Social Issues.

FROM THE PREFACE TO THE FIRST EDITION

Every teacher is, in a sense, a frustrated actor-performer. The longer he works at his craft the more convinced he becomes that he has uncovered a successful formula to convey to students something of the excitement and fascination of the particular intellectual pursuits that have occupied his own intellectual life. In this sense, every textbook is a kind of well-intentioned ego-trip by a professor who honestly believes he can come closer to target center than did those who wrote before him. Thus, if I am to be honest with you, it is necessary to confess that this book was written for many of these same reasons.

This book is about psychology in the manner that I would say to you, "I'd like you to meet a very good friend of mine. I think you will like one another, and this may well be the beginning of a beautiful and permanent friendship." If your thoughts run in the same direction as mine, this ought to be a book that holds your interest, that answers a great many questions that have rattled around in the back of your mind for some time now—a book that makes psychology come alive for you and become a meaningful part of your daily life.

The text has been written in a narrative fashion that attempts to communicate the flavor of psychology while minimizing its jargon. It is designed to be read by any interested person, with or without previous knowledge of the field. It is intended for the student who might stop at one course in psychology, as well as for the student who will need a solid background for more advanced courses. In addition, as the title suggests, this text has been written for human beings who are interested in and capable of achieving their full potential of being human.

To all readers of this text, may I say that I hope the study of psychology will provide as much pleasure for you as it has for me.

Elton B. McNeil

PREFACE TO THE SECOND EDITION

Psychology is a dynamic science that continues to change and to affect our lives and our society. To keep up with these changes, I have revised *The Psychology of Being Human.* I have expanded the treatment of *Learning,* developed new chapters on *Memory* and *Male and Female,* and brought the social psychological content together into two chapters, *Attitudes and Influence* and *Interpersonal Relationships.* Yet, there is not a chapter I have not edited in order to clarify and more fully explain the basic principles and concepts of psychology.

Even though there is a great deal of new material in this revision (and, to keep the book to a reasonable length, an equivalent amount of material from the first edition has been deleted), I have remained faithful to the basic concept, tone, and format of the first edition. In *The Psychology of Being Human,* Elton McNeil wanted to share with his readers his own personal fascination with and enthusiasm for the science of psychology. Dr. McNeil wrote as a person with a full range of feelings about psychology—respect for its historical foundations, excitement about its research frontiers, bemused skepticism about its fads and foibles, faith in its ability to better people's lives, and apprehension about its possible abuses. He saw no need to hide these feelings—although Dr. McNeil took psychology seriously, he also found the whole enterprise to be fun. I myself share those feelings about psychology, and in preparing this revision I have tried to follow Dr. McNeil's example—and in the process, to make psychology come alive for you.

To help him achieve his aims for *The Psychology of Being Human,* Dr. McNeil made use of several special features in the text—boxes, teasers, and Psychological Issues. These features served their purpose well, and have been retained in this revision.

Each chapter of the text contains several boxes. Each box is a brief, self-contained treatment of some extension, application, or sidelight of topics covered in the body of the text. Some boxes deal with current research frontiers, such as "Memory Drugs." Other boxes discuss areas of social concern, such as "Remote Control of the Brain," and still other boxes provide inside glimpses of the profession of psychology, as "The Personal Side of Psychological Research."

Scattered through the margins of the text are paragraphs that Dr. McNeil called teasers. "For the most part," Dr. McNeil noted in his preface to the first edition, "these are composed of anecdotal information that professors (myself included) often use to 'spice up' their lectures, and I wanted a way to share in a textbook some of the material that my students have found fascinating over the years." Many of the teasers simply contain interesting bits of information. Read and enjoy them when you're in the mood, and ignore them when you're not.

Among the most distinctive aspects of the first edition of *The Psychology of Being Human* were the series of Psychological Issues that came at the end of each chapter. These Psychological Issues are essays, presented in a magazine format, that center on the links between psychological research and social issues. Many of the Psychological Issues confront current social questions, such as "Men's and Women's Liberation," "Morality," and "Marriage and Divorce." The Psychological Issues on "Meditation," "Behavior Control," and "Memory and the Law," speak for the potential uses and abuses of psychology. Finally, some issues delve into areas that are subjects of considerable excitement and controversy, such as research on "Our Two Brains" and "Extrasensory Perception." In every case, there is a direct link between the Psychological Issue and the material in the chapter that precedes it. Thus, the Psychological Issues emphasize the many applications of psychology in today's world.

Although I never had the opportunity to know Elton McNeil well, our paths did cross. I arrived in Ann Arbor, Michigan in September of 1965 to begin graduate training in psychology. At that time Dr. McNeil was the Department of Psychology's director of Graduate Studies, and his responsibilities included the official welcoming of new students. I remember him greeting me and the other new graduate students warmly, enthusiastically, and with a relaxed sense of humor that made all of us feel at ease in what otherwise might have been an intimidating new situation. I hope that this second edition of *The Psychology of Being Human* will continue Dr. McNeil's tradition of providing a warm and enthusiastic welcome to the fascinating field of psychology.

Many people contributed to this revision of *The Psychology of Being Human.* I would like to express my appreciation to each of the following people for their help: Joseph Dewhirst, a graduate student in psychology at Harvard University, worked closely with me throughout the course of this revision and prepared preliminary drafts of various portions of the manuscript. Jackie Estrada, as developmental editor for the revision, helped to coordinate the final preparation of the entire manuscript and also prepared the summaries at the end of each chapter and the glossary at the end of the book. Carol Rubin provided sensitive criticism of many portions of the manuscript, as well as the emotional support that every human being needs. Richard McGlynn of Texas Tech University provided valuable assistance in the planning of Chapters 5 and 6. Connie Franklin contributed valuable research assistance. Myra Burnett, Steven Dudley, and Mari Tavitian provided important secretarial help.

I'm also grateful to the board of consulting reviewers who provided prompt and incisive comments on drafts of each chapter of the revision, drawing from their own experience as instructors of introductory psychology courses: Marina Estabrook, University of California, Davis; Michael Hughmanick, West Valley College; Terry Maul, San Bernardino Valley College; Barbara Strait, Portland Community College; and Georgia Witkin-Lanoil, Westchester Community College. Thanks also go to Richard McGlynn and Terry Maul for coordinating the preparation of the Instructor's Manual, Study Guide, and Test Bank that accompany the text.

Many other people assisted by providing reviews of chapters of the first edition or of drafts of the revised chapters. These included the following:

Leonard Blau, Chabot College
Lynn Brokaw, Portland Community College
Richard Cahoon, Cape Cod Community College
Lerita Coleman, Harvard University
James Cook, Mt. San Antonio College
Alice Crichlow, Massasoit Community College
Robert Cusick, Massasoit Community College
Anne Louise Daily, Allegheny Community College
Michael Flynn, North Texas State University
Bernadine Chuck Fong, Foothill College
Lucy Freund, Loop College
Louis A. Fusilli, Monroe Community College
Reid Hastie, Harvard University
Ralph W. Hood, Jr., University of Tennessee, Chattanooga
James Howell, Portland Community College
Susan L. Kaplan, Stanford University Medical Center
John P. Keating, University of Washington
Benjamin Kleinmuntz, University of Illinois
L. D. Korella, Mount Royal College
John R. Korte, University of Dayton
Gary Lesnik, Portland Community College
Margaret Lloyd, Suffolk University
Al Mayer, Portland Community College
Daniel McGillis, Harvard Law School
Bert Moore, Wellesley College
George Mount, Mt. View Community College

Jack R. Nation, Texas A&M University
Thomas R. Newton, Pennsylvania State University, McKeesport
Letitia Anne Peplau, UCLA
Jane Platt, Harvard University
Mary Wenker Platt, Genesee Community College
Donis Price, Mesa Community College
Frank Rosekrans, Eastern Washington State College
John Rybush, Mohawk Valley College
Alfred Stone, Edinboro State College
Michael Saks, Boston College
Arthur Seagull, Michigan State University
Michael Sewell, Mohawk Valley College
Barbara L. Short, Chabot College
Paul Sorrells, Texas Women's University

I want to thank John Miller, Ted Ricks, Jonathan Baker, and other members of the editorial and production staffs of Canfield Press for their extensive work on this revision. I am also grateful to Marjorie McNeil for her cooperation and support.

Zick Rubin

CONTENTS

PART

1

The Science of Psychology

Psychology is both one of the most familiar and one of the most mysterious of sciences. Psychology is the science of behavior—especially of human behavior—and what could be more familiar to all of us than that? Psychologists are concerned with the same phenomena that all of us are concerned with in our daily lives, from remembering names to falling in love. But even though our own behavior is close at hand, the underlying causes of our behavior often elude our grasp. And as psychologists explore the commonplaces of everyday life, they discover that this familiar territory is full of puzzles and mysteries.

In introducing psychology, we will look at both the familiar and the mysterious faces of this science. In Chapter 1, *What is Psychology?*, we will examine the methods that psychologists employ in order to study behavior objectively. We will try to convey a sense of the adventure of psychologists' efforts to extend our knowledge of the mind and behavior. We will also consider some of the ways in which psychologists apply the results of their research to the solution of personal and societal problems. In the Psychological Issue on *Parascience* that follows Chapter 1, we will look at some of the alternative approaches to human behavior that people have taken through the ages in their attempt to understand human behavior, from counting the bumps on people's heads to charting the movements of the planets.

In Chapter 2 we will explore the workings of *The Brain and the Nervous System*, the anatomical structures that underlie all of our thoughts and actions, but that most of us know relatively little about. In the Psychological Issue on *Our Two Brains* we will survey one of the current frontiers of brain research, the discovery that each of us has, in a sense, not one but two brains—a "left brain" and a "right brain" that specialize in different sorts of functions and that sometimes can even operate quite independently of one another.

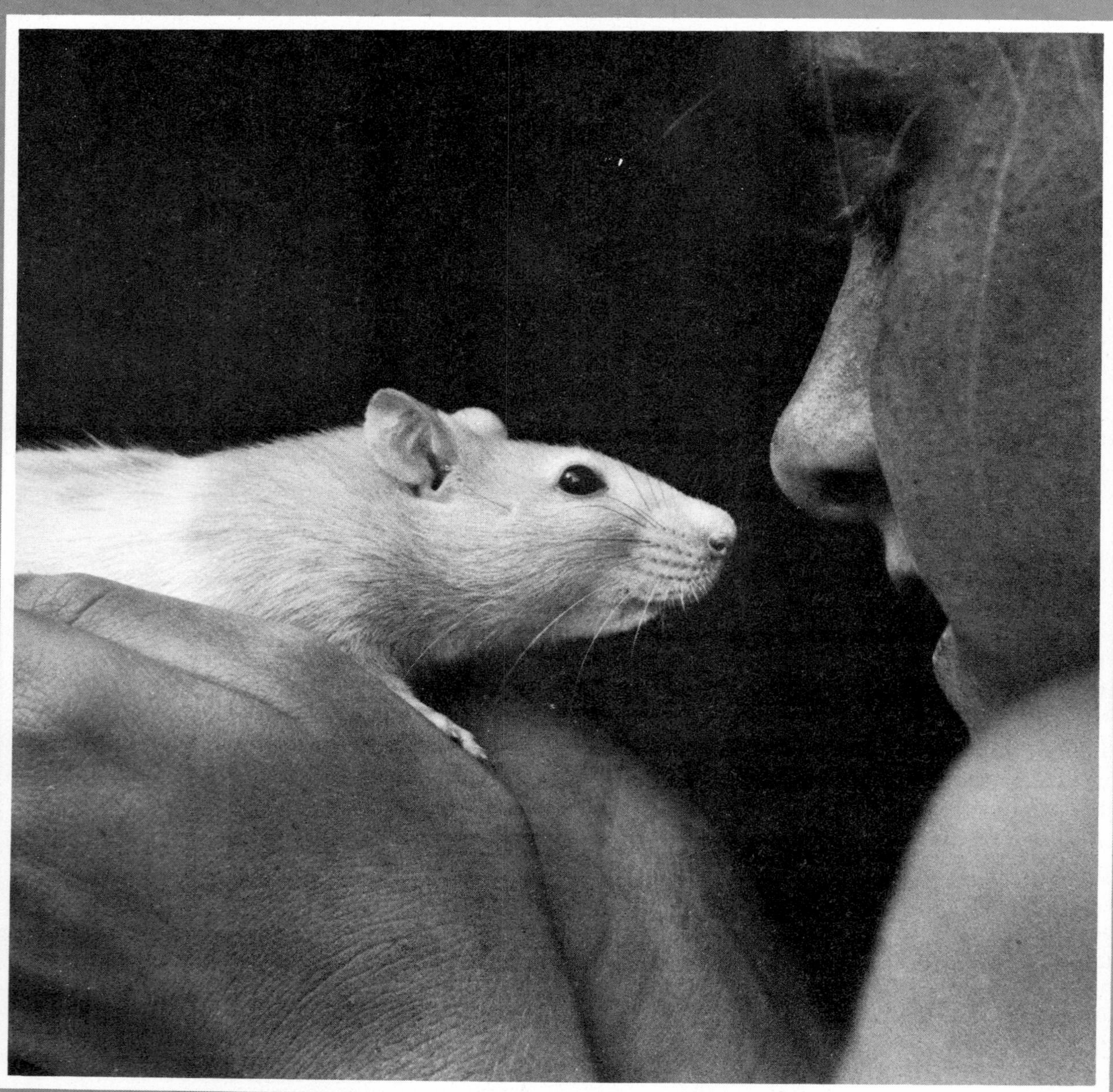

What is Psychology?

CHAPTER 1

What Is Psychology?

Even though this is probably your first course in psychology, you are a psychologist already. That's because the kinds of questions that psychologists ask and try to answer are very similar to the kinds of questions that all of us ask and try to answer in our everyday lives. The essential difference between you, the "everyday psychologist," and the professional psychologists lies in the specific ways in which the questions are posed and in the specific techniques that are used to answer them.

For example, here are a few questions that you might have asked yourself at one time or another:

Why is it that you sometimes feel that you can *almost* remember something but can't quite come up with it—that the word or name is on the tip of your tongue?

Why is it that people who witness an emergency—say, a person who seems to be having a fainting spell—sometimes rush over to help but at other times walk right on by?

How does a person's birth order in a family affect his or her personality? Is it true, for example, that first-borns are more likely to become leaders than later-borns or that only children are likely to be shy and lonely?

Why is it that some people keep slim without much apparent pain or effort, while others find weight control to be a terrible ordeal? Is it simply a matter of "self-control," or does it reflect other fundamental psychological differences?

What leads two people to fall in love, and two other people to feel nothing but disdain for each other? And, vows of love notwithstanding, what are the reasons for the soaring divorce rate in America today?

Why do some people need to sleep 9 or 10 hours every night, while others seem to get along on 4 or 5 hours? And why in the world do we all need to spend such a large portion of our lives sleeping, anyway?

Is it essential for a preschool child's mother or father to devote full time to the child's care? Are children who spend weekdays in day-care centers likely to be any less well adjusted than children who are cared for by a parent (usually the mother) at home?

How can we possibly explain the many crimes of violence that we read about in the newpapers everyday, such as the assassination of President Kennedy, the massacre at the Munich Olympics, or the killing of innocent civilians at My Lai? Were these the acts of deranged individuals, or do they reflect some fundamental characteristics of the human species?

These are the sorts of questions that people are likely to ask themselves at one time or another in their lives, even if they have never heard of the academic discipline called "psychology." But they are also the sorts of questions that are the professional psychologist's bread and butter.

There is a simple explanation for the fact that most people ponder the same sorts of questions that psychologists do. *Psychology* is the science of behavior—and, most importantly, of human behavior. And human behavior is nothing less than the substance of our lives: our actions, our thoughts, our attitudes, our moods, even our hopes and dreams. It is no wonder, then, that psychology is a subject that all of us are likely to ask questions about. The purpose of psychology as a science and profession is twofold: first, to provide better answers to psychological questions than the "everyday psychologist" is likely to come up with; and second, to help people make use of these answers in shaping their own lives.

Psychology is still a very young science (there were virtually no psychology courses or psychologists before the twentieth century), and we psychologists are still a long way from having all the answers. Nevertheless, the approach that psychologists take in asking and trying to answer questions about human behavior is one that represents a significant advance from the approaches that have been taken by "everyday psychologists" throughout history. (For a glimpse at some other approaches to explaining and predicting human behavior, see the Issue on parascience following this chapter.) Because the psychologist's methods of research are so central to understanding what psychology is all about, most of this chapter will be devoted to examining these methods.

SOUL, MIND, AND BEHAVIOR

The term "psychology" (actually *psychologia* in Latin) was apparently first used around 1530 by a German scholar, Phillip Melanchthon, as a title for some lectures. Its original meaning—from the Greek *psyche* (or soul) and *logos* (or study)—was "the study of the soul." Later *psyche* became translated as "mind" rather than "soul"; and in this century, psychology was redefined as "the science of behavior."

THE RESEARCH ADVENTURE

What does the word "research" mean to you? Perhaps it brings to mind a white-coated scientist scurrying around a laboratory with test tubes in hand. Or perhaps it evokes memories of sitting in the library, surrounded by a pile of almanacs, encyclopedias, and other reference works, trying to gather the information you need for a report or term paper. Psychologists do a good deal of work in the laboratory (where some of us even wear white coats) and in the library. But neither the laboratory nor the library is essential to psychological research. In fact, research can be done in a wide variety of locales—in boardrooms and bars, as well as in laboratories and libraries. And, regardless of where it is done, there is a sense in which psychological research is like a detective story. As researchers, we begin with a mystery that we want to solve, and then we gradually trace a series of clues that, we hope, will ultimately lead to a solution.

To help give you the flavor of this research adventure, we will trace two psychological detective stories in some detail. Each of them comes from a different area of psychology: the first deals with a troublesome aspect of people's behavior toward their fel-

low human beings; the second, with a puzzling aspect of human memory.

The Case of the Good Samaritan

Have you ever walked down the street and watched a person collapse on the sidewalk? Or seen a fight break out between two children, with one of them really seeming to hurt the other? In some such cases, a bystander will immediately come to the aid of the victim. If the incident seems too difficult for the one helper to handle, he or she might recruit other people or call the police for assistance. In other cases, however, incidents like these—or worse—occur in the presence of many bystanders, yet nobody does anything at all. Some years ago, for example, a young woman named Kitty Genovese was attacked by a male assailant one night as she returned to her home in New York City. Thirty-eight of her neighbors watched from their apartment windows without doing anything to intervene—even though it took her attacker over half an hour to murder her (Rosenthal, 1964). Since that time, many similar cases have been played up in the news, usually in urban locations.

What determines whether or not a person will come to the aid of a victim in an accident or emergency? It was the desire to answer this question that motivated two psychologists, John Darley and C. Daniel Batson (1973), to investigate the case of the Good Samaritan. In setting up their study of factors that affect helping, Darley and Batson got *their* help from an unexpected—well, perhaps not so unexpected—quarter: the Bible. "Fortunately," Dr. Batson later recounted, "Jesus showed us the way—with his parable of the Good Samaritan" (1976 page 207).

In the parable of the Good Samaritan, Jesus described the situation of a man who had been robbed, beaten, and left half dead along the road from Jerusalem to Jericho. A priest came down the road but walked right on by without stopping. Later a Levite (a member of the group who assisted the priests in the temple) came down the road, but he did not stop to help either. Finally, a Samaritan—a member of a group of religious outcasts—stopped, took care of the man's wounds, and took him to an inn where he could recover. The message of the parable, of course, is that we should not be like the priest or the Levite, so-called religious people who did not stop to help; instead, we should emulate the Good Samaritan, an "irreligious" person who nevertheless had compassion for a fellow human being.

The parable of the Good Samaritan suggested to Darley and Batson two factors that might have an effect on whether a person would offer to help in a crisis: first, what the person happens to be thinking about when he or she notices the victim, and second, the person's time schedule. Darley and Batson speculated that the priest and Levite, as religious functionaries, were likely to have had their heads full of prayers, rituals, and Biblical passages; they may have been so preoccupied with "religious" thoughts that they could not pay attention to the plight of the victim. Darley and Batson also reasoned that the priest and Levite, as prominent public figures, might have been in more of a rush than the Samaritan and that this, too, might have decreased their willingness to help.

Finally, the parable of the Good Samaritan suggested to Darley and Batson a concrete way of setting up an experiment. They selected as their experimental site a narrow, usually deserted alley that ran between two campus buildings at Princeton University. The subjects in the study were sent from one building to the other. As a subject walked along the deserted alley, he encountered the victim—a young man slumped in a doorway, with head down and eyes closed. As the student went by, the victim coughed twice and groaned, keeping his head down. Darley and Batson's main interest was in whether or not the student offered to help the victim. The victim, of course, was an accomplice of the researchers who went into his act on a signal from the experimenter. If the subject stopped and offered help, the victim assured him that he was actually all right and thanked the subject for stopping and offering help.

Since Darley and Batson's study had a religious theme, they decided to recruit divinity school students as their subjects. The students were told that they would be sent to the other building to tape-record a short talk. Half of the subjects were asked to

TROUBLE IN THE ALLEY

The course of a psychological experiment doesn't always run smooth—especially when it is done in a natural setting, where all sorts of unpredictable events can take place. Batson (1976) has recounted several of the unforeseen problems that beset his and Darley's study of helping behavior, which took place in an alley running between two buildings. On one occasion, for example, the experimenters found a telephone truck blocking the alley at a crucial moment, and it was moved out of sight just in time for the first subject. "The janitor also presented a problem. On the second day of running, just as the subject entered the alley, he came out of a side door and cheerily called over to our 'victim' huddled ready and waiting, 'Feeling better today?' One subject's data, $2.50, and over an hour of experimenter time evaporated" (Batson, 1976 page 209).

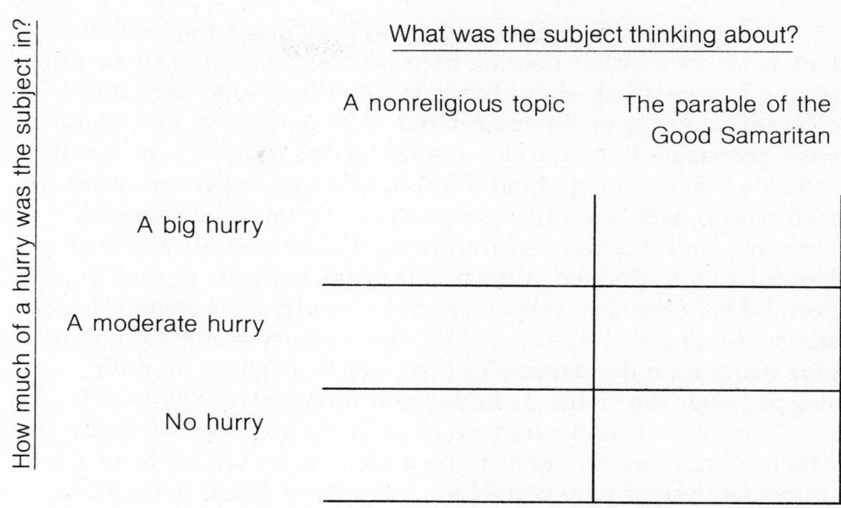

FIG. 1 · 1 The experimental conditions in Darley and Batson's Good Samaritan study. There were approximately seven subjects in each of the six conditions.

give a talk on a nonreligious topic. The other half of the subjects were to give a talk that was not only religious but specifically relevant to the ideal of helping victims: they were to talk on the parable of the Good Samaritan. All of the students were given a chance to think about their talk briefly before being sent over to the other building. We can assume, therefore, that subjects in the two different experimental conditions had rather different thoughts on their minds as they walked along the narrow road.

The experiment had another variation, cross-cutting the first one (see Figure 1.1). One-third of the subjects were told that the experiment was running late and that they would have to get over to the other building in a hurry. Another one-third of the students were simply told to go right over to the other building. The remaining one-third were told that they could take their time, since it would be a few minutes before the assistant in the other building would be ready for them. Thus, some subjects were in a big hurry as they walked down the road, some were in a moderate hurry, and some were in no hurry at all.

What was the evidence in the case of the Good Samaritan? All told, 40 percent of the subjects helped the victim, either by stopping and offering help directly or at least by telling someone else about the emergency; 60 percent did not. But these rates were markedly affected by the experimental variations. How much of a rush the subjects were in clearly affected their behavior: 63 percent of the no-hurry subjects offered help, compared to 45 percent of the moderate-hurry subjects and only 10 percent of the big-hurry subjects. This factor probably has an effect on helping in other situations as well. For example, the fact that city-dwellers are often less likely to help others than are country-dwellers (Milgram, 1970) does not imply that people who live in cities are a less compassionate breed of human beings than people who live in the country. Rather, it may be a consequence of the fact that city-dwellers are more likely to be in a rush, which in turn tends to narrow their focus of attention.

The subjects' thoughts as they walked along the road also had an effect on their helping behavior: 53 percent of those preparing to give a talk about the parable of the Good Samaritan offered aid to the victim, compared to 29 percent of those who were preparing to talk about a nonreligious topic. These results indicate that thinking about the religious ideal of compassion for victims can itself promote compassion. It should be stressed, however, that thinking helpful thoughts does not always lead to helpful action—indeed, almost half of the subjects in this condition did *not* offer any assistance to the victim. "On several occasions," Darley and Batson report, "a seminary student going to give his talk on the parable of the Good Samaritan literally stepped over the victim as he hurried on his way" (page 107).

The case of the Good Samaritan is by no means closed. Much more research needs to be done before we will have a full understanding of why people are sometimes Good Samaritans and sometimes not. A great deal of research into this question is now being conducted, and we will discuss some of it in Chapter 18. Darley and Batson's study made an important contribution to this line of investigation.

The "Tip of the Tongue" Solution

Like Darley and Batson's study, our second research adventure also has its roots in everyday experiences. Not long ago, one of us (Zick Rubin) was watching a news reporter on television. I had seen him before, and I knew that I knew his name, but I couldn't quite remember it. I struggled to get the name off the tip of my tongue and into my consciousness. Was it John Calhoun? That was close, it seemed, but it wasn't quite right. Was it John Coltrane? That seemed even closer, but it still wasn't the name I was groping for. I remained for some time in what Brown and McNeill (1966) have described as a state of "mild torment, something like the brink of a sneeze." When I finally managed to get the right name into my mind, I felt a tremendous relief; the sneeze had finally come. (It was John Cochran.)

This "tip of the tongue" phenomenon—the feeling of almost but not quite being able to recall a word—is one that most people are familiar with but have difficulty explaining. The phenomenon involves an essential puzzle: How can you know that you know something without actually knowing what that something is? This was the puzzle that intrigued two psychologists at Harvard University, Roger Brown and David McNeill.

Like most of us, Brown and McNeill had experienced the "tip of the tongue" state (TOT, for short), and they had even formed some personal guesses about its causes. In order to check out their guesses, or *hypotheses,* Brown and McNeill needed to study a large number of TOT states, as they occurred, among a large number of people. But studying TOT states is a lot like catching butterflies; these states fly into people's heads only occasionally and unpredictably, and not necessarily when the psychologist who is collecting them happens to be standing by with a net. Brown and McNeill (1966) came up with an ingenious way to get around the problem, however. Instead of waiting for TOT states to come to pass of their own accord, they devised a way to *create* them. To do this, they read the definitions of obscure words to a large group of college students. For each definition, there were some students who immediately recalled the word being defined, and there were others who had no inkling of what it was. Still other students, however, were thrust into a TOT state—they said they knew the correct word but couldn't quite recall it. Students in the TOT state were then asked to do several things: to guess the number of syllables in the "target word," to guess what its first letter was, and, most importantly, to write down all the words that came to mind as they were groping for the target word.

Brown and McNeill found that the words that the students wrote down while in the TOT state could be divided into two categories: those resembling the target word in meaning, and those resembling the word in sound. For example, one of the definitions that Brown and McNeill read to their subjects was "A navigational instrument used in measuring angular distances, especially the altitude of the sun, moon, and stars at sea." The correct answer, or target word, was *sextant.* The words of similar meaning that subjects in the TOT state thought of included "astrolabe," "compass," "dividers," and "protractor." The words of similar sound included "secant," "sextet," and "sexton." The similar sounding words were of particular interest to Brown and McNeill. The fact that these words came to mind made it clear that the subjects knew a great deal about the target word even though they could not quite remember it. As further evidence of this knowledge, subjects in the TOT state were remarkably accurate in identifying the first letter and the number of syllables of the target word.

What, then, is the solution to the "tip of the tongue" mystery? In fact, the solution is not a simple or final one. On the basis of their results, however, Brown and McNeill were able to construct a model of the process by which people store words in their memories. Brown and McNeill proposed that this storage resembles a complex cross-referenced filing system. One part of the filing system is arranged something like a thesaurus, indexed in terms of word meanings. The definition of a "navigational instrument" calls forth the mental file drawer for that category, including words like astrolabe and compass as well as sextant. The other part of the filing system is organized something like a conventional dictionary, but with a difference: it is organized not only according to the way words are spelled but also according to the ways they sound. The meaning-filing system helps us to recall the right word when speaking or writing: we retrieve the appropriate file from the appropriate file drawer and then search through it for the word we want. The sound-filing system is especially helpful in enabling us to recognize and understand words—if someone says something remotely like "sextant," we can usually figure out what he or she means. But the sound-filing system is not a perfect one. If we think of our storehouse of words as a set of file cards, some parts of the cards seem to be written more legibly than others. In particular, the beginnings of words are written more clearly, the endings somewhat less clearly, and the middles least clearly of all. (See Figure 1.2.) That is why we are likely to have the feeling that we're after a two-syllable word that begins with C and ends with N, or a two-syllable word that begins with S and ends with T, even though we still

Box 1

Psychology's Roots

People have been asking questions about why they behave the way they do since ancient times. But the first people to formally speculate about the nature of human beings and their behavior were the early Greek and Roman philosophers. They were concerned with the question, "What is the mind?" and came up with some interesting answers. Aristotle, for example, thought that mental functions were located in the heart. Centuries passed before this view was corrected and mental functions were assigned to the brain. Meanwhile, questions that today would be considered psychological were left to the realm of philosophy, and college courses concerned with the mind and behavior were confined to philosophy departments. It is only within the last 80 years that psychology has become recognized as a distinct discipline.

Two streams of thought, one in philosophy and the other in the physical and biological sciences, eventually led to the early development of psychology as a separate area of study. The first stream was the concern in British philosophy of the nineteenth century with the nature of ideas and how ideas are associated in the mind. This approach had come out of the writings of John Locke (1632-1704), who attempted to answer questions about how we can obtain valid information about the physical world. Locke concluded that at birth a person's mind is a *tabula rasa*—Latin for a "blank slate"—on which sensory experience (vision, hearing, and so on) makes its marks. All knowledge, Locke believed, no matter how complex or abstract, derives from sensory encounters with the physical world.

The second stream was in the biological and physical sciences of nineteenth-century Germany. In 1879 Wilhelm Wundt, a German physiologist and philosopher, opened a psychological laboratory in Leipzig. For this reason, many psychologists consider Wundt to be the "father of scientific psychology." (In fact, William James had established a laboratory a few years earlier at Harvard University, but his lab was used solely for class demonstrations, rather than research.) Wundt's studies were aimed at discovering the nature of consciousness. Subjects were asked to describe sensations, images, and feelings as they were exposed to various experiences. Wundt's psychology was thought by the German psychologists to be a "pure science" because there was no practical application of the findings. It was Wundt's students in America—James, Dewey, Cattell, and

others—who became interested in finding ways for practical application of the study of conscious processes. Early American psychology became an applied discipline that developed into the fields of child psychology, educational psychology, and mental testing, among others. Wundt and his followers were called *structuralists,* because they were interested in the anatomy or structure of conscious processes, whereas the practical Americans were called *functionalists.*

John B. Watson, a former functionalist, founded *behaviorism* as a reaction to the structuralists, who were then occupied with such undecidable questions—it seemed to Watson—as "Do all thoughts

FIG. 1 · 2 Brown and McNeill suggested that words are stored on "mental file cards," with the beginnings and endings of the words written more legibly than the middles.

involve images?" Watson asserted that the only proper subject matter for psychology was observable behavior. This assertion, coupled with the development of objective experimental methods, brought the study of conscious processes to a virtual end. The behaviorist approach, carried on by B. F. Skinner and others, has been the predominant one in American psychology for the past fifty years. We'll hear more about this approach in Chapter 5.

Quite recently—during the last 10 to 15 years—things have come full circle. Although behaviorism is still strong, many psychologists have returned to questions about consciousness, mental imagery, thought processes, and other aspects of "the mind." Only now such research is done with more sophisticated scientific tools than those employed by the early structuralists.

While structuralism, functionalism, and behaviorism were developing, mainly in the universities, another crucial development in psychology sprang from medicine and treatment of mental illness: Freud and his psychoanalytic theory. Freud emphasized unconscious motives and the importance of early life experiences in shaping personality. We'll have a lot to say about Freud and his theory in Chapter 13.

Aristotle

John Locke

Wilhelm Wundt

William James

can't put our finger on the exact word. To support this part of their model, Brown and McNeill note that spelling errors are most commonly made in the middle of words, next most commonly in the endings, and least commonly in the beginnings (Jensen, 1962).

Needless to say, we don't really have file cards in our heads. The question of just what physical or chemical form memory takes is a mystery that has yet to be solved. Nevertheless, the tip of the tongue solution, as proposed by Brown and McNeill, made an important contribution to this continuing search. More recent models of memory have been aided by Brown and McNeill's results (see Chapter 6). Their study provided a fine example of how adventurous researchers can go beyond their own personal experience in search of the processes that underlie human behavior.

Where Do Psychologists Get Their Ideas?

As the two cases we have just examined suggest, psychologists get their ideas about research questions and ways of answering them from a wide variety of sources:

Our own personal experience is one of the most important sources of research questions, whether it concerns our memory for names, the effects of meditation, or the factors that lead people to like each other.

Events in the news may also suggest important research questions. The case of Kitty Genovese and her 38 neighbors directly inspired many valuable studies of helping behavior. Similarly, the horrors of the Nazi era in Germany led psychologist Stanley Milgram to conduct important experiments on people's obedience to authority (see Chapter 18).

As the case of the Good Samaritan indicates, psychologists can sometimes get important insights from religious, philosophical, or literary writings. For example, the research of Christie and Geis (1970) on people's tendencies to manipulate other people was inspired in large measure by the writings of the sixteenth-century Italian diplomat Nicolo Machiavelli (from whom we get the adjective "machiavellian").

Sometimes a psychologist's insights arise by accident, as an outgrowth of other work that the psychologist happened to be doing. For example, the Russian physiologist Ivan Pavlov was studying the process of salivation in dogs when they were fed. He noticed that after a while the dogs began to salivate even before they were fed, as soon as they saw the experimenter who was about to feed them. This unexpected observation led Pavlov to discover the type of learning known as classical conditioning (see Chapter 5).

Research is often prompted by the desire to find ways of solving pressing psychological and social problems. In Chapter 16, for example, we will explore research that has been conducted in an effort to better understand the causes of mental illnesses such as depression and schizophrenia.

And at many points in this book we will examine research that has attempted to learn more about such social problems as violence, prejudice, and divorce.

Although psychologists get research ideas from all these sources, you should not be led to think that psychological research is largely a matter of happenstance. Psychologists do not in fact get out of bed each morning, slap some cold water on their faces, and say to themselves, "Let's see, what interesting new thing can I study today?" One of the hallmarks of scientific research is that it is a *cumulative* process, in which each researcher builds on the work that has already been done in a particular area. For example, Brown and McNeill got their ideas about the tip of the tongue phenomenon not only from their own experience but from talking to colleagues, from the work of earlier psychologists; and from existing theories of language and memory. And their work, in turn, has been built upon by more recent researchers.

The Importance of Theory

A key word to understand in connection with the sources of psychologists' ideas is *theory.* You have probably heard of some theories in other sciences, like Darwin's theory of natural selection or Einstein's theory of relativity. Each theory, whether in biology, physics, or psychology, is a set of ideas and principles that fit together to provide a perspective on some aspect of the world. One of the widest ranging psychological theories is Freud's psychoanalytic theory (discussed in Chapter 14), which provides a perspective on such diverse phenomena as dreams, slips of the tongue, personality development, sexuality, mental illness, and psychotherapy. Other theories, like the model of memory that was developed in part on the basis of Brown and McNeill's research, are much more narrowly focused and specific. Regardless of how broad or narrow they may be, theories serve the important functions of organizing our knowledge in a coherent way, of suggesting specific studies that will help to test or refine the theory, and of providing a common language that scientists can use to communicate with one another about their findings.

Even before studying psychology, each of us is likely to have his or her own theory about human behavior. For example, you may have a theory of personality that suggests that people can be sorted into categories like "leaders and followers" or "introverts and extraverts." This theory may lead you to conduct informal research of your own. Whenever you meet a new person, for example, your first thought might be to determine which category the person belongs to. And your theory of personality may also provide a language that you can use to describe people to your friends—"He's a jock," or "She's a brain."

Psychologists have developed their own theories of personality (see Chapter 14), some of which are quite similar to the sorts of typologies that nonpsychologists use. But there are some fundamental differences between everyday theories and psychological theories. Whereas everyday theories are usually left unstated or implicit, psychological theories are stated clearly and publicly. And whereas everyday theories are often based on one person's intuition and experience, psychological theories are continually checked and rechecked by many researchers, on the basis of systematic observations. That doesn't mean that psychological theories can't be wrong. In fact, psychological theories are quite likely to be wrong in some respects. An essential part of the process of psychological research is to test and refine theories, and to replace inadequate theories with better ones.

In short, psychological research is a methodical, painstaking process, with each study extending our knowledge a tiny step farther, usually by helping to test or refine a theory. What makes this gradual accumulation of information so exciting to us—and we hope to you as well—is that it is knowledge that is directly relevant to our lives as human beings.

THE METHODS OF PSYCHOLOGY

To understand how psychologists go about the process of accumulating knowledge about human behavior, we need to look more closely at the methods they use. Although psychological researchers may derive important insights from their personal

---

Box 2

The Personal Side of Psychological Research

Why do psychologists decide to do particular sorts of research? The reasons they usually give are scientific ones—the desire to test a theory or to continue the work of other researchers in a given area. Although underlying reasons are usually not stated in research reports, the decision to investigate particular topics has its personal roots, too. Frequently, something about a psychologist's own life and personal concerns motivates him or her to explore particular questions. The following first-hand accounts by three researchers provide good examples.

Howard Schuman is a social psychologist at the University of Michigan who conducted extensive surveys on the sources of antiwar sentiment in America. Several years later, he recounted the set of events that led him to do this research:

> *In November of 1969 my wife and 14-year-old son prepared for an overnight bus trip to join what turned out to be the largest protest ever held in Washington against the Vietnam war. Many of my friends and colleagues were also traveling to the capitol for the same purpose. I shared their opposition to the war and felt the pull to participate in the demonstration, but at the same time I had vague doubts about the effect of such a mass demonstration on the broader public. . . . The upshot of these considerations—plus the quite practical need for someone to take care of our two younger children—was that I stayed home. I wished my wife success and promised to spend the time trying to locate data that would cast some light on how effective mass demonstrations were. So I spent the period of the Washington demonstration watching children, looking at television coverage of the protest, and rummaging through old files for survey data on public attitudes toward the war. I had no intention of becoming involved in research on war attitudes, but in fact that avocational work provided the start for* [my research on the sources of antiwar sentiment]. *(Schuman, 1976 page 287–288)*†

†From "Two Sources of Anti-War Sentiment in America" Howard Schuman, American Journal of Sociology, Vol. 78, 1972. © 1972 by The University of Chicago Press. Reprinted by permission.

experience, such experiences are likely to be casual and sketchy and to be based on a rather small and unsystematic body of evidence. Our own experiences are also likely to be colored by our motives and moods, so that what one person sees in a particular situation may be quite different from what another person sees. Depending on how you feel about yourself and what sort of mood you are in, for example, you may interpret the expression on another person's face as either a friendly glance, a puzzled look, or a hostile stare. In contrast, psychologists strive to study behavior in ways that are *systematic* (based on a thorough and well-organized search for facts) and *objective* (based on careful observations that different observers can agree on, rather than one person's intuitions).

In their efforts to gather systematic and objective information, psychologists may use a wide variety of methods. No single method, such as the laboratory experiment or the nationwide survey, is *the* best method for psychological research, any more than a hammer is the best tool for the carpenter or a putter is the best tool for the golfer. The particular method a researcher chooses will depend on the nature of the problem, the methods that previous researchers have used, and the researcher's own personal tastes and preferences. Here we will consider some of the most commonly used methods of the psychological researcher.

Kelly Gersick is a social-clinical psychologist at the Yale Medical School who recently wrote a dissertation (one of the requirements for a Ph.D.) about the characteristics of "fathers by choice"—men who seek custody of their children following divorce. In the preface to his dissertation, Gersick explains that he chose his research topic because of personal, as well as scientific, reasons:

This dissertation grows out of two closely related developments. One is my growing intellectual sense that something important is happening to the relationships between men and their children in our society, and as psychologists we know very little about it. The other development is my own new paternity. The pretesting and literature review for this thesis was done while my wife and I were expecting our first child, Andrew; the data gathering and analysis were completed during his early months, and the writing by his first birthday. (Gersick, 1975, page ii)

Dan Batson, one of the psychologists who conducted the Good Samaritan study discussed earlier in this chapter, also had personal reasons for deciding to study helping behavior, stemming from his religious concerns and his prior training as a minister. When one of us asked him about this, Batson wrote back:

It's true that I had some designs on "tending the flocks" before being called by the Lord of Wundt, James, and Watson [see Box 1]. *Actually, I carried through to the point of being ordained (still am—Presbyterian), getting a Ph.D. at Princeton Seminary, and teaching part-time while I completed my Ph.D. in psychology. Bizarre, perhaps, but really quite enjoyable and overall a solid educational experience. My difficulty with the Seminary was that I kept wanting to know what religion actually did in people's lives (quite apart from whether it was true or not). Did it, as advertised, encourage them to be more caring? Or the opposite? Both, neither, etc.? Pursuit of these questions led me across campus to psychology—and research on helping behavior.*

So, as you see, psychologists' decisions to study particular aspects of other people's lives have a great deal to do with their own lives as human beings.

Whom Does the Psychologist Observe?

The psychologist's business is to make systematic observations of behavior. But no psychologist can study *everyone's* behavior. Instead, the researcher chooses a *sample* of people to study. Just as a geologist may attempt to determine the composition of the moon by analyzing a small sample of rocks, so the psychologist attempts to discover principles of human behavior by studying a small but representative sample of humans. In some cases, the nature of the psychologist's sample is dictated by the problem being studied. If the researcher is interested in alcoholism, he or she will study a sample of alcoholics—and, preferably, a sample that reflects as closely as possible the characteristics of alcoholics more generally. Similarly, a psychologist interested in child development will study children; one interested in mental illness will study schizophrenics.

The psychologist's choice of a sample of subjects is also likely to be dictated by convenience. By one count, fully 80 percent of psychological research with humans has made use of college students as subjects (Schultz, 1969). This is not too surprising: Since most psychological researchers work in colleges and universities, students—especially those taking psychology courses—provide their most readily available supply of subjects. The heavy reliance on college students as subjects presents certain problems, however. Since most college students are young, white, and middle-class, it may not always be possible to generalize from the behavior of college students to the behavior of people from other segments of society. For example, a large number of studies have shown that people often devote a great deal of effort to making sure that their behavior seems *consistent* to themselves and others. As a result of these studies, consistency has been viewed by many psychologists as a fundamental human motive (see Chapter 9). But this conclusion needs to be taken with a grain of salt. In fact, the large majority of studies demonstrating the consistency motive were conducted with college students. It may well be the case that in the course of writing papers and giving class presentations students are taught that consistency is a virtue and inconsistency is a vice. As a result, college students may be especially likely to behave consistently in experiments. If the same experiments were done with people who are not college students, considerably less evidence for a "fundamental human motive" of consistency might be found.

In fact, the degree to which the results of research can be generalized from one group of people to another depends in large measure on the particular problem being studied. Whereas basic processes of learning and memory may work in much the same way for almost all human beings, patterns of social behavior are more likely to depend on people's social and cultural background. There is no easy answer to the problem of selecting subjects for psychological research. Being aware of this difficulty, you should ask yourself when reading about a psychological study: "Who were the subjects? Are their responses typical of what my own would be? Do their findings apply to me?"

YOUR OBEDIENT SUBJECT

People—or other animals—who take part in psychological research are generally called *subjects*. However, some psychologists object to the connotations of the word "subject." It suggests that people are subjected to the whims of the researcher, much in the way that a king's subjects are under the control of the king. The word "subject" may also perpetuate an impersonal attitude toward the people who take part in research. Instead of saying, "I interviewed two men and two women yesterday," psychologists sometimes catch themselves saying, "I ran four subjects yesterday." As a result, some psychologists would like to do away with the word "subject"—at least for humans—and to replace it with a less objectionable word, such as "participant."

In most cases, the psychologist includes a fairly large number of subjects in any given study. By observing the behavior of 30 or 50 or 100 people, the researcher can look for common patterns, as well as individual differences, in their behavior. Sometimes, when researchers are trying to describe the behavior or attitudes of a large group of people, they conduct surveys of hundreds or even thousands of subjects. At the other extreme, the psychologist can sometimes learn a great deal about human behavior by closely observing a single subject. In his pioneering studies of memory, Hermann Ebbinghaus made use of only one subject—himself (see Chapter 6). Similarly, clinical psychologists can often learn and communicate a great deal about personality from intensive *case studies* of individuals.

Since most psychologists are ultimately concerned with human behavior, it may seem surprising that much of our research is conducted with nonhumans. The best-known animal subjects are pigeons, monkeys, and, most popular of all, white rats. But psychologists have also conducted research with many other species, including houseflies, worms, elephants, kangaroos,

and even cockroaches. Psychologists use nonhuman subjects for a variety of reasons. For one thing, animals can be kept captive in laboratories for long periods of time, so it is easier to observe their behavior. Animals are also less likely than humans to try to second-guess the experimenters or to be suspicious of the researcher's stated intentions. There are also certain techniques, such as brain surgery or severe electric shocks, that cannot ethically be used with humans but that sometimes can be used with animals.

Some critics argue that human beings are a unique species able to human behavior. It certainly is true that some human problems have no known parallels among other animals. As Robert Zajonc (1972) notes, "No amount of experimentation with animals would tell us whether the possession of handguns by private citizens enhances crime and violence, or what to do about industrial conflict or how to deal with poverty" (page 2). On the other hand, there are often striking continuities between animal and human behavior. Much of what we know about human learning, for example, is based on studies of parallel processes in pigeons, rats, and other animals (see Chapter 5). In addition, as Zajonc points out, studying other animals helps to keep us honest about our own behavior. Human beings are a unique species in many ways, but we must remember that we, too, are members of the animal kingdom, and we cannot be viewed in isolation from other animals.

UNOBTRUSIVE MEASURES

When people know that their behavior is being observed, they are likely to behave differently than they might otherwise. And when they are asked direct questions about their attitudes or actions, they do not always provide objective reports. To get around these problems, psychologists sometimes make use of "unobtrusive measures"—that is, measures that are unlikely to have any effect on the attitude of behavior being measured. For example, one investigator wanted to find out how much liquor was being consumed in a town that was officially "dry." He didn't want to ask people directly about this illegal behavior, however. His solution: count empty bottles in trashcans. In a study of another delicate topic, researchers investigated cultural differences in sexual attitudes by comparing the inscriptions on toilet walls in the Philippines and the United States (Webb, Campbell, Schwartz, and Sechrest, 1966).

What Does the Psychologist Observe?

Psychologists cannot observe everything about a person's (or animal's) behavior at once. They must instead devise ways of observing and measuring those specific aspects of behavior that they are most interested in. In many instances, the researcher will record particular aspects of a subject's overt behavior—for example, the number of times a baby smiles or cries, the amount of food a person eats in a given situation, the length of time it takes a cat to figure out how to open the door of its cage. In addition, researchers sometimes use special equipment to record a subject's physiological responses, such as heart rate, blood pressure, or sweat gland activity. Finally, researchers often record people's responses to questions put to them, whether in the form of personal interviews, questionnaires, or tests of personality, intelligence, or ability. This points to one respect in which human subjects are clearly superior to other animals. Whereas we can observe the overt behavior of both people and other animals, only humans can provide the researcher with their own assessments, or *self-reports,* of their thoughts and feelings.

As with methods of research more generally, there is no single best measure for the psychologist. In many cases, the researcher will do best to use several different measures simultaneously, to find out how they compare with one another. For example, one of us once attempted to define and measure one of the more mysterious facets of human behavior, romantic love (Rubin, 1973). My primary approach was to obtain college students' self-reports of their attitudes and feelings toward their boyfriends or girl friends. To do this, I asked the students to indicate how much they agreed or disagreed with statements like, "If I were lonely, my first thought would be to seek ___ out," or "I would do almost anything for ___." In each case, the blank space denoted the student's boyfriend or girl friend. In addition, I obtained a behavioral measure of love by recording the amount of time couples spent looking into each others' eyes while they were waiting for an experiment to begin. I found, as I had hoped, that the two measures related to each other: The more people indicated that they loved each other on the attitude scale, the more eye contact they tended to make.

Where Does the Psychologist Observe?

A large proportion of psychological research is conducted in laboratories. There are many different sorts of psychological laboratories. For example, an animal learning laboratory may have rooms full of cages in which the animals are kept and special boxes and mazes in which the animals are tested. A human group laboratory may have rooms in which groups of people can meet around a table and equipment for observing and videotaping group discussions. Laboratories are of great importance to psychologists because they help us to study behavior under precise, well-regulated conditions. There are also certain problems with laboratory research, however. Because the laboratory is a rather artificial environment, it is sometimes difficult to generalize from the ways subjects behave in the laboratory to the ways they would behave in other situations. For example, studies of aggression in the laboratory can never give us a complete understanding of the determinants of violence in the streets. An additional problem is that when people are studied in the laboratory, they are aware of the fact that they are being studied. This awareness may lead people to be on their best behavior or to respond in ways that are not typical of their usual behavior. To get around these problems, many psychologists conduct research in nonlaboratory settings. Although it may be difficult to do so, it is often worthwhile to study an animal's behavior in its natural habitat, whether jungle, marsh, or stream. Psychologists often study human behavior in natural settings as well, including dormitory rooms, hospitals, parks, churches, subways, factories, and even elevators.

What Is an Experiment?

Oliver Wendell Holmes Jr., a great justice of the United States Supreme Court, once declared, "All life is an experiment." What Holmes meant was that throughout life we try out different courses of behavior: We attend particular schools, enter particular occupations, marry particular people, raise our children in particular ways, and then assess the consequences of these actions. Sometimes we make these decisions for ourselves; in other cases our environments leave us with little choice in the matter. Psychological researchers also do experiments, albeit on a smaller scale, in which they treat sets of subjects in different ways and then observe what impact the treatments have on the subjects' thoughts or behavior.

Box 3

Finding What You're Looking For

One of the pitfalls of psychological research is the possibility that the researcher may sometimes inadvertently produce precisely the results he or she expects to find.

Robert Rosenthal (1966) has conducted many studies that demonstrate the existence of such *experimenter expectancy effects*. In one study, ten advanced undergraduate and graduate students were recruited to serve as experimenters. Each experimenter was assigned a group of 20 students to serve as subjects. The experimenters were to show the subjects a series of photographs of people's faces. The subjects were to guess the degree of "success" or "failure" expressed in each face, on a scale that went from minus 10 (extreme failure) to plus ten (extreme success). The experimenters were all given the same set of instructions about how to conduct the experiment and were told not to deviate from them. Finally, the experimenters were given an idea of the average ratings they could expect to obtain in the study, on the basis of previous research. Half were told that most people tended to rate the faces in the photos as quite successful; the other half were told that people tended to rate the faces as quite unsuccessful. After this briefing, the experimenters began their research. The results of the Rosenthal study were clearcut: The experimenters who were led to expect "success" ratings in fact obtained much more "successful" ratings from their subjects than did the experimenters who were led to expect failure ratings.

How do experimenter expectancy effects work? The best guess is that experimenters do not intentionally set out to

An *experiment,* then, is a study in which the researcher exerts direct control over some aspect of the subjects' environment and then assesses the effects. Not all psychological studies are experiments. In many cases, the researcher observes behavior or asks questions without trying to have a direct impact on the subjects. Such nonexperimental studies are often called *correlational studies,* because the researcher is usually trying to discover the relationship (or correlation) between two or more aspects of

---

shape their subjects' responses. Nevertheless, subtle nonverbal cues such as facial expressions and tone of voice can provide signals to the subject as to what sort of response is expected. And once they have picked up on these cues, subjects may unconsciously shift their responses in the direction that the experimenter seems to expect. You can probably demonstrate similar effects yourself. Go up to a friend with a smile on your face and ask, in a bright tone of voice, "How often do you get depressed?" Go up to another friend and ask the same question, but this time wear a sorrowful expression and use a somber tone. There's a good chance that the way you ask the question will affect the response you get.

The fact that researchers may unintentionally affect the results of their research presents a problem for psychologists. It suggests that our results may not always be as objective and reliable as we would like them to be. As a result of the work of Rosenthal and others, however, psychologists have become aware of this problem, and they have taken measures to combat it. One device is to present instructions to subjects in writing or on tape, so that the experimenter will not be able to behave differently toward different subjects. Another precaution is for the researchers to keep themselves in the dark about the experimental condition being run. The less the experimenters know about what to expect from subjects, the reasoning goes, the less likely they will be to unwittingly influence the results. In the Good Samaritan study, for example, the "victim," who had to record the subjects' helping responses, remained unaware of (or "blind" to) the experimental condition of the subjects who came down the road.

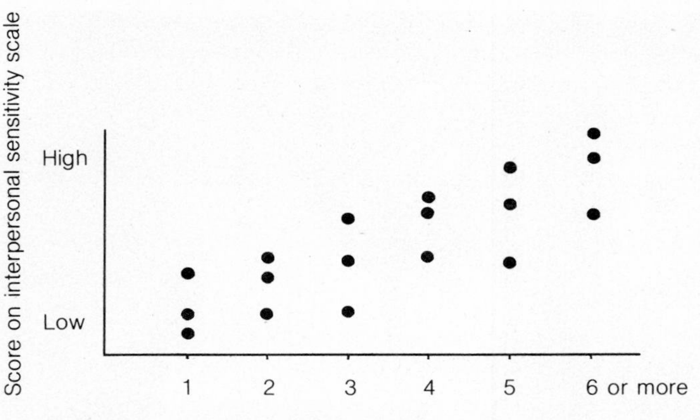

FIG. 1 · 3 The results of a hypothetical study relating training in psychology to scores on a test of interpersonal sensitivity. Each dot represents one subject. The results show a high correlation between the two variables.

people's background, attitudes, or behavior. Suppose, for example, that you were interested in determining the relationship between people's training in psychology and their sensitivity to other people's feelings. You might go about such a study by choosing a sample of students, asking each one how many psychology courses he or she has taken, and finally giving them a test of interpersonal sensitivity. You would be able to chart the relationship between your two measures. Figure 1.3 presents one possible set of results from such a study, suggesting that the two measures (sometimes called *variables*) are in fact related to one another. (For more on correlations and how they are computed, see the Appendix.)

As far as we know, this particular study has never been done, but it would certainly be an interesting one to do. Such a correlational study has its limitations, however. Although our hypothetical study demonstrates that training in psychology and interpersonal sensitivity are related to each other, it does not tell us which of the variables is the cause and which is the effect. One hypothesis would be that training in psychology has the effect of increasing people's sensitivity to others. But the causal link might also go in the other direction: People who are sensitive to others may be especially interested in taking psychology courses. It is even possible that neither of the variables has any effect on the other and that both of them are caused by a third factor that we neglected to measure. For example, it is possible that students who come from particular family backgrounds are especially likely both to be interpersonally sensitive and to take psychology, while people who come from other family backgrounds are likely to lack sensitivity and to avoid psychology like the plague. The moral of this story is that *correlation does not imply causation.* In other words, simply knowing that two variables are related does not in itself tell us what is causing what.

In order to learn more about the causes of behavior, psychologists turn to experiments. In the case of our example, one might set up an experiment in the following way: First, select a sample of incoming freshmen who have not yet taken psychology. Next, randomly divide your sample into two groups (you can do this by putting the subjects' names on slips of paper, mixing them up, and then dividing the slips into two piles). Give the students in both groups a test of interpersonal sensitivity. Now give the students in one group a weekly assignment from a psychology textbook. (We hope you'll choose this one!) Give the students in the other group a weekly reading assignment of the same length but in some other field, such as history or economics. Finally, at the end of the term, give all the students another test of interpersonal sensitivity. If the psychology training increased sensitivity to others' feelings, you should find that the average sensitivity scores of the first group increased significantly more than the average sensitivity scores of the second group. (A statistically significant difference is one that is highly unlikely to have come about by chance, and therefore can be attributed to the impact of your experimental treatments. For a discussion of statistical significance and how it is determined, see the Appendix.)

Because in this experiment you had direct control over your subjects' psychology training, it is now possible for you to find out whether it actually *caused* increases in social sensitivity. In experiments, the variable that the researcher has control over (in this case, training in psychology) is called the *independent variable,* and the variable that may be affected by the independent variable is the *dependent variable* (in this case, interpersonal sensitivity). The group of subjects who receive the special treatment (in this case, the training in psychology) is called the *experimental group,* and the group of subjects that one compares them with (in this case, the ones who were assigned reading in some other field) is called the *control group.* The control group plays a vital function in an experiment by ruling out the effects of extraneous factors on the dependent variable. It is possible, for example, that college students generally tend to become more interpersonally sensitive over the course of a year as the result of their increasing maturity and their accumulating experiences with other people. If our experiment did not include a control group, we would not know whether changes in interpersonal sensitivity were caused by the independent variable (training in psychology) or by the increased maturity that would have taken place anyway. By including the control group, whose subjects also got older during the year but who did not get training in psychology, we can determine whether the psychology training in fact made the difference.

It is not always easy, or even possible, to conduct experimental studies of particular hypotheses. This is because it is often difficult or impossible to gain control over the independent variable. For example, you might be interested in assessing the impact of a person's sex on his or her aggressiveness, or the effects of physical appearance on marital happiness. But it would be difficult, to say the least, to conduct experimental studies along these lines. It is impossible to randomly assign subjects to "male" and "female" subgroups or to randomly decide that some subjects will henceforth be physically attractive and that others will be unattractive. In these instances, the researcher would have to settle for doing a correlational study.

RESEARCH AND APPLICATION

Psychological research has been applied to a wide range of practical issues, from helping people to make better career decisions to suggesting more effective policies of environmental control. The translation from research to application is by no means easy or automatic, however. Whereas some psychological research has obvious and immediate applications, other research has no apparent application at all. To understand more fully the links between research and application, it is useful to think of two sorts of psychological research: *basic research* and *applied research.*

The purpose of basic research is to advance our understanding of behavior without any immediate concern for the practical uses of this understanding. Brown and McNeill's study of TOT states and Darley and Batson's Good Samaritan study are both examples of basic research. But although basic research seldom has any direct application, in the long run it may prove to be of great practical importance. For example, studies of verbal learning, such as Brown and McNeill's, may eventually lead to better techniques of teaching and learning languages. Similarly, basic research on helping behavior may eventually lead to ways of encouraging people to be more responsive to the plight of others. It is unusual, however, for any single basic research study to have important applications. Rather, the research gradually accumulates to help build a theory or model of some aspect of behavior, and it is the theory, in turn, that is likely to suggest new applications. In Chapter 5, for example, we will explore some basic research on principles of learning, much of it done with rats and pigeons, that might seem at first to have no practical usefulness; in Chapter 17, we will discover that the theoretical framework that grew out of this research has proved to be of great use in treating psychological and emotional disorders.

Applied research is work that attempts, from the outset, to help solve a practical problem. For example, psychologists have conducted a good deal of research on the effectiveness of different modes of psychotherapy (see Chapter 17). This research may be of direct use to therapists who must decide what approach to take in a particular case. Other applied research has dealt with the effectiveness of newly designed equipment, from the standpoint of human perceptual and motor abilities. In still other cases, psychologists have done research that has direct bearing on court cases or on decisions about government programs. For example, Bem and Bem (1973) conducted experiments that demonstrated that certain newspaper want ads are worded in such a way as to steer women into particular sorts of jobs and men into others. Their findings played an important role in a court decision that one of the largest American corporations had engaged in discriminatory hiring practices.

In addition to conducting basic and applied research, many psychologists are also involved in the *practice* of psychology—that is, in making direct applications of psychological knowledge. These activities include providing psychological help for individual clients, working with groups and organizations, and playing a

GIVING PSYCHOLOGY AWAY

"Our responsibility is less to assume the role of experts and try to apply psychology ourselves than to give it away to the people who really need it—and that includes everyone. The practice of valid psychology by nonpsychologists will inevitably change people's conception of themselves and what they can do. When we have accomplished that, we will really have caused a psychological revolution" (Miller, 1969, page 16).

role in the development of social policies and programs. In the following section, we will take a closer look at the variety of activities, including both research and practice, that psychologists are involved in.

SUBFIELDS OF PSYCHOLOGY

Many people have a specific image of what psychologists do. One popular conception is that psychologists, like television's Bob Newhart, spend most of their time talking to people about their personal and emotional problems. Another is that psychologists can usually be found showing people inkblots and asking them to make up stories about them. Still another image is that of people with stopwatches and clipboards who unceasingly watch rats run mazes until, after a while, they begin to look a little like rats themselves. All these images have a grain of truth to them in that psychotherapy, psychological testing, and research with laboratory animals are all among the activities of psychologists.

As you probably realize by now, however, each of these images provides an inaccurate picture of the psychologist. In fact, not all psychologists are alike. Rather, different psychologists specialize in different subfields of the discipline. Some do psychotherapy, some give tests, some study laboratory animals, and some engage in a wide range of other activities. In this section we will provide a brief tour of the different psychology subfields (as categorized by Lipsey and Brayfield, 1975) in order to give you a fuller idea of what psychologists do.

Box 4
Some Assorted Facts About Psychologists

How Many Psychologists Are There? There are currently about 50,000 psychologists in the United States. Since its beginnings in this country around 1870, psychology has been expanding at a rapidly escalating rate, with the number of living psychologists doubling every dozen years. In 1951, E. G. Boring, a noted historian of psychology, calculated that if this rate of growth continued, by the end of the twenty-first century every man, woman, and child in the United States would be a psychologist (Lipsey and Brayfield, 1975).

Where Do They Work? Almost half of the psychologists in America (46 percent) work primarily in colleges and universities; 18 percent work in governmental agencies, 13 percent in schools, 7 percent in business, 6 percent in clinics, and 3 percent in nongovernmental agencies. Seven percent are self-employed (Cates and Dawson, 1971).

Psychologists and Psychiatrists Psychologists and psychiatrists differ in their training and in their professional activities. Psychologists are trained in graduate schools, where they receive M.A. or Ph.D. degrees. Psychiatrists go to medical schools and earn M.D. degrees, after which they go on to do additional work in psychiatry. Both psychiatrists and one group of psychologists—clinical psychologists—are concerned with the diagnosis and treatment of psychological problems and mental illness. Clinical psychologists more often use psychological tests as part of this work, and they are more likely to draw on theory and research from other areas of psychology. Psychiatrists, because they are M.D.s, are able to make use of drugs and other medical treatments.

Experimental psychology. Although psychologists in several different subfields conduct experiments, the term "experimental psychology" is generally reserved for research on the most fundamental psychological processes, such as perception, learning, memory, motivation, and emotion. Experimental psychologists do much of their work in laboratories, using both animal and human subjects. In this category are comparative psychologists, who compare the behavior patterns of different animal species, and physiological psychologists, who study the operation of the brain and nervous system. One experimental psychologist may be engaged in studying the physiological effects of meditation; another may be conducting research on how loud noises affect people's ability to solve problems; and a third may be concerned with explaining why it is that lesions in particular areas of the brain cause rats to overeat and become fat.

Clinical, counseling, school, and community psychology. These subfields of psychology are all concerned with helping people deal with psychological problems. Clinical psychologists work in schools, hospitals, and mental health centers and in private practice; they diagnose psychological difficulties and provide therapy for those who need it. Counseling psychologists work with people who are trying to decide on a career (vocational counseling), who are pondering whether or when to get married (marriage counseling), or who are trying to readjust their lives after a severe illness or injury (rehabilitation counseling). School psychologists work with children who are having difficulty in school, consult with teachers and parents, and help to design special school programs, such as those for retarded or gifted children. Community psychologists specialize in preventing and treating psychological problems at a community level—for example, by working with organizations of elderly people or with youth groups. All of these specialties are primarily concerned with the practice of psychology rather than research. Nevertheless, many psychologists in these fields do research—for example, on the effectiveness of particular modes of therapy or of particular school programs.

Personnel, organizational, engineering, and consumer psychology. Psychologists in these areas generally work in commercial or industrial settings. Personnel psychologists are concerned with selecting workers for particular jobs and with handling questions of morale and job satisfaction. Organizational psychologists are called upon to develop ways for businesses and other organizations to function more effectively. For example, an organizational psychologist might meet with managers and employees in a large company and develop a plan for the employees to have more say in designing their own jobs or in arranging their own work schedules. Engineering psychologists are concerned with making sure that the design of equipment, from telephone systems to space capsules, takes into account the abilities and limitations of the people using it. Consumer psychologists are concerned with the application of psychology to questions involving the purchase

WHAT'S IN A NAME?

A questionnaire administered to 376 college students on three campuses found consistent differences in student reaction to hearing the names "Counseling Center" and "Psychological Center." The name "Counseling Center" was associated with the treatment of minor problems. "Psychological Center" was associated with the treatment of more serious problems. The "Psychological Center" was seen as more medical, expensive, professional, embarrassing to go to, and competent than the "Counseling Center" (Sieveking and Chappell, 1970).

One way psychologists study human behavior is to administer standardized tests (see Chapter 8).

and consumption of goods and services. A consumer psychologist might help to decide what kind of package would maximize the sales of a new brand of shampoo or might help to develop a campaign to encourage people to conserve gas and electricity.

Developmental and educational psychology. Developmental psychologists are concerned with the development of human capacities and behavior, from conception and birth through old age and death. A developmental psychologist might conduct research on the effects of day care on children's adjustment and personality, and this research might lead to recommendations about the ways in which day-care centers should be set up. Another developmental psychologist might conduct research on the way in which people adjust to retirement and the necessity for finding new ways to keep busy and active in old age. Educational psychologists are involved with the design of educational settings and techniques and with the training of teachers. For example, an educational psychologist might take part in the planning of a television show for preschool children and then might do an evaluation of the show's impact on the children's intellectual development. In developmental and educational psychology, research and practice are often closely intertwined. Research on human development, for example, often leads directly to recommendations about child rearing, teaching, and dealing with childhood problems.

Personality and social psychology. Psychologists in these related fields are concerned with the nature and dynamics of human personality and with the ways in which people's behavior is affected by other people and by the social environment. Personality and social psychologists are primarily basic researchers, but they often apply their research to such areas as education, psychotherapy, organizational management, and intergroup relations. For example, someone specializing in personality might study the function that religious or racial prejudice plays for some people, while a social psychologist might examine the processes that take place when groups—such as a jury in a court case—have to arrive at joint decisions.

It should be clear by now that even though psychology consists of a diverse set of specialties, these specialties are often closely related. An educational psychologist, for example, may call upon research generated in experimental psychology (on principles of learning), organizational psychology (as it relates to the workings of a school system), clinical psychology (on disorders that may affect the educational process), developmental psychology (on the development of intellectual abilities), and social psychology (as it relates to group instruction among students). Because of these many interconnections, there are in fact no absolute dividing lines between the various specialties. And the careers of individual psychologists often span several of the subfields. For example, Elton McNeil began as an experimental psychologist, was then trained to be a clinical psychologist, worked as an educational consultant to school systems and as a school psychologist, directed a training center for persons planning to work with emotionally disturbed and delinquent boys, worked on psychological aspects of disarmament proposals, and was a field selection officer for the Peace Corps.

Before concluding, a final activity of psychologists should be mentioned: the role of *teaching* psychology. People who teach psychology often engage in other psychological work as well, such as research, counseling, or psychotherapy. But teaching remains the primary activity of 23 percent of all psychologists (Cates, 1970), including both authors of this book. For us, as for most teachers of psychology, teaching is another way of putting research into practice. By presenting psychological theory and research to our students, we hope to inspire them to think about how this work applies to their own lives.

SUMMARY

1. *Psychology* is the science of behavior. Psychologists attempt to systematically ask and answer questions about why people act, think, and feel the way they do.
2. Darley and Batson designed an experiment to see what factors affect helping behavior. In their Good Samaritan study, they learned that people's mental preoccupations and hurriedness can influence whether or not they will stop to help someone who is in trouble.
3. Brown and McNeill set up an experiment to study the "tip of the tongue" (TOT) phenomenon. They developed guesses, or *hypotheses,* about TOT states and they tested their hypotheses by creating such states in experimental subjects. Their results led them to theorize that words are stored in memory on the basis of both meaning and sound.
4. The science of psychology is relatively new; prior to the late nineteenth century psychological questions were relegated to philosophy. With the founding of the first psychological laboratory by the German Wilhelm Wundt and with the influence of English philosophical thought, the discipline of psychology came into its own. Wundt's *structuralism,* which focused on conscious processes, became an applied science for *functionalists* in America. As a reaction against structuralism, Watson developed *behaviorism,* in which mental processes were discounted. Now things seem to have gone full circle with renewed interest in the conscious mind.
5. Psychologists get their research ideas from a variety of sources: personal experience, events in the news, philosophical and literary writings, a need to solve an urgent psychological or social problem—even by accident.
6. Psychological *theories*—sets of ideas that fit together to provide a perspective on some aspect of behavior—serve to organize knowledge and to provide a common language for psychologists to use in communicating their findings.
7. Psychologists use a wide variety of methods for systematically gathering objective and reliable information about human behavior. These methods range from laboratory experiments to nationwide surveys.
8. The subjects in a psychological study may be chosen on the basis of appropriateness, convenience (most subjects are college students), and the nature of the problem being studied. The *sample,* or group of subjects representing a larger population, may range from a single person to thousands. Animal subjects are widely used in psychological research, but the applicability of results to humans depends greatly on the aspect of behavior being studied.
9. Psychologists must narrow down the focus of their study; they may choose to measure overt behavior, to record phy-

siological responses, or to gather self-reports in the form of interviews, questionnaires, or tests. Often more than one type of measure is used in examining a single phenomenon.

10. One problem in psychological research is the influence of *experimenter expectancy effects.* It seems that if a researcher expects an experiment to turn out a certain way, that expectation can subtly influence the outcome of the experiment.
11. Research may take place in a variety of settings, from different types of laboratories to factories, parks, and subways. Because the laboratory is an artificial environment, it is often difficult to be sure that subjects are behaving "normally" there.
12. *Correlational studies* are those in which a researcher tries to discover a relationship between two factors by measuring each separately and comparing the results. The problem with such studies is that a high correlation does not necessarily imply that one factor has caused the other.
13. In an *experiment,* the researcher exerts direct control over one factor (the *independent variable*) to see what effect, if any, it will have on another factor (the *dependent variable*). The group from whom the independent variable is being manipulated is called the *experimental group;* the results for the experimental group are then compared with those for a second group, called the *control group.* Some phenomena lend themselves to experiments; others are accessible only through correlational studies.
14. *Basic Research* is work that aims to advance our understanding of behavior without any immediate concern for its practical implications. *Applied research* attempts, from the outset, to help solve a practical problem. The *practice* of psychology involves making direct applications of psychological knowledge.
15. Psychology contains numerous subfields, each devoted to research and practice of psychology in a specific area. However, a working psychologist is likely to draw from many of the subdisciplines in doing his or her own work. In addition, nearly a quarter of all psychologists are principally teachers of the discipline.
16. Psychology is a growing field, with more and more professionals joining the ranks each year. The majority of psychologists work in educational institutions; most others work in government and business jobs. Psychologists generally have an M.A. or Ph.D. degree, whereas psychiatrists are M.D.s.

Parascience

Indeed, errors in scientific theories often originate in errors of fact.

The science of psychology is based on the traditional approaches and methods of science in general. But there are alternative ways of looking at the world that are not based on the scientific view of reality. The world of mysticism and the occult, for example, begins with a set of premises that differ sharply from those of the scientific world. Such alternative views are often referred to as being pseudoscientific or parascientific. The term *parascience* (*para* meaning "beside, apart from, or accessory to") is a fairer choice of terms than the traditional derogatory label *pseudoscience* (meaning "false science"). As Kaufmann (1968) observed, "Some aspects of science itself developed out of magic, and whatever the dissimilarities, it shares with magic the urge to know the . . . world, and the belief that Man can be more than a passive, uncomprehending thing in it" (page 7).

In 1865, Claude Bernard insisted that if the *facts* used for the basis of reasoning are ill-established or erroneous, everything will crumble. Indeed, errors in scientific theories often originate in errors of fact. But it is this disagreement about what is or is not "fact" that triggers most of the hostile dialogue between parascientists and scientists.

Scientists may seem unreasonable to parascientists, but, as Martin Gardner (1952) pointed out, this very stubbornness of science "forces the scientist with a novel view to mass considerable evidence before his theory can be seriously entertained. If this situation did not exist, science would be reduced to shambles by having to examine every new-fangled notion that came along. Clearly, working scientists have more important tasks" (page 11).

The Psychologist and Personal Bias

The realm of parascience is a particularly difficult one to treat in an objective, impartial manner. This is true for me (Elton McNeil) not only because it is an area of study usually defined as *outside* science but also because of the personal convictions I have accumulated over a period of many years. I label these convictions scholarly conclusions. Those who disagree with me would call them personal biases.

Do I have an open or closed mind about parascientific phenomena? Questions like this are at the center of much scientific controversy. In the scientific method, objectivity—impersonal concern with "the facts and only the facts"—has long been a professional watchword. There are areas of experimental endeavor, however, in which "the facts" are hard to come by and the argument over trustworthy facts is fueled more by emotion than by incontrovertible evidence.

What I have labeled "parascience" is only one of many

There are areas of experimental endeavor, however, in which "the facts" are hard to come by. . . .

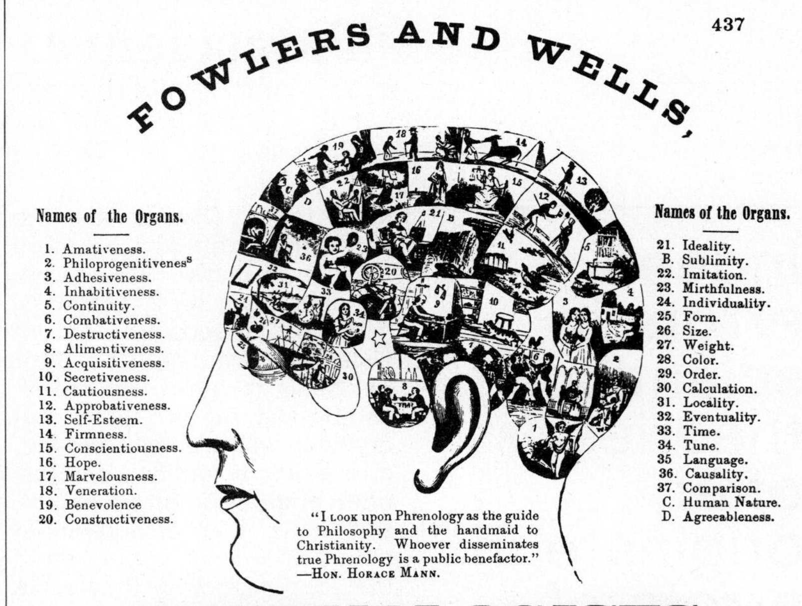

PHRENOLOGISTS,

142 WASHINGTON ST., BOSTON,

308 BROADWAY, NEW YORK,

231 ARCH ST., PHILADELPHIA.

OUR CABINETS OR MUSEUMS

Contain Busts and Casts from the heads of the most distinguished men that ever lived; alsc Skulls, human and animal, from all quarters of the globe—including Egyptian Mummies, Pirates, Robbers, Murderers and Thieves; also numerous Paintings and Drawings of celebrated Individuals, living and dead.

Strangers and citizens will find our Phrenological Rooms an agreeable place to visit.

PHRENOLOGICAL EXAMINATIONS

AND ADVICE, with Charts and full Written Descriptions of Character, given, when desired. These MENTAL portraits, as guides to self-culture, are invaluable.

THE UTILITY OF PHRENOLOGY.

Phrenology teaches us our natural capacities, our right and wrong tendencies, the most appropriate avocations, and directs us how to attain self-improvement, happiness, and success in life.

VALUABLE PUBLICATIONS,

Fowlers and Wells have all works on Phrenology, Physiology, Phonography, Hydropathy, and the Natural Sciences generally.

such areas of marked disagreement among dedicated researchers. In other scientific areas, personal bias is harder to detect, and often a psychologist is unaware that his views of "the facts" may appear distorted or blurred to others. If you one day join the ranks of behavioral scientists, you will be confronted with the same challenges to your objectivity. As a behavioral scientist you will be forced to decide when, or if, you will personally declare certain directions of exploration to be "unscientific." You can begin this decision-making process now by examining your current convictions to see which can be easily changed if adequate proof is presented, which would require a remarkable level of unarguable evidence, and which would be nearly impossible to abandon, even in the face of startling "facts" to the contrary.

Since we are all human, this is what the pursuit of science is all about—the making of imperfect humans into more perfect instruments of factual discovery. In what follows, my own bias with regard to parascientific phenomena will be apparent—I am very skeptical about them. More psychologists share my position than disagree with it, but each of you must decide these issues for yourself. History tells us with great certainty that the "facts" of the year 2000 will most assuredly not correspond with the facts of the mid-1970s.

So read the rest of this Issue, subtract what you take to be the author's personal bias, and keep your options open so that tomorrow can be significantly better than today. You are well advised to retain your skepticism about what you read and to consider the possibility that those of us who have gone before you have figured it out all wrong.

The Varieties of Parascience

The parasciences are too numerous to describe in detail, but a brief outline of a few of them can serve as an illustration of the ways people have sought to unlock the secrets of the universe. First we will look at a few approaches that are closely aligned with psychology. Then we will look to the occult parasciences.

Phrenology Phrenology was thought to be a major key to personality in the early nineteenth century. This discipline began with Franz Joseph Gall's (1758–1828) curiosity about a possible relationship between the physical characteristics and psychological qualities of people. Gall concluded that the mind was composed of 37 powers or propensities (firmness, reverence, acquisitiveness, and combativeness, for example.) Physician Johann Kaspar Spurzheim (1776–1832) modified some of Gall's theories and made a number of further observations.

Phrenology was based on the following series of assumptions: (1) the brain is the physical organ of the mind; (2) the shape and size of the various parts of the growing brain represent the overdevelopment or underdevelopment of personality traits; and (3) the bumps and hollows of the skull reflect the shape of the brain it contains. It followed logically that the phrenologist need only measure head bumps to determine the shape of the brain and diagnose the subject's personality.

By 1840 phrenology had become a popular craze, offering a quick, "scientific," inexpensive way to get vocational guidance and assure happiness. There were phrenology parlors scattered across the country, and traveling phrenologists crisscrossed the nation on lecture tours. Phrenology had a reasonable ring to it in that day and age, even though today's scientists reject the notion that the brain is like a muscle that becomes weak or strong depending on how much it is exercised.

Graphology The practitioners of graphology—the analysis of handwriting—have made astonishing claims about its uses. One modern advocate, Daniel Anthony (1967), maintained, "I am convinced that in the hands of a skilled practitioner, graphology can assist corporations in the selection of productive and reliable employees, can aid therapists in evaluating their patients, and can help youths choose their careers by pinpointing talents and personality traits. I believe that graphology could aid in difficult medical diagnosis" (page 30).†

Anthony insists that graphology is a legitimate subdiscipline of psychology, but few psychologists would agree with him. And, few psychologists study handwriting analysis enough to do effective research on its claims.

In one appraisal of a series of handwriting studies, McNeil and Blum (1952) revealed a number of experimental weaknesses, including failure to consider consistency of an individual's handwriting and reliability of raters' judgments; lack of specific criteria for evaluating handwriting; and dubious character of some of the personality variables.

Psychological research in graphology continues to languish today, but popular fascination has not diminished accordingly. As Anthony puts it, "The 'easy art' of handwriting analysis has answered the needs of the drawing room psychologizers who seek a dramatic new path to personal popularity" (page 76).

†*From "Is Graphology Valid?" D. S. Anthony,* Psychology Today, *August 1967. Copyright © 1967 Ziff-Davis Publishing Company. REPRINTED BY PERMISSION OF PSYCHOLOGY TODAY MAGAZINE.*

Recent times have seen the rise of astrology, numerology, witchcraft, Satanism, Ouija boards, Tarot cards. . . .

The Occult Parasciences

Recent times have seen the rise of astrology, numerology, witchcraft, Satanism, Ouija boards, Tarot cards, and a multitude of other approaches to the mysteries of human life. An estimated 90 percent of American newspapers carry daily astrological forecasts, and as many as two million Ouija boards are purchased each year in this scientifically sophisticated society. Let us look at a few of the systems that people tend to rely on to guide their daily lives.

Astrology. Astrology long has captured the interest of persons of all ages in our society. It "seeks to blend in varied proportions the fundamental methods of astrology with the broad

psychological knowledge which has been spread throughout the United States" (Rudhyar, 1968, page 7). The information astrologers offer to believers is often related to mysterious and ancient wisdom amassed over the centuries. What precisely this wisdom was and what exactly the ancients achieved with their knowledge somehow never gets discussed. The facts are probably not really relevant if people believe that the patterns they observe in the sky give order to the apparent chaos and confusion of daily life.

Astrology is one way to convince ourselves that we are not alone and unnoticed in this life. The belief in astrology (or in any parascientific phenomenon) is an emotional rather than a rational one. What *feels* right and true to an individual *is* truth to him or her, and no massive accumulation of so-called scientific data can shake the foundation on which such belief is based. The belief itself is comforting and probably harmless, if it does not become the sole focus of existence.

The Ouija Board. The name *ouija* is a combination of the French *oui* and the German *ja* and literally means "yes-yes". The Ouija board has the letters of the alphabet, the words "yes" and "no," and the numbers 1 through 10 printed on it. The tiny Ouija table (a small surface with three short legs) moves about the larger board spelling out words, answering yes or no, or adding up numbers, in response to the pressure of the fingertips of the participants. Believers are convinced that answers to their questions are furnished by supernatural forces that guide their fingers to the truth. Nonbelieving psychologists are convinced that this phenomenon is less ghostly and more an instance of the simple physical expression of an unconscious wish for evidence of a guiding force in the universe. It is a harmless pastime as long as you don't begin to take it too seriously and guide your life and decisions according to "messages" received from the spiritual world.

Satanism and Other Mysteries. Recently a major airline offered a "Psychic Tour" of Great Britain that included a visit to a psychic healing center, a séance, and a day at Stonehenge with the chief of Britain's Most Ancient Order of Druids. Each tourist received a personalized astro-numerology chart, and flight dates were astrologically planned to be favorable. The current popularity of such attractions attests to the nature of our times. In an age in which everyone except computer cards gets duly stapled, folded, and mutilated, one boon is the feeling that one is the manipulator instead of the one who is eternally manipulated. Many of the occult "sciences" are aimed at making humans attain a godlike position—masters of the world.

"Blessed are the strong, for they shall possess the earth. If a man smite you on one cheek, SMASH him on the other!" This inverted gospel—from Anton Szandor La Vey's *The Satanic Bible*—sets the tone for today's leading brand of Satanism, the San Francisco-based Church of Satan. Founded in 1966 by La Vey, a former circus animal trainer, the Church of Satan offers a mirror image of most of the beliefs and ethics of traditional Christianity. La Vey's sinister balderdash reaches hundreds of thousands through the black gospel of *The Satanic Bible* and his second book, *The Compleat Witch* (*Time,* June 19, 1972).

In addition to Satanism, occult groups include witches' covens, voodoo cults, and other such strange assemblages. The organizers of these groups have been accused of being either intellectual frauds, financial swindlers, or disturbed invidividuals who frequently mistake psychoses for psychic phenomena.

Flying Saucers. The flying saucer phenomena of the 1950s provide additional insight into the emotional and social aspects of belief in the occult. According to Buckner's (1966) analysis of flying saucers, excitement about Unidentified Flying Objects (UFOs) began in 1947, producing a period of public sensitization to the notion that there were mysterious things flying around our planet. From April through July 1952, *Life* magazine carried articles about flying saucers, which increased the number of UFO sightings about tenfold. Before long, the flying saucer craze entered a new phase Buckner calls "occult colonization"—people began to report UFOs landing and making contact with humans. By the mid-1950s, a large body of publications had appeared suggesting the possibility that we were being watched by aliens from outer space. Flying saucer clubs were formed. National UFO conventions were held, and a lecture circuit was established.

The Air Force went out of the UFO business after a blue-ribbon study by University of Colorado scientists concluded the UFO reports were mostly hokum. There have been 25,000 UFO reports in the last 25 years. With the accepted range of 10 to 20 percent unexplained sightings, 100 to 200 out of an average of 1,000 reports each year simply cannot be brushed off as hoaxes, conventional aircraft, meteors, reflections on clouds, or other natural phenomena. That is a big enough margin to keep the believers hoping and a small enough margin for the nonbelievers to dismiss flying saucers as a figment of someone's overactive imagination.

An interesting aspect of the recent upsurge in interest in UFOs and the occult parasciences is the fact that believers often belong to several different cults. As Buckner

(1966) observed, "The pattern of membership is one of continuous movement from one idea to another. Seekers stay with a cult until they are satisfied that they can learn no more from it, or that it has nothing to offer, and then they move on" (page 11). Much of the parascience that some young people are involved in today is an open rather than closed cult. That is, the believer need not adhere to a fixed dogma or doctrine but only respect the mystic beliefs of others and share the common mood of mystery.

Much of parascience that some young people are involved in today is an open rather than a closed cult.

Summary

1. The parasciences provide a view of reality quite different from that offered by the regular sciences. Because facts are hard to come by in the parasciences, much of the debate in this area is clouded by emotion and personal bias.
2. Parasciences related to psychology include phrenology—examination of personality by feeling the bumps and hollows of a person's skull—and graphology—handwriting analysis.
3. The occult parasciences include astrology, numerology, witchcraft, Satanism, spiritualism, and related mystical systems that people rely on to give order to their lives. A related phenomenon is the belief in UFOs.

The Brain and the Nervous System

CHAPTER 2

The Brain and the Nervous System

Compared to our animal neighbors, we human beings are creatures of modest physical endowment. We have a poor sense of smell, just average hearing, only passable vision, thin skin, weak jaws and teeth, unimpressive muscular strength, middling running speed, and so-so stamina. Our one saving grace, the one that distinguishes us from the rest of the animals and allows us to master our environment, is the human brain.

This remarkable organ allows human beings to do things unparalleled in the animal kingdom: create works of art, compose symphonies, build machines, communicate by means of highly abstract forms of language, wrestle with mathematical problems, contemplate the meaning of life, and, not least of all, explore the mysteries of the brain itself.

Most of us have not thought much at all about our brains, since we seldom think of any part of the body unless it malfunctions. A headache makes us acutely aware of the housing that holds our brain; the pain from touching a hot pan makes us well aware of the nerve endings in our fingertips. But the brain and nervous system function at all times—not only at those moments that strike our awareness. Our thoughts, our emotions, our actions are all governed by processes occurring in the brain.

The brain is the central part of the nervous system, the complex apparatus that provides the once mysterious links between the "mind," the body, and behavior. These links were once considered to be in the domain of religion or philosophy and not a proper subject for scientists to study. But now biologists and psychologists have gotten up the nerve (if you'll forgive the pun) to examine these links, and they have already discovered a great deal about how brain functioning influences behavior.

To begin to explain the brain and its workings, we will start by examining the smallest part of the nervous system: the nerve cell. Then we'll explore the overall operation of nerves and the nervous system, the way messages are transmitted through the system, and, finally, the central switchboard, the brain itself.

NERVES AND THEIR MESSAGES

Specialized cells called *neurons* are the basic building blocks of the nervous system. A neuron consists of three principal parts: the *cell body,* which contains the nucleus; the *dendrites,* which are many short fibers that project from the cell body and that receive activity from nearby cells; and the *axon*, a long fiber that extends away from one side of the cell body and transmits messages to other neurons or to muscles and glands. (See Figure 2.1.)

Nerve messages normally move in one direction—from the dendrites, through the cell body, and along the axon to the dendrites or cell body of the next neuron, or to a muscle or gland. While all neurons have these general features, they differ greatly in their dimensions. A neuron in the spinal cord may have an axon two or three feet long, whereas neurons in the brain may cover only a few thousandths of an inch.

Different neurons carry different sorts of messages: Some of them collect information from inside or outside the body (for

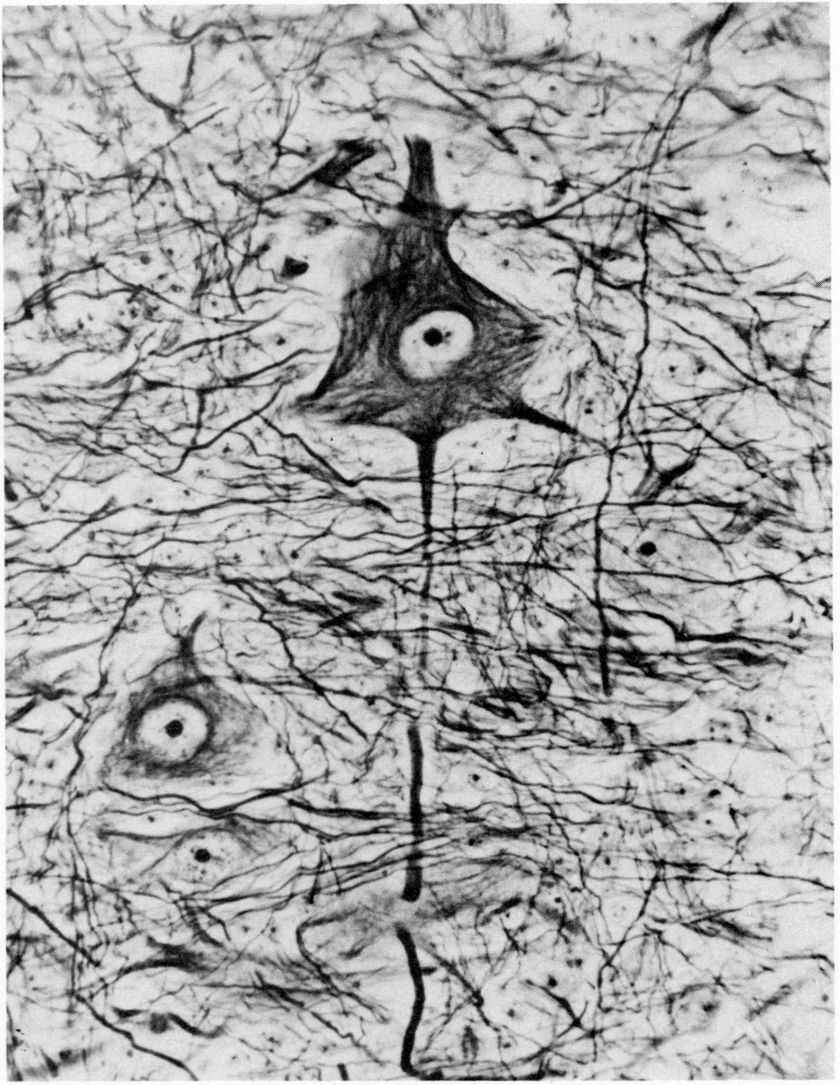

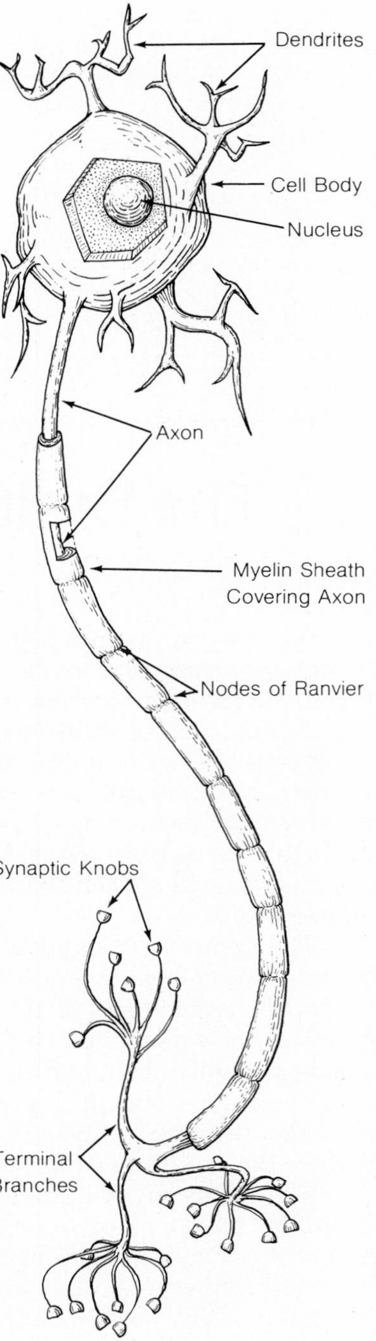

FIG. 2 · 1 The neuron, the basic unit of the nervous system.

FINDING THE BRAIN

It took scientists most of human history to pinpoint mental functioning in the brain. Aristotle believed that the mind (or soul) resided in the heart, for if the heart was pierced, a person almost always died. The brain was often considered to be little more than a radiator where hot blood was pumped to be cooled off. Another view, sometimes attributed to the early Egyptians, was that a "little man," or homunculus, lived in the skull and pulled the strings that operated the muscles. The problem couldn't be solved scientifically until we found out enough about electricity and chemistry to understand how the brain actually functions. It took until the late 1700s before the set of consciousness was fixed within the confines of the skull.

example, from the eyes or ears) and transmit this information to the spinal cord or to the brain. Other neurons carry messages from the brain or spinal cord to other parts of the body (for example, to the legs when one is walking). And still others, usually located within the brain or spinal cord, make the connections between the incoming and outgoing messages.

Messages are transmitted through the nervous system in two ways. There is *axonal* transmission—the movement of nerve impulses along the surface of a neuron. And there is also *synaptic* transmission—the transfer of impulses *between* neurons. A nerve impulse in the human body may travel anywhere from 2 to 200 miles an hour, depending on the diameter of the axon and a number of other factors.

Axonal transmission is primarily an electrical process. Let's see how the process works by looking at the membrane that surrounds an axon. This membrane is selectively permeable, which means that some substances may pass through the membrane but others are blocked out. When the cell is not firing, the cell membrane acts like a dam to keep positively charged sodium ions out of the cell and positively charged potassium ions in. Electrically, the inside of the cell is negatively charged, for althought it has a high concentration of positive potassium ions, it is filled with other molecules (such as chloride) that tip the scales to the negative side. In this resting state, in which the inside of the neuron is negative and the outside positive, the axon is said to be *polarized.*

Now, an outside disturbance—such as stimulation of the dendrite—may cause the cell membrane to temporarily lose its selectiveness and to become *depolarized.* First, the membrane becomes permeable to sodium ions, which come pouring into the cell. As these positive ions enter the cell, the inside becomes electrically positive. Then, the membrane becomes permeable to potassium ions, and potassium flows out of the cell, so that eventually, the original balance of the cell is restored (negative inside, positive outside), and the membrane once again becomes selectively permeable. Only now the cell is filled with sodium instead of potassium. To restore the cell to its resting state, a process known as the *ion pump* must take over, pumping potassium into the cell and sodium out. Now the cell is prepared for another depolarization, should another message come along.

So far, we've discussed these changes in the nerve cell as if they occur in only one place. Actually, when one part of the axon membrane becomes permeable, it causes a chain reaction that ripples down the surface of the cell to the other end. All along the axon, the cell membrane becomes permeable, first to sodium and then to potassium, and the electrical voltage inside the cell changes from negative to positive and back again. When the chain reaction is complete, the neuron is said to have *fired.*

Toward the end of each axon, a great many small fibers called *terminal branches* extend, each ending in a tiny synaptic knob. A microscopic gap separates the end of each terminal from the dendrite or cell body of another neuron. This tiny space is called a *synapse,* and if a message is to travel between neurons it must cross this gap. The gap can be bridged because axon terminals usually contain many tiny sacs called *synaptic vesicles.* When a nerve impulse reaches the end of the axon, it causes some of these vesicles to burst and to release a chemical *transmitter substance* that travels across the gap. (See Figure 2.2.) In some cases, this chemical stimulus makes it more likely that the next neuron will fire. In other cases, the opposite occurs: the chemical acts to inhibit the neuron from firing for a short time. In either case, the effect is that a message is "passed on" from one neuron to the next.

Each axon requires a certain minimum level of stimulus intensity before a nerve impulse can be produced in it. (The stimulus might be a message from a sense organ or from another neuron.) If the strength of the stimulus is below this minimum

THE SQUID'S NEURON

Most of what scientists know about the structure and function of neurons has come not from studies of human neurons but from studies of the neurons of a totally different creature—the squid. In the early 1930s a British scientist named John Z. Young found that the squid has, in its body walls, certain giant nerve fibers, nearly one millimeter in diameter. At that time scientists had been frustrated in their studies of neurons because the nerve fibers in mammals were too small for their instruments to handle. But the giant neurons could be removed from a squid and kept alive for analysis and experimentation. With the squid's giant neurons two British scientists, Alan Hodgkins and Andrew Huxley, were able to develop the first microelectrodes to probe a single nerve cell and record its electrical signals.

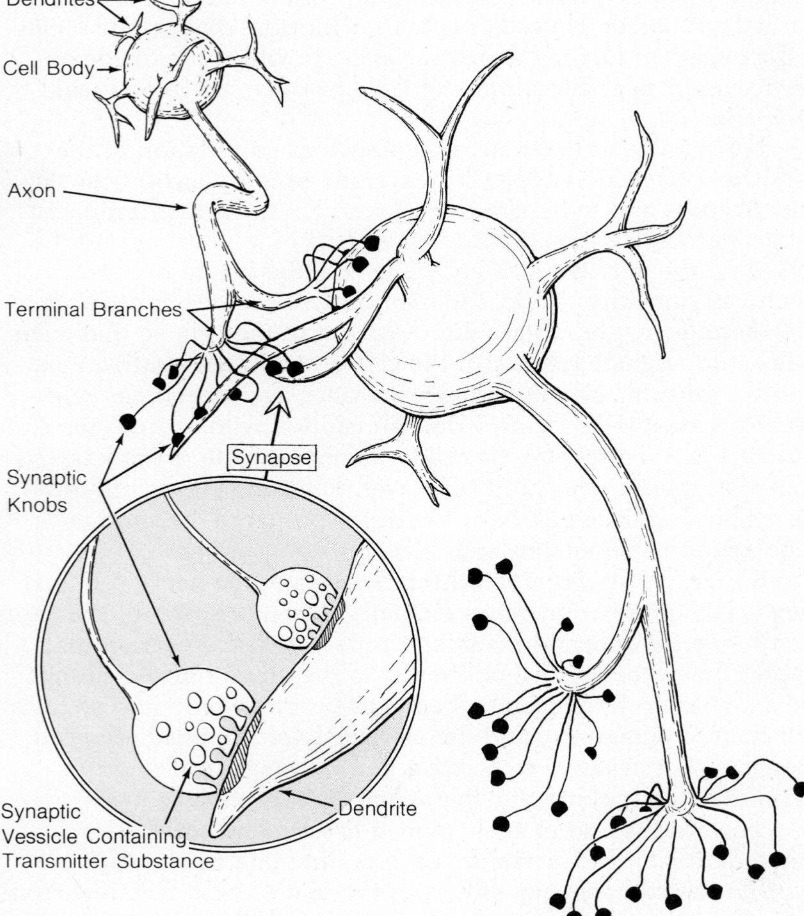

FIG. 2·2 Messages pass from one neuron to another through the release of chemical transmitter substances into the *synapse* (inset) between the synaptic knobs of one cell and the dendrites or cell body of the other.

ELECTRIC FROGS

"In the late 1700s . . . Italian physiologist Luigi Galvani and his wife, Lucia, conducted a variety of experiments with frogs, in which they demonstrated that some force present in the atmosphere could provoke nerve action and muscle movement. In one of their most significant experiments, they took a dissected frog out to an upstairs porch, attached a lightning rod to its head, and stretched a wire from its foot to a well filled with water. In due time, a storm developed; and during the course of it, while lightning crackled, the muscles of the frog, in Galvani's words, 'fell into violent and multiple contractions.'

"Galvani's explanation for this phenomenon was that he had discovered an atmospheric force yet unknown to science. He called it 'animal electricity.' What he had actually discovered was the existence of an electrophysiological force present in all animals, a force now commonly referred to as the *neural impulse.*" [Schneider and Tarshis, 1975, page 121]

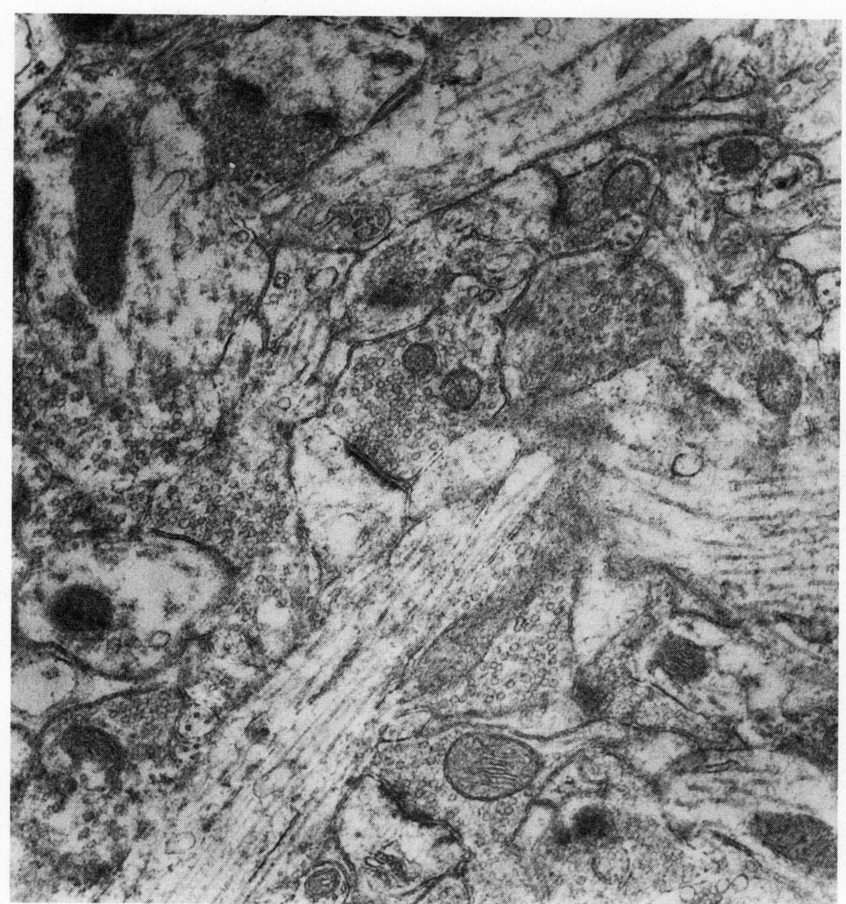

level, no firing of a nerve impulse occurs. However,if the stimulus goes anywhere above this level—just barely or very far above—the axon fires. Thus, the axon fires either completely or not at all, which is known as the *all-or-none principle.* The strength of the nerve impulse is always the same for any particular axon, regardless of the size of the stimulus. In some ways, it is like firing a gun. You must pull the trigger hard enough to fire, but pulling harder on the trigger will not cause the bullet to travel any faster or any farther.

Some nerve fibers are insulated by a *myelin sheath.* The sheath of these myelinated fibers is interrupted about every two millimeters by little pinched-off places called nodes, where the sheath is very thin or totally absent. The nerve impulse jumps along the fiber from node to node, and thus transmission of messages is much more rapid. The myelin sheath acts as insulation and helps to keep the impulse from straying away from the right path. The myelin sheath of many nerve fibers in the brain is partial or incomplete at birth. This suggests that the maturation of some of the infant's sensory and motor apparatus may be

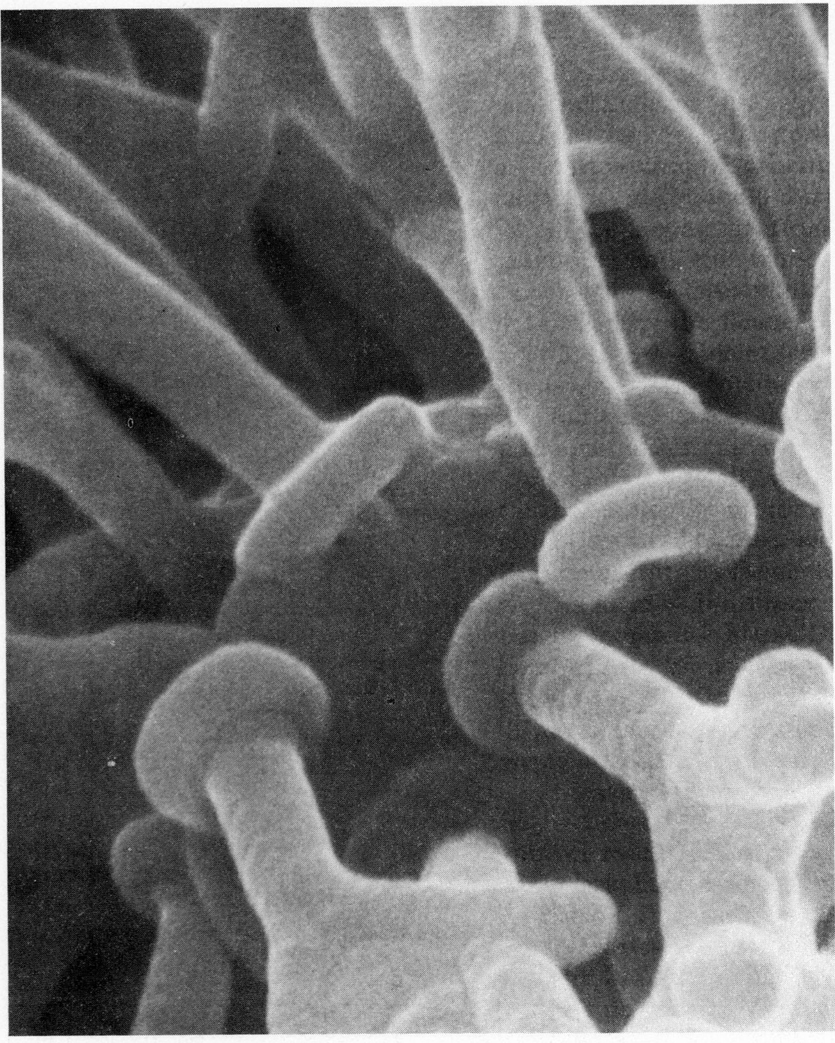

Synaptic knobs (greatly enlarged).

related to the gradual process of myelination as the child grows older. For example, infants cannot be toilet-trained until they have grown the myelin sheath to insulate neurons from being short-circuited and miscommunicating messages to the wrong muscles.

THE NERVOUS SYSTEM

Now that we know something about how nerves communicate, we can consider the network of nerves making up the human nervous system. Our nervous system is a miracle of complexity when compared to forms of life much lower on the evolutionary scale. Animals such as the one-celled amoeba, for example, don't have a nervous system—the entire cell body is responsive to stimulation. In slightly more advanced species, such as the jelly fish, neurons are spread throughout the body in a primitive sort of net. Stimulation of one neuron spreads to all others. A further stage in the evolution of the nervous system appears in some flatworms (planaria). In these tiny animals the nerves form a system closer to that of humans, with the neurons arranged in a bundle called a nerve cord. This is a kind of primitive spinal cord with the cell bodies of the neurons concentrated in the head to form something similar to the brain. In higher animals, the vertebrates, the concentrations of nerves that form the spinal cord and brain are more complex and are protected by a bony case.

The Nervous System Divisions

The human nervous system consists of the brain, the spinal cord, and the nerves that connect them to *receptors* (cells in the sense organs) and *effectors* (muscles and glands). The brain and spinal cord make up the *central nervous system,* while other nerves make up the *peripheral nervous system.* The peripheral nervous system, in turn, contains two kinds of nerves: *afferent,* or *sensory,* neurons that collect messages from inside and outside the body and transmit them *to* the spinal cord or the brain; and *efferent,* or *motor,* neurons that carry messages *from* the spinal cord or the brain to the muscles and glands. Some neurons (usually in the brain and spinal cord) make the connection between incoming and outgoing messages. These are called *association* neurons.

The peripheral nervous system is further divided according to the parts of the body it serves. Voluntary muscles, which control most body movements, are controlled by the *somatic nervous system.* Glands and involuntary muscles are controlled by the *autonomic nervous system.* The autonomic nervous system has two branches: the *sympathetic* and *parasympathetic* divisions. (See Figure 2.4.) Both divisions are directly involved in controlling and integrating the actions of the glands and blood vessels within the body, but they do so by waging a constant tug-of-war. The nerve fibers of the sympathetic division are busiest when the body is responding to stress, as when one is frightened or angry. They

FIG. 2 · 3 Divisions of the nervous system

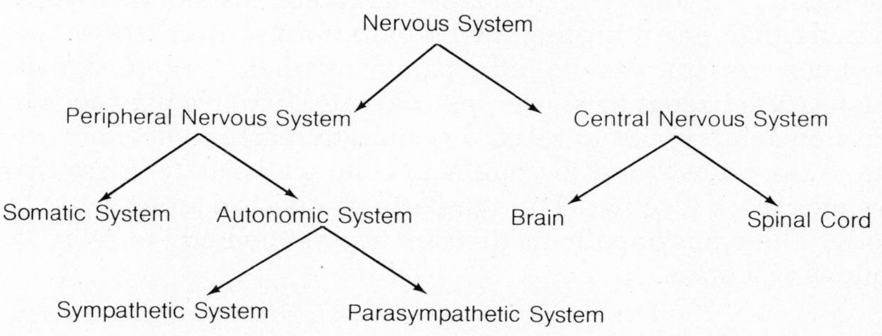

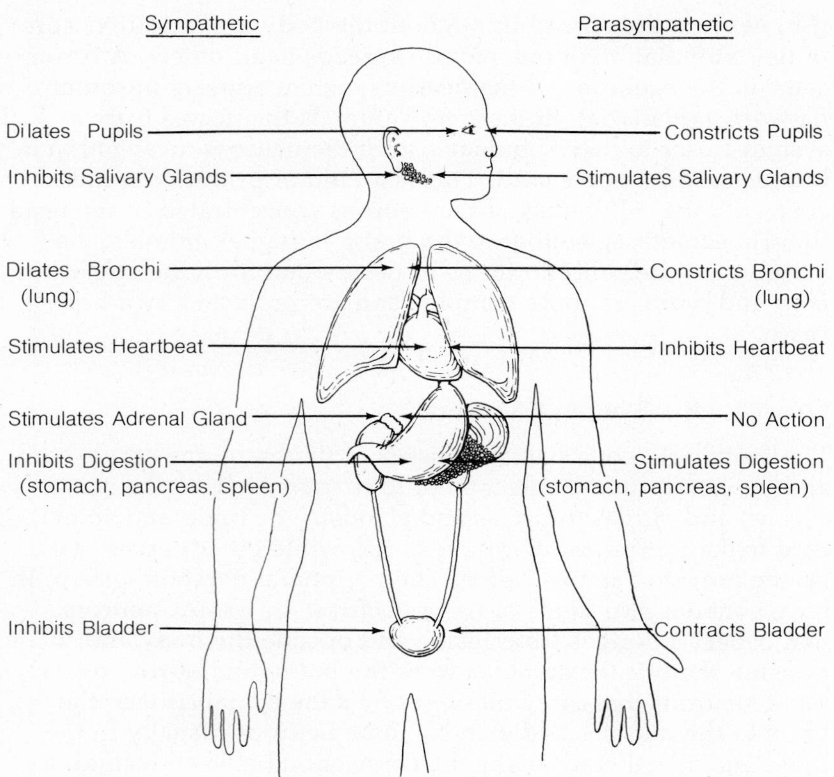

FIG. 2 · 4 The sympathetic and parasympathetic divisions of the autonomic nervous system have opposing effects on many parts of the body.

carry messages telling the body to prepare for an emergency, to get ready to act quickly and decisively. In response to messages from the sympathetic division, the heart pounds, breathing becomes faster, the pupils enlarge, digestion stops, and blood is redistributed through the body. When one reacts to sudden stress, almost all the body becomes involved.

The nerve fibers of the parasympathetic system are connected to most of the same organs as the sympathetic nerve fibers, but their messages often tell the organs to do just the opposite of what the sympathetic division directs. The parasympathetic division most often sends messages that reduce the emergency reaction, but the parasympathetic division is involved in more than just returning the body to normal after stress. Following a stressful situation, the parasympathetic system signals the heart to beat at its slower, normal rate. It relays messages for the stomach muscles to relax, digestion to recommence, breathing to slow down, and the pupils to contract. Usually, these two systems work together. The sympathetic division arouses the body. The parasympathetic division allows the body to relax following a crisis.

The nervous system is far from complete at this point. We have yet to describe the spinal cord and brain, without which we would not be able to sense and respond to our environment—much less write or read a psychology textbook.

The Spinal Cord

Through the hollow center of the backbone's connected vertebrae runs the major nerve of the body, the *spinal cord.* It provides basic connections between motor and sensory neurons and serves as the pathway for nerve impulses traveling from the outlying portions of the body to the brain. As Wooldridge (1963) describes it:

> *Starting from the periphery of the body, fibers from neighboring individual neurons are first grouped together as a nerve. . . . The fibers of the nerves are sorted out on arriving at the backbone, entering the spinal column at various levels, where they join with many thousands of fibers from other levels, forming together the main cable between the input/output devices and the brain. . . . This main cable of the spinal cord reaches the brain with an accumulation of several million conducting nerve fibers. About half of these fibers are busy bringing information to the brain while the other half are busy transmitting to the muscles and glands the instructions that constitute the results of the brain's data-processing and computing activities.*

A cross section of the spinal cord shows that it comprises two different regions. The dark tissue forming the H at the center of the cord is known as *gray matter.* It consists of cell bodies and nerve fibers without myelin sheaths. The nearly instantaneous reflex connections of sensory and motor nerves are found in the gray matter. The *white matter,* which derives its name and color from the myelin sheathing of its nerve fibers, surrounds the gray matter and carries messages to and from the brain.

If someone hands you a scorching hot potato, you will drop it without stopping to think about it. The action is accomplished in the spinal cord without involving the higher brain centers. The impulse moves along the sensory nerve to the spinal cord and out along a motor nerve to the hand. Such an automatic action is called a *reflex.* (See Figure 2.5.) Any action more complex than the reflexive withdrawal of the hand would involve higher brain centers. Thus, if the potato is fairly hot but not hot enough to produce a reflex action, your brain may tell you to pass the potato from hand to hand until you can safely set it down somewhere.

How does the brain control such actions? And what part of the brain controls, for example, hand movements as opposed to vision, or thinking? We now turn to the brain itself, the central headquarters and commander-in-chief of the entire system.

THE BRAIN

At first glance, the brain seems an unlikely candidate for commander-in-chief. The organ has the consistency of soft cheese,

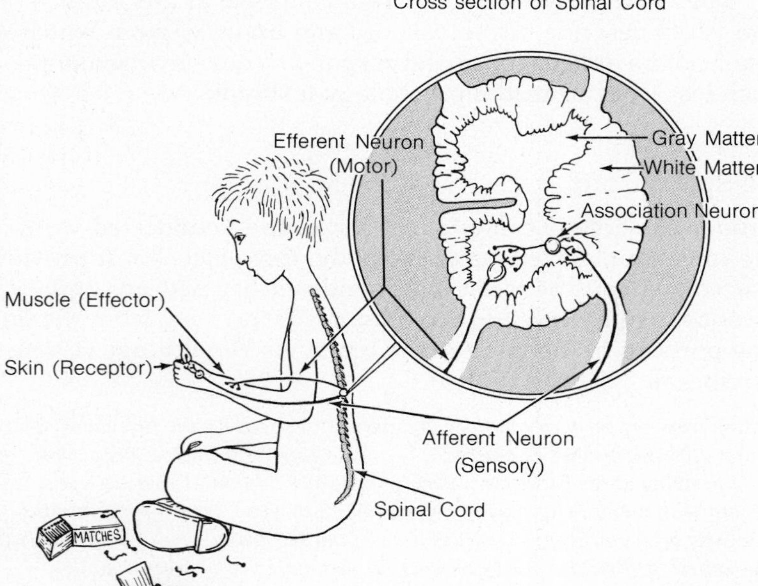

FIG. 2 · 5 *An example of a reflex:* 1. Skin receptors send a "hot" message along an afferent (sensory) neuron to the spinal cord. 2. The message is relayed within the spinal cord to an efferent (motor) neuron. 3. The efferent neuron sends a "drop" message to muscles in the hand. 4. The child drops the match—fast!

The knee-jerk response is another example of a reflex.

and with its many convolutions and ridges it looks and feels something like a giant mushy walnut. But in cellular terms the brain is impressive. It contains about 110 billion cells—10 billion neurons and 100 billion *glia,* which provide nourishment and support for the neurons. In terms of relative size, (i.e. in proportion to body weight) the human brain is the largest of all brains. For the sake of comparison, a dog, a gorilla, and a man of the same body size would have brains of one-half, one, and three pounds, respectively.

The simplest brains, found in certain primitive animals, are nothing more than bulbous swellings at the end of the spinal cord, and this description essentially fits the human brain. The brain is composed of three basic structures. (See Figure 2.6.) The enlarged and knobby protrusion of the spinal cord is the *brain stem.* Behind the brain stem sits the ball-like mass of the *cerebellum.* Enveloping the entire brain stem and most of the cerebellum is the *cerebral cortex.* The wrinkles and folds of the surface layer of the cerebral cortex give the brain its characteristic appearance.

THE HEAVY HEAD

There is a correlation between the brain size of various animal species and the ability of those species to solve problems. The correlation is not perfect and there are a number of crude exceptions such as elephant brains that weigh 13 pounds and whale brains at 19 pounds. The principle of brain weight and ability holds true, however, if brain weight is figured as a proportion of body weight. Thus, an elephant's brain, compared to its size, is 1/1,000 of its weight. The ratio for the whale is 1/10,000. The ratio for humans is 1/60 (Asimov, 1965). Within the human species, however, there is no evidence that brain size and intelligence are correlated.

The Brain Stem

From an evolutionary standpoint, the brain stem is the "oldest" part of the brain, and it resembles the brains of lower animals. In

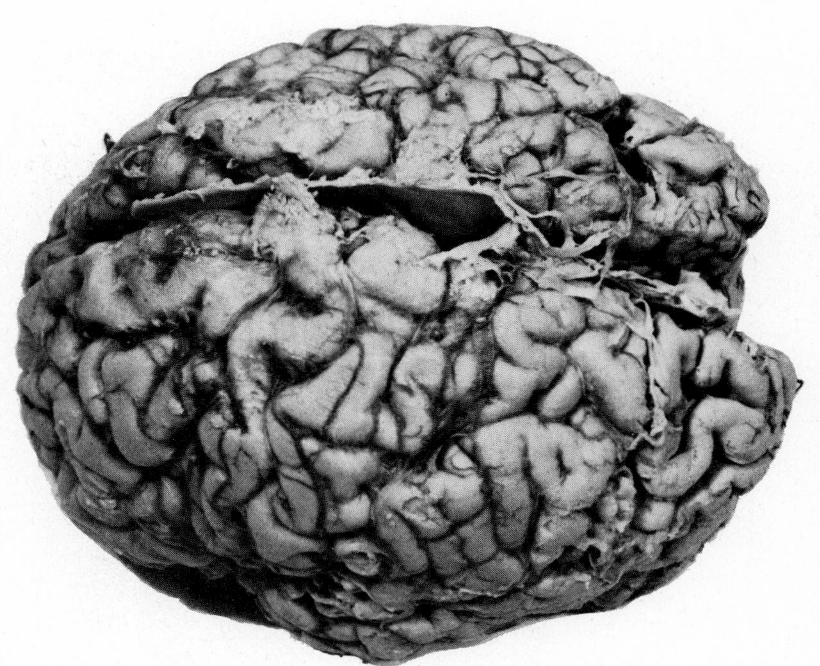

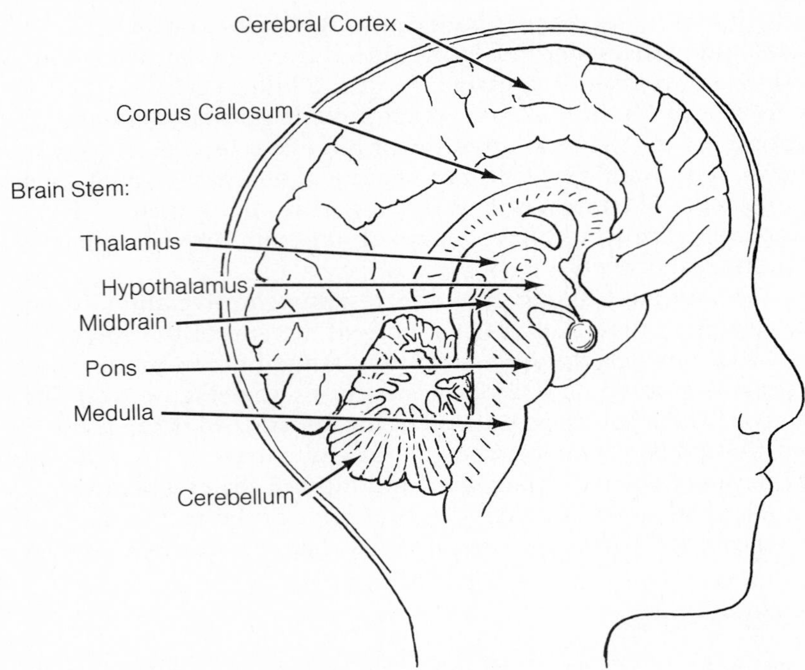

FIG. 2 · 6 A cross-section of the brain, showing its major structures.

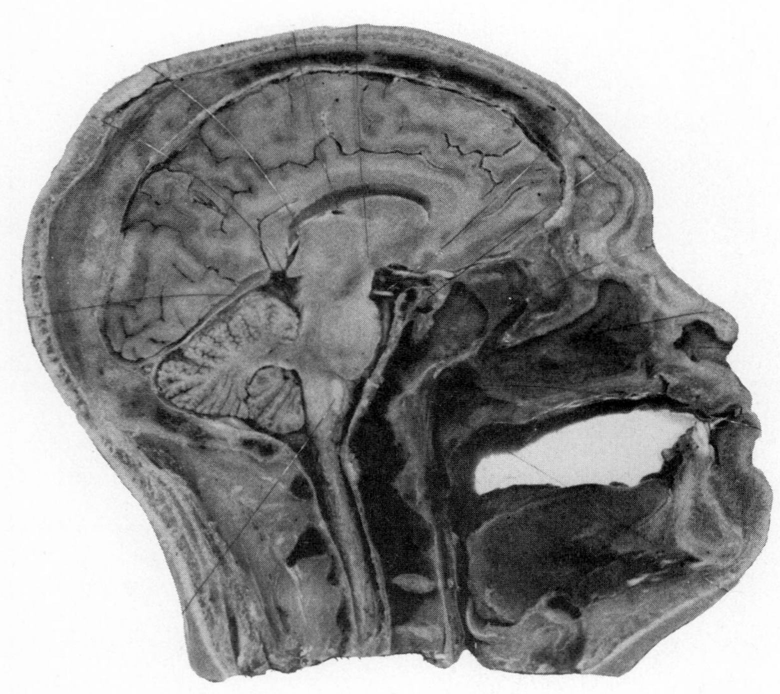

keeping with the brain stem's primitive origins, its functions are connected to the fundamental processes of survival and to emotions, or "gut reactions."

The brain stem comprises several connected structures, each with its own distinct functions. The *medulla,* at the base of the brain stem, controls such basic physical rhythms as heartbeat and breathing, and it contains the reflex centers for vomiting, sneezing, coughing, and swallowing. Above the medulla is the *pons,* which houses ascending and descending nerve tracts and a cross-connection between the brain stem and the cerebellum. The *midbrain* acts as a relay center in complex reflexes involving hearing and vision and in the reception of pain. The exact role of the *thalamus* is not well understood, but it seems to sort incoming sensory messages and to route them to the appropriate region of the cerebral cortex. The *hypothalamus,* to the front and underside of the thalamus, is the most important automatic control point in the brain. It monitors particular activites such as eating, drinking, sex, sleeping, and temperature regulation, and plays a direct role in the patterns of emotional behavior we call rage, terror, and pleasure.

Messages coming into the brain pass through nerve fiber tracts along the backside of the brain stem, while outoing information follows neural pathways on the front side. Between these two regions lies a core of nerve tissue known as the *reticular activating system,* which runs the entire length of the brain stem. The reticular system monitors incoming information, decides what is important, alerts higher brain centers that significant information is coming, and discards insignificant messages to keep them from jamming neural pathways. Thus, the reticular activat-

ing system is responsible for deciding how the brain will use its time to deal with the environment.

The Cerebellum

The cerebellum is positioned behind the brain stem and is largely concerned with automatic controls of body position and motion. For example, it monitors the tension of arm muscles and keeps track of where the arm is in relation to the rest of the body and its surroundings. When you make a conscious effort to move your arm, the cerebellum acts as an intermediary between command and execution, translating the order into a series of specific motor impulses that results in a coordinated and controlled movement.

The Cerebral Cortex

As one comes up the evolutionary scale from the simple to the complex animals, the cerebral cortex grows markedly in size. In a shark, for example, the cerebral cortex is a very small portion of the brain. In contrast, the cerebral cortex takes up 80 percent of the human brain. As the cortex has grown larger, it has assumed many tasks originally performed by the brain stem. For example, if you cut away the section of the cerebral cortex associated with vision in a rat, the rat can still see, although it will be unable to distinguish patterns. Do the same to a man, and he will become blind. The midbrain of the rat performs basic visual functions, but in humans these functions have been passed on to the more developed cerebral cortex.

In humans, the cerebral cortex is the place where sensory impulses concerning sight, sound, taste, smell, and touch are interpreted. It is the site of thought, intelligence, and memory. Portions of the cerebral cortex integrate the sensory and motor systems, acting as a sort of final switchboard between what comes in and what goes out.

Two prominent grooves, or *fissures*, run through the cerebral cortex: the *central sulcus* passes through the top of the cortex, and the *fissure of Silvius* runs from the bottom toward the top at an oblique angle. Using these fissures as reference points, the cerebral cortex can be divided into regions, or *lobes*. (See Figure 2.7.) Ahead of the central sulcus is the *frontal lobe*, which is believed to be the seat of personality and to be concerned with some aspects of speech. Behind the central sulcus lie the *parietal* and *occipital* lobes. The parietal lobe is involved in the skin senses and in the sense of bodily position. The occipital lobe is the site of the visual cortex and may also be involved in memory. Beneath the fissure of Silvius lies the *temporal lobe*, which contains the hearing area, centers for speech, and possibly sites for memory and learning.

A narrow band of cortex at the rear of the frontal lobe controls the motor responses of the whole body. Just across the

---

THE CEREBELLUM STEERS THE SHIP

"The kind of work done in the cerebellum is made painfully clear when it is damaged. The patient may suffer from ataxia, a loss of control of movements. In a typical case, he will reach out to take another person's hand but swing his own hand wildly around it. It is a succession of errors closely similar to those of an inexpert helmsman who cannot hold the ship on course but swings her from port to starboard and back again; the essence of helmsmanship is to start checking the ship's swing *before* her head has come back on course, otherwise she will swing past it. In terms of movement in the human limbs, good control requires an orchestrated stream of signals to many muscles, telling each of them to pull or relax at just the right moment. In well-practiced, purposeful movements, and in the 'instinctive' movements which help us to retain our balance, we rely primarily on the cerebellum for such control." [Calder, 1970, page 148]

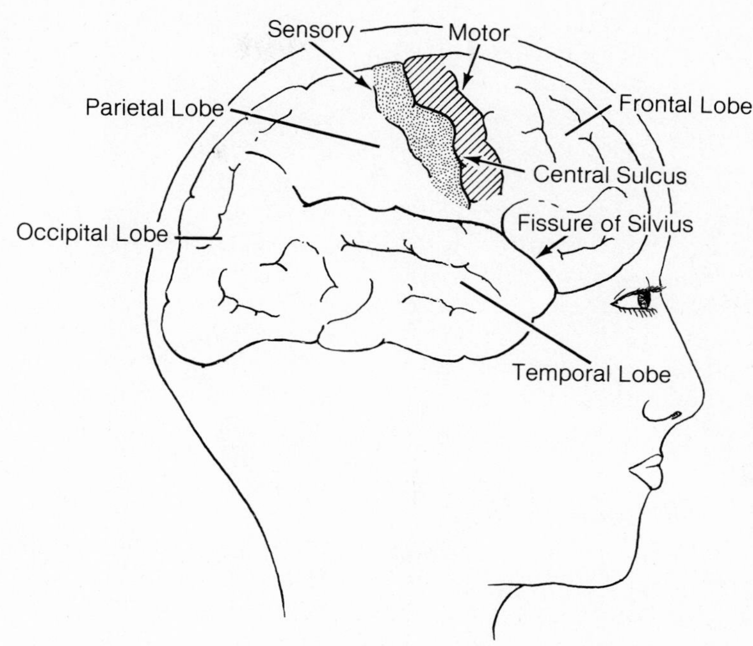

FIG. 2 · 7 The *cerebral cortex* is responsible for sensation, body movement, speech, memory, and other higher mental functions. The functions of the sensory and motor areas (shaded portions of the illustration) are shown in detail in Figure 2 · 8.

central sulcus into the parietal lobe is another strip of cortex, which controls the sensory responses of the whole body. The amount of sensory and motor tissue devoted to a particular part of the body is not related to the size of that particular portion of the anatomy; for example, the hands and mouth make up only a small percentage of the volume of the body, but they merit almost half of the motor cortex. (See Figure 2.8.)

PHINEAS P. GAGE

In 1868, the foreman of a road gang, Phineas P. Gage, was in a dynamite accident. The explosion rammed a four-foot long, one-inch thick crowbar through his jaw, up through the frontal lobe of his brain, and out the top of his head. Gage survived the accident, but there was a marked change in his personality. He became like a child. He had fits of temper when he didn't get his way, made elaborate plans and then changed his mind suddenly, and swore a blue streak at any time or place. Gage's experience illustrates that to a large extent the frontal lobes are responsible for what we call social control and personality.

UNLOCKING THE BRAIN

The brain is a difficult organ to study. It is locked up inside a bony skull and is protected by several layers of membrane and cushioning fluid. In the early days of brain study, the brain was removed after death and sliced into sections for examination, but very little valuable information was gained through this method. Today, a variety of approaches to research on the brain are beginning to unlock some of the secrets of its functioning. To understand these methods it helps to know something of the electrical properties of the brain.

Brain Waves

The presence of electrical current in the brain was discovered in 1875. But it wasn't until 1924 that Hans Berger, a German neurologist, used his ordinary radio equipment to amplify the brain's electrical activity and recorded it on graph paper. The flunctuations of current into the brain appeared on this first *electroen-*

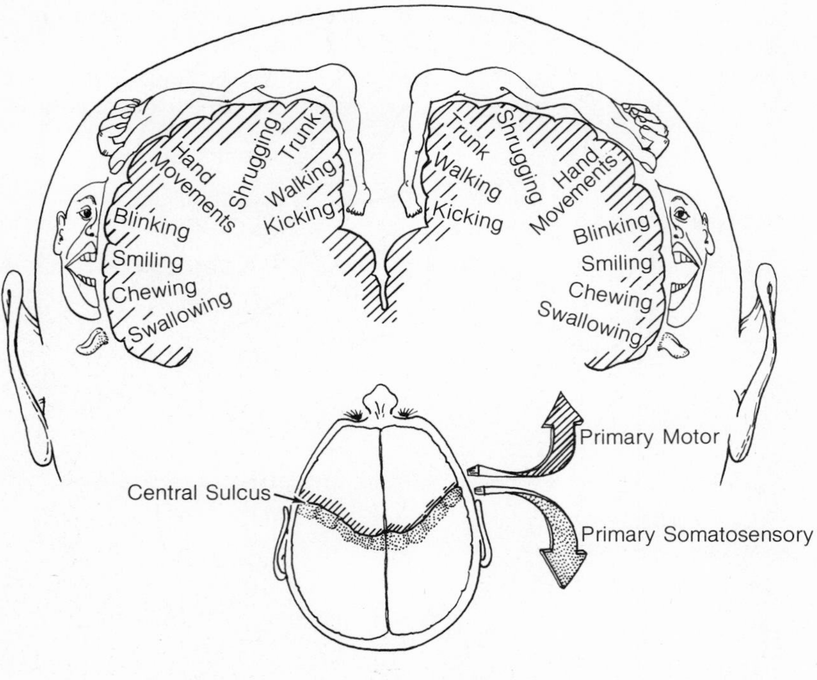

FIG. 2 · 8 Specific areas of the sensory and motor areas of the cerebral cortex are responsible for sensation and movement of different parts of the body.

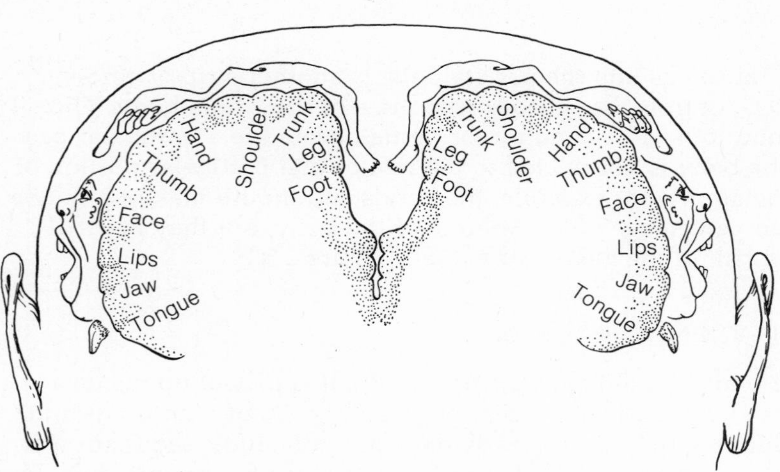

cephalogram (EEG) as a bunch of squiggly lines. On closer examination, however, Berger noted that the fluctuations were regular. They changed in a consistent manner corresponding to the person's state of mind. We now call these rhythmic fluctuations of brain impulses *brain waves.*

Researchers have been able to distinguish four basic brain waves, each with a characteristic pattern that shows up on the EEG. These are alpha, beta, theta, and delta waves. Although none of these waves is ever emitted exclusively by the brain at any one time, one wave may be more pronounced than the others, depending on the individual's state of mind. By attaching electrodes

BRAIN WAVES

To try to determine the emotional state associated with different brain waves, Barbara Brown devised an experiment in which she used lights of three colors to represent three different kinds of brain waves. Whenever a subject was producing alpha waves, for example, a blue light would shine. Brown then asked 26 subjects to write down their feelings as they observed each color. She found that most of the subjects described their experience during the alpha state as pleasant and tranquil, while in the beta state many of the subjects reported feelings of worry, anger, fear, and excitement. In the more mysterious and rarer theta state, only a few of the people could identify definite feelings, although eight subjects indicated that their minds were involved in some sort of problem solving process (Pines, 1973). The fourth type of brain wave, delta, was not tested, being characteristic of deep sleep or the infant mind.

from an EEG machine to the skull of a patient, doctors are able to tell whether an individual's brain waves indicate brain tumors or epilepsy, and psychologists can use EEG readings to learn about dreams, sleeping, and different types of consciousness (see Chapter 4).

Box 1

Biofeedback

There has been an enormous interest in recent years in the phenomenon of *biofeedback*—the use of electronic devices to amplify various physiological measures so that the individual can monitor and perhaps alter certain aspects of bodily functioning. For example, biofeedback is used in monitoring brain waves, heartbeat, blood pressure, and muscle contractions. In many biofeedback experiments, subjects are asked to try to consciously alter the aspect being measured—to try to lower blood pressure, for example.

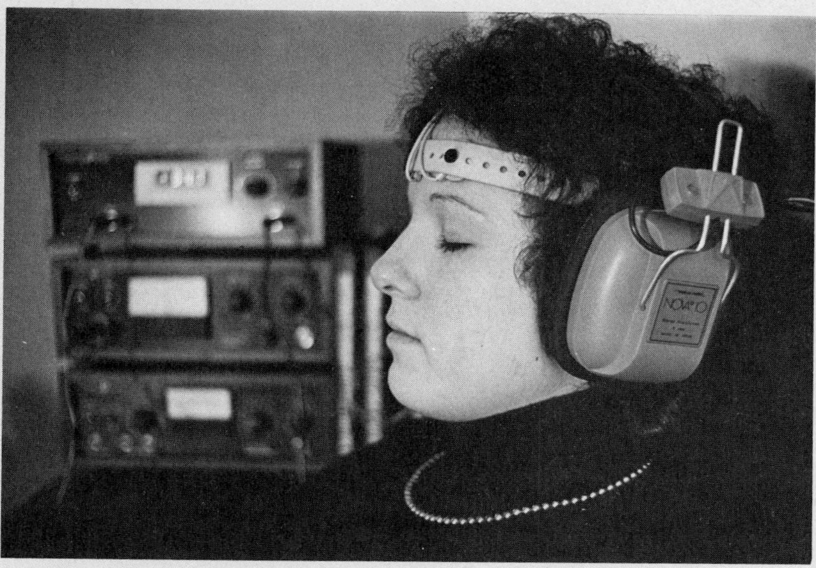

Some of the most interesting studies with biofeedback have involved efforts to control brain waves. Electrodes are attached to the subject's skull, and changes in the brain are indicated by signals in the instruments (such as a sound or a light). The signals allow the individual to identify internal changes and perhaps learn to control them. Just as you learn to ride a bicycle by feeling your body move and correcting your movements to keep balance, so people in these experiments learn to relax and alter their brain waves by getting feedback from an EEG machine (Luce and Peper, 1971). Using EEG readings to guide them, biofeedback experimenters are trying to learn to manipulate the brain from states of high alertness to states of rest.

In this way, people can learn to sit with their eyes closed and "will" certain brain-wave patterns to occur. The alpha rhythm in particular has stirred a great deal of interest since subjects report they are relaxed and feel like they are floating on air when the alpha rhythm appears. Subjects have reported that it is as if a force were flowing through them or they have a "lonely, serene feeling of being in harmony with the universe" (Hoover, 1972). Other subjects reported a state of "alert tranquillity and calm," closely resembling that described by practicers of Zen and Yoga meditation. In fact, masters in Zen and Yoga learn control of their alpha waves far more rapidly than the average person. People who have practiced meditation for six months to a year all show the same EEG characteristics: high alpha while meditating, low alpha when not (Kamiya, 1968).

It has been suggested that conscious production of alpha waves may one day increase people's creativity and lead them to ways of controlling internal states of mind. Some of the more enthusiastic advocates of biofeedback think that it is a greater invention than the wheel and that it may open the door to the secrets of inner space or be the next step in human evolution (Rorvik, 1970). The implications of biofeedback have yet to be fully explored, but it opens a new area for research and raises an interesting question: Can those aspects of our functioning that we've always considered to be beyond our control now come within the realm of conscious regulation?

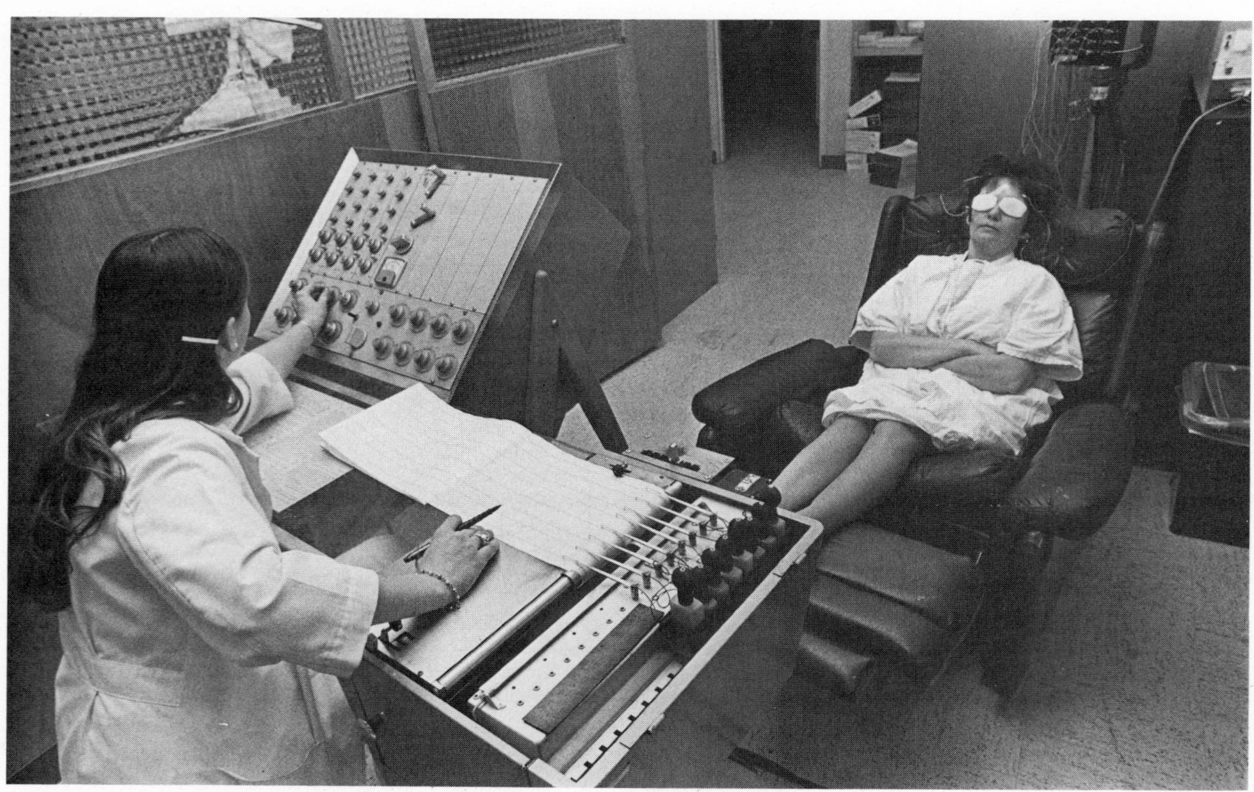

Box 2
Remote Control of the Brain

Would you stand in a bullring without cape or sword while an enraged bull charged at you? You might if you were José Delgado and if you had a radio transmitter with which to send a "stop" message to the bull through electrodes implanted in its brain. Although it may sound a bit like science fiction, Delgado has demonstrated that electrical stimulation of the brain can be done by remote control and can be used to direct an animal's behavior.

Delgado's method of electrical brain stimulation (ESB) involves drilling a small hole in the skull of an animal, introducing fine insulated electrode wires into precise, preplanned locations in the brain, and connecting the wires to sockets anchored in the skull. Some of the chimpanzees Delgado first used as subjects have had up to 100 electrodes implanted for more than four years. Each wire is attached to a generator capable of transmitting minute electrical impulses to the brain. Depending on the placement of the electrodes, a chimp can be made to open or shuts its eyes, turn its head, hop, yawn, sneeze, stick out its tongue, or flex its limbs, merely at the flick of a switch.

Not all ESB reactions are as simple as these. One of Delgado's monkeys, when stimulated, would stop what she was doing, change expression, turn her head to the right, stand up on two feet and circle to the right, climb a pole and descend, and growl and attack another monkey. Through the course of 20,000 stimulations, the monkey repeated this behavior in the same order every time.

Delgado developed the "stimoceiver," a one-ounce transmitter-receiver able to stimulate the brain by remote radio command and record the electrical activity of the brain. The bullring escapade was the most dramatic of Delgado's remote-control demonstrations. In another experiment, one monkey in a colony learned to activate the radio stimulator to inhibit the aggressiveness of the mean-tempered boss-monkey of the group.

ESB and the stimoceiver

Electrical Stimulation of the Brain

Scientists have developed devices called microelectrodes, which are very tiny wires that can be implanted in the brain. These devices record the electrical activity of a single neuron, which allows researchers to track an impulse from neuron to neuron in response to a specific stimulus. In addition to recording impulses with such electrodes, researchers can *stimulate* individual neurons or small areas of the brain. Through such stimulation scientists can discover the functions of very specific brain areas. Work with human patients during brain surgery and on experimental animals with permanently implanted electrodes has made possible "mapping" sensory and motor activity of the brain.

Electrical stimulation of the brain (ESB) is a technique in which scientists apply electricity to portions of the brain in order to learn about brain functioning. As early as 1870 Fritsch and Hitzig discovered that when a certain area of the exposed brain was touched with an electrode an involuntary response occurred. For example, when the motor area was touched, there was movement in the subject's arms, legs, or trunk.

More recently, neurosurgeon Wilder Penfield (1959) discovered that memory can be stimulated in this way, too. By touching an electrode to a specific portion of the brain during brain surgery, Penfield caused a patient to relive—as if in a movie or a dream—a part of his past life: a childhood birthday party, an exciting trip, or some other major incident. As long as the electrode was in place, the patient continued to relive the incident as

---

may be good for more than entertaining demonstrations. For example, people suffering from constant and incurable pain, perhaps the result of back injuries or cancer, are now walking around with tiny pain-killing radio receivers implanted in their chests. When the patient switches on this device, it feeds a signal into his or her spinal cord. The signal seems to raise the pain threshold by canceling out pain impulses in the spinal cord before they reach the brain. In most cases, this relieves the pain for as long as the signal remains on. The pain-blocking effect is not great enough to prevent the person from feeling any pain, but it blocks the dull pain that can linger for hours.

Delgado's experiments also suggest that unwanted patterns of brain activity—those associated with epilepsy, for example—might be recognized by a computer-at-a-distance and might be inhibited before reaching the critical phase that produces an epileptic seizure. The epileptic could have a cerebral pacemaker installed that would work something like a brain-wave thermostat. When brain activity of a preseizure sort begins to appear, the signals could be flashed to a preprogrammed computer that would react instantly, by radio, to stimulate those areas of the brain that would counteract and forestall the seizure. Epilepsy as well as other disorders triggered by brain activity might then be brought under control without drugs or conscious awareness on the part of the patient.

ESB might also be used to alter life-long patterns of behavior, such as anxiety, fear, and violence, by stimulation of precisely selected parts of the brain. ESB might prove to be an efficient and easy procedure for assuring socially acceptable behavior, but people are understandably uneasy about other people controlling their minds. For most of us, walking through life with electrodes implanted in our brain may be a bit repulsive. But Delgado sees it differently. As he puts it, "We now have the capacity to plan our future destiny . . . to direct our own evolution" (Restak, 1975, page 25).

if it were stored on videotape inside the brain. When the electrode was removed, the "movie" stopped. If Penfield was able to penetrate the exact same spot again, the movie continued where it had left off.

Because the nervous system is chemical as well as electrical in nature, parts of the brain can also be stimulated with certain chemicals in order to see how the organism reacts. For example, applying certain hormones to a spot in a rat's brain can cause the rat to feel very thirsty or very hungry.

Brain Damage

Because of accidents, strokes, tumors, or similar injuries to the brain, certain brain areas may become destroyed or inactivated. Gardner (1975) considers brain-damaged individuals to constitute "a unique experiment in nature" because such damage is selective—rather than affecting overall functioning, brain damage results in the loss or impairment of very specific functions. Psychologists can study brain-damaged individuals in order to see how the injury or illness has altered their functioning. Through such research, scientists have received insights into such mental activities as reading, writing, speaking, drawing, working mathematical problems, and making music. (In Chapter 6 we will examine the links between certain sorts of brain damage and memory loss.)

Brain Surgery

Brain surgery is occasionally resorted to for dealing with severe mental illness as well as for such brain diseases as epilepsy and tumors. In such surgery parts of the brain may be removed or severed. By observing people who have undergone such surgery, researchers have been able to determine some of the effects of tampering with specific parts of the brain and to see the behavioral effects of the surgery. For example, some fascinating things have been learned about the brain as a result of a special operation known as split-brain surgery (see the Psychological Issue that follows this chapter). Such brain surgery is highly controversial, especially when used for psychiatric purposes (see Chapter 17). More commonly, scientists perform brain surgery on rats and other animals in order to study brain function.

EFFECTS OF EXPERIENCE ON THE BRAIN

Scientists have long thought that whatever we learn or remember must somehow be reflected in changes in the brain—perhaps physical changes, perhaps chemical changes. Until recently, however, they did not have the tools to detect such changes.

Perhaps the earliest scientist who tried to show that the brain changes as a result of experience was an Italian anatomist named Michele Gaetano Malacarne. Back in the 1780s Malacarne

DAMAGING STROKES

By far the most common injury to the adult brain is the cerebral vascular accident, or *stroke.* In the United States each year, approximately 300,000 people suffer strokes when the blood vessels leading to their brains are blocked by fat deposits, or when a clot forms in an artery, or when an artery bursts. These blockages deprive the brain of oxygen and glucose and lead to damage or destruction of brain tissue. And once brain tissue is destroyed, it cannot be regenerated. The result is a loss of those functions controlled by the portions of the brain that are destroyed. Sometimes the stroke victim's sensory capacities are impaired, sometimes the ability to move certain parts of the body, and sometimes the ability to speak or to understand language (Gardner, 1975).

raised several pairs of animals—dogs, parrots, goldfinches, and blackbirds—with each pair being from the same litter or clutch of eggs. In each pair he trained one member and left the other untrained. After a while, Malacarne killed the animals and examined their brains. He found that the trained animals had more folds in the cerebellum than did the untrained ones.

In the 1870s, the French physician Paul Broca measured the heads of medical students and of male nurses and found that the medical students had larger heads. He concluded that the difference was the result of the extra training the medical students had received. Other scientists pointed out, however, that skull size bears no relation to brain size, and they found other problems with Broca's conclusions as well. Fifty years passed before scientists seriously addressed the question again.

In the early 1950s, Mark Rosenzweig and his coworkers conducted experiments with rats that demonstrated definite brain changes as a result of experience (Rosenzweig, Bennett, and Diamond, 1972). These researchers began by taking three males from each of about a dozen litters of rats. Of each group, one rat

Box 3

Nutrition and the Brain: You Are What You Eat

Everyone knows that nutrition can affect physical development and resistance to disease, but few stop to consider its potential effects on psychological development and behavior: how we think, feel, and act. The brain and nervous system are parts of the body just like the muscles and bones, and their demands for nutrition are stronger than those of any other part of the body.

Recent research illustrates the devastating effects of malnutrition on brain development (Lewin, 1975). One effect of malnutrition is to reduce the number of brain cells in the cerebellum, the portion of the brain responsible for fine motor control and coordination. Another effect is on the quality of nerve cells: Axons in malnourished animals shrink in diameter in many parts of the brain. Finally, malnutrition has an enormous impact on the connections (synapses) between nerves in the brain. Researchers have found reductions of up to 40 percent in the cortexes of undernourished animals. Malnutrition may well have similar effects on humans. It is not surprising, then, that tests on undernourished children show them to be retarded in many physical and intellectual skills.

Malnutrition can have subtler effects on behavior. For example, pellagra (a deficiency of niacin, one of the B vitamins) produces symptoms resembling schizophrenia. The unexplained successes of orthomolecular (megavitamin) therapy in the treatment of certain psychiatric disorders suggests that some mental illnesses may have a nutritional base (Ross, 1974).

Researchers have pinpointed the mechanisms for some very intricate nutritional effects. Fernstrom and Wurtman (1974) have shown that synthesis of the transmitter substance serotonin is directly affected by the body's production of insulin. In turn, production of insulin is affected by consumption of carbohydrates (sugars and starches). Levels of serotonin in the brain seem to affect motor activity, food consumption, hormone secretion, and other important processes and functions.

Some effects of malnutrition may also be mediated by reduced activity. If a person is too weak to move around, variations in experience are reduced. As Rosenzweig and his associates (1972) learned in their studies with rats, variations in experience enhance many aspects of brain development. Thus, the inactive malnourished individual is twice handicapped. However, current research suggests that some of the effects of malnutrition may be offset by programs of environmental stimulation, in which the animal is provided with more varied experiences.

was placed in a standard laboratory cage with some other rats, the second rat was placed in an "enriched" environment, and the third rat was put in an "impoverished" environment. The enriched environment consisted of a large cage in which several rats were able to interact with each other and to play with a variety of toys that were changed daily. In the impoverished condition a rat was confined alone in a cage. At the end of the experimental period (from a few days to several months), the researchers killed the three littermates and examined their brains. They found several key changes in the brains of the rats that had lived in the enriched environment: greater weight and thickness of the cortex, greater total activity of certain transmitter substances, more glial cells, and larger cell bodies and nuclei. The greatest differences were found in the occipital lobe, which is primarily related to vision.

The experimenters consistently found that the enriched rats had brains in which the weight of the cortex had increased in relation to the weight of the rest of the brain. This finding is particularly significant, since the cortex is the location of all the

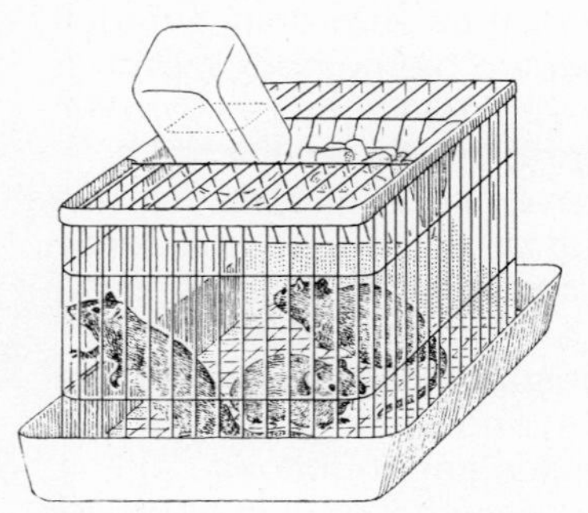

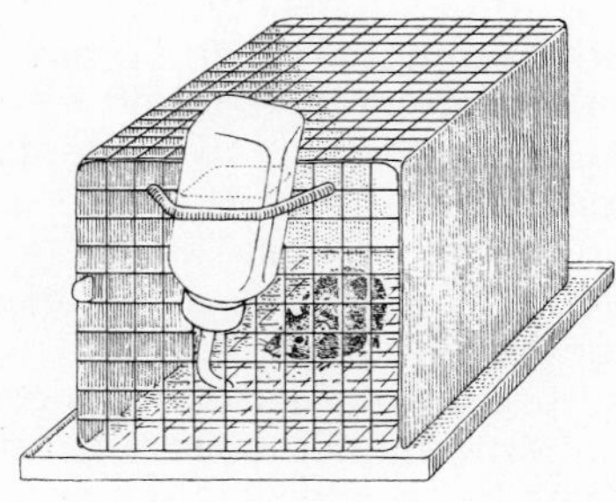

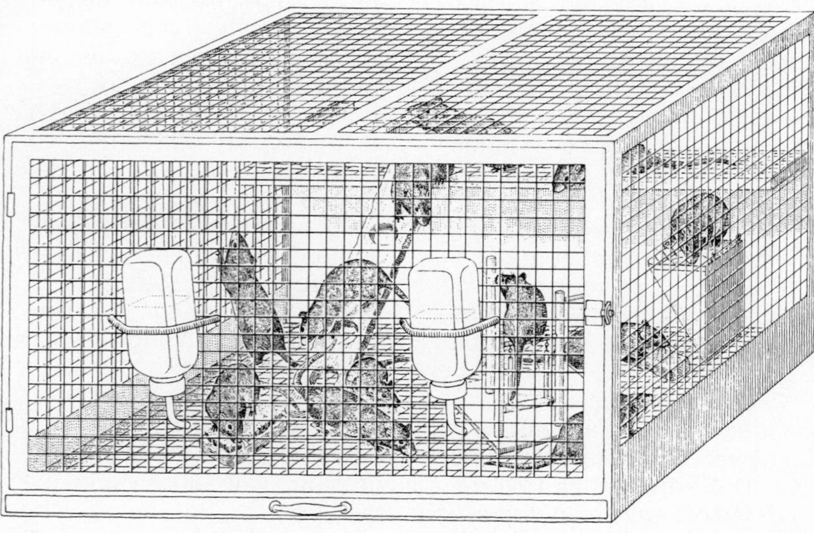

Rosenzweig's experiment showing three environments having different effects on the brain anatomy of rats. Upper left, standard laboratory environment. Upper right, impoverished environment. Center, enriched environment.

brain's higher functions: learning, memory, thinking, and creativity.

Another significant finding was that the enriched rats in at least one study showed 50 percent increase in the size of the synaptic junctions in the brain. As you will recall, the synapse is where messages pass from one neuron to another. Perhaps the larger such "message centers" are, the more information the brain can handle. What this experiment seems to imply is that experience with varied objects in the environment allows rats to handle even more information.

Does this experiment tell us anything about the human brain? Obviously, the same sort of experiments cannot be done on human beings. But the more we learn about how other animals' brains work, the more clues we will have about the functioning of our own brains. These kinds of experiments could have important implications for research into human learning, memory, intellectual development, mental retardation, and senility.

The experiments by Rosenzweig and his associates also raise some interesting questions. One such question is whether it would be possible to bring about greater development of a specific brain region by exposing it to a great deal of stimulation. For example, could listening to or playing a great deal of music enhance the development of the auditory cortex? Another question deals with the "critical periods" of brain development. How early in life must experience be obtained for it to have an effect on brain development?

SUMMARY

1. The basic unit of the nervous system is the *neuron,* a cell specialized for the transmission of impulses through the body. Nerve impulses in the neuron move from the *dendrites,* through the *cell body,* and along the *axon* to another neuron or to a muscle or gland.
2. *Axonal transmission* of impulses along the surface of a neuron is an electrical process. First the neuronal membrane becomes *depolarized*—it temporarily loses its selective permeability, and positively charged sodium ions pour into the usually negatively charged cell, causing the cell to briefly be positively charged. Positively charged potassium ions then flow out of the cell, returning the cell to its negative, or *polarized,* state. Finally, the original balance of potassium and sodium ions inside and outside the cell is restored by the *ion pump.*
3. *Synaptic transmission* of impulses between neurons is a chemical process. An impulse traveling along an axon reaches the *axon terminal,* causing a *transmitter substance* to be released from the *synaptic vesicles.* This substance crosses the gap, or *synapse,* to the next neuron.

4. The *all-or-none principle* refers to the fact that neurons will fire only if the impulse they pick up is of a certain minimum intensity. The neuron will fire at its maximum intensity as long as this minimum level is reached.
5. Some nerve cells are insulated by a *myelin sheath* that tends to speed up transmission of impulses through these cells.
6. The human nervous system consists of the *central nervous system* (brain and spinal cord) and the *peripheral nervous system.* The peripheral system contains two kinds of nerves. *Afferent,* or *sensory,* neurons collect messages from *receptors* and transmit the messages to the central nervous system. *Efferent,* or *motor,* neurons carry messages to the *effectors*—muscles and glands.
7. The peripheral nervous system is made up of two subsystems: the *somatic,* which controls voluntary body movements, and the *autonomic,* which controls involuntary muscles and glands. The autonomic system is further divided into the *sympathetic* and *parasympathetic* systems, which seem to work in opposition to each other—the first to speed things up, the second to slow things down.
8. The *spinal cord* is made up of bundles of long nerve fibers. The *white matter,* on the outside of the cord, conducts messages to the brain. The *gray matter,* on the inside, is responsible for reflex action.
9. The brain is essentially a bulbous swelling at the end of the spinal cord. It is comprised of three basic structures: the brain stem, the cerebellum, and the cerebral cortex.
10. The *brain stem* contains the *medulla, pons, midbrain, thalamus, hypothalamus,* and *reticular activating system.* The brain stem's functions are the most basic and primitive, relating to control of bodily organs, routing of messages within the brain, and the experiencing of such basic emotions as fear and pleasure.
11. The *cerebellum,* located behind the brain stem, is in charge of balance and coordination.
12. The *cerebral cortex* contains centers for sight, hearing, taste, smell, and touch. It is the site of thought, intelligence, and memory. Two major fissures serve to divide the brain into four functionally separate lobes: the *frontal, parietal, occipital,* and *temporal.* Two narrow strips of cortex along the central sulcus control the sensory and motor responses of the body.
13. The *electroencephalogram* (EEG) is a record of the electrical activity in the brain known as *brain waves.* Researchers have identified four basic patterns of brain waves (alpha, beta, theta, and delta) that appear to be related to different states of mind.
14. Among techniques being used to learn about the functions of specific brain areas are electrical stimulation (ESB),

chemical stimulation, brain surgery, and study of brain-damaged individuals.

15. Studies with rats raised in various environments have shown that those rats raised in enriched conditions experience key changes in their brains. These findings appear to indicate that experience produces definite changes in the brain.

psychological issue

Our Two Brains

Imagine what it would be like to have two brains. . . .

Imagine what it would be like to have two brains, one controlling the left side of your body, the other controlling the right side. Each brain would control one hand and one leg, and each brain would have a separate consciousness. You could think with one brain, daydream with the other; or you might write a paper with one brain while playing the harmonica with the other. Quite literally, your left hand might not know what your right hand is doing.

Actually, this description isn't far from the truth. The brain—or more precisely, the cerebral cortex—is composed of two separate halves, or hemispheres. Each hemisphere is capable of functioning independently of the other, and each hemisphere controls one side of the body.

But the two hemispheres of the cortex are not identical twins. Somehow, during the course of evolution of the human species, the two halves began to specialize. In right-handed people, the left hemisphere has primary control over verbal abilities, such as reading and writing, whereas the right hemisphere has primary control over nonverbal skills, such as grasp of spatial relationships. In left-handers, these functions seem to be more evenly distributed between hemispheres. Generally, the left hemisphere of the brain is involved with activities of the right side of the body, while the right hemisphere is involved with the left side of the body. This may seem strange, but it is due to the fact that most afferent nerve fibers cross over when they reach the brain. As a result, everything touched with the right hand is registered in the left hemisphere, and everything touched with the left hand is registered in the right hemisphere.

How does the left brain know what the right brain is doing? The two hemispheres are connected by the *corpus callosum,* a body of nerve fibers. These fibers form an important communication network, referred to as the "transfer area" because it transfers information received by one half of the brain over to the other half. Through these fibers, the two hemispheres let each other know what they are up to.

Box I-1

Doing Two Things at Once

"Ask a friend to balance a wooden dowel on the index finger of each hand, one hand at a time. Generally, the preferred hand is more adept at this balancing. Ask the person then to speak while balancing this dowel, and time the length of the balancing. In [the original] experiment, the balancing time of the right hand decreased, as would be expected, since the addition of a task interferes with performance in most situations. But the balancing time of the left hand *increased* with concurrent verbalization.

". . . When the left hemisphere is engaged in speech, its control of the right hand suffers. While the left hand is balancing, the left hemisphere may still intrude on its performance. When the left hemisphere is occupied in speech, it no longer seems to interfere with the left hand and the balancing time of the left improves." [Ornstein, 1972, page 62]

The Split Brain

In an early experiment with cats, researchers cut the corpus callosum and also the optic chiasm, the place where visual information crosses to reach the opposite side of the brain. Cats that underwent this

Box I-2

It's a Right-Handed World

For the almost 94 percent of us who are right-handed, the left hemisphere is "dominant." Unfortunately for the left-handers among us, we seem to live in a right-handed world. Try playing the violin, cutting with scissors, or opening a refrigerator door with your left hand; you will learn just how right-handed our culture is. A lefty who eats dinner with a right-hander requires extra caution to avoid bruised elbows. Pilots find that most of the aircraft controls are on the right. The same thing is true of TV sets. There are only a few settings, such as professional baseball, in which left-handers seem to get an even break.

operation behaved normally, but now visual information went directly to the same side of the brain as the eye that saw it. Thus, if one eye was covered, all visual information went to only one side of the brain. To prove this, the experimenters put a patch over a cat's left eye and taught the cat to respond in certain ways to seeing a square. When they moved the patch to the right eye, the cat acted as if it had not encountered a square before. Thus, the right brain had learned something, while the left brain was still ignorant.

A number of human patients have also had their hemispheres completely separated. Brain surgeons have cut the corpus callosum of people afflicted with uncontrollable epilepsy in hopes of confining seizures to one hemisphere. The operation has proved to be remarkably successful, producing an almost total elimination of attacks. And the side effects are much less chaotic than you might expect, considering the fact that after this operation people in effect have two separate brains. The operation produces no noticeable change in the patients' temperaments, personalities, or general intelligence. Split-brain patients appear to be so normal that special laboratory experiments were required to reveal the unusual effects of this operation.

Roger Sperry and Michael Gazzaniga devised several experiments to determine how cutting the corpus callosum had affected their patients (Gazzaniga, 1967). At first Sperry and Gazzaniga thought that the right hemisphere in these people was "blind" because when they were shown visual displays they reported only what they saw in the right visual field (the area seen by the right half of each eye). Objects in the right visual field are "seen" by the left hemisphere. Then the researchers realized that only the left hemisphere could "speak"—that is, the speech centers are located in this side of the brain. The right hemisphere saw the display but was unable to say so.

Split-brain patients appear to be so normal that special experiments were required to reveal the unusual effects of this operation.

The experimenters then set up situations in which information would be sent to only one side of the brain. For example, pictures would be flashed in only the right or left visual field, or objects would be placed (out of sight) in the right or left hand. Whenever items were shown or given to the left hemisphere, the person could verbally describe what he or she had seen. But when objects were presented to the right hemisphere, the person was unable to identify them verbally. Instead, the person would guess at what had been shown or would deny that he or she had seen anything. However, if the person was asked to point to or pick up the object that had been shown, the right hemisphere had no problem picking the right one.

For example, some patients were shown the word "heart," with the "he" positioned in the left of the visual field and "art" in the right. When asked to pronounce the word they had seen, the patients would say "art," for that is what the speaking left hemisphere saw. But when the patients were asked to point with their left hand to the word they had seen, they pointed to the word "he," for that is what the right hemisphere (which controls the left hand) saw. (See Figure 2.9.)

The reason that these differences didn't handicap people in normal life was that the hemispheres were able to interact through "cross-cuing." Gazzaniga (1967) described how this happened:

We had a case of such cross-cuing during a series of tests of whether the right hemisphere could respond verbally to simple red or green stimuli. . . . After a few trials, [*the patient's*] *score improved whenever the examiner allowed a second guess. We soon caught on to the strategy the patient used. If a red light was flashed and the patient chanced to guess red, he would stick with the answer. If the flashed light was red and the patient by chance guessed green, he would frown, shake his head and then say, "Oh no, I meant red." What was happening was that the right hemisphere saw the red light and heard the left hemisphere make the guess "green." Knowing that the answer was wrong, the right hemisphere precipitated a frown and a shake of the head, which in turn cued the left hemisphere to the fact that the answer was wrong and that it had better correct itself!*†

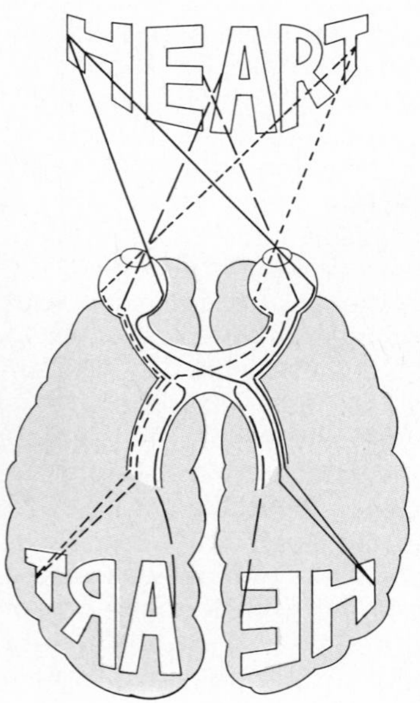

FIG. 2 · 9 The left hemisphere of the brain "sees" material presented to the right visual field ("ART"), and the right hemisphere "sees" material presented to the left visual field ("HE").

The experimenters were also interested in finding out whether the two hemispheres experienced emotions separately. To do so, they showed a series of pictures to a woman patient and then suddenly flashed the photo of a nude woman. If the photo was shown to the left hemisphere, the patient laughed and said she saw a picture of a naked lady. But if the picture was shown to the right hemisphere, the patient said she saw nothing—but smiled and began to chuckle. When the experimenters asked her what was funny, she said, "I don't know . . . nothing . . . oh—that funny machine."

†*From "The Split-Brain in Man," M. S. Gazzaniga,* Scientific American, *August 1967, p. 27. Copyright © 1967 by Scientific American, Inc. All rights reserved.*

In fact, when the right hand failed at solving the problem, the patient's left hand could not restrain itself and corrected the right.

These experiments may make it seem as though the "verbal" left hemisphere is the superior one. However, there are tasks at which the right hemisphere seems more competent, especially when spatial relations and "visual-constructional" tasks are involved. For example, one of Sperry's split-brain subjects was asked to construct a two-dimensional geometric figure using a set of cubes with each face painted a different color. The left hand could perform this task very well; the right hand could not. In fact, when the right hand failed at solving the problem, the patient's left hand could not restrain itself and corrected the right (Ornstein, 1972).

All these experiments converge on the conclusion that split-brain operations produce individuals who have two separate brains, each with special abilities. The implications of this fact are fantastic, for already Gazzaniga has shown that split-brain patients can sometimes carry out two tasks in the same amount of time needed for a normal person to carry out one. It may be possible for people with split brains to handle twice as much information as the rest of us. It is also possible that if the operation is done early enough in life, each of the hemispheres could develop a fuller set of capacities.

Two Forms of Consciousness

Robert Ornstein (1972) has speculated that the differences between the two hemispheres are even more striking than the split-brain experiments seem to imply. He describes the left brain as being more logical and analytical, especially predominant in verbal and mathematical functions, whereas he characterizes the right brain as being more artistic and intuitive, primarily responsible for spatial orientation, crafts, body image, and recognition of faces. Ornstein describes the left hemisphere as performing its functions sequentially and logically, whereas the right hemisphere must integrate many inputs at once to produce a whole movement or action. (See Figure 2.10.)

In ordinary life, these two hemispheres—or these two modes of functioning—seem to alternate with each other. When the brain waves of people engaged in verbal tasks are recorded on the EEG, the left hemisphere shows activity, whereas the right hemisphere is at rest. But when spatial activities are involved, the right hemisphere is more active. As Ornstein (1972) explains it:

> *The two modes of operation* complement *each other, but do not readily substitute for one another. Consider describing a spiral staircase. Most would begin using words and quickly begin to gesture in the air. Or consider attempting to ride a bicycle purely from verbal instruction* [page 63]

People may develop one mode at the expense of the other. We all know someone who is highly logical but lacks coordination and artistic sense, or someone else who is very creative but has poor verbal skills. Much of Western culture seems to focus on the left mode; much of Eastern philosophy makes more of the right mode. Ornstein hopes that eventually people may learn to use *both* modes to their fullest capacity.

Summary

1. The cerebral cortex is composed of two hemispheres, each of which has specialized functions. The left hemisphere has control over verbal abilities, while the right hemisphere controls nonver-

---

Box I-3

Taking Sides

Here is an exercise, suggested by Robert Ornstein (1972), that should help you become more aware of the differences between the two sides of your consciousness. First, close your eyes and try to get in touch with each side of your body. Examine its strengths and weaknesses and the feelings that arise as you explore yourself. Now take each of the following questions in turn and ponder it with your eyes closed, and sense within for the answer:

1. Which side of you is more feminine?
2. Which is more masculine?
3. Which do you consider the "dark" side of yourself?
4. Which side is the "lighter"?
5. Which is more active?
6. Which is more passive?
7. Which side is more logical?
8. Which more "intuitive"?
9. Which side of you is the more mysterious?
10. Which side is the more artistic?

Right-handers are more likely to see the right side of their body as being more masculine, lighter, active, and logical and their left side as more feminine, dark, passive, intuitive, mysterious, and artistic.

Box I-4

Left-Looking and Right-Looking

1. Do you use the word "logical" or "rational" more often?
2. For you, is anger or hate a stronger emotion?
3. On the face of a quarter, does the face of George Washington look to the right or the left?
4. If you were crossing a street from west to east, and a car from the south smashed into you, which leg would be shattered first?

Ask a friend each of the above questions. As your friend answers, watch his or her eyes carefully and make a note of the direction in which they shift (right or left). This initial shift, known as a "lateral eye movement" (LEM), provides us with clues about the nature of the brain and about personality differences between people.

Spontaneous lateral eye movements reflect relative levels of activity in the two hemispheres of the brain. Left movements indicate greater involvement of the right hemisphere; right movements indicate greater involvement of the left hemisphere. When a question produces movements in one direction, we know that the opposite side of the brain is involved in answering it. It is possible to construct all sorts of questions, examine the direction of LEMs in large numbers of subjects, and come to some general conclusions about the functions of the two hemispheres of the brain.

The four questions above were taken from a study by Schwartz, Davidson, and Maer (in press). The first two questions are primarily verbal, whereas the second two are spatial-visual. Similarly, questions 2 and 4 are emotional, while 1 and 3 are nonemotional.

If your friend is like most of the subjects tested by Schwartz, Davidson, and Maer, he or she looked to the left more often than to the right. However, looking to the left was probably a response to the spatial and emotional questions. Looking to the right was most likely associated with the verbal and nonemotional questions. This is because, for right-handed persons, the right hemisphere of the brain is primarily involved in spatial and emotional reasoning, while the left hemisphere is involved in verbal and nonemotional reasoning.

If the person looked to the left on at least three of the questions, he or she is called a "left mover." If the person looked to the right most often, he or she is a "right mover." Left and right movers seem to be different kinds of people. Left movers (who seem to prefer using the right hemisphere of their brains) may be more artistic and aesthetic; they are more readily hypnotized; they tend to be humanities or social science majors; and they seem more emotional. Right movers (who seem to prefer the use of the left hemisphere) may be more analytical and mathematical; they tend to be physical science majors; and they seem more rational.

These differences are only relative. Everyone uses both hemispheres almost incessantly. Nevertheless, a distinct tendency to left movement or right movement may indicate that one is more right-brained or left-brained than most other people.

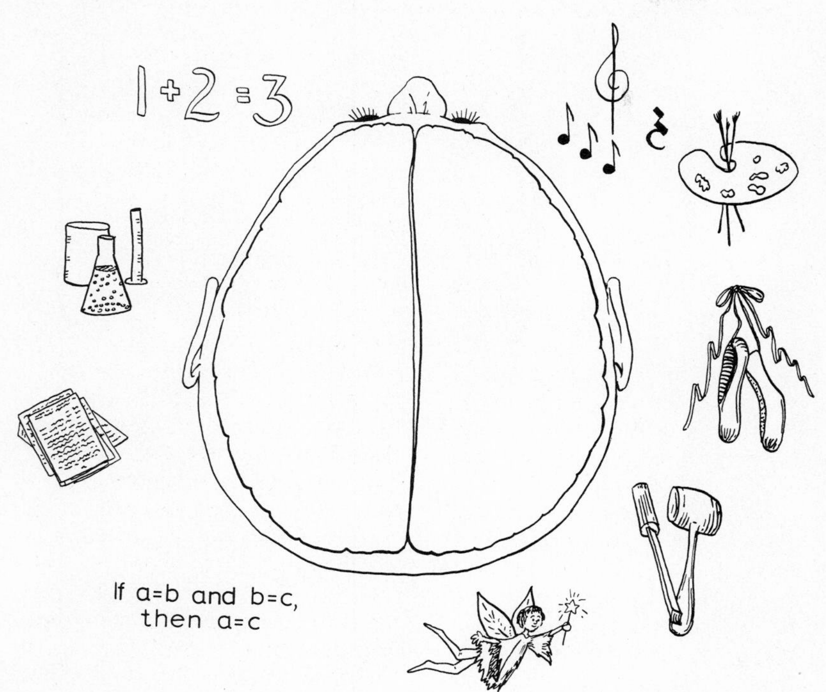

FIG. 2 · 10 The right and left hemispheres of the cerebral cortex tend to specialize in different functions. Ornstein suggests that the left hemisphere is especially concerned with rational, logical activities, while the right hemisphere is especially concerned with intuitive, artistic functions.

bal skills, such as grasp of spatial relations. Information received by the right side of the body is registered in the left hemisphere, and vice versa.

2. The hemispheres are connected by a band of fibers called the corpus callosum. When this band is severed, the individual in effect has two separate brains. In split-brain patients, each half of the brain processes information separately, in its own way. For example, information shown only in the right visual field is experienced by the left hemisphere, while the right hemisphere remains ignorant.

3. In split-brain patients, the left hemisphere can communicate by speaking or writing, whereas the right hemisphere can communicate only by pointing, gesturing, or drawing. The two hemispheres are able to interact through the process of cross-cuing.

4. Ornstein describes the left brain as logical and analytical and the right brain as artistic and intuitive. These two modes alternate with each other in daily activities.

PART 2

Experiencing the World

A central part of being human is our experience of the world. There is more than one world of experience, however. Chapter 3, on *Sensation and Perception,* deals with the ways in which we come to experience the outer physical world, through our eyes, ears, and other sense organs. We will discover that experiencing the outer world is not a passive process, but an active one that is shaped by our own needs and values. What we "see" when we experience the world depends a great deal on what we are looking for. In the Psychological Issue following this chapter we will consider the possibility that there are still other ways of experiencing the outer world that do not rely on our senses. Whether such *Extrasensory Perception* exists is a matter of considerable controversy among psychologists. Because of its far-reaching implications, extrasensory perception is an area in which research methods must come under the closest scrutiny.

In addition to the outer physical world, we also experience an inner world, the world of our own *Consciousness,* to be explored in Chapter 4. We will pay special attention to states of consciousness that differ from our usual waking state—in particular, our experiences when we are asleep and when we are under the influence of drugs. In this connection we will return to the remarkable workings of the brain and the ways in which it regulates our experience. In the Psychological Issue that follows we will look into the psychology of *Meditation,* which has recently gained great popularity as a means of expanding and enriching our inner experience.

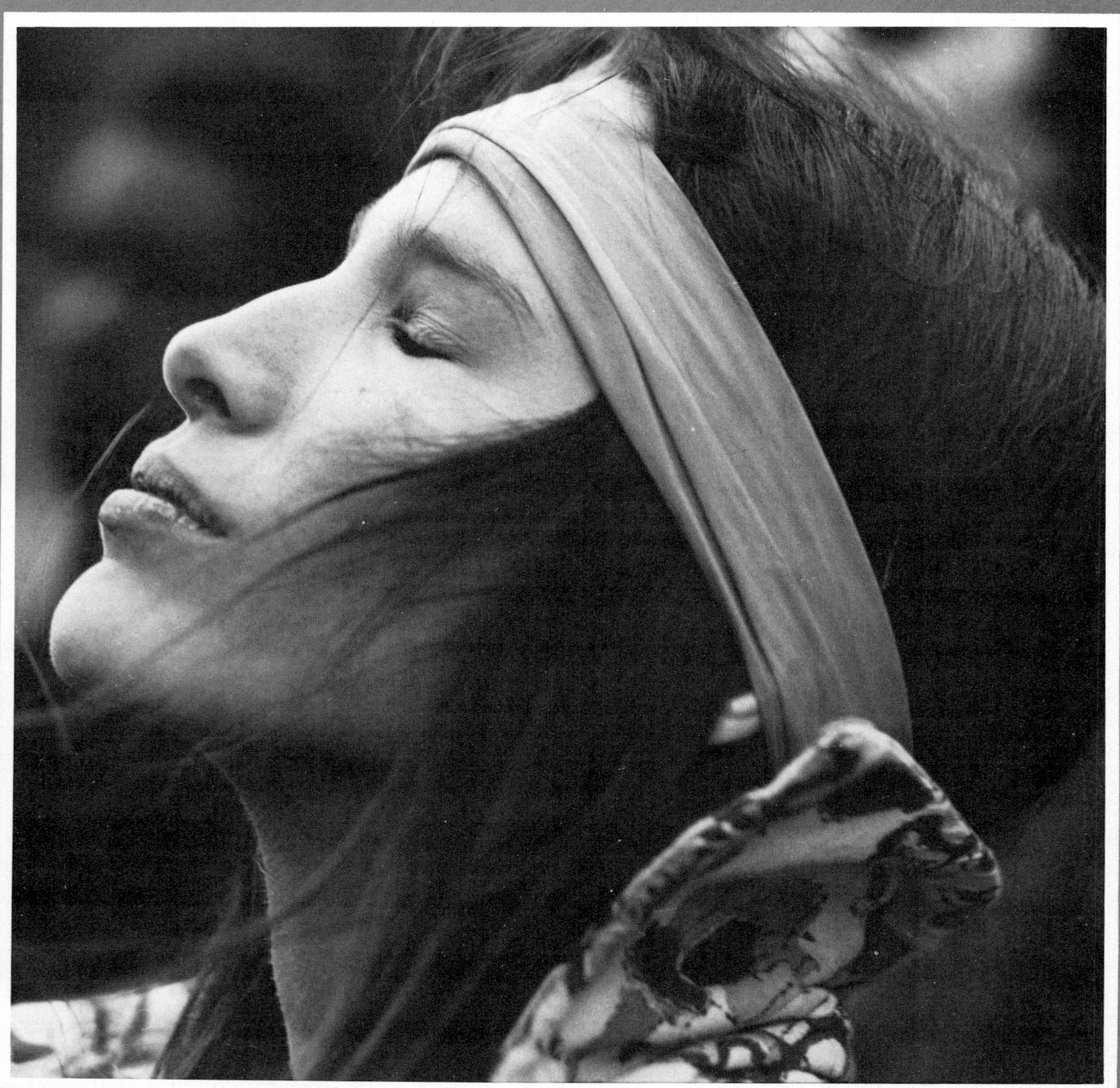

Sensation and Perception

CHAPTER

3

Sensation and Perception

So here we are, each of us with our own brain and nervous system, in a world filled with a dazzling array of objects—houses and sidewalks, plants and dogs, hamburgers and roses, ballpoint pens and computers, not to mention billions of other people. Or at least that's where we think we are. But how do we really know? How does the complex and diverse set of things "out there" get inside our brains so clearly and vividly? Philosophers have grappled such questions throughout the history of civilization. Now, within the past century, these issues have become central ones for psychologists.

Sensation and *perception* are the processes by which people come to experience the stimuli in their environment. Our study of these processes will begin with a discussion of the human *senses,* the organs and neural pathways through which information about our environment is received. Our senses include vision, hearing, the skin senses, smell, and taste. When we say we "sense" something, we are actually experiencing activity in our brain and nervous system. Physical energy (such as light, sound waves, heat) emanating from objects must be transformed by the sense organs into a code that can be transferred to and interpreted by the brain. The first step in this process is the work of the *receptor cells,* which respond to particular forms of energy. These receptors include cells in the retina of the eye that are particularly sensitive to light and structures in the ear that are sensitive to sound waves. The energy is next converted into electrical impulses, which travel from the sense organs along nerve fibers to the central nervous system and eventually to the appropriate area of the cerebral cortex (see Chapter 2). Here in the brain, the information is collated, processed, and interpreted to yield our experienced perceptions. Although the line between the two terms is somewhat arbitrary, *sensation* typically refers to the direct reception and transmission of messages, whereas *perception* refers to the active process of integrating and organizing these sensations.

VISION

About two-thirds of all we know about the outside world comes to us through our eyes. Indeed, vision dominates our life. Vision has played a dominant role for researchers as well: Scientists know more about sight than they do about all the other senses combined. For these reasons, our discussion of the senses will focus primarily on vision.

The Eye

In many ways the human eye is like a color television camera. The eye admits light through a small hole and passes it through a lens that focuses an image on a photosensitive surface. In the eye, light first passes through the *cornea,* a transparent protective coating over the front part of the eye. Light next passes through the *pupil,* an opening that can be widened or narrowed to let more or less light in by contractions in the muscles of the *iris,* the colored part of the eye. Light passes through the pupil to the *lens,* which can be adjusted to bring near or far objects into focus. The light is focused through the lens onto the inner lining of the back of the eyeball, the *retina;* there the light stimulates receptor cells that will transmit the information to the brain via the *optic nerve.* (See Figure 3.1.)

More than 6 million cones and 100 million rods are distributed on the retina. (See Figure 3.2.) *Rods* are slim nerve cells; *cones* are thicker, with a cone-shaped tip at one end. Both types of cell contain chemicals that are sensitive to light. When light strikes a rod, it causes the breakdown of a chemical called *rhodopsin* (visual purple). The cones contain different photosensitive chemicals, which break down when struck by other light waves. These processes in the rods and cones trigger activity in the optic nerve and, subsequently, in the brain.

The rods are colorblind and are located mainly at the edges of the retina. The cones are the color receptors and are packed together in the center of the eye. The *fovea,* a depressed spot on the retina directly behind the lens, is packed with millions of cones, but no rods. A few cones are mixed with rods all the way to the outer edges of the retina, but the center of the eye is the most color-sensitive portion.

When you first go into a dark movie theater, you stumble around, barely able to make out the shapes of the people or seats. After you have been in the theater for a while, you are able to see quite well. As you go from bright to dim light, the rods and the cones adapt to the change in illumination. In dim light, the chemicals in the rods and cones are built up faster than they

THE WING OF A BEE

A sensory threshold is the smallest amount of stimulation that can be detected by one's sense organs. Here are some approximate human thresholds (Galanter, 1962):

Vision	A candle flame seen at 30 miles on a dark clear night.
Hearing	The tick of a watch under quiet conditions at 20 feet.
Taste	One teaspoon of sugar in two gallons of water.
Smell	One drop of perfume diffused into a three-room apartment.
Touch	The wing of a bee falling on your cheek from a distance of about half an inch.

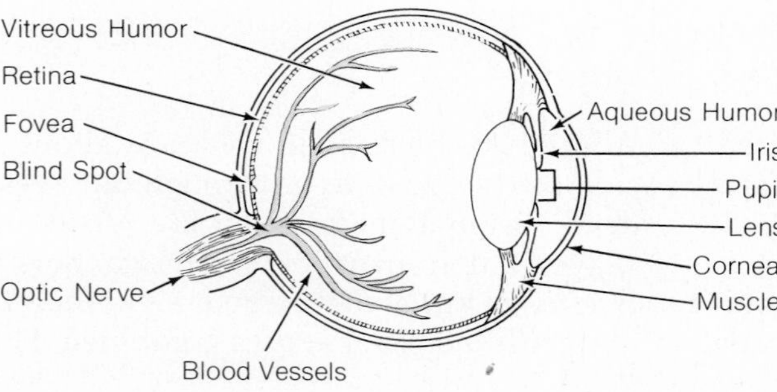

FIG. 3 · 1 Cross-section of the eye.

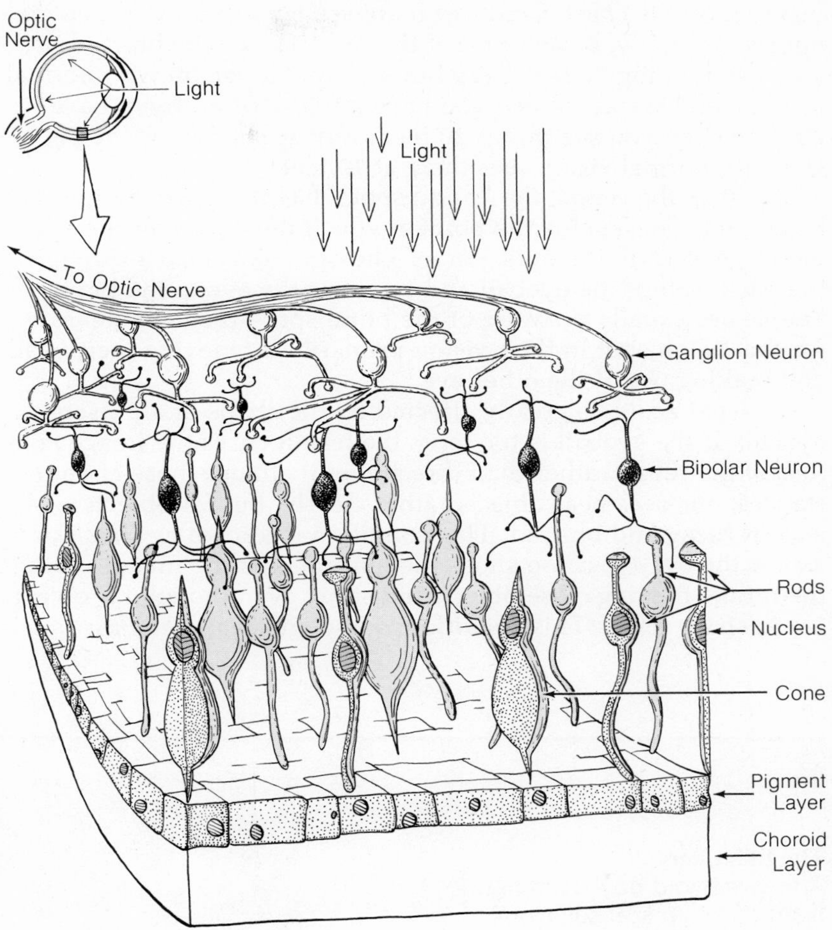

FIG. 3 · 2 A magnified, three-dimensional illustration of a portion of the retina.

are broken down by light stimulation. The greater the concentration of these chemicals, the lower the *visual threshold* (the smallest amount of stimulation the rods and cones will respond to). Thus, adaptation to darkness is a matter of building up a surplus of rhodopsin in the rods and of other chemicals in the cones.

The cones adapt quickly in the dark (10 minutes or so), but the rods adapt slowly and continue to adapt even after 30 minutes or more of darkness. When completely adapted, the rods are much more sensitive to light than the cones. Thus, if you want to see a dim light in pitch darkness, do not look directly at it, since the center of the eye contains only the less sensitive cones. If you look away from the object, the image will fall on the edge of the retina, where the rods are. You will be much more likely to see the dim light in this manner.

Visual Acuity

Visual acuity is the ability to discriminate the details in the field of vision. One way this ability can be measured is by using the familiar eye chart. Standard perfect vision is often called 20/20 vision. If you stand 20 feet from a standard eye chart and see the material on the chart clearly, you are seeing normally. If you do not see normally, some or all of the material will be blurred. If you are standing 20 feet away but see what a person with normal vision could see at 50 feet, you have 20/50 vision. If you have 20/10 vision, you see things 20 feet away as sharply as the person with normal vision sees them at 10 feet.

Part of the retina, the "blind spot," has no visual acuity. (See Figure 3.3) This spot is the point at which the nerves of the eye converge to form the optic nerve. The optic nerve exits through the back wall of the eyeball and connects the eye to the brain. People are usually unaware of the blind spot—they compensate for this blank spot in their vision primarily by moving their head and making use of the other eye.

Visual acuity is greatly affected by the shape of a person's eyeball. If the eyeball is too long, the lens focuses the image *in front of* the retina rather than directly on it. Under these circumstances, one sees near objects rather clearly, but far objects appear fuzzy and blurred. This condition is known as *nearsightedness.* If the eyeball is too short, the lens focuses the image *behind* the retina, making close objects indistinct even though far objects are in sharp focus. This condition is known as *farsightedness.*

Box 1

The Eidetikers

A ten-year-old boy is sitting in front of a blank easel, from which a picture (from *Alice in Wonderland*) he has been looking at has just been removed.

Experimenter: Do you see something there?

Subject: I see the tree, gray tree with three limbs. I see the cat with stripes around its tail.

Experimenter: Can you count those stripes?

Subject: Yes (pause). *There's about 16 . . . .*

Experimenter: What is the cat doing with its paws?

Subject: Well, one of them he's holding out and the other one is on the tree.

Experimenter: What color is the sky?

Subject: Can't tell.

FIG. 3 · 3 Close your right eye and look at the magician. Move the page closer or further away until the rabbit disappears and the wand appears unbroken. It's not really magic—the images of the rabbit and of the break in the wand are now falling on your blind spot, where the optic nerve connects to the eye and there is no retina.

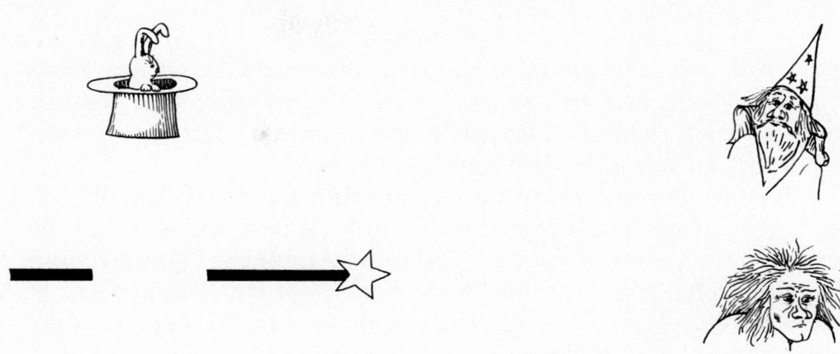

As people grow older, their lenses gradually become brittle and cannot focus as readily on near objects. This condition is called *presbyopia.* Since we all become more farsighted as we grow older, nearsighted individuals may actually find their vision improving somewhat with age. Farsighted people fare less well. Their vision not only deteriorates with age, but they also are subject to severe headaches, resulting from eyestrain.

Experimenter: Can't tell at all?

Subject: No. I can see the yellowish ground, though . . . . (The subject looks away from the easel and back again.)

Experimenter: Is the image gone?

Subject: Yes, except for the tree.

Experimenter: Tell me when it goes away.

Subject: (pause) *It went away.*

(from Haber, 1969)†

The boy is being tested for his ability to see, or at least to report that he sees, sharp visual images that persist for many seconds or even minutes after the source of the images has been removed. Some people, like this boy, claim that the image is projected in space in front of their eyes, almost as if the original were still there. Such images have been called *eidetic,* from the Greek *eidētikos* (which means "pertaining to image"). People who are thought to have this ability, sometimes labeled "photographic memory," are called *eidetikers,* and they are almost always children.

Several hundred studies have been published about eidetic imagery, but there is still some question as to whether the phenomenon exists at all. Stromeyer (1970) studied an adult eidetiker named Elizabeth, who could, among other things, often bring back an eidetic image several days after the original was first presented to her. Even more striking, she could mentally superimpose two meaningless patterns of dots that she had been shown to see a meaningful composite picture. This test helped to rule out the possibility that Elizabeth simply had an unusually good memory.

But Elizabeth remains a unique case in the annals of research on eidetic imagery. A recent review of the research has come to the skeptical conclusion that eidetic imagery is not basically different from visual memory (Gray and Gummerman, 1975). According to this view, the picture is not really seen "out there," even though children, with the help of subtle suggestions from eager psychologists, may sometimes claim that it is. In addition, very few, if any, eidetikers are accurate enough to justify calling the phenomenon "photographic memory." Many people who do not claim to see things "out there" can describe pictures they saw more accurately than eidetikers can.

†*From "Eidetic Images," Ralph Norman Haber,* Scientific American, *April 1969, p. 39.*

Color Vision

We cannot see ultraviolet rays, x-ray, radio and television waves, or radar waves. But we can see the *spectrum* of color that occurs when we pass sunlight through a prism, where light is converted into bands of red, green, yellow, and blue.

Any color can be created by combining three different colored lights in different proportions (mixing light is shown in the endpapers). A similar process apparently underlies color vision. We don't have separate receptors for each of the hundreds of colors we perceive. Instead, we have three types of cones—one sensitive to red, one to green, and one to blue. Each cone contains a single type of photosensitive pigment and, in combination, their stimulation gives us the experience of color. Just how the messages from the three types of cones combine in the brain remains a subject of some controversy. It does *not* appear that the three messages simply add together to produce a new color sensation as in the case of light mixtures.

About 7 percent of the people in the world cannot see one or more colors (Haber and Fried, 1975). Most of these partially colorblind people are men, since color blindness is an inherited, sex-linked characteristic. The most common type of color blindness is *dichromatic*: Color vision is normal in two of the three primary colors but deficient in the third because one of the three types of cones is deficient or missing. In one type of dichromatic color blindness—red-green deficiency—the person sees the world almost entirely in blues and yellows. A red fire engine appears dull yellow, and grass is blue. The person with yellow-blue color blindness, in contrast, sees a world of reds and greens. Red-green color blindness is by far the most common, and blue-yellow is the least common (Haber and Fried, 1975).

People with *achromatic* color blindness see nothing but black, white, and shades of gray, because they have no cone cells. We all have some experience of a world without color—we've seen lots of movies and TV shows in black and white. But it is not easy to understand what it means to be truly colorblind. If you look at the pictures in the endpapers, you begin to get some idea of what it is like to experience the world without a full range of colors.

Although colorblind people may miss out on one sort of experience that other people have, they can still function quite well without color cues—so much so that some people don't even know they're colorblind. For example, it's not hard for a red-green colorblind person to know whether a traffic light is green or red, since the red light is always at the top and the green light is at the bottom. Colorblind people can also discriminate between different colors because there is usually a perceivable difference in brightness. Special tests have been devised to eliminate such cues when determining whether a person is colorblind. Most commonly these tests consist of buried figures composed of dots of different colors but of equal brightness to surrounding dots. A person who is red-green colorblind, for example, won't

THE ELECTROMAGNETIC WORLD

The world is filled with waves of energy called electromagnetic radiation. Radio and television waves are types of electromagnetic energy. Other types are ultraviolet rays, x-rays, cosmic rays, infrared heat rays, and radar. Some radio waves have wave lengths of 20 miles or more. Cosmic rays have a wave length of approximately one millimicrons of an inch and occupy only a small part of the electromagnetic energy spectrum. Light waves vary from 16 millionths of an inch (the blue end of the spectrum) to 32 millionths of an inch (the red end of the spectrum).

be able to distinguish the red dots from the green ones and won't be able to see the figure (see the endpapers).

Depth Perception

How do we know how close or how far away objects are? How can we tell that objects are three-dimensional just by looking at them, when all that is recorded on the retina is a two-dimensional image? For one thing, objects overlap, which gives us a cue that one is in front of another. Another clue to depth is the size of objects—if one tree is larger than another, we assume that the larger one is closer. And all art students know about perspective—the fact that lines converge when stretched into the distance, such as the lines that form railroad tracks. The patterns of shadowing on and around an object also tell us about its three-dimensionality. All these clues—overlap, relative size, perspective, and shadows—are called *monocular cues* because they work even when we use only one eye.

Seeing depth also depends on the positioning of the two eyes. The right and left eye each gets a slightly different image of the object being looked at. If you cover your right eye and then your left, you will see the object you are focusing on jump from left to right. When both eyes look at an object they see a unified three-dimensional image. Humans are among the many animals who have the benefit of *binocular vision,* in which the two eyes cooperate to give solidity and distance to objects. Binocular cues add to the monocular ones. If you close one eye and survey a scene, you will perceive depth less clearly. And if you squint that one open eye, the scene may begin to look like a two-dimensional canvas rather than a three-dimensional world.

Some of the cues for depth perception, such as the evaluation of the relative sizes of objects, seem to result from experience. Psychologists used to believe, in fact, that learning is necessary for depth perception to occur at all. But studies with the *visual cliff* have provided convincing evidence that at least some depth perception is innate—that the brain seems to be wired to infer depth from the available cues.

Gibson and Walk (1960) devised the original visual cliff apparatus, consisting of a large tabletop with a wide wooden board down the center. On one side of the board was a glass-covered checkerboard pattern. On the other side was a clear sheet of glass, and the same checkerboard pattern was painted on the floor three-and-a-half feet below the table. When viewed from above, the entire tabletop appeared to contain the checkered pattern.

Human infants were then placed on the tabletop and allowed to crawl about. In one experiment only 8 percent of the infants ventured onto the "deep" side even when urged. When babies from six to fourteen months old were placed on the table and encouraged to crawl over the fake cliff, they would not go beyond the perceptual "edge" of the cliff (Gregory, 1966). The

THE SOUND OF BORSCHT

Most of us see with our eyes, hear with our ears, and taste with our tongue. But there are people who report occasional mixups in links—when, for example, sounds may be experienced as colors or tastes. This experience of sensory blending is called *synesthesia.* The French writer Théophile Gautier reported such an experience: "My hearing was fantastically developed. I heard the clamor of colors. Green, red, blue, yellow sounds came to me in perfectly distinct waves." The Russian psychologist Alexander Luria gave an account of a person for whom a pure tone of 1,000 cycles per second produced "a brown stripe against a dark background that had red, tonguelike edges [and] the taste . . . of sweet-and-sour borscht." Many psychologists are skeptical of such reports, but others believe that synesthesia may result from a mechanism in the nervous system that connects the senses with each other (Marks, 1975).

The visual cliff. Infants as young as six months old will not crawl beyond the perceptual "edge" of the cliff, indicating that they have depth perception.

fact that six-month-old babies have depth perception does not in itself prove that this ability is innate—a good deal of learning might have taken place during the first six months of life. But other experiments, using animals such as lambs and chickens that can walk within a day after birth, demonstrated that newborn animals also avoid the deep side of the cliff, suggesting that the reaction is in fact innate. Nevertheless, depth perception does require learning in order to be developed and improved.

HEARING

Ears are surprising organs. They are not as magnificent or as delicate as the eyes, but they are nonetheless fascinating instruments. The ears can almost detect single molecules moving in the air, yet they can withstand the shock of rock music and jet planes, at least for a short period of time.

The sensation of hearing is produced by changes in air pressure caused by vibrations or movements of the sound source. *Loudness* is the amplitude of the sound wave—the amount of expansion and contraction of the pressure changes that form a sound wave. When you turn up the volume of a radio, you increase the amplitude of the vibrations and therefore the sound is louder. *Pitch* refers to the high or low quality of a sound. It is determined by the frequency of wave vibrations—the faster the vibration, the higher the pitch. Another property of sound is *timbre,* the richness or quality of a sound that comes from a particular sound source. A note played on a violin will not sound exactly like the same note played on a trumpet or a piano.

To understand hearing, imagine throwing a stone into a pool of water. What happens? Wave after wave of ripples circle out from the center. The waves strike the edge of the pool and bounce back. Similarly, whenever any object is struck, it tends to vibrate. As it does so, the molecules of air around it are pushed away—just as a stone thrown into a pool pushes water molecules away from it. If you threw a number of stones into the pond, you would set up a series of waves on the water's surface. If these were waves in the air, they would reach your ear and set your eardrum moving back and forth in rhythm with the vibrating object. The vibration of your eardrum would eventually trigger impulses in the auditory nerve. These impulses would travel to your brain and would there be experienced as sound.

The ear receives and amplifies the vibration movements of the air in order to give information to the nervous system. The structures of the ear that do so are the outer, middle, and inner ears. (See Figure 3.4.) The *outer ear* is composed of an inch-long

FIG. 3 · 4 The anatomy of the ear.

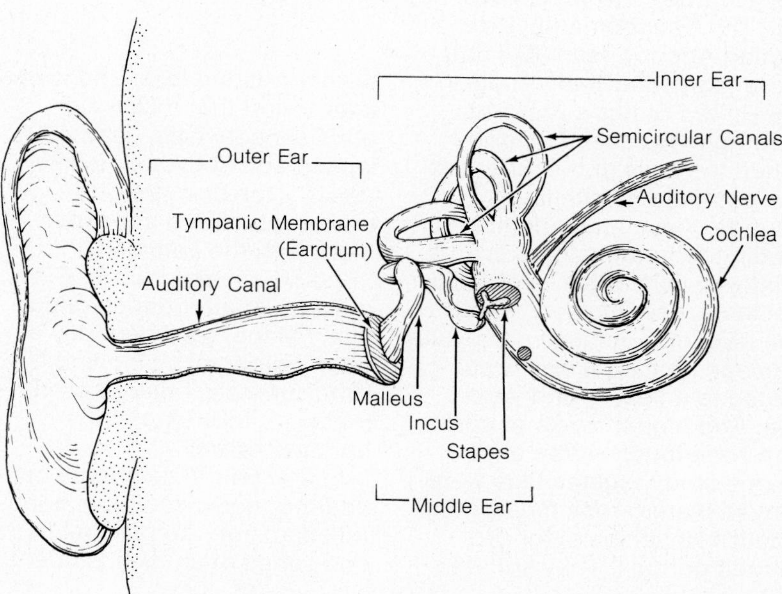

canal and the *tympanic membrane* (the eardrum). Changes in air pressure are channeled to this flexible membrane, which moves in response to the pressure changes. The *middle ear* is composed of three bones: the *malleus,* the *incus,* and the *stapes.* (These terms are Latin and mean "hammer," "anvil," and "stirrup"; the names are derived from the shapes of these three bones.) These bones make up a mechanical system that conducts sound waves to the inner ear. In the *inner ear* the vibrations are transmitted to the fluid inside the *cochlea,* a snail-shaped structure. There the sound waves reach the receptor cells for hearing and

Box 2

Noise Pollution

American cities, with their screeching cars, thundering trucks, roaring subways, wailing sirens, blaring horns, and bellowing factories, are tremendously noisy places, and they are getting noisier. Because of the devastating effects that sustained high levels of noise can have on human functioning, noise pollution has become one of modern society's greatest environmental hazards.

For one thing, high levels of noise can literally be deafening. The Environmental Protection Agency estimates that more than 16 million people in the United States suffer from hearing loss caused by noise. When the cells of the inner ear are bombarded with loud sounds, they can be damaged, leading to hearing loss. Even a relatively mild noise level of 70 decibels (see Table A), about the level of a cocktail party, can damage hearing if one is subjected to it year in and year out. And higher levels of noise can have much worse effects. In one study, guinea pigs were played blaring rock music (at about 110 decibels) for prolonged periods. They suffered severe hearing loss, and it was later found that their inner ear's sensory cells "had collapsed and shriveled up like peas." One discotheque owner reacted to the experiment with the comment, "Should a major increase in guinea-pig attendance occur at my place, we'll certainly bear their comfort in mind." Unfortunately, analogous effects can take place in humans as well.

In addition to its effects on hearing, noise can have harmful effects on the psyche. In one series of studies, students heard tape-recorded bursts of either extremely loud (110 decibels) or soft (56 decibels) noise over a period of 20 minutes (Glass and Singer, 1973). After a short while, the subjects adapted to the noise, and they were able to perform clerical tasks successfully. But the loud noise had unwelcome aftereffects. Immediately after the noisy period, subjects who had heard the loud noise were impaired in their ability to work efficiently on problem-solving and proofreading tasks.

In this and other studies, Glass and Singer found that

are translated into nerve impulses, which travel to the brain by way of the *auditory nerve.*

The ears are far enough apart to allow people to locate the position of a sound source. If a noise is two or three feet away from your left ear, it will reach that ear a fraction of a second before it reaches your right ear. The sound will also be louder in your left ear than in your right ear. The time lag and difference in loudness allow you to localize the sound as being on your left. Thus, to properly locate a sound, both ears are necessary.

---

the predictability and controllability of the noise made a big difference in subjects' reactions to it. When subjects knew when the loud noise was coming, its harmful aftereffects were greatly reduced. And when subjects knew they could stop the noise if they wanted to, the effects were also reduced—even though they didn't actually make use of their "stop" button. You are probably much less bothered by the clatter of your own typewriter than you are by that of your roommate's, since in the former case you have direct control over the noise. Unfortunately, most of the noise that pervades our cities is of the worst kind—it comes in unpredictable bursts, and it comes from sources over which we have no control.

When noise continues over a period of years, it can have adverse effects on intellectual abilities. In four New York City apartment buildings spanning a noisy highway, elementary school children who lived on the lower floors (where noises were loudest) were found to have less ability to discriminate between sounds than children who lived on higher floors (Glass, Cohen, and Singer, 1973). Children on the lower floors also had poorer reading skills than those on the higher floors. In interpreting these results, the researchers considered the possibility that wealthier and better-educated families might live in the choice apartments on the higher floors and that this factor, rather than the noise, might underlie the reading differences. But the same differences were found even when possible differences in parents' educational level were accounted for statistically. Glass and Singer suggest that in tuning out a noisy environment, children may fail to distinguish between speech-relevant sounds and speech-irrelevant sounds. The unhappy result is that the longer children must endure noise, the more likely they are to ignore all sounds, and this, in turn, may make reading more difficult.

The sound of all this is not very encouraging. And the noise levels of our cities—and, increasingly, of the countryside as well—are getting worse and worse. By one extreme estimate, the urban sound level is increasing at the rate of 10 percent a year, enough to make us all deaf by the year 2000 (Dempsey, 1975). It is possible to combat this trend. One way is by encouraging the production of quieter jets, trucks, cars, and appliances. As things stand, however, people don't necessarily want quieter machines. One manufacturer found that people would not buy his newly designed, quieter vacuum cleaner—since it didn't make a lot of noise, consumers assumed that it couldn't be doing a good job!

Approximate Intensity of Some Common Sounds

Rustling Leaves	12
Human Whisper	30
Normal Conversation	50
City Traffic	80
Subway Train	95
Motorcycle	110
Rock Band (amplified)	110
Snowmobile	115
Pain Threshold	*130*
Sonic Boom	130

The column on the right shows the decibel intensity of some common sounds (Dempsey, 1975). A decibel is the smallest difference in intensity of sound that the human ear can detect. The scale is a mathematical power function. At around the middle of the scale, every increase of 10 decibels represents approximate doubling of sound intensity.

THE SKIN SENSES

The importance of the skin senses is reflected in our everyday language. As Montagu stated:

> *We speak of "rubbing" people the wrong way . . . "a soft touch." . . . We get into "touch" or "contact" with others. Some people have to be "handled" carefully ("with kid gloves"). Some are "thick-skinned," others are "thin-skinned," some get "under one's skin," while others remain only "skin-deep." . . . Some people are "touchy."* [*1971, page 5*]

The sense of touch is actually a combination of at least three sensations: pressure, temperature, and pain. If you unbend a

SKIN LANGUAGE

Is it possible to communicate with the skin, using some system of symbols such as Morse code or even English? Geldard (1968) explored the idea of "body English" with a language called *vibratese*, consisting of 45 separate signals with three intensities (weak, medium, strong) and three durations (short, medium, long), delivered to five different spots on the chest. He found that the vibratese alphabet could be mastered in a few hours. Before long, two- and three-letter words could be introduced, and then short sentences. Geldard has begun experimentation with vibratese scattered all over the body. The skin may soon have a language all its own.

paper clip and probe an area of your skin lightly, you will feel pressure at certain points where the wire contacts your skin, but not at *every* point. If you do the same thing with a cold wire, you will feel cold at various specific points. If you probe your skin with a warm wire, you will feel warmth at various points. A pin point will produce spots of pain. Thus, different points on the skin are serviced by receptors that are sensitive to different kinds of stimuli.

The experience you have when you are touched lightly with a single hair is called *pressure* or *touch.* The amount of pressure required to produce this experience varies for different parts of the body. The tip of the tongue, the lips, the fingers, and the hands are the most sensitive areas. The arms, legs, and body trunk are less sensitive. People experience pressure not only when an object touches their skin, but also when the hairs on the body are slightly moved.

In addition to pressure receptors, the skin contains receptors for both *heat* and *cold.* There are about six times as many cold receptors as heat receptors in the skin. These temperature receptors are more concentrated along the trunk of the body, which is why the hands and feet can withstand greater temperature extremes than can the bare back. "Hot" and "cold" are relative terms: Anything that you touch that is colder than your skin will be perceived as cool; anything you touch that is hotter than your skin will seem warm. Interestingly, a really hot stimulus excites both cold and warm receptors.

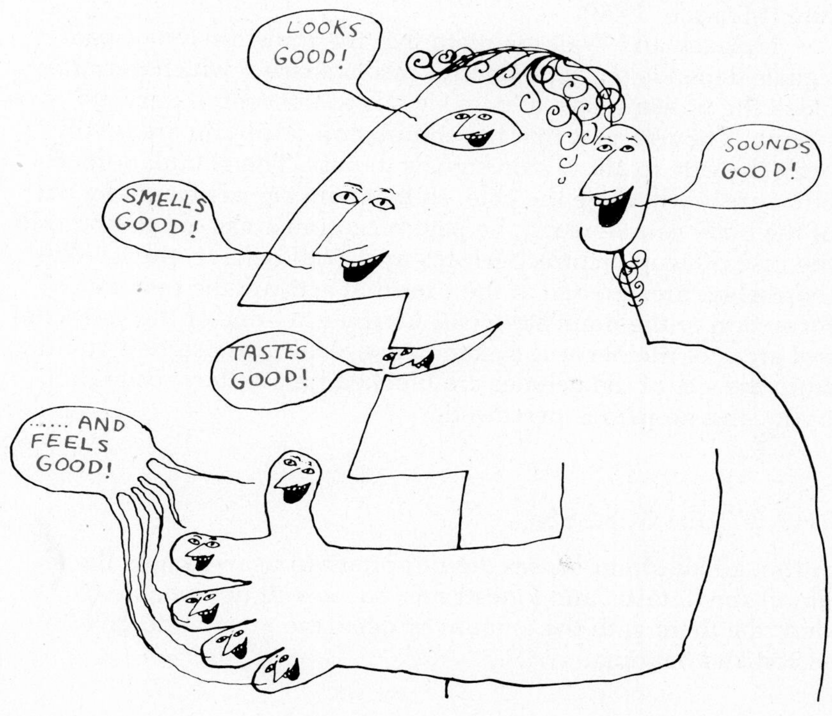

Here's an experiment you can try. Place one hand in a bucket of cold water and the other hand in a bucket of warm water. In a little while you will be aware that the feeling of warmth or cold comes only from the area where the hand meets both water and air. Now, put both hands in a third bucket filled with lukewarm water. This water will feel warm to the hand that was in cold water and cold to the hand that was in warm water. The sensation from the hand depends on the temperature to which the skin was previously adapted.

A third type of receptor in the skin is the *pain* receptor. Psychologists are still debating whether pain is a separate sense with its own nerve structures or whether it results from a pattern of intense stimulation from any of a number of receptors. Pain seems to be received by a variety of nerve endings—not only in the skin but in other organs as well. Interestingly, pain can arise from extreme stimulation of any kind: Very bright lights, loud noises, high or low temperatures, or great pressures all yield pain sensations. Pain serves to warn us of tissue destruction. However, most internal organs of the body do not have sense receptors for pain and are unable to inform us when they are in trouble.

How do we experience pain? According to the *specificity theory* there are specific pain receptors that relay signals of pain directly to the brain. A person should therefore feel pain exactly where the stimulation occurs, and the amount of pain felt should depend on the amount of stimulation at the pain site. But this theory does not account for the phenomenon of *acupuncture,* in which the insertion of needles into various sites on the body surface sometimes relieves pain in body regions quite distant from the needle site. Melzack and Wall came up with a new theory of pain that would account for the effects of acupuncture (Melzack, 1973).

Melzack and Wall maintain that the transmission of pain signals depends on "gate-control mechanisms," which permit or block the transmission of pain signals to the central nervous system. They suggest that the stimulation of certain areas will open the gate to allow pain signals to pass. The stimulation of other areas will close the gate, so that pain signals from any part of the body cannot reach the pain reception areas of the brain. In the case of acupuncture, Melzack and Wall believe, the needles themselves are inserted at the sites that activate the reticular formation of the brain stem (see Chapter 2)—one of the gate-control areas of the nervous system. As a result, pain signals coming from the site of the needles are blocked before they reach the brain, and no pain is perceived.

THE WOMAN WHO COULDN'T FEEL PAIN

McMurray (1950) reported a case of a woman who never experienced pain:

At no time had she ever reported any form of ache or pain such as headache, earache, toothache, or stomachache. . . . The hands, legs, and feet showed multiple scars which had been produced by cuts, bites, and scratches, many of which were unnoticed. After a day on the beach she had to inspect her feet carefully for cuts. It is also interesting that she reported never having felt the sensation of itch. [page 161]

THE OTHER SENSES

Although all of our senses are important to us, we know the least about smell, taste, and kinesthesis, so we will not be able to describe them with the amount of detail we are able to give vision and hearing.

Kinesthesis and Equilibrium

Close your eyes and raise your hand. You still know where your hand is. Now touch your nose with your finger. You know where both parts are. The sense that tells you the positions and movements of your muscles and joints is called *kinesthesis.* Some kinesthetic receptors are embedded in the muscles and send information to the brain about the load on the muscle and its state of contraction. Other receptors are in tendons and joints. With these sensors you can detect a movement of one-third of a degree in the shoulder and wrist. In the ankle more than a full degree of movement is needed for detection.

The kinesthetic senses provide information about active body movement. Thus, you can tell the relative weights of objects by lifting them. You can walk along the streeet without watching what your legs are doing. And you can talk without thinking about moving your tongue and jaw.

Kinesthesis is extremely important to daily life. When kinesthetic sensitivity is destroyed somewhere along the spinal cord, impulses coming into the spinal cord below the point of damage cannot find a path to the brain. If this were to happen to you, you would sway and have trouble keeping your balance with your eyes closed. You might not be able to lift your foot onto a curb without first looking at the foot, and you would walk with a peculiar gait.

The sense of balance, or *equilibrium,* works in conjunction with kinesthesis. These senses keep track of body motion and body position in relation to gravity. The sense organs for equilibrium are in the inner ear. The *semicircular canals,* which are oriented in different directions, are filled with a fluid that moves when the head rotates. The fluid movement allows perception of the body's movement. If movement is extreme, the individual gets dizzy.

Smell and Taste

The sense of *smell* results from stimulation of receptor cells in the nose. Most of what we smell comes from gaseous chemical molecules that are heavier than air. These molecules tend to collect on the floor or ground. When you stand erect, your nose misses most smells. Human beings have to sniff when they want to smell things. Breathing through the nose increases the number of molecules that hit the olfactory membrane, where smells are detected.

Molecular action also accounts for how a male dog can tell at a distance whether a female dog is in heat. The female dog in heat secretes a special odor, and a mere whiff of this smell will sexually excite the male dog. Fortunately for dogs and humans, we adapt to even the most powerful smells. Since our noses are mostly used to detect changes in the environment, they will eventually stop sending urgent messages to the brain and ignore even a persistent smell.

STEAK IS TASTELESS

Steak has almost no taste at all—if taste is limited to the message your tongue can send to the brain. It may smell good, look good, and have an interesting chewy texture, but these experiences have nothing to do with the taste of steak, which is neither salty, sweet, sour, nor bitter. If taste were the only sensation you got from steak, it would hardly be worth paying for. If you find this hard to believe, try closing your eyes and holding your nose the next time you eat some steak.

According to some theories, there are four basic odors: acid, fragrant, burnt, and caprylic (like limburger cheese). Other theories hold that there are six odors: fruity, flowery, burnt, spicy, resinous, and putrid. Most often, in fact, we describe smells as being "like" some familiar odor. We say "it smells like burning rubber"or "it smells like a locker room."

To a great extent, *taste* depends on smell. If you could not smell food, you could not tell what you were eating. After the first bite of food, you no longer perceive as much flavor as you

---

Box 3
Sensory Deprivation

During practically all of our waking lives, we are constantly bombarded with stimulation to our senses. What would happen if we were deprived of this sensory stimulation? For one thing, we would no longer obtain information about what is going on around us. There is evidence that such sensory deprivation can have devastating psychological effects. Until recently, psychologists have generally warned against the perils of sensory deprivation. In the past few years, however, another view has been expressed—the idea that although sensory deprivation has its dangers, it may have important benefits as well.

Psychologists became interested in studying the effects of sensory deprivation in the early 1950s. One spur to this research was the report that the Chinese and North Koreans had used sensory deprivation to brainwash prisoners of the Korean War (Smith, 1976). To study the effects of sensory deprivation, researchers enlisted volunteers to spend days at a time in environments that permitted virtually no sensory stimulation. In one well-known study, Woodburn Heron (1957) paid male college students $20 a day to lie on a bed in a lighted cubicle, around the clock, for as many days as they could. The subjects wore translucent plastic visors, permitting them to see only constant, diffuse light, but no objects or patterns. They wore gloves and cardboard cuffs to restrict skin sensation. Hearing was limited by a U-shaped foam rubber pillow and by the unchanging hum of air-conditioning equipment. There were only brief timeouts for meals and for going to the toilet.

A marathon swimmer experiences near total sensory deprivation.

After one or more days in this setting, subjects' performance on a variety of intellectual tasks was markedly impaired. In addition, they were found to be highly persuasible: When a tape recording arguing for the reality of ghosts was played, the subjects found it to be much more believable after the period of sensory deprivation than before it. Some students reported that they were afraid of seeing ghosts for several days after the experiment.

The most dramatic results of Heron's experiment were the hallucinations subjects experienced while in the chamber. At first, they "saw" dots of light, lines, or geometrical patterns. Later, they began to see more complex images, such as marching squirrels with sacks over their shoulders or processions of eyeglasses walking down the street. Initially, these cartoonlike visions were entertaining, but as they continued, they became more frightening. One subject reported, "My mind seemed to be a ball of cotton wool floating above my body." After emerging from several days of isolation, subjects experienced perceptual distortions—straight lines seemed curved, and stationary rooms seemed to be in motion.

did when you first began eating. If you pause long enough between bites, however, the taste returns.

Your taste buds are scattered across the upper surface and side of the tongue. They respond to four basic taste qualities: sweet, sour, bitter, and salty. The number of taste receptors on your tongue is limited, and your taste experiences are mixtures of these four basic qualities. All in all, the sense of taste is a quite restricted sensory experience.

Heron concluded: "A changing sensory environment seems essential for human beings. Without it the brain ceases to function in an adequate way." It has been speculated that the brain structure called the reticular activating system (see Chapter 2) sends advance warnings of incoming stimulation to the higher brain centers. These warnings are needed if the brain is to function efficiently. When we are deprived of sensory stimulation, however, the reticular activating system slows down. As a result, brain functioning is disturbed.

These effects of sensory deprivation point to real dangers. Many crucial jobs are typically done in highly monotonous, unchanging settings. If radar operators scanning screens for enemy missiles were to begin to see nonexistent blips—or if they were to miss real ones—the consequences could be disastrous. Truckers on long hauls sometimes report seeing nonexistent animals running across the road. It may be in part to reduce the monotony of these hauls that truckers make such extensive use of their Citizens Band radios.

But the effects of sensory deprivation are not all negative. On the basis of recent research. Peter Suedfeld (1975) has reported that sensory deprivation does not necessarily harm intellectual functioning. In fact, it sometimes even improves it. Suedfeld adds that severe emotional reactions to sensory deprivation experiments are extremely rare. One of the reasons that negative reactions have been reported in some studies may be that the subjects were swayed by their expectations. As long as researchers assumed that sensory deprivation was harmful—an image that was fostered by psychology textbooks and brainwashing film scenarios—subjects may have approached the situation apprehensively and may have proceeded to react negatively. When sensory deprivation is administered in calm surroundings, there seem to be few such negative effects.

Suedfeld suggests that the hallucinations of sensory deprivation subjects are caused by the spontaneous firing of nerves in the retina and are not signs of mental disorganization. Subjects may also experience sensations of hearing or smell from stimuli within their own body, including such stimuli as yesterday's dinner. After experiencing sensory deprivation for several hours, Adam Smith (1976) had the following advice: "I would counsel future deprivation subjects to stay away from sardines or smoked oysters immediately before the experiment, unless they plan to spend some hours communicating with the very essence of their sardineness."

Suedfeld suggests that sensory deprivation may also have some unexpected benefits. It leads to greater openness to new experiences, and thus may help to foster artistic creativity. In some cases, sensory deprivation may sharpen subjects' visual and auditory acuity. Finally, Suedfeld and his colleagues have successfully used sensory deprivation to help people to stop smoking. Once people discover that they can do without cigarettes for hours in the sensory deprivation room, which contains none of the usual smoking cues, they are more likely to be able to do without them on the outside. Researchers have also begun to make use of sensory deprivation for other purposes—to treat overeating, hypertension, and fears, for example.

Whereas Heron called his 1957 article about sensory deprivation "The Pathology of Boredom," Suedfeld called his 1975 article "The Benefits of Boredom." It is still too early to evaluate fully the new research on the benefits of sensory deprivation, but there seem to be considerable grounds for optimism.

The number of taste buds on the tongue decreases with age. As a result, older people are less sensitive to taste than children are. In general, sensitivity to salt is greatest on the tip and sides of the tongue. Sour is detected on the sides, and bitter is detected on the back of the tongue.

PERCEPTION AS AN ACTIVE PROCESS

Perception was once thought to be a passive and more or less automatic process. All you had to do was keep your eyes and ears open, and the world would magically represent itself in your head. We now know that this view was mistaken. In fact, the achievement of meaningful perceptions is an active process, with the individual perceiver playing a major role in determining his or her own experiences. This role goes far beyond simply deciding where to look or what to touch. We rarely experience just one sensation at a time. Instead, we are constantly being bombarded with a multitude of messages that must be sorted out, identified, and interpreted. We must select certain messages from the incoming array, identify them, and figure out how they relate to one another, in order to construct a meaningful picture of reality. As we will see, this process depends not only on the impinging sensations themselves but also on our past experiences, our needs, and our values. We will focus here on two aspects of this process: *perceptual selectivity* and *perceptual constancy.*

THE INVERTED WORLD

To learn how a reversal of sensory perception affects us, psychologists have had subjects wear special goggles that reverse the images of the outside world. Kohler's (1962) subjects wore such goggles for weeks, and observations were made on how they adapted. At the beginning, they were very clumsy and would bump into people and things. After a while they adapted, and the world began to look normal. Kohler reported that the subjects had to go through an adaptation period to adjust to a "new" environment when the goggles were removed.

Seeing What You're Looking For: Perceptual Selectivity

If we paid equal attention to all the thousands of messages being sent by our sense organs to the brain at any particular moment, our world would be a hopeless jumble, full of sounds and colors and twinges, signifying essentially nothing. We could not survive in such a world of raw sensations. Fortunately, perception is selective. We pay attention to only a very small portion of the stimuli around us. While you are reading this sentence, stop for a moment and attend to some of the other stimuli that are present in your environment—the sounds in the next room, the pressure of the shoes against your feet, the clutter on your desk. The process of selecting out certain stimuli while suppressing others is called *attention.* As we all know, it is sometimes difficult to pay attention to a particular task and easy to get distracted by other stimuli. Nevertheless, the ability to attend to some stimuli while filtering out others is something all of us develop.

Another aspect of perceptual selectivity is the tendency to see (hear, smell, or taste) what we expect to, while remaining unaware of things we do not expect. This phenomenon is called *perceptual set.* Siipola (1935) demonstrated this phenomenon in his studies of individuals' responses to words. He told one group of people they would be shown words that referred to animals. He then showed them combinations of letters that really did not spell anything ("sael," "dack," or "wharl"). Most of the group perceived the letters as the words "seal," "duck," and "whale." He told a second group he was going to show them words pertaining to boats. He showed this group the same combinations that the first group saw. This group reported seeing the words "sail," "deck," and "wharf." Each group perceived what they expected to perceive.

You can demonstrate the phenomenon of perceptual set using Figure 3.5. Show a friend picture A and ask what he or she sees. Then present picture C and ask what he or she sees. Most likely the friend will say that A shows an old woman and that C is another picture of the same woman. Now show another friend picture B and then picture C. Most likely, he or she will report that B is the picture of a young girl and that so is C. Thus, each friend will see something different in picture C—and, of course, each will be right, since C includes both an old woman and a young girl, depending on how you look at the picture (Leeper, 1935). But the particular image that each friend sees depends on what he or she expects, based on previous experience. Researchers have shown that once a person is primed to see a picture in a particular way, it is very hard to change that set and see things differently. (You can try this with your friends: Ask them whether they see anything *else* in the picture, and find out how long it takes for them to come up with another possibility.)

The effects of our expectations help to demonstrate that perception is an active process, involving a great deal of learning and experience. What we perceive is also influenced by our physical and psychological needs. A hungry person, for example, is especially likely to notice signs saying RESTAURANT or FOOD. Similarly, researchers have found that people who have not eaten for long periods display the "mirage effect" of identifying hazy objects as food or as eating utensils (McClelland and Atkinson, 1948).

SPEED READING

Although advertisements for speed-reading courses sound like scientific reports on a major advance in human education, the ads are closer to science fiction, according to Carver (1972). The ads claim that an average person can triple reading speed with no loss in comprehension. But the evidence suggests that people cannot increase their reading speeds without affecting comprehension. Speed-reading courses do not increase *reading* speed. They teach people to *skim* or *scan* material—to control what they attend to. Most people read between 150 and 300 words per minute with complete comprehension of the written material. Researchers have shown that an intelligent individual reading very easy material cannot comprehend most of it at rates above 500 to 600 words per minute.

FIG. 3 · 5 An illustration of perceptual set (see text).

A

B

C

Our perceptions can also be colored by values—what we consider to be important or desirable. Some studies have suggested that people tend to perceive objects they value highly as being larger than objects they value less highly. For example, poor children—for whom we may speculate that the value of money is particularly great—were found in at least one study to perceive coins as being larger than rich children did (Bruner and Goodman, 1947). A similar effect was observed in a study involving people's perception of other people. Two-thirds of a sample of Californians who planned to vote for John F. Kennedy in 1960 perceived him as being taller than Richard M. Nixon, whereas more than half of those planning to vote for Nixon perceived their candidate as being at least as tall (Kassarijan, 1963). (In fact, Kennedy was slightly taller.) The tendency to see valued objects as larger or as more vivid is called *perceptual accentuation.*

Bruner (1957) has suggested that these phenomena of perceptual set and perceptual accentuation reflect people's need to predict their environment and to get what they want. As a result, people tend to pay attention to stimuli that conform to their expectations, needs, and values. We find in our environment things we are looking for, and we overlook or avoid things that do not fit our interests. Sometimes this process leads to misperceptions or to ignoring information of great importance. But se-

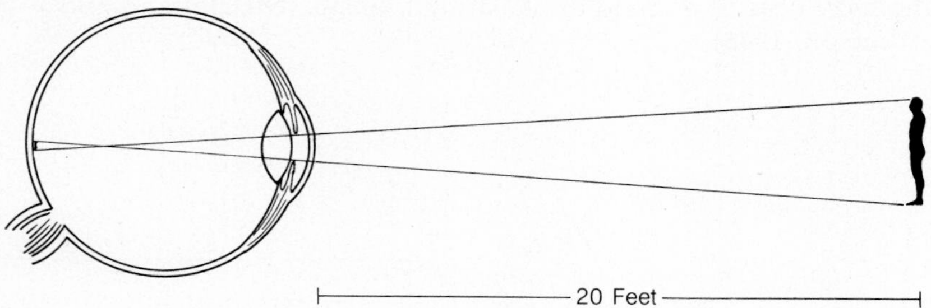

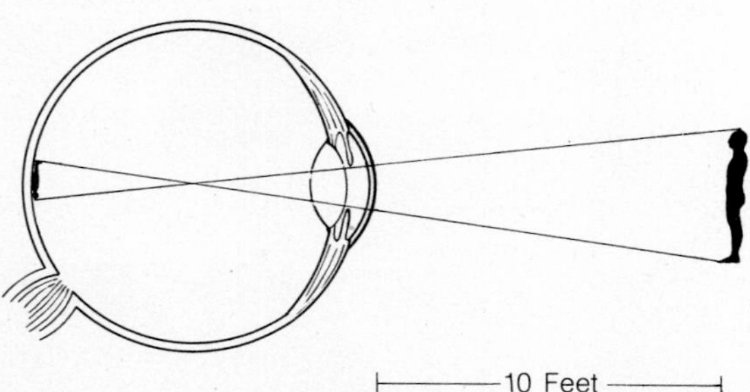

FIG. 3 · 6 As you move closer or farther away from an object, the size of the image on your retina gets larger or smaller. But you still perceive the object as being the same size. This phenomenon is known as *size constancy.*

lectivity is unavoidable, and we are apparently selective in an efficient way that reflects our best bets about what will happen and what is important.

Experiencing a Stable World: Perceptual Constancy

Consider the following situation (suggested by Hastorf, Schneider, and Polefka, 1970). You are sitting in a chair in your living room. A man walks into the room, moves over to a table by the window, picks up a newspaper, and then goes across the room to sit down and read. What are the successive patterns of visual stimulation that register on your retina as you watch this scene?

Every time the man moves closer to you, the image on the retina gets larger (see Figure 3.6). In fact, if he moves from 20 feet away to 10 feet away, the height of the image on your retina doubles. The opposite occurs if the person moves away from you. In addition, as the man moves nearer the window, more light is available, and his image on your retina gets brighter. When the man moves away from the window, the image gets darker. That is what your retina senses. But what do you actually perceive? A changeable chameleon of a person who constantly gets larger and smaller, lighter and darker? Not at all. Instead, you see the same man, who remains more or less the same size and brightness, regardless of the games his retinal image may be playing. We learn to make adjustments in our perception of objects that take into account changes in the distance and lighting. By so doing, we manage to convert what would otherwise be a bewildering pattern of stimulation into a stable and meaningful world.

The process by which we take into account changing distances and other cues in order to perceive objects as staying the same size is known as *size constancy.* Some aspects of this process may be innate, but it also seems to depend on experience. Size constancy may be especially difficult to achieve when distance cues are not available or when we are dealing with unfamiliar objects. Turnbull (1961) tells of the Bambuti Pygmies who live in the forests of the Congo and are not familiar with wide-open spaces. Turnbull took a Pygmy to a vast plain, and when the Pygmy looked at a herd of buffalo several hundred yards away, he asked what type of insects they were. He refused to believe they were buffalo. The Pygmy had to learn to take distance as well as retinal image into account, since he rarely looked at objects more than a few yards away.

The studies of Zeigler and Leibowitz (1957) indicate that eight-year-old children do not show the same degree of size constancy that adults do. Adults tend to perceive objects as being their real size when the objects are as far as 100 feet away. Eight-year-olds perceive the same objects as smaller than life size at that distance. This finding suggests that size constancy develops as a result of learning.

THE MOON ILLUSION

The moon appears larger when it is near the horizon than when it is higher in the sky, despite the fact that its image on the retina remains the same size. One possible explanation: An object that is far away appears smaller to us than it does when it is closer. We compensate for this by assuming that a distant object is actually larger than it appears to be. Most people perceive the horizon as being further away than the sky overhead. Therefore, when the moon is on the horizon, we compensate for its apparently greater distance by perceiving it as larger than its retinal image would suggest (Rock and Kaufman, 1962).

In addition to size constancy, we also see the world in terms of *brightness constancy* and *color constancy.* As was noted earlier, objects appear to be the same brightness no matter what the lighting conditions. Similarly, objects maintain their color no matter what the lighting or what other colors they are near.

Perceptual Illusions

Magicians are sometimes known as masters of illusion because they can make us "see" things (rabbits coming out of hats, cut ropes joining back together) that are not really there. Psychologists have a special interest in perceptual illusions—instances in which perception and reality do not agree—not only because of their intrinsic fascination but also because such illusions can help us to understand the process of perception.

One of the best known illusions is the Müller-Lyer illusion, named after the person who devised it in 1889 (see Figure 3.7). The illusion is an extremely powerful one. Even after you mea-

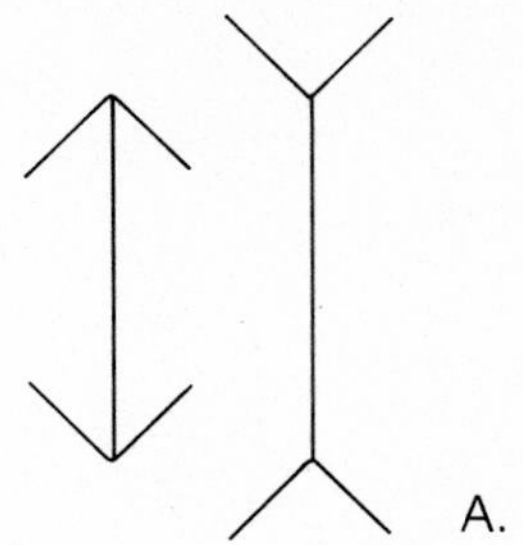

FIG. 3 · 7 *The Müller-Lyer illusion.* Why does the vertical line on the right in Figure 3 · 7A appear to be longer than the vertical line on the left? (They're really the same length.) The photograph (Figure 3 · 7B) may help provide the answer (see text).

FIG. 3 · 8 *The Ponzo illusion.* Why does the top horizontal line in Figure 3 · 8A appear to be longer than the bottom horizontal line? The photograph of railroad tracks in Figure 3 · 8B may help solve the mystery.

B.

sure the two lines and prove to yourself that they are equal, you will still perceive the line with the reversed arrowheads (B) as being longer than the line with the standard arrowheads (A). What causes this illusion? Many hypotheses have been offered, but the most likely explanation has to do with the phenomenon of size constancy (Gregory, 1968). The pattern of lines in A looks like the lines in a photograph of the outside corner of a building whereas the lines in B resemble those of an inside corner of a building. To maintain size constancy, we reason that the vertical line in B must be longer than in A, since it seems to be more distant from the viewer. Because we know that more distant objects produce smaller retinal images, we compensate and see the "distant" object as *larger* than the retinal image. Normally, this correction enables us to see a world that corresponds to reality. But when three-dimensional objects are represented on a two-dimensional surface, as in drawings and photographs, these corrections can in fact lead us astray. These correction processes are not conscious ones. Indeed, they are so deeply ingrained that we keep using them even when we know them to be inappropriate.

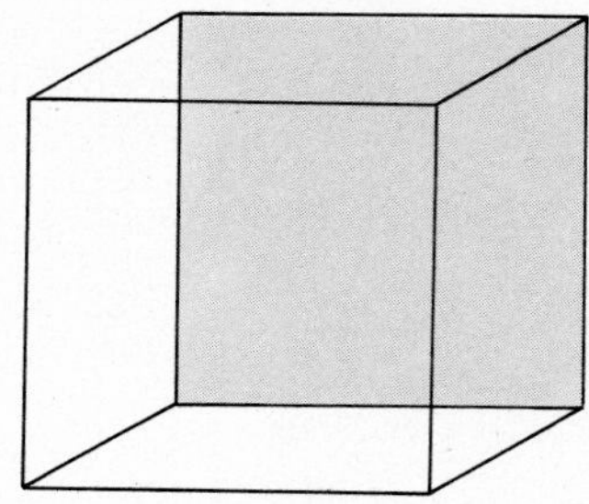

FIG. 3 · 9 The Necker cube.

Other perceptual illusions can similarly be understood as special cases in which the corrections that usually insure accurate perception are inappropriately applied. One of these is the Ponzo illusion (also known as the railway lines illusion), in which the top line (the one that would ordinarily be seen as more distant) appears larger than the bottom line (see Figure 3.8). Another famous illusion is the Necker cube, devised in 1832 by a Swiss scientist named L. S. Necker. He noticed that a cube drawn in two dimensions (as in Figure 3.9) will spontaneously reverse its direction. The tinted area can appear as either an outer surface or an inner surface of a transparent box. When such three-dimensional figures are drawn in two dimensions, they become ambiguous. Our perception reflects this ambiguity, alternating back and forth between one interpretation and another.

The perceptual illusions we have discussed here have all been devised by scientists. Our senses and our perceptual processes function so well in ordinary circumstances that it took a great deal of ingenuity to come up with ways to trick our perceptions. So don't let magicians and psychologists make you begin to doubt your senses—they're amazingly trustworthy!

SUMMARY

1. *Sensation* is the direct reception and transmission of messages from the sense organs. *Perception* is the active process of integrating and organizing sensations.
2. The first step in the process of sensation is for *receptor cells* in the sense organs to respond to energy in the environment. In the sense organs the energy is then converted to electrical impulses that can be transmitted to and interpreted by the brain.

3. *Vision* is the dominant human sense. The eye admits light (through the *pupil*) and focuses it (via the *lens*) onto the light-sensitive cells of the *retina.* These cells, the *rods* and *cones,* contain chemicals that break down when struck by light. The breakdown of chemicals triggers the sending of messages to the brain along the *optic nerve.*
4. The cones, which are packed together in the center of the retina, are the color receptors. The rods, which spread to the outer edges of the retina, are essentially colorblind. Adaptation to dim light occurs because chemicals in the rods and cones build up faster than they are broken down when there is little light stimulation. With more chemicals, the *visual threshold* is lowered, and less light is needed to stimulate the cells.
5. *Visual acuity* is the ability to discriminate the details in the field of vision. Poor visual acuity may be the result of *nearsightedness* (in which the eyeball is too long and the lens focuses the image in front of the retina) or of *farsightedness* (in which the eyeball is too short and images fall behind the retina). The *blind spot* is an empty spot in one's vision corresponding to the place on the back of the eye where the optic nerve exits to the brain.
6. *Eidetikers* are people (primarily children) who are able to see sharp visual images of things that have been removed from their field of vision. This ability has also been called "photographic memory." Many researchers believe that eidetic imagery is basically the same as a well-developed visual memory and is not a special ability at all.
7. Color vision is thought to result from the "mixing" of stimulation of three types of cones, each sensitive to a different primary color. Defects in cones result in *color blindness,* which may be *dichromatic* (in which only two of the three types of cones are functioning) or *achromatic* (in which none of the cones are functioning).
8. *Monocular cues* to depth perception include overlapping of objects, size differences, perspective, and shading. Depth perception is also aided by *binocular vision,* in which the images received by the two eyes combine to give objects three-dimensionality. Experiments with the *visual cliff* indicate that depth perception is innate, but improves with learning.
9. *Hearing* occurs when a sound wave causes the eardrum to vibrate, which in turn sets the three bones of the middle ear into motion. These bones transmit the vibrations to fluids in the *cochlea* in the inner ear, where receptor cells are stimulated, causing messages to be sent along the *auditory nerve* to the brain.
10. Among the qualities of a sound are *loudness* (determined by the amplitude of the sound wave), *pitch* (determined by the frequency of wave vibrations), and *timbre* (determined by the nature of the sound source).

11. Locating the source of a sound generally requires two ears: Sounds reach one ear a fraction of a second before the other, and they are also louder for the first (and closer) ear they reach.
12. *Noise pollution* can be harmful not only physically, but psychologically as well. Noise has been shown to impair performance on intellectual tasks, although the ability to predict and control the noise reduces the impairment. Prolonged noise over a period of years is also thought to have adverse effects on the intellectual abilities of children.
13. The *skin senses* include receptors for pressure, temperature, and pain. The experiencing of warmth and cold is relative, depending on the temperature of the skin. Psychologists are uncertain whether pain is a sense in itself or a result of the intense stimulation of any of a number of receptors. The phenomenon of *acupuncture* has led psychologists to reassess their theories of pain to account for the fact that needles inserted in one part of the body can relieve pain in a distant part.
14. Studies of *sensory deprivation* in the 1950s showed that students who were placed in a room without sensory stimulation experienced hallucinations, were impaired in performance of intellectual tasks, and were more susceptible to persuasion. More recent research suggests that sensory deprivation can have benefits, such as increasing self-awareness and helping people with such problems as smoking and overeating.
15. *Kinesthesis* is the sense of body movement and position. Receptors for this sense are located in the muscles, tendons, and joints. The sense of balance, or *equilibrium* (based in the *semicircular canals* in the inner ear), works in conjunction with kinesthesis to make one aware of body position in relation to gravity.
16. The sense of *smell* involves the reception of chemical molecules by cells on the olfactory membrane of the nose. According to differing theories, there are either four or six basic smells. There appear to be four basic *taste* qualities: sweet, sour, salty, and bitter. Actually, it is the sense of smell that provides much of our eating enjoyment because taste receptors adapt very quickly.
17. Perception is an active process. It is *selective*—people pay attention to only a small percentage of the stimuli in their environment. Furthermore, people tend to perceive what they expect to perceive; this phenomenon is called *perceptual set.* Perception is also influenced by a person's needs and values. The tendency to see valued objects as larger or more vivid, for example, is called *perceptual accentuation.*
18. People learn to make adjustments in perception of objects in order to take into account changes in distance and lighting. The process of perceiving objects as staying the same size no matter what the distance is known as *size constancy.*

Size constancy apparently requires some learning and experience to be accurate.

19. Perceptual *illusions* are instances in which perception and reality do not agree. Famous illusions include the Müller-Lyer illusion, the Ponzo illusion, and the Necker Cube.

Extrasensory Perception

Many people believe they can receive impressions of distant realities that do not reach them through their regular sense organs. They report catching impressions of catastrophes involving distant loved ones, or they have had curiously exact premonitions of future events (Murphy, 1961).

Since the impressions apparently do not come through any of the senses that scientists know about, they have been called phenomena of *extrasensory perception* (ESP). They are studied as part of the general enterprise of *parapsychology*—the study of phenomena that are beyond the usual bounds of psychology.

The study of parapsychology includes *clairvoyance* (in which extrasensory perception allows one to know about an object or event without employing the usual senses), *telepathy* (being aware of another person's thoughts without communicating through the normal sensory channels), and *psychokinesis* (the ability to influence a physical object by a sheer exercise of will).

ESP seems to be considered a legitimate area of inquiry in

ESP seems to be considered a legitimate area of inquiry in the Soviet Union.

the Soviet Union. Krippner and Davidson (1972) traveled there to observe some of the research of Russian psychologists. When they returned to the United States, they reported, "The Russian parapsychologists seem to harbor no doubts about the existence of parapsychological phenomena. Instead, they are seeking practical applications and an understanding of how these

Skeptical Attitudes

The attitude of most American psychologists toward ESP is much more skeptical. Wayne Sage (1972) has observed that with ESP one either believes it or one doesn't. It depends on what one is willing to accept as proof. Correctly or incorrectly, this form of "perception" has thus far failed to be accepted as legitimate by most American psychologists. The physiologist Hermann von Helmholtz (1821–1894) expressed a sentiment that still seems evident among present-day psychologists. When asked what evidence would convince him of the reality of extrasensory phenomena, he said that not even what his own eyes recorded would convince him of the existence of telepathy. He held that ESP was manifestly impossible. In 1951 a similar view was expressed by D. O. Hebb, a former president of the American Psychological Association, who stated, "Personally, I do not accept ESP for a moment, because it does not make sense . . . my own rejection of [ESP] is—in the literal sense—a prejudice" (page 45).

Zick Rubin recently asked one of the nation's leading researchers on "ordinary" perception how scientists in this area view the continuing research on extrasensory perception nowadays. His answer: "We look the other way."

Warner (1952) concluded, in a survey made 25 years ago, that fewer than 3 percent of psychologists felt ESP was an established fact, and a higher percentage (10 percent) believed ESP was impossible. There is little likelihood that the attitudes of psychologists have changed drastically since then. As Gertrude Schmeidler (1969) noted, "A glance at the Psychological Abstracts indicates that by the criterion of number of published articles, parapsychology is only a minor topic; and ESP is only one of its subtopics" (page 1).

> A scientist's answer: "We look the other way."

Those most firmly set against ESP insist it is an illusory phenomenon that is no different from the superstitious beliefs of primitive and nonliterate people. The skeptics believe that scientific inquiry into ESP's nature is of no more value than the ghost hunting that has occupied unscientific humanity for centuries. The disbelievers point out that discovering dependable ESP subjects is rare. Between 1938 and 1954, despite active research in the field, no such subjects appeared in America (Soal and Bateman, 1954). In England, researchers credited only three persons with the capacity to maintain their ESP ability over a sustained period. Even this sustained ability was often a marginal one.

Statistical Arguments

To understand further why psychologists are skeptical, let us consider an experiment performed in J. B. Rhine's laboratory at Duke University (Rhine, 1942). Rhine was trying to determine whether a subject might, through some combination of ESP and willpower, influence the positions of cards in a mechanical shuffler. In all, 50 persons predicted the order in which cards would come out of the shuffler. The experiment was performed carefully. In more than 50,000 trials, the results were at chance level. Further statistical analyses were then made, but they failed to

. . . the critical problem is the failure of experi- menters to produce an ESP experiment that can be replicated in the laboratory. . . .

yield significant results. Finally, an analysis based on a complex statistic called a covariance of salience ratio produced a better-than-chance finding.

The statistical argument is a futile one, according to Crumbaugh (1969). It starts with the premise that ESP exists, and its proof relies on some demonstration of a human capacity to violate the laws of mathematical expectancy. Crumbaugh feels that the critical problem is the failure of experimenters to produce an ESP experiment that can be replicated in a laboratory with the same results. (To replicate an experiment is to repeat it using identical procedures to see whether one gets the same results.) In Crumbaugh's experience, only 25 to 50 percent of the experimental replications attempted in parapsychological experiments have been successful. For example, Layton and Turnbull (1975) submitted the results of their research to a psychological journal. They had apparently discovered certain complex, but nonchance, effects of people's own belief in ESP on their performance of a clairvoyance task. The editors of the journal agreed to publish the findings on the condition that the researchers attempt an exact replication. They did, but this time there were no ESP effects of any kind. The most reasonable explanation seems to be that the first set of findings was a fluke.

Crumbaugh found that the published reports that made the most convincing case for ESP were conducted by researchers who had doubtful reputations among working parapsychologists. He concluded that it is impossible for scientists to decide the merits of the case for ESP solely on the basis of published reports.

Sheep and Goats

An unsettling observation is found in the work of Schmeidler and McConnell (1958). They separated research subjects into two categories: "sheep" (believers in ESP) and "goats" (nonbelievers). They found that the sheep regularly scored beyond chance expectation in ESP experiments. The goats, however, consistently scored at only chance or a little below. To the many goats among professional psychologists, these research findings suggested that the study of ESP has always been unwittingly biased in its design because it has traditionally been conducted almost exclusively among sheep.

In spite of the prevalent criticism, research in ESP continues, and some of it has received the serious attention of psychologists. Research on clairvoyance has been quite disappointing, but evidence for telepathy continues to be found under certain conditions. It may be, for example, that telepathy is most likely to take place when the stimuli being "sent" and "received" have strong emotional connotations. McBain et al. (1970) had two-person teams of subjects sending and receiving emotional symbols (such as "home," "sorrow," "peace"). Also, they hypnotized the subjects in order to enhance their ability to express and sense the emotional content. On the average, over many series of trials, their eleven teams scored about 27 "hits" out of 125 trials—above chance, but just barely. Same-sex teams produced about 29 hits for 125 trials, while opposite-sex teams scored only 24 hits. Furthermore, senders who were more susceptible to hypnosis tended to produce higher scores, although there was no comparable effect for receivers. Similar effects of hypnosis on telepathic performance have been reported by Krippner (1968), and success in telepathic transmission of emotional stimuli was also reported by Moss and Gengerelli (1967).

ESP may well exist, but it still has to be demonstrated conclusively according to the rules of established science. If ESP does exist, it will eventually enter the halls of science, despite the strong resistance by the scientific establishment.

Box I-1

The Think Tank and the Magician

The Stanford Research Institute (SRI) is one of America's largest and best-known think tanks. In addition to numerous other projects, the institute has been investigating the psychic powers of an Israeli named Uri Geller. Geller claims to be able to communicate by telepathy, to detect and describe objects hidden from view, and to distort metal implements with his psychic energy.

Among those observing Geller were psychologists Ray Hyman and Robert Van de Castle and Department of Defense investigator George Lawrence. Although Van de Castle concluded that Geller was "an interesting subject for further study," neither Lawrence nor Hyman was impressed. Hyman said that he could spot "loopholes and inconclusiveness" in each of Geller's feats of ESP and psychokinesis. Hyman also said that he caught Geller in some outright deceptions.

Geller, for instance, asked Lawrence to think of a number between one and ten and to write it down, as large as possible, on a pad. While Lawrence wrote, Geller made a show of concentrating and covered his eyes with his hands. But Hyman, carefully observing Geller, noticed that the young man's eyes were open and visible through the fingers. Hyman concluded that Geller was able to see the motion of Lawrence's arm as he wrote and could therefore correctly identify the number. In another case, Geller caused a compass needle to turn about five degrees. Lawrence, noting that Geller had moved his body and vibrated the floor, did the same, and the needle deflected even more.

Despite the skepticism, Geller volunteered to demonstrate his powers to the editors of *Time* magazine. After Geller performed his feats, a professional magician, James Randi, duplicated each one. In its story on Geller, *Time* called the psychic a fraud.

Only a few days after the *Time* article appeared, however, SRI reported its findings on Geller to a physics symposium at Columbia University. Their report described some of the feats Geller had performed in foolproof laboratory tests at SRI. Although they did not claim that Geller had psychic powers, the researchers stated, "We have observed certain phenomena . . . for which we have no explanation. All we can say at this point is that further investigation is warranted."

Curious about Geller, Andrew Weil, a physician and author, met the young man and was overwhelmed by his feats. He wrote glowingly of the encounter in *Psychology Today* (Weil, 1974). As a follow-up, Weil visited the magician James Randi, who demonstrated his ability to do all the things Geller had done. In a second *Psychology Today* article, Weil declared that Geller was an extremely good hoax and that in fact Geller had learned the skills of magic while growing up in Israel.

Geller has continued to demonstrate his abilities before the public and before interested researchers, and the debate is still on as to whether his feats are mere magic tricks or real demonstrations of ESP powers.

And then we will be faced with the mind-boggling task of explaining how it works.

Summary

1. *Parapsychology,* is the study of phenomena that is beyond the usual bounds of psychology, encompasses clairvoyance, telepathy, and psychokinesis.
2. American psychologists remain skeptical about parapsychology and its subbranch, *extrasensory perception* (ESP). They want solid scientific proof, and although ESP experiments have been conducted for years, such proof is yet to be established.
3. Laboratory studies of ESP have been criticized because they are based on statistical probability, because they are difficult to replicate, because some experimenters have reputations which are doubtful, and because they may be unwittingly biased.

Consciousness

CHAPTER 4

Consciousness

What is consciousness? Who cares?

These are probably the two questions that have been asked most often during psychology's brief history. For some psychologists, such as the "structuralists" described in Chapter 1, the nature of consciousness has been a primary concern. Others have doubted that consciousness or the mind exists at all.

What is consciousness? Even for psychologists, the question is difficult. Sometimes the term implies awareness, as in "self-conscious"; at other times it connotes a certain deliberateness: a "*conscious* decision." Even if we can't define consciousness, it seems easy to recognize when we experience it. Most of us feel quite conscious of learning a new skill or of making a difficult choice. Consciousness appears important for dealing with new and unfamiliar stimuli or for producing novel behavior patterns. Consciousness is not essential for all behaviors, however. Most of our routine activities—tying shoes, descending stairs, speaking English—are quite automatic and unconscious. Consciousness may even interfere with these kinds of behaviors. Try running down a flight of stairs thinking about what your feet are doing (but bring along bandages!). Perhaps consciousness can best be considered a level of thought that integrates and regulates our experience and that is sometimes necessary for normal activities but often is not.

Who cares? Today even that's not clear. For many decades, the study of consciousness was considered unscientific. After all, no one can see or touch consciousness, and no one can really get inside another person's head. As a consequence, scientists who wanted to study consciousness were compelled to gather data from people's verbal reports. Unfortunately, that's somewhat like studying digestion by listening to stomach growls: You're never entirely sure how the noises coming out relate to the processes within. This situation has improved in recent years, with the advent of techniques such as electrical recording of brain activity. But the suitability of consciousness for scientific investigation is still a topic of debate.

Much of psychology is about conscious processes. Many aspects of thought, language, attention, and interpersonal relations are conscious in every sense. Thus, it is somewhat artificial to use "consciousness" as the title for a single chapter of this book, and it is difficult to decide what materials belong here. Nevertheless, one can often learn what something *is* by studying what it is *not*. So, like early psychologists who attempted to learn about personality by studying people who seemed crazy, modern psychologists often try to learn about "normal" consciousness by studying its altered states—states that seem markedly different from our usual waking state. For this reason, the present chapter focuses on three altered states of consciousness: sleep, hypnosis, and drug states. And the Psychological Issue following this chapter is concerned with meditation, another altered state of consciousness that has recently gained tremendous popularity.

SLEEP

We spend about one-third of our lives in the altered state of consciousness called sleep. By age 60, you will have slept the same 20 years that Rip Van Winkle slept. People are seldom aware of the exact moment they slip into sleep, and they rarely know how long they have slept. You can't judge the amount of sleep you've had by how rested you feel or how alert you are when you wake up. If you sleep too long, you may feel even more tired than you did before you went to bed, and you may perform poorly on tasks requiring alertness (Taub and Burger, 1969).

If you go without sleep for a long time (say, 48 hours), staying awake will require a tremendous effort. But when you finally do go to sleep, you won't need to make up for all the lost sleeping time. Even after many days without sleep, it takes only about 12 hours of sleeping to get even. If you go without sleep for 100 hours or more, you will drag around physically and start to lapse every so often into moments of lost awareness called

FEELING GOOD AND FEELING BAD

"A man at 10 A.M. is not the same man at 4 P.M. or midnight. Indeed, the same man is radically different at 2 A.M. One of the obvious signs of this daily rhythm is the body temperature. It varies about two degrees in 24 hours. With great regularity the body temperature rises during the day and falls at night, dropping to its lowest point between 2 and 4 A.M.

"Ordinarily a person will feel at his best during the hours when his temperature is high, and if he is awake when it falls to its low point he will feel frankly terrible. This is the time when night workers and railroad people have most accidents, the time when a doctor will receive the most calls reporting night coronaries." [Luce and Segal, 1966, page 199]†

†*From "What time is it? The body clock knows," Gay Gaer Luce and Dr. Julius Segal, in* The New York Times Magazine, *April 3, 1966. © 1966 by the New York Times Company. Reprinted by permission*

Box 1

Little People Inside Our Heads

We all know what the *brain* is, but what is the *mind?* How do people consider alternatives, select courses of action, and reflect on their own thoughts and behaviors? In answering these questions, scientists are tempted to think about consciousness as if there were a little man, or *homunculus,* inside each person's head, pulling strings and pushing buttons. Popular expressions such as "So I said to myself . . ." or "I couldn't let myself do it!" reinforce this way of thinking. Nevertheless, psychologists don't usually

find these concepts very helpful in explaining behavior.

One problem is that even if we could locate and study such a homunculus we would have to wonder about a little man within *his* head. Furthermore, we would have to argue that split-brain patients (see Psychological Issue, Chapter 2), who have two separate consciousnesses, have two homunculi. Women, needless to say, would have heads populated by little women.

The idea that the *mind* (or consciousness, or will) is separate from the *brain* is known as "dualism," a philosophical position popularized by René Descartes. Modern psychologists find such a perspective unhelpful. Instead, they attempt to understand the physical and chemical processes within the brain that account for consciousness.

microsleep. If you stay awake much longer, you may begin to hallucinate.

People don't really have much choice about sleeping, since sleep seems to be an automatic behavior necessary for survival. The amount of sleep one needs does not vary greatly with the amount of mental work one does; hard thinking does not make one sleepy. In fact, the lack of mental activity—boredom—is more likely to make a person sleepy.

Is nightly sleep nothing but a habit? As far as we know, people all over the world sleep 5 to 8 hours in every 24 hours and generally do so at night. If this pattern were totally habit, we might expect to find some groups that get along on short naps during different parts of the day. But so far, no such culture has been reported, not even in the northernmost regions of Canada, Norway, and Russia where winter means months of uninterrupted night and summer brings unending daylight.

There is probably no absolutely necessary relationship between when people sleep and the day-night cycle. Lower animals, like humans, can reverse their typical cycle in response to a change in environmental conditions. Physiologist Nathaniel Kleitman (1939) concluded that there are actually two kinds of wakefulness. One, called *wakefulness of necessity,* is controlled by portions of the brain stem (the more "primitive" part of the brain). The other, *wakefulness of choice,* is superimposed on the sleep cycle and is controlled by the cerebral cortex.

Though psychologists have searched at length for a "sleep center" in the brain, no such structure appears to exist. Instead, portions of the brain stem (especially the reticular activating system, described in Chapter 2) are to some extent involved in the regulation of sleep and wakefulness. Destruction of parts of some of these structures can lead to states of permanent wakefulness; destruction of other areas can lead to permanent sleep. Both conditions are ultimately fatal.

Stages of Sleep

Scientists who have studied sleep in the laboratory have discovered that the sleeping person actually goes through several stages of sleep (See Figure 4.1.):

Stage 1 is falling asleep. This is a very short stage, usually occurring a few minutes after bedtime. Brain waves become irregular. The heart rate begins to slow, and muscles relax. The person in Stage 1 is easy to waken and may not realize that he or she has been asleep.

Stages 2 and 3 are deeper stages of sleep. In Stage 2, brain waves show bursts of activity called "spindles." In Stage 3,

WHO NEEDS AN ALARM CLOCK?

Some of us claim we can wake up at a predetermined time just by setting the "alarm clock" in our head. Believe it or not, it's true. In one experiment, subjects were sent to bed with a target time to wake up. The subjects were offered a pay bonus if they could hit the target (give or take 10 minutes). They found that they could do it, no matter what stage of sleep they were in before waking. They didn't do it by "sleeping with one eye open," either. They slept as deeply as they usually did (Zung and Wilson, 1971).

Box 2

Long and Short Sleepers

Napoleon Bonaparte apparently flourished on only 4 to 6 hours of sleep each night. Albert Einstein, on the other hand, was a very long sleeper. Recent evidence suggests that the contrasting sleep preferences of eminent and ordinary people alike may be related to differences in both personality and brain function.

Of course, most of us are not extremely long- or short-sleepers. Furthermore, it is difficult for us to tell which we are, because many aspects of our environments interfere with the expression of our natural sleep preferences. However, Ernest L. Hartmann (1973) studied groups of extreme short- and long-sleepers under carefully controlled conditions, in which late-night movies and early-morning classes could not get in the way. Free to sleep as little or as much as they pleased, the short-sleeping subjects averaged only 5½ hours of sleep each night. They usually fell asleep within about 15 minutes and spent little time awake in bed. The long-sleepers, in contrast, averaged about 8½ hours of sleep each night, took over 30 minutes to fall asleep, and spent at least another 30 minutes awake each night in bed. Long-sleepers seemed to regard sleep as a luxury, while short-sleepers considered it almost a chore.

Hartmann carefully monitored the sleep patterns of both groups. The two groups showed approximately equal durations of the four stages of non-REM sleep. However, long-sleepers spent almost twice as much time each night (2 hours as compared to only 1 hour for short-sleepers) in REM sleep. Their REM periods were longer, more frequent, and more intense. Further-

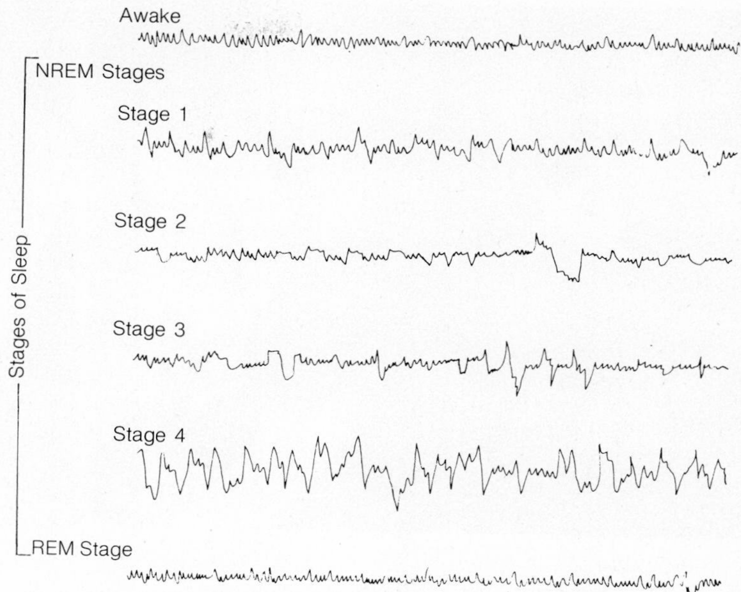

FIG. 4 · 1 Tracings of brain waves during different stages of sleep.

more, when long and short-sleepers had been awakened repeatedly to deprive them of REM periods, long-sleepers compensated more strongly by sleeping even longer than usual. This response to REM deprivation implies that long-sleeping is not just a habit but rather is a response to a basic physiological need.

The personalities of long- and short-sleepers also seem to differ. Obviously, no sleeper was a carbon copy of the others. Nevertheless, on the average the short-sleepers seemed more extraverted, carefree, and confident. However, they also appeared to be both politically apathetic and social conforming. In contrast, the long-sleepers tended to be more introverted, anxious, and unsettled. Politically and socially, however, they seemed concerned and unconforming. While short-sleepers may have been more productive, long-sleepers appeared to be more creative. To Hartmann, eminent short-sleepers seemed like extremely efficient and practical persons—leaders in business and government, administrators, and applied scientists. Famous long-sleepers, on the other hand, resembled the "tortured genius."

According to Hartmann, REM sleep may help restore the effectiveness of certain pathways in the brain in which norepinephrine is a transmitter substance. For some unknown reason, some people may have more norepinephrine—or may restore it more quickly—than others. Conversely, some people may need more REM sleep to replenish their norepinephrine. Since brain levels of norepinephrine appear to be related to motor behavior, memory, attention, and mood, suggestions of an association between REM requirements and personality may be reasonable. In the years to come, this pioneering research may further clarify the relationships between brain function and behavior.

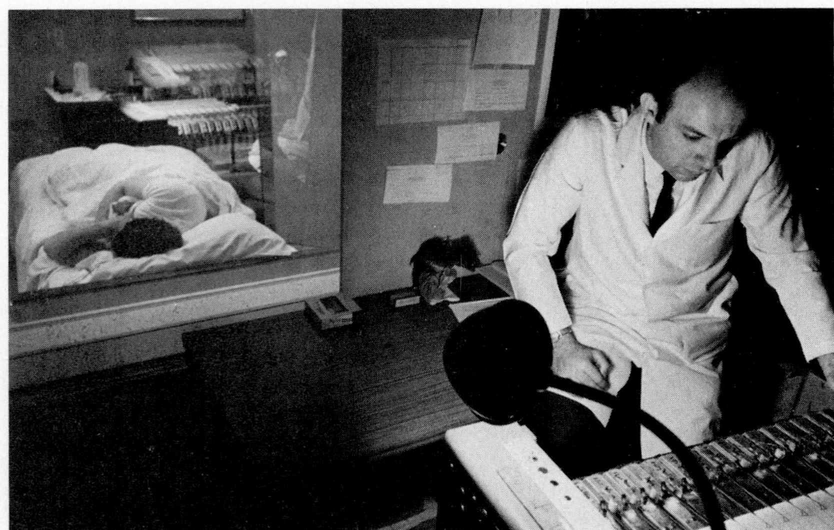

A researcher monitors a subject's brain waves in a sleep research laboratory.

the spindles disappear, and brain waves become long and slow (about one wave per second). At this stage, the sleeper is hard to waken and unresponsive to stimuli. Heart rate, blood pressure, and temperature continue to drop.

Stage 4 is the deepest stage, and is called *delta sleep.* In young adults, delta sleep occurs in 15- or 20-minute segments (interspersed with lighter stages) during the first half of the night. Delta sleep lessens with age.

These four stages, which recur in a regular pattern throughout the night, occupy about 75 percent of our sleeping time. Collectively, they are known as "slow-wave" sleep. For reasons that will become clear shortly, these stages are also known as non-REM (NREM) sleep.

Perchance to REM

There is another stage of sleep that seems qualitatively different from the other four. Approximately every hour and a half during sleep, our eyes dart and roll around under their lids in what is called REM (rapid eye movement) sleep. The REM periods are easily visible to anyone who looks at the closed eyelids of the sleeping person. An hour or so after the person has gone to sleep, the first REM period of the night usually starts and lasts for about 5 to 10 minutes. Later in the night REM periods last as long as 25 minutes. Such eye movements do not occur in stages 1 through 4, which is why they are referred to collectively as NREM sleep.

REM and NREM sleep are different in more respects than the presence or absence of rapid eye movements. Some physiological processes that are connected in the normal waking state appear to be disconnected during REM sleep. Although most muscles are relaxed during REM sleep, some muscles show a great deal of spontaneous twitching. In addition, during REM

NIGHTMARES AND NIGHT TERRORS

A bad dream in the form of a nightmare is pretty bad, but night terrors are even worse. Night terrors scare the hell out of most people. When you are caught in the middle of one, your heart rate may speed up from 64 beats a minute to as high as 152 beats every minute. When such terrors visit you in your sleep, they often arrive early in the night, sometimes within 45 minutes after you have dropped off to sleep.

Nightmares raise your heartbeat only slightly (10 to 16 beats a minute) and may be forgotten with the morning light. A full-blown night terror, however, propels you into a wide-awake state directly from the deepest stage of sleep. Such terrors are actually massive anxiety attacks, which also include rapid increases in breathing rate and calls for help. Scientists are not fully certain what triggers these attacks.

sleep pulse and respiration are a bit faster, blood pressure is higher and all three processes are more irregular than during NREM sleep. Males often experience erections during REM periods, with no necessary relationship to the content of dreams occurring at the same time.

Most importantly, the mental activity that occurs during sleep varies greatly between REM and NREM sleep. Researchers have found that almost every time a person is awakened during an REM period he or she has been dreaming. But people who are awakened during NREM sleep rarely report that they have been dreaming. And the dreams they do report seem more like random thoughts than real dreams. Many researchers have therefore concluded that REM sleep and dreaming are almost synonymous. The reason that the sleeper's eyes dart around during REM sleep may be that he or she is looking at the various people and events of the dream.

Dreaming

The need to dream appears to be as basic as the need to sleep. People dream about two hours a night on the average—whether or not the dreams are remembered. In one experiment, people were consistently awakened for five consecutive nights just as the periods of REM sleep began (Dement, 1965). These people became anxious, irritable, and angry; they had difficulty concentrating, and some began to hallucinate. There seems to be a strong need to compensate for dreaming time that has been lost (Dement, 1960). People who lose dreaming time because of sickness or worry say they compensate by dreaming more intensely. Often they have nightmares when their worries have passed.

The longer you sleep, the more likely you are to remember a dream. Since the later periods of sleep are light, you may be partly awake and become aware of the fact you have been dreaming (Taub, 1970). Although many people do not recall their dreams in the morning, they appear to dream as often as those who do remember. Interestingly, those who cannot recall dreams in the morning also find it hard to recall them when awakened just after an REM period.

Young children can't tell the difference between what is real and what they dream. They finally learn the difference, of course, and the stages of this learning have been described by Piaget (1950). In the first stage, the child does not know what a dream is and doesn't understand the distinction that adults make between real and unreal. Young children will report that a dream is in the bedroom where everyone can see it. Or they will say the dream disappears when the lights are turned on or when they hide under the covers. Before long, children begin to think of the dream as being inside their head, very much like a tiny TV show. If you could look inside, they believe, you would see the dream, too. Eventually, children achieve an adult understanding of the difference between dreams and reality. They do so because adults keep telling them which is which.

BLIND DREAMING

Sighted persons may follow dreams with their eyes because their dreams are strongly visual, but people who have been blind for a long time do not use their eyes in this way. Many of them report that their dreams are not visual in content. If rapid eye movements serve only the purpose of following dream activity, such movements should be absent in persons who have been without sight for many years. Berger, Olley, and Oswald (1962) found rapid eye movements were present during dreams only for those subjects who had been blind for less than 15 years. Measurements with instruments attached directly to the eyelid (Gross, Burne, and Fisher, 1965) revealed that tiny eye movements do occur in the blind. REM therefore seems to be a universal phenomenon in sleep, even when visual dreaming does not occur.

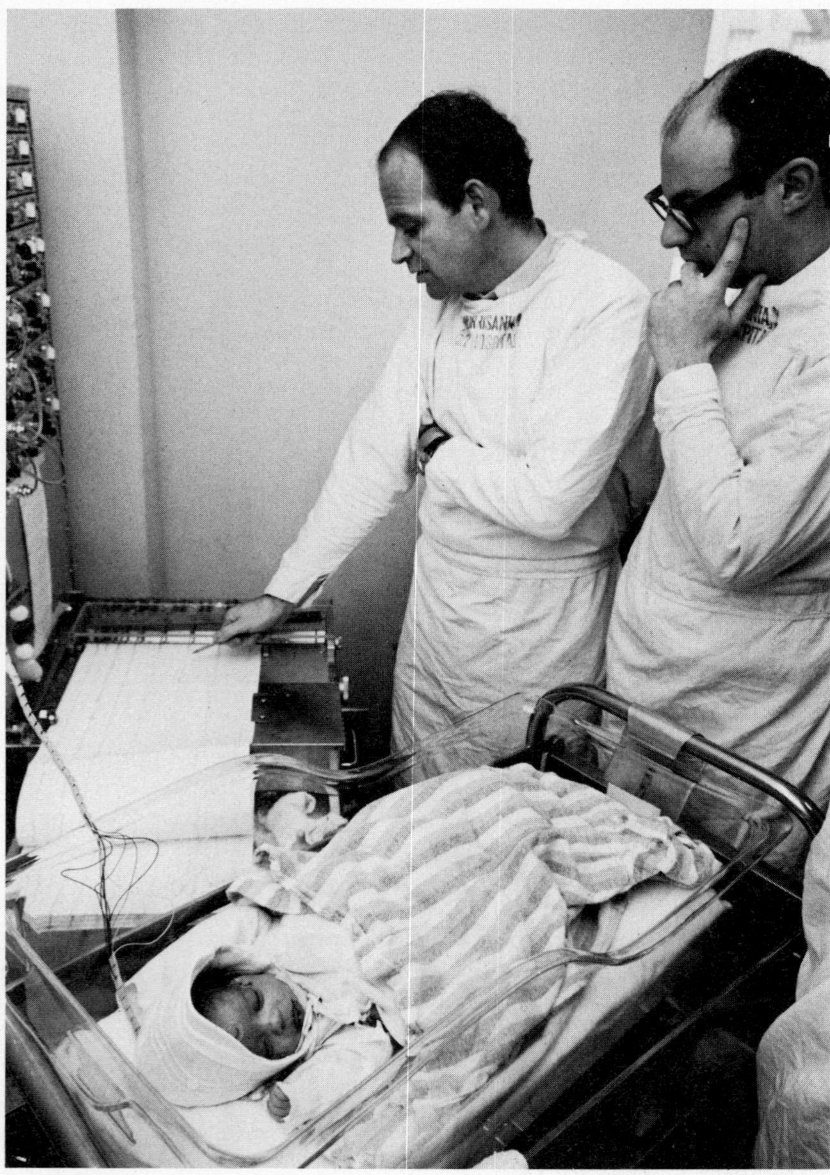

"Sleeping like a baby". The researchers are trying to figure out how the baby does it.

The Function of Dreams

The most influential theorist about the meaning of dreams was Sigmund Freud, who presented his theory in *The Interpretation of Dreams* (1900). There, Freud stated that unconscious impulses, unacceptable on a conscious level, are responsible for dreams and that the aim of the dream is the reduction of tension created by these impulses. The underlying meaning of the dream is called the *latent* content. The meaning is not expressed directly but rather appears in disguised form. What is remembered is the *manifest* content of the disguised form of the dream.

Freud declared that dreams represent pent-up emotional stresses and basic desires that we repress or deny. In sleep, with

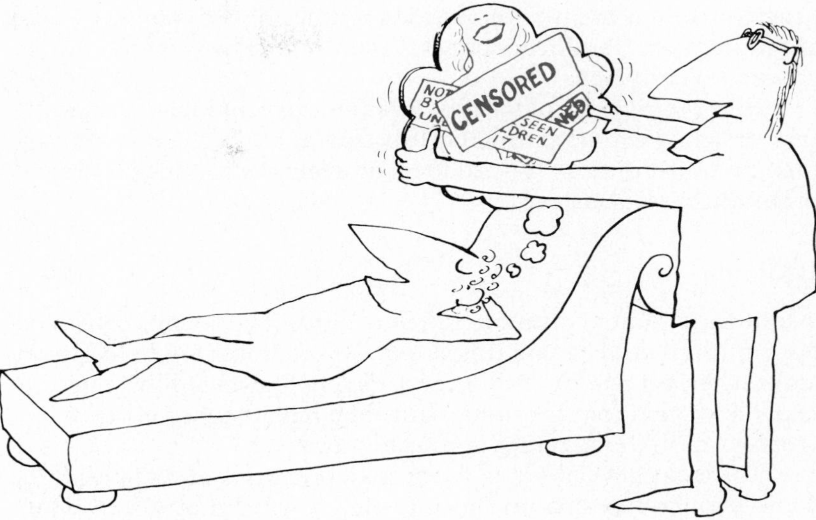

the "social censor" off guard, these repressed forces thrust to the surface as dreams. We can see, then, why psychoanalysis attaches such great importance to the content of dreams. According to psychoanalytic theory, dreams are clues to a person's true psychological concerns (Evans, 1967).

To Freud, much of our impulsive life centers around sexual wishes that are associated with taboos. Since these sexual wishes are suppressed, we can expect them to be symbolized in our dreams. Freud also thought that the dream is the guardian of sleep. Dreams get rid of unfulfilled impulses that might otherwise disturb sleep. Disguising these impulses is necessary so that the guilt associated with the disturbing impulse will not perturb the sleeper. If the meaning of the dream were to become known to the dreamer, he or she might awaken in order to get rid of such unacceptable thoughts. In Freudian theory, a nightmare is a dream that has been unsuccessful. The sleeper awakens because his or her thoughts have become so dangerous that conscious defenses must be brought into play to keep them under control.

Of course, Freud's is not the only interpretation of the function of dreams. Other psychologists have developed different explanations. For example, Jung (1964) argued that "the general function of dreams is to try to restore our psychological balance by producing dream material that reestablishes, in a subtle way, the total psychic equilibrium." Wish-fulfillment may sometimes be part of this balancing mechanism. In other cases, however, dreams warn us of personal weakness. Jung provides the example of a stubborn and stupid woman who ignored all reasonable argument. He wrote:

One night she dreamed she was attending an important social occasion. She was greeted by the hostess with the words, "How nice that you could come. All your friends are here, and they are waiting for you." The hostess then led her to the door and opened it, and the dreamer stepped through—into a cowshed! [1964, pages 49–50]

DAYDREAMS

Although psychoanalysts have long used patient's daydreams in diagnosis and therapy, psychologists have devoted surprisingly little effort to these waking fantasies. Daydreaming is more than just an escape from reality. It is our way of exploring possibilities and rehearsing our reactions to them.

Men and women daydream equally, but there is a difference in their fantasies. Women's daydreams may show an interest in fashions, whereas men tend to think about heroics and sports. The frequency of fantasies changes as people grow older. The peak of daydreaming occurs in midadolescence and seems to fall off gradually into old age (Singer, 1969).

Jung concluded that the dream was telling the woman something about her own "bullheadedness," pointing out a weakness that should be corrected.

Still other, physiologically oriented, psychologists suggest that dreams have no particular function at all; instead, dreams may be taken only as by-products of events occurring in the brain during REM sleep.

Insomnia

Insomnia is rather common. In some cities insomniac clubs have been formed and, as you might expect, meetings are held late at night when no one can fall asleep. Psychologists still do not know enough about insomnia, but they have begun to make progress in understanding and testing it.

To begin with, there is more than one kind of insomnia. Some people may toss and turn restlessly until they get to sleep but then sleep well the rest of the night. Others seem to sleep and wake up and then sleep and wake up all night long. There is also a type called "postdormitional insomnia," in which the individual wakes up in the early morning and is unable to go back to sleep.

Why are some people unable to fall asleep? The answer depends on which psychologist you ask. Some will explain insomnia as "sleep phobia"—the person is afraid of what will happen if he or she goes to sleep. Such people are afraid that they will have a nightmare or that an emergency will arise after they have fallen asleep. Other psychologists say insomnia arises from anxiety or fear. And it may be depression and worry that wake the individual too early and won't allow him or her to go back to sleep (Karacan and Williams, 1971).

Many people who claim to be insomniacs may not really be ones, of course. They might have "imaginary insomnia." Most so-called insomniacs get a lot more sleep than they think they do. With daytime naps they get as much sleep as the rest of us.

Beating Sleeplessness

Insomniacs can do something about their problem if they really want to. The most prominent causes of sleeplessness are tension and worry. Thus, methods of relaxing the mind and muscles are often successful in not only reducing tension but also improving sleep. Kahn, Baker, and Weiss (1968) used relaxation training to help Yale students sleep better prior to final exams. The method they used was simple (Schultz and Luthe, 1959). The subjects were instructed to lie comfortably on mattresses with their eyes closed. The students were told to visualize themselves in a peaceful situation, such as lying on a beach, while thinking the words, "I am at peace." This sentence was alternated with another repetition such as "My right arm is heavy." For 30 to 45 seconds, the leader repeated the instructions aloud: "I am at peace; my right arm is heavy. My right arm is heavy; I am at

SLEEPING WITHOUT BREATHING

Your breathing naturally becomes shallow while you are sleeping, but some sleepers stop breathing altogether for periods up to a minute and a half at a time. This disorder, known as *sleep apnea,* lowers the oxygen level of the blood, changes the blood's acid-base balance, and may lead to chronic hypertension. People suffering from sleep apnea don't stop breathing just once or twice; stoppages recur throughout the night. One patient studied by Mitler and his associates (1975) actually stopped breathing 534 times in one night. Even if each stoppage was only 10 seconds, this patient spent about 3 hours that night not breathing!

peace." The subjects were then asked to say the same thing silently for an additional 30 to 35 seconds. Next, the subjects were asked to practice the technique at home three times a day, using three one-minute trials, with short breaks in between. They were also asked to use the technique for 5 to 10 minutes after going to bed. When these instructions were followed, nearly everyone in the experiment reported clear improvement in sleeping. In a follow-up study nearly a year later, the improvement still continued.

Many people in today's drug-conscious society use sleeping pills in an effort to beat sleeplessness. When used occasionally and under medical supervision, such pills may help to relieve anxiety and thereby help the individual to sleep. But sleeping pills do not provide a permanent solution to sleeping problems. In fact, sleeping pills tend to interfere with REM sleep. As a result, the sleep that comes from pill-taking may not have the same value as natural sleep, and is less likely to leave the person feeling rested the next day.

FOR BETTER SLEEP, TRY COUNTING SHEEP

The idea of counting sheep in order to get to sleep is an old and much ridiculed one. Traditionally people thought that if this method was effective at all it was because of the pastoral setting in which the sheep leaped. But now two psychologists have suggested that the setting has nothing to do with it and that counting sheep can indeed be successful in dealing with insomnia. Richard Davidson and Gary Schwartz provide a strong scientific explanation. They point out that visualization of the sheep appeals to the brain's right hemisphere and prevents it from processing anxiety-provoking imagery. Similarly, counting sheep comes to occupy the left hemisphere and to keep it from becoming preoccupied with verbal problems. In this way, both hemispheres are lured away from the day's distractions.

DRUGS

Throughout history human beings have taken various chemical substances to change their mood, perception, and thought processes. The urge to use chemicals to alter the mind has spread to modern times with a vengeance (Evans, 1971). Contemporary observers can imagine a future in which chemicals will cushion everyone against headaches, frustration, and self-doubt. Whenever one's tranquility is threatened, one may simply swallow a pill and enjoy a brief, but satisfying, hallucination.

Drugs can alter consciousness in a number of ways. Depending on which drug is taken and on who takes it, drugs can cause (1) disturbances in thinking (altered attention, memory, and judgment); (2) a changed sense of time (time may speed up, slow down, or seem suspended); (3) feelings of loss of control (helplessness, as in a nightmare when you run but never seem to get anywhere); (4) alteration of emotional expression (unexpectedly intense or primitive emotional outbursts); and (5) distortions of perception (illusions, hyperacute perceptions, or hallucinations) (Ludwig, 1966).

Drugs may also produce changes in the meaning or significance of events. Drugs may bring on a sense of profound insight or discovery of ultimate truth, and this experience may trigger a sense of rejuvenation or renewed hope. There may also be a feeling of depersonalization. The usual perception of the body image may be distorted so that parts of the body seem shrunken or enlarged or seem to be floating. There may also be bodily effects in the form of numbness, weakness, dizziness, tingling, and the like.

Before discussing the effects of different types of drugs, we should define exactly what a drug is. Stroebel (1972) provides a definition that includes any substance of any type that is "eaten, injected into, inhaled, or absorbed by a living organism." Of course, by this definition everything from oxygen to a pepperoni pizza is a drug. Unfortunately, it may be impossible to devise a better definition. (Try coming up with one yourself.)

When we talk about drugs in this chapter, we will be focusing on substances that have a noticeable impact on consciousness and on behavior. These *psychoactive* drugs include hallucinogenic drugs (LSD, mescaline, psilocybin), amphetamines (Dexedrine, Benzedrine), narcotics (opium, morphine, heroin), barbiturates, cocaine, alcohol, marijuana, and a host of other compounds. In this chapter we will be focusing on only a few of the psychoactive drugs to develop a picture of their effects on human consciousness.

THE MEDICAL PUSHERS

Our medical men are drowning in commercial advertisements that push psychoactive drugs as the treatment of choice for emotional disorders of all kinds (Seidenberg, 1971). The drug industry spends nearly a billion dollars a year advertising directly to doctors. Rogers (1971) insists that the epidemic of legal drug abuse is just what the doctor ordered:

"Depression, social inadequacy, anxiety, apathy, marital discord, children's misbehavior, and other psychological and social problems of living are now being redefined as medical problems, to be solved by physicians with prescription pads" (page 16).

Why Do People Take Drugs?

There is a long list of reasons why some people choose to try drugs and others abstain. The possibilities listed by Lipinski and Lipinski (1970) are:

Curiosity.

The feeling of missing something or not being "with it."

Box 3

Hypnosis

Don't look up while you are reading this. There may be someone nearby whose piercing eyes are waiting to catch your attention, hypnotize you, destroy your willpower, and make you a slave. At least that's what you might believe if you watch too many old movies. The mystery surrounding hypnosis was inevitable, since it can produce so many unusual phenomena. Naturally you have some questions about this unusual state of consciousness, and we will try to answer a few of them for you.

What Is Hypnosis? Hypnosis is a state of increased suggestibility (or willingness to comply with another person's directions) that is brought about through the use of certain procedures by another person, the hypnotist. (Hypnosis can also be self-induced, using relaxation training techniques.) There is some controversy among psychologists concerning whether hypnosis is an altered state of consciousness or a state of heightened motivation that does not involve an alteration of consciousness.

How Is Hypnosis Done? The usual methods of hypnosis are having the person focus on an object or telling the person that he or she is getting sleepy. The point is to get the subject to relax, use his or her imagination, attend closely to what is said, and stop fighting it. The rest is up to the hypnotic subject and his or her

A need to prove one's intellectual depth and emotional maturity (particularly for shy people who don't relate easily to others).

A search for meaning (failing to find a clear answer in the outside world, the quest turns inward).

Escape from feelings of inadequacy (the hope for a magical cure for personal, emotional turmoil without the embarrassment of revealing "weakness" to others).

An end to isolation (drugs may give the feeling of greater closeness with others).

In addition to these motivations, drug use also depends on people's social environment and on the examples set by others. For example, Smart and Fejer (1972) obtained information about the drug use patterns (including alcohol and tobacco as well as other psychoactive drugs) of 8,865 Toronto students and their parents. They found a positive association between the students' use of drugs and that of their parents. Their data suggested that young people may often use their parents as models in deciding whether or not to try drugs.

---

willingness to go along with the suggestions.

Can You Be Hypnotized? Probably. Most people can. But it is easier for some than for others. The difference may be a question of personality and learning—it helps if you have a vivid imagination and feel comfortable accepting commands from others (Hilgard, 1965). But a genetic component may be involved as well. Studies of hypnotizability suggest that this ability is at least partly inherited. If your father and mother are easily hypnotized, chances are you're easily hypnotized, too (Morgan, 1973). Perhaps people inherit the ability to produce the vivid imagery that hypnosis requires.

How Does Hypnosis Work? The first thing to realize is that hypnosis is not something done to you by a hypnotist; it is a state you produce for yourself. The important questions are *how* and *why.*

No one really knows how this state is produced. This vagueness has led some researchers to doubt whether a unique condition called the "hypnotic trance" even exists. Barber (1970) claims that there is no scientific support or reliable test for it. For instance, hypnotized subjects don't exhibit a certain sort of EEG pattern the way people do when they are asleep.

Investigators are just beginning to learn why hypnotized subjects behave the way they do. Barber suggests that hypnosis has two important ingredients: the hypnotized person is motivated to cooperate with the hypnotist's suggestions, and the hypnotized person is able to involve his or her imagination in those suggestions. In fact, Barber insists that anything you can do while hypnotized, you can do in a wide-awake state. If both motivation and involvement are present, Barber says, the "hypnotic trance" and its induction are unnecessary. Of course, other experts disagree with this assessment. While admitting that motivation and imagination are important, Hilgard (1972), for example, argues that the hypnotic trance adds something extra.

Can Hypnosis Get Rid of Pain? Pain is a peculiar thing. Sometimes just a sugar pill can make pain disappear, if you believe that the pill will help. Hypnosis may be like this—reducing pain only because we believe it will. Then again, hypnosis may actually reduce pain through some more complex process relating to the hypnotic trance. At this point, we really don't know how hypnosis works. One thing is clear, however: hypnosis can produce pain relief. Hypnosis is commonly used to control pain in dental patients, and it has even been used to relieve pain in terminal cancer patients (Sacerdote, 1966).

LSD

LSD has been called a "utopiate" by Blum (1964) and a "nightmare drug" by Louria (1966). LSD-25 (lysergic acid diethylamide) produces a profound alteration of sensory, perceptual, cognitive, and emotional experiences. Louria has described such experiences in these terms:

They [colors] swirl around the individual with great vividness. Fixed objects fuse and diffuse; there is often a perceptual flowing of geometric designs and one sensation merges into another and one sense into another so that the individual may say he can taste color; touch sound. The body image is distorted and ordinary sounds increase profoundly in intensity. There is a sense of intense isolation and depersonalization so that "me" as an individual disappears and the user feels he is fused with all humanity and with his environment. Time stands still, and many give themselves up to what they describe as an experience of inexpressible ecstasy [pages 45–46]

The term *hallucinogenic* implies that the characteristic effect or action of the drug is to produce hallucinations. *Psychotomimetic* is a similar term, implying that the drug imitates or mimics psychosis. The terms *psychedelic* and *consciousness-expanding* imply that the person who takes the drug can expect a positive, creative, mind-expanding experience (Fort, 1970). None of these terms is precisely accurate, since the effects of the drug depend to a great extent on the personal characterstics of the user. The effect also depends on the setting in which the drug is taken and on the purity of the product that is being used.

LSD was originally used in research on social problems. It was tried with alcoholics to help them stop drinking and with autistic children to increase their contact with people in the real world (Ungerleider and Fisher, 1970). LSD has also been used by persons dying of cancer, in an effort to produce greater pain tolerance and a calmer acceptance of death. For some patients, LSD produces a dramatic improvement, but for others it only makes things worse. LSD not only eases pain, but for some it also relieves depression, anxiety, and a sense of psychological isolation. Pain relief alone may be a sufficient justification for its use.

There are other substances that produce psychological effects similar to those of LSD. *Peyote* (a Mexican cactus) is made up of alkaloids (one of which is mescaline) that produce intense color awareness and hallucinations. Reflexes seem heightened, time is overestimated, and spatial perception is altered. Hearing and sight seem intensified, and ideas flow rapidly (Nabokov, 1969). Some Indian tribes have used mescal buttons (from the peyote cactus) for centuries in religious ceremonies. Another drug, *psilocybin,* is derived from mushrooms that have been used in Indian religious rites since pre-Columbian times. Psilocybin is not nearly as potent as LSD, but it produces similar hallucinogenic effects.

Though the consciousness-expanding effects of hallucinogenic drugs have been expounded at great length, their effects will inevitably be explained in mundane and unromantic terms. For example, Barron, Jarvik, and Bunnell (1964) point out apparent similarities in the chemical structures of LSD, psilocybin, and serotonin, a substance used for communicating between neurons. Similarly, mescaline resembles the neural transmitter substance norepinephrine. The "mystical" effects of these drugs may result, it seems, from their interference with normal processes of neural transmission within the brain.

No psychedelic retains popularity for very long. Certainly, no drug can provide a packaged answer to the complex riddle of being human. In recent times the most popular drugs have been mood-changers of a different sort.

SPEED ON THE GRIDIRON

Though most of us are familiar with the common uses of amphetamines (to fight fatigue, depression, hunger), these drugs have invaded other areas of life as well. For example, Arnold Mandell (1975), former team psychologist for the San Diego Chargers, reports that about 50 percent of all professional football players use amphetamines during football games. Mandell writes, "One professional explained the practical facts. 'Doc,' he rumbled, 'I'm not about to go out there one-on-one against a guy who is grunting and drooling and coming at me with big dilated pupils unless I'm in the same condition.'"

The Amphetamines

In 1887 a German pharmacologist synthesized the first amphetamine (Benzedrine), but he was not interested in exploring the pharmacological properties of the drug and put the project aside. In 1932, the Benzedrine inhaler was made available to the public in drugstores across the country. It was taken as a medicine for hay fever, asthma, and other disorders involving nasal congestion. The American Medical Association gave this new drug the generic name *amphetamine,* from *a*lpha-*m*ethyl-*phe*thyl-*amine.* The only caution for the drug at that time was that "continued overdose" might cause "restlessness and sleeplessness." Physicians were assured that no serious reactions had been observed. By the end of World War II, at least seven different inhalers containing large amounts of amphetamine were on the market. All of them could be purchased without prescription. As Grinspoon and Hedblom (1972) note:

World War II probably was responsible for spurring both the legal medically authorized use and the illegal black-market abuse of the amphetamines. When German Panzer troops overwhelmed Poland, then Denmark and Norway, and drove through Belgium and France, they were taking huge doses of methamphetamine to eliminate fatigue and maintain physical endurance. But the Wehrmacht was by no means the sole large-scale consumer of amphetamines during World War II; Japanese soldiers and factory workers used as much or more. Nor was use of these stimulants confined to the Axis powers. According to British war statistics, seventy-two million standard-dose amphetamine tablets were distributed to the British armed forces alone. [page 36]†

In recent years, the use—and abuse—of amphetamines has reached frightening proportions. In 1971, legal amphetamine production in the United States had reached 12 billion tablets per year (Grinspoon and Hedblom, 1972). People who abuse amphetamines—"speed freaks"—usually inject the drug rather than take pills. They may spend several days on a "run," keeping a continuous high by injecting the drug every few hours. When the amphetamine high is over, the physical and psychological effects can be quite uncomfortable. The user may suffer extreme lethargy, fatigue, anxiety, terrifying nightmares, severe depression, disorientation, bewilderment, and confusion. The user may become extremely irritable and demanding, and may lose self-control or act out aggressive impulses. As Grinspoon and Hedblom describe the user, "His head aches, he has difficulty in breathing, he sweats profusely, and his body is racked with alternating sensations of extreme heat and cold and with excruciating muscle cramps. He characteristically suffers violently painful gastrointestinal cramps" (1972, page 40).

The amphetamines can also lead to psychosis-like episodes called *amphetamine psychosis.* Snyder (1972) has described this state as follows:

*Signs of amphetamine psychosis first develop while the speed-freak is under the influence of the drug. . . . The harbinger is vague fear and suspicion—*What was that? I heard something. Is somebody trying to get me? *Soon the paranoia centers around a specific delusion—for example, that the FBI is out to get him. An amphetamine party may begin with everyone very elated and talkative and may end with each person stationed silently at a window, peeking through the curtains for signs of the police. . . . Acting on his delusions the speed-freak may become violent—*to get them before they get me. *It is in this sense that the*

†*From "Amphetamines Reconsidered," L. Grinspoon and P. Hedblom,* Saturday Review, *July 8, 1972. Reprinted by permission.*

THE COPILOT

Grinspoon and Hedblom (1972) report that some of the early slang names for amphetamines originated among truck drivers, who called them "cartwheels," "coast-to-coasts," "West-Coast turnarounds," "truck drivers," and "copilots." "The last term presumably was derived from the now-legendary accident that occurred when one exceedingly lucky driver, who had stayed behind his wheel for more than two days on speed, decided to take a brief nap in his sleeping berth while moving at 60 miles per hour. When finally extricated from his totally demolished vehicle, he stated that he had been sure that his assistant was competent to handle the truck in broad daylight. The 'copilot,' however, was an amphetamine-induced illusion; the driver had been alone for the entire forty-eight hour period." [page 38]†

[3]*From "Amphetamines Reconsidered," L. Grinspoon and P. Hedblom,* Saturday Review, *July 8, 1972. Reprinted by permission.*

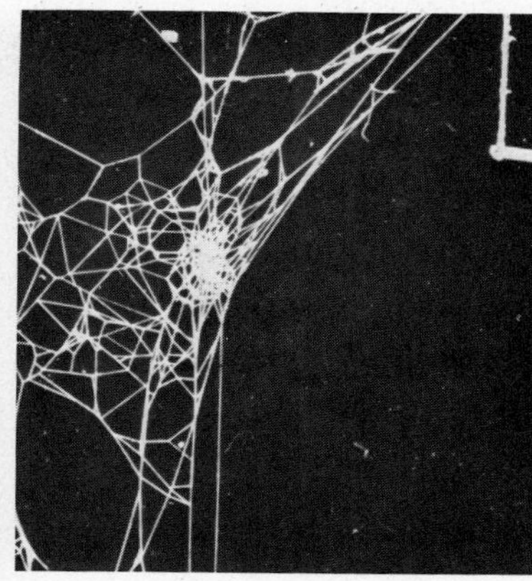

The effect of dextro-amphetamine (speed) on the web building of an adult female spider is shown here.

slogan SPEED KILLS is most accurate: more persons die from senseless and brutal violence associated with amphetamine delusions than from overdoses of the drug itself. . . . Another unique feature of amphetamine psychosis is compulsive, stereotyped behavior that the victim repeats hour after hour, apparently without fatigue or boredom. [*page* 44]

As with the hallucinogenic drugs, amphetamines produce their psychological effects by influencing neural transmission. During normal transmission of nerve impulses, transmitter substances are removed or destroyed immediately after being used,

Box 4
The Common Drugs

A nation of drug addicts? Well, not quite, but most of us do use drugs a great deal more than we are aware.

Cigarettes, for example, are a common source of nicotine, a drug that acts by blocking transmission in the sympathetic nervous system. Nicotine causes constriction in the peripheral blood vessels, elevates heart rate and blood pressure, and increases stomach activity. Perhaps for this reason smokers usually find cigarettes after meals quite pleasurable.

Caffeine, in coffee, tea, and cola drinks, acts as a central nervous system stimulant. People who consume too much caffeine may experience tremors, rapid heartbeat, overactivity, restlessness, and nausea. Strangely enough, caffeine is the "extra ingredient" in many common pain relievers, though its effects on pain are not clear.

Ethyl alcohol is consumed in huge quantities in beer, wine, and liquor. Alcohol abuse is, in fact, the biggest drug problem in America today, in all age groups. Small doses cause dilation of the pupils, slight increases in blood pressure, and temporary elevation of blood sugar level. Larger doses interfere with fine discrimination, motor control, and self-restraint. Excessive doses can cause coma and death. Alcohol appears to interfere with REM sleep, and chronic consumption leads to hallucinations and delirium (see Psychological Issue, Chapter 15).

Finally, there are a large number of drugs that are not quite as popular but are by no means uncommon. Codeine, a narcotic, is used for pain relief and for remedy of coughs. Amphetamines are consumed in the form of "diet pills" and "pep pills." Sedatives and tranquilizers are used by thousands of people to promote relaxation, reduce anxiety, and induce sleep. Surprising numbers of people trap themselves in a vicious cycle, taking one pill for pep in the morning, various other stimulants and anxiety-reducers during the day, and a sleeping pill at night, to the potential detriment of their physical and psychological well-being.

thereby keeping the neural pathways "free" for future messages and also indicating that the previous message is "over". Amphetamines not only cause the release of at least one neural transmitter (norepinephrine), they also impair the transmitters' removal. As a result, nerve transmission is altered in people who take amphetamines. Nerves that otherwise might not have fired do so because norepinephrine is released and maintained by amphetamine. Since norepinephrine is a transmitter for nerves involved in attention, wakefulness, memory, and mood, it influences all these psychological processes.†

Marijuana

Marijuana is made from the flowering tops of the hemp plant, *Cannabis sativa,* and except for alcohol it is probably mankind's oldest drug (Grinspoon, 1969). The earliest record of its use is found in a Chinese medical text of Emperor Shen Nung, dated 2737 B.C. Marijuana's use as an intoxicant spread from China to India, to North Africa, and eventually to Europe in about 1800 A.D. In fact, it may have been brought to Europe by Napoleon's troops returning from Egypt. Marijuana has been used for centuries in South America and Central America, but only became important in the United States after 1920.

During the 1930s and 1940s an aggressive law enforcement and publicity campaign condemning marijuana as "the assassin of youth" helped restrict its use to the poor and the eccentric. But during the past decade marijuana has enjoyed an explosion of popularity, and in 1972 an estimated 36 percent of American college students had tried the drug (Gergen and Morse, 1972). Of course, some groups use marijuana more than others. Males are more likely to have used it than have females, and students at schools in the Northeast and West are more likely to have tried it than those in the South and Midwest. Students at more selective colleges, students with higher grade point averages, and students with graduate ambitions are more likely to have tried the drug, although they may not be heavy users. Marijuana use also seems to be more common among students who are politically active.

Marijuana has only two easily observable physiological effects: it increases the pulse rate, and it enhances the appetite. Many of its other effects—including mild pupilary dilation, slight impairment of coordination, and even tremors—are less severe and less frequent (Grinspoon, 1969). But like all drugs that alter consciousness, marijuana does have effects on the brain. According to Maugh (1974), marijuana alters brain levels of the transmitter substances norepinephrine and serotonin, and it also produces changes in the EEG. Still, these effects seem only temporary, at least in light users (marijuana is not physically addicting).

†*From "The True Speed Trip: Schizophrenia," S. H. Snyder,* Psychology Today, *January, 1972, p. 44. Copyright © 1971 Ziff-Davis Publishing Company. REPRINTED BY PERMISSION OF PSYCHOLOGY TODAY MAGAZINE.*

The psychological effects of marijuana are even less obvious than the physiological effects: the drug seems to have little or no impact on sensory acuity, judgments of short time periods, or reaction times to simple stimuli. However, marijuana does seem to have an influence on hand steadiness, judgments of long time periods, and response times to complex stimuli. As a result, marijuana may impair performance on complex tasks. Nevertheless, it seems to cause less of an impairment of driving ability than alcohol (Grinspoon, 1969).

More serious consequences of marijuana use are still the subject of heated debate. Maugh (1974) argues that while light and occasional use of marijuana has no serious physiological or psychological effects, heavy and continued use may produce permanent deterioration in mental health. Some researchers have noticed a chronic lack of motivation in people who have used marijuana heavily, as well as in experimental animals given heavy doses of the drug. Though the evidence is by no means clearcut, some scientists believe that heavy use of the drug may produce irreversible brain damage.

The New Drugs

In the past, drugs that dominated the drug scene were psychedelics, amphetamines, and opiates (especially heroin). Now downers (barbiturates and other depressant drugs) are rapidly becoming the nation's number one abused drug (after alcohol, of course).

Most popular among the downers are the short-acting barbiturates (secobarbital and pentobarbital) and much newer soporifics. Users seem to prefer short-acting downers because they take effect in only 15 to 30 minutes and last from 2 to 4 hours. The immediate effect is that of a heavy, euphoric rush that can be sustained for some time if the urge to fall asleep is successfully fought off.

The change to these newer drugs seems motivated by the bad side effects produced by drugs such as LSD and the amphetamines. With LSD, even a simple experience can become diffi-

Box 5

Truth Drugs

Drugs with sedative or hypnotic effects have been used to stimulate people to talk. The technique, sometimes called *narcoanalysis,* proved useful to physicians who confronted large numbers of emotional casualties in the armed forces during World War II and the Korean War. In the twilight state induced by sodium pentothal and other drugs, even the usually uncommunicative patient talks easily and without inhibitions. This approach helps speed up treatment by supplying the therapist with diagnostic material that might not otherwise have been forthcoming or might have taken a long time to uncover.

The use of chemical assistance in interviews began in 1922 when physician Robert House employed scopolamine in the interrogation of suspected criminals. He tried it on two prisoners and enthusiastically reached the conclusion that the person under the influence of scopolamine "cannot create a lie . . . and there is no power to think or reason." This experiment and House's erroneous conclusion attracted wide interest, and the myth of the truth drug came into being.

The theory behind using truth drugs is that, by stripping away the conscious controls of behavior, the "truth" will come out. It is not quite as easy as that, as Freedman (1970) reports in an experiment on sleep at the Yale Medical School. He injected the "truth drug" sodium amytal very slowly into a large number of volunteer medical students. Previously, Freedman had attached electrodes to the subjects' heads and chests in order to take measurements related to sleep cycles. Since he was concerned with getting the students to sleep, he simply informed them of what he was doing. But the method and rate of injection were otherwise identical with the techniques regularly used for psychiatric interviews. Freedman recalls that in only one instance was there any talking, and the subject revealed no spontaneous "truths" about himself or his experiences.

Limitations in the use of truth serum became apparent in the case of the Boston Strangler, who killed 13 women in the early 1960s. In the frantic search for a guilty party, one man was put under a "truth" drug and made a very elaborate confession—which later turned out to be entirely false (Frank, 1966).

Even more destructive to the "truth drug" myth was an experiment in which sodium amytal was administered to volunteers after they had revealed shameful, guilt-producing episodes of their past and had then invented stories to cover up the episodes. Under the influence of the drug, the subjects were cross-examined about their cover story by a second investigator. The results suggested that normal individuals with no overtly pathological traits could stick to their invented stories. On the other hand, some neurotic individuals not only tended to confess more easily but also to substitute fantasy for the truth, confessing to offenses never actually committed.

These experimental and clinical findings indicate that only individuals with reasons for doing so are inclined to confess under the influence of drugs. Of course, if you *think* you are being given a truth drug that is impossible to resist, you may confess because you are convinced that there really isn't much point in lying.

cult to handle. With amphetamines, physical and mental activity are accelerated to the point of exhaustion. The newer drugs are cheap, available, and bring on a much pleasanter, uninhibited euphoria similar to that of alcohol.

Apparently, there is no end to ways of achieving drug-induced consciousness alteration. In fact, some legislators have suggested that American society abandon attempts to legislate how individuals treat or mistreat themselves—for one thing, it's an impossible job.

The psychiatrist Thomas Szasz (1972) suggests that in an open society the government has no business regulating which drugs a person puts into his or her body. According to Szasz, all drugs should be decriminalized and unrestricted if we are to be consistent with the principles of personal liberty. At the moment, we reserve that liberty for alcohol. As Szasz notes:

Our present practices with respect to alcohol embody and reflect this individualistic ethic. We have the right to buy, possess, consume alcoholic beverages. Regardless of how offensive drunkenness might be to a person, he cannot interfere with another person's "right" to become inebriated so long as that person drinks in the privacy of his own home or at some other appropriate location, and so long as he conducts himself in an otherwise law-abiding manner. In short, we have a right to be intoxicated—in private. [1972, page 77]†

There is no easy answer to the drug problem. Evidently the drug issue is an important factor in the direction our society will take in the future. The argument rages not about the issue of altering consciousness but about the question of which methods are acceptable and which are not.

SUMMARY

1. Although psychologists have trouble defining consciousness—and some insist that it may not really exist—this concept can best be defined as a level of thought that integrates and regulates one's experience and that is sometimes necessary for normal activities but often is not.
2. Sleep is an altered state of consciousness that appears to be universal. Lack of sleep for long periods of time can lead one to experience brief losses of awareness called *microsleep.*
3. There is probably no necessary relationship between when people sleep and the day-night cycle, although the human propensity to sleep at night appears to be universal. Kleitman suggests that our ability to alter sleeping patterns is due to the fact that there are two kinds of wakefulness: *wakefulness of necessity,* which is controlled by the brain stem, and *wakefulness of choice,* which is controlled by the cortex.
4. Each night's sleep session involves several levels of altered consciousness, each having a characteristic brain wave pat-

†*From "The Ethics of Addiction," T. S. Szasz,* Harper's, *April 1972, p. 77. Reprinted by permission.*

tern. Of the four stages of sleep, the fourth, *delta sleep,* is the deepest and occurs primarily in the first part of the night.

5. In addition to these four stages, called non-REM (NREM) sleep, there is a qualitatively different type of sleep characterized by rapid eye movements and by dreaming. REM and NREM sleep differ in several physiological respects.
6. Hartmann found that short-sleepers tend to be extraverted, carefree, confident, politically apathetic, and socially conforming, while long-sleepers tend to be introverted, anxious, unsettled, politically concerned, and nonconforming.
7. Everyone dreams, although some people may not be able to recall their dreams. Apparently, we have a real need to dream. People prevented from dreaming soon become anxious and irritable, and have difficulty concentrating.
8. Piaget pointed out that children's concepts of what a dream is and how dreams differ from reality change as children grow older.
9. Sigmund Freud proposed that dreams fulfill the need to express unconscious, forbidden impulses. The expression is disguised, however, so the sleeper won't be disturbed. Freud thought that nightmares are unsuccessful dreams that have allowed forbidden wishes to become too explicit. Jung suggested that dreams function to produce psychological equilibrium in the individual.
10. Insomnia may have a number of causes and occurs in a number of forms. One method of dealing with insomnia is to use relaxation training in order to reduce tension and thereby encourage sleep. Sleeping pills may bring sleep, but they tend to interfere with REM sleep and therefore are not really helpful.
11. Hypnosis is a state of increased suggestibility that may or may not be an altered state of consciousness. Some people seem to be more easily hypnotized than others, and this may be genetically influenced. Hypnosis has been used in a number of areas, including relief of pain.
12. Drug-altered states of consciousness differ from ordinary consciousness in a number of ways. The user experiences disturbances in thinking, a changed sense of time, feelings of loss of control, alteration of emotional expression, and distortions of perception.
13. *Psychoactive* drugs are those having a noticeable impact on consciousness and behavior. Use of drugs may result from a variety of motivations—from curiosity, to escape, to a need to fit in. There is also a strong relationship between patterns of drug use by parents and by children.
14. LSD is a psychedelic drug that produces profound alterations of sensory, perceptual, cognitive, and emotional experiences. Therapeutically, it has been used to help alcoholics, autistic children, and terminal cancer patients. Similar

psychological effects are produced by mescaline (or peyote) and psilocybin.

15. Psychedelic drugs are thought to achieve their effects by interfering with the transmission of messages between neurons in the brain.

16. Amphetamines are drugs that stimulate the central nervous system. People who use amphetamines for dieting or for staying awake usually take pills, whereas true "speed freaks" inject the drug while on a several-day "run." Excessive use of amphetamines can lead to *amphetamine psychosis*, in which the user has episodes of hallucinations and paranoia.

17. Like the psychedelics, amphetamines are thought to achieve their effects by interfering with nerve transmission. Amphetamines may cause neurons to fire when ordinarily they wouldn't.

18. Among other drugs commonly used in America are nicotine (in cigarettes), caffeine, alcohol, and narcotics. Americans often get caught in a cycle of taking stimulants and depressants to pick them up and bring them down during the day.

19. Marijuana's effects are mild compared to those of most other drugs. Its few physiological effects include increased pulse rate, increased appetite, changes in the EEG, and slight impairment of coordination. Psychological effects are less easily measured but appear to include impaired judgment of long time periods and longer reaction times to complex stimuli.

20. Downers seem to have replaced other drugs as the most popular in the drug community. Downers include barbiturates and soporifics. Users enjoy the pleasant euphoria downers provide.

21. "Truth drugs" have sometimes been used in psychiatry and police work to get people to volunteer information truthfully and without inhibitions. Various experiments and true-life examples seem to show, however, that truth drugs do not really provide the desired effects.

Meditation

The search for the meaning of life and for some way to cope with life's pressures is as ancient as mankind itself. Recently, this quest has led to a widespread interest in meditation as a possible answer.

What is meditation? According to Naranjo and Ornstein (1971):

Meditation has been described as a process of calming the ripples on a lake; when calm, the bottom, usually invisible, can be seen. In another metaphor meditation is likened to the night: stars cannot be seen during the day, their faint points of light overwhelmed by the brilliance of the sun. In this image, meditation is the process of "turning off" the overwhelming competing activity that is the light of the sun, until . . . the stars can be seen quite clearly. [*page 214*]

Meditation has been described as a deep passivity combined with awareness—a suspension of the usual rat race of mental and physical activity in order to *experience* things rather than just *do* them. Usually, your mind bounces

Meditation has been described as a deep passivity combined with awareness. . . .

Box I-1
You Take the High Road . . .
Like the roads to Scotland, the roads to altered consciousness are varied. One surprise finding concerning meditation is that it appears to reduce interest in drugs. A study of nearly 2,000 practitioners of transcendental meditation (TM) reported dramatic decreases in the use of marijuana, LSD, amphetamines, barbiturates, narcotics, alcohol, cigarettes, and other nonprescribed drugs after meditation. Perhaps meditation makes drugs unnecessary; it may be a cheaper, more reliable, and more direct route to altered consciousness (Benson and Wallace, 1972).

from one idea to another, reacting to every sensation, thought, or stimulus. But in order to reach new and unusual experiences, you must learn how to ignore the usual, familiar stimuli.

Learning to Meditate

The position used in meditation is important. It should let you relax, yet not allow you to fall asleep. The cross-legged "lotus" positions used by some meditators are very difficult and quite uncomfortable for most beginners. These positions are not absolutely essential to the meditative state. You can meditate while sitting up straight but relaxed in a regular chair. In that position you can practice concentrating and eliminating distractions. You don't fight to prevent them. You just bring your attention back again to the object of your meditation every time your attention wanders. If you try too hard to prevent distractions, you can get distracted by the very task. Most meditators sit alone or with a small group in a special room set aside for meditation. Some meditators burn incense to give a consistent odor to the place of meditation and to mask other odors that might break concentration. Typically, meditation is practiced for 20 minutes twice a day.

In psychological terms there are two general kinds of meditation. One kind involves restriction of awareness by focusing attention on an object or repeated word. The second type involves opening up awareness to experience everything in greater depth. To achieve these goals, meditators practice various exercises. They may decide to concentrate on one part of their body, to focus on their breathing, or to stare at an object without blinking. One form of meditative practice uses the *mantra*. A mantra is a series of words used as the focus of awareness. The mantra is repeated over and over, aloud or silently, while all other thoughts and stimuli are excluded. "Mantras are sonorous, mellifluous words, which repeat easily. An example is OM. This mantra is chanted aloud in groups, or used individually in silent or voiced meditation. Another is OM - MANI - PADME - HUM." (Naranjo and Ornstein, 1971, page 150).

The simpler forms of meditation can be learned quickly. In an experiment conducted by Maupin (1965), college students volunteered to concentrate on the natural process of

A mantra is a series of words used as a focus of awareness.

breathing. They were told to relax and then focus their attention on their breathing and the movement of their belly. The students were to avoid being distracted by other thoughts or stimuli. Not all subjects were equally good at the task. In a two-week period, however, a group of "high-responders" reported reaching a deeply satisfying state of altered consciousness. They described this altered state in terms of extreme detachment from the outside world, intense concentration, and pleasant bodily sensations.

Transcendental Meditation

One form of meditation that has become especially popular recently is called transcendental meditation (TM), a system developed by an Indian guru (or Holy Man) named Maharishi Mahesh Yogi. TM advocates include quarterback Joe Namath, singer Stevie Wonder, and perhaps as many as 600,000 other Americans. TM includes a number of exotic elements, including an initiation ceremony in which the initiate brings an "offering" of a white handkerchief, several pieces of fruit, and a bunch of

"A good time for the world is coming. . . ." Maharishi Mahesh Yogi

flowers, symbolizing, respectively, the cleansing of the spirit, the seed of life, and the flowers of life. In a private room, the initiate's guru or teacher places the offering on an altar under a picture of Guru Dev (Maharishi's teacher). The teacher then introduces the meditator to his own personal mantra, on which he is to meditate for the rest of his life (*Time,* October 11, 1975).

The Maharishi Mahesh Yogi is the only one in the TM movement who is not expected to meditate on a regular basis. "He doesn't have to," one of his secretaries explained. "He long ago achieved a perpetual fourth state of consciousness. The clarity of his mind is awesome." *Time* magazine reports that the Maharishi believes that if only 1 percent of the population of any community or country is meditating, the other 99 percent of the population will feel the good effects and crime will be reduced. If 5 percent meditates, great things will begin to happen, says the Maharishi. "A good time for the world is coming. I see the dawn of the Age of Enlightenment. I am only giving expression to the phenomenon that is taking place." (*Time,* October 13, 1975)

Transcendental meditation is, of course, only one meditative technique. Other methods are possible and, throughout history, have produced similar effects. In addition, some nonmeditative techniques, such as progressive relaxation (used in systematic desensitization, described in Chapter 17) and hypnosis (described in Box 3 of Chapter 4) appear capable of yielding many of these effects. Benson, Beary, and Carol (1974) have suggested that there may be an integrated physiological pattern, which they label the "relaxation response," that results from TM, progressive relaxation, hypnosis, and a number of other procedures.

Benson and others suggest that four elements are necessary to elicit the relaxation response: (1) A quiet environ-

Box I-2

The Blue Vase
To study the phenomenon of meditation, Deikman (1963) had a research subject practice staring at a blue vase. The subject was told not to analyze the different parts of the vase but rather to try to see the vase as it existed in itself. The subject was supposed to exclude all other thoughts, feelings, or sounds. As the experiment progressed, the subject reported an increasingly intense perception of the vase, a more rapid passage of time, less distractibility from outside events, and the achievement of a pleasant, rewarding new state of consciousness.

ment; loud noises should be absent and the eyes should be closed. (2) Decreased muscle tone; the posture should be comfortable and the muscles relaxed. (3) A passive attitude; distracting thoughts should be ignored and anxiety about performance should be eliminated. (4) A "mental device"; attention should be shifted from logical thought to an object or sound (such as a mantra).

Transcendental meditation and other techniques would appear to be successful because they incorporate these four elements. The mystical and religious overtones of these methods may be mere icing on the cake.

Meditation and Body Control

For a great many years psychologists dismissed the claims made in favor of meditation as unscientific and mystical. In recent years, however, research has proven that meditators can alter their bodily metabolism and even the patterns of their brain waves.

Wallace and Benson (1972), for example, found that powerful metabolic changes were produced during transcendental meditation. These changes were different from those produced by either hypnosis or sleep. In meditators, less oxygen was consumed, the heartbeat was slowed, respiration was retarded, and brain waves changed. Various bodily measures indicated that the meditators were extremely relaxed, but awake. Other investigators have learned that experienced meditators show improved cardiovascular efficiency, faster reaction times, lower blood pressure, decreased anxiety and irritability, and increased self-assurance and emotional stability. Wallace and Benson suggest meditation might prove to be a valuable tool for maintaining psychological health—especially for those caught up in the bustle of industrial society.

Practicing yogis have made much more fantastic claims of body control. It is said that they can be buried alive or walk on hot coals. Until now, such actions have been considered impossible, since the yogi would have to control parts of the nervous system traditionally thought to work only on an autonomic basis. We have known for some time, of course, that the mind can produce incredible and mysterious changes in the body. The fact is now evident that yogi masters, with years of practice, can accomplish astonishing control over what happens to their bodies. We don't know what limits are really possible. We can only guess at the final effect that meditative experience will have on psychology and the study of consciousness.

Summary

1. In meditation one experiences a detachment from the outside world and very intense concentration. Meditators try to create an atmosphere in which they will not be subject to distractions.
2. Meditation may involve a restriction of awareness to one object or word (such as a mantra) or it may mean opening up awareness to experience the world in greater depth.
3. Transcendental meditation (TM) is practiced by the followers of Maharishi Mahesh Yogi. Techniques such as progressive relaxation and hypnosis seem to produce results similar to those of TM.
4. Some skilled meditators are able to alter many of their physiological mechanisms, including heart rate, breathing, and brain waves. Meditators have shown that many processes previously thought to be beyond voluntary control may actually be within conscious direction.

PART 3

Learning and Thinking

Worms can learn to wriggle their way through mazes, dogs can remember people and places, and there is even some evidence that chimpanzees can be taught to use language. Nevertheless, human beings have taken the abilities to learn and to think farther than any of their animal relatives. Indeed, learning and thinking are often viewed as the hallmarks of being human. The official name for our species, *Homo sapiens*, can be translated from the Latin as "thinking man." In the next four chapters we will explore the rational, information-processing aspect of human beings. Chapter 5 will be devoted to the principles of *Learning*, Chapter 6 to the mechanisms of *Memory*, Chapter 7 to the interrelated processes of *Thought and Language*, and Chapter 8 to the nature of *Intelligence*. We often take these capacities for granted, but their importance is pointed up when we consider cases in which they are impaired. Chapter 6, for example, will include a discussion of memory disorders, and Chapter 8 will discuss mental retardation.

Learning and thinking not only play a major role in our lives as individuals, but they are also central to the workings of society as a whole. We will consider some of these implications in the Psychological Issues that follow each of the chapters in this part. After Chapter 5, we will discuss the ways in which our knowledge of the principles of learning can lead to *Behavior Control*—the regulation of some people's behavior by other people, whether for good or evil purposes. We will follow our examination of memory in Chapter 6 with a discussion of the role of *Memory in the Courtroom*. After Chapter 7, we will deal with the nature and sources of human *Creativity*. And after Chapter 8, we will consider our system of *Education*, including some of the charges that have been leveled against it and some of the educational innovations now appearing on the horizon. Through the course of these chapters, it will become increasingly clear that human learning, memory, thought, language, and intelligence are not only fascinating psychological processes, but also powerful weapons. Depending on how we use these capacities, they can be the instruments of our betterment or of our destruction.

CHAPTER 5

Learning

Is this something like your typical day? You wash, brush your teeth, get dressed. You walk or ride or drive to school. You go to the correct rooms for your classes, and you make your way to the library almost without thinking. There, you read a book effortlessly. On your way to the student union you see someone you know and say, "Hi, Sue!" When you get home, you prepare yourself a snack and do some studying. Later, you play cards with some friends.

How is it that you can do all these things? When you were much younger, you couldn't do any of them. Gradually, over time, you've come to be able to do more and more. The basic process underlying all of these changes (from not being able to do something to being able to) is called *learning.* Learning is defined in psychology as a relatively permanent change in behavior as the result of experience or practice. Because so much of our behavior is learned—and because this simple fact has so many implications—learning has long been the cornerstone of American psychology.

In this chapter and the next, we will deal with learning and with the related process of memory. To be able to say "Hi, Sue!" you must have learned Sue's name in the first place and you must have been able to remember it over some period of time. To be able to play cards, you must remember the rules of the particular card game. And to do well in classes you need to learn and remember course material. The processes of learning and memory are thus closely interrelated. Each brings up separate issues and problems, however, so we will take them up in separate chapters.

BIOLOGICAL INFLUENCES ON LEARNING

American psychologists, especially those in the *behaviorist* tradition, have placed such a heavy emphasis on learning that the impression is sometimes created that *all* behavior is learned and that anyone can learn virtually anything, if he or she only works at it long enough. Learning is tremendously important for all of us, but we should not fall into the trap of believing that learning is everything. Our behavior is also influenced by heredity in a number of important ways. There are some patterns of behavior that animals are born with (often called instincts) and other patterns that are genetically preprogrammed to develop at particular critical periods of an animal's life. In addition, different animals (including humans) are limited biologically in what they can and cannot learn. With the possible exception of Dumbo, for example, elephants cannot learn to fly—their anatomy makes it impossible. Before we focus on the types and principles of learning, therefore, it will be useful for us to consider some of these hereditary influences that limit learning.

Instinct

Some behaviors do not have to be learned. Such automatic, inborn activities are referred to as *instincts.* Patterns of instinctive behavior are found in many species, particularly in birds, insects, and fish. Mother birds build nests, lay eggs, secure food, and return to the nest to feed the young without having learned to do so. A cat bearing her first litter will instinctively eat the placenta (the afterbirth membrane), kill any kittens that have been born deformed, and nurse the healthy young. Behaviors such as these are instinctive because they conform to three conditions: (1) all members of the species (of the appropriate age and sex) exhibit them, (2) they are not learned, (3) they are not mere reflexes (simple automatic responses to a specific stimulus).

The term "instinct" is often used inaccurately in referring to human behaviors. We may talk about the "maternal instinct" in a new mother or a "killer instinct" in a mass murderer. But by doing so we are confusing behaviors that are impulsive with those that are in fact instinctive—that is, inborn and unlearned. When you get right down to it, the concept of instinctive behavior appears to have little relevance to the behavior of higher animals, especially human beings. For example, there is such a wide variation in human maternal behavior that it cannot be called instinctive—many human parents take special parenthood preparation courses to learn how to care for their expected children, while other humans choose not to have children at all. However, humans' apparent lack of instincts should not lead you to assume that inherited characteristics play little role in human behavior. In fact, our actions and thoughts reflect the combined effects of our inherited capacities and what we learn from experience.

A PARENTAL INSTINCT?

Konrad Lorenz has suggested that there is at least one possible area in which humans have an "instinct." He noticed that people all share a similar response whenever they see young animals, whether bunnies, kittens, puppies, or babies—they smile and remark on the cuteness of the animal or child. Lorenz noted that the young of many species share similar characteristics: short faces, prominent foreheads, large round eyes, and plump cheeks. He identified these characteristics as a stimulus that arouses the "parental response." Whether this type of response would be considered "instinctive" is still a matter of debate.

Critical Periods

The interaction between heredity and environment is dramatically illustrated in the case of *critical periods.* For some organisms, particular behaviors must be learned at a certain early time in the animal's development or the behaviors will not be learned at all. There are many examples of critical periods in learning, but the now-classic example is the process of *imprinting,* first identified by Konrad Lorenz ((1937). Lorenz noted that soon after ducklings are born they start following the mother duck around, and he wondered why this response occurred. By arranging things so that he would be the first moving object a group of newly hatched ducklings would see, Lorenz found that they would follow him around instead of the mother. These ducklings

Soon after ducklings are born, they start following the mother duck or anyone else, even Konrad Lorenz. This is an example of the process called *imprinting.*

had imprinted the response during a critical period, in which any object that fit certain characteristics became the "mother" figure to be followed. Other experimenters used a wooden duck and a recording of a duck call during imprinting (Hess, 1959) and confirmed that ducks are imprintable only at a certain time shortly after hatching.

In a different sort of study, J. P. Scott (1969) raised a newborn female lamb on a bottle and kept it in his house for ten days. The lamb quickly became attached to family members; everywhere the Scotts went, the lamb was sure to go. When the lamb was introduced to other sheep, it paid them no attention. Three years later, it was still wandering around the field by itself while the rest of the flock stayed together as sheep normally do.

Such controlled experiments would be unthinkable with human infants. As a result, there is still controversy over whether there are critical periods in human development. It has been suggested, for example, that there is a critical period for making social attachments, since infants who are confined to institutions during the first six months of life, and who are deprived of motherly love, tend to become maladjusted more often than infants institutionalized at a later age (Goldfarb, 1947).

A stronger case for critical periods in human beings has been made in the area of language development. Eric Lenneberg (1967) studied the language skills of deaf children and related them to the age at which the children had become deaf. He found that children who did not become deaf until age three or four had an easier time at learning language than childen who had lost their hearing at an earlier age. He also found that deaf children stopped improving their language skills at about age fourteen. From such findings Lenneberg concluded that the critical period for language development begins at about age two and ends at about age fourteen. Lenneberg's conclusions coincide with the language theory of Noam Chomsky (see Chapter 7), who believes that humans are born with a biological predisposition toward learning language.

WILD CHILDREN

Several cases have been recorded of children who have grown up in the wilderness in the absence of other human beings. One of the most famous cases involved the "Wild Child of Aveyron," immortalized in Francois Truffaut's film *The Wild Child.* This boy was found living in the forests in the south of France and was brought to Paris and put in an institution for deaf-mute children. A doctor took on the job of trying to teach the boy, who seemed to be about 12 years old, to behave in a civilized manner. Although the doctor succeeded in teaching the boy manners and cleanliness, the child never did learn more than a few words, despite persistent efforts to teach him to talk and understand language. Although there is some speculation that the boy might have been mentally retarded, it may simply be that he had gone beyond the critical period for learning to use language.

Predispositions

A further biological influence on learning is the fact that organisms seem to have *predispositions* to learn certain behaviors—particularly actions that have survival value. Animals of a particular species (such as rats) seem to prefer certain kinds of responses to danger (such as running rather than fighting), and it is difficult to teach them other kinds of responses for avoiding the danger (Bolles, 1970).

An example of a built-in predisposition to learn certain responses and not others was provided by Garcia and Koelling (1966). Using a clever experimental setup, they were able to show that rats have a predisposition to associate sickness with taste but not with sounds, sights, or other types of stimuli. They gave rats water with a distinctive taste, and as the rats drank they were exposed to flashing lights and clicking sounds. The animals were then subjected to x-rays that made them sick about eight hours later. Despite the fact that the novel multimedia experience had occurred only once, and despite the fact that the sickness had occurred many hours afterward, the rats almost totally avoided the novel taste in later tests. However, they showed no aversion to the flashing lights or clicking sounds. On the basis of this and other experiments, Revusky (1971) has suggested that there is a sort of biologically programmed "rat logic"—a predisposition to learn associations that make sense biologically. After all, a rat is more likely to get sick from something that it eats or drinks than from something that it sees or hears.

As is the case with instincts and critical periods, the significance of these findings for the more complex and flexible human organism is difficult to assess. Psychologists have speculated, however, that such biological predispositions have an influence on human fears. Ask yourself which of the following things you are more likely to be afraid of: electrical outlets, spiders, scissors, fire, snakes, broken glass. You have learned that all these things are potentially dangerous, and yet you are likely to be most wary of the naturally occurring phenomena (fire, insects, etc.). Humans may be predisposed (perhaps originally for the purpose of survival) to fear some things and not others (Scarf, 1974). We are not born with these fears; they must still be learned. Once again, experience interacts with what one has inherited to produce specific learning.

CONDITIONING: CLASSICAL AND OPERANT

Psychologists who study learning have focused on two basic processes that seem to underlie much of the learning that we do: *classical conditioning* and *operant conditioning.* The word "conditioning" is used because it indicates that in each case particular *stimuli* (objects or events in the world) set up the conditions for the occurrence of our *responses* (the behaviors we perform). Classical (or respondent) conditioning focuses on the way in which *involuntary* responses (such as heart rate, blood pressure, or aspects of emotion that we have no direct control over) may be linked to particular objects or events. Operant conditioning focuses on the way in which *voluntary* responses (such as walking, writing, or talking) may be linked to the rewards and punishments we receive for making them. Let us consider each of these types of learning in turn.

Classical Conditioning

The story of conditioning begins with the work of the Russian physiologist Ivan Pavlov (1849–1936). A Nobel prize winner in physiology, Pavlov was experimenting on the salivary and digestive glands of animals—primarily dogs—to measure the effect of gastric juices and to learn how digestion works. He noticed that when food was put directly into a dog's stomach it did not produce enough digestive juices to allow for normal digestion. He also noted that digestive juices would begin to flow when the dog

Ivan Pavlov

merely *saw* food. But his most surprising discovery was that laboratory animals would begin to salivate as soon as the experimenter who had previously fed them entered the room. The same thing happens when you pick up your dog's feeding dish; he starts to respond as if it were time to eat. Pavlov's curiosity was aroused by this phenomenon, and he began a long series of experiments on it because he thought it could serve as the basis for a theory of brain functioning. His theory has long since passed into obscurity, but his experiments demonstrated the basic principles of what is now called classical conditioning.

We will use a typical experiment in Pavlov's laboratory to analyze classical conditioning. The animals were prepared so that their saliva flowed into a small glass funnel outside the cheek, allowing their salivation to be measured. (See Figure 5.1.) During the experiment the dog was placed in a harness while the experimenter sat on the other side of a partition, presenting stimuli to the dog and recording its responses. At this point in the experiment, before conditioning, two things could be observed: (1) Food presented to the animal elicited salivation. This is a reflex; it occurs automatically. Since no conditioning had yet taken place, Pavlov called food the *unconditioned stimulus,* and he called salivation the *unconditioned response.* (2) Other stimuli that were irrelevant to salivation would evoke other responses from the dog. A bell, for example, would cause the dog to prick up its ears and orient itself toward the sound but would not cause saliva to flow. At this point, the bell would be called a *neutral stimulus,* and the dog's response would be called the *orienting response.*

The next part of the experiment was the conditioning phase, which took place over a period of several days. During conditioning, a bell was rung and a few seconds later a small amount of food was placed near the dog's mouth, causing it to salivate. After about thirty such presentations of the bell and food together, the bell alone was sufficient to elicit a strong flow of

CONDITIONING BEFORE BIRTH

Spelt (1948) discovered that he could condition a fetus in the mother's uterus during the last two months of pregnancy. He used a very loud noise as the unconditioned stimulus and vibration of the mother's abdomen as the conditioned stimulus. After pairing the noise and the vibration about 15 or 20 times, the fetus would move in response to the vibration alone. Spelt also found that he could extinguish this conditioned response, that spontaneous recovery occurred, and that the conditioned response could be retained over a three-week period.

FIG. 5 · 1 Laboratory apparatus similar to that used by Pavlov. The tube, connected to the salivary gland, collects any saliva secreted, and the number of drops is recorded on a revolving drum outside the chamber.

FIG. 5 · 2 Classical conditioning

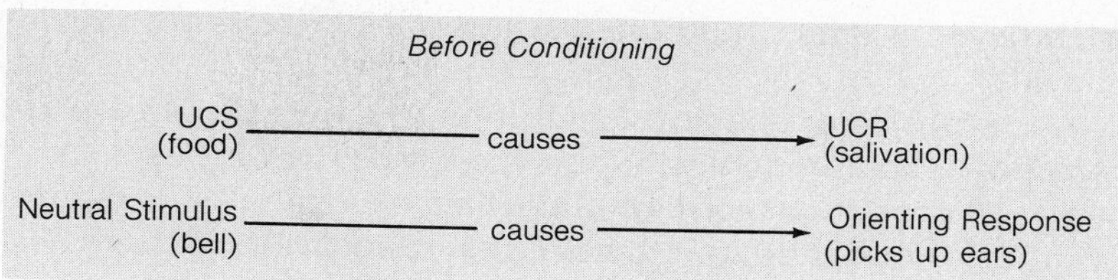

An unconditioned stimulus (UCS) produces an unconditioned response (UCR). Similarly, a neutral stimulus produces an orienting response.

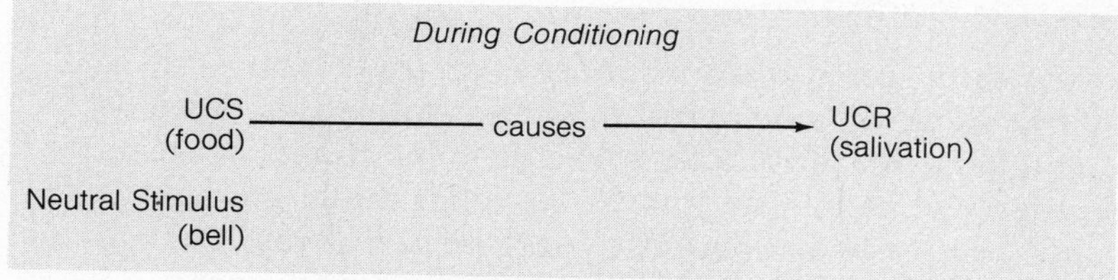

The unconditioned stimulus is presented along with the neutral stimulus. The unconditioned stimulus continues to produce an unconditioned response.

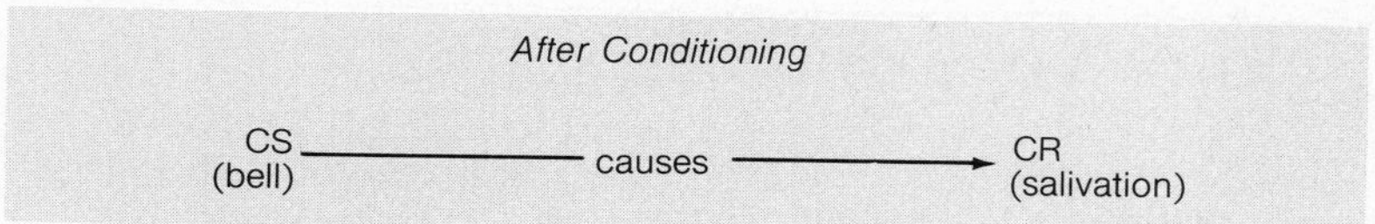

The neutral stimulus has become a conditioned stimulus (CS). It is now capable of producing a conditioned response (CR) —the same response which was previously produced by the unconditioned stimulus.

saliva. The bell was now called the *conditioned stimulus,* and the salivation was called the *conditioned response.* The essence of classical conditioning is thus that the subject learns to attach an existing response (such as salivation) to a new stimulus (such as the bell)—a dog would never, under normal circumstances, salivate at the sound of a bell. For a summary of the classical conditioning process, see Figure 5.2.

Although it is a very simple form of learning, classical conditioning reveals many facets of learning that have direct and important implications for human beings. For example, suppose Bob and Fred are acquaintances. Bob is insulted by Fred one day, and he gets angry, causing his blood pressure to rise alarmingly. This is an involuntary, physiological response that occurs with many strong emotions (see Chapter 10). The next time Bob sees Fred, his blood pressure may automatically begin to rise. Fred becomes a conditioned stimulus for Bob; he is linked in Bob's mind to the insult, and as a result he can have effects on Bob's physiology without even doing anything. Some employees have developed classically conditioned responses of this sort to their bosses. As soon as the boss comes into the room, the employee may begin to experience an upset stomach or other symptoms, which have become conditioned as a result of the boss's previous behavior.

An example of classical conditioning in humans is the case of the boy who automatically puts his hands over his ears as soon as he sees a flash of lightning. This was initially a response to thunder, not lightning. But once the boy found out that thunder immediately follows lightning, the response became linked to lightning as well.

Operant Conditioning

A classically conditioned response is an involuntary one—Pavlov's dogs had no control over their salivation. But most human behavior is voluntary. We do some things because we feel they will benefit us, and we do other things so that we can avoid having a bad experience. And we can always change our behavior if we stop receiving the benefits or if we get punished for it. It is this capacity to change or shape behavior on the basis

---

Box 1

Learning To Be Superstitious

Old-time Dodger pitcher Alan Foster forgot his baseball shoes on a road trip and borrowed a pair from a teammate. That night he pitched a no-hitter and later, needless to say, bought the shoes from his friend. They became his most prized possession.

Rube Waddel, a Philadelphia Athletics pitching great of long ago, always had a hairpin in his pocket when he pitched. However, the hairpin was only powerful as long as he won. If he lost a game, he would look for another hairpin (which had to be found on the street), and he would not pitch until he found one (Gmelch, 1971).

Most people who act superstitiously defend their actions by saying that they don't really believe that an object causes good or bad luck, but they're just not taking any chances. So there are a great many unsuperstitious people who carry lucky charms, knock on wood, avoid black cats, don't walk under ladders, wear a lucky shirt to a tough interview, and get a little nervous when they break a mirror. Why do so many seemingly trivial acts continue to hold so much importance for so many individuals? It's simply a matter of operant conditioning, say the learning theorists.

In 1957, Morse and Skinner demonstrated how superstitious behavior can be produced in animals. They put hungry pigeons in small cages and fed them every so often. The animals were fed regardless of what they did in the cage. Yet most birds (but not all) developed patterns of "superstitious" behavior. They began to repeat certain behaviors in order to get more food, even though feeding was not at all contingent on the behavior. One bird learned to make two or three counterclockwise turns about the cage trying to cause the food hopper to drop more food. Another bird learned to jerk its head repeatedly, and still another learned to make pecking or brushing movements toward the floor. Whatever the pigeon happened to be doing when the food was delivered became a reinforced response and thus was likely to occur more often subsequently.

Skinner (1953) argues that humans resemble pigeons in forming superstitions. If you say, wear, or do something just before a good experience (reinforcement), there is a chance that you will associate the reward with your actions. In the reverse case, if you *expect* bad luck to follow the appearance of a black cat, you will be especially sensitive to any event that can be interpreted as unfortunate. If such an event occurs, it will confirm your belief about bad luck and black cats.

All of this is based on the principles of learning. When the reward is meant to follow your actions, your subsequent repetition of the reinforced response makes a good deal of sense. But even when a reward is only coincidental, you may still respond to it as if someone were trying to reinforce your behavior.

of its consequences that is explained by the principles of operant conditioning.

Let's take a simple situation: A woman is learning to play golf. She finds that if she swings the putter in a particular way, the ball is likely to go into the hole. As a result, she will become more likely to swing the putter the same way on future holes. In the language of operant conditioning, the golf swing is an *operant* response—it operates on the environment to produce some effect. If an operant response is closely followed by a reward (such as the golf ball's dropping into the hole), the response is said to have been *reinforced*, and the response is more likely to be repeated. However, if the response is followed by something unpleasant or painful (such as the ball's flying into a pond), the behavior is less likely to be repeated.

This basic idea, and the principles that follow from it, is well known by animal trainers who teach animals from pigeons to whales to obey by selectively rewarding and punishing their behaviors. On the same principle, any number of human responses can also be altered. Greenspoon (1955) demonstrated that the use of certain words (such as *I*, *me*, or plural nouns) can be increased simply by having the experimenter say "mm-hmm" whenever the subject uses the words. One group of psychology students decided to turn the tables on their instructor in order to demonstrate this effect (Sanford, 1965). On alternate days they either laughed at anything remotely funny in the instructor's lecture or did not crack a smile throughout the entire period. They reported great day-to-day variation in the amount of humor or attempted humor in the lectures. On days when humor was rewarded, there were many attempts to produce it. On days when even the best jokes were met with only grim silence, lectures become dedicatedly serious.

TRAINING YOUR HEART

For years learning psychologists made a strict distinction between classical conditioning of involuntary responses (such as salivation, heart rate, blood pressure) and operant conditioning of voluntary responses (such as moving one's arms and legs). A few years ago Neal Miller challenged this assumption. Miller and Banuazizi (1968) trained rats to modify heart rate and intestinal contraction. One group of rats was rewarded for an increase in heart rate and another for a decrease. Any increase or decrease at all was rewarded at first; then reward was given only for marked increases or decreases. The experimenters were able to slow a rat's heart rate from 350 beats per minute to 230 in a short period of time and to increase or decrease intestinal contractions to roughly the same degree. There is some controversy about these results, and Miller and others have not always been able to replicate them. Nevertheless, attempts are being made to apply the technique of operant body control to humans—to help people keep their own blood pressure under control, for example.

REINFORCEMENT AND PUNISHMENT

From the examples of operant conditioning we have given so far, you can see that there are two major ways to alter a behavior—to increase its occurrence and to decrease its occurrence. Increasing a behavior, such as joke telling, requires *reinforcement*—in this case by laughing. Decreasing a behavior, on the other hand, requires either withdrawing reinforcements or else administering punishment. If, for example, the students had groaned and booed at the instructor's attempts at humor, his joke telling would probably have decreased. Let's take a closer look at each of these fundamental principles of operant conditioning.

Reinforcement

Reinforcement is any event following a response that strengthens it or that increases the probability of the response occurring again. There are two kinds of reinforcement: positive and negative. In *positive reinforcement*, a rewarding stimulus is presented after a response in order to strengthen the response. Thus, the students' laughter is an example of positive reinforcement. In *negative reinforcement,* a response is strengthened by the *removal* of an unpleasant stimulus. For example, the students could also have tried whispering to each other whenever the lecture was serious, ceasing this undesirable behavior whenever the instructor told a joke. The end of the whispering would have served as a negative reinforcement, and it, too, would have tended to increase the instructor's attempts at humor.

Psychologists use both positive and negative reinforcement in studying learning in animals. A dog can learn to jump over a barrier in order to get food (positive reinforcement) or to avoid or escape an electric shock (negative reinforcement). In either case, the response of jumping over the barrier is strengthened.

For reinforcement to be effective, it must be well timed. That is, it must come immediately after the response it is meant to reinforce. If the reinforcement comes before the response, it

A psychologist records the responses of a pigeon in a Skinner box.

cannot serve as a reward for the response, and if it comes too late, the person or animal will not realize what behavior is being rewarded. Thus, timing is an important aspect of operant conditioning.

The systematic study of operant conditioning was greatly facilitated by the introduction of the Skinner box, an apparatus developed by B. F. Skinner. A Skinner box is a chamber with enough room to allow an animal to move about somewhat, and it contains devices to deliver food and water. The animal must perform specific responses in order to trip the mechanism that delivers reinforcement. For example, the box may contain a small bar or lever for a rat to press or a circular key for a pigeon to peck, in order to receive a food pellet. The animal's rate of responding (such as number of bar presses per minute) can then be recorded automatically. The Skinner box makes it possible to demonstrate the effects of positive and negative reinforcement under highly controlled conditions. If a rat presses the bar and receives a food pellet each time, the rate of bar-pressing increases. This is positive reinforcement. The rate of bar-pressing will also increase if the bar press turns off a painful electric shock. This is a case of negative reinforcement.

Positive and negative reinforcers play a vital part in our daily lives. We study to become educated. We adjust the environment when it irritates us. We buy food that tastes good and that fills us. We read books by authors who have pleased us in the past. We avoid parking in a place where we previously received a ticket. In each instance, we behave in a way that will produce rewards and avoid unpleasantness. Of course, people differ in what reinforces them. Some people find horror movies rewarding; others find horror movies painful and much prefer comedies. Some people love spinach but would never touch an artichoke; others have exactly the opposite reaction. As they say, "Different strokes for different folks."

GUIDED MISSILES—FOR THE BIRDS?

During World War II, B. F. Skinner came up with the idea of using pigeons to control guided missiles. As *Time* magazine (September 20, 1971) explains it:

Three birds were conditioned to peck continuously for four or five minutes at the image of a target on the screen. Then they were placed in harness in the nose of the missile, facing a screen on which the target would appear when the missile was in flight. By pecking at the image moving on the screen, the pigeons would send corrective signals that moved the missile's fins and kept it on target. The missile, called the Pelican, was never used in warfare: the pigeon-aided equipment was so complex and bulky that the missile could carry little high explosive. Furthermore, Skinner mourns, "our problem was no one would take us seriously."†

†From "Skinner's Utopia: Panacea, or Path to Hell," Time, September 20, 1971. Reprinted by permission from TIME, The Weekly Newsmagazine; Copyright Time Inc.

B. F. Skinner in his laboratory.

Punishment

Suppose we have taught a rat in a Skinner box to press a bar in order to receive food. If we now shock the rat each time it presses the bar, the rat will quickly learn to decrease its bar-pressing behavior. We have thus used punishment to decrease a response.

Although reinforcement increases the probability of a response and punishment decreases the probability of a response, the effects of punishment are not simply the opposite of those produced by reinforcement. Not all responses are affected by punishment in the same way, the effectiveness of punishment depends on the way in which the response was established in the first place. Responses that have been established by positive reinforcement can be temporarily suppressed by mild punishment,

---

Box 2

How To Be an Operant

If you want to try operant conditioning on others, the first thing you must figure out is how to get the individual to make the first correct response so you can reinforce it. This can be done in many ways, and each of the ways has some advantages and some disadvantages.

Motivate your subject. Increase your subject's motivation to make a lot of responses so that you can get the one you want to reinforce. If the subject is a rat, you can use batteries to electrify the floor of its cage to keep the rat moving. If you have a human subject, you can promise a future reward or threaten punishment or deprivation.

Eliminate old reinforcers. If motivation alone doesn't work, you may decide to search for something that is inhibiting the response you are looking for and to try to eliminate the inhibitor. If, for example, your subject doesn't want to dance, she may perhaps be easily embarrassed in public. In a private place she may be able to dance up a storm. Removing the reinforcers that are maintaining the inhibitions helps to produce the response you are looking for.

Act as a model. If you are getting nowhere, you might try telling your subject exactly what you want him or her to do—either by verbal instruction or, sometimes more successful, by acting as a model. When Elton McNeil learned to fly, the instructor (often in despair) would execute the maneuver and have McNeil follow him by doing what he did rather than what he tried to explain.

Limit your subject's responses. Sometimes you have to structure the environment if you want to encourage a particular type of response. If you want an animal to learn to pull a lever, you can make it more likely to happen if you put the animal in a box where a lever is the only thing available.

Shaping. Try to shape the behavior so that any response that is even roughly close to what you want can be reinforced. Then, one step at a time, reward responses that are progressively more like the desired response. In time these partial behaviors will be shaped into a sequence that will produce the action you want.

Force the response. If shaping isn't fast enough, you can force the response. When you teach your dog tricks, you often do so by saying "shake hands" and then lifting his paw and rewarding him until he learns what the words mean. In a way, then, you can not only lead a horse to water, you can also make him drink, if you need to.

Much of our behavior has been influenced by the operant techniques of the people around us—particularly our parents. Once they got us to perform the desired response, the rest was easy. They simply reinforced us with praise each time we said "thank you" or ate everything on our plates. It may seem a little frightening how easy it is to operant condition someone. Most of us, however, including parents, have neither the time nor the patience it takes to purposefully condition the more significant and complex behaviors of thought and emotions.

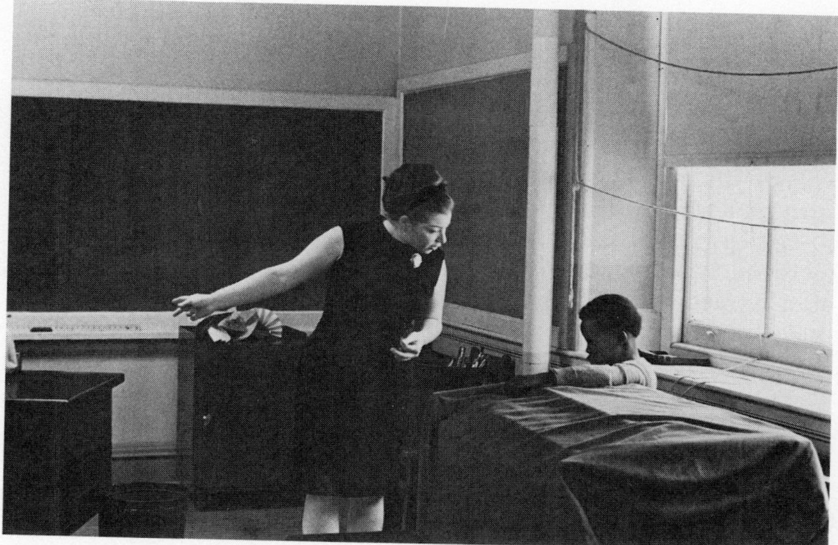

but the response will not be completely eliminated unless an alternative response is provided. In housebreaking a dog, for example, merely punishing urination inside the house is ineffective unless the opportunity to urinate outside is provided and reinforced. Millions of housebroken puppies will attest to the effectiveness of the judicious use of punishment and positive reinforcement.

Other kinds of responses are affected differently by punishment. Responses such as eating and sexual behavior, for instance, are remarkably suppressed by punishment—at least in some animals. Dogs and cats will starve to death rather than eat if they have been subjected to mild electric shock for eating. On the other hand, responses that were originally established by punishment are surprisingly resistant to punishment. Dogs who have learned to jump a barrier in order to avoid an electric shock do not respond to being punished for jumping. In fact, some experiments have shown that punishment actually increases the strength of such responses.

As with reinforcement, the effectiveness of punishment depends greatly on timing. Punishment delivered immediately after a response is most effective; the longer the delay between the response and the punishment, the greater the chance that the punishment will become associated with other intervening events. Thus, the traditional procedure of mother asking father to punish little Johnny at the end of the day doesn't work too well. By the time father spanks him, Johnny may no longer have a clear notion of what he is being spanked for.

The use of punishment has some built-in problems. Some responses that are temporarily suppressed by punishment may reappear again and again. The usual reason is that the punishment has actually become rewarding to the animal or person. If little Johnny is ignored whenever he is being a good boy but is scolded whenever he does something wrong, he may find that doing "bad" things is an effective way of getting the attention he wants. Another unfortunate side effect of punishment is that the individual being punished comes to associate negative emotional responses with the situation and agent of punishment. A child will do his best to avoid parents who punish him a lot, which in turn makes it more difficult for the parents to have opportunities to employ positive reinforcement. For these reasons, psychologists much prefer to use positive and negative reinforcement in altering behaviors. They recommend, for example, that parents make a point of rewarding a child's good behavior and ignoring the child's misbehavior.

PRINCIPLES OF LEARNING

So far, we have had only a bare outline of the two basic types of learning. In this section, we will try to put some flesh on the skeleton by considering a few of the many principles of learning that psychologists have studied. Most of the principles that we will consider in this section are relevant to both classical and operant conditioning, although the principles must sometimes be interpreted somewhat differently in each case.

Extinction

We learn many responses in the course of our lives, but not all of them remain strong. The weakening of learned responses is called *extinction.* When you were a young child, you may have been acutely afraid of going to bed in the dark and insisted that your parents keep a light on outside your room. This fear was probably learned through a process of classical conditioning, in which you learned to associate darkness with thoughts of animals, ghosts, or other scary objects. Some of you may still be afraid of the dark, but for most of you the learned response has been *extinguished* and you no longer feel a need for a light on at night. Or, to take another example, many people learn to pray every night when they are children. In some cases this is a response that is operantly conditioned: Children may learn that when they pray they are praised or otherwise rewarded by their parents. What's more, they may sometimes discover that the things they pray for come true. Many adults continue to pray every day (and some start praying for the first time), but many others discontinue the practice; for them, the response of daily prayer has been extinguished.

As these examples show, the process of extinction is slightly different for the two types of conditioning. In the case of classical conditioning, a response tends to die out when the conditioned stimulus is repeatedly presented without the unconditioned stimulus. Thus, when Pavlov would ring his bell (the conditioned stimulus) over and over without giving his dogs food (the unconditioned stimulus), the dogs salivated less and less. After a while the bell no longer elicited the salivation response—the response was now extinguished. In operant conditioning, extinction involves the discovery that the learned response no longer leads to reinforcement. In a Skinner box, if a rat is no longer reinforced with food for pressing a bar, the bar-pressing will eventually cease. Similarly, if a slot machine never pays off, you will stop putting your money into it. You will stop shopping at a store that gives you bad service, and you will avoid a former friend who has caused you grief.

Although extinction is the gradual decrease in the strength of a response, it is important to note that the response does not just fade away. Rather, it becomes weaker because of an active process of unlearning, requiring repeated occasions on which the conditioned stimulus is withheld (if the response has been classically conditioned) or on which the behavior goes unrewarded (if the response has been operantly conditioned).

Many responses are never completely extinguished. Pavlov observed this with his dogs. Sometimes after a conditioned response had been extinguished it would suddenly reappear during a rest period. Pavlov called this phenomenon *spontaneous recovery*. (See Figure 5.3.) Children who have apparently conquered their classically conditioned fear of the dark, for example, may have it suddenly return on a stormy night. Spontaneous recovery also occurs with operantly conditioned responses. You may go back to the nonpaying slot machine, shop at the store with bad service, or speak to your former friend—perhaps in hopes that they have somehow changed during the interval.

Generalization and Discrimination

Situations are never repeated in the environment in exactly the same form. How do learning principles account for the fact that we can get along in a constantly changing environment? To understand how we respond to new situations and how we learn to distinguish similar situations from each other, we must consider the complementary processes of generalization and discrimination.

Pavlov found that a dog that was conditioned to respond to the sound of a bell would also respond to the sound of a tuning

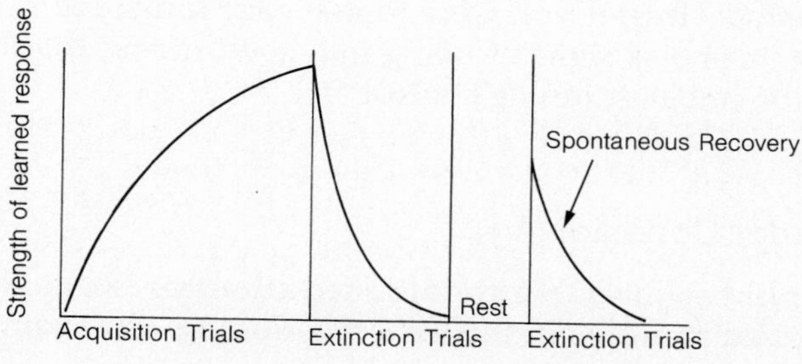

FIG. 5 · 3 Over a series of trials, learned responses may gain strength when they are reinforced (acquisition), lose strength when they are not reinforced (extinction), or regain strength after a rest period (spontaneous recovery).

fork, a buzzer, a metronone, or a variety of other stimuli. The finding that stimuli similar to the conditioned stimulus can elicit the same conditioned response is called *generalization.* As you might guess, the more similar the new stimulus is to the original conditioned stimulus, the more similar (stronger) will be the response.

Generalization also occurs with operantly learned responses. If you have been to several films directed by Alfred Hitchcock and have found most of them to be rewarding to you, you may generalize the response and attend future Hitchcock films with the expectation of reward. Similarly, if you have learned that kicking a soft drink machine a certain way often gets you a free drink, you may generalize the response and start kicking other food-dispensing machines.

Generalization is valuable—it would be terrible to have to learn how to respond anew in each and every situation slightly different from the last. But together with generalization, you need to be able to *discriminate* between stimuli so that you can respond in ways that are appropriate to the particular situation. Pavlov found that he could teach his dogs to make such distinctions between stimuli. Using classical conditioning methods, he taught a dog not to salivate at the sight of a piece of dyed bread, which it was never allowed to eat. However, the dog continued to salivate to the stimulus of undyed bread—it had learned to discriminate between the two similar stimuli. One way to think of discrimination is that it involves conditioning of a response to one stimulus while extinguishing the response to a similar stimulus.

Discrimination is very important in operant conditioning. Imagine the operant response of asking your father for money. In such a situation it is important to be able to tell whether or not your father is in a good mood: A good mood signals reinforcement (money), while a bad mood signals nonreinforcement. In this example, your father's mood would be called a discriminative stimulus. A discriminative stimulus is one that becomes associated with the delivery of reinforcement because reinforcement is forthcoming in its presence. In a Skinner box an animal can learn that bar-pressing leads to reinforcement only when a light is turned on. Under these conditions, the animal does very little bar-pressing when the light is off but is quite active when the light is on. When a behavior such as bar-pressing occurs consistently in the presence of a discriminative stimulus such as light (but not in its absence), the behavior is said to be under *stimulus control.* Thus, if you were to ask your father for money only when he shows signs of being in a good mood, that behavior would be under stimulus control.

Higher-Order Conditioning

In *higher-order conditioning,* a conditioned stimulus is used as an unconditioned stimulus in further conditioning. For example,

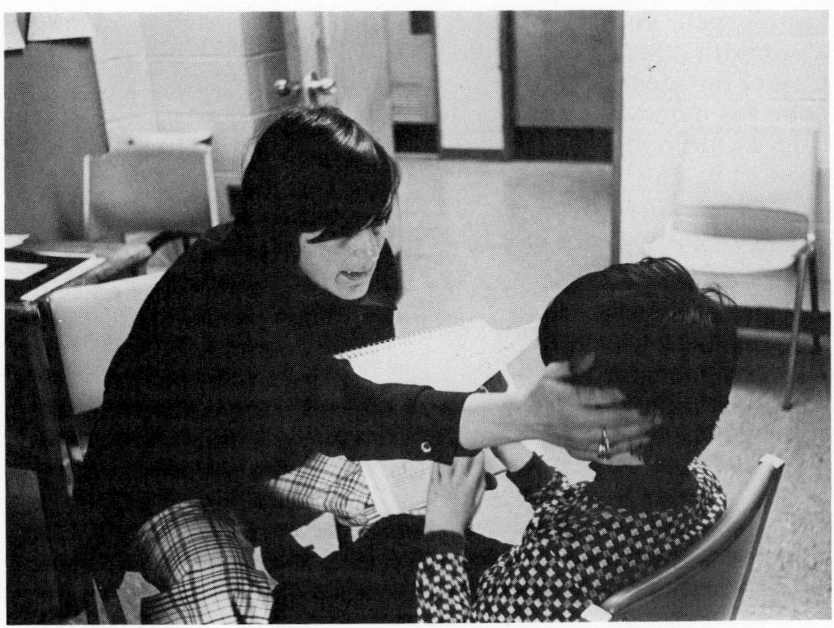

Pavlov found that once the conditioned response of salivation to the sound of a bell had been firmly established, the sound of a bell could be presented to the dog along with the sight of a black square, and after a number of such pairings, the dog would salivate at the sight of the black square alone. The bell (which was a conditioned stimulus) had become an unconditioned stimulus, and the black square (which had been a neutral stimulus) had become a conditioned stimulus.

Higher-order conditioning helps explain why we respond to so many different events in the way we do. If a child is seen reaching toward an electric socket, a parent might firmly say "no" and then pull the child's hand away. After a while the word "no" becomes a conditioned stimulus for a response of fear or of withdrawal. Later the word can be used as an unconditioned stimulus so that the child learns to respond to something as simple as a parent's frown, which has been linked to the word "no." In the same way, many of our responses to the expressions and gestures of other people have been established by higher-order conditioning.

Higher-order conditioning is also seen with operant responses. Any stimulus that becomes associated with reinforcement may become reinforcing itself—the stimulus acquires the ability to increase the probability of a response. Reinforcers that naturally increase a response are called *primary reinforcers,* such as food, water, and affection. Stimuli that become reinforcers as a result of association with primary reinforcers are called *secondary reinforcers.* Secondary reinforcers play a big part in shaping our behavior: Think of all the behaviors we engage in to earn awards, pats on the back, and grades. We have learned that the awards, pats, and grades are rewarding, because they tend to go along with other more basic rewards like affection and esteem. One of the most important secondary reinforcers for human beings is money. Consider a dollar bill. To a child or to a person from a culture that does not use paper money, a dollar does not seem to be much of a reinforcement. It doesn't taste particularly good, it's not much fun to rub against, and the expression on George Washington's face looks, if anything, rather forbidding. But dollar bills become reinforcers once we have learned that with a dollar bill (or with many of them) it is posssible to obtain food, clothing, and other items that are primary reinforcers. Similarly, poker chips, which in themselves have little value, are highly reinforcing to gamblers who know that they can change the chips for money—and that they can later exchange the money for whatever it is that they really find rewarding. Even monkeys can be taught new behaviors using poker chips as a reward, as long as the monkeys have previously learned that the chips can later be exchanged for food (Wolfe, 1936).

BARNABUS PERFORMS

Pierrel and Sherman (1963) taught their rat Barnabus to climb a spiral staircase, cross a narrow drawbridge, go up a ladder, pull a toy car over by a chain, get into the car and pedal it to a second ladder, climb this ladder, crawl through a tube, board an elevator, pull a chain to raise a flat, and lower himself back to the starting platform where he would press a lever to get a food pellet. After the pellet was eaten, the remarkable sequence of behaviors began all over again.

Another type of higher-order conditioning involves combining of classical and operant conditioning to produce chains of learning. In such chains each act may serve as a stimulus for the next act to be performed. A good example of such behavioral *chaining* is driving a car. In sequence, you take out your keys, unlock the car, open the door, sit down in the driver's seat, fasten your seatbelt, put the gear in neutral, turn on the ignition, shift into gear, check the traffic, and press down on the accelerator. These acts become an automatic sequence that occurs in a well-established order. In this way learning is built upon learning to produce complex behaviors.

Schedules of Reinforcement

The principles of learning described up to this point have applied to both classical and operant conditioning. Here we will be talking about an aspect of learning that occurs primarily with operant conditioning and involves the various ways in which responses can be reinforced.

Some of our behaviors are reinforced every time we produce them. When you press the elevator button, the elevator stops at your floor. When you go to a cafeteria for lunch, you get food. This is called *continuous reinforcement.* But it is much more common for responses to be rewarded on some occasions and not on others. If you are familiar with a soft drink machine that works only intermittently, you will understand the concept of *partial reinforcement.*

Since no one gets rewarded or reinforced all the time for everything he or she does, experimental work in learning has focused on partial reinforcement. If you use partial reinforcement to train an animal, for example, you could decide to schedule reinforcement so that it is delivered after every third response the animal makes, after every fifth response, or whatever.

In other words, a certain number of responses must occur before each reinforcement. This is called *ratio* schedule of reinforcement. On the other hand, you could schedule the reinforcement according to the clock, so that a certain amount of time must pass before a response is reinforced. When time is the main factor, the schedule is called an *interval* schedule.

For both ratio and interval schedules another distinction can be made. If either the ratio or the interval is constant, the schedule is referred to as *fixed;* if the ratio or interval is not constant and varies somewhat each time, the schedule is called *variable.* Thus, there are four basic schedules of reinforcement based on these two distinctions (see Figure 5.4):

Fixed-ratio schedules involve reinforcement after a fixed number of responses—after every tenth response, for example. In this case there would be nine unreinforced responses followed by one reinforced response. If you had a job in which you were paid for every 20 pieces of work that you turned out, you would be working on a fixed-ratio schedule.

Variable-ratio schedules also involve reinforcement after a certain number of responses, but the number varies around some average. For instance, suppose that making a free throw is reinforcing for Jim, a basketball player, and that on the average he will make one of every two shots. Jim can never know whether a particular shot will be reinforced, but he can be fairly certain

FIG. 5 · 4 A variety of schedules can be used to reinforce people's responses.

Interval Schedules

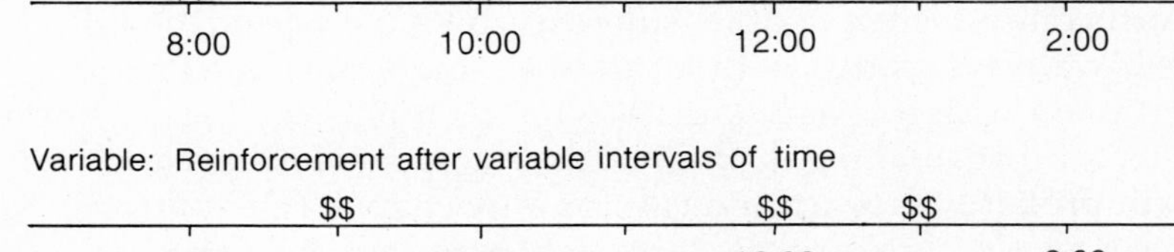

Ratio Schedules

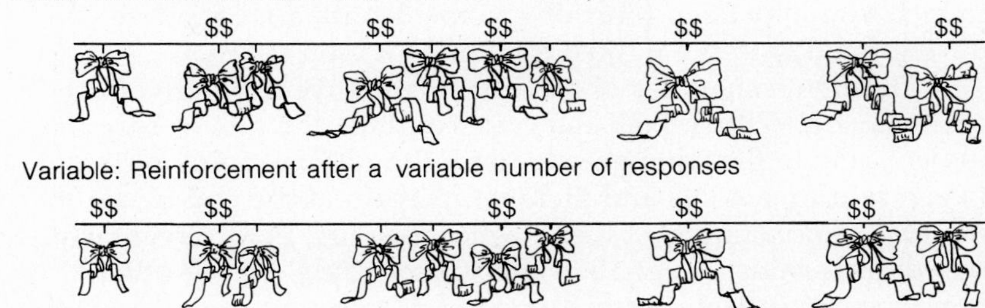

that the reinforcement will come about half of the time . Slot machines also reward gamblers on a variable-ratio schedule.

With *fixed-interval schedules,* it is the first response after a set period of time that gets reinforced. The number of responses made during the interval does not matter. Animals such as rats do not learn time the way humans do, but a rat in a Skinner box will increase the number of bar presses as the time for reinforcement draws near. Students are likely to respond to the fixed intervals at which examinations take place. They tend to cram just before the exam, lay off right afterward, and start to study again as the next exam approaches. Jobs with salaries on regular paydays are reinforced on a fixed-interval schedule.

With *variable-interval* schedules, the only response reinforced is the first one after a time interval has passed, but the length of the interval varies around some average. An animal in a Skinner box might be rewarded after intervals that average out to five minutes, with some intervals as short as a minute and some as long as fifteen minutes. Similarly, an instructor might have you on a variable-interval schedule for studying by giving surprise quizzes. The quizzes don't come at regular intervals; time is the main factor.

An interesting aspect of partial reinforcement schedules is that they tend to make a response more resistant to extinction. When responses are first acquired, continuous reinforcement is most effective in producing a strong response. However, such responses are easily extinguished. But if a response is reinforced on one of the intermittent schedules, it takes much longer for the response to extinguish when reinforcement is withdrawn. Why is this the case? With partial reinforcement, the person or animal comes to learn that not every response will be reinforced. As a result, the individual may keep trying even when reinforcement is withheld, in the hope that sooner or later reinforcement will be forthcoming. For example, suppose you have a very reliable car. It has always started without trouble, and you've never had a problem with it. Then one morning it simply won't start. You try to start it several times, but nothing happens. In this case, you will probably give up and call for a mechanic. But suppose you have an old clunker that starts right up some days and is sluggish on others. Again, one morning you try to start it and nothing happens. Because you know that this car is erratic, you will probably spend a much longer time trying to start this car. With the reliable car your starting response is likely to extinguish rather quickly, but with the clunker extinction may take hours. In fact, you may keep returning to the car at various points during the day to see if "just this time" it won't start.

Different schedules of reinforcement have different effects on behavior. With a fixed-interval schedule, the rate of responding is likely to fluctuate greatly, with the rate dropping off between reinforcements and picking up again at the end of the interval—for example, students who cram just before regularly scheduled exams. A variable-interval schedule, on the other hand, produces a more steady rate of responding—you have to

OPERANT CULTURAL CONDITIONING

In his novel *Walden Two*, B. F. Skinner (1948) fictionally employed operant conditioning techniques, which he called "cultural engineering." Intermittent reinforcement was used in Skinner's fictional community to develop frustration tolerance in children. Beginning at about age six months, babies were given certain toys designed to build perseverance. In order for the toy to be rewarding—for a music box to play a song or for a pattern of flashing lights to go off—the child had to give a certain response, such as pulling a ring. At first every pull of the ring was rewarded, but then the reward came every second response, every third, or even every tenth response, on a variable-ratio schedule. As Skinner stated, "It's possible to build up fantastically perseverative behavior without encountering frustration or rage" (1948, page 101).

study regularly to be prepared for pop quizzes. On the whole, both kinds of interval schedules result in lower response rates than those produced with ratio schedules. Both kinds of ratio schedules tend to produce high rates of responding. Pigeons in a Skinner box will peck the response key up to several hundred times a minute on ratio schedules. And why not? The more pecking, the more food; if the pigeon slows down, so does the reinforcement.

In real life it is difficult to find pure examples of these four basic schedules, since the schedules of partial reinforcement that most often occur are *mixed* schedules that are combinations of ratio and interval, fixed and variable. You may be paid on the first and fifteenth of every month (fixed interval), but pay raises are more likely to be determined by the number of responses, or how hard you work (variable ratio).

LEARNING BY OBSERVATION

So far we have focused on the ways in which people's behavior is shaped by reinforcements and punishments that are administered to them directly. Especially among human beings, however, a great deal of learning takes place without any direct reward or punishment, simply as a result of our observing the behavior of other people. For example, a boy who is beginning nursery school may learn how to fingerpaint or to build block castles simply by watching the activity of other children in the class. And if the newcomer observes that other children are rewarded for certain sorts of behaviors, he will be more likely to engage in such behaviors. Similarly, a person who is beginning to work at a new job will learn a great deal by watching veteran workers. Such *learning by observation* (also known as *learning by imitation,* or *modeling*) plays a major role in human learning, alongside learning by direct reinforcement and punishment (Bandura, 1971). We will return to both kinds of learning at several points in this book. In the Psychological Issue after Chapter 10, we will consider the roles of reinforcement and observation in connection with aggression and violence. In Chapter 13, we will examine the processes of reinforcement and observational learning that influence the development of sex roles. And in Chapter 14, we will discuss both kinds of learning as they contribute to the shaping of an individual's personality.

SUMMARY

1. *Learning* is a relatively permanent change in behavior as a result of experience or practice. Learning is tempered to some extent by biological influences, including instincts, critical periods, and predispositions.
2. Animals have certain innate patterns of behavior that occur naturally, regardless of the animal's experience. Such inborn patterns of behavior are called *instincts.* It appears that humans have few, if any, instinctive patterns of behavior.

3. A *critical period* is a time during an organism's development in which a behavior must be learned or it may never be learned at all. For example, geese and ducks have a critical period for *imprinting* the response of following their mother. Humans may have a critical period for language development.
4. Animals appear to have biological *predispositions* to learn behaviors that have survival value. Such predispositions have been demonstrated in other animals, and it has been suggested that humans have similar built-in propensities to learn some behaviors more easily than others.
5. In *classical conditioning,* a neutral stimulus is paired with an *unconditioned stimulus* that elicits an *unconditioned response.* After repeated pairings, the neutral stimulus alone comes to elicit the response, and it is then called a *conditioned stimulus* and the response is called a *conditioned response.* Classical conditioning applies only to involuntary responses, such as salivation, blushing, and heart rate.
6. In *operant conditioning,* an *operant response* (one that operates on the environment to produce some effect) that is rewarded is more likely to be repeated, whereas a response that is not reinforced or that is punished is less likely to be repeated.
7. Skinner has suggested that superstitious behavior occurs when a reinforcement is accidentally paired with a particular response. Since learning principles work whether or not they are purposeful, the subject will view the desired event as being contingent on his or her performing the "reinforced" behavior.
8. *Reinforcement* is any event following a response that strengthens it or that increases the probability of the response happening again. In *positive reinforcement,* a reward is used to increase the response. In *negative reinforcement,* an unpleasant stimulus is removed in order to increase the response. To be effective, reinforcement must be applied immediately after the response.
9. The Skinner box is a specially designed chamber in which animals can be limited in their behaviors and can be taught new behaviors using operant conditioning techniques.
10. One task of operant conditioning is to get the subject to perform the response so that it can be reinforced. This may be accomplished by eliminating interfering behaviors, modeling the desired behavior, limiting the subject's responses, shaping existing responses, or forcing the response.
11. *Punishment* is any event following a response that decreases the probability of that response occurring again. Its effectiveness depends on the way in which the response was originally established. Eliminating a response acquired with positive reinforcement requires not only punishment but provision of an alternative response. Responses originally established by punishment are very difficult to remove

using punishment. As with reinforcement, timing of punishment is important. One side effect of punishment is that it may actually be rewarding in certain instances.

12. *Extinction* is the weakening of a learned response. In classical conditioning, extinction is accomplished by repeatedly presenting the conditioned stimulus without the unconditioned stimulus. In operant conditioning, a response is extinguished by withdrawing reinforcement. Sometimes an extinguished response suddenly reappears; this is called *spontaneous recovery.*
13. *Generalization* is responding in the same way to more than one stimulus with similar characteristics. *Discrimination* involves responding to one stimulus while not responding to a very similar stimulus. These two processes occur in both classical and operant conditioning.
14. A *discriminative stimulus* is one that becomes associated with the delivery of reinforcement because reinforcement occurs in its presence. When a behavior consistently occurs only in the presence of a discriminative stimulus, the behavior is said to be under *stimulus control.*
15. In *higher-order conditioning,* a conditioned stimulus is used as an unconditioned stimulus in further conditioning. A similar process is seen in operant conditioning, in which stimuli associated with *primary reinforcers* (food, water) become reinforcers, too. They are called *secondary reinforcers.* Another type of higher-order conditioning is *chaining.* Each act in a behavioral chain serves as a stimulus for the next act to be performed, producing a smooth sequence.
16. In *continuous* reinforcement, every response is rewarded. In *partial* reinforcement, responses are rewarded after a certain number have been emitted (*ratio schedule*) or after a certain amount of time has elapsed (*interval schedule*). Responses are more resistant to extinction when reinforced on a partial schedule than on a continuous schedule.
17. When reinforcement is delivered only after a fixed number of responses, the reinforcement is on a *fixed-ratio schedule. Fixed-interval schedules* are those in which reinforcements are given only after a certain amount of time has passed. With *variable-ratio schedules,* the subject never knows how many responses it will take to get the reward. With *variable-interval schedules,* the interval between rewards changes from trial to trial.
18. A fixed-interval schedule produces an erratic rate of response, while responding is more steady on a variable-interval schedule. However, both kinds of ratio schedules produce higher and steadier rates of response than interval schedules.
19. In addition to conditioning, people learn by watching how other people behave and by emulating that behavior. This is called *learning by observation.*

Behavior Control

Behavior control is not just an idle fantasy.

"Today's behavioral psychologists are the architects and engineers of the Brave New World." The behavioral psychologist James McConnell said it, we didn't. But what seems to have people worried is that he may be right. As we learn more and more about why people behave as they do, we become more capable of controlling *how* they behave. Scientific behavior control could have great practical benefits. But it also could present serious threats to individual freedom and autonomy.

Behavior control is not just an idle fantasy. Behavioral psychologists—those who focus on the principles of learning—began to move out of campus psychology laboratories some 25 years ago. Now, they are likely to be found in mental hospitals, rehabilitation wards,

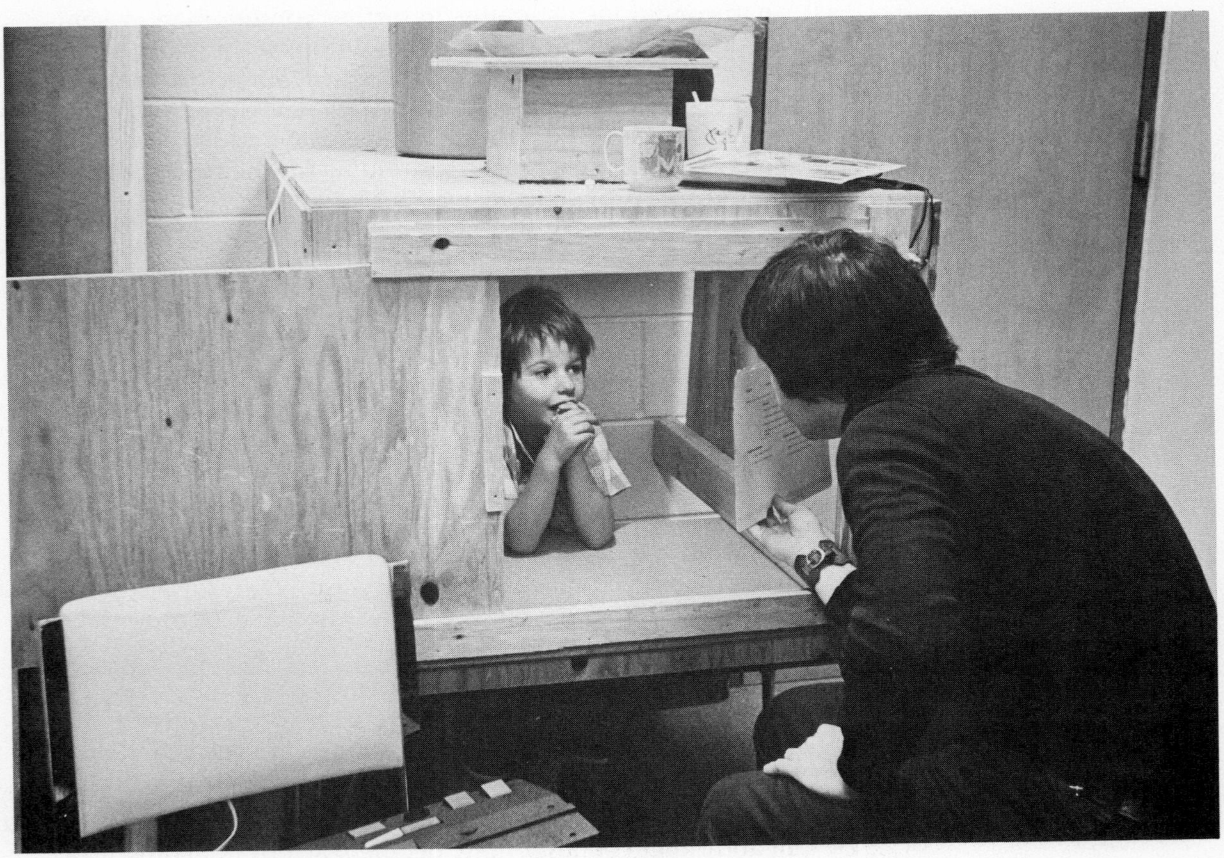

prisons, nursing homes, day-care centers, factories, movie theaters, national parks, and community mental health centers (Goodall, 1972).

For example: Chronic psychotic patients in a mental hospital were given reinforcement in the form of tokens, such as poker chips, whenever they engaged in constructive behavior (see Box 2 Chapter 17). These tokens could be used, in a system known as a "token economy," to buy various rewards, such as cigarettes, a walk outside, or a chance to watch TV. Eventually, these previously helpless patients were taught to care for themselves, to do housekeeping chores, and to perform a number of jobs around the hospital (Ayllon and Azrin, 1968).

In a quite different application of behavior control, littering in a theater (measured by the amount of trash not deposited in trash cans) declined from 81 percent to 6 percent when patrons were given litter bags and were offered a dime for each bag of litter turned in after the show. In another theater, littering declined from 84 percent to 5 percent when patrons were offered free tickets to a special children's show (Burgess, Clark, and Hendee, 1971).

A group of seven "incorrigible" junior high students were the subjects in another approach to behavior control. They were taught to use rewards such as smiles, praise, eye contact, and shows of interest to shape their teachers' behavior. During a five-week conditioning period, positive teacher-student contacts increased 400 percent, while negative contacts dropped to zero. In the end, the teachers were happy because the students were learning, and the students were happy because they could control their relationship with the teachers (Gray, Graubard, and Rosenberg, 1974). This example also suggests that, contrary to popular impression, techniques of behavior control can be used effectively by relatively powerless people (such as the students) as well as by powerful groups.

Although the work of behavioral psychologists has changed over the years, its focus has always been on techniques of controlling behavior, and its roots still lead back to the basic principles formulated by B. F. Skinner and his associates on the basis of their work with laboratory rats and pigeons. For the behavioral psychologist, the real question is not *whether* we should be controlled, for we are all controlled by our past histories and by our present environments. Instead, the question is *how* we should be controlled: by the erratic forces of nature, by our accidental encounters with people and situations, or by a scientifically programmed pattern of reinforcements.

. . . the question is *how* we should be controlled. . . .

The thought of controlling human behavior has ignited widespread argument among professionals and lay persons alike. Since people are less likely to be disturbed by the controlling influences of rewards, public comment and debate have been particularly heated when the control involves punishment. In addition, there has been a great deal of controversy—and a great deal of confusion as well—about the ethics of "behavior modification."

Punishment

In recent years, some behaviorists have used punishment—sometimes called *aversive control*—as a therapeutic tool. In some cases, they have found punishment to be a fast, effective technique for ridding people of severe behavior problems, such as self-injury or addiction. But the public response has frequently been one of outrage. "How," people ask, "could psychologists be so callous as to administer electric shocks to fellow human beings?"

Baer (1971) has argued that public resistance to the use of punishment is based on ill-considered emotional grounds. "Had the findings been a vaccine against some disease," he writes, "there would have been headlines and congratulations. But the treatment is not called 'vaccination,' it is called 'punishment.' The word brings with it images of anger, whips, screams. So instead of celebrating a new scientific advance, we feel apprehensive; we look for a hint of sadism

. . . somehow, pain inflicted by a human being seems different—barbaric and repellant" (page 33).† Critics have argued that pain is bad and should always be avoided, but Baer contends that it is immoral *not* to inflict pain if it can correct and eliminate undesirable (and painful) behaviors. And, as Baer points out, punishment often works.

In most human situations punishment does not need to be harsh to be effective. Mild punishments such as criticism and frowning can designate undesirable behavior quite clearly; and most people respond to mild punishment as a signal to begin new response patterns. If an alternative, correct behavior is pointed out, mild punishment can teach avoidance of the undesirable behavior in favor of the desirable one.

Behavior Modification

In the behaviorist view, from the time we are born until the time we die, each of our responses is followed by either positive or negative consequences. Initially our reinforcements are primarily physical: We are rewarded with food, water, and physical comfort, and we are punished with hunger, thirst, and pain. Later on, we experience social rewards and punishments, such as approval or criticism. Still later, we begin to administer rewards and punishments to ourselves; we feel proud of our accomplishments and ashamed of our failures. Life, to the behaviorist, is an unending series of rewards and punishments. If we wish to control human behavior, the behaviorists contend, we need only to systematize and regularize the forces of learning. This process has become known as *behavior modification.*

Life, to the behaviorist, is an unending series of rewards and punishments.

The term "behavior modification" may seem confusing or ambiguous. Therefore, in addition to defining what it is, we must clarify what it is *not.* In particular, behavior modification does not include a number of techniques that may be effective in controlling or modifying behavior but that do not derive from the principles of learning. So, behavior modification does *not* include the use of brain surgery, drugs, or electroshock therapy to treat psychiatric symptoms or to subdue patients and inmates. Neither does it include electrical stimulation of the brain in order to influence behavior (see Chapter 2). When we discuss behavior modification, we refer only to behavioral control through the scientific use of reward and punishment.

Even people who understand perfectly well what behavior modification is sometimes object to it on ethical grounds. Some critics have argued that behavior modification is dehu-

†*From "Let's Take Another Look at Punishment," Donald M. Baer,* Psychology Today, *October 1971, p. 33. Copyright © 1971 Ziff-Davis Publishing Company. REPRINTED BY PERMISSION OF PSYCHOLOGY TODAY MAGAZINE.*

manizing because it requires treating people like animals or like machines. In part, this attitude may result from the fact that so much of the early work on learning was conducted with animals. But even more, this attitude seems to derive from a fear that we can be conditioned without even realizing it. As Bandura (1974) points out, however, this fear is largely unfounded. In general, people won't behave a certain way just because they have been reinforced. Rather, a key element in behavior modification is that people *recognize* that a particular behavior will result in more reward, and they change the way they act accordingly.

Once we recognize that people are not likely to be conditioned against their will, behavior modification loses much of its dreadful appearance. As one of the high school students who had been trained to shape his teachers' behavior noted, "If the person knows you're doing it [and, we should add, if the person doesn't want it to work], it won't work. At least not very well. He'll figure, 'Oh, he's trying to do it to me. He's not going to change the way I am!'" This student had attempted to condition his little brother not to curse. But the child found out about the conditioning techniques. Instead of learning not to curse, the boy simply turned to his older brother and said, "Oh, you dumb little psychologist!"

At this point, you may be wondering why people who are aware that they are being conditioned would ever go along with it. In fact, behavior modification is often used for therapy (see Chapter 17), in which the patient knows about the conditioning because he or she has specifically requested it. The patient says to the therapist, in effect, "You condition me to stop smoking, or to stop eating so much, and I'll not only go along with it, I'll pay you for it."

Most of the time, behavior modification involves a behavioral bargain: "I'll do what you want if you'll do what I want."

There are many other situations in which people go along with the conditioning because it works to their advantage. As an example, suppose your father wants you to wash his car. Naturally, you're not too interested. But if he offers you $5 as a reward for doing it, chances are you'll do the job, and technically this is behavior modification. Previously you wouldn't wash the car, but now you will. And, you've modified your father's behavior, as well, because now he's paying you. In everyday behavior modification situations one can't always tell who is conditioning whom. Most of the time, behavior modification involves a behavioral bargain: "I'll do what you want if you'll do what I want."

Some critics of behavior modification contend that it promotes a manipulative outlook on interpersonal relations and that eventually it may spawn mistrust and suspicion. They suggest that effective behavior control requires that people sometimes praise or smile at one another when they don't really mean it. The critics fear that, pretty soon, everyone will be cold and calculating rather than genuinely positive. Defenders of behavior modification are quick to point out, however, that this method need not be manipulative or destructive. They contend that in any serious behavior modification program designed to benefit someone, the reinforcers are usually quite sincere and surely more genuine than the average compliment. In one commune based on behaviorist techniques, for example, the emphasis is on sincere communication and feedback as to both positive and negative sides of a person's behavior. The commune's focus is on behavior rather than on personality; instead of saying "You're lazy," members would say, "You have missed your turn doing the dishes twice in a row now." Supporters of behavior modification point to such applications of learning principles as an indication that rewards and punishments can be meted out honestly and sincerely in an effort to help people make desirable changes in their behavior.

Behavior modification is useful in a wide range of settings Anyone who wants to modify some aspect of his or her behavior can make use of learning techniques. One need not surrender one's control to others—rewards and punishments can easily be administered by oneself. In this way, people can take on the responsibility for changing their diet, stopping smoking, improving study habits, or otherwise altering undesirable parts of their lives. So, although behavior modification may seem on the surface to require a surrendering of freedom, those who recognize its possibilities can actually use behavior modification to make their lives freer.

The Controlled Society

The most compelling criticism of behavior control is that it could be used in ways that are contrary to the principles of a free society. A free society upholds people's right to be treated in the ways that they themselves choose. But there are many persons who might benefit from behavior modification who are unable to give their consent to such treatment. Many children, mental patients, and retarded individuals fall into this category. Can we justify the use of behavior modification with such people? An even thornier issue concerns prisoners. Given the totally controlled environment of the prison, is it possible to be a true volunteer? Imagine a prison official telling a sex offender, "Submit to behavior modification or spend ten more years in jail." The choice may belong to the prisoner, but is it free? Finally, in both prisons and hospitals it is difficult to distinguish between behavior modification designed for the welfare of its recipients and behavior modification used as a tool by the institutional administration to keep the inmates in their place.

Ordinary citizens, who are neither in prisons nor in mental hospitals, are probably most afraid of the use of behavior modification by a malevolent, totalitarian government. Of course, the use of techniques for behavior control by governments would not be anything new. Governments have been using a wide variety of control mechanisms, including reward, punishment, and coercion, throughout recorded history. Perhaps we are most frightened by the possibility that these efforts will become more effective as they become more scientific.

The most difficult dilemmas revolve around the use of behavior control within democratic societies. In societies such as our own, the government is supposed to defend freedom, and the people have some freedom to lose. In this connection, two related questions have taken center stage in the long debate over social control of behavior: Is this freedom real? And is it worth maintaining? Opposing positions on this issue were perhaps best outlined in the 1956 debate between behaviorist B. F. Skinner and humanist Carl Rogers.

Skinner argued that freedom is a myth.

Skinner argued that freedom is a myth. What we are and what we do depend entirely on our genetic heritage and, most importantly, on the reinforcements provided by our environment. Therefore, none of us is really free. Since society would be more orderly, productive, and peaceful if we controlled our own reinforcements, it would actually be beneficial if we gave up the myth of freedom altogether. Skinner stated:

> *What is needed is a new conception of human behavior which is compatible with the implications of a scientific analysis. All men control and are controlled. The question of government in the broadest possible sense is not how freedom is to be preserved but what kinds of control are to be used and to what ends.* [Rogers and Skinner, 1956.]

In rebuttal, Rogers suggested that we should use our scientific knowledge to make people more free, rather than less. He said:

> *We can choose to use our growing knowledge to enslave people in ways never dreamed of before, depersonalizing them, controlling them by means so carefully selected that they will perhaps never be aware of their loss of personhood. . . . Or, at the other end of the spectrum of choice, we can choose to use the behavioral sciences in ways which will free, not control . . . which will facilitate each per-*

Extensive scientific control over behavior might require a dramatic change in our form of government.

son in his self-directed process of becoming; which will aid individuals [and] groups . . . in freshly adaptive ways of meeting life and its problems. [Rogers and Skinner, 1956]†

Clearly, Rogers doesn't feel that freedom of choice is a myth. Instead, he views freedom as a prerequisite for human growth.

Even if these philosophical issues are resolved some day, there are still other problems. Who, for example, decides which behaviors will be controlled and how? In the past, we have awarded the power of social control to elected officials. Legislatures decide whether to punish people who murder or steal or smoke marijuana. But legislatures may be incapable of exercising scientific behavior control. In that case, nonelected scientific experts might be given the job. But these experts may not have the right to tell us when we should be rewarded and when we should be punished. Extensive scientific control over behavior might require a dramatic change in our form of government.

†*From "Some Issues Concerning the Control of Human Behavior," C. R. Rogers and B. F. Skinner,* Science, *Vol. 124, pp. 1057–1066, 30 November 1956. Copyright 1956 by the American Association for the Advancement of Science. Reprinted by permission.*

Summary

1. Behavior control has been applied in a wide variety of settings over the last 25 years, from helping patients in mental hospitals to cutting down on littering in movie theaters.
2. The use of punishment, or aversive control, as a therapeutic tool has caused many people to criticize behavior control. But defenders of punishment point out that the punishment used in therapy is usually mild and that its value in eliminating undesirable responses outweighs its negative aspects.
3. Behavior modification is the systematic application of rewards and punishments to alter or control behavior. Critics of behavior modification argue that it is dehumanizing, that it promotes cold manipulation in interpersonal relationships, and that it takes control away from the individual. Advocates of behavior modification contend that people are not likely to be conditioned against their will, that behavior control programs are based on sincere and honest rewards and punishments, and that individuals can apply learning principles in their own lives without surrendering control to others.
4. Social control of behavior in a democratic society is a matter of great debate. Skinner argues that social control is necessary for a productive, peaceful society. Rogers, on the other hand, calls for less control and more individual freedom.

Memory

CHAPTER 6

Memory

Of all the remarkable mental capacities of the human being, the ability to remember is perhaps the most remarkable of all. As with many of our capacities, we tend to take memory for granted. The fact that we can recall a news item that we read in the newspaper yesterday, or a conversation that we had with a friend two months ago, or even the name of a grade-school teacher we haven't seen for more than ten years is taken as a matter of course. Since these are experiences we once had, why shouldn't they still be with us now? But consider for a moment how incredible this ability to recall information from the past really is. It means that we are not only capable of recording information but also of storing it in some form that will make it available to us days, months, or years later, when we need it. In fact, the human brain's capacity for information storage and retrieval is considerably more efficient than that of any computer system yet developed.

In this chapter we will explore the workings of human memory. First, we will consider two basic types of memory, short-term and long-term, and the way they work together to register, store, and retrieve information. Then we will look at some of the research on learning of words and syllables that has helped psychologists to understand the workings of memory more fully. After that, we will delve into the mysterious brain mechanisms that underlie the processes for memory. Next, to make sure that we don't take memory too much for granted, we will examine some memory disorders, including cases of people who have lived without the capacity to form new memories. Finally, we will draw from psychological research on memory to provide some concrete tips on how you can improve your own memory.

SHORT-TERM AND LONG-TERM MEMORY

Almost a century ago, the pioneering American psychologist William James noted that there seem to be two distinct types of memory, one sort that is fleeting and another sort that appears to be permanent and indestructible. James wrote:

> *The stream of thought flows on, but most of its elements fall into the bottomless pit of oblivion. Of some, no element survives the instant of their passage. Of others, it is confined to a few moments, hours, or days. Others, again, leave vestiges which are indestructible, and by means of which they may be recalled as long as life endures. Can we explain these differences?* [James, 1890]

James's analysis agrees with everyday experience. Some thoughts—such as a telephone number we've just looked up—seem to be immediately present in our consciousness but do not stay there for very long. Other thoughts—such as the capital of Kansas—may be somewhere in our memory stores but we can't bring them to consciousness without an active search; such memories seem to be quite permanent, however.

The two-component model of memory was discarded by behaviorists, who dealt primarily with animal learning and didn't see the need to make that sort of distinction. But research on verbal learning and memory over the past several decades has suggested that James was in fact right about the existence of two distinct sorts of memory—*short-term* and *long-term.* A model of memory that includes these two types has been proposed by Atkinson and Shiffrin (1968). If the model of memory that we are about to describe reminds you of a computer program, it is no accident. (See Figure 6.1.) In fact, this model was developed as a direct analogy to the ways in which computers register, store, and retrieve information.

THE MAGICAL NUMBER SEVEN (PLUS OR MINUS TWO)

"My problem is that I have been persecuted by an integer. For seven years this number has followed me around, has intruded in my most private data, and has assaulted me from the pages of our most public journals." Although psychologist George Miller opened his 1955 address to a psychological convention with these words, he was not publicly confessing his paranoia but was referring to the fact that we are able to process only about five to nine items of information at a time. What Miller (1956) calls the "magical number seven" is the limit of immediate memory to seven plus or minus two items, whether the items are digits, letters, or words.

Short-Term Memory

Asimov (1967) reports that the brain, in a lifetime, probably absorbs as many as one quadrillion—1,000,000,000,000,000—separate bits of information. At any moment, thousands of pieces of information impinge on our eyes, ears, and other sense organs. Very little of this information actually reaches our consciousness, however. From all of the incoming sensory stimulation, most is held in a stage of *sensory storage,* lasting but a fraction of a second,

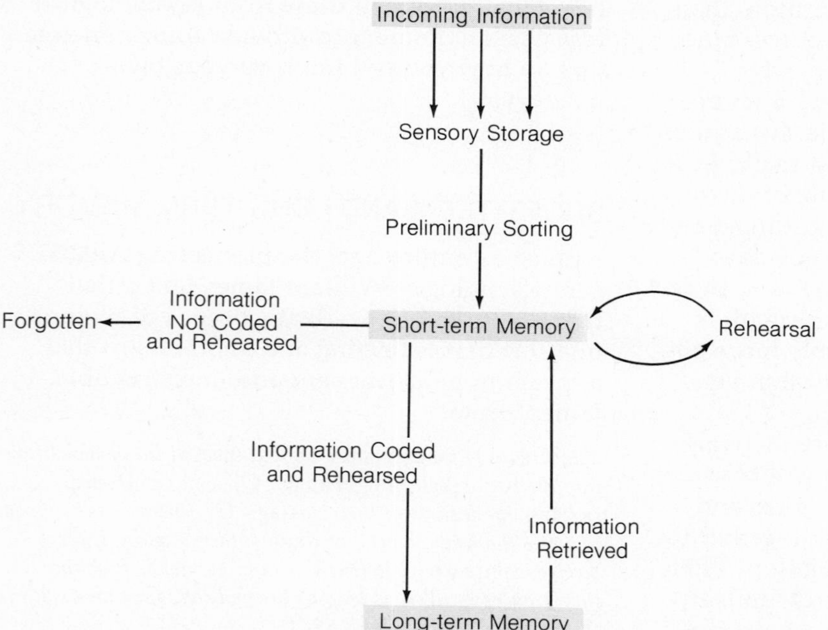

FIG. 6 · 1 A model of memory

Short term memory is important in many of our everyday activities.

and then is lost. The sensory storage system acts as kind of a filter—it sorts out a small fraction of the information to go into *short-term memory.*

Short-term memory lasts much longer compared to sensory storage. But it, too, is limited, for it can hold only a limited amount of information. For example, if you recite a list of letters or numbers to someone and ask that person to repeat the list, he or she can usually handle lists of up to seven (or sometimes eight or nine) items, but not much more. Thus, short-term memory appears to have a limited capacity of about seven items (Miller, 1956). Maybe that's one reason why telephone numbers have seven digits.

Although short-term memory is limited, its span can be increased by organizing inputs into larger "chunks." Short-term memory is not limited to seven letters or numbers but rather to about seven pieces of information. If we can manage to code a set of letters or numbers into a single piece of information (such as a word or phrase), the amount of information we can hold in short-term memory will be increased. To illustrate this point, Miller reported that one highly practiced subject could recall up to 40 binary digits (such as 1010001001 . . . by mentally organizing them into eight "chunks" of five digits each. The subject did so by learning a simple coding system in which, for example,

10100 equals 20, 01001 equals 9, and so on. Listening to the sequence 1010001001 . . . , he needed only to remember 20, 9, and so on and then to recode back to the binary numbers when being tested. The real limitation, then, is in the number of chunks that can be recalled. The size of the chunk can vary considerably, though, depending on the coding system used. That is why the span of immediate memory is approximately seven, whether the items are letters, words, sentences, or even larger units. After all, language is a coding system that we have had a lot of practice with.

Although short-term memory can be expanded in this way, its capacity remains limited, and the information is kept in mind for only a short time. Sometimes the information doesn't stay in mind for as long as we need it. You've surely had the experience of looking up a phone number, then being distracted before dialing, and forgetting the number by the time you turn to dial. Or, when you are introduced to a lot of people, you may forget their names at almost the same rate that new names are introduced. In this instance, new information is arriving in short-term memory at a time when the storehouse is already full. In such a case the new information may bump the older information out of short-term memory before it can be readied for long-term storage.

In general, short-term memory can hold items fairly well for the first few seconds. After about 12 seconds, however, recall is poor, and after 20 seconds the information has disappeared entirely, unless we have kept rehearsing the material in our minds. A phone number that we look up and dial is often forgotten by the time the call is answered. But a certain relatively small proportion of the material that enters short-term memory is not lost along the way. Instead, we manage to transfer this material to long-term memory for later reference. Thus, there are some telephone numbers that we once had to look up but that now we know without looking. These are the numbers that are important enough for us to have taken pains to record them in our long-term memory store.

Long-Term Memory

Sherlock Holmes, the fictional detective who was, among other things, a master of memory, once gave Dr. Watson the following advice:

> *I consider that a man's brain originally is like a little empty attic and you have to stock it with such functions as you choose. A fool takes in all the lumber of every sort that he comes across . . . now the skilled workman is very careful indeed as to what he takes into his brain-attic. He will have nothing but the tools which may help him in doing his work, but of these he has a large assortment, and all in the most perfect order. It is a mistake to think that that little room has elastic walls and can distend to any extent. Depend upon it that there comes a time when for every addition of knowledge you forget something that you knew before.* [*Doyle, 1927, page 21*]

What Holmes referred to as the "brain attic" is what today's psychologists call *long-term memory*, the process by which we can retain information for days, years, or even a lifetime. Holmes's model of memory does not agree in all respects with that suggested by recent psychological research. In fact, the "attic" of long-term memory does seem to have elastic walls, in that its capacity seems to be unlimited. But Holmes was quite correct in emphasizing the importance of stocking that attic carefully. Unless information is carefully coded and filed, it will become impossible for us to retrieve the information when we need it—the task would be like trying to find a book in a large library where the books are arranged randomly and the card catalog is disorganized.

How do we get information from short-term memory into long-term storage? There are two basic processes: rehearsal of the information (repeating it to yourself) and coding it (linking it to concepts and categories that you already have learned). Coding is like filing things in a complicated, cross-referenced file system. The coding of information for storage may take different forms, depending on the type of material to be remembered. The coding process may either simplify or elaborate on the information or change it into a different form (Bower, 1972). The process may be thought of as analogous to marking books, cross-listing them on cards, and storing the material in specified places in a library. All this is done in order to make information easier to retrieve. In the same way information is coded in long-term memory so that it may be available when needed.

As Atkinson and Shiffrin (1968) emphasize, memory storage is not a passive process. Rather, we must decide what information we would like to store in long-term memory by selecting the items to rehearse and code. *How* we code material is particularly important because, as we will see, our success at retrieving material from long-term memory depends in large measure on the efficiency with which it is stored.

SILVER
LETTUCE
TYPEWRITER
TOMATO
DESK
COPPER
CELERY
FILE CABINET
BRONZE

As part of our attempt to stock our brain attics carefully, we have all learned to package the material in meaningful clusters. To demonstrate this process, you can do the following simple experiment, using a friend as your subject. Read the adjacent list of words to your friend, telling him or her to remember as many of the words as possible. After you've read the list of words, ask your friend to start with the number 42 and count backward by threes to zero. The purpose of this counting task is to provide some mental interference so that the memory task won't be too easy. Now ask your friend to tell you as many of the words as possible, in whatever order he or she likes. If your friend is like most subjects in this sort of experiment, he or she will remember a large proportion of the words—but he or she will report them in a different order from the order that you read them. Your friend will probably report them in clusters or categories—for example, by vegetables, office furniture, and then metals. This finding illustrates that it is much easier to learn and remember a list of words that includes meaningful clusters than it is to learn a list of words that bear no relation to one another.

While most information needs to be rehearsed and coded to get into long-term storage, there seem to be exceptions: certain visual images—such as faces—seem to go directly into long-term storage. Haber (1970) showed subjects a series of 2,560 photographic slides of people, objects, and scenes, each for 10 seconds. An hour after the subjects had seen the last of the slides, they were shown 280 pairs of pictures. One member of each pair was from the series the subjects had seen; the other was from a similar set that had not been shown to the subjects. When the subjects were asked to say which of the two pictures they had seen before, about 90 percent of their choices were correct. Although this sort of experiment shows that we can record a large quantity of visual material directly into memory, our visual memories are by no means perfect (see the discussion of eyewitness testimony in the Psychological Issue at the end of this chapter).

Paivio (1971) has proposed that there are actually two systems for coding information into memory, one verbal and one visual. Under some conditions, such as learning a set of pictures or a list of concrete words that are easy to visualize (like "cat, dog, monkey . . ."), the visual system predominates. In a number of experiments, Paivio has demonstrated that recall is best when conditions favor using both visual and verbal coding processes simultaneously. The presence of both a name and a picture of an object or person helps us to get a better handle on the information than we would have with only the name or only the picture. Such *dual coding* may also enable people to bring more "brain power" to bear on a memory problem: both the verbal processes dominated by the left brain hemisphere and the visual processes dominated by the right hemisphere come into play (see Psychological Issue following Chapter 2).

Once information has been coded and stored in long-term memory, the next problem is being able to retrieve the information at the moment that we need it. As we noted earlier, the best way to improve information retrieval is to store and code things carefully in the first place. In addition, it may sometimes help to return to the situation in which we originally stored the material (it would be like remembering the day we first put something in the attic and trying to figure out where we might have put it). This return can be done mentally (by thinking back) or physically. For example, police take victims and witnesses back to the scene of a crime, and they often find that this helps to sharpen the witnesses' recollections.

An interesting example of a retrieval problem comes from Brown and McNeill's (1966) research on the "tip of the tongue" phenomenon: the feeling that you know a word you want to use but are unable to recall it (their study was described in detail in Chapter 1). To study this phenomenon, the researchers read the definitions of obscure words to their subjects and recorded the words that came to mind for subjects who said they knew the

A MEMORY FOR CHESS

"There have been chess players who obviously had fantastic memories. Among these is Paul Charles Morphy, born in New Orleans in 1837. He was world-renowned and often played championship games blindfolded. It would seem to tax the memory to remember just the game at hand, but Morphy claimed he could recall every move of every one of the hundreds of games he played in championship matches! In fact, he later recorded about four hundred of these games, play by play." [Halacy, 1970, page 83]

correct word but could not quite recall it. Although the words the subjects thought of were similar to the correct word in a number of ways, most of them were similar in sound to the correct word.

When subjects were given the definition of the word "sampan," for example, those in the tip-of-the-tongue state brought to mind both words that were similar to it in meaning, such as "barge," "houseboat," and "junk," and words that were similar to it in sound, such as "Saipan," "Cheyenne," "sarong," "sanching," and "sympoon" (some of which are not even words). Brown and McNeill's research seems to indicate that our verbal storage system is cross-referenced by both meaning and sound. We use the meaning reference system to retrieve the word we want to use in a particular context; we often use the sound reference system (something like an alphabetically organized dictionary) to help us recognize words in spoken language.

REMEMBERING AND FORGETTING

Now that we have an overall view of the information storage and retrieval mechanisms that make up human memory, we are in a better position to examine some of the basic features of remembering and forgetting. In this section, we will examine the methods and results of a wide range of psychological studies, some conducted in the earliest days of psychological research in the late nineteenth and early twentieth century, and some conducted much more recently.

Verbal Learning

Most of the research on processes of remembering and forgetting has involved *verbal learning*—the ways in which we remember or forget words, letters, or other verbal material. Laboratory studies have taught us a great deal about the conditions that are most conducive to recall and the conditions that are most likely to impede it and thus lead to forgetting.

Box 1

Those Unforgettable High School Days

How many of the people in your high school class do you think you will be able to remember twenty-five years from now? A recent study of long-term memory suggests that it may be more than you think, especially if your memory in the year 2000 is given the right sorts of prods.

This study, conducted by Harry P. Bahrick, Phyllis O. Bahrick, and Roy P. Wittlinger (1974), was an ingenious approach to the measurement of long-term memory. In most studies of long-term memory, people are taught material in the laboratory and are then tested a few hours, days, or weeks later. Although these studies have been valuable, Bahrick and his colleagues wanted to explore people's memories over much longer periods of time. To do this, they needed to find a standard set of material that subjects could be assumed to have learned reasonably well at one point in their lives and that they would not have much opportunity to relearn after that time. Their solution was to test people with names and pictures taken from their high school yearbooks. Their subjects were 392 high school graduates between the ages of 17 and 74 who had been out of high school for anywhere from 3 months to 40 years or more.

The subjects were first given a *free recall* test, in which they were simply asked to list as many of their classmates as they could in an eight-minute period. (In preliminary testing the researchers had found that after eight minutes, people had more or less exhausted the names they could recall without prompting). On the free recall test, the most recent graduates could recall an average of 47 names. Surprisingly, the size of the subject's high school class made little difference on this measure; subjects could recall as many names whether they graduated from classes of 90 or 900. Free recall performance declined steadily with age, with people who had been out of school for 40 years or more being able to recall an average of only 19 names.

Subjects were then given a *picture recognition* test, in which they were shown ten cards with five pictures on each. One of the five was a classmate. The other four were foils, selected from other yearbooks of the same era. The procedure was something like a police lineup: The sub-

Some of this research might, at first glance, seem like a lot of nonsense. For what could be more nonsensical than a psychologist spending a good deal of his life trying to memorize meaningless syllables like KEJ, GOK, and PUM? The researcher was a German psychologist named Hermann Ebbinghaus (1850–1909), who invented *nonsense syllables* as a means of studying verbal learning and memory. From these nonsense syllables (all consisting of a vowel between two consonants), he made up random lists, which he memorized, systematically varying the amount of practice and the length of time between learning and testing.

Actually, Ebbinghaus's choice of materials to learn was not really nonsensical at all. While some research on learning (like

---

jects were asked to look at the five pictures and to pick out their classmate. Subjects performed extremely well on this test. Recent high school graduates could correctly identify nine out of ten of their classmates' pictures—and, quite remarkably, so could people who had graduated 35 years earlier. Even those subjects who had graduated from high school 40 years earlier—men and women in their late 50s and early 60s—could identify an average of three-fourths of their classmates. Subjects were also given a *name recognition* test, in which they had to pick out classmates' names from sets of five, and did almost as well.

The researchers also found that subjects' recall of their classmates' names was significantly improved if they were "prompted" with classmates' pictures. On a *picture prompting* test, subjects were shown a series of ten pictures, drawn at random from their yearbook, and were asked to provide each person's name. On this test, the youngest group of subjects recalled almost 70 percent of their classmates' names. Performance declined steadily over time, with people in the oldest group being able to recall fewer than two out of ten names. For all groups, however, the "prompting" led to the recall of many classmates who had otherwise been "forgotten."

These results emphasize that long-term memory has tremendous capacity and endurance—subjects remembered the large majority of their high school classmates well enough to pick them out of a crowd even after 40 years had gone by. The results also emphasize, however, that much of the information in long-term memory is not ordinarily accessible to us. In order to be able to retrieve this information, we need to enter our mental filing system with the proper visual or verbal cues. Without these cues, we are left to stumble around our mental storeroom more or less at random. With them, we can much more efficiently find the information we are looking for. That is why performance on tests of *recognition,* in which we simply have to match up cues that we are given with our mental images, tends to be so much better than *recall,* in which we must come up with our own cues and probes to aid in retrieval.

In this connection it is noteworthy that on the free recall test, in which subjects were left to their own devices to bring to mind classmates' names, they could rarely recall someone unless they also remembered the type of association they had with that person—for example, as a close friend, a date, or a teammate. On the other hand, subjects could recognize many classmates' names and faces without remembering their association with them.

The effectiveness of picture prompting in improving recall points to the value of simultaneous visual and verbal coding in memory storage. During the course of four years of high school, we repeatedly learn and relearn linkages between particular names and particular faces. As a result, when we see the picture—even if it is a picture of someone we haven't seen or thought of for years—it is likely to elicit the name that goes along with it.

Ah, those bygone high school days, muses one mellowing alumnus, now 16 years out. The Bronx High School of Science, Class of 1961, what has become of you? Costas Hercules, Richard Rocco, Delores Mack, Barbara Friedlander, Fred Fay, Deeday LaRene, and good-old-what's-his-name, where are you?

Hermann E. Ebbinghaus

the experiment you did with your friend) is concerned with the effects of meaningfulness, Ebbinghaus wanted to focus on basic features of learning and memory that did *not* involve meaning—what is sometimes called "rote learning." To do this he had to find stimuli that did not have any special meaning or significance—hence, the nonsense syllable. Although somewhat more sophisticated methods have been developed in the last hundred years, Ebbinghaus's basic finding that forgetting occurs rapidly at first and slows down greatly as time passes remains basically unchallenged.

Ebbinghaus's principle is referred to as the *learning curve.* The typical learning curve shows that the greatest memory loss happens soon after learning and that the rate of loss declines as time passes. Thus, memory losses are slower after the initial forgetting, but they still occur. Forgetting is also influenced by the strength of the original learning—the greater the degree of original learning, the greater the retention. When material is well-learned, the retention is the same for material of varying difficulty and for individuals with varying learning abilities. Slow learners and fast learners both forget at the same rate, and easily learned material is probably not retained any longer than difficult material.

SLEEP LEARNING

Wouldn't it be great if we could turn on a language record before going to sleep and wake up able to speak a new tongue? People have been interested in sleep learning for a long time, but an experiment by Emmons and Simon (1956) seems to indicate that people cannot learn while they are asleep. The researchers played a recording of ten one-syllable words to sleeping subjects. (If the subjects showed signs of waking, as indicated by their EEG, the recording was turned off.) To test learning, the subjects were asked to choose, from a list of 50 words, those words that had been played during sleep. They didn't do any better than the control subjects. The conclusion drawn from this and similar studies is very simple: if you want to learn and remember, you'd better be awake.

Recall, Recognition, and Relearning

Researchers studying verbal learning have used three basic measures of memory (or retention): recall, recognition, and relearning. In *recall,* the individual must recount or reproduce something

EXERCISING MEMORY

If muscles get stronger and become more developed with use, it seems reasonable that the brain could be developed in the same way. Or at least that's what William James hypothesized. He tried an experiment to see whether he could improve his memory by exercising his brain cells. First he learned a certain amount of material and kept track of how long it took him. Then he spent 20 minutes a day for 38 days diligently exercising his memory cells by memorizing information. Finally, he retested his ability to learn a specific amount of material—and found he was even slower at learning than he had been before the exercise. Subsequent studies have had similar results—muscle-building doesn't work on the brain (Halacy, 1970).

previously learned, with the help of only the barest of cues. In *recognition,* the individual must simply identify something that he or she has encountered before. As you might expect, people's recognition of people or events tends to be considerably better than recall (see Box 1). For example, ask a friend to tell you the name of the capital of Kansas (or, if you live in Kansas, the capital of some other state, like Florida). Some of your friends will recall the answer right away, but others will be stumped. Now give these stumped friends another chance. Ask them, "Which is it: Lincoln, Topeka, Kansas City, Lawrence, or Jefferson City?" Now, the chances are that most of your previously stumped friends will immediately recognize the right answer (it's Topeka). In such cases, the person clearly has the correct information stored somewhere in memory. The problem is that he or she can't find the item in the mental storehouse, much as we may sometimes be unable to find an item in a cluttered room, even though we know it's there. But if you present the right answer as part of a list, the retrieval problem is solved and the answer is recognized.

A third measure of retention is *relearning.* With this measure, a researcher sees how quickly the subject can learn material that he or she learned previously. The number of trials required to master the relearned material can be compared with the number of trials it took to master it originally. The difference between the first and second learnings is the *savings* in trials or time. (For this reason, the relearning method of measuring memory is sometimes called the savings method.) Of the three measures, relearning generally shows the greatest amount of retention over the longest period of time. Often individuals who have once learned something find it impossible to recall or even recognize the material at a later time, yet they are still able to relearn the material much more quickly than if they had never learned it in the first place. This ability to relearn material quickly can be of great practical value later in life—when, for example, one wants to brush up on French before taking that long-awaited trip to Paris, or one needs to relearn shorthand to move into a desired job.

Interference

Verbal learning can often be hindered by activities that interfere with what has been learned. There seem to be two types of interference—the influence of activities prior to the learning and of activities following the learning. The first type is called *proactive interference* because material learned earlier interferes with something learned more recently. For example, students who have learned the French words for certain objects often have trouble learning Spanish words for the same objects (and vice versa) because the previous learning interferes with the learning of new information. Underwood (1957) described the effects of proactive interference in the laboratory. Subjects learned nine different lists of words on successive days and were asked each day to recall the list learned the previous day. Subjects remembered 71 percent of the first list but only 27 percent of the last list. Apparently, the previously learned lists interfered with the ability to recall the newer lists.

Interference may also occur because the new material is so similar to the old that it produces conflict. Thus, when you have been driving a standard-shift car and then drive one with automatic transmission, you may keep moving your foot to a nonexistent clutch. This mistake is not forgetting; it is interference with new learning that causes you to have the difficulty (Ceraso, 1967).

The second kind of interference is called *retroactive* because a newly learned piece of information tends to hinder the recall of an earlier learned piece. It's like the professor of ichthyology who refused to learn the names of his new students because, as he put it, "Whenever I learn a new student's name, I forget the name of a fish" (Lindzey, Hall, and Thompson, 1975, page 218). In a typical verbal learning experiment retroactive interference can be demonstrated by comparing the recall of a list of nonsense syllables by two groups, the first group consisting of subjects who are required to learn only this list, and the second group made up of subjects who must learn a second list before trying to recall the first. In such experiments, subjects in the second group do not recall as many words from the list because retroactive interference from the second list makes the task more difficult.

The interfering activity does not have to be another laboratory learning task. A number of experimenters have tested the effects of retroactive interference by comparing subjects who sleep during the retention interval with those who remain awake. The assumption is that there will be fewer interfering activities during sleep. In the classic experiment of this type (Jenkins and Dallenbach, 1924), as well as in more recent studies (Ekstrand, 1967), greater retention has been shown for subjects who sleep between learning and recall. For years students have used these results to justify abandoning their books and going to sleep the night before an exam. One should recognize, however, that the benefits of sleep in reducing interference occur only when the material has been well learned in the first place.

The process of interference, whether proactive or retroactive, may possibly be explained by the need to rehearse material in order to store it in long-term memory. If something happens to prevent rehearsal or repetition once an item is in short-term memory, recall may be greatly impaired. Peterson and Peterson (1959) conducted an experiment that demonstrated this phenomenon. They read a three-letter combination, such as CTX, to their subjects and varied the retention interval (the time between presentation of the item and the recall test) from 3 to 18 seconds. Normally, of course, you would be able to remember CTX for 18 seconds. But the Petersons had the subjects count backward by threes during the retention interval in order to prevent rehearsal. The results were dramatic: the longer the interval, the less likely subjects were to remember the item. After 18 seconds correct recall had dropped to less than 10 percent. A similar thing may

UNFINISHED BUSINESS

In a classic study of memory, Zeigarnik (1927) gave her subjects a number of simple tasks to do. She allowed some of the tasks to be completed, but she interrupted others. Several hours later, when the subjects were asked to recall the tasks, they recalled more of the incomplete tasks than the complete ones. This tendency to recall incomplete tasks is now called the Zeigarnik effect. It apparently stems from our greater need to remember things that are still unfinished so that we can go back and finish them. Usually, there is less need to remember completed tasks.

happen to you if you study with the radio on. Switching your attention away from the book to the radio for a moment may prevent you from rehearsing an item of information you thought you had registered. If you don't go back to the item, you may not be able to recall it. To ensure that material *is* rehearsed and stored, many people use special memory tricks as ways of coding the material effectively (some of these tricks will be described later in the chapter).

Why Do We Forget?

Given the impressive capacities of human memory, we can ask a different sort of basic question: Why do we forget things at all? Several different reasons for forgetting have been identified. For one thing, as we noted earlier, some information is forgotten almost as soon as it is learned. This is information, such as a telephone number, that is held for a brief period in short-term memory but is never transferred to long-term memory. Once such information drops out of short-term memory, it is lost to us forever.

When we talk about forgetting things, however, we are usually talking about information that we once knew—that was once part of our long-term memory store—but that we can no longer bring to mind. Psychologists once believed that information in long-term memory would "decay" over time if it was never used or that it would fade as the result of interference from new material—which would correspond with Sherlock Holmes's idea that "for every addition of knowledge you forget something that you knew before." But recent research suggests that this is not the case. In fact, long-term memories remain in permanent storage, embedded in physical-chemical codes that scientists are just beginning to understand. When we talk about "forgetting" such material, we are usually talking about a retrieval problem. Especially when a great deal of information in long-term storage is not carefully coded, it may be extremely difficult for the person to find it. With the right sort of prompting, however, even such long-lost information can eventually be dredged up from our memories (see Box 1).

We sometimes forget material that is in our long-term memories not only because we *can't* retrieve it but also because we don't really want to. That is, we may sometimes forget things on purpose because remembering them would be embarrassing or painful. This process is called *motivated forgetting.* The existence of this type of forgetting often comes out in family discussions in which members reminisce about days gone by. Someone will bring up an incident in which another family member appears in a bad light, and the second person will say, "Did I do that?" and will profess to no memory of the event. In fact, the "accused" family member may have a totally different recollection of the same event, even if all other family members remember the embarrassing version.

Sigmund Freud's conception of *repression* deals with motivated forgetting on a deeper level. According to Freud, we are

THE SERIAL-POSITION EFFECT

3 8 5 6 2 9 4 2 7 1 4

Read this list of digits aloud, just once. Then turn away from the book and write down the list, as well as you can remember it. The chances are that you will remember the first and last numbers correctly but have some errors for digits near the middle of the list. This tendency to remember the first and last items in a list better than the ones in the middle is called the *serial-position effect.* It occurs with all sorts of lists—numbers, letters, words.

Why is this so? For one thing the items at the beginnings and ends of lists seem to be particularly noticeable. Also, the first item may be remembered because it is stored in long-term memory before other items start getting in the way. And the last few items are probably remembered because they are still in short-term memory. The middle items, however, may never have made the jump into long-term memory and may have been bumped out of short-term memory by items later on the list.

unable to retrieve some memories because they are related to emotional conflicts. If we remembered certain feelings and events, such as our early sexual and aggressive feelings, we would experience severe anxiety. To avoid this anxiety, we manage to repress this material and keep it from coming to the surface. In this way "forgetting" serves to protect one's self-concept.

MEMORY AND THE BRAIN

Psychologists and physiologists are just beginning to discover the brain mechanisms that underlie the processes of memory. For a long time it was thought that long-term memory depended on electrical circuits in various parts of the brain that laid down lasting patterns, called "engrams." Karl Lashley, a noted neurophysiologist, spent a good part of his life searching for such engrams in the brains of laboratory animals. One procedure he used was to teach a rat a new skill—to run a particular maze, for example—and then to remove portions of the rat's cortex. He would then put the rat back into the maze to see whether it still remembered the skill. Lashley found, to his dismay, that no matter how much of the rat's cortex he removed, memory still re-

Box 2

Memory Drugs

At his laboratory at the University of Michigan, biochemist Bernard Agranoff was teaching goldfish a new task—to cross an underwater barrier whenever a light was flashed in order to avoid a mild electric shock. Normally, goldfish that have learned this skill will remember it for at least a month. But this time Dr. Agranoff injected some puromycin, a chemical that blocks the formation of protein, into the fishes' skulls immediately after they had learned the task. Suddenly, the newly learned skill vanished. On subsequent tests, the goldfish behaved as if they had never learned to cross the barrier at all. Further research confirmed that the puromycin interfered with the chemical processes that cause new learning to be consolidated, or "fixed," in long-term memory. For this interference to take place, the puromycin had to be administered soon after the training session. If Dr. Agranoff waited as long as an hour, it was too late—the memory had already been consolidated.

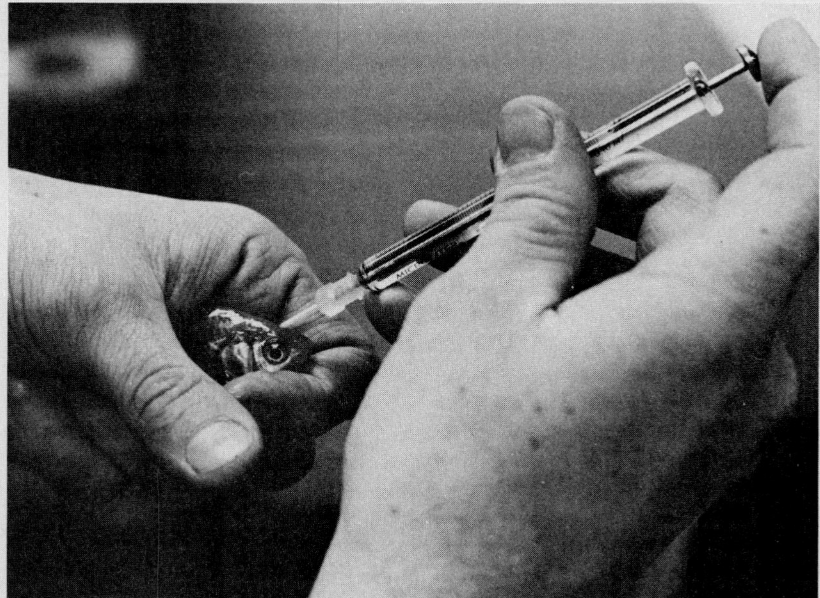

At another laboratory, at the University of California at Irvine, physiological psychologist James McGaugh gave rats mained. Looking back over his research, Lashley came to the tongue-in-cheek conclusion, "I sometimes feel, in reviewing the evidence on the localization of the memory trace, that the necessary conclusion is that learning is just not possible" (1950, pages 477–478).

In the mid-1960s, researchers began to turn from the search for localized electrical circuits to an emphasis on the chemical aspect of memory. It is now believed that memories are created by chemical changes that affect neurotransmitters (the chemicals that carry messages across synapses from one neuron to another) or that affect nerve cells' sensitivity to neurotransmitters. It is believed that as learning progresses these chemical changes cause particular synapses in the brain to become more efficient at passing messages (Deutsch, 1968).

Apparently, it takes time for such chemical changes to have a permanent impact on the nervous system. This period of time is called the *consolidation* phase. If brain processes are disrupted during this period, the memory is lost. If no disruption occurs, the message consolidates into long-term memory. For example, people who suffer brain injury often have amnesia for the events that occurred just before the accident. This loss of memory, called *retrograde amnesia,* may cover a period from several minutes

---

injections of strychnine shortly after they had learned to run a maze. He discovered that this drug, too, had an effect on memory—but this time in the opposite direction. The larger the dose of strychnine, the better the rats' memory for what they had learned. Whereas puromycin seemed to interfere with the consolidation process In Dr. Agranoff's goldfish, strychnine seemed to cause a quicker or stronger consolidation in McGaugh's rats. As in the case of puromycin, however, timing was crucial—the drug had to be administered within an hour of learning for it to have its effect.

These studies are part of an exciting new wave of research on the chemistry of memory. Such studies are demonstrating that memory is governed by the action of chemical neurotransmitters in the brain and that the formation of new memories can be locked or improved by giving animals chemicals that affect these neurotransmitters (Pines, 1975).

Might these "memory drugs" ever be used to treat human beings? The possibility is an intriguing one. Memory loss is frequently suffered by old people, perhaps because of the breakdown of chemical processes in the brain. As scientists learn more and more about these processes, it is conceivable that new drugs will be developed that could reduce memory loss in people with certain neurological diseases.

Memory drugs that block or facilitate the consolidation process could have other uses as well. As Maya Pines (1975) speculates, "In the future we may be able to select either one of these alternatives at various times: We may decide to take amnesic drugs [drugs that cause forgetting] before events so horrible that we want no permanent record of them, or we may seek a heightening of experience through drugs that sharpen our memory for special occasions" (p. 20).

At the moment, memory drugs for humans are still a long way off. All of the drugs that have been used to affect memory in animals either are poisonous, are addictive, or lead to convulsions. It is quite possible, however, that within the next decade or two memory drugs that can safely be administered to humans will be developed. But no matter how safe the drugs may be, we will have to keep a careful eye on their use—and possible abuse. Although memory drugs might prove to be a great boon to humanity, they might also present grave dangers if they are used indiscriminately.

to more than an hour before the accident (Russell and Nathan, 1964). The injury apparently interferes with chemical changes in the brain before the changes have a chance to consolidate.

Memory loss of this sort can also be produced in the laboratory. If an electroconvulsive shock—an electric current that produces temporary unconsciousness—is passed through the brain of a laboratory animal shortly after it has learned a new task, the new learning will be forgotten. The important finding for consolidation theory is that the electroconvulsive shock causes the greatest memory loss when administered shortly after the learning; the longer the delay, the less forgetting. This is because the formation of memory is susceptible to disruption only during the consolidation phase. On the other hand, the injection of certain drugs just after learning seems to speed up the consolidation process and to make memory less subject to disruption. Research with such drugs is proceeding rapidly right now. Such research is providing further information about the chemical basis of memory. And it is also raising the possibility that in the not-too-distant future drugs may be available to improve memory in humans and to reduce its decline in old age (see Box 2).

DISORDERS OF MEMORY

One way in which we can learn more about the workings of memory is by studying cases in which it does not work normally. For example, brain-damaged patients sometimes experience a condition of *transient global amnesia,* in which they are unable to hold on to any information for more than a few seconds. The patient retains all memories that were formed up to a few hours before the attack, but he or she cannot remember what is happening from one moment to the next. Such a patient can drive a car, but he doesn't know where he started from and has a hard time remembering where he is going. The patient can't boil an egg unless he is watching a clock and has written down the time the egg was placed on the stove. The attack usually lasts about a day, and then it gradually clears up. In most cases, Gardner (1975) reports, the patient eventually returns to normal, except that he can't remember anything that happened during the period of the attack.

This condition is similar to the sort of retrograde amnesia that can be caused by a head injury. Retrograde amnesia is apparently caused by a disruption of the chemical processes by which new learning becomes consolidated into long-term memory. In the case of transient global amnesia, however, the disruption is caused by attacks within the brain that can recur periodically. In another, even more serious condition, called *Korsakoff's syndrome,* the patient's inability to place new information in long-term storage is a lasting one. Named for S. S. Korsakoff, a Russian psychiatrist, this syndrome results from excessive intake of alcohol over a period of many years. Korsakoff patients can remember their lives up to the time the syndrome took hold, but they remember little else since that point. To illustrate the

FOOD FOR THOUGHT

Some researchers have had the notion that memories are stored in specific molecules in the nervous system. To test this idea, James McConnell (1962) devised a classical conditioning experiment in which he taught planaria (flatworms) to respond to a flash of light. The conditioned planaria were then chopped up and fed to untrained planaria, which were then put through the same learning process. McConnell reported that these planaria learned to react to the light faster than did ordinary planaria. They had, McConnell suggested, incorporated the "memory molecules" from their food and had thus acquired the memories they contained. The original excitement over McConnell's findings has died down, however, because other experimenters have had a hard time replicating the research. Most of the research on the chemical basis of memory is proceeding in different, noncannibalistic directions.

nature of the problem, Gardner (1975) recounts the following conversation he had with a man suffering from Korsakoff's syndrome:

"How old are you?"

"I was born in 1927."

"Which makes you . . . "

"Let's see, Doctor, how I always forget, the year is . . . "

"The year is what?"

"Oh, I must be thirty-four, thirty-five, what's the difference?" He grinned sheepishly.

"You'll soon be forty-six, Mr. O'Donnell, the year is 1973."

Mr. O'Donnell looked momentarily surprised, started to protest, and said, "Sure, you must be right, Doctor. How silly of me. I'm forty-five, that's right, I guess." [*pages 178–179*]

A famous case of brain disorder is that of a man who has been referred to as "H. M." in the scientific literature. H. M. had both temporal lobes of his brain removed to treat a severe epileptic condition. The surgery succeeded in curing the epilepsy, but the particular operation has never been done again because it caused H. M. to have a profound memory deficit. Like patients with Korsakoff's syndrome—but to a more complete degree—H. M. lives only in the present. He lacks the capacity to store any new information in memory. As a result, H. M. reads the same magazine over and over again, never realizing that he has seen the material before. He could not remember his new address, even after six years of residence.

Although researchers initially thought that H. M. could not learn anything at all, later tests showed that he was in fact capable of motor learning (Milner, 1966). With practice, for example, he steadily improved in his ability at "mirror drawing," a task that involved drawing a line around the border of a star, when he could only observe what he was doing through a mirror. (See Figure 6.2.) (If you've ever tried such mirror writing, you know that it takes a good deal of practice to get it right.) Did H. M. "remember" the mirror-drawing task? Each time H. M. was asked to do the task, he reported that he had never seen it before, and it had to be explained to him anew. At the verbal level, therefore, he didn't remember it at all. But his performance got steadily better, suggesting that at a motor level he came to remember the task quite well. This discrepancy suggests that our verbal memory and our motor memory are in fact quite different systems.

At the other extreme from H. M. is the famous case of the mnemonist called S., described by the Russian psychologist A. R. Luria (1968). Whereas H. M. could not remember anything, S. was a man who could not forget anything, down to the most trivial detail.

He could remember lists of numbers or words of any length, reciting them either frontwards or backwards on request; years later he could produce the entire copies of previous lists, without ever confusing any two of them. . . . His faithful

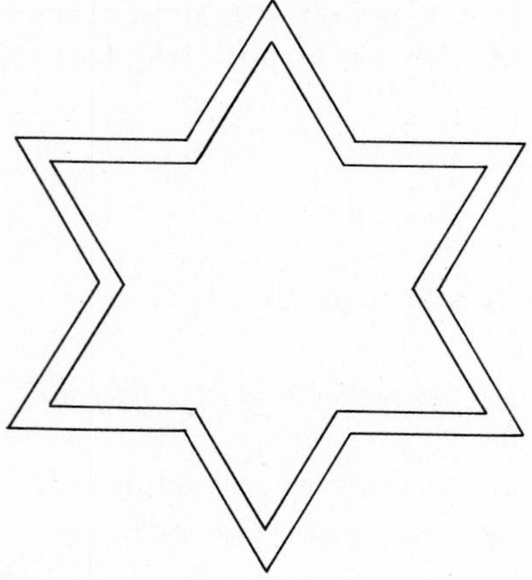

FIG. 6 · 2 Figure used in mirror-drawing task, to assess H.M.'s motor learning.

memory extended back to earliest childhood: he recalled being placed in his crib, lying there and staring at the wallpaper, feeling sensations of comfort and warmth, when less than a year old. [*Gardner, 1975, pages 210–211*]

S.'s astounding memory was apparently due to extraordinarily powerful sensory imagery that accompanied all of his activity. Every letter, number, or scene evoked an array of colors, sounds, and feelings that fixed the experience in his mind. S.'s condition may have been caused in part by a chemical imbalance in the brain. While H. M. and other amnesic patients may have an insufficiency of those chemicals that facilitate the consolidation of memory, S. may have had an excess of such chemicals (Pines, 1975). But S.'s rare talent was really no blessing. Because he remembered every concrete experience, S. was unable to ab-

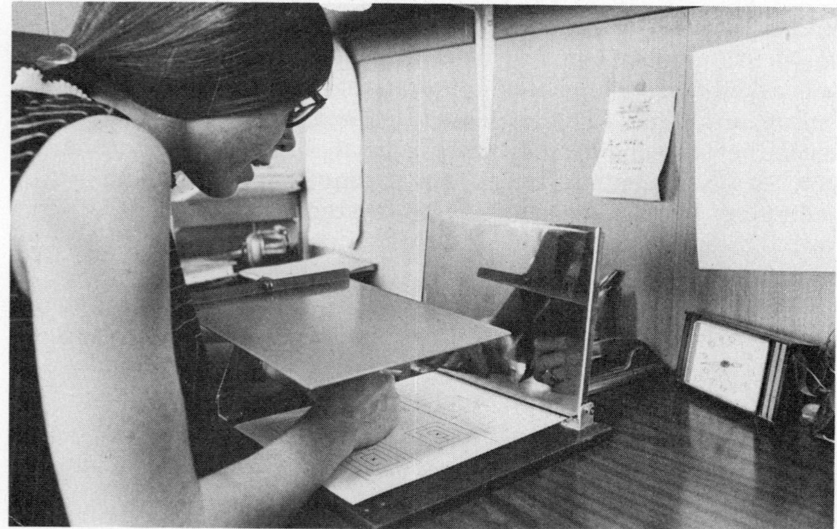

Subject performs a mirror-drawing task, similar to the one used to assess H.M.'s memory for motor skills.

stract or generalize across situations. He could not hold any job that required the abilities to organize, classify, or evaluate. As a result, the only way he could make a living was as a professional mnemonist—a performer treated by most people as something of a freak.

The cases of H. M. and S. show that most of us are doubly blessed. We not only have the ability to store new information in our memories, we also have the ability to sift through the information available to us and to decide what *not* to store. Both the ability to remember and the ability to forget are important prerequisites for our functioning as human beings.

IMPROVING MEMORY

When you want to remember something important, what do you do? Tie a string around your finger? Write it down? Say it over and over to yourself? Ask a friend to remind you? We all have our own ways of insuring that we remember certain things, but some ways are better than others. Thus, when some people say they have a "bad memory," they probably are just using an inefficient method of remembering. By applying some of the principles psychologists have discovered in their study of memory, recall can be improved.

Study Strategies

The strategy you use in studying information to be remembered is an important factor in memory. Experiments indicate, for example, that *spacing study periods* is more efficient than learning material all at once. This is because your attention tends to wander after long periods of time, and fatigue is more likely to set in. In addition, long study periods do not allow an opportunity to consolidate what you have learned. New material is likely to bump old material out of short-term memory before it can be rehearsed and transferred into long-term storage. The appropriate length for study periods varies with the nature of the material being learned and with different people, but the principle of spaced practice is well established. For most students, four one-hour intervals of study would result in better recall of the material in this chapter than would one four-hour session.

Simply putting in time in front of an open book, of course, will not improve recall. As you read and learn information, it is useful to stop every so often and repeat to yourself what you have just learned. This procedure, called *active recitation,* focuses your attention on the material at hand and gives you repeated practice in retrieving information that has been stored. As a result, it helps to insure that you will be able to recall (not merely recognize) the material when it is needed. In one early study, subjects who spent up to 80 percent of their reading time in reciting what they were learning recalled three times as much of the material as subjects who read without recitation (Gates, 1917).

If you must learn a list of items, you are better off if you do not stop at the point at which you can recall the complete list without error. You should keep practicing beyond that point—in other words, make a habit of *overlearning* the material. Continued practice beyond the point of bare mastery increases the amount of material that you will be able to remember later. An experiment by Krueger (1929) showed that subjects who continued practice on a list of words well beyond the point at which they first recited the list without errors exhibited superior retention when tested anywhere from 1 to 28 days later. Overlearning may account for the fact that in real life people seem to remember a lot more than laboratory experiments might suggest. In the study described in Box 1, Bahrick, Bahrick, and Wittlinger (1974) found that people could correctly match the names and faces of 90 percent of their high school classmates 15 years after graduation. Clearly, such information is greatly overlearned during a four-year period.

Finally, following the principle of *savings* introduced earlier in the chapter, it is easier to remember material that has been relearned. Therefore, if you know you will be tested on material learned early in the term, it pays to review the material every so often to refresh your memory about the parts you know and to learn those parts you had trouble with the first time. The more you review during the term, the less time you will have to spend going over old material for the final examination.

Memory Systems

Psychologists have begun to study the sometimes elaborate techniques—or *mnemonic* devices—used by memory performers to dazzle audiences. Unlike S., who was a rather special case, most of these performers have mental capacities that are not essentially different from those of "ordinary" people. They have developed their remarkable memories by making use of tricks and systems that are related to a basic principle of memory that we discussed earlier: Careful and systematic coding can greatly increase our ability to store and retrieve information. You can use similar devices yourself to improve your memory.

The best way to organize material to be remembered is to think of ways to give it meaning. As we saw earlier, when we learn lists of words, we are likely to code them in meaningful clusters or categories. There are other ways, however, in which meaning can be given to a list of words. Suppose you were asked to learn the following list of unrelated words: tree, magazine, swimming pool, shoelace, hospital, faucet, potato chips, stocking, convertible, cigarette. Instead of saying the words over and over to yourself, try to make up a story in which all of the words are used in the proper order. For example:

> *Susan was sitting under a* tree, *reading a* magazine *with a* swimming pool *on the cover. As she leaned over to tie her* shoelace, *she developed a sprained back and had to be taken to the* hospital. *In the hospital, she was kept awake by the sounds of a dripping* faucet *and of her roommate's crunching on* potato chips *all night long. To make things even worse, a man wearing a* stocking *over his head broke into her room the next day and carried her off in a* convertible. *Most unpleasant of all, he kept blowing* cigarette *smoke into her face.*

The story doesn't have to be a particularly plausible one. It still serves the purpose of placing the list of words into a meaningful framework. Now when you are asked to recall the list of words, you simply run the story through your mind and report the key words as you get to them.

An experiment by Bower and Clark (1969) demonstrated the tremendous effectiveness of this method. Subjects were asked to learn twelve lists of ten unrelated nouns. Half the subjects were instructed to learn the words by making up a story that included the ten words in the proper order. The other subjects (the control group) merely studied the words for an equivalent amount of time. On the average, subjects using the narrative method recalled 94 percent of all the words, while subjects in the control group recalled only 14 percent.

An additional reason for the effectiveness of this memory system is that it adds vivid visual images to the verbal material to be recalled—for example, the man with the stocking over his head, driving a convertible, and smoking a cigarette. As we noted

MNEMONIC TRICKS

Students have been using mnemonic tricks for memorizing standard facts for centuries. A popular device is to develop an acronym for the material to be learned—using the first letters of each word. Conversely, letters that must be remembered in sequence, such as the spelling of a word, can be used to make up a sentence, such as Every Good Boy Does Fine for remembering musical notes, and George Eliot's Old Grandmother Ran A Pig Home Yesterday for the spelling of geography. Another common method is to develop a rhyme—"I before E except after C," or "Thirty days hath September . . ." What is your favorite mnemonic trick?

earlier, recall tends to be best when we can make use of verbal and visual coding systems simultaneously. A number of other effective memory systems are also based on the principle of simultaneous verbal and visual coding. Miller, Galanter, and Pribram (1960) suggest the following system of using visual and verbal codes together to improve memory. First, memorize this nursery rhyme: One is a bun, two is a shoe, three is a tree, four is a door, five is a hive, six are sticks, seven is heaven, eight is a gate, nine is a line, ten is a hen. Got it? OK, now take a list of ten objects such as: 1, car, 2. typewriter, 3. pencil, and so on. For each object, form a vivid visual image of it interacting with the code word for the appropriate number—for example, "typewriter" is number 2 on the list, so you might visualize a shoe-typing. Once you have followed this procedure for each object on your list, you will be able not only to remember the words in order but also to recite them backward or to answer such questions as, "What is the fifth object?" and "What number is the word 'typewriter'?"

The one-is-a-bun system is just a simple example of what is known as the *pegword method,* in which the words in the rhyme serve as pegs to which the images of the word to be learned are attached. The rhyme can be elaborated and extended to include numbers beyond ten and thus extend the range of the system.

The pegword method is by no means a new discovery. In fact, it is closely related to a memory system called the *method of loci* that is said to have been used by the ancient Greeks. This system depends on a vivid image of a set of familiar locations that follow in some logical order. You might imagine a familiar walk between two points on campus and identify ten or twenty distinctive locations along the way. The second step is to form images of the items you want to remember and mentally place each object in a distinctive location. As with the pegword method, the important thing is that the images of the items vividly interact with the images of the locations. If, for example, the first location on your walk is a mailbox and the first item on your list is a *neuron,* you might form a mental image of one neuron mailing a letter (presumably containing a vital message) to another neuron. When it is time to recall the list of items, you need only take a mental walk through your familiar mental image and pick up the images of the items one by one.

Groninger (1971) designed an experiment to determine just how effective this ancient method is. Half of his subjects learned a 25 item list by the method of loci while the other half were given no instructions. The method of loci resulted in better recall after one week (92 percent to 64 percent) and after five weeks (80 percent to 36 percent). Bower (1975), who has also studied the method, lists three reasons for its success: 1. the mental image provides a ready-made route to guide you effortlessly from one item to the next; 2. when you find an empty location or one with a vague image, you know that you have forgotten something; and 3. arriving at the end of your mental walk is a signal that recall is

ABSENTMINDEDNESS

Harry Lorayne and Jerry Lucas, authors of *The Memory Book* (1974), suggest that many cases of absentmindedness (forgetting where you put your glasses, etc.) are simply matters of not having fully registered the information in the first place. They advise you to grab your mind "by the scruff of the neck" and force it to think of a specific thing at a specific moment. For example, have you ever gone to the refrigerator and then forgotten what you wanted? Lorayne and Lucas have a simple solution: "Just make an association the moment you think of what it is you want from the refrigerator. If you want a glass of milk, see yourself opening the refrigerator door and gallons of milk flying out and hitting you in the face! Try this idea, and you'll never stare into a refrigerator again" (page 79).

complete. Bower views the method of loci as taking advantage of our vital ability to make mental maps of our environment.

Similar kinds of memory systems have been developed for specific purposes. For example, Atkinson (1975) describes a procedure that has proved effective in the learning of a foreign language vocabulary. Called the *keyword method,* it consists of two steps: 1. the foreign word (such as the Spanish word "pato") is linked to an Engish keyword on the basis of similar sound ("pato" = "pot"); and 2. the keyword is then linked to the correct English translation (duck) by an interacting mental image (a duck in a pot). In one test subjects using the keyword method had 88 percent correct recall, while subjects who learned by rote had only 28 percent correct recall.

We should note here that when we talk about improving memory we are not really talking about the *ability* to remember. That ability is a given, and it seems to be the same for all normal humans. What we *are* talking about is improving our methods of putting information into memory in the first place, so that we can insure that it's there and that we can retrieve it easily. People are fascinated with the idea that there may be some secret method or drug that will suddenly render them able to remember anything that enters their consciousness or impinges upon their senses—that taking a pill will allow them to recall everything from the birth trauma to the exact wording of every book they've ever read. Aside from the inherent disadvantages such an ability would bring with it, the ultimate truth is that memory just doesn't work that way.

SUMMARY

1. There appear to be two distinct sorts of memory—short-term and long-term. Information from the environment is first held in *sensory storage* for a fraction of a second and is then either discarded or passed on to short-term memory.
2. *Short-term memory* appears to have a limited capacity of about seven items. The amount of information held in short-term memory can be increased by organizing inputs into "chunks." Short-term memory lasts about 20 seconds at most without rehearsal. Information is either then forgotten or is passed on to *long-term memory.*
3. Information can be transferred from short-term memory to long-term memory by rehearsal or by coding. The way material is coded is a major factor in its later accessibility for retrieval. One useful coding method is to package information in meaningful clusters.
4. There are probably two systems for coding information into memory, one verbal and one visual. Visual information often goes directly into long-term memory. Recall is best when both methods are used simultaneously; this is called *dual coding.*

5. Retrieval of information is often aided by returning, mentally or physically, to the setting in which the material was originally learned. One interesting retrieval problem—the tip-of-the-tongue phenomenon—seems to indicate that our verbal storage system is coded according to both meaning and sound.
6. In a study of long-term memory, researchers found that people were able to recognize pictures and names of most of their high-school classmates as long as 35 years after graduation. Recall of classmates' names improved when subjects were prompted with photographs from high-school annuals. This study illustrates that recognition tends to be better than recall and that memories can be remarkably enduring.
7. Studies of *verbal learning,* such as those done by Ebbinghaus, have given us the *learning curve,* which demonstrates that the greatest memory loss happens soon after learning and that the rate of loss declines with time.
8. The three basic measures of retention are recall, recognition, and relearning. In *recall,* one recounts or reproduces something previously learned. In *recognition,* one identifies something that one has encountered before. In *relearning,* one is able to quickly relearn material that was learned at some earlier time.
9. Verbal learning can be hindered by interference. In *proactive interference,* previously learned material interferes with something learned more recently. In *retroactive interference,* new learning interferes with old. Interference may cause its disruptions by preventing rehearsal of material.
10. "Forgetting" of long-term memories may result from poor coding—the information is there but it's difficult to retrieve. Or, forgetting may be *motivated*—a memory may be unaccessible because the individual has *chosen* to "forget" it. Freud called such forgetting of unacceptable memories *repression.*
11. Memory appears to be a chemical process, involving chemical changes in neurotransmitters or in neurons in the brain. These changes require about an hour to consolidate. If the *consolidation phase* is disrupted, the memory is lost, producing *retrograde amnesia.* Disruption may take the form of brain injury, electric shock, or chemical interference.
12. Research with goldfish and rats has shown that some drugs can prevent consolidation of memories while other drugs seem to speed up the process. Memory drugs for humans are still a long way off, however.
13. Among unusual disorders of memory are *transient global amnesia,* in which the victim is temporarily unable to hold onto new information for more than a few minutes, and *Korsakoff's syndrome,* in which the victim has a lasting inability to

put new information into long-term storage. A different sort of memory disorder was seen in the case of S., who seemed unable to forget anything.

14. Among methods of improving memory that are particularly helpful in studying are space practice, active recitation, overlearning, and relearning (savings).

15. Careful and systematic coding of information can be accomplished with several methods. One approach is to make up a story containing the information to be remembered. Another, called the *pegword method,* requires memorizing key words to serve as pegs for associations. This is similar to the ancient *method of loci,* in which one imagines the items to be remembered as being placed in a set of familiar locations. One memory system developed for a specific purpose is the *keyword method,* used for learning foreign words.

psychological issue

Memory and the Law

"Where were you on the night of August 22nd?"

"Is this the man you saw running from your house?"

"What happened immediately after the man took your wallet?"

As these questions illustrate, memory plays an essential role in criminal investigations and trials. Courtroom proceedings place heavy emphasis on eyewitness testimony. This emphasis is based on the assumption that witnesses can see and hear accurately—and, what's more, that they have a clear memory of what they saw and heard, even when the event occurred a year or more before the trial. If they do not testify accurately on direct examination, it is further assumed that cross-examination will straighten them out.

Unfortunately, these assumptions are not fully justified. Despite the heavy reliance on eyewitness testimony, such reports are often much less complete and much less accurate than is commonly believed. In the Warren Commission Report on the assassination of President John F. Kennedy, for example, there was conflict between eyewitnesses as to the number of shots fired, the direction from which the shots were fired, the size of the rifle bag Oswald carried, and other details (Marshall, 1969). There are also many tragic cases on record in which innocent people were mistakenly identified by eyewitnesses as the perpetrators of crimes (Loftus, 1974).

Eyewitness testimony has been demonstrated in classroom exercises to be unreliable. In one study, 141 students witnessed a staged attack on a professor. After seven weeks had gone by, the students were asked to pick out the assailant from a set of six photographs. Even though the incident had been highly dramatic, 60 percent of the witnesses, including the professor himself, picked out the wrong man. Further, 25 percent of the students identified as the assailant a person who had been an innocent bystander at the scene of the crime (Buckhout, Figueroa, and Hoff, 1972).

What accounts for the discrepancy between the law's heavy reliance on eyewitness testimony and the actual unreliability of such recollections? In criminal proceedings, it is often assumed that memory is complete, easily accessible, and totally accurate. The fact of the matter, however, is that memory has none of these qualities. It is not complete, since many aspects of events are not noticed or transferred into long-term storage. Furthermore, memory is not always easily accessible—it is often

In criminal proceedings, it is often assumed that memory is complete, easily accessible, and totally accurate.

quite difficult to retrieve material from long-term memory. And, above all, memory is not always fully accurate.

We sometimes talk about memories for past events as if they were located on videotapes in our brain. To recall the event (in terms of this metaphor), all we need to do is replay the tape. But that metaphor is not a very appropriate one. It would be more accurate to think of memory for past events as a kind of blurry slide show—a loose assortment of images and phrases that often requires a good deal of interpretation before it makes sense. Bartlett (1932) had this sort of interpretation in mind when he characterized remembering as "an imaginative reconstruction" of experience.

Imaginative Reconstruction

Erlich (1974) provides a good example of imaginative reconstruction, from another classroom demonstration:

Some twenty students sit in a classroom, their heads bent over examination papers. Suddenly the door pops open, and a young woman, above five feet tall and dressed in levis, a plaid hunting skirt, and green tyrolean hat, bursts into the room. She quickly levels a carrot at a student seated in the first row and shouts, "Federal herring! You stole my marks!" Outside in the corridor, a popping sound is heard.

A student in the front row clutches his breast, screams and falls to the floor. As the assailant runs out, two men dressed as ambulance attendants enter the room, drag the victim to his feet, and quickly carry him away.

The whole scene has taken almost one minute from the time the assailant enters until the victim is removed.

The students in this class were immediately asked to write a complete description of the events they witnessed. Considering that these witnesses were all graduate students in psychology, the results are enlightening:

Who was the assailant? One student wrote, " . . . a big Germanic type . . . like a Hollywood storm trooper."

What did the assailant wear? Another student described her dress as " . . . a European-style railroad conductor's uniform."

What was the weapon? And the motive? According to one account, the murderer "used a switch-blade knife on the victim . . . and said . . . 'You are a Marxist and are working to destroy our republic.' "

Who was the victim? "A white male dressed in khaki trousers and a blue sweater," testified one witness. Actually, the victim was a black male in an ROTC uniform.

In all of these reports, we see how the students gave structure and meaning to their recollections of the event they saw—and, came up with quite distorted reports. Such reconstructions of observed events are likely to take place in the courtroom as well.

One factor that may have a large impact on eyewitnesses' recollections is the wording of the questions that investigators and lawyers put to them both before and during the trial. To demonstrate such effects, Elizabeth Loftus (1974) showed students a short film depicting a traffic accident. Some of the student-witnesses were subsequently asked, "About how fast were the cars going when they hit each other?" For other witnesses, the verb "hit" was replaced with "smashed," "collided," "bumped," or "contacted." It turned out that the witnesses' estimates were influenced by the particular verb used. Those questioned with "contacted" gave the lowest speed estimates (31.8 mph on the average), while those questioned using the verb "smashed" gave the highest (40.8 mph).

In a follow-up study, Loftus brought subjects back to the laboratory a week after viewing an accident and asked them some more questions about it. A critical question was whether the witness had seen any broken glass—although in fact there had been none in the film. Loftus reasoned that if the verb "smashed" really influenced witnesses to remember the accident as more severe than it had been, they might also "remember" details that would be congruent with a high-speed accident—like broken glass. This is just what she found. Over 30 percent of the subjects who had been questioned a week earlier with "smashed" reported seeing the nonexistent glass, compared to 16 percent of those who had been questioned with "hit." On the basis of this and other studies, Loftus concludes that human memory is much more changeable than is often assumed to be the case. The witnesses in her study were not lying to the questioner. Rather, the form of the questions influenced their recollections—or, in Bartlett's terms, reconstructions—of the events.

Mistaken Identification

The changeability or *malleability* of memory is also demonstrated in cases of mistaken identifications of "criminals." The following examples (cited by Loftus, 1975) are just a few of the many such cases on record:

> In November 1972, Lawrence Berson was arrested in Queens, New York, on multiple rape charges. The 17-year old college freshman was identified by five different women as their attacker. Berson was released only after Richard Carbone, a 20-year old "gypsy cab driver" from the Bronx, was arrested for the same crimes. Carbone was later convicted. Then, in 1974, George Morales was arrested for rob-

George Morales Richard Carbone Lawrence Berson

Clearly, lineups in which one person sticks out like a sore thumb are not fair.

bery, only to be cleared when the same Richard Carbone admitted the crime. Both Berson and Morales had the great misfortune of looking like Carbone.

In 1973, Assistant District Attorney William Schrager was arrested for sexual assault. Four different women identified him as their assailant. Schrager was released only after a similar-looking postman, the same height but 40 pounds heavier, confessed to some of the crimes.

Gregory Boyd was arrested for robbery and was identified by two gas station attendants as the man who held them up. Boyd couldn't establish an alibi because he couldn't remember where he had been the night of the crime. On the witness stand, Boyd recalled that he had been in jail that night—and it turned out to be true! He was then promptly released.

Mistaken identifications of this sort are especially common when the mistaken suspect, like Berson and Morales, happens to look a great deal like the person the witness had seen. But even less striking resemblances can lead to mistaken identifications. This is especially likely when the witness is asked to select an assailant from a lineup that is biased or "stacked" in particular ways. In one case, the suspect was at least ten years older than the other men in the lineup. In another case, the suspect was at least four inches shorter than any of the others. And in still another case, the suspect was the only man in the lineup not wearing a tie and glasses. In such cases, the witness is likely to pick out the distinctive looking person in the lineup, even if that person resembles the actual criminal only slightly. The witness might think to himself, "The person who attacked me was not wearing glasses or a tie. And neither is that man over there—so it must be him." Clearly, lineups in which one person sticks out like a sore thumb are not fair (Social Action and the Law Newsletter, 1975). Such lineups increase the likelihood that witnesses will make "imaginative reconstructions" that are far from the truth.

In spite of the unreliability of eyewitness testimony, jurors often appear to be heavily influenced by it. In another of Loftus' studies, 68 percent of student-jurors in a mock trial voted to convict a defendant in a murder case on the basis of a single eyewitness report, even when it was proved that the eyewitness had 20-400 vision, was not wearing his glasses, and therefore could not possibly have seen the face of the murderer from where he stood. (When there was no eyewitness, only 18 percent of the jurors voted for conviction.) Given the malleability of human memory and the skillfulness of attorneys, jurors might well take eyewitness testimony with a larger grain of salt.

Summary

1. Eyewitness testimony in trials and criminal investigations is not as reliable as is commonly believed. This discrepancy arises from the fact that memory is incomplete, not always easily accessible, and not always accurate.
2. People often give structure and meaning to their recollections—a phenomenon by Bartlett called "imaginative reconstruction." A person's memory of an event is often influenced simply by the way he or she is questioned about the event.
3. The malleability of memory is further demonstrated by the fact that mistaken identification is a common occurrence in criminal cases.

Thought and Language

CHAPTER 7

Thought and Language

First Student: What is this stuff they're serving us?

Second Student: I *think* it's beef.

First Student: But it's orange. Beef is supposed to be reddish-brown!

Second Student: I *think* the beef here is always orange.

First Student: But what was the brown stuff we had last night?

Second Student: The brown stuff they serve is chicken. I *think* that must have been chicken, too.

First Student: Are you going to eat this mess?

Second Student: I don't *think* so.

First Student: What can we do about these meals?

Second Student: We'd better *think* of something!

As this conversation suggests, the word "thinking" (or "thought") can have several different meanings, but all of them converge on the mental methods by which we process information, make decisions, and solve problems. In this chapter we will discuss several types of thinking that psychologists have been studying: the use of concepts or categories to organize our experience; inductive and deductive reasoning; and problem solving. (You might note that each of these types of thinking is represented in the above dialogue.) We will also learn that thinking, as a distinctively human phenomenon, is also highly related to another human phenomenon: language. Indeed, some theorists contend that without language it would be virtually impossible to think at all.

CONCEPTS

Imagine yourself walking in a park with a friend. Suddenly an object flashes through the air, startling you both. Shortly your friend says, in relief, "Oh, it's only a bird." In those few seconds between the initial perception and the ultimate labeling of the bird, some very complex psychological processes have occurred. In order to use the label, your friend has had to recognize important attributes of the flying object and then to categorize it among thousands of similar objects. This same categorization occurs when you call apples, peaches, and plums "fruits" or when you call Barbra Streisand, Paul Simon, and Ray Charles "singers." Categories such as these are called *concepts*—the concept of "bird," the concept of "fruit," and so on. Such concepts play a central role in our thought processes and in our experiencing of life.

How Concepts Are Learned

People are not born with ready-made concepts. Concepts have to be learned. Some concepts are communicated through explicit definitions, as when your physics instructor defines "gravity" or your psychology instructor defines "neuron." But this kind of explicit concept learning is rather uncommon, and among small children it is rare indeed. Most concepts are learned from examples. When a boy is told, "Go feed the birdie," he learns that the particular object hopping around on the ground is an instance of the concept "bird." And when the boy is later scolded for throwing crumbs to a cat, he learns that not all objects hopping around on the ground are birdies. Psychologists call examples that fit within a concept *positive instances;* robins, sparrows, eagles, and chickens are all positive instances of the concept "bird." Cats, dogs, rocks, and trees would be *negative instances.* Given enough encounters with both positive and negative instances, the child develops a refined picture of the attributes that characterize a bird. In other words, the child learns the concept. Concept learning is vitally linked to language, since it involves developing a vocabulary—words are necessary for use as labels for categories of objects, actions, and attributes (see Box 1).

Psychologists have put forth several different explanations of the processes involved in concept learning. One theory suggests that concepts are learned through *stimulus-response associations.* According to this approach, the attributes of an object can be considered the stimuli and the labeling of the object can be seen as a response. Presumably, when an object is identified as an example of a concept, a mental association between the attributes and the label is strengthened. So, when a child sees an animal identified as a "dog," the child begins to associate a number of the animal's characteristics with the concept "dog." In time, with exposure to more and more animals that are called "dogs," the concept should become most strongly associated with the most typical attributes of the dogs the child has observed. For example, if all the dogs in a girl's experience have cold noses, then she will incorporate the attribute "cold nose" as an integral part of the concept "dog."

Although the idea of stimulus-response associations seems a logical explanation for how concepts are learned, it does raise a few questions. Are associations between attributes and categories really that direct? The verbal-mediation theory suggests that they are not. This theory suggests that associations between certain attributes and concepts develop only when a verbal response focuses attention on those attributes. These verbal responses may take the form of tentative guesses, or hypotheses. For example, a child might think, "Maybe barking is related to being a dog," or "Maybe all dogs have four legs," ignoring the possible importance of other characteristics such as noses, teeth, hair, and tails. According to this theory, the hypothesis "mediates" between the observed attributes and the conceptual label.

One experiment designed to test these two theories involves shifts in concepts. Imagine being in a concept-learning study in which you are required to learn the concept "glick." You would probably be presented with a succession of objects differing in color, size, shape, and so on. After viewing each object, you would be told by an experimenter, "Yes, that's a glick," or "No, that's not a glick." Pretty soon you would be able to tell the experimenter just what attributes are characteristic of the glick. Suppose that at first the experimenter identifies all the blue objects as glicks and all the white objects as nonglicks (see Figure 7.1). You might decide rather quickly that all glicks are blue.

FIG. 7 · 1 Examples of reversal and nonreversal shifts (see text for explanation).

However, a conceptual shift would be required if the experimenter then started identifying all white objects as glicks and all blue objects as nonglicks. Since the relevant dimension (color) remains the same, but the significant values (blue and white) are reversed, this change is known as a *reversal shift.* To learn a reversal shift, you would have to reverse your old concept and decide that all glicks are white.

A different conceptual shift would be required if the experimenter started identifying all large objects as glicks and all small objects as nonglicks, regardless of color. Since the relevant dimension is changed (from color to size) rather than reversed, this is known as a *nonreversal shift.* To learn a nonreversal shift, you would have to abandon your old concept and decide that all glicks are large.

Which sort of shift should be easier to learn? According to the association theory, the nonreversal shift should be easier, since it should involve building new associations rather than totally reversing old ones. According to mediation theory, however, the reversal shift should be easier, since subjects have already learned to pay attention to the color dimension. It turns out that for adults reversal shifts are simpler than nonreversal shifts (Kendler and D'Amato, 1955). But for animals (Kelleher, 1956) and for young children (Kendler, Kendler, and Wells, 1960) the opposite is true. It appears that verbal-mediation theory fits best for learners who have substantial verbal skills (such as adults) whereas the association theory fits best for learners who do not have such skills (such as animals and young children).

Concepts and Culture

There is no single, objectively correct way to classify most of the objects in our experience. Classifications are socially and culturally determined and depend to a great extent on such factors as the physical environment and the culture's level of social and technological development. As Whorf (1956) pointed out, we who speak English have only one word for snow, but the Eskimos have separate words for falling snow, fallen snow, packed snow, slushy snow, wind-driven snow, and still other varieties. Such distinctions make good sense in an environment where snow of all types is an everyday occurrence. In contrast, the Aztecs reportedly used variations of a single word to communicate the concepts "snow," "cold," and "ice." In their hot climate, more extensive categorization was unnecessary. In a similar vein, Conklin (1954) reported that the Hanunoo of the Philippines have 92 different names for rice. Rice is a staple of the Hanunoo diet, so 92 names may be valuable. In the United States, on the other hand, rice is rice.

Because concepts are culture-specific and necessarily learned, people can disagree about them. Even people within a single culture may categorize objects differently. This disagreement can occur because concept learning depends to a great extent on the particular instances a person happens to observe.

COLORFUL LANGUAGE

Bassa (a Liberian language), Shona (a Rhodesian language), and English designate the color spectrum in different ways (Gleason, 1961). In English, we identify six basic color ranges: purple, blue, green, yellow, orange, and red. Bassa contains only one word for the purple-blue-green end of the spectrum, and one word for the yellow-orange-red end. Shona groups purple and red, blue and green, yellow and orange. Roger Brown (1965) suggests one possible reason for these cultural differences. Many color names derive from specific objects. The English color word "orange" is one example. In other cultures, other objects are important sources of color names. Many coastal cultures that combine green and blue, for example, derive that color name from their word for the sea. An object that is "sea-color" can, after all, be blue, green, or any shade in between.

For example, a person who has seen only robins and sparrows might look at a penguin and say, "That can't be a bird—it doesn't fly!" On the other hand, a person who has seen only ducks and geese might encounter a sparrow and exclaim, "That can't be a bird—it doesn't swim!" Scientists who have observed many different birds—including penguins and ostriches, which don't fly, and the kiwi, which doesn't even have wings—have developed a concept of "bird" that includes attributes relating to anatomy and physiology rather than relying on such abilities as flying or swimming. Because science requires extensive observations, it often results in refinement or revision of everyday concepts.

How Concepts Affect Our Lives

Once concepts are learned, they affect the way we interpret the world. As a result, they have a large impact on our everyday lives. In particular, concepts help us to predict and control events. For example, until we learn to incorporate "sharp teeth" into our concept of "dog," we risk being bitten. But concepts

Box 1

What's in a Label?
the influence of language on our perceptions, Carmichael, Hogan, and Walter (1932) showed two groups of subjects stimulus figures similar to the ones in the middle column of this illustration. Each group was given a different set of words as the figures were presented, and later the subjects were asked to redraw the figures from memory. Consistently, the redrawn figures looked more like the words associated with them than like the original figures themselves.

This study shows us that the label we give to an object (the category we put it in) primes us to see a picture of that object, which in turn affects the way the picture is stored and recalled. The study also suggests that we may sometimes distort reality when we attempt to place new experiences in pre-existing categories.

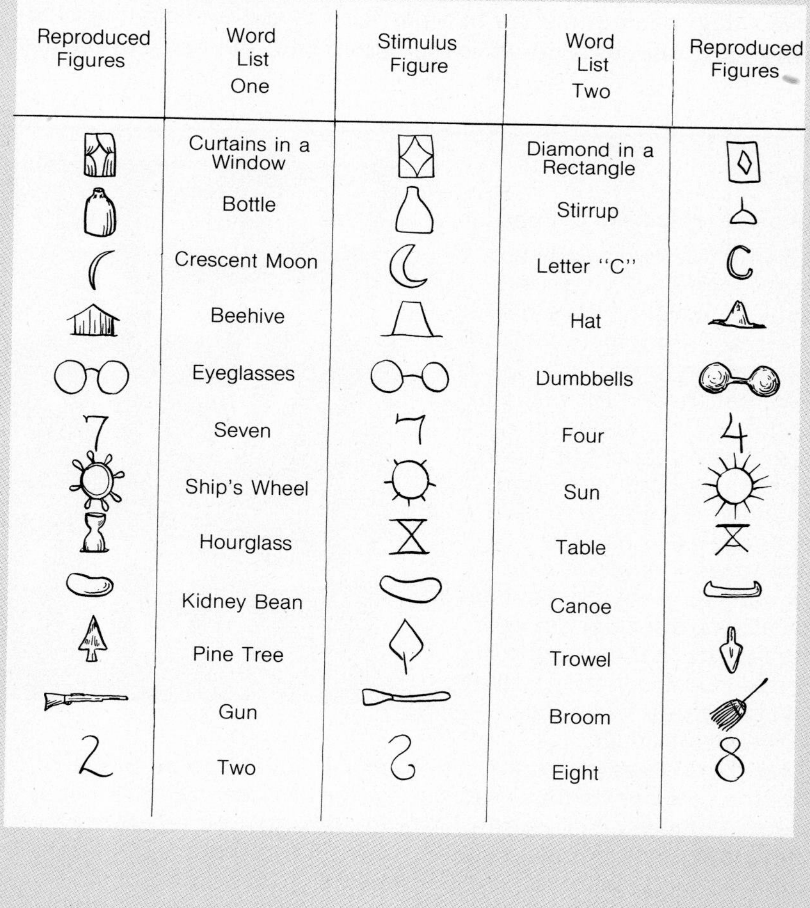

Reproduced Figures	Word List One	Stimulus Figure	Word List Two	Reproduced Figures
	Curtains in a Window		Diamond in a Rectangle	
	Bottle		Stirrup	
	Crescent Moon		Letter "C"	
	Beehive		Hat	
	Eyeglasses		Dumbbells	
	Seven		Four	
	Ship's Wheel		Sun	
	Hourglass		Table	
	Kidney Bean		Canoe	
	Pine Tree		Trowel	
	Gun		Broom	
	Two		Eight	

help us only if they *appropriately* organize our experience. The child who thinks that a rat is a "kitty" or that orange-flavored aspirins are "candy" is clearly in danger. Similarly, problems may arise for the adolescent who interprets a grimace as a type of smile or a friendly joke as an insult.

Psychologists are especially interested in how people form concepts of each other and the impact of such social concepts. *Stereotypes* are concepts about groups of people. When you have a stereotype that blacks are musical or that women are emotional, it means that being musical or emotional is part of your concept of a black person or of a woman, in the same way that having feathers may be part of your concept of a bird. As we have already pointed out, concepts are not necessarily correct. And, in fact, because stereotypes are so often based on small numbers of observed instances (and sometimes on no observed instances at all), they are particularly prone to error. (We will come back to stereotypes and their effects in Chapter 13 when we discuss sex roles, and in the Psychological Issue following Chapter 18, when we look at racial prejudice.)

In addition to concepts about other people, we develop concepts about ourselves. One person may think of herself as a "genius," another as a "romantic," another as a "failure." These self-concepts also have a large impact on our lives. Once we have categorized ourselves in a particular way, we may try especially hard to behave in ways that agree with our self-concept.

THE THINKING CHESS PLAYER

Most of us would think of the chess master who can play 12 boards of "blindfold" chess simultaneously as a model of intense thought and concentration. Psychologist and master chess player Reuben Fine (1965) has commented on the skills and thought processes of such people. He observes that, as a result of long experience with the game, both the board and the pieces acquire so many associations for the player that it becomes impossible for him to think of the board separately from the pieces or of the pieces with no relationship to the board. The master player also thinks in terms of symbols, and it is impossible for him to think of the moves without the symbolic language that chess players use to describe their plays.

Box 2

Solving Problems in Groups

Is it true that two heads are better than one? Or do too many cooks spoil the stew? There are arguments for both sides of the issue. Thousands of scientists and technicians worked harmoniously to conquer outer space, but Albert Einstein worked alone and announced the theory of relativity at age 26. Since the decision to work alone or with others has great practical implications, consider some of the factors that make group performance superior or that hamper group solutions.

The major advantage of solving problems in groups is that the unique talents of each group member can be combined into a new whole. Also, when working in a group it is easier to see other people's

mistakes than to be aware of your own. Annoying as it may be, having your errors corrected by others is frequently helpful. Not only can the group filter out errors, but it may also stimulate ideas that would not have occurred to individuals working alone.

The most obvious disadvantage of group problem solving is the familiar temptation to let somebody else take the responsibility and slack off in your own effort. Also constructive group efforts may be hampered by status differences. A group member may not want to criticize the ideas of high-ranking individuals, and low-ranking individuals may not want to speak out at all.

These disadvantages may be reduced when groups use *brainstorming* to tackle their problems. The technique of brainstorming started with the assumption that creative ideas will be greatest when everyone feels free to communicate suggestions about a problem at hand. When a group is assembled to solve a problem, it is

PROBLEM SOLVING

As we go through life, we are constantly faced with problems, from small ones like arithmetic problems to much larger ones like planning a family budget or deciding how to patch up an argument with a close friend. Problems themselves can be categorized, just like birds and fruits and persons. In fact, it is deciding how to categorize a problem that often brings the first step to its solution. In arithmetic, for example, there are problems of addition, subtraction, multiplication, and division. For example: "How many beers in three six-packs?" The first step in solving this problem is to recognize that it is a problem in multiplication. This seems easy to most of us, since we've had a lot of experience with similar problems. But someone new to arithmetic might have a harder time categorizing it and as a result would find it much more difficult to solve.

Problem solving can be approached in a number of different ways. Here we will be looking at inductive and deductive reasoning as methods of problem solving; at the trial-and-error approach, and at the contribution of insight. We will also be examining some of the factors that interfere with our ability to solve problems.

asked to follow some specific ground rules. During the initial phase of brainstorming (the green-light stage), group members can put forth any idea they wish—no matter how impractical or ridiculous it may at first appear. In this stage "killer thoughts" are forbidden: "We tried that before and it didn't work"; "You will never get people to cooperate"; "It's too expensive." All of the ideas are recorded until the flow of ideas dries up.

In the next phase (the red-light stage), all the suggestions are examined, evaluated, and criticized until a solution agreeable to the group is found.

Brainstorming does not always work, however. In an early study by Taylor, Berry, and Block (1958), subjects were assigned at random to work alone or in five-member groups. In both conditions five problems were posed, and 12 minutes were allowed to work on each one. The comparisons of individuals and groups in terms of the quantity and originality of ideas showed that individuals working alone did better than the groups.

Are two—or more—heads better than one? The best available answer is, "It depends"—on the kind of problem and on the membership of the group.

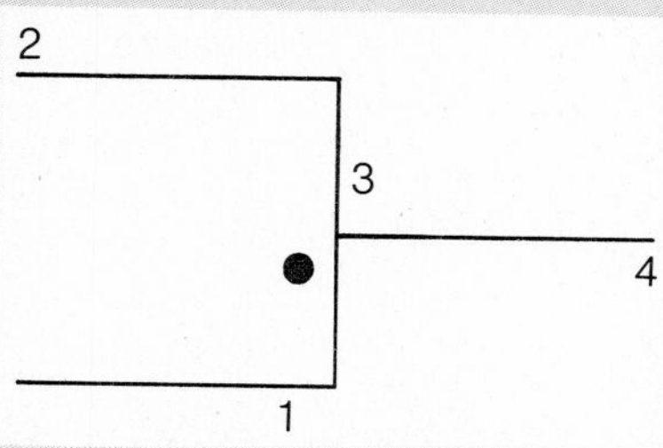

FIG. 7 · 7 Can a group solve this puzzle faster than an individual? Set up a mini-test by giving the puzzle to several of your friends together and to others individually. The rules: Arrange four matchsticks as shown above and place a piece of "dirt" in the "shovel." By moving only two matchsticks, get the dirt out of the shovel. Solution appears at the end of the box.

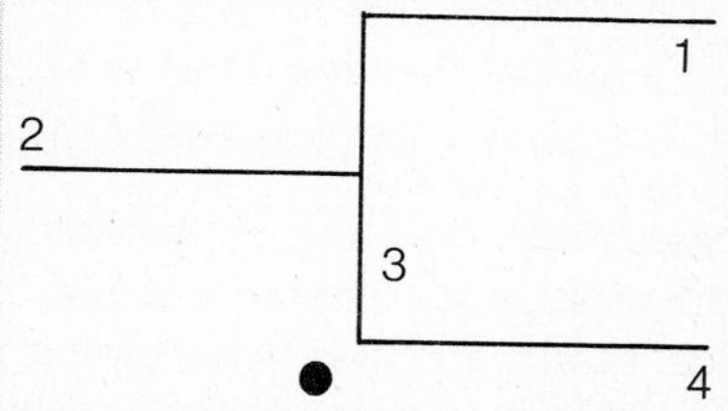

FIG. 7 · 7 Solution To solve the matchstick problem, slide match 2 up so that the end of it touches the end of match 1. Then move match 4 so that it is above and parallel to match 1. Match 3 thus becomes the handle and the dirt is out of the shovel.

Inductive and Deductive Reasoning

An important aspect of thinking is the way we evaluate evidence about the world and draw conclusions from it. Such reasoning is classified as either inductive or deductive. *Inductive reasoning* involves observing particular objects and then proceeding to draw general conclusions. For example, a person who has observed thousands of crows, all of them black, may reason inductively that *all* crows are black. As with concept learning, it is very hard to be sure that propositions derived inductively are true. After all, somewhere there may be a crow that is white.

Deductive reasoning, instead of going from particular instances to general propositions, goes from the general to the particular. The general proposition is sometimes called the *major premise,* while the statement that identifies the particular object as appropriate is called the *minor premise.* For example:

Major Premise: All crows are black.

Minor Premise: That bird is a crow.

Conclusion: That bird is black.

Naturally, deduction produces incorrect conclusions if either premise is incorrect (if some crows are not black or if that bird is not really a crow). Interesting problems result from the faulty use of deductive reasoning. For example:

Major Premise: All crows are black.

Minor Premise: That telephone is black.

Conclusion: That telephone is a crow.

This reasoning may be intriguing, but it is not logical. Although this particular *syllogism* (combination of major premise, minor premise and conclusion) is clearly absurd, subtler examples of faulty deduction abound in our daily lives.

Try this one, for example: "Motorcycles have only one headlight; the vehicle I see coming this way has only one headlight; therefore, that vehicle must be a motorcycle." Sound like good logic to you? If so, be careful crossing the street at night—you might wind up in a hospital. People who think like this learn the hard way about broken headlights. (You might say they learn from close, personal contact.) The syllogism is clearly a faulty one. For the conclusion to follow logically, the major premise would have to be "All vehicles with only one headlight are motorcycles." Despite this, people are frequently startled by one-headlighted cars that they "logically" deduced were motorcycles.

FEEDBACK

More often than not, problem solving is an activity that involves at least one other person. The degree to which feedback from another person is important becomes evident when it is restricted. Bavelas (1957) gave a subject a diagram for the arrangement of some dominoes. The subject's partner had the dominoes and tried to follow directions given over the telephone by the subject. The communication was one-way so there could be no feedback. The partner receiving instructions soon found himself bewildered. No pair of problem solvers managed to get the problem solved. When the second person could react with a push-button for "yes" or "no," the problem was solved and the subjects no longer felt they had been stuck with a stupid coworker!

Trial and Error

When we are not sure about how to categorize a problem, we are most likely to resort to *trial and error.* This approach involves trying many possible solutions one by one until the correct solution appears—we hope. The trial and error method can be useful in solving simple problems such as finding the right key to open a door. But it would take forever to use trial and error for finding the proper numbers to open a combination lock.

More than 75 years ago, E. L. Thorndike (1898) experimented with trial and error by putting cats in a puzzle box (like the one in Figure 7.2) and watching them make a variety of futile attempts to open the cage before they finally managed to escape. The animals could not solve the problem of escape simply by sitting back and thinking about it. The door-release mechanism was not visible, so the cats couldn't have figured out how the doors worked even if they had been smart enough to do so. Only after persistent trial and error did they finally stumble on the way to get out.

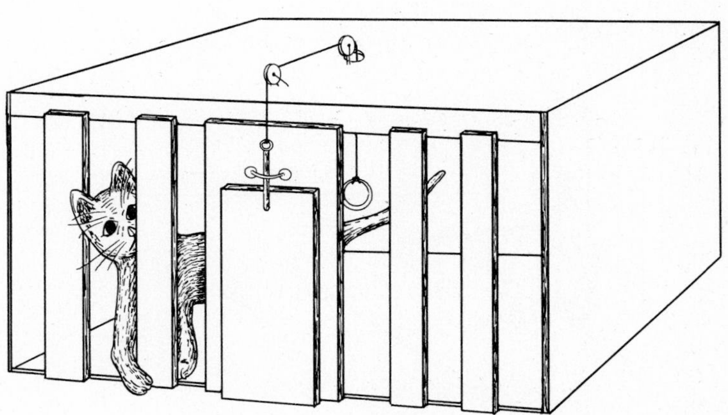

FIG. 7 · 2 A puzzle box similar to the one employed by Thorndike. The cat must make use of persistent trial and error in order to escape from the cage.

Insight

When a problem seems impossible to solve, sometimes the answer appears unexpectedly in the form of an awareness known as *insight.* Often the problem solver has set aside the problem for a while when the answer finally strikes him or her, seemingly out of nowhere. During the period when the problem is set aside, the thinker may be unconsciously reshuffling his or her past experiences and searching for the solution. During this search the thinker tries to fit the present problem into categories provided by past problems. Imagine trying to figure out how to eat a coconut if you had never seen or heard of one before. At first you might try to bite it like an apple, peel it like a banana, or slice it like a grapefruit. At long last it might suddenly dawn on you that a coconut is more like a pecan or a walnut than an apple or a banana and that to eat it you must first crack it open. Having done so, you would have insightfully solved the problem and satisfied your hunger.

Köhler (1925) conducted a famous series of experiments with apes to demonstrate insight in problem solving. The task was for the apes to get food that had been placed out of reach in a basket suspended from the roof of the cage. The basket would swing back and forth when a string was pulled, and nearby was a scaffolding that the ape could use to reach the basket as it swung by. Köhler's apes appeared to solve the problem suddenly rather than to stumble on the solution while making random, trial-and-error responses. Once they had the solution, they used it every time thereafter. (See Figure 7.3.)

Archimedes, the Greek physicist, provided one of the most famous examples of insight. He had been wrestling with a difficult problem: The king, suspecting that a golden crown contained more silver than it was supposed to, had commissioned Archimedes to devise a method for determining the crown's purity. While sitting in his bathtub one day, Archimedes noticed that the bath water was overflowing. All of a sudden he came up with an ingenious method for solving the king's problem, involv-

THE TWO-STRING REASONING PROBLEM

Imagine this situation: You're in a room with two strings hanging from the ceiling, a chair, and a table on which are a six-inch piece of wire, a cup, a pair of pliers, and some paper. You are told that you must tie the two pieces of string together, but no matter how much you stretch, you can't reach the second string while you're holding on to the first. Your arms need to be two feet longer, or you need to figure out a different way to solve the problem. Think about it for a bit before looking at the answer on the next page.

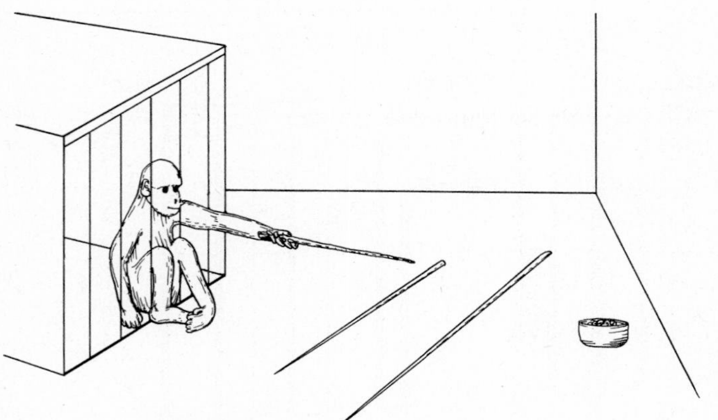

FIG. 7 · 3 How can the ape get access to the food in the dish? Köhler demonstrated that problems such as this one are likely to be solved in a sudden flash of insight.

SOLUTION TO TWO-STRING REASONING PROBLEM

If you can tie a weight on the second string and set it in motion, it will swing toward you while you are grasping the first string. Only one object on the table is heavy enough to do this—the pliers.

ing the amount of water that would be displaced by a pure gold as opposed to an adulterated crown. According to legend, Archimedes was so excited by his discovery that he rushed out naked into the streets of Syracuse shouting "Eureka!" (I've found it!) In the process, Archimedes had discovered a general principle for determining the purity of a wide variety of objects. As in this case, insight into one problem often leads to solutions of similar problems.

Functional Fixedness

Sometimes our use of particular concepts has the effect of blinding us to other concepts that might in fact be more useful to us. We keep trying solutions that worked for old problems, instead of discovering solutions appropriate for the new one. This hazard is known as *functional fixedness.*

Functional fixedness is especially likely to affect our use of tools. If you think of an object in terms of its normal use, you remain "fixed" to that expectation and have trouble thinking of it in a different way. Thus, the more you use an object, the harder it is to think of novel uses for it. This fixation may be less powerful when the object is not used for a while. If, for example, you had not used a hammer for some time, you might be more likely to use it creatively to prop something up than if you had just used it to bang a nail into the wall (Adamson and Taylor, 1954). Similarly, dimes and butterknives make passable screwdrivers, but we use them so often to buy things or to butter bread that this novel use may not occur to us.

Rigidity in thinking may result from ingrained, habitual ways of thinking or behaving. This explains why you can sometimes labor over a problem for hours and get nowhere, whereas someone who is new to the problem can walk in and see the solution at once. A classic story illustrates this case. A semitrailer was too tall for a bridge that it tried to go under. Its top crashed into the bottom of the bridge, and it became hopelessly stuck. As the story goes, a great many elaborate solutions were tried to get the truck out. For example, some engineers suggested that a huge hydraulic crane be used to lift the bridge. None of these elaborate solutions worked, however. Finally, a little boy came along and asked the people why they didn't let the air out of the truck's tires. They did and it worked. Their functional fixedness in problem solving had made them blind to the possibility of the tires.

Mathematical formulas are also tools that we use to solve problems, and the problem of functional fixedness applies to these tools as well. In one study, Scheerer (1963) presented a series of problems to several subjects (see Figure 7.4). Each subject was asked to measure out a given quantity of water using only three pitchers, labeled *a, b,* and *c.* In each problem, the subjects were told how much water each pitcher could hold. In one problem, for example, pitcher *a* held 21 units, *b* held 127

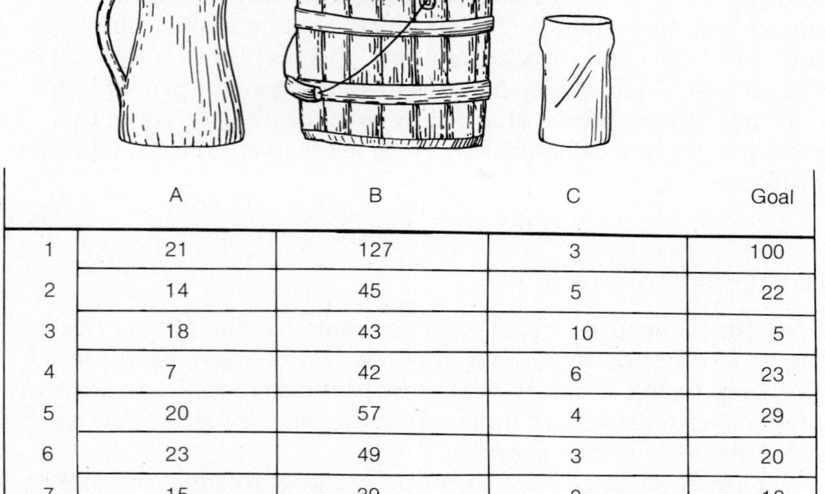

	A	B	C	Goal
1	21	127	3	100
2	14	45	5	22
3	18	43	10	5
4	7	42	6	23
5	20	57	4	29
6	23	49	3	20
7	15	39	3	18

FIG. 7 · 4 In each of the problems, your task is to measure out a given quantity of water (the "Goal"), using only the three pitchers (A, B, and C). Scheerer (1963) used this series of problems to demonstrate functional fixedness (see text for explanation).

units, and *c* held 3 units. The problem was to measure 100 units. Most of the subjects soon discovered that the formula for solving the problem was $b - a - 2c$. They followed this same formula for all the subsequent problems, and it worked. Once they were hooked on this formula, they continued to follow it, even when (as in problems 6 and 7) a much simpler solution was available.

Like everyone else who attempts to solve problems, scientists suffer from functional fixedness. Often they spend years trying to solve new problems with old methods. Sometimes they are successful, but on other occasions novel approaches are necessary. This shift in problem solving is essentially what occurs in a scientific revolution (Kuhn, 1970). But because it is so easy to fall victim to functional fixedness, many of the most important

FIG. 7 · 5 A test of functional fixedness. How can you mount the candle vertically on the wall, using the equipment provided? If you can't figure out how to do it, the solution appears on page 215.

breakthroughs are made by young scientists who are still flexible in their approach. For example, Pascal's theorem, a great mathematical discovery, was published when Pascal was only 17 years old. And Einstein's most revolutionary work appeared when he was still in his twenties.

LANGUAGE

If you were to estimate the number of words you speak in a day, a month, or a year, you would find that even if you are not a particularly talkative person you will speak a billion words in a lifetime. The number of words that you hear during the same lifetime is even more tremendous. According to Carroll's (1964) calculations, an average college student might hear 100,000 words in a day and read about 90,000 words a day. That would mean that such a student would be exposed to 750 million words a year (although many of the words would be the same, of course).

Language is the means by which we communicate with other people—the way we give and receive instructions, learn and teach, entertain and create, share and socialize. What's more, as we noted earlier, without language we would have a hard time doing any thinking.

REPEATED LANGUAGE

Statistical counts of word usage indicate that we repeat ourselves on the average of 1 word in every 10 to 15 words. There are 50 commonly used words that make up about 60 percent of all the words we speak and about 45 percent of all the words we write. We repeat a very few words and arrange and rearrange them in a great number of ways and thus express an almost infinite number of ideas. (Brief exercise: What word is used most often in the above paragraph?)

Theories of Language Development

A ruler of Egypt in the seventh century B.C. wanted to discover the original, universal language of humankind. To find out, he conducted the first controlled psychological experiment in recorded history—an experiment in developmental psycholinguistics, reported by Herodotus. The ruler took two infants and gave them to a shepherd. They were to be brought up with his flock, and the shepherd was to make sure that no one uttered a word in their presence. The king wanted to learn whether isolated children would speak Egyptian words first and thereby "prove" that the Egyptians were the original race of mankind. We don't know for sure how the experiment turned out, but it would be astonishing if the infants had developed any language at all.

A perspective quite different from that of the Egyptian king has been advocated by the learning theorists (Mowrer, 1958; Skinner, 1957), who feel that language, whether Egyptian or any other, is not "built into" the developing child. Instead, they contend, language is learned behavior, and it follows the principles of operant conditioning discussed in Chapter 5. According to this theory, the infant acquires language skills largely by reinforced imitation of models. That is, every time the child copies an adult word or group of words, he or she is given a reward, such as attention, an immediate response, or a smile. Short language units are combined into larger units, which are also reinforced if they are correct. There is some evidence to support the idea that vocalizations in three-month-old infants can be increased by reinforcements (Rheingold, Gewirtz, and Ross, 1959). But simple reinforcement theories do not seem to provide a sufficient explanation of language learning. For example, questions were raised by Wahler (1969), who found that mothers in a natural situation do not reinforce vocalizations selectively. In order words, they don't reinforce only the sounds that resemble adult speech. They reinforce one sound as much as any other. Nevertheless, children somehow learn to make sounds that are appropriate to the language of their family and community. The evidence suggests that although a completely genetic theory, such as that of the Egyptian king, cannot explain language learning, a completely environmental theory cannot explain it either.

A middle position is advocated by Noam Chomsky (1969; Chomsky and Halle, 1968). Chomsky acknowledges that the particular language you learn is determined by your environment—put an American baby in China and he will learn to speak flawless Chinese. But Chomsky argues that people's *capacity* for language is innate. It is based on principles of organization that are "intrinsic to the mind"—the same principles that organize perception, learning and thought.

According to Chomsky, learning a language involves learning rules; these rules allow a speaker to generate novel sentences and a listener to understand them. For example, some of the rules in English deal with word order. The sentence "The dog bites John" means something quite different from the sentence

"John bites the dog," even though the words are all the same. In this kind of sentence, we employ a rule stating that the agent appears before the action, which in turn appears before the object. So, we can tell from the word order which of the two is biting and which is being bitten. And once we know this rule we can generate other sentences that we have never heard before: "The dog bites Mary," "John feeds the dog," and so on.

Another linguistic rule in English governs the formation of the past tense of a verb. The past tense is usually created by adding "-d" or "-ed" to the end of the verb. Thus, a child may learn to say, "I play*ed* in the park this morning," or "I bake*d* a mudpie yesterday." The use of such a rule becomes most apparent when it leads to mistakes. Children who are learning the past tense rule often *overregularize* it—they apply it in instances when it is incorrect, such as "I goed to the zoo with Mommy" or "I maked my bed all by myself." Even though the children are doing some violence to the language, their mistakes prove that they are learning the rule.

If Chomsky is right and the capacity for language is innate, then language learning should proceed in a similar manner in widely different cultures, even though the specific rules may differ. And so, Chomsky's theory has led to a search for universal characteristics of language and language acquisition.

Stages of Language Acquisition

In fact, it appears that children everywhere develop language in a fairly stable sequence. Although there is a good deal of individual variation, most children begin to babble at about six months. They say their first word at about one year and begin to combine words when they are a year and a half or two. By the age of about four and a half, the basic grammar of adult speech is in use.

Vocalization is very limited during the first months of life, but by about six months infants are producing a great variety of sounds and putting them together in various combinations. During this babbling phase, infants can produce all the sounds that form the basis of any language. At this stage you can't tell the babbling of an American baby from that of any infant the world over (Atkinson, MacWhinney, and Stoel, 1970). The sounds in the infant's environment seem to have little bearing on the infant at this stage. Lenneberg (1969) found that infants who had two deaf parents and who had few other sounds in their homes (from TV, radio, or voices) produced the same sorts of vocalizations as babies with "noisier" environments.

At around nine months, the range of babbled sounds starts to narrow. The child has seemingly completed his experiments with sounds and has begun practicing syllables that will make up his first words. As Slobin (1972) indicates, "In all cultures the child's first word generally is a noun or proper name, identifying some object, animal, or person he sees every day."

At about two years (give or take a few months), the child begins what Roger Brown (1973) calls Stage I language, by combining strings of two (or occasionally three) words to form rudimentary sentences. During this two-word stage grammatical devices are simple. For example, the child indicates possession by combining a person's name or a personal pronoun with a noun: "Adam ball" or "Jill cup"; action is indicated by placing a name or pronoun in front of a verb: "Adam cry" or "Jill run." Stage I seems universal. At least, there is evidence for it in a dozen different languages. This cross-cultural consistency provides support for Chomsky's view that people's capacity to acquire language is innate.

As children get older, their grammatical tools become more and more complex. In English, Stage II (Brown, 1973) involves the use of inflections to indicate possession, number, or tense (John*'s* ball, those cup*s*, we walk*ed*), the use of the prepositions "in" and "on," and the use of the articles "a" and "the." Later stages (III through V) incorporate questions, clauses, compound sentences, and all the other forms of adult language.

There is little evidence that these later stages of language development are universal. This is not too surprising, since the rules of grammar differ in different languages. Nevertheless, there doesn't seem to be anything intrinsically more difficult about the rules of one language when compared to others. All languages seem to be equally easy for young children to learn.

Linguistic Communication

Language is, above all else, a form of communication. And like any other form of communication, it makes use of certain basic equipment. Radio communication, for example, requires both a receiver and a transmitter. Analogously, linguistic communication depends on both reception and transmission. Language *reception* takes place through the sense organs: Speech is received through hearing and written communications are received through sight. Naturally, people with defects in one sensory system—for example, those who are blind or deaf—must receive communications through another system instead. Thus, deaf people may receive sign language through sight, and blind people receive Braille communication through the sense of touch.

Linguistic communication also depends on *transmission.* The main way in which language is transmitted is through speech. Human speech is made possible by the coordinated use of the diaphragm, lungs, chest muscles, vocal cords, mouth, lips, and tongue. Of these body parts, the vocal cords (two membranes stretched across the inside of the larynx) are critical since we could not speak above a whisper without them. The lungs are used like bellows that, when squeezed by the chest muscles, force air up the windpipe and past the vocal cords, making them vibrate. But vibration alone is not enough. To produce high and low tones (and all the tones in between), we must be able to raise

THINKING WITHOUT LANGUAGE

It is possible to think without using language. Einstein reported that some of his thoughts came to him in visual terms. Some composers claim they "hear" the music before they write it down or play it on an instrument. You can visualize physical activities without really using language, but most of your thinking is dependent on language.

NONVERBAL COMMUNICATION

Nonverbal communication can convey some kinds of information that would take a great many words to describe. And, perhaps, part of the meaning would still be lost in translation. Most of us can comprehend a great number of gestures and nonverbal signs even if they are made by persons speaking a different language. In one study, several hundred high school and college students were asked to guess the meanings of some gestures used by American Indians. Both groups showed a better-than-chance understanding. Students with higher IQ scores were able to decode the gestures better than others. In general, deaf students performed better than students with normal hearing (Rowe, Brooks, and Watson, 1960).

or lower the larynx (the voice box). Certain language deficits may result from poor control over these muscles and organs (see Box 3). It is not surprising that the child's first spoken words are likely to be relatively easy to pronounce, including front-of-the mouth consonants (p, m, b, t) and back-of-the-mouth vowels (e, a). This may explain why the words "mama" and "papa" are similar in many languages and are so often the first pronounced by infants everywhere.

Like a radio, which can work properly only when its circuits are in order, linguistic communication is possible only when the brain is properly "wired." A wide variety of disturbances in language are due to brain malfunction. For example, language may never develop in those who are severely retarded, simply because they never develop the mental capacity to understand and produce language. In addition, *aphasia* (loss of language ability because of brain damage) may occur in those who have already mastered speech. The exact nature of an aphasia depends on which area of the brain has been damaged. Some aphasics—those who have suffered large-scale damage to parts of the brain most related to conceptual thought—may lose the use of language entirely. Other aphasics, with more localized lesions, may be able to use one form of language, but not another. In *receptive aphasia,* for example, patients can speak and write, but they cannot read or understand the speech of others. In *expressive aphasia,* patients can understand written or spoken language, but they cannot write or speak (Milner, 1970).

Since the left hemisphere of the brain seems to bear primary responsibility for language (see Chapter 2), damage to the left hemisphere has more serious effects on the learning and production of language. It is sometimes impossible, however, to train the right brain to take over some of these linguistic functions. These attempts are usually most successful when the brain damage has occurred during childhood, before the two hemispheres have become completely specialized. The right brain of the adult is more fixed in its functions and capabilities; it can be taught to take over language functions only slowly, if at all (Lenneberg, 1966).

Even among people who possess all the necessary biological equipment, communication depends on a commonly understood code. Words—labels for categories of objects, actions, and attributes—are a basic part of that code. As we have seen, the code also includes intricate rules about how words are put together in sentences. The failure to learn linguistic rules can sometimes present serious problems. Violations of word order, for example, have been known to produce such ambiguous (and potentially dangerous) sentences as, "Throw Mama from the train a kiss."

Box 3

Stuttering

When we consider the complexity of learning to speak clearly and coherently in a smooth, uninterrupted flow, the wonder is that so many of us master the task and so few of us end up stuttering or stammering. Everyone stutters a little, but some people stutter almost every time they speak.

Stuttering usually begins early in life (at three to four years of age), but it is most often diagnosed in school settings at age seven or eight. Boys stutter more than girls, and rough estimates suggest that stuttering occurs in 1 to 3 percent of the children in our school population. Only rarely is a physical basis found for this disorder. Attempts to demonstrate clear personality differences between stutterers and nonstutterers have failed more often than they have succeeded.

Freudian explanations of stuttering stress the presence of a mixture of sexual and aggressive motives for these mild disorders of speech. Stuttering is thought to reflect tension and conflict on the part of the speaker. For example, if you wish to harm the person to whom you are talking, your stutter could be an attempt to hold such impulses in check by halting or hesitating when you communicate. A less complicated explanation suggests that when a child is tense and anxious for any of a number of reasons, his or her speech may be disrupted as an expression of inner feelings. A pattern of stuttering can, of course, be self-perpetuating once it is firmly established. The experience of failing to communicate can sensitize the child to anticipate more failure later on.

Behavioral theorists view speech problems—how they begin, how they continue—as imperfectly learned behavior. The speech behavior may have suffered interference because of perceptual defects that scramble the feedback control we use to think, speak, hear ourselves, and then speak some more.

An equally popular theory holds that stuttering occurs when circumstances make a young child anxious about speaking—afraid of being unable to speak properly. According to this approach, parents and teachers unwittingly foster the development of stuttering out of the normal speech errors that children usually make (Carroll, 1964). If such a theory were true, then all stutterers should be anxious about their speech and a reduction in anxiety should diminish stuttering. Although clearly demonstrated, stutterers do have great speech anxiety; there is little systematic evidence that stuttering is reduced with a reduction in anxiety.

This kind of ambiguity is avoided once the grammatical rules of a language are well learned.

Other linguistic rules are social, rather than grammatical. For example, some languages use different forms of the pronoun "you" depending on the degree of intimacy or the status difference between the person speaking and the person being addressed. In French, the pronoun *tu* has traditionally been used for friends or subordinates, while *vous* has been used for strangers and superiors (Brown, 1965). English doesn't employ different pronoun forms, but it makes similar distinctions with respect to names. Friends and subordinates are called by their first names; strangers and superiors are referred to by their title (Mr., Ms., Dr.) and last names. That crusty English professor, Reid A. Bookaday, probably refers to his students as "Laurel" and "Joel"; it is difficult to imagine those students calling him "Reid."

Our language, then, is made up of many different elements, and an alteration of any of these elements can cause a breakdown in communication. We need to be able to transmit, to receive, and to use rules in order to make use of the complex phenomenon we call language.

PHONEMES

Language is based on a number of basic sounds called *phonemes.* The English language has about 45 phonemes (such as *sh, fl, cr*), which reflect the different ways we pronounce the vowels and consonants of our alphabet. Some languages have as few as 15 phonemes, and others have as many as 85.

When phonemes are correctly combined, they give language a form and structure. The correct combination of phonemes makes nonsense words easier to remember. Brown and Hildum (1956) reported that it is easier to remember nonsense words that have correct phoneme combinations (stroop, skile) than nonsense words that do not have correct combinations (zbax, xrop, gtbil).

IF I COULD TALK LIKE THE HUMANS

Language has traditionally been regarded as a distinctively human capacity, something that separates us from all the other members of the animal kingdom. But is it really? As one approach to answering this question, a number of investigators have attempted to do what others said couldn't be done—to teach language to chimpanzees. In the 1930s, Winthrop and Luella Kellogg raised a female chimpanzee named Gua along with their infant son Donald. By the age of 16 months, Gua could understand about 100 words, but she never tried to speak to the Kelloggs. In the late 1940s, Keith and Cathy Hayes (1951) raised a chimpanzee named Vicki in their home. She understood a large number of words and with some difficulty could mouth the words "mama," "papa," and "cup." But she never got beyond that rather primitive level of speech. It may be unfair, though, to expect chimpanzees to speak. After all, their vocal apparatus is not as well developed as ours. Recognizing this fact, other investigators have attempted to teach chimpanzees languages that do not involve speech.

Since 1966, Ann and David Premack (1972) have been teaching a chimpanzee named Sarah to read and write using various shapes and colors of plastic to represent words. In 1972 Sarah had a " vocabulary" of about 130 terms. The first step for the Premacks was to exploit knowledge that was already present:

In teaching Sarah we first mapped the simple social transaction of giving, which is something the chimpanzee does both in nature and in the laboratory. Considered in terms of cognitive and perceptual elements, the verb "give" involves a relation between two individuals and one object, that is, between the donor, the recipient, and the object being transferred. . . . Once she wrote "Give apple Gussie," and the trainer promptly gave the apple to another chimpanzee named Gussie. Sarah never repeated the sentence. At every stage she was required to observe the proper word sequence. "Give apple" was accepted but "Apple give" was not. When donors were to be named, Sarah had to identify all the members of the social transaction: "Mary give apple Sarah." [page 95]†

The Premacks' objective was to reduce complex notions to a series of simple and highly learnable steps. But a key question remains: Did Sarah actually learn a language? Or was she merely trained to associate the plastic shapes with actions, as a dog may learn to associate commands with particular behaviors? The answer is unclear. Roger Brown (Brown and Herrnstein, 1975) points out that Sarah never initiated communications on her own and that she never produced really novel sentences. A human child who learns sentences like "I eat apple" and "Give me carrot" will often produce new sentences like "I eat carrot" and "Give me apple." There is no evidence that Sarah ever did so. It is uncertain whether Sarah learned general grammatical rules. She may have learned only specific sequences of words to which she had been exposed and for which she had been reinforced, rather than the ability to use general rules.

More convincing evidence—convincing, at least, to some psychologists—comes from the work of Gardner and Gardner (1969) with a female chimpanzee named Washoe. The Gardners began their study of Washoe in 1966, when she was about one year old. Washoe would spend most of each day interacting with humans speaking to her in American Sign Language (Ameslan), a language that is used by deaf people in America. At first, Washoe learned signs slowly—after six months of training, she could use only a few. By age four, however, she had a vocabulary of 85

VICKI AND ME

In 1950, I (Elton McNeil) became acquainted with Vicki, the chimpanzee raised by Keith and Cathy Hayes, when she visited the University of Michigan Psychological Clinic. At that time the possibility was being considered that Vicki was unable to speak English, in part, because she simply was not intelligent enough. Just for the fun of it, we tried administering simple intelligence tests suited for a child that might be Vicki's mental age. The testing room was soon in a shambles as Vicki romped around, played with all the "toys," swiped my wallet out of my back pocket, and climbed out the window to the fire escape to make faces and screeching noises at the passing Ann Arbor citizens. From the test items Vicki completed (none of which involved speech), it was clear that stupidity was not her problem.

†*From Ann James Premack and David Premack, "Teaching Language to an Ape."* Scientific American, *October 1972, p. 95.*

signs, and by age five it had nearly doubled to 165. Furthermore, she was regularly combining signs into sequences up to five signs long. Some of the words Washoe regularly used are described in Table 7.1.

Washoe's use of Ameslan was crude, but she did seem to be using it as a language. She often initiated communication. In addition, she separated her sign sequences with pauses, just as we would separate sentences. Most importantly, she sometimes seemed to produce novel expressions. For example, on one occasion she signed, "Open food drink" while gesturing toward the refrigerator. The Gardners believe that Washoe had never encountered this particular sentence before. Though we cannot be certain, since sufficiently detailed records of her training were not kept, Washoe was probably being "productive" in her use of language.

Recently, even greater success has been achieved with the infant chimpanzees Moja and Pili. They have been interacting since soon after birth with trainers who are deaf and fluent in Ameslan. Moja learned four signs by her thirteenth week, Pili by his fifteenth week. After six months, Moja knew 15 signs and Pili knew 13 (Gardner and Gardner, 1975).

Psychologists were once reluctant to admit that chimpanzees could use any language at all. Now Moja's and Pili's performance has made some psychologists start to worry that, during infancy at least, chimpanzees can use language better than humans! Meanwhile, important research continues. In one laboratory, for example, psychologists are waiting to see whether an adult chimpanzee familiar with Ameslan will spontaneously teach it to an infant. Taken in sum, the available evidence suggests that chimpanzees are capable of learning language at a rudimentary level similar to that of a young child. There is no evidence—yet—that their use of language can advance past those first stages.

Table 7.1 Some Signs Used by Washoe

Sign	Description	Context
Tickle	The index finger of one hand is drawn across the back of the other hand.	For tickling or for chasing games.
Hurry	Open hand is shaken at the wrist.	Often follows signs such as "come-gimme," "out," "open," and "go," particularly if there is a delay before Washoe is obeyed. Also, used while watching her meal being prepared.
Hear-listen	Index finger touches ear.	For loud or strange sounds: bells, car horns, sonic booms, etc. Also, for asking someone to hold a watch to her ear.
Sorry	Fisted hand clasps and unclasps at shoulder.	After biting someone, or when someone has been hurt in another way (not necessarily by Washoe). When told to apologize for mischief.
Funny	Tip of index finger presses nose, and Washoe snorts.	When soliciting interaction play, and during games. Occasionally, when being pursued after mischief.

Source: Adapted from Gardiner, R. A. and Gardiner, B. T., "Teaching Sign Language to a Chimpanzee," Science, *Vol. 165, pp. 664–672, Table 1, August, 1969, Copyright 1969 by the American Association for the Advancement of Science.*

FIG. 7 · 5 **Solution** Solution to the test of functional fixedness. When the tacks are shown in the box, many people think of the box only as a container and not as a possible candleholder.

SUMMARY

1. *Concepts* are categories that we use to group a variety of objects or ideas according to their similar characteristics. A concept is learned by discovering *positive instances* and *negative instances* in which the concept applies.
2. According to the *stimulus-response association theory,* concepts are learned through associating a stimulus (an attribute of an object) with a response (the label for the object). But according to the *verbal mediation theory,* associations between attributes and labels (concepts) occur only when a verbal response focuses attention on these attributes.
3. Concepts are to a great extent socially and culturally determined. Once learned, concepts can also influence our behavior. For example, concepts about groups of people—stereotypes—can influence the way we behave toward people in these groups. And concepts can influence our perceptions—putting a label on something can influence the way we perceive it and remember it.
4. The first step in solving a problem is determining the kind of problem it is. Problems may be approached using *inductive reasoning*—generalizing on the basis of a few instances—or using *deductive reasoning*—going from a general proposition to a particular instance.
5. Trying to solve a problem in a group has advantages and disadvantages. Sometimes the disadvantages can be overcome by *brainstorming*—everyone suggesting whatever comes to mind without fear of ridicule. Later, the suggestions are evaluated. With some kinds of problems, however, it is better for individuals to solve them on their own rather than in groups.
6. One simple method of problem solving is *trial and error*—trying every possible solution until one finally works. Sometimes the answer to a problem occurs to a person unexpectedly in the form of *insight.*
7. The ability to solve problems is sometimes hampered by *functional fixedness,* in which the individual gets "stuck" on old methods of problem solving and ignores novel or new methods that may be more appropriate to a new situation.
8. *Language* is the means by which we communicate with other people. Learning theorists believe that children learn language by being reinforced for imitating the speech patterns of people in their environment. Other theorists, such as Chomsky, contend that humans have an innate capacity to use language and that, like the capacity to use concepts, this ability "unfolds" with learning as the child grows.
9. Children all over the world develop speech in a fairly stable sequence. They start with babbling, then go to single-word utterances, and by the age of two are combining words into two- and three-word sentences. By the age of four and a

half, the child has learned the basic grammar of adult speech.

10. Linguistic communication depends on *reception* (through the senses) and on *transmission* (by speaking, writing, using hand signals). *Aphasia* is a condition in which brain damage interferes with the ability to use or to understand language. Poor ability to communicate may also be caused by the failure to obey linguistic rules.
11. Stuttering is a speech problem that rarely has a physical basis. The Freudian explanation is that stuttering is an attempt to hold in harmful impulses. Behaviorists see stuttering as the result of improper learning of speech behaviors. Another theory is that stuttering comes from the speaker's high level of anxiety and fear of making mistakes in speaking. None of these theories has been substantiated.
12. Many attempts have been made to teach chimpanzees to use language. The Premacks taught Sarah to use plastic symbols to represent words. The Gardners taught Washoe American Sign Language, and she has been able to create novel sentences in Ameslan. However, no chimpanzee has been able to use language at a level higher than that of a young child.

Creativity

We are often astonished by past examples of extremes in human creativity. The list of musical prodigies, for example, is long. Handel played the clavichord "when but an infant" and was composing by the age of 11. Haydn played and composed at the age of 6. Mozart played the harpsichord at 3, was composing at 4, and was on a tour at age 6. Chopin played in public at the age of 8; Liszt, at 9; Verdi, at 10; Schubert, at 12; and Rossini, at 14. Mendelssohn was playing and composing at the age of 9, Debussy, at 11, Dvorak, at 12, and Berlioz, at 14. Wagner conducted one of his own compositions in public when he was 17.

As if this information were not oppressive enough, John Stuart Mill began the study of Greek at the age of 3, and by the age of 8 he had read Xenophon, Herodotus, and Plato and had begun to study geometry and algebra. At 12 he began logic, reading Aristotle in the original Greek. The next year he began the study of political economy, and at 16 he was publishing controversial articles in that field (Pressey, 1955). In more modern times the mathematician Norbert Weiner entered college at 11 and completed his doctorate at Harvard by age 18.

...John Stuart Mill began the study of Greek at the age of 3....

Those of us who are more average sometimes feel comforted by the notion that creative people are strange, deviant, and perhaps a little crazy. But, unfortunately, the evidence suggests otherwise.

Creativity and Madness

Vincent Van Gogh cut off his ear and later took his life. Edgar Allen Poe frequently wrote under the influence of drugs. Indeed, some creative works have come from the "mentally disturbed," but only a few truly creative people are seriously disturbed, even if many seem quite eccentric. For one thing, creative people do not always conform to society; this may account for studies showing that highly creative people lean toward the abnormal on personality tests. The appearance of abnormality may go along with the tendency to be different from others, but this is not necessarily a sign of mental disturbance. Creative people seem to be able to enjoy the bizarre while still maintaining a grasp on reality.

Frank Barron (1972) clarified

this issue in his comparison of a group of young creative artists with a group of hospitalized mental patients diagnosed as schizophrenic. He found the following distinguishing characteristics:

1. *Clinical schizophrenia, in contrast to artistic unconventionality or oddness, is marked by apathy, despair, dread, and a sort of spiritual death.*
2. *In schizophrenia there is confusion, bizarre ideation, delusion of control by others, and loss of stable self-regulation of mood.*
3. *The artist, by contrast, finds joy in life, is not self-pitying, is reasonably worried about practical matters, and functions well physically.* [*page 44*]†

There were also similarities between the artists and the patients. About an equal number of artists and schizophrenic patients reported odd sensations such as ringing in their ears, peculiar odors, and unaccountable numbness in parts of their bodies at times. Both groups preferred solitude to the company of other persons, and they shared a feeling of lack of love from parents and a rejection of home and many common social values. Both groups also expressed high levels of tension, restlessness, strain, and impulsive outbursts.

†*From Frank X. Barron, "The Creative Personality Akin to Madness,"* Psychology Today, *July 1972, p. 44. Article originally appeared in Frank X. Barron, ARTISTS IN THE MAKING, (New York. Seminar Press, 1972). © 1972 by Academic Press. Reprinted by permission.*

Barron concluded that his findings suggest an unusual state of psychic affairs in creative artists. They seem to be able to incorporate emotionally disturbing experiences and then combine them with rationality, very high conceptual intelligence, and honesty. Artists, Barron says, are capable of "dreaming awake," and this makes the difference in their personal adjustment.

The fact that creative people are often individualistic and independent is not surprising. Truly creative work is characterized by its distinctiveness and originality. The scientist or writer who is unduly sensitive to the opinions of others would find it difficult to create anything.

The Creative Process

The stages in the creative process have been described as: (1) preparation, (2) incubation, (3) illumination, and (4) verification or revision. Preparing for creative thinking may involve making a great many false starts. Preparation is a process of "sorting out" and organizing that may amount to more than arriving at a clear statement of what the problem is.

The next possible step is an unexpected one—some scientists stop working on the problem or stop consciously thinking about it. Some creative thinkers deliberately put the problem out of mind and simply let the issue incubate for a while as they relax, play, read, or go to sleep. While their attention is thus diverted, some part of their mental apparatus is probably still turning over and continuing to examine the problem. Dreams may reflect this process:

Inventor James Watt had been working on lead shot for shotguns. The standard process, a costly one, involved cutting or chopping metal. About this time Watt had a recurring dream. He seemed to be walking through a heavy storm; instead of rain, he was showered with tiny lead pellets. The next morning he interpreted his dream to mean that molten lead, falling through the air, would harden into small spheres. Watt melted several

Box I-1

The Creative Classroom
How can we educate exceptional children if we do not understand them? This vital question can be emphasized with a bizarre example. Imagine a teacher who has to design the curriculum for the following group of gifted children: Bach, J.; Bronte, E.; Curie, M.; DaVinci, L.; Darwin, C.; Einstein, A.; Freud, S.; Kant, I.; Lincoln, A.; Marx, K.; Newton, I.; Rand, A.; Shakespeare, W.; Stein, G.; and Whitman, W. The sense of helplessness one would feel in such a situation is mute evidence of the mismatch of methods and goals that probably would occur. Undoubtedly, the teacher would resort to a solution that characterizes current plans for special education. He or she would "enrich" and "accelerate" with the unspoken hope that creativity would somehow emerge.

pounds of lead and flung it from the bell tower of a church that had a waterfilled moat at its base. Hastening down the stairs, he scooped tiny lead pellets from the moat and revolutionized the leadshot industry. [Krippner and Hughes, 1970, page 42]†

†*From S. Krippner & W. Hughes, "Genius at Work,"* Psychology Today, *June 1970, p. 42. Copyright © 1970 Ziff-Davis Publishing Company. Reprinted by permission of PSYCHOLOGY TODAY MAGAZINE.*

The sudden appearance of an idea after the period of incubation is the "illumination" regularly reported by creative thinkers. These periods of incubation and illumination in creative thinking are identical to the process of insight, which we described for normal problem solving. Insight is an essential part of the creative process. Illumination triggers the intensive work necessary to check out the idea or invention. As Thomas Edison once said, "Genius is 1 percent inspiration and 99 percent perspiration." The evaluation and testing process may then stimulate new ideas that allow the basic invention to be modified or improved.

Lehman (1953) contends that creative contributions in the sciences are most regularly produced by people between the ages of 30 and 40. In most fields gifted contributors not only produce their best work at a relatively early age, but are most productive (counting the total number of works produced) during these same early years.

This timing of creativity may be related to the high energy level of young people. Regardless of age, the more productive the creative individual is, the more likely he or she is to create a work of outstanding significance. In nearly all fields of intellectual endeavor, eminent workers tend to produce more works than their less distinguished colleagues.

People's creativity may also be affected by their society and culture. Some cultures may encourage creativity; others may stifle it. Simonton (in press) studied the lives of about 5,000 eminent, creative people in science, philosophy, art, literature, and other fields, scattered over the past 26 centuries. His data suggest political instability may retard the development

Box I-2
Fostering Creativity
To foster creativity, early plan of intellectual growth must demand the following characteristics from its students:

an insatiable urge to inquire into the nature of the world;

a willingness to be skeptical of our most cherished beliefs;

a capacity to pursue this inquiry in the face of opposition.

Henry (1963) suggests that if we truly want to induce completely creative thinking, we should teach children to question the Ten Commandments, patriotism, the two-party system, monogamy, and the laws against incest.

and expression of unusual creativity. Political takeovers, military revolts, and conflicts between royal dynasties all tend to precede periods when creative eminence is rare. On the other hand, political fragmentation seems to enhance creative expression. The prevalence of small, independent states—as in Classical Greece or Renaissance Italy—may support diverse perspectives and, hence, creative insights. All in all, creativity may be favored when governments are stable and when they allow a diversity of cultural and social pursuits.

...political fragmentation seems to enhance creative expression.

Intelligence and Creativity

Although many outstanding creative people have also been quite intelligent, creativity and intelligence are actually independent aspects of thought. To determine the relationship between these two dimensions, Wallach and Kogan (1967) did an extensive study of 151 fifth-grade, middle-class children. They used measures of creativity that would allow a creative child to be of either low or high intelligence. By their measures, a child who was relatively low in creativity could also be of either high or low intelligence. Their descriptive accounts of children with various combinations of intelligence and creativity make fascinating reading.

High creativity–high intelligence. In the classroom, these children tend to be particularly high in their degree of attention span and concentration on academic work. They also are the most socially "healthy" of the four groups. They have the strongest inclination to be friends with others, and others also have the strongest inclination to be friends with them.

Low creativity–high intelligence. These children, in the classroom, are least likely to engage in disruptive activities. They tend to hesitate about expressing opinions and seem rather unwilling to take chances. They are characterized by a coolness or reserve in relations with their peers. The possibility of making an error seems particularly painful to these children.

High creativity–low intelligence. Such young people tend to exhibit disruptive behavior in the classroom. They are the least able to concentrate and pay attention in class, the lowest in self-confidence, and the most likely to express the conviction that their case is a hopeless one. They are relatively isolated socially. Not only do they avoid contact with others, they are shunned by their peers more than any other group.

We seem to want creativity in the young—but only if it follows all the rules, isn't too noisy, pleases the adults, and doesn't rock the boat....

Box I-3
Measuring Creativity

There is no single, agreed-upon measure of creativity, but psychologists have tried various methods of getting at people's ability to relate ideas and objects that would otherwise be unrelated. We can see how this might aid creativity—people might be able to find new uses for old tools, for example. One measure of this ability is Mednick's Remote Association Test (Mednick, 1962). Subjects are given a group of three words and are asked to give a fourth word that can be meaningfully linked to the first three. Sample items are: rat, blue, cottage; surprise, line, birthday; out, dog, cat; wheel, electric, high (answers are at the end of the box.)

Another method of assessing this ability is to ask for new uses for common objects. For example, Guilford (1954) asked subjects to name as many uses as they could for such common objects as a brick, a toothpick, or a paper clip.

To get at a person's ingenuity, researchers have also asked for solutions to problems or completions of stories. Flanagan (1963) tried to measure ingenuity in response to stories such as the following:

A very rare wind storm destroyed the transmission tower of a television station in a small town. The station was located in a town in a flat prairie with no tall buildings. Its former 300-foot tower enabled it to serve a large farming community, and the management wanted to restore service while a new tower was being erected. The problem was temporarily solved by using a ________.

Along similar lines, Getzels and Jackson (1962) had subjects write endings for fables such as "The Mischievous Dog":

A rascally dog used to run quietly to the heels of every passerby and bite them without warning. So his master was obliged to tie a bell around the cur's neck so that he might give notice wherever he went. This the dog thought very fine indeed, and he went about tinkling it in pride all over town. But an old hound said ________.

There are, of course, no *right* answers or stories. Rather, the solutions are rated according to how novel—yet appropriate—they are.

Answers for the Mednick Remote Association Test items: cheese; party; house; chair.

Low creativity–low intelligence. Despite this combination of apparent handicaps, these children seem to make up for it to some degree in the social sphere. They are more extraverted socially, less hesitant, and more self-confident than the children of low intelligence, but high creativity.

Farson (1967) insists that if we seek creativity, education must not be limited to activities that seem to involve thinking. We must develop the other dimensions of humanness—the senses, feelings and emotions, taste and judgment, and an understanding of how humans relate to one another. We seem to want creativity in the young—but only if it follows all the rules, isn't too noisy, pleases the adults, and doesn't rock the social boat—conditions sure to kill all creativity in children.

Summary

1. Creative people may have an unusual state of psychic affairs. Unlike the mentally ill, they can use their mental oddities with reason and for a purpose. Because creative people must be somewhat insensitive to criticism in order to produce anything unusual or new, they often seem eccentric and mindless of society's rules.
2. The creative process appears to involve four stages: preparation, incubation, illumination, and verification of the idea.
3. Creativity is related to age in some fields of endeavor and also seems to be related to productivity—creative people tend to be more productive. Creativity also seems to be influenced by the time period in which one lives.
4. A number of studies have been done to identify creativity in children and to determine its relation to intelligence and to personality.

CHAPTER

8

Intelligence

In some animal species the most important and admired attribute is physical size and strength; in others, it is speed and agility. Among humans, size and speed are also valued, at least on the football field. For the human animal, however, these attributes are overshadowed by *intelligence*. Our mental ability has made us unique in the animal kingdom and has made possible our survival. Thus, there is probably no greater compliment you can pay to a person than to say, "She's a really intelligent person" and no greater insult than, "He's a nice guy, but kind of dumb."

In spite of its acknowledged importance, intelligence is also an elusive and controversial concept, and psychologists differ among themselves as to what exactly it is. But most would agree with the general notion that intelligence is "the capacity to acquire and apply knowledge" (American Heritage Dictionary, 1969). David Wechsler, the developer of one of the most frequently used intelligence tests, recently offered a similar definition: Intelligence is "the capacity of an individual to understand the world about him and his resourcefulness to cope with its challenges" (1975, page 139). A key feature of these definitions is that intelligence is a *capacity*, rather than the possession of particular information or skills. It is possible for someone to have a great deal of information drummed into him or her without knowing what to do with it—and, therefore, without being particularly intelligent. On the other hand, it is possible for someone to lack a great deal of knowledge, perhaps as a result of limited experience, and still be highly intelligent.

Our definition of intelligence does raise one problem, however. How do we go about measuring a capacity, as opposed to the ability to retain information or to perform specific skills? For in practice, most of what psychologists know about intelligence is based on the scores people obtain on intelligence tests—their intelligence quotients, or IQs. As we will see in the next section, IQs are based on people's performance on particular measures of their skills, mainly those involving the ability to manipulate words and numbers. Whereas IQ scores tend to be highly related to school grades, there is some question about their relevance to people's capacity to acquire and apply knowledge in other areas of life. We will return to this issue after describing the essential features of intelligence testing.

MEASURING INTELLIGENCE

First we will look at two major tests used to measure intelligence—the Stanford-Binet and the Wechsler—and then we will explore some of the uses and misuses of IQ tests and their scores.

EDUCATIONAL IQ

Cronbach (1960) reviewed studies on the relationship between intelligence and educational attainments; he found that people with Ph.D. degrees had IQs averaging about 130. The average IQ for all college graduates was 120, and for high-school graduates it was 110. These IQ scores are for groups and tell us little about any individual case. Educational attainment depends on more than just intelligence, but these test scores do reflect relevant intellectual abilities in academic work.

The Stanford-Binet Test

In the early 1900s the Minister of Public Instruction in Paris, France, needed to know which students required special instruction and which should go to a regular school. Since guessing someone's intelligence was hardly an accurate way to make such an important decision, he sought more objective methods. In 1904, a commission was established to determine ways to distinguish between bright and dull children. It was led by Alfred Binet and his co-worker Theodore Simon. In setting up the first intelligence tests, they began using four factors as a rough guide: direction (the ability to set up a goal and work toward it); adaptation (the ability to adapt oneself to the problem and use appropriate means to solve it); comprehension (the ability to understand the problem); and self-evaluation (the ability to evaluate one's performance and determine whether one is approaching the problem correctly).

Binet assumed that the nature of intelligence changes with age, and thus the items selected must be graded by both age and difficulty. To each test item he assigned a certain number of months' "credit" of mental age. Each test item would count as two months' credit of mental age, and a group of six items would total one year of mental age if all were answered correctly by the child.

Binet thus introduced the concept of *mental age* (MA). If a child can pass the items on which the average six-year-old child is successful, he or she is said to have a mental age of six years. And, if a six-year-old can come up with the correct answers to the tests passed by the average nine-year-old, he or she is considered accelerated in mental development. But, if a ten-year-old can pass only the items passed by a nine-year-old, he or she is considered below average in intelligence.

Using a child's mental age and chronological age, we are able to compute an *intelligence quotient* (IQ) using the formula:

$$\text{IQ} = \frac{\text{MA (mental age)}}{\text{CA (chronological age)}} \times 100$$

When mental age is greater than chronological age, the IQ is greater than 100. When chronological age is greater than mental age, IQ is less than 100. Perhaps a few samples of these calculations will make the idea of IQ clearer. Suppose a ten-year-old passes only enough tests to get a mental age of eight. Then (MA 8/CA 10) $\times$ 100 = 80. Suppose another ten-year-old has a mental age of twelve. Then (MA 12/CA 10) $\times$ 100 = 120.

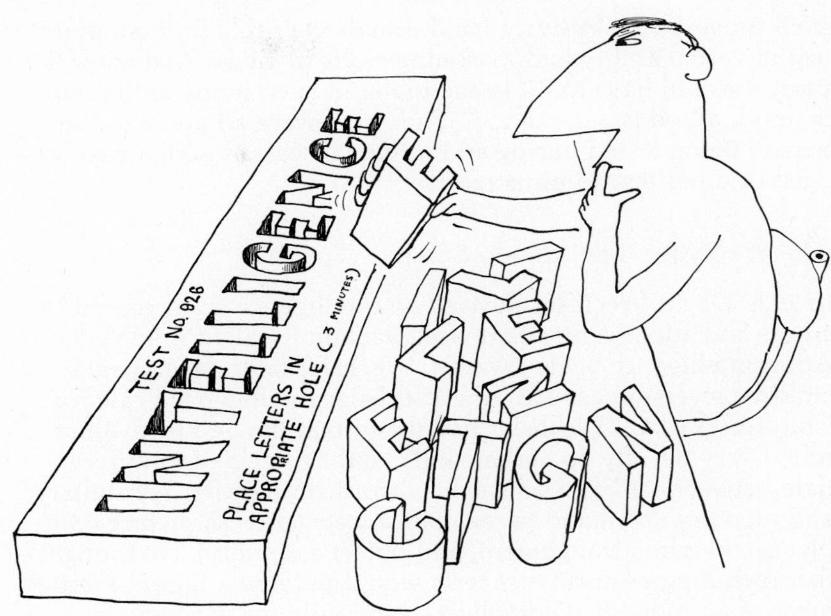

For adults, the MA/CA formula is not relevant—we certainly would not want to say that a 20-year-old woman has twice the IQ of a 40-year-old woman who answers the same number of questions correctly. For adults, an IQ of 100 is equal to the average score of a large sample of adults of all ages, and higher or lower scores mean that one did better or worse than this average (as will be discussed further when we delve into test standardization).

Lewis M. Terman of Stanford University tested almost 3,000 American children with Binet's tests and arranged the tests by mental-age levels. In 1916 he published a revision of Binet's tests that became known as the *Stanford-Binet test.* This revised version of the test emphasized the scholastic aspects of intelligence: reading, writing, arithmetic. This emphasis can be seen in the types of items included (Terman and Merrill, 1937). For seven-year-olds, for example, a typical task was to discover the absurdity in a picture, such as of a man trying to cut wood with an upside down saw. Another task was to be able to tell the similarities between a pair of words, such as "wood and coal," "apple and peach," or "ship and automobile." Eight-year-olds were asked to give not only the similarities, but also the differences between two words such as "orange and baseball" and "ocean and river." Children's memory was tested in different ways at different age levels. For example, children might be asked to reproduce a geometrical figure they had been shown earlier. Or they might be asked to repeat the main points of a story they had been read.

In adult tests, more difficult items were included. For example, the person would be asked to distinguish words that differ in subtle ways, such as "laziness and idleness" or "character and reputation." Another adult test was to analyze the meaning of such proverbs as "A burnt child dreads the fire." Still another test of verbal ability and reasoning skills involved analogies; the person would have to fill in the blank in such items as "A rabbit is timid, a lion is ________." The items were all given to the person being tested during an individual session with a psychologist or other test administrator.

The Wechsler Intelligence Scales

In 1939 David Wechsler devised an intelligence scale geared to adults and adolescents; its revised version is called the Wechsler Adult Intelligence Scale (WAIS). Wechsler later developed a children's version as well—the Wechsler Intelligence Scale for Children (WISC). Wechsler had noted that the Stanford-Binet relied very heavily on verbal skills, and he decided to differentiate between verbal tests (such as word similarities, vocabulary, and memory span) and performance tests (such as picture completion, picture arrangement, and object assembly). He thought that including performance tests would provide a fairer assessment of an individual's intellect—especially for individuals whose social backgrounds did not promote verbal skills. (See Figure 8.1.)

The WAIS is one of the most widely used scales for measuring adult intelligence. Its general features are similar to those of

FIG. 8 · 1 Items such as those used on the Wechsler Adult Intelligence Scale.

A FLASH OF BRILLIANCE: THE NEURAL EFFICIENCY ANALYZER

A scientist named John Ertl has invented a machine that popular magazine articles have billed as the successor to the IQ test. His machine, the neural efficiency analyzer, is supposed to measure one component of intelligence: speed of information transmission within the brain. The person being tested wears a helmet lined with electrodes and is made comfortable in a seat opposite a strobe light. A compact unit containing a computer and an EEG measures the time it takes for flashes of light to register as changes in the subject's brainwave patterns. After a minute, and more than 100 flashes, the device reads out an average score in milliseconds. The shorter the interval, the greater the efficiency of information processing, Ertl claims (Asher, 1973). Although such a device sounds intriguing, most psychologists would not consider this flashy machine a serious alternative to intelligence tests.

the Stanford-Binet, but it is broken down into eleven subtests. The items within each subtest are arranged in order of difficulty. On some subtests, the score is the number of correct responses. On other subtests, the score is determined by the amount of time taken to solve the problem or complete the task. The overall IQ score is derived by combining the scores from all the subtests, but it is also possible to look at the individual subtest scores to see which areas the person does particularly well or poorly in.

Both the Wechsler and Stanford-Binet are individually administered, but schools, industry, and government require tests that can be administered to large groups of people simultaneously. The beginning of widespread *group testing* took place during World War I, when nearly 2 million men were tested for intelligence and assigned to various army jobs accordingly. During World War I psychologists constructed two group intelligence tests: one for literates (the Army Alpha), and the other for illiterates (the Army Beta). These tests have evolved into the Army General Classification Test and the Armed Forces Qualification Test. Among civilians some of the most widely used group tests are the California Test of Mental Maturity, the Cooperative School and College Ability Tests, and the Scholastic Aptitude Tests.

Test Standardization

The *standardization* of intelligence tests such as the Stanford-Binet or the Wechsler consists of administering the test to large, representative samples of children and adults of various ages and calculating their scores. The construction of intelligence tests is done so that the distribution of scores obtained by a large group of people is usually "normal" in shape. That is, a bell-shaped curve is produced in which the majority of the test takers achieve scores in the middle range while increasingly fewer achieve scores toward the lower and higher ends of the range (see Figure 8.2 and Table 8.1).

IQ	Classification	Approximate Percentage in Standardization Sample
140 and above	Very Superior	1
120–139	Superior	10
110–119	High Average	18
90–109	Average	47
80–89	Low Average	15
70–79	Borderline	6
69 and below	Mental Defective	3

Source: From L. M. Terman & M. A. Merrill, MEASURING INTELLIGENCE: A GUIDE TO THE ADMINISTRATION OF THE NEW REVISED STANFORD-BINET TESTS OF INTELLIGENCE (Boston: Houghton-Mifflin). copyright © 1960, 1937.

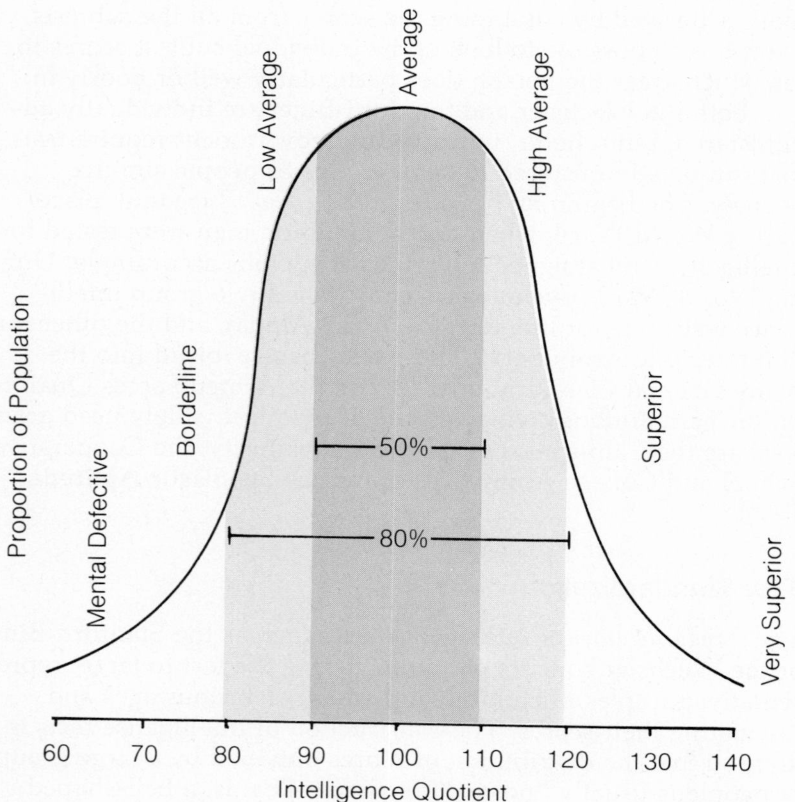

FIG. 8 · 2 When we plot the distribution of IQs listed in the table, we come up with a curve like the one above. Note that 80 percent of the population falls within the range described as "average."

If the distribution of IQs is normal, then the odds of having a given IQ score may be determined. The average score on most IQ tests is around 100, and 50 percent of a large sample of persons will fall below. About half the people taking a test will fall within 10 points of the average (between 90 and 109), and about 80 percent will fall within 20 points of the average (between 80 and 119).

It should be clear that one's IQ is a relative matter—it expresses one's standing in comparison to those in the group used to standardize the test. David Wechsler was once criticized for taking this approach, in which IQ levels are classified in terms of the amount they deviate from an established norm. By this procedure, his critic pointed out, the topmost 2 percent of people in an institution for mental defectives would have to be labeled as of superior intelligence. "My reply," Wechsler recounted, "was that this stricture was quite correct but would have to be supplemented by a statement to the effect that it applied only to subjects in an institution for mental defectives. 'Among the blind the one-eyed man is king' " (1975, page 138).†

The Structure of Tested Intelligence

Just what is the capacity called intelligence? Is it a single, unitary entity, or is it a mixed bag of abilities that are not closely related to one another? Based on data from intelligence tests, psychologists have tried to settle this difficult question. Charles Spearman, (1904), a British psychologist, took the view that intelligence is a single entity. He proposed that a single general-intelligence factor (which he labeled *g*) accounted for the correlations that are regularly found between different measures of mental ability. He described *g* as a kind of well or spring of mental energy that flows into everything an individual does.

In contrast, L. L. Thurstone (1938) felt that intelligence consists of eight primary abilities that are relatively independent of one another. He identified these eight abilities as verbal comprehension, perceptual speed, numerical ability, rote memory, word fluency, spatial visualization, inductive reasoning, and deductive reasoning. Excelling in any one of these, Thurstone believed, has little to do with excelling in any other.

Most of the evidence suggests that a compromise between these two positions is probably closer to the truth. That is, intelligence—at least as it is measured on intelligence tests—seems to include a general ability that underlies scores on a wide variety of subtests (such as those of the WAIS). The higher a person scores on any one subtest, the higher he or she will probably score on any of the other subtests. But there also seem to be clusters of intellectual abilities that are somewhat independent of

†*D. Wechsler, "Intelligence Defined and Undefined: A Relative Appraisal,"* American Psychologist, *1975, 30, p. 138–39.*

one another; thus, some people may be better at visual skills, others at verbal ones. For example, a psychology professor we know is good at crossword puzzles (a verbal skill) but has a miserable sense of direction and often finds himself driving around in circles.

THE USES AND MISUSES OF INTELLIGENCE TESTING

The first intelligence tests in this country were greeted with tremendous enthusiasm. Within two and a half years of the first publication of a group IQ test, immediately after World War I, some 4 million children had been tested (Cronbach, 1975). The expansion of public education made it seem especially important to identify children's abilities so they could be given appropriate attention, whether this meant developing their special gifts or providing extra help where it was needed. As a result, the tests were eagerly snatched up by the school systems and colleges as a basis for student classification and guidance and for college admissions. As Cronbach notes, "The momentum of the tests overrode all criticism."

Today, however, criticism of IQ tests is on the rise. For example, the California legislature has voted to prohibit group mental testing in the schools, on the grounds that such tests limit

The blinded woman is trying to put the right pieces into the right holes. This form board test is used to measure mechanical ability.

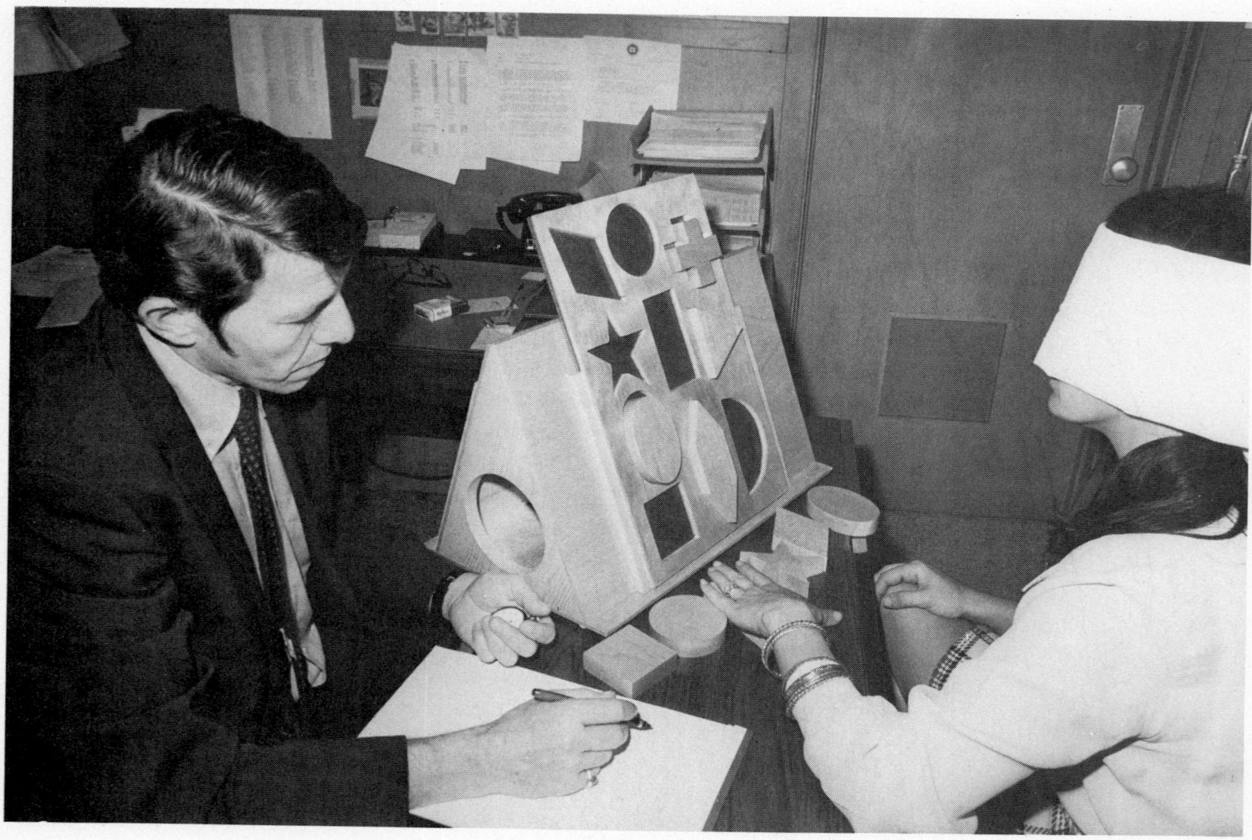

the education that black children receive (Cronbach, 1975). Many psychologists have also advocated a halt to testing, maintaining that the tests have done great harm by introducing irrelevant and unfair considerations into the way people are treated and by putting the students into "fast" or "slow" classes or categories that can influence their self-concepts and the attitudes of others toward them.

The most important use of IQ tests remains their ability to predict success in school. In fact, IQ tests are the single best predictor of scholastic success in the United States (McCall, 1975). Not everyone with a high IQ does well in school, of course, but few people do really well in school without having an above-average IQ. The fact that IQ scores predict school success suggests that a person's IQ might reveal other things as well, such as the sort of job that might be appropriate for that person or the sorts of interests that the person is likely to have.

On the other hand, it has been pointed out—with considerable justification—that extensive use of IQ tests may discriminate against blacks, Mexican-Americans and other minorities, and people from lower socio-economic backgrounds. On the average, people from these groups score lower than whites, Anglos, and people from more privileged socio-economic backgrounds. But this difference may not reflect fundamental intellectual differences so much as cultural differences. The tests are aimed primarily at traditional academic skills that are emphasized in white, middle-class culture. What's more, they were developed by middle-class whites and were standardized on middle-class white populations (Garcia, 1972). Critics contend that to use such "culture-specific" measures as a basis for making educational decisions about members of other cultural groups, such as blacks and the poor, is inappropriate and discriminatory.

Robert L. Williams, a black psychologist, has mounted a convincing argument against IQ testing, based in part on his own personal experience: "I was almost one of the testing casualties. At 15, I earned an IQ test score of 82, three points above the track of the special education class. Based on this score, my counselor suggested that I take up bricklaying because I was 'good with my hands.' My low IQ, however, did not allow me to see that as desirable" (1974, page 32). Instead Williams went to college, ultimately to earn a Ph.D. and become a professor of psychology. But, he adds, "Other blacks, equally as qualified, have been wiped out." To help remedy the situation, Williams and others have called for federal laws to regulate strictly—and in some cases to eliminate—the IQ testing of minority children. At the same time, Williams has been working on the development of new IQ tests that would be based on black rather than on white culture (see Box 1).

It must also be kept in mind that although IQ tests are rather good predictors of success in school, they do not necessarily predict success in other areas of life. IQ scores and school grades have been found to relate to how well people do their jobs in some occupations (such as being a stockbroker, which

INTELLIGENCE OR WORD GAMES?

"Suppose you are a ghetto resident in the Roxbury section of Boston. To qualify for being a policeman you have to take a three-hour-long general intelligence test in which you must know the meaning of words like 'quell,' 'pyromaniac,' and 'lexicon.' If you do not know enough of these words or cannot play analogy games with them, you do not qualify and must be satisfied with some such job as being a janitor for which an 'intelligence' test is not required yet by the Massachusetts Civil Service Commission. . . . Psychologists should be ashamed of themselves for promoting a view of general intelligence that has encouraged such a testing program, particularly when there is no solid evidence that significantly relates performance on this type of intelligence test with performance as a policeman" (McClelland, 1973, page 4).

Robert L. Williams

Box 1

The BITCH Test

"Scientific racism is part of the silent racial war," writes psychologist Robert Williams, "and the practitioners of it use intelligence tests as their hired guns" (1974, page 32).†

Williams believes that standard IQ tests, such as the Stanford-Binet and the Wechsler, are biased in favor of white values and white culture. It is not surprising, from this perspective, that on the average whites score higher than blacks on these tests. To make his point, Williams set out to develop an intelligence test that was biased in favor of black culture. He assembled 100 vocabulary items from the Afro-American slang dictionary and from his own knowledge of black culture. He called the test the Black Intelligence Test of Cultural Homogeneity (the BITCH test, for short).

†From R. L. Williams, "Scientific Racism and IQ: The Silent Mugging of the Black Community," Psychology Today, *May 1974, p. 32, 37. Copyright © 1974 Ziff-Davis Publishing Company. REPRINTED BY PERMISSION OF PSYCHOLOGY TODAY MAGAZINE.*

Here are some items from a later version of the BITCH test (known as the S.O.B. test). Check the letter with the correct meaning of each phrase as black people use it:

1. *the bump*
   a) a condition caused by a forceful blow
   b) a suit
   c) a car
   d) a dance
2. *running a game*
   a) writing a bad check
   b) looking for something
   c) directing a contest
   d) getting what one wants from another person or thing
3. *to get down*
   a) to dominate
   b) to travel
   c) to lower a position
   d) to have sexual intercourse
4. *cop an attitude*
   a) leave
   b) become angry
   c) sit down
   d) protect a neighbor
5. *leg*
   a) a sexual meaning
   b) a lower limb
   c) a white
   d) food

Not surprisingly, when Williams administered the BITCH test to 100 black and 100 white adolescents, he found that the blacks got much higher scores than the whites. He concludes: "Clearly, if black children are given a culture-specific test that is representative of their backgrounds, they will do better than white children taking the same test" (page 37).

Answers: 1—d; 2—d; 3—d; 4—b; 5—a.

requires verbal and mathematical skills), but not in others (such as being a factory worker or an air traffic controller).

David McClelland (1973) found that college grades had little relation to success in careers after college. He studied sixteen men from a class at Wesleyan University in the late 1940s. Half these men were top students while the other half had been poor students. About twenty years after these men had left college there seemed to be no differences in their career success. There were lawyers, doctors, research scientists, and teachers in both groups. The men with better grades did get into better law schools and medical schools, but even this supposed advantage did not produce notably more successful careers. Similar findings have been produced in the research of Holland and Richards (1965) and Elton and Shevel (1969). These researchers have shown that no consistent relationships exist between SAT scores of college students and their actual accomplishments in social leadership, the arts, science, music, writing, speech, and drama.

And yet businesses and industrial firms continue to use IQ tests as a basis for hiring and promotion, sometimes with discriminatory effects. The U. S. Supreme Court has recently spoken out against such unfair use of IQ tests. In 1971, Willie S. Griggs and twelve other black employees at the Duke Power Company argued in court that they could not move up in the company unless they got high school diplomas or else scored well on a pair of intelligence tests. Their lawyer did not charge that the company intended to discriminate against blacks. Nevertheless, they argued that in practice the tests had the effect of discriminating against employees who grew up in Southern black communities. The Supreme Court decided unanimously in favor of Griggs. No test or educational requirement can keep a person out of a job, the Court ruled, unless the test measures the specific talents needed to do that job (Harris, 1973).

Because of the undeniable limitations and misuses of IQ tests, some psychologists want to do away with them. McClelland (1973) suggests that educational testers stop talking about "intelligence" altogether and instead test for more specific sorts of competences that are relevant to effective performance in particular areas, such as communication skills, patience, and the ability to set reasonable goals for oneself. He also notes that reliance on paper-and-pencil tests is often inappropriate: "If you want to know how well a person can drive a car, sample his ability to do so by giving him a driver's test. Do not give him a pencil-and-paper test for following directions" (page 7).†

Most psychologists believe, however, that IQ tests do have important uses, especially in diagnosing learning problems and in helping provide the best possible education for all children. The important thing, they feel, is to make sure that the tests are used for appropriate purposes. For example, the California legis-

ARTIFICIAL INTELLIGENCE

Artificial intelligence is the name of a new science that is on the border between psychology and computer programming. Its major goal is to program computers to do "intelligent" things—to converse with human beings, play chess, recognize objects, solve abstract problems, and use common sense. Work in this field has practical importance; for example, developing computers of this type can help with such tasks as medical diagnosis. In the process of developing these computer programs, artificial-intelligence researchers are also learning more about the nature of human intelligence. So far the computers are not threatening to displace human beings. Even the most "intelligent" sophisticated machine cannot understand English nearly as well as a four-year-old child can (Winograd, 1974).

†*From D. C. McClelland, "Testing for Competence Rather Than for 'Intelligence,'"* American Psychologist, *1973, 28, p. 1–14.*

lature recently dropped one test for grades 6 through 10 that was thought to have no proper function, but at the same time they instituted a new, carefully safeguarded test for first graders to provide needed baseline information for reading instruction (Cronbach, 1975). As Cronbach states, "Sound policy is not for tests or against tests; what matters is how tests are used" (page 1).

THE HEREDITY-ENVIRONMENT ISSUE

One extreme view of intelligence is that it is a part of one's inheritance, transmitted from one's parents through the genes, much like eye color or blood type. Another extreme view is that heredity has nothing to do with one's intelligence—that it is totally a function of one's environment and experience. But neither of these extreme views is correct. In fact, intelligence is a product of both heredity and environment. But although virtually all psychologists would agree with this statement, there is still a great deal of controversy—and some confusion—about the relative importance of each of these factors in determining intelligence. To understand this issue, we first need to examine the concept of heritability.

Heritability of IQ

The *heritability* of any trait, whether eye color, height, or intelligence, is a statistic that reflects the amount of variation of that trait that is associated with differences in the genetic composition of the members of a particular group. Heritability is calculated on the basis of correlations between the traits of individuals who stand in different degrees of kinship to one another. A correlation expresses the degree to which two sets of measurements are associated with one another. If there was a perfect match between the IQs of parents and those of their children—the higher the parents' IQs, the higher the child's—the correlation between the two measures would be 1.00. If there were no relationship at all, the correlation would be .00. The higher the correlation, the higher the degree of positive association. (See the Appendix for a full explanation of the concept of correlation.)

The correlation between the IQs of parents and their children in fact falls at about .50 (Jensen, 1969; Erlenmayer-Kimling and Jarvik, 1963). This correlation suggests that there may be some hereditary component to IQ. But this, of course, is not the only interpretation of the correlation. It is also possible that the correlation reflects the fact that parents with high IQs are likely to create an intellectually stimulating environment for their children. Because of the interference of such environmental influences, some scientists have argued that it is impossible to calculate the heritability of IQ with any degree of accuracy.

Most scientists conclude, however, that IQ has a substantial heritability (at least within the white samples from which most of the data were obtained). One revealing comparison is between

correlations of IQ scores for pairs of identical twins and for pairs of fraternal twins. Identical twins develop from the same fertilized ovum and have all the same genes (see Chapter 11). Fraternal twins, in contrast, develop from two different fertilized eggs and are no more similar genetically than ordinary siblings. If IQ were highly heritable, therefore, we would expect the IQs of identical twins to be more highly correlated than the IQs of fraternal twins. This turns out to be the case. Combining results from various studies, the average IQ correlation for identical twins reared together is .87, and that for fraternal twins reared together is .56 (Jensen, 1969; Erlenmayer-Kimling and Jarvik, 1963). Moreover, the correlation between the IQs of identical twins reared apart (because one or both was put up for adoption) still tends to be higher (about .75) than the correlation between IQs of fraternal twins reared together, suggesting that common genes may be more important than common environment. On the basis of data like these, it is generally agreed that heredity accounts for at least 50 percent (and perhaps as much as 80 percent) of the variation in people's IQ scores within the populations that have been studied. As we will see, however, this does not imply anything at all about the reasons for differences in IQ scores *between* different groups.

WHEN BIGGER IS SMARTER

Even though identical twins tend to have very similar IQs, one or the other twin usually scores slightly higher than the other. Churchill (1965) discovered that the twin who weighs more at birth usually has a higher IQ. His explanation is that both body size and brain maturation may be stunted before birth as a consequence of unequal sharing of nutrients in the placenta.

The Effects of Environment

The fact that IQ has a substantial heritability does *not* imply that environment does not also have a large impact on IQ or that one's IQ cannot be changed. In fact, there is strong evidence that environmental factors can have a tremendous effect on IQ. One dramatic example was reported by psychologist H. M. Skeels (1966) in the 1930s. Skeels was working at an orphanage in Iowa. The infants lived in a bleak, unstimulating environment. Their cribs had white sheets draped over the sides, which prevented them from seeing other children, and there were no toys to play with. Human contacts were limited to overworked nurses. At two years of age, the child joined 30 to 35 other children in cramped quarters where they ate, slept, and played according to a rigid schedule.

Skeels noticed two baby girls who were "pitiful little creatures." They were undersized, sad, inactive, and spent most of their days whining and rocking back and forth in their beds. Some time later, he observed "two outstanding little girls. They were alert, smiling, running about, responding to the playful attention of adults, and generally behaving and looking like any other toddlers." He was surprised to learn that these were the same two babies he had seen before. He tested them and found they had almost normal IQs. He waited a year and tested them again. They now had a measured intelligence in the range of normal children their age.

Skeels found out that these little girls had each been "adopted" by an older retarded woman in the institution who devoted many hours each day to caring for the children. The employees of the institution also spent time with them doing a number of activities not available to the other children.

Skeels then decided to try an experiment with ten more orphans who had been rated as retarded. Each child was lodged with older retardates who could provide love, attention, and stimulation. The children were tested regularly for several years afterward. In every case, the children improved in health, happiness, maturity, and intelligence. They showed an increase in intelligence ranging from 7 to 58 IQ points, with an average increase of 28 IQ points. All but one of the children in Skeels's control group (who stayed in the orphanage) showed a loss in tested intelligence ranging from 8 to 45 IQ points, with the average loss close to 30 points.

When Skeels returned to study the children in both groups 30 years later, he found that the groups were even more different than before. The children who had been "mothered" by the older retardates were healthier, happier, better adjusted, and more productive than those who had not had the advantage of such human contact.

In much the same manner, it has been found that placement in a good home tends to raise the IQ of the adopted child beyond what would have been predicted from the IQ of the biological parent (Skodak and Skeels, 1949). Thus, the importance of environment cannot be underestimated in the development and improvement of IQ.

Social Class and IQ

A great many studies on social-class differences lead to the general conclusion that the average intelligence-test performance of children from upper-class and middle-class families is better than that of children from lower-class families. Such differences exist in almost all the studies, regardless of the tests and groups used. Coleman and his colleagues (1966), for example, reported that children of lower socio-economic status scored below the national averages on both verbal and nonverbal tests at all grades tested.

To what extent are these social-class differences attributable to hereditary factors, and to what extent are they attributable to the different environments and experiences of the different classes? Most of the evidence points to the importance of environment. The equal opportunity of the Israeli kibbutz (communal settlement) and the great diversity of the cultural backgrounds of its members present an opportunity to examine what can happen to IQ if social factors are equalized. Outside the kibbutz, Israeli children of European parents have a mean IQ of 105, but the mean IQ of children born to first-generation, "Oriental" Jews (from North African and Middle Eastern countries) is only 85. Some would suspect that the difference is genetic. However, when children of both groups were raised for four years in the kibbutz nursery, they achieved exactly the same mean IQ score—115 (Garcia, 1972). Just what is the cause of this change? In pursuing this question, Garcia speculated that the kibbutz environment was more likely than the Oriental home to emphasize the sorts of intellectual skills that IQ tests measure.

Race and IQ: The Jensen Controversy

The fact that cultural differences in IQ scores exist is well known. It is also known that there are racial differences in IQ scores. Many psychologists have observed that *on the average* the tested IQ of blacks is about 15 points lower than that of whites. Both blacks and whites score at all points along the IQ continuum, but there are proportionately more blacks at the lower end of the scale and more whites at the higher end of the scale. What accounts for these differences? Arthur Jensen exploded this issue into a major controversy when he asserted that the difference is accounted for primarily by heredity. It is his belief that heredity is responsible for about 80 percent of the IQ differences among individuals and that innate differences may exist between blacks and whites.

Jensen does not dispute that environmental factors play a part in the obtained differences. As he stated, "No one, to my knowledge, questions the role of environmental factors, including influences from past history, in determining at least some of the variance between racial groups in standard measures of intelligence, school performance, and occupational status" (1969b, pages 79–80). But Jensen also feels that genetic factors in racial behavioral differences have been greatly ignored because of a social taboo against even discussing such possibilities.

The concepts of genotype and phenotype (see Chapter 11) help in understanding Jensen's argument. Genotype refers to the gene structure of an individual—his or her fixed genetic makeup. Phenotype refers to the actual physical, anatomical, and psychological characteristics of a person and always reflects a *combination* of genetic and environmental influences. Jensen attempted to determine the relative proportion of these two influences in determining the phenotypic trait we call intelligence. He estimated that environment accounts for approximately 20 percent of the variability in IQ and that genetic factors account for the remaining 80 percent. He made his case with statistics derived from the studies of identical twins reared apart and of unrelated children reared together.

Jensen's view stirred up a cyclone of controversy that has not yet died down. Many psychologists condemned his findings on the grounds that his statistics were faulty, his evidence inadequate, and his conclusions illogical. In an attempt to demonstrate the error in Jensen's logic, Whitten and Kagan (1969) used the example of height. They point out that children who live in Central or South American countries are much shorter than children who live in the urban areas of those countries. According to Jensen's theory, the shorter stature of the rural children must be due to differences in genetic constitution. The truth is, however, that the reason these rural children are shorter is that they are subjected to disease and malnutrition. As a matter of fact, the heights of children in most areas of the world have increased substantially during the past 20 years, because of better nutrition and mass immunization against disease. Thus, the differences in height between individuals who have had the same nutrition and health may be largely hereditary, but differences in height between two groups that have had different levels of nutrition and health may be due primarily to environmental differences. The same argument would apply to racial or other group differences in IQ.

Jensen's critics further point out that when blacks and whites from similar cultural backgrounds are compared, differences in IQ scores diminish greatly, and the more similar in background, the smaller the difference. What all this adds up to is that although IQ has been shown to have substantial heritability within white populations, this data doesn't really tell us anything about the reason for the differences between white and black IQ scores. In fact, there is no direct evidence that the black-white difference in IQ is genetic in origin.

One recent study helps to emphasize the enormous role that environment can play in black-white differences. Scarr-Salapatek and Weinberg (1975) measured the IQs of black children who were adopted and raised by white families in Minneapolis. In all cases, the children were reared in a more affluent environment than the one they were born in. The researchers found that the children's IQs were considerably higher than would have been expected if they had remained in an impoverished environment. Moreover, the earlier in life the children were adopted, the higher their IQs tended to be, pointing to the importance of early-life experiences. These researchers were not suggesting that trans-racial adoption itself is a good thing. Indeed, many black action groups feel that it is not good for the child's sense of identity and are putting pressure on adoption agencies to stop this practice. But Scarr-Salapatek and Weinberg's data provide additional evidence for the contention that black-white IQ differences are not inevitable.

INTELLIGENCE THROUGH THE LIFE CYCLE

Intelligence develops most dramatically in the earliest years of life. Benjamin Bloom (1964) has estimated that half of a child's intellectual potential is established by age 4 and most of it before age 8. Some psychologists believe that the critical time period for the development of intelligence is even earlier—between 8 and 18 months. This is the period during which children learn to get around the house on their own, begin to use language, and acquire basic skills of interacting with others. During this period the child's experience may play a major role in the development of intellectual abilities. This is why many psychologists and educators are now stressing the need for extremely early educational programs, beginning at birth (Pines, 1975).

It is very difficult to predict what a child's IQ will be in later years on the basis of IQ tests administered in the first few years of life. This may partly be due to the fact that intelligence is developing so fast during the early years and that its development depends greatly on experience. Another reason for the lack of predictability is that preschool intelligence tests cannot include school-type verbal or mathematical questions. Instead, they rely mainly on nonverbal abilities, such as visual-motor coordination (for example, the baby's ability to grasp an object). These measures may reflect a different sort of intelligence than the paper-and-pencil measures used in later years.

From the time the child enters school until early adulthood, his or her intellectual skills continue to increase, although not quite so dramatically as in the earlier years. In general, it is possible to predict an adult's IQ fairly well from his or her IQ score at age 6 or 7. The correlation between IQs at ages 6 and 18, based on studies in which people were tested at both points in their lives, is .77, indicating a good deal of consistency in people's performance on such tests (Brown and Herrnstein, 1975). But in spite of this general consistency, some people's IQs change markedly during the childhood years and during adolescence. Large shifts can and do take place, and they can go upward or downward on the scale. In fact, between the ages of 6 and 10, 15 to 20 percent of all children's IQ scores change by at least 15 points, and some children's scores change by as much as 60 points (Whitten and Kagan, 1969). As Brown and Herrnstein (1975) point out, IQ is a statistical trait and thus carries with it an amount of uncertainty. It is not a fixed characteristic like eye color, but rather is somewhat flexible, like one's state of health.

Until very recently, psychologists believed that people's intellectual capacity leveled off in their twenties and thirties, and then started to decline gradually in middle age and more rapidly in old age. Those people now in their thirties and forties should therefore be gratified by recent research suggesting that in fact intelligence does not generally decline with advancing years. According to these studies, intelligence actually increases on many measures well into the seventies (Baltes and Schaie, 1974).

Most of the earlier studies of intelligence in adulthood and old age may have been misleading, because they were *cross-sectional*; that is, they were conducted at a single point in time and measured a group of people of differing ages. Using this approach, the younger people tested higher in general than the older ones. But the younger people were also born in a time of greater educational opportunities and this may have been a factor in their higher intelligence. When a *longitudinal* study was done, in which individuals were tested at two points in time (in

THE WISE IDIOT

"Idiot savant" is a misleading label given to retarded persons who are neither wise nor idiots. They are most often slightly or moderately retarded people who display a single, incredible mental talent totally different from their otherwise limited intellectual capacity. A number of idiot savants are "calendar calculators" who can accurately tell the day of the week on which any date in history fell. Other idiot savants possess specialized knowledge of trivial facts (batting averages over the years, positions of the planets in time, and so on). Since accurate early histories of idiot savants are not usually available, little is known about the causes of such capacities.

1956 and 1963), people at all age levels showed increases in verbal comprehension, numerical skills, and inductive reasoning. On the average, people's visual-motor coordination skills did decline with advanced age, perhaps as a result of a biological slowing-down. On the basis of their overall results, Baltes and Schaie concluded that "intellectual decline [throughout adulthood and old age] is largely a myth."

THE MENTALLY RETARDED

The size of the challenge of mental retardation in our society is enormous. Hormuth (1963) estimated there are nearly 6 million mentally retarded adults and children in America—about 3 percent of the total population. This means there are only four seriously disabling conditions that are more prevalent than retardation—mental illness, heart disease, arthritis, and cancer.

Technically, degrees of retardation are determined by performance on a standardized intelligence test. In fact, however, an implicit judgment is made of the degree to which the retardate will be able to manage self-care and live in a technologically advanced society.

Degrees of Retardation

Retarded people used to be given different labels based on the degree of their retardation: "idiots" were the most seriously retarded, "imbeciles" were at the next level, and "morons" were the least seriously retarded. But these terms came to be used in ways that went beyond their original technical meaning. Phrases such as "You idiot!" are now used as general insults, more often than not directed at people of at least average intelligence. As a result, a less derogatory set of categories for classifying levels of retardation is now in use.

The following is a description of individuals at each level of mental retardation (Robinson and Robinson, 1970).

Borderline mental retardation. The persons in this category have tested IQs in the range of 68 to 83. Children in this group are often placed in "slow learner" classes in school and are able to achieve some degree of education, even though the majority do not graduate from high school. With some education and training they are able to become self-sufficient adults, with jobs and adequate social adjustment. Few people in this IQ range are actually diagnosed as mentally retarded (they are not included in the estimate of 6 million retarded people in the United States).

Mild mental retardation. People are placed in this category if their tested IQs fall in the 52 to 67 range. About 90 percent of persons with IQs lower than 67 fall in this category. Children in this IQ range are eligible for special classes for the educable mentally retarded. As adults they are usually able to handle unskilled jobs, and only a very small percentage are institutionalized.

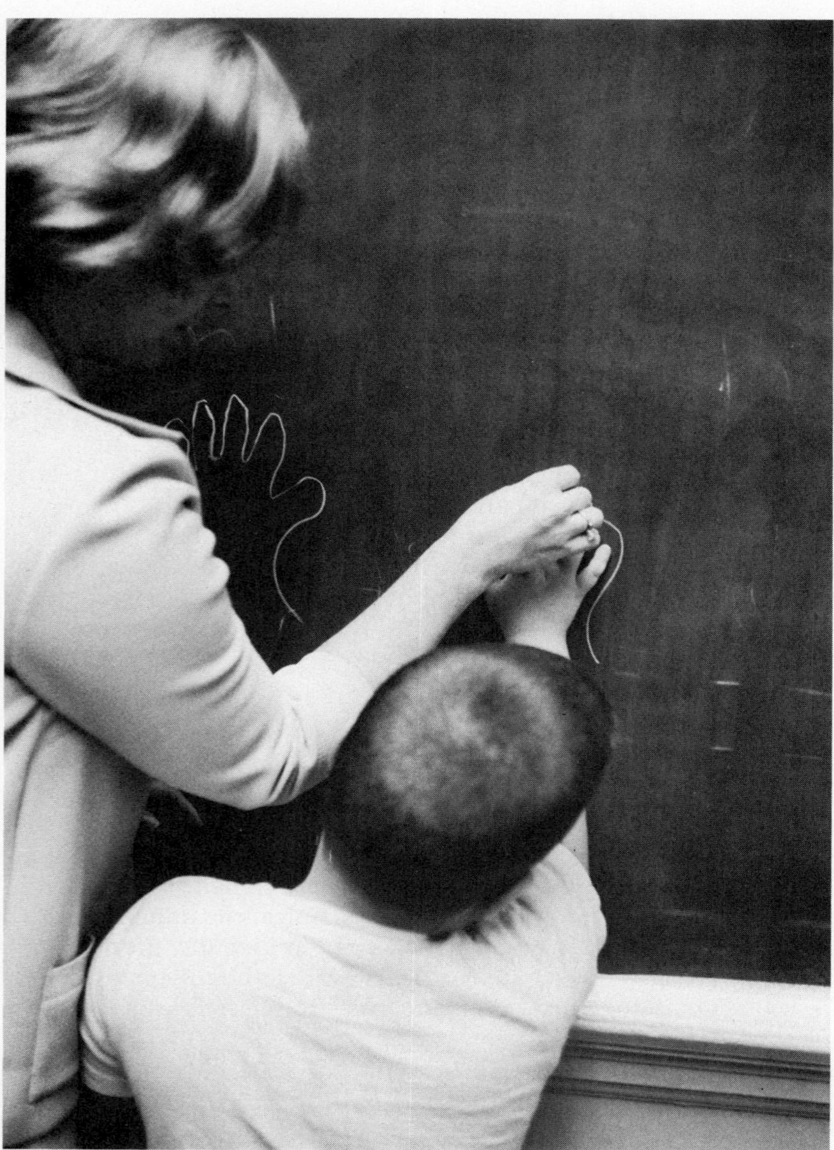

Moderate mental retardation. Persons whose IQs fall in the 36 to 51 range are placed in this category. Their retardation is often associated with brain damage and other physical problems. They have poor sensorimotor coordination and in early childhood are noticeably slow in learning verbal and social skills. They can be trained to take care of themselves and may be capable of doing useful work. Many people in this category have been institutionalized.

Severe mental retardation. This category contains those persons who score in the 20 to 35 range on IQ tests. Most people in this group require constant care and supervision, although some can learn to handle various self-needs with extensive training. For this reason most people in this group are institutionalized, whereas those in the higher IQ groups are usually cared for at home. As adults the severely retarded may be friendly, but they are capable of only limited communication.

Profound mental retardation. This group contains the small minority (1.5 percent of the retarded) whose intellectual level is so low (below 20 IQ) that they must have their needs attended to by others throughout their lives. They seem capable of very little learning besides how to walk, say a few words, feed themselves, and go to the toilet. Many have other disabilities as well, and the mortality rate in childhood for this group is quite high.

A distinction is often made between those children who are *educable* mentally retarded and those who are *trainable* mentally retarded (Davison and Neale, 1974). In general, those in the mildly retarded category (IQ of 52 to 67) are considered educable; they are expected to be able to reach an academic level equal to a sixth-grade education. Those in the moderately retarded category (IQ of 36 to 51) are considered trainable in that they can be taught to care for themselves and to carry out routine tasks that do not require "academic" sorts of learning.

Causes of Retardation

In the first decade of this century, scientists viewed "feeblemindedness" as the stunted development of the brain's intellectual capacity. They thought the chief cause of this problem was the absence of cells in some layers of the cerebral cortex ("lack of

Box 2

Brothers and Sisters of Retarded Children

Frances Kaplan Grossman (1972) explored the way brothers and sisters were affected by living with their retarded sibling. She recruited 83 college-student volunteers who had a retarded brother or sister. One-half of this sample was selected from a highly competitive, expensive eastern college (Private U), and half came from a much less expensive local college (Community U). Grossman and her coworkers found that a number of students apparently benefited from the experience of growing up with handicapped siblings, but they also identified a number who had been harmed. Those who seemed to have been harmed often manifested bitter resentment toward their family situation. They had guilt about the rage they felt toward their parents and the retarded sibling, and they had feared that they themselves might be defective. Often they had been deprived of the personal attention they needed, because so much family time and energy had to be given to their handicapped sibling.

For the Community U students, lack of money was often a serious limitation that affected their manner of caring for the retarded child. The parents were often poorly educated and, in the eyes of their children, unable to cope with the burden of a retarded child. The primary goal of many of these families was simple financial survival. As each child became old enough to help out, he or she was expected to share the burdens of family life.

Overall, the effect of a retardate in the family was much the same for brothers and sisters in Community U as for those in Private U. There was, however, a significant difference in the role of girls in well-to-do families and in poorer families. The young women whose financial circumstances were modest had been expected to assume a major share of responsibility for handicapped siblings. From an early age, they spent enormous amounts of time with the retarded child. In the well-to-do families, affluence removed some of the burden of direct care from the sisters.

gray matter"), and this defect was assumed to be a hereditary condition in most cases. The feeling then was that feeblemindedness was irreversible (Bucklew, 1969). We now know, however, that a number of factors, including some that are preventable or reversible, are involved in mental retardation.

Organic causes. In about 25 percent of the cases of retardation, the condition can be traced to specific organic or physiological causes. These tend to be the most severe cases. Organic causes of retardation are of three main types: genetic, prenatal environment influences, and physical damage during birth.

Few of the genetic puzzles of retardation have been solved. Two exceptions are *Down's syndrome,* which is apparently produced by certain chromosomal abnormalities, and PKU (phenylketonuria), a relatively rare metabolic disorder. PKU can be brought under control by establishing a proper diet early in life; otherwise, the victim becomes severely limited in intellectual development (see Chapter 11).

Among the many prenatal environmental influences on the child's mental development are maternal health, maternal use of various drugs or exposure to radiation, physical trauma (automobile accidents, for example), and endocrine disorders. It has been found, for example, that if a woman contracts German measles (rubella) during the first three months of pregnancy, the child is likely to develop mental defects.

The infant's birth may also be hazardous, since brain damage can occur as a result of inappropriately administered anaesthesia, prolonged delivery, asphyxia (lack of oxygen), or injury from mechanical instruments (forceps) used to assist a difficult delivery.

Cultural-familial factors. About three-fourths of retardates—typically those with the least severe retardation—do not have any known physiological defects (Zigler, 1967). These cases of retardation are generally considered to result from deprived family conditions and are called *cultural-familial retardation.* Although the relative importance of heredity and environment in these cases is difficult to determine, it seems clear that poverty can contribute to retardation. Davison and Neale (1974) suggest many possible conditions in the deprived child's environment that might contribute to retardation: poor diet of the mother during pregnancy; the child's eating of lead-based paint or plaster chipped off the walls in old apartment buildings; lack of intellectual stimulation by other family members; and lack of stimulation in the neighborhood, which the child seldom leaves. We do not yet understand very well which of these factors may be most crucial and precisely how they work to limit intellectual development. What is clear, however, is that many such cases of retardation could be prevented if poverty conditions were reduced or eliminated.

HIDDEN TALENT

Yoshihiko Yamamoto is a mentally retarded young man in Japan. He was diagnosed as suffering from hydrocephalus, an abnormal accumulation of fluid on the brain. He has never scored more than 47 on an IQ test (the Japanese version of the Stanford-Binet). And he has a hearing defect that has caused his speech to be nearly unintelligible. But Yoshihiko Yamamoto is also an outstanding artist and printmaker who has won prizes in artistic competitions and has gained a wide reputation. Although his verbal skills are poor, his visual perception and memory are above average. When encouraged by a special education teacher, his talent blossomed (Morishima, 1975).

Training the Mentally Retarded

Regardless of whether a case of retardation involves a physiological defect, retarded individuals remain responsive to rewards

and punishment in their environment. Thus, learning theorists, such as Ullmann and Krasner (1975) stress the role of rewards and punishments in shaping a retardate's behavior; in fact, parents' uses of reinforcements may actually limit the retardate's development of skills. For example, once parents find out that their child is retarded, they might fail to reinforce the child for asking simple questions or for performing simple tasks, even though these behaviors are an important part of the learning process. They might also reinforce the wrong behavior, such as being very quiet all the time, or they might inflict punishment that is so severe that the child stops engaging in all sorts of other behaviors besides the one that is being punished.

But learning principles, when used knowledgeably, can be extremely effective in training retarded people. Behavior therapists have used operant conditioning to get responses from even the most severely retarded children and adults—those who had previously emitted very few responses. They have taught some of these persons to respond to the environment at a very simple level such as that of toilet training. A variety of self-help behaviors such as feeding and dressing have been taught to persons once thought unteachable.

Using positive reinforcement (in the form of token rewards that can be exchanged for various privileges) has produced some striking results in the retarded. Girardeau and Spradlin (1964), for example, worked with institutionalized girls with IQs ranging from 20 to 50 and trained them to acquire the skills needed to live successfully in their home community. The researchers used bronze tokens (which could be traded for candy, pop, fancy underwear, cosmetics, records, and so on) to reinforce the girls when they displayed desirable behavior (making their bed, setting their hair, showering properly, being on time). The girls were mildly punished for disapproved behavior—for a fixed period of time they were not allowed to earn tokens. The program not only succeeded with the girls, but also provided a tremendous boost to the morale of the staff members at the institution, since they could see clear evidence of the girls' progress.

The Retardate in Society

The mentally deficient child, despite an intellectual handicap, is still a sensitive human being who experiences anger and resentment as well as love and acceptance. Such children can sense the mood of the people they depend on. McKinney and Keele (1963) reported that severely retarded boys responded positively to extra attention from others. If the retarded child has an accepting and supporting environment during the growing years, he or she may later obtain employment, get married, and become a productive member of society.

At the moment, only 4 percent of retarded cases are institutionalized. These retardates are often the products of broken homes, homes that could not provide for them, and homes legally judged to be grossly inadequate (Benda et al., 1963). Whatever the degree of their retardation, few of these children receive visitors or gifts during their years of hospitalization (Zigler, 1967). It seems that some parents respond to retarded children not as the "infants of God," as they were viewed in the Middle Ages, but as the "infants of the Devil," as they were regarded in the times of the Protestant Reformation.

THE INTELLECTUALLY GIFTED

At the other end of the range of intellectual capacity are those people who have extremely high intellectual potential—the intellectually *gifted.* As we noted earlier in the chapter, people's measured intelligence may have relatively little to do with their success in nonscholastic aspects of life. It remains true, however, that people who achieve eminence in science, law, politics, literature, the arts, and other fields are likely to have unusually high intelligence. The signs of future intellectual achievements are sometimes seen early in life. For example, Macaulay began his career as a historian at age 6 with what he called a "Compendium of Universal History," filling about 25 pages before losing interest in the project. At age 11, Pascal was so interested in mathematics that his father deprived him of books on the subject until he had first learned Latin and Greek. But Pascal proceeded

AND NOW WE MEASURE FAMOUS MEN

Cox (1926) made use of extensive biographical information to estimate the IQs in early life of 300 famous people. The average of the estimated IQs was 155. The following are some of her estimates:

Sir Francis Galton	200
John Stuart Mill	190
Johann W. von Goethe	185
Samuel Taylor Coleridge	175
Voltaire	170
Alfred, Lord Tennyson	155
Sir Walter Scott	150
Wolfgang Amadeus Mozart	150
Henry Wadsworth Longfellow	150
Thomas Jefferson	145
John Milton	145
Benjamin Franklin	145
Napoleon Bonaparte	135
Charles Darwin	135

secretly to construct a geometry of his own—getting as far as the 32nd proposition of Euclid. And at 14, Leibnitz was writing on logic and philosophy and composing what he called "An Alphabet of Human Thought" (Terman, 1954).

The most famous study of gifted children was begun by Lewis M. Terman in the early 1920s. He located almost 1,500 children with IQs of 140 or higher to use in his study. The purpose of the research, in his words, was "first of all, to find what traits characterize children of high IQ, and secondly, to follow them for as many years as possible to see what kind of adults they might become" (Terman, 1954). After carefully choosing a representative sample of high-IQ children and a control group of normal-IQ children, Terman and his associates examined the children through physical measurements, medical examinations, achievement tests, interest tests, and other information provided by parents and teachers.

In fulfilling the first purpose of his study, Terman found that the gifted children were, in general, healthier, better adjusted, superior in moral attitudes (as measured by certain tests of character), and far more advanced in mastery of school subjects than children in the control group.

The other part of Terman's study is still continuing (even though Terman died in 1956). The gifted individuals in the study have been subject to follow-up interviews and questionnaires several times since the 1920s. These follow-up studies have shown that the incidence of death, illness, insanity, and alcoholism is lower for this group than for the overall population. These gifted individuals have been well-educated and have pursued professional careers, despite the fact that they spent their young adult lives weathering the Depression. Terman was particularly pleased that these studies indicated that the gifted person does not fit the stereotypical picture of the mental giant with a withered body and poor social abilities. The "bright children" in Terman's study not only continued to be bright into late adulthood, but they were also healthy and socially adjusted.

Studies such as Terman's give rise to the question: Just what makes someone intellectually gifted? And going beyond high intelligence, what makes someone a "genius"—someone who makes creative and lasting contributions to civilization? Surely both heredity and environment are involved. But just what sort of environment is needed to nourish particular sorts of intellectual potential? This is a challenging question for which psychologists do not yet have a full answer.

SUMMARY

1. *Intelligence* may be defined as the capacity to learn about and understand the world and to apply this knowledge in order to cope with life's challenges.
2. Among the first tests developed for assessing intelligence were the Binet, the Stanford-Binet, and the Wechsler. The

Stanford-Binet is still in use; it emphasizes primarily verbal skills. The *Wechsler tests,* also in use today, focus on both verbal and performance skills. Both tests are administered individually; other kinds of tests have been developed for group testing.

3. A child's IQ score is computed by dividing *mental age* (as measured by an intelligence test) by chronological age and multiplying by 100. An adult's IQ score is determined by comparing his or her test results with those of a large sample.
4. The *standardization* of an intelligence test involves obtaining test scores from a large representative sample. An effort is made to develop a test that will produce a bell-shaped curve, or normal distribution, when administered to a large number of people.
5. Spearman considered intelligence to be a single factor (which he called *g*), while Thurstone thought intelligence comprised eight primary abilities. Most likely, a combination of these two theories is closer to the truth.
6. Intelligence testing has been criticized as discriminatory toward blacks, minorities, and people from lower socioeconomic backgrounds. It has been suggested that the tests are aimed primarily at skills and knowledge emphasized in white, middle-class culture.
7. IQ test scores are the single best predictor of scholastic success. However, IQ scores don't necessarily predict success in other areas of life, such as in a career. Nevertheless, employers have come to rely so heavily on testing that they have unintentionally become discriminatory toward blacks and minorities. To avoid such abuse, intelligence tests should be given only in appropriate situations.
8. The *heritability* of a trait is a statistic that reflects the amount of variation of that trait that is associated with differences in the genetic composition of the members of a particular group. It is based on correlations between traits of individuals who are related to each other in varying degrees.
9. Most scientists conclude, on the basis of correlational studies of fraternal and identical twins, that IQ has a substantial heritability. It is generally agreed that heredity accounts for at least 50 percent of the variation in people's IQ scores within the populations that have been studied.
10. The influence of environment on IQ has been seen in studies such as that of Skeels, who found that orphans given special attention, love, and stimulation grew up healthier and happier and showed increases in IQ scores, whereas orphans who did not receive the special treatment actually showed decreases in measured IQ. Other evidence of environmental influences comes from the Israeli kibbutz. Children from disparate cultures and backgrounds have

achieved similar mean IQ scores in the kibbutz environment.

11. Arthur Jensen has suggested that heredity is responsible for about 80 percent of the IQ differences that are known to exist between racial and cultural groups. His suggestion has raised a storm of controversy. Jensen's critics cite data that demonstrate the important effects environmental differences can have on what are considered highly heritable traits. They also point to data showing that blacks and whites of similar backgrounds score similarly on IQ tests and to other studies showing that black-white IQ differences are not inevitable.
12. It is estimated that half a child's intellectual potential is established by age 4 and most of it before age 8—and the critical learning period may be even earlier. Most people's IQs stay consistent between the ages of 8 and 18, but some people's IQs change markedly during this period.
13. Contrary to popular belief, intelligence does not generally decline with advancing years. In fact, intelligence actually increases on some measures well into the seventies.
14. Intelligence tests are used to help classify levels of mental retardation. Current categories of retardation are: Borderline (68–83 IQ), mild (52–67 IQ), moderate (36–51 IQ), severe (20–35 IQ), and profound (below 20 IQ).
15. Children with IQs in the mild mental retardation range are considered *educable* and are expected to reach an academic level equal to a sixth-grade education. Those in the moderately retarded category are considered *trainable*—they can be taught to care for themselves and to perform routine tasks.
16. Among organic (physical) causes of mental retardation are genetic defects, prenatal environmental influences, and physical damage during birth. Most retardates, however, have no known physical defects. Their problem, called *cultural-familial retardation,* results from deprived family conditions.
17. Operant conditioning techniques have been used to teach even the most severely retarded individuals to respond to their environment. Systems of reinforcement and mild punishment have been highly successful in teaching such people simple behaviors. However, only a very small percentage of retarded cases are institutionalized. With love and support during childhood, most retardates can grow up to work, marry, and become productive members of society.
18. Lewis Terman found that *intellectually gifted* children—those who scored extremely high on IQ tests—grew up to be healthier, better adjusted, and more successful than people from similar backgrounds with lower IQ scores.

Education

Almost everyone would agree that a society's educational system—its schools—is one of its most vital resources. A tremendous amount of time, energy, and money is devoted to education in America. However, American schools have in recent years been subjected to a tremendous barrage of criticism. The schools have been accused of failing to do their job and of being in a state of crisis. In this Issue we will take a look at some of these criticisms. Then we'll examine some of the alternatives and innovations that are being proposed as ways of improving education, ranging from "free schools" such as Summerhill to the use of computers in teaching.

Schools in Crisis

Critics of today's educational system point to some basic problems in today's schools. Silberman (1970), for example, has decried the oppressiveness of American schools, their barren atmosphere, and the contempt that teachers and principals unconsciously display toward children. Postman and Weingartner (1969) charge that our educational system is a poor guide for leading the young into the future. They say that the educational establishment is not daring enough or vigorous enough to furnish ideas for a new approach to education, and they invoke the names of other educational critics in their cry for reform:

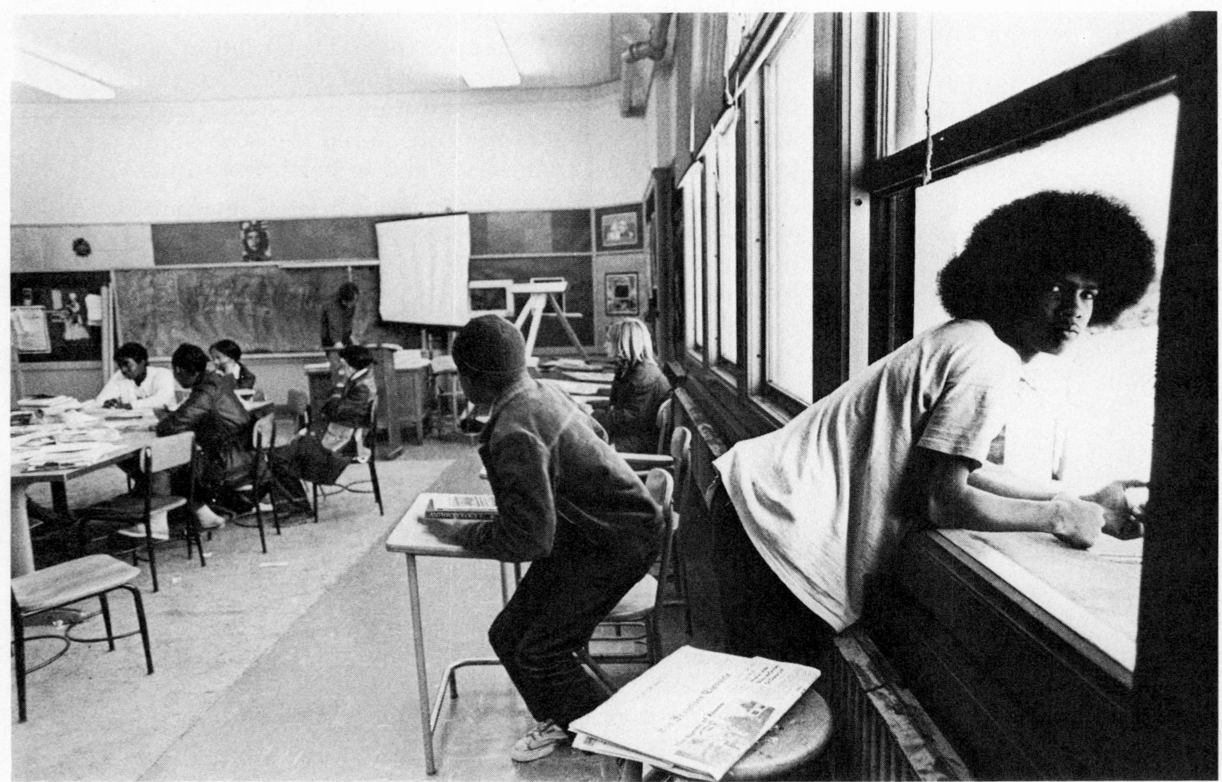

The institution we call "school" is what it is because we made it that way. If it is irrelevant, as Marshall McLuhan says; if it shields children from reality, as Norbert Wiener says; if it educates for obsolescence, as John Gardner says; if it does not develop intelligence, as Jerome Bruner says; if it is based on fear, as John Holt says; if it avoids the promotion of significant learnings, as Carl Rogers says; if it induces alienation, as Paul Goodman says; if it punishes creativity and independence, as Edgar Friedenberg says; if, in short, it is not doing what needs to be done, it can be changed; it must be changed. [*page xiv*]

Others have pointed out that none of these problems are new. Colin Greer (1972) notes that it is fashionable these days to talk of the decline of the public school—as if there was a time in some golden past when schools made equal opportunity available to children of every economic and social class. The truth is that our public schools have always failed the lower classes—both white and black. Current educational problems stem not from the fact that the schools have changed, but from the fact that schools continue to do precisely the job they have always done.

Echoing this view is Peter F. Drucker (1972), who says, "Today's school does no poorer a job than it did yesterday; the school has simply done a terribly poor job all along. But what we tolerated in the past can no longer be tolerated." What today's educational crisis really involves, then, is a heightened awareness of the shortcomings of our educational system and a major concern over what to do about the problems that seem inherent in it.

The truth is that our public schools have always failed the lower class—both white and black.

Self-Fulfilling Prophecies

Many of the criticisms of education in America are general and are hard to document. But there are several areas in which studies have shown specific difficulties in the system. One such problem was brought to light in some famous studies on "self-fulfilling prophecy" in the classroom.

Self-fulfilling prophecy refers to the fact that our expectations can influence or bring about the thing we expect to happen. Robert Rosenthal (1966) demonstrated this effect in the laboratory when he carried out experiments with groups of rats that were designated either "bright" or "dull." In one experiment, twelve psychology students were each given five laboratory rats of the same strain. Six of the students were told that their rats had been bred for brightness in running a maze. The other six were informed that their rats, for obscure genetic reasons, would probably be poor at running a maze. When the two groups of students taught the rats to run the maze, the rats expected to be good at maze running actually turned out to be better performers. Expectations alone, it seems, can produce positive changes in "learning" ability. (This phenomenon was described in the box on experimenter effects in Chapter 1.)

Expectations alone, it seems, can produce positive changes in "learning" ability.

How did this come about? Apparently, the experimenters handled the rats differently depending on what they had been told about them. That is, the rats were treated more or less roughly, taken out of the maze more or less quickly, and so on, depending on the expectations. This difference obviously influenced the performance of the rats.

Rosenthal and Lenore Jacobson, an elementary school principal, decided to see whether this sort of effect held true for teachers dealing with children in schools (Rosenthal and Jacobson, 1968). In their experiment, they led teachers to believe (at the beginning of a school year) that certain of their pupils could be expected to show a marked academic improvement during the year. These pupils were called "late bloomers." The teachers assumed these predictions were based on tests administered to the students the previous school year. They did not know that the children designated as late bloomers were chosen at random from the class. Intelligence tests administered after the experiment had been in progress several months then revealed that these later bloomers had indeed improved more than other children—evidently because their teachers expected them to.

How do these effects take place in the classroom? Rosenthal and Jacobson do not believe that teachers bring them about intentionally. Most likely, they result from the subtle ways in which teachers interact with students—their facial expressions, tone of voice, and manner—all of which may have the effect of conveying the expectation to the student. For example, if a teacher thinks that a student has hidden intellectual potential, he or she may wait for a longer time, wearing an encouraging expression, while the child fumbles for the answer to a question. If the teacher's expectations were lower, he or she might give up quickly, with a gesture of resignation. The result may be that the first child develops a more positive attitude about himself and works harder than the second.

One conclusion that many have made from this study is that the problem of poor learning in the schools might rest not so much with the children as with the expectations the teacher has for them. Just as a teacher may subtly act to help a student become a "late bloomer," so, too, may a teacher's expectations of failure influence the child to do poorly.

Free Schools

One solution to the stagnant educational system is an alternative type of school, such as the various "free schools" which have sprung up across the country. The prototype for this type of school is Summerhill, a school founded by A. S. Neill in England in 1921. Neill later wrote a highly influential book about the school and its philosophy. Neill felt the book *Summerhill* (1960) had impact because it voiced what so many of the young felt but had not been able to put into words. The theme of the book was freedom in education for all to grow at their own pace, freedom from indoctrination, and freedom for children to live in their own community, making their own social laws. Neill would abolish nearly every school subject in favor of only creative pursuits, such as art, music, and drama.

Writing in a foreword to Neill's book, Erich Fromm described this radical approach to education and child rearing in terms of these principles:

> A firm faith in the essential goodness of children.
>
> A belief that education must be both emotional and intellectual and must have happiness as its aim.

A conviction that punishment creates fear and fear creates hostility.

A declaration that freedom does not mean license.

A belief that education must help children cut their primary ties to parents and other authority figures, if they are truly to become individuals.

A dedication to rearing children to become happy human beings rather than to fit into the existing social order.

Neill's Summerhill children were not required to do things they did not wish to do. And they were allowed to do almost anything they wished, as long as they did not infringe upon the rights of others. Neill's principles have been adopted as a basis for many American free schools, which have been touted as the ideal form of education upon which public education should be patterned. But free schools are not without drawbacks. Jonathan Kozol recently expressed some pointed criticisms of free schools after having observed many of the schools in operation. One problem is that students are not quite sure how to deal with the freedom in order to actually learn something. Says Kozol (1972):

"We're into a new thing," I hear the high-school students say. "We're into ecology," or "into women's liberation," or "into communes." It isn't that each of these items might not be a thing worth being "into." The trouble is the fantasy these students have: (a) that they are freely choosing each thing they go "into"; (b) that to be "into" something only for the length of time it takes to try and fail is of any real worth to other human beings. [*page 10*]

Some critics suggest that schools may not work as well as they should, because they start too late.

Preschool Education

Some critics suggest that schools may not work as well as they should, because they start too late. As we noted in Chapter 8, most of a child's intellectual potential seems to be developed before he or she even enters school. The Head Start program, which offered instruction to children between the ages of three and five, was one approach to the need for preschool education. But many psychologists now believe that even this age may be too late. Developmental psychologist Burton White believes that the present educational system is misdirected: "We spend nothing on a child's most important years [especially the first three], when the foundations of his educational capacity are being set. Then we spend more and more as he grows older, when he needs it less and less" (quoted by Pines, 1975). White and others are trying to reverse these priorities, by launching large-scale preschool educational programs. An essential part of these programs is to teach the parents of infants how to promote their children's

intellectual development—for example, by encouraging them to actively explore their environment. If these programs prove successful, White believes, it will lead to a total reevaluation of our educational priorities.

Another sort of preschool education has been under way for some years now and seems to be quite successful. This is the teaching that takes place through children's television programs, such as the pioneering *Sesame Street* and *Electric Company.* As a result of these programs, there are many two-year-olds who are learning to identify letters of the alphabet, three-year-olds who can spell words, and four-year-olds who are beginning to read. Their parents may decide that these children are brilliant, but that is not necessarily the case. They are merely taking advantage of the learning resources that are being made available to them.

My Teacher, the Computer

One of the most exciting innovations in education is *computer-assisted instruction* (CAI). Richard Atkinson (1974) has used computers with great success to help children learn to read. His system makes use of simple teletypewriters and audio headsets. First-, second-, and third-graders in different parts of the country get CAI reading instruction for 15 to 30 minutes a day—all linked to a central computer at Stanford University. The instruction begins when the student types in R (for "reading"), an ID number that he or she has learned, and his or her first name. The computer responds by typing out the child's last name and automatically goes to the point in the curriculum where the child finished on the previous day.

The curriculum includes several different components of reading skills, from letter identification to sentence comprehension. The following is an example of an exercise in word recall:

	Teletypewriter Display	Audio Message (taped voice)
PROGRAM OUTPUT:		Type crept.
Student responds:	CREPT	
PROGRAM OUTPUT:	+	That's fabulous!†

Thus, the child gets immediate feedback from the computer and is rewarded for correct answers. In addition to typing "+" for a correct answer, every so often the program will give an audio feedback message, from simple ones like "great," "fabulous," and "you're doing brilliantly" to some that have cheering, clapping, or bells ringing in the background. The messages are not random. They depend on the student's performance that day. If the child's performance

†Adapted from R. C. Atkinson, "Teaching Children to Read Using a Computer," American Psychologist, 1974, 29, 169–178, Table 2. Copyright 1974 by the American Psychological Association. Reprinted by permission.

And when the child does not get the right answer, the computer gently corrects him or her.

is above that of the preceding three days, he or she will be rewarded with frequent audio messages. And when the child does not get the right answer, the computer gently corrects him or her.

The CAI reading program has proven extremely effective. It has been used with students in schools where the average reading level at the end of the third grade when CAI is *not* used is at a grade level of 2.9. In contrast, the average reading level of children using CAI is 4.1 (compared to a national average of 4.0). Thus, students with CAI are slightly above grade level by the end of the third grade, while those without it are one year behind.

Atkinson stresses that *individualizing* instruction is a critical factor in successful teaching of reading. The computer is ideally suited to provide this individual attention. It has a complete response history for each student, and it uses this information to make trial-by-trial decisions about which instruction to present next. A teacher interacting with a student on a one-to-one basis may well be more effective than a computer in providing this sort of individualized treatment. But when working with a group of students—even as few as four or five—the teacher is unlikely to match the computer's effectiveness in this regard.

Atkinson notes that psychologists and educators still have a great deal to learn about how to sequence instructional procedures in such a way that they are most effective, given the student's current state of knowledge. Before the computer, there was no real individual flexibility in managing the flow of information in school. As a result, whether or not we understood how to individualize learning was of little practical consequence—we couldn't do much about it anyway. "Now, with the computer," Atkinson believes, "a new dimension of school learning has emerged" (pages 177–178).

Some psychologists and educators still have reservations about the usefulness of CAI. They suspect that it would be too expensive to institute on a widespread basis (although Atkinson claims that the costs are in fact quite reasonable), and they feel that the computer may have the effect of depersonalizing the learning process. But in spite of such reservations, it seems almost certain that computers will play an increasing role in the classroom in years to come.

Summary

1. Today's educational system has been criticized for its oppressiveness, barren atmosphere, poor preparation of the young for future lives, and many other deficiencies. It has been pointed out that most of these problems have always been around—we are just becoming more aware of them now.
2. Studies of self-fulfilling prophecy in the classroom have shown that a teacher's expectations for students can influence their academic performance. Thus, the problem of poor learning may be a problem of low expectation on the part of teachers, rather than one of a poor system or of defective students.
3. Among suggested solutions to the current educational system are "free," schools, preschool education, and computer-assisted instruction (CAI). Each of these approaches has its advocates and its critics.

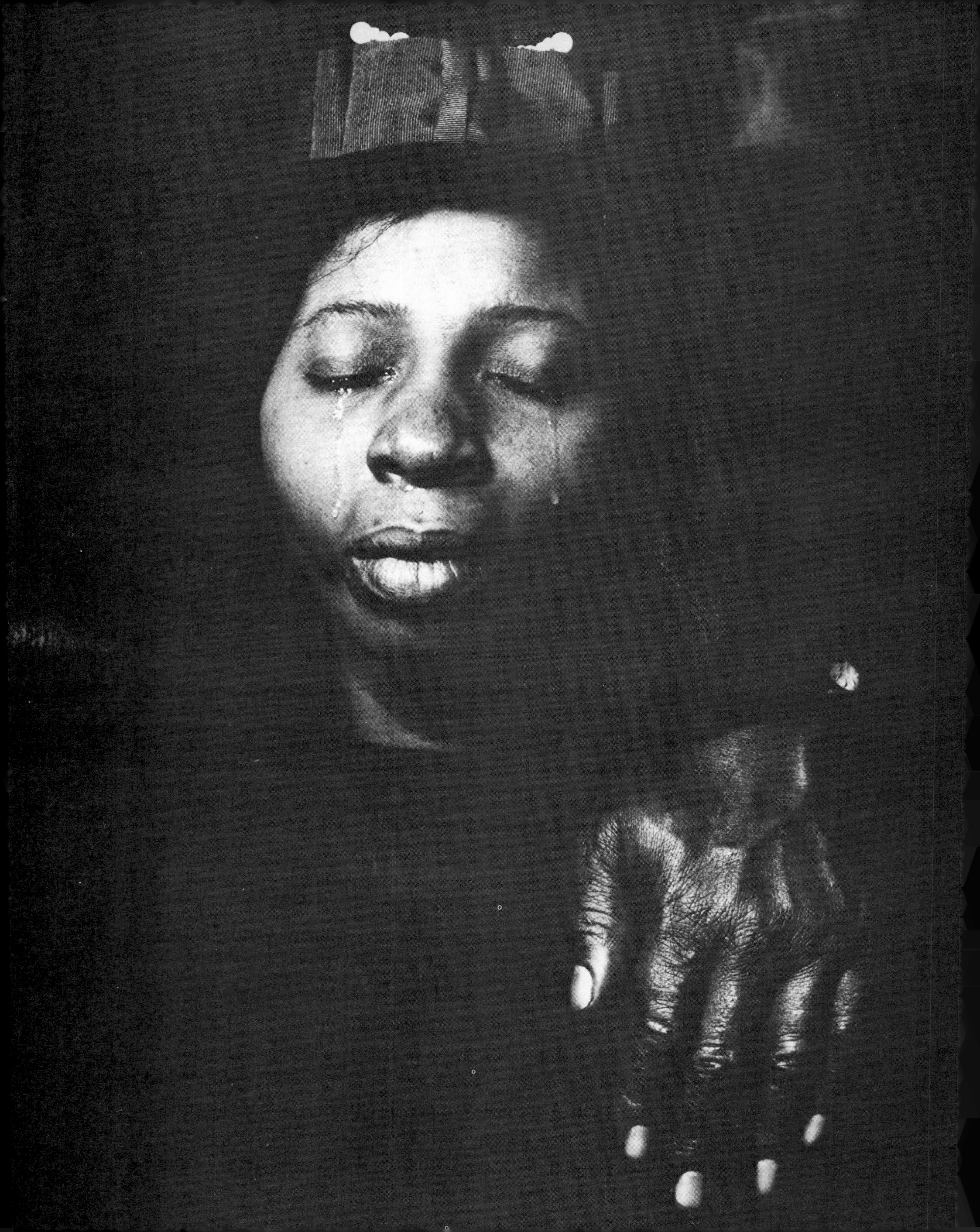

PART 4

Motivation and Emotion

The previous four chapters focused on the rational side of being human. These chapters examined the person as learner, thinker, information processor, and problem solver. In the next two chapters, we turn to aspects of being human that are less "rational"—to the impulses and drives, goals and aspirations, joys and sorrows that are all central parts of our existence. Chapter 9 delves into the processes of *Motivation,* the inner needs and desires that direct much of our behavior. Chapter 10 explores the phenomena of *Emotion,* the bodily changes and experienced feelings that not only spur many of our actions, but also provide the greatest highs and lows of human life.

The Psychological Issues that follow these chapters consider some specific ways in which motivation and emotion affect life in society. After our discussion of motivation in Chapter 9, we will examine the impact of human motives in the spheres of *Work and Achievement.* And after our consideration of emotion in Chapter 10, we will investigate the increasing level of *Violence* in today's world.

Although motivation and emotion can be contrasted to the more "rational" processes of learning and thinking, these realms are by no means independent of one another. We will see throughout these two chapters that there is a close interplay between people's rational, cognitive processes and their desires and feelings. We humans are many-sided creatures and if we are to understand ourselves more fully we must continually probe the ways in which our different sides relate to each other.

Motivation

CHAPTER 9

Motivation

In trying to solve a murder case, one of the detective's first questions is, "What was the *motive*?" Was the crime committed for money, for revenge, for sexual satisfaction, or for the "thrill" of it? The detective is not unique in wanting to know why people do things. In fact, we are always asking questions about the underlying *why's* of human behavior—in other words, about *motivation.*

In a sense, the entire study of psychology concerns the underlying causes of human behavior. But *motives* are certain kinds of causes, the internal factors that arouse and direct a person's behavior. These include such forces as hunger, thirst, sex, and curiosity, among many others. These are all forces that *move* a person to act in certain ways; in fact, the word "motive" comes from the Latin word for "move." Actually, no one has ever seen a motive with the naked eye, or even under the microscope. Rather, it is a hypothetical concept that psychologists employ to help understand the immediate causes of behavior.

Even without the help of psychologists, most people come up with the idea of motives on their own. If you think about it for a minute, you will discover that you already know a great deal about human motivation. For example, you watch the enthusiastic way Bill is eating lunch one day, and you say to yourself, "Bill is really hungry today!" You might also speculate about the reason for Bill's unusual hunger: perhaps he missed breakfast that morning, or perhaps he had an especially active workout on the basketball court. Or you listen to Sally ask a foreign student a series of questions about his country, and you decide that she has a strong motive of curiosity. Perhaps that goes along with the fact that she reads so much about unusual places and peoples.

In addition to asking questions about other people's motives, we often ask questions about our own. After the Watergate incident, for example, several of President Nixon's advisers publicly questioned their own motives. They decided that they had been motivated by the desire for power and prestige and perhaps had let these motives get the better of them. We are not always aware of our own motives at the time we are behaving in certain ways, but we can sometimes figure out what our motives were afterward.

Psychologists have studied many different motives, from the need to eat to the need to fulfill or actualize oneself. One famous psychologist, Henry Murray (1938), listed twenty different human motives (although he called them "needs"), and other psychologists have added dozens more, from the need for autonomy to the need for social approval. There are also many different typologies or schemes for dividing up those motives. In this chapter, we will consider a sampling of the motives that psychologists have postulated, and we will organize them in terms of two major categories: *survival motives* (such as hunger and thirst), which must be satisfied if the organism (whether human or animal) is to survive, and *competence motives,* which are more distinctively human motives, such as the needs to understand, explore, and control our environment. Different people may be more influenced by some motives than by others, and these differences in priorities are a central part of people's distinctive personalities.

A MOST STIMULATING EXPERIENCE

Research done by James Olds (1958) provides some leads into what might be the physiological basis for motivation, at the level of brain function. In his studies Olds has demonstrated that rats that normally press a bar 25 times an hour for food will press it more than 200 times an hour to receive electrical stimulation to the lateral hypothalamus in the brain. Olds also used an "obstacle course" technique. He placed a rat in a box and let it press a lever three times to receive brain stimulation. Then this lever stopped working and the rat had to cross an electrically charged floor to get to another lever. Olds found that the rat would not only cross the electrified floor to receive stimulation, but that it would endure twice as much pain as that endured by a rat trying to obtain food after going hungry for 24 hours. The experiments by Olds and others seem to suggest that there are "pleasure centers" in the brain and that rewards in everyday life (whether food, drink, sex, or whatever) may have effects on these brain centers.

THE SURVIVAL MOTIVES

The most important survival motives are hunger, thirst, sex and pain avoidance. The survival motives are needs that we share with other organisms. All organisms must eat, drink, and be able to avoid pain if they are to survive. And sex, although not necessary for the survival of the individual organism, is of course necessary for the survival of the species. All these motives have a clear physiological basis. They are regulated, in most cases quite directly, by the primitive portions of the brain (see Chapter 2).

Drive Reduction Theory

The survival motives can be understood in terms of a *drive reduction theory* of motivation. According to this theory, motivation begins with a physiological *need,* such as for nutrients (hunger) or for water (thirst). Through different biochemical mechanisms,

this need is experienced as a psychological *drive.* The drive is an internal tension or pressure that becomes increasingly more uncomfortable. The drive leads the organism to act in a certain way—for example, to find and eat some food or drink some water. The food or water is the *incentive* toward which the drive is directed. When this is done, the physiological deficit is corrected and the unpleasant drive is reduced.

Hunger

Hunger comes from the body's need for food used in growth, bodily repair, maintenance of health, and manufacture of energy. One way that we know we are hungry is through hunger pangs caused by contraction of the stomach muscles. In fact, an early theory of hunger, put forth by Cannon (1911), held that the stomach and its contractions were primarily responsible for the experience of hunger and for motivating us to eat. He theorized that the hunger drive was associated with the stomach pangs and that food reduced the drive by stopping the pangs. But, as Cannon himself realized, there are problems with trying to explain hunger and eating solely in terms of stomach activity. For one thing, people in affluent cultures like our own rarely experience hunger pangs. We fill ourselves up too often for such feelings of hunger to occur more than once in a while. So hunger pangs themselves can't explain why we eat when we do. In addition, there is evidence that humans whose stomachs have been surgically removed (for medical reasons) still feel hungry and that rats whose stomachs have been removed still behave like hungry rats.

Although the fullness or emptiness of the stomach plays a role in regulating our eating patterns, other mechanisms, involving the hypothalamus in the brain (see Chapter 2), seem to play a more important role. First of all, the hypothalamus monitors the level of sugar in the blood. When blood sugar is low, the hypothalamus causes one to feel hungry and to eat more. Conversely, when the blood sugar level is high, the hypothalamus inhibits eating. Second, the hypothalamus keeps track of the fat content of the body and apparently inhibits us from eating when the fat content goes above a certain "set point." This regulatory mechanism enables humans and other mammals to maintain a remarkably stable weight. If you were to eat slightly more every day than you usually eat, your weight would rise quite rapidly, and if you were to eat a little less every day your weight would soon begin to plunge. But because of the hypothalamus's regulatory activity, most people's weights stay within a fairly narrow range.

When the functioning of the hypothalamus is impaired, an animal can no longer monitor blood sugar levels or fat content, and weight no longer remains stable. This has been demonstrated dramatically in an experiment in which portions of the hypothalamus were destroyed in laboratory animals (Teitelbaum, 1967). This operation has startling effects: The animal begins to eat compulsively over an extended period of time, ultimately assuming monstrous proportions—often from two to three times

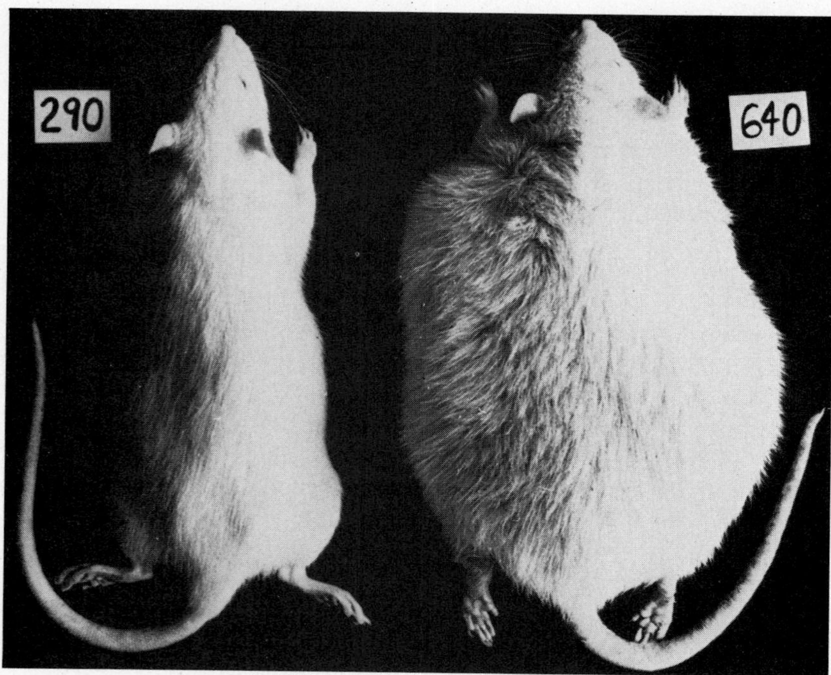

When portions of the hypothalamus in the brain are destroyed, a rat (such as the one on the right) may become *hyperphagic* and grow to two or three times its normal body weight.

greater than normal body weight. These animals are called *hyperphagic,* from the Greek words for overeating. Such effects have been obtained in rats, dogs, cats, monkeys, and chickens, among others.

The taste of food seems to play an unusually large role in regulating the eating behavior of these lesioned rats. Whereas most animals will eat even bad-tasting food if they are hungry enough, the hyperphagic rat won't. If such rats are given only distasteful food (their regular chow with quinine added), they go on a hunger strike and become underweight (Teitelbaum, 1955). It has been speculated that the hypothalamic lesions reduce the rats' sensitivity to internal cues of satiation (like blood sugar level and body fat level) and instead they are at the mercy of external cues (like taste). Recently, Schachter (1971) has found some remarkable similarities between the eating behavior of obese or overweight humans and that of hyperphagic rats (see Box 1). Like the hyperphagic animals, overweight humans seem to pay little attention to internal cues (like hunger pangs) and base their eating habits more on external cues (like the food's availability and taste). There is no evidence of impaired functioning in the hypothalamus of overweight humans, but since the hypothalamus apparently plays a major role in regulating eating behavior, it is quite possible that some of the differences between "thin eaters" (people who eat in a way that keeps their weight at normal levels) and "fat eaters" will be eventually traced to differences in the functioning of this part of the brain.

We usually think of hunger as a very general drive that can be satisfied by just about any kind of food. However, food preferences may arise from specific bodily needs, and a diet that is deficient in some esssential food may cause specific drives that can be satisfied only by the appropriate foods. When rats are put on a fat-free diet and then offered a choice between fat, sugar, and wheat, they show a marked preference for fat. Similarly, rats deprived of sugar will prefer sugar. Rats can also have specific hungers for protein, thiamine, riboflavin, salt, phosphorus, sodium, and calcium. We are not certain how specific hungers are regulated in the body, but it is assumed that the needed foods must taste better to the animal than unneeded foods do. When the taste nerves of the rats are cut, the animals will not select a balanced diet (Richter, 1943).

For most animals, the mechanisms of hunger and of eating are, as we have seen, pretty automatic. The animal responds to physiological drives without giving a great deal of thought to the matter. Humans are animals, too, and the same physiological mechanisms of hunger seem to operate in humans as in rats. But, as you know, among humans there's more to it than that. Why do some people eat a great deal and others very little? Why do some people love ice cream while others go crazy for potato chips? Why is it that some days you can go without food for long periods of time without feeling deprived, while other days you can't seem to keep yourself from snacking constantly? Why do some people love to eat meat and others refuse to eat it at all? It seems that among humans, cognitive factors—thoughts, attitudes, and values—have a great deal to do with eating behavior. We will return to the role of cognitive factors later in this chapter.

Thirst

We can go without food substantially longer than we can go without water. People who have been deprived of both food and water for long periods of time report that the sensations of thirst soon become maddening, but the pangs of hunger tend to disappear after a few days. Experiments with rats reveal that thirsty animals will learn to find a reward of water more quickly than hungry ones learn to find food. Thus, thirst seems to be an even stronger motive than hunger.

It is obvious when we are thirsty: a dry throat and mouth tells us we need water. But easing this dryness is only one factor in alleviating the thirst drive. Dogs subjected to different degrees of water deficit will drink amounts of water directly proportional to the known deficits (Adolph, 1941). Such precise estimation of the need for water cannot be explained in terms of dryness in the mouth and throat alone. The brain seems to exert major control over the amount of drinking in various species (Andersson, 1953).

The thirst drive is controlled by delicate biochemical balances within the body and has been linked to the level of salt in the bloodstream. Salt causes water to leave the body cells. A high level of salt in the blood will cause the cells to become dehydrated. When the level of salt in the blood reaches a certain point, a thirst center in the hypothalamus is stimulated and activates the thirst drive. Drinking returns the system to normal.

Box 1

Thin Eaters and Fat Eaters

Dieticians estimate that 10 to 25 percent of the American public is overweight, and medical experts report that only 12 percent of overweight patients who seek a physician's help actually lose weight. Worse yet, almost all of the people who lose weight gain back their excess pounds within a year or two. Nutrition expert Jean Mayer summarized the problem succinctly. "Never in history," he said, "nowhere else in the world, have such huge numbers of human beings eaten so much, burned away so little of the food by activity and accumulated so much of the surplus in their bodies as fat. . . . The evidence is disturbing" (Mayer and Harris, 1970, page 43).

Why are so many people overweight? For some, malfunctioning glands are the problem; these people have either too much or too little of the hormones that help regulate weight. But for most overweight people the answer is simpler: they eat too much. This is an obvious generalization and it doesn't really explain obesity. But it does pose another question: Why do overweight people eat so much? Recent research suggests that there may be basic differences in the eating patterns of normal-weight and overweight people. Normal-weight people seem to regulate the amount they eat through *internal* cues—how hungry they feel. In contrast, overweight people seem to respond more to *external* cues—the taste of food, its availability, and its visibility (even on billboards and on television).

One sort of evidence for this difference comes from the work of Stunkard and Koch (1964). They had both normal-weight and overweight subjects skip breakfast one day and arrive at the lab by 9 A.M. For the next four hours, Stunkard and Koch recorded the subjects' stomach contractions. Every 15 minutes, they asked each subject, "Do you feel hungry?" Then they compared the record of the stomach contractions with the reports of hunger. For normal-weight subjects, stomach contractions and reports of hunger coincided closely. For overweight subjects, however,

this wasn't true. The fat subject's feelings of hunger had surprisingly little to do with his or her stomach contractions.

Schachter, Goldman, and Gordon (1968) wondered whether these differences for reported hunger applied to eating as well. They scheduled their study for a time of day when their subjects—both normal-weight and overweight students—would probably be hungry. Immediately after the subjects arrived, some of them were given roast beef sandwiches, while others were not fed at all. Thus, some of the subjects now had full stomachs, while the others still had empty stomachs. Then the subjects engaged in a "taste test." Their job was to be cracker tasters and to judge how salty, cheesy, and garlicky each type of cracker was. They could taste as many or as few of the crackers as they wished before making up their mind on each trial. Schachter, Goldman, and Gordon weren't really studying taste, of course; they were interested in the number of crackers each subject consumed. But they couldn't tell this to the subjects beforehand, because such an explanation would influence the subjects' eating. After all, no one wants to be viewed as a glutton or a slob. So, as the subjects tasted and rated crackers for 15 minutes, the researchers simply counted the number they ate.

The results were just what the researchers had predicted. Normal-weight subjects ate fewer crackers when their stomachs were full of roast beef sandwiches than when their stomachs were empty. But the overweight subjects ate just as much, or slightly more, when their stomachs were full than when they were empty. It seems as if the eating behavior of the overweight subjects had little to do with the condition of their stomachs.

Although overweight subjects do not seem to be greatly affected by internal cues, Schachter (1971) has found that they are highly responsive to external cues. In one study, Schachter offered both normal-weight and overweight subjects milkshakes to drink. Some subjects received good-tasting milkshakes, but others received milkshakes spiked with quinine, which is quite bitter. Both normal-weight and overweight subjects drank more good-tasting milkshake than bitter milkshake. But the difference was much greater for the overweight subjects: They drank lots of milkshake when it was good and very little when it was bad. Apparently, the taste of the food had a larger influence on the eating behavior of overweight than of normal-weight subjects.

In another Schachter study, both normal-weight and overweight subjects were offered sandwiches. For some of the subjects, the sandwiches were left on a table. For the rest of the subjects, the food was left out of sight. Normal-weight subjects ate about the same number of sandwiches in both conditions. Overweight subjects, however, ate many sandwiches if they were directly in view, but very few if they were out of sight. Here, the eating behavior of the overweight subjects seemed to be influenced by the visibility of food.

In a third study, both normal-weight and overweight subjects were left alone in a room for a half-hour with a rigged clock. The experimental sessions began at 5:05 in the afternoon, just before dinner. For half the subjects, the clock ran at twice the normal speed. At the end of their half-hour session it read 6:05. For the rest of the subjects, the clock ran at half the normal speed; at the end of the session it read 5:20. When each session was over, the subjects were offered some crackers and were asked to fill out a "personality inventory." The researchers found that the phony elapse of time stimulated eating among the overweight subjects, but it didn't have such an effect on the normal-weight subjects. The overweight subjects seemed to reason, "If it's 6:05, I must be hungry," rather than to depend on internal cues of hunger.

The evidence from these and other studies seems to point to a general conclusion. When overweight people overeat, it's not because they're hungry. They eat in response to external cues—they eat when food is visible and available, when it tastes good, and when the time is right.

So what do you do if you're overweight? One approach, suggested by the Schachter studies, is to stay away from food cues. Don't cook big meals or eat in cafeterias, if you can help it, because if there's a lot of food around you'll probably eat it. Keep your soda pop in a cabinet and your bread in a bread box. Above all, never leave jellybeans or chocolate kisses sitting out in a candy dish. For you, at least as far as food is concerned, out of sight is out of mind.

As with the case of hunger, however, people's thoughts and attitudes can affect their thirst (we will return to this later when we discuss cognitive dissonance).

Sex

Sex, as you probably already know, is a much more complex motive than hunger or thirst. Even including it among the survival motives may be misleading. Clearly, sexual intercourse is necessary for animals or humans if the species is to survive. On the individual level, however, sexual activity is not necessary for survival. In fact, there is no good evidence that abstinence from sexual activity is detrimental to a person's health (Katchadourian and Lunde, 1975). It is also debatable whether sex in humans can be considered a "drive" analogous to hunger and thirst.

It may be useful to compare human sexual motivation with that of lower animals. In both cases, sex is often quite pleasurable, and the anticipation of this physical pleasure may strongly impel the animal to engage in sexual activity. For example, when male rats are deprived of food for up to six days and are then given a choice between food and a receptive female, they commonly choose the female (Sachs and Marsan, 1972). You can probably think of similar cases among humans, where other rewards are foregone for the sake of sexual pleasure.

But sexual motivation is less clearly related to physiological needs for humans than it is for lower animals. Among lower mammals, such as rats, sexual behavior is strongly controlled by the sex hormones—*testosterone* produced by the male testes, and *estrogen* produced by the female ovaries. If the ovaries or testes of rats are removed, sexual activity decreases or stops. In humans, on the other hand, there is no clear relation between hormone level and sexual desire. Men and women whose testes or ovaries have been removed for medical reasons do not necessarily show changes in their sexual desires or behavior (Katchadourian and Lunde, 1975).

In humans, psychological and social motives play a large role in regulating sexual behavior. Sex may be engaged in as an expression of love, as a means of gaining popularity, or even as an economic transaction. Some people engage in sexual behavior to calm their nerves; others use it as a form of self-expression. Moreover, the motives that encourage sex, as well as the forces that inhibit it, take different forms in different cultures. On Mangaia Island in Polynesia, making love is the predictable outcome of social contact between the sexes, and parents encourage their children to have varied sexual experiences in order to find the most compatible mate (Marshall, 1971). On a particular Irish island, in contrast, sex is never discussed in the home, most girls are unprepared for their first menstrual flow, and the female orgasm is unknown or considered a deviant response (Messenger, 1971). These cultural differences have a strong impact on the sexual desires that people feel (or don't feel) as well as on the behavior they engage in. Even in America, there are large differ-

NEVER EAT IN PUBLIC!

Our sexual motivation is influenced by our society's attitudes and values about sex. Baron, Byrne, and Griffitt (1974) make this point by describing a hypothetical society in which attitudes about sex and about food are reversed. People engage in public sex acts in sexaurants, and fast-sex stores dot the highways. But people *never* eat in public, and children are not taught the proper words for "knife" and "fork." Taking this idea a little further, one might guess that in such a society all eating is done "behind closed doors," although there may be movie houses that feature "food flicks" that appeal to "perverts" who often hide food items under their raincoats and sneak them into the theater. Well, you get the idea.

ences between the sexual motives and behaviors of members of different social and cultural groups.

> **WHY MEN GIVE BLOOD**
>
> Ernest Dichter (1964), a famous motivational researcher, once lent his talents to a Red Cross Drive for blood donations. He concluded that many men were reluctant to give blood, because it aroused unconscious anxieties about the loss of strength and virility. He recommended, therefore, that the campaign focus on masculinity, implying that each man in the audience had so much virility that he could afford to give away a little. Dichter also suggested that the Red Cross try to make the men proud of any suffering. Each donor should be given a pin in the shape of a drop of blood—the equivalent of a wounded soldier's Purple Heart. Dichter reported that these techniques produced a sharp increase in blood donations by men.

THE COMPETENCE MOTIVES

Whereas the survival motives are shared by humans and other animals, the *competence motives* are more distinctly human. Robert White (1959) suggests that the "master reinforcer" that keeps most of us motivated over long periods of time is the need to confirm our sense of personal competence. White defines competence as one's capacity to interact effectively with the environment. Being able to master our environment is rewarding, whether it involves learning to ride a bike, bringing up a child successfully, or keeping one's head when everyone else panics. It is rewarding or reinforcing to feel that we are capable human beings. It is punishing or negatively reinforcing to see ourselves as helpless, ineffective people. In this section we will consider three sorts of competence motives: the curiosity motive, the need for cognitive consistency, and the need for control over the environment. The three are closely related in that they all concern our desire to understand, predict, and control the world we live in.

These competence motives have sometimes been viewed in terms of the drive reduction theory that we discussed earlier. For example, some psychologists have postulated the existence of a "curiosity drive," which we must reduce by exploring our surroundings. But the notion of "drive" doesn't really seem to be the most useful way of viewing the competence motives. For one thing, they are not the sort of needs that we can satisfy and then do without for a while. To the contrary, acquiring knowledge about our environment often motivates us to seek still more knowledge, not less. For another thing, these motives are not rooted in specific physiological needs, as in the cases of hunger and thirst. Competence seems to be a continuing, expanding motive, rather than one like hunger that comes and goes.

Curiosity and Exploration

Question: What do Christopher Columbus, Sir Edmund Hillary (who conquered Mt. Everest), and an infant beginning to crawl have in common?

Answer: They all have a strong motive to explore their environment. To put it another way, they are all curious.

Some of us seem to have a stronger urge to explore the environment than others. Scientists exemplify this motive, whether they probe the inner workings of the atom or the outer reaches of the universe. But the same desire to explore—and hence, to master—the environment can be seen in every human infant. In the first few months of life the baby learns to manipulate objects, apparently for their inherent interest value. A rattle or a finger can be fascinating to the infant at this stage. Between five and seven

months of age the infant will remove a cloth covering his or her face and play peekaboo. By eight to ten months the child will begin to look behind or beneath things. In fact, much of what we call "play" in infants and children is part of the enterprise of exploring the environment (Piaget, 1952). Such "learning through play" is a necessary part of becoming a competent and effective adult.

We should hasten to add that curiosity is not an exclusively human motive. Anyone who has spent time with a playful puppy or kitten knows that they are also motivated to explore their environment. Monkeys, too, will explore their surroundings and manipulate objects, apparently just for the fun of it. Butler (1954) gave monkeys mechanical puzzles involving a pin, a hook and eye, and a clasp. To solve the puzzle the monkeys had to manipulate the parts in an exact order. The monkeys soon learned how to do it, and if the experimenter presented the puzzle again, the monkeys would rework it hour after hour with no reward except the joy of solving the puzzle (perhaps this is where the expression "monkey around" came from). Even rats will work for the opportunity to explore a new environment. When deprived of food and water for several days, they will still prefer to explore a new environment rather than stop to eat or drink (Welker, 1961).

ANYONE FOR GRASSHOPPERS? OR, DISSONANCE OVER LUNCH

Zimbardo and his colleagues (1965) performed an experiment in which subjects were persuaded to eat grasshoppers. In one experimental condition, the experimenter was a pleasant, relaxed, and friendly person who presented his arguments in an attractive manner. In the other condition, the experimenter was cold, aggressive, distant, and came across as unpleasant. Some subjects in each group agreed to eat the grasshoppers. After they had done so, they rated how much they liked them. Those who had the unpleasant experimenter said they liked grasshoppers more than those who had the genial experimenter. How would the theory of cognitive dissonance account for this result?

The Need for Cognitive Consistency

In addition to our desire to explore the environment, we have a need to experience a world that makes sense. One aspect of this is the need to believe that our own attitudes and behaviors are consistent with one another. Leon Festinger (1962) coined the phrase *cognitive dissonance* to refer to our internal state of unease when we perceive inconsistencies between our attitudes or between our attitudes and our behavior. Festinger conceived of cognitive dissonance as being an unpleasant feeling and as operating very much like a drive. Just as hunger motivates us to eat, thus reducing the hunger drive, cognitive dissonance motivates us to change our opinions or behavior in such a way as to restore consistency, thus reducing the dissonance.

A man who smokes a pack of cigarettes a day, even though he knows that cigarette smoking is harmful to his health, can be expected to experience a good deal of cognitive dissonance. The best way to reduce this dissonance, of course, is to stop smoking. This will reduce the inconsistency as well as reduce the threat to health. Unfortunately, many people choose a different means of dissonance reduction in this situation. Instead of refraining from smoking, they decide that smoking is not really harmful to *them.* They may proceed to bolster this conclusion by thinking of a dozen people who smoked heavily and still lived long lives. Or smokers may underestimate the amount that they actually smoke, fooling themselves into believing that it is not enough to be harmful. All of these cognitive contortions have the effect of restoring consistency and thus serve to reduce the smoker's inner tension. In Chapter 18 we will return to the ways in which the desire to be consistent can affect our attitudes.

The need for cognitive consistency may sometimes be so powerful as to outweigh other drives like hunger or thirst. In one study (Mansson, 1968), students were first given some "hot" crackers to eat, which made them very thirsty. (The crackers were served with a specially prepared sauce that created the sensation of a hot, dry mouth and the accompanying sensation of extreme thirst. The recipe, for you gourmets, was two parts catsup, one part tabasco, and one part horseradish.) Some of these subjects were then persuaded to agree to go for an additional 24 hours without drinking. This agreement probably created a good deal of cognitive dissonance on the part of the subjects, since it seems quite inconsistent (if not masochistic) to agree to abstain from drinking when one's tongue and mouth are burning and one's throat is parched. Having made the commitment to go without drinking, however, these subjects proceeded to reduce the dissonance in perhaps the only way that was available to them: they decided that they really weren't that thirsty after all. Compared to subjects who had not made so great a commitment, these subjects reported being less thirsty, and when given the opportunity to drink shortly thereafter (the 24-hour deprivation was called off), they drank considerably less. Apparently our need to be consistent can have strong effects on our other motives, including physiological ones. Other studies have demonstrated that the need for cognitive consistency can affect hunger and even the experience of pain (Zimbardo, 1968).

We have introduced the need for cognitive consistency as one of the competence motives. It should be acknowledged, however, that dissonance reduction does not always make for "effective interaction with the environment"—not, for example, when it leads us to rationalize away real dangers, such as those of cigarette smoking. The world does involve some real inconsistencies and it is not always helpful to think them away. Nevertheless, human beings apparently do have a predisposition to understand their world in consistent, predictable terms, and the search for these consistencies plays an important part in our efforts to master the environment.

The Need for Control

One of the most important of all human motives is the desire to be in control of one's own fate, rather than remaining at the mercy of external forces. Although we enter the world in a helpless state, one of the central themes in growing up is the attempt to gain more and more control over our environment and our lives. As we will see in later parts of this book, people who do not have control over their environment may find it difficult to cope with stress (see Chapter 10) and often fall victim to depression (see Chapter 16). When we do feel "in control," on the other hand, we are more likely to feel secure, competent, and effective.

The need for control is very closely associated with the need for freedom—that is, to be free from the controls and injunctions of other people. As Brehm (1966) writes, an individual is motivated to feel "that he can do what he wants, that he does not have to do what he doesn't want, and that . . . he is the sole director of his own behavior" (page 9). When our freedom to behave the way we want is threatened, we are likely to react by reasserting the freedom in question. Brehm calls the motive to restore or reassert a threatened freedom *psychological reactance.* If a parent tells a child that he can't play with a particular toy, for example, the child may make even more of a fuss about the toy than he would have otherwise. The same principle was illustrated in an experiment on people's reactions to censorship. Subjects were told that they would be able to choose whether or not to listen to a certain speech. They were later informed that the speech had been censored and that they would not be able to listen to it. As Brehm's theory of reactance would predict, these subjects now wanted to hear the speech more than they did before they learned about the censorship (Worchel and Arnold, 1973).

The desire to reassert one's freedom provides an explanation for the effectiveness of "reverse psychology": If you want someone to do something, it is sometimes quite effective to tell him that he *must* do the opposite. The person may be so eager to reassert his freedom and control that he or she will defy you and,

THE HUNTER'S MOTIVES

"If you ask a nonhunter why hunters hunt, you'll get answers like 'a big macho trip,' or 'working off their aggressive instincts.' If you ask hunters, you'll often get a blank look, as if you asked a fish why it swims." In fact, there seem to be many motives for hunting, including escape from frustrating work, overcoming the challenges of nature, and bagging symbols of success. A sample of duck hunters interviewed by Copp (1975) gave many such reasons, but not one mentioned the desire to kill or to obtain food as a principal reason.

as a result, do exactly what you really want. Parents have been known to use this somewhat sneaky tactic as a means of child control. In the musical play *The Fantasticks,* two fathers use this technique to get their children—a boy and a girl—interested in one another. They forbid the two to see each other and, sure enough, they quickly fall in love.

Older people probably have just as much need for control over their environment as younger people do. Unfortunately, older people often lose such control, and as a result feel a loss of competence and of self-esteem. Retirement from the occupational world causes the loss of one area of mastery, and the loss of the parent role when children are old enough to leave home results in the loss of another sort of control. When older people move to retirement homes, their control declines still further, since many of the things they used to do for themselves are now taken over by others.

The psychological well-being of residents of old-age homes can probably be improved if efforts are made to give them a

Box 2

Ideological Motivation

All the competence motives that we have considered—curiosity and exploration, cognitive consistency, and the need for control—may also be categorized as *cognitive* motives. They are based in people's higher mental processes—their thoughts and attitudes—rather than in their physical needs. As we go up the evolutionary ladder, from lower animals to humans, thoughts and ideas play a progressively more important role in motivation. The strongest form of such cognitive motivation is that provided by religious or political *ideologies,* systems of belief to which people may become strongly committed.

Dember (1974) reminds us of several striking examples of such ideological motivation:

> Diana Oughton, daughter of a wealthy midwestern family, described as sensitive and warmhearted, was killed with two Weatherman companions when bombs they were constructing in a Greenwich Village apartment exploded.
>
> An assistant pastor and a layman of the Holiness Church of God in Jesus Name of Carson Spring, Tennessee died in agony after drinking a mixture of strychnine and water. They were testing their faith in the Bible, where it is said of those who believe, "if they drink any deadly thing, it shall not hurt them" (Mark 16:16–18).
>
> Countless religious martyrs and political prisoners have undergone torture and death in the service of their faith, their party, their country.

Ideology is sometimes so potent that it can override all our other motives and emotions.

greater degree of control over their own lives. Even if the control involves relatively small things, or "tokens," it may still do a great deal for the old person's morale. Langer and Rodin (1976) demonstrated this in an experiment conducted in an old-age home. Half of the subjects, all between the ages of 65 and 90, were told by the home's administrator that they still had a good deal of influence over their own lives and that they should be deciding for themselves how to spend their time. For example, they were told that they could decide which night to see a movie that was to be shown. And they were given personal responsibility for taking care of a plant. The other half of the subjects were told that the home staff was concerned about their well-being, but the old people were not encouraged to exert greater control over their lives. They were to be informed by the staff when they would see the movie, rather than deciding for themselves. And they, too, were given a plant, but they were told that the nurses would take care of it for them. Later, Langer and Rodin obtained ratings of the residents' happiness, alertness, and activity, both from the nurses and from the residents themselves. They found striking increases in the morale and activity level of the people who had been encouraged to take more control, while the people in the comparison group showed lower morale and reduced activity.

UNCONSCIOUS MOTIVES

We are quite conscious of many of our motives. We usually know when we are hungry, when we are curious about something, or when we are trying to achieve a good grade in a course. Often, however, we are unaware of our own motives. We seek goals that, for one reason or another, we don't consciously know we are seeking.

The psychologist who first gave major emphasis to unconscious motives was Sigmund Freud (see Chapter 14). Freud believed that certain of our motives were *repressed,* or banished from consciousness, because they are too anxiety-arousing for us to deal with. But these motives still have clear effects on our behavior. Freud paid special attention to people's slips of the tongue as one reflection of unconscious motivation. In his honor, these are commonly referred to as "Freudian slips." Although these slips are often passed off as accidental, Freud believed that they are not accidental at all. One of Freud's colleagues, a Dr. Brill, provided the following example:

> *"While writing a prescription for a woman who was especially weighted down by the financial burden of the treatment, I was interested in her saying, 'Please do not give me any* big bills *because I cannot swallow them.' Of course she meant to say pills." (Freud, 1915, page 103)*

Freud also noted that people sometimes express unconscious feelings toward others by "accidentally" mispronouncing their names. What would you conclude, for example, if your professor were to begin his or her next lecture with, "Today we will consider the contributions of the great psychologist Sigmund Fraud"? Such a slip might betray the fact that the professor really doesn't think that Freud was that great after all.

MOTIVES IN CONFLICT

A single motive seldom operates in isolation, and sometimes our motives interfere with one another. Motives can conflict in several ways. The major types of conflict have been termed *approach-approach, avoidance-avoidance,* and *approach-avoidance* conflicts.

Approach-Approach Conflict

An approach-approach conflict is one in which there are two goals competing with each other that seem to be equally attractive. For example, two of your favorite TV programs may be on at the same time, so you can watch only one. Or you may have trouble deciding what to order in a restaurant, because two items on the menu are equally enticing. On a grander scale, people must make choices about how to spend large amounts of money (buy a car, take a trip) or what to do with their lives at a major choice point: continue on in college and get that advanced degree, or take a job offer that seems promising. These conflicts may seem pleasant to the outsider, but they can be agonizing to

Approach-Approach Conflict

the person who is torn in two different directions and must make a decision that will result in the loss of something that is desired.

Avoidance-Avoidance Conflict

In a second type of conflict, avoidance-avoidance, there are two goals, neither of which is desirable, but one of which must be chosen. This was the kind of conflict faced by war protestors when, for reasons of conscience, they had to choose between the

Avoidance-Avoidance Conflict

draft and going to prison. Neither choice was attractive, but no other real alternatives were available. Similarly, a man who has been in a serious accident may have to decide between having his leg amputated or risking gangrene. And voters in an election may have to choose between equally undesirable candidates. A decision in such cases is often based on choosing the "lesser of two evils."

Approach-Avoidance Conflict

In this final type of conflict there is one goal, but two motives. One motive leads us to approach the goal-object, and the other tells us to avoid it. Such conflict is seen in the hungry dieter who wants to eat and also wants to leave food alone. This conflict may be visible as the person alternately approaches and avoids the refrigerator, unable to decide which impulse to follow. Or consider the case of a young man standing against the wall at a party:

He sees an attractive young woman near the opposite wall. His emotions are mixed. On the one hand, he would like to move toward her and strike up a conversation. On the other, he is afraid of being rejected and hence would like to stay away. At first his approach tendency is the stronger, and he begins to move across the floor. As he gets closer to his goal, the avoidance tendency gains in strength. Like a rat heading toward a goal box where it has sometimes been fed and sometimes been shocked, the young man slows down and vacillates. If he is outgoing and secure, the approach tendency will win out. If he is shy and insecure, the avoidance tendency will be the victor. In borderline cases, the young man may spend much of the evening glancing at his watch and looking foolish in the middle of the floor. (Rubin, 1973, pages 64–65)

Approach-Avoidance Conflict

It is the same with every approach-avoidance situation. When we are tempted to do or think of the act, we feel guilty or anxious. This often keeps us from actually reaching the goal, but it also leaves us in conflict.

Box 3

A Pyramid of Human Needs

Many psychologists have come up with lists of basic human "needs" and with ways of classifying those needs. One of the most famous and most useful is the "pyramid of human needs" developed by humanistic psychologist Abraham Maslow (1962).

Maslow viewed the person as having an inner nature that is constantly unfolding and growing, even if this growth is not easily visible to others. The human capacity to develop, for Maslow, is like that of a tiny seed that contains a tremendous potential for growth. Even in adverse circumstances, it will grow despite the odds against it. Seeds differ in their ability to survive, and so do humans. Maslow (1943) felt there are certain basic needs humans must meet before they can be concerned with satisfying other needs. Maslow's theoretical pyramid of human needs included (from the bottom going up): the basic physiological needs of food, air, and the like; stimulation needs, including sex, activity, and exploration; safety and security needs; love and belonging needs; self-esteem needs; and the need for self-actualization.

Maslow said we must first satisfy one set of needs before we can become involved with satisfying the next set. He felt that some people may live their entire lives stuck on just one set of needs. There are millions of people who live out their lives at the bottom of the pyramid, barely able to keep themselves and their families alive. Some people move beyond safety and security needs only to fashion a life style that is devoted entirely to the search for love from others. These people never have enough time or energy left to actualize the full potentials they were born with.

The ultimate need on Maslow's pyramid is the need for self-actualization—the need to realize all of one's innate capacities and talents. According to Maslow (1962), the self-actualized person has certain qualities, including: efficient perception of reality; spontaneity and unconventionality of thought; acceptance of oneself, of others, and of nature; independence from the environment; concern for basic philosophical and ethical issues; and a new appreciation for ordinary events. Self-actualized people are those who have been able to satisfy all their other needs in order to fulfill themselves as human beings.

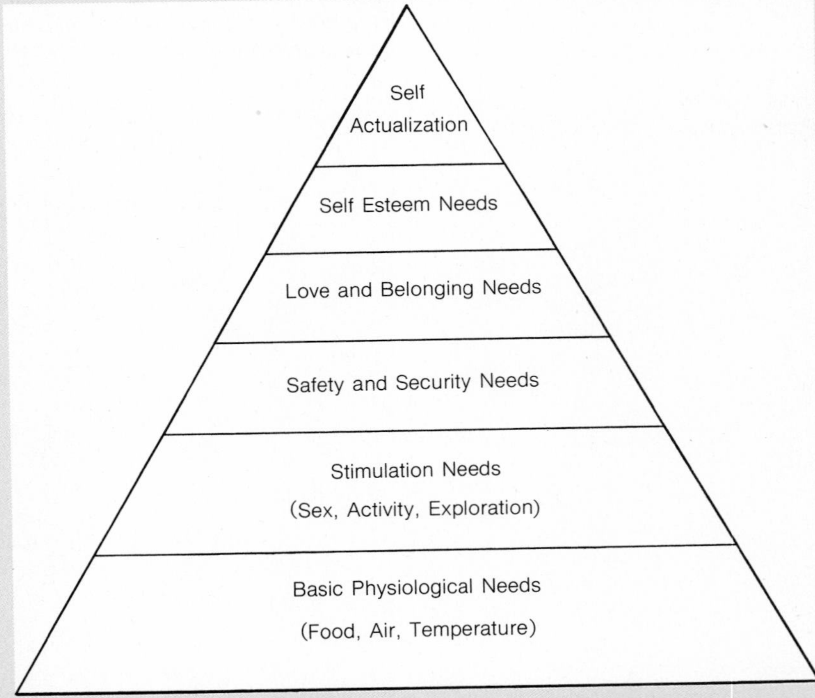

FIG. 9 · 1 Maslow's pyramid of human needs.

SUMMARY

1. *Motives* are internal forces that arouse and direct a person's behavior. Two major categories of motives are *survival* motives (such as hunger and thirst) and *competence* motives (such as the needs to explore, understand, and control one's environment).
2. According to *drive reduction theory,* motivation begins with a physiological *need* that is experienced as a psychological *drive.* The drive leads the individual to satisfy the need and is thereby reduced.
3. *Hunger* is a basic physiological motive. Although stomach emptiness and hunger pangs play some role in regulating eating patterns, the major role is played by the hypothalamus in the brain. It monitors blood sugar level and body fat content and stimulates or inhibits the hunger drive in order to keep these levels in the normal range.
4. Animals who have had portions of their hypothalamus destroyed become compulsive eaters and double or triple in weight. These *hyperphagic* animals are no longer able to respond to *internal cues* for eating so instead depend on such *external cues* as the presence and taste of food. Schachter has suggested that, like hyperphagic rats, overweight humans base their eating habits on external cues, such as food taste and availability, rather than on internal cues, such as hunger pangs.
5. Food preferences may come from specific bodily needs. If an animal's diet is deficient in some essential nutrient, foods containing that nutrient come to taste better and the animal eats more of them. In humans, cognitive factors seem to play a much greater role in food preferences and eating habits.
6. *Thirst* seems to be an even stronger motive than hunger. The thirst drive is regulated by centers in the hypothalamus that monitor the level of salt in the bloodstream.
7. In lower animals the *sex drive* is strongly controlled by sex hormones, and it may even be stronger than the hunger and thirst drives. Psychological and social factors play a greater role than hormones in regulating human sexual behavior.
8. The drive reduction theory does not seem to apply to the competence motives. White sees competence as effective functioning in one's environment, which is reinforced by the feeling that one is a worthy human being. Competence seems to be a continuing, expanding motive rather than one like hunger, which comes and goes.
9. The desire to explore and master one's environment is seen in the play of human infants and even in the behavior of monkeys and rats. The desire to understand and make sense of the environment is seen in the need for cognitive consistency—the need to resolve any *cognitive dissonance* be-

tween one's attitudes or between one's attitudes and behavior. The desire to control one's own life is seen in the phenomenon of *psychological reactance*—doing the opposite of what others want one to do.

10. The competence motives may also be categorized as *cognitive* motives, because they are based in people's higher mental processes. The strongest form of such cognitive motivation is that provided by *ideologies,* or systems of belief to which one has a strong commitment. Such a commitment may override all other motives.
11. Some motives are unconscious. Freud felt that such *repressed* motives are sometimes revealed through slips of the tongue or by other "accidental" means.
12. Maslow developed a pyramid of human needs, with physiological needs at the bottom and actualizing needs at the very top. He suggested that needs at each lower level must be satisfied before one can begin to satisfy needs at the next higher level.
13. Motives may conflict with one another in several ways. The major types of conflict have been identified as: *approach-approach* (in which there is a choice between two desirable goals), *avoidance-avoidance* (in which there are two undesirable goals), and *approach-avoidance* (in which there is one goal with both advantages and disadvantages).

psychological issue

Work and Achievement

At the very heart . . . is the assumption that people can find pleasure in work.

Most adult Americans spend at least one of every three waking hours working. We are part of a culture that weans us on fierce individualism, independence, the rags-to-riches myth, and a deep-rooted absolute belief in achievement via imagination, energy, self-denial, and stick-to-itiveness. At the very heart of these characteristics is the assumption that people can find pleasure in work. Thomas Carlyle declared in 1843, "Older than all preached Gospels was this unpreached, inarticulate, but ineradicable, forever-enduring Gospel: Work, and therein have well-being."

Why Work?

How does work provide this sense of well-being? If you can answer that question, you understand a lot about human motivation. To start with, a person who works can purchase adequate food, shelter, and clothing and can also provide for his or her family. So, people can be motivated to work, because work enables them to satisfy their basic physical needs.

But work can contribute to psychological well-being as well. Work is the prime arena in which many adults develop skills and show competence—and this, in turn, may lead to increased self-esteem. There are many other motives that may underlie a person's desire to work, including the inherent interest of the work, the opportunity to learn or use new ideas, and the opportunity to socialize with others.

Morse and Weiss (1968) asked a sample of workers what they would do if they inherited enough money to let them stop working. About 80 percent answered that they would continue to work anyway. Two-thirds of these workers mentioned positive satisfactions with work, while about one-third felt that joblessness would make them feel lost, useless, and unable to decide what to do with their time. It seems that work is vital for many people; the job often becomes the organizing center of one's life.

Theory X and Theory Y

Not everyone would agree that work is intrinsically satisfying. In fact, as McGregor (1960) notes, most of the people who hire and manage workers have traditionally assumed that people work only because they have to. McGregor suggests that a particular theory of human nature underlies most industrial organizations. This

attitude includes the following assumptions: that everyone dislikes work and will try to avoid it; that the average person prefers to be directed and wants to avoid responsibility; that as a consequence the industrialist must find a way to coerce or entice people to do their work. McGregor called this set of assumptions *Theory X.*

McGregor put forth an alternative set of principles, which he called *Theory Y.* The assumptions of this theory of human nature are that the expenditure of energy is natural, that external control is not the only way to ensure good performance, that people like responsibility, that people are creative, and that, under present industrial conditions, only part of the human potential is fulfilled.

It should be apparent that if you are the manager of a business, it will make a great deal of difference whether you subscribe to Theory X or Theory Y. The current movement to humanize the nature of work makes a lot of sense to a Y theorist, but seems like coddling workers to an X theorist. You might briefly suppose that the educational institution you are attending right now is the work setting and you are an employee. Are your professors X or Y theorists?

Intrinsic and Extrinsic Motivation

When you do an activity solely for the pleasure of it, psychologists say you are *intrinsically motivated,* since the activity is its own reward. If you do something for an outside reward, such as money, good grades, or avoidance of punishment, you would be described as *extrinsically motivated.* People often receive both intrinsic and extrinsic rewards for doing a job; for example, they are paid for it, but they also enjoy the work itself. Sometimes, however, the promise of extrinsic rewards can reduce or undermine one's intrinsic motivation. For example, who do you think is likely to enjoy playing basketball more—a person who plays on an amateur team without pay, or a superstar who has just signed a five-year, $3 million contract with a professional team? If you guessed that it is the amateur, there is evidence from laboratory studies that you are probably right.

Edward Deci (1972) used an experimental puzzle called Soma to explore intrinsic and extrinsic motivation. He gave each subject four puzzle problems to solve. After completing the four puzzles, each subject was left alone to do whatever he wished: read magazines, solve more puzzles, or do whatever interested him. If he spent his free time playing with the Soma game, this became a measure of intrinsic motivation for that activity. In one experiment, half of the subjects were told they would get a dollar for each correct solution to a puzzle, while the other half were not paid for getting the right answers. Deci discovered that the money made a big difference. Subjects who were paid spent significantly less time with the puzzles when they were alone than did subjects who had worked the same puz-

Why does external reward decrease intrinsic motivation?

zles for free. Intrinsic motivation decreased when subjects were given an external reward.

Why does external reward decrease intrinsic motivation? One explanation deals with people's interpretations of their own behavior. Imagine asking one of Deci's subjects why he was working on the puzzle. The subjects who were not being paid would probably say, "Because I like to." The subjects who *were* being paid might say both "Because I like to" and "Because I earn money." In the later sessions when no reward was present, the unrewarded subjects would continue to play with the puzzle—after all, they "like to." But the rewarded subjects might not—after all, this time they wouldn't be rewarded. For similar reasons, a highly paid professional athlete may paid professional athlete may be less likely than an amateur to play "just for fun" during the off season.

This *overjustification* explanation suggests that the presence of *any* extrinsic motivation or pressure should weaken existing intrinsic motivations. For example, if a little boy's behavior is monitored by an adult, he may become less interested in what he is doing, since he can say to himself, "I'm only doing it because the teacher's watching" (Greene and Lepper, 1974).

How do we resolve the problem of extrinsic pressures? As Deci (1972, 92) has put it:

If we want individuals to enjoy what they do, to derive joy and satisfaction from their work as well as their play, we must do two things. We must create more activities that are inherently interesting and gratifying; and we must not use extrinsic rewards in a way that will lower the interest level of those activities that are intrinsically motivated.†

The Achievement Motive: Do a Job Right!

The achievement motive can be characterized as the striving to maintain or increase one's competence in activities in which a standard of excellence is thought to apply. One can either succeed or fail in such activities. The person who is highly motivated to achieve is one who will keep trying to succeed, by matching or exceeding his or her existing standard.

People's achievement motivation has been measured by asking them to make up stories about a series of pictures. (These pictures are part of a measuring device called the TAT—Thematic Apperception Test.) The four pictures originally used by McClelland and colleagues (1953) depicted a work situation (a man at a machine), an academic situation (a boy at a desk, a father and son, and a boy who appeared to be day-dreaming. Subjects are shown these pictures and are asked to tell what is happening at the moment, what led up to the situation, what is being thought, and what the outcome will be. Then the subjects' responses are scored for the number of achievement-related ideas or themes that their stories contain. For example, if a subject were to write the following as part of his or her story about the boy who appears to be day-dreaming, it would be coded as an achievement-related theme: "He is thinking about his ambition to become an astronaut and become the first man to visit Mars." As a contrast, the following story would not be judged as achievement-related theme: "He is thinking about his ambition to become an astronaut and become the first man to visit Mars." In contrast, the following story would not be judged as achievement-related: "He is thinking about how much fun he had when he went to the beach with his family."

People may not always be aware of their own achievement needs. . . .

†*From E. Deci, "Work: Who Does It and Why,"* Psychology Today, *August 1972, p. 92. Copyright © 1972 Ziff-Davis Publishing Company. REPRINTED BY PERMISSION OF PSYCHOLOGY TODAY MAGAZINE.*

It is interesting to note that when the subjects are given a questionnaire about their desire for achievement, their answers do not agree very closely with the themes that emerge in the stories they make up. People may not always be aware of the extent of their own achievement needs—and, if they are, they may not always want to admit them. McClelland believes that the assessment of people's fantasies about achievement, as reflected in the stories they make up, provides a less direct, but more useful measure of the strength of their achievement motives.

Why are some people high in the need for achievement, while others are low? Culture is clearly an influence. Some cultures put a greater emphasis on performance and excellence than others. In fact, McClelland (1965) uncovered the fact that the amount of achievement imagery in children's textbooks of 30 countries in the 1920s was related to the economic development in those countries 20 years later. The more achievement imagery in the textbooks, the greater the economic development. The cultural emphasis on achievement apparently led to harder work, which, in turn, led to greater economic progress.

There also seems to be a relation between the learning of the achievement motive and the nature of childhood training. Winterbottom (1953) found that the mothers of eight- to ten-year-old boys who were high in the need for achievement reported that their children were expected to have mastered at an early age such independent behaviors as obeying traffic signals, entertaining themselves, earning their own spending money, and choosing their own clothes. In contrast, mothers of boys low in need for achievement reported that they expected the same level of independence, but at a significantly later age. It may well be that many adults who have strong needs to achieve were subjected to rigorous training for independence when they were young.

Level of Aspiration

What are the effects of the achievement motive on people's behavior? The most obvious effects relate to one's *level of aspiration,* the goal that one hopes to achieve when undertaking a task. Individuals who are high in the achievement motive tend to be realistic about setting levels of aspiration. They avoid tasks in which they are almost sure to succeed, but receive little reward. On the other hand, they also avoid tasks in which they are almost sure to fail, but could gain very high rewards. For example, McClelland (1958) performed a study in which subjects participated in a ring-toss game. They received points for throwing a ring onto a peg, with more points awarded for successful throws from greater distances. Subjects with a high need for achievement generally tossed from moderate distances. They had a preference for moderate risks with moderate rewards. People with a low need for achievement—especially when combined with a high fear of failure—were more likely to set goals that were either unrealistically high *or* that were very low risk and presented no challenge. In the ring-toss game, they tended to stand either very close to the peg or very far from it.

These differences between people with high and low needs for achievement also seem to be reflected in their choice of occupations. People who have a strong achievement motive and relatively little fear of failure are likely to prefer challenging jobs in which they have a fairly good chance of success and can obtain reasonable rewards. People with the opposite pattern of motives are more likely to settle for an easier and less challenging job or else to aspire unrealistically to a job that is beyond their abilities.

The Female Achiever

Most of the research on the achievement motive was done with male subjects. When researchers conducted the same studies on women, they rarely got the same results—in fact,

> **...recent studies have indicated that nowadays men are just as likely as women to fear success....**

they didn't get any understandable results at all. Horner (1969) identified one possible reason for this failure: that the woman motivated to achieve finds herself in a classic approach-avoidance conflict situation: For her, success may mean failure:

Consciously or unconsciously the girl equates intellectual achievement with loss of femininity. A bright woman is caught in a double bind. In testing and other achievement-oriented situations she worries not only about failure, but also about success. If she fails, she is not living up to her own standards of performance; if she succeeds she is not living up to societal expectations about the female role. . . . For women, then, the desire to achieve is often contaminated by what I call the motive to avoid success. [*Horner, 1969, pages 37–38*]†

Horner and associates found that women with a strong motive to avoid success will sometimes unconsciously do badly on academic tasks, presumably to avoid the threatening implications of success. Certainly not all women fear success, however. In fact, some recent studies have indicated that nowadays men are just as likely as women to fear success (Tresemer, 1974). We will return to this issue of men's and women's achievement in Chapter 13.

Is the need for achievement a good thing? Your answer will depend on your own set of values, which in turn depends on your culture and upbringing. Most of us have been taught that achieving is a good thing. But, it may also be that, like other good things, the achievement motive can be overemphasized, at the expense of other human goals and motives.

†*From M. Horner, "Fail: Bright Woman,"* Psychology Today, *Nov. 1969, p. 37–38. Copyright © 1969 Ziff-Davis Publishing Company. REPRINTED BY PERMISSION OF PSYCHOLOGY TODAY MAGAZINE.*

Summary

1. The motivation to work comes from the desire to fulfill both physiological and psychological needs. Those who believe that basically people dislike work, are uncomfortable with responsibility, and must be coerced adhere to the assumptions of Theory X. Those who are more confident in the human desire to work, to take on responsibility, to be creative, and to fulfill one's potential embrace the assumptions of Theory Y.
2. Work motivation may be intrinsic (the activity is its own reward), extrinsic (an outside reward is required), or both. In some cases, an extrinsic reward may decrease intrinsic motivation.
3. The achievement motive has been measured with the Thematic Apperception Test. The level of one's need for achievement appears to be influenced by one's culture and by one's childhood training.
4. Individuals high in the achievement motive tend to be realistic about setting levels of aspiration, whereas people low in the achievement motive are more likely to set unrealistic goals or to attempt only low-risk, unchallenging tasks.
5. Many women who are motivated to achieve find themselves in a classic approach-avoidance situation. They want to be successful, but they are afraid that success in academics or in a career will mean failure in the female role and the disapproval of society.

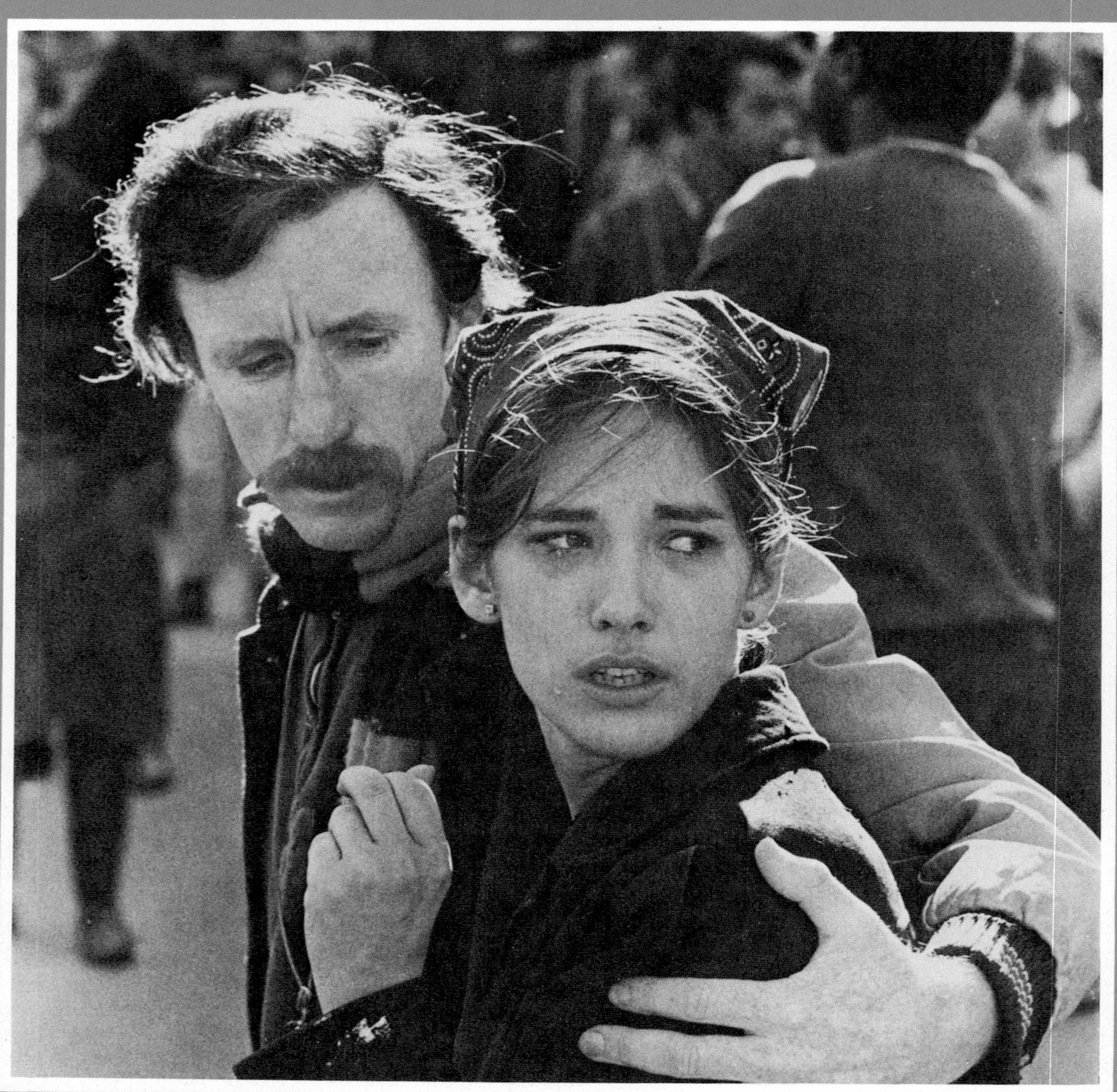

Emotion

CHAPTER 10

Emotion

Suppose, when human beings finally explore the distant reaches of the universe, we stumble on a planet occupied by beings much like ourselves, with one major exception: they are incapable of experiencing what we call emotion. Suppose these beings exist without the feelings of triumph or failure, joy or sorrow, pleasure or disgust. To us, it would be like life with all the juices wrung out of it—a colorless, monotonous, one-dimensional existence.

It would be difficult to relate to these beings; to do so would be like making friends with a computer or a television set. They could think, react, and respond, but they would have no feelings. Imagine for a moment what it would be like if a person close to you had absolutely no feelings about you one way or another. Suppose your friend were to give only a logical reponse to "the facts" and no more. Before long, you would begin to have an emotional reaction to the *lack* of emotion in your friend.

Spock, one of the characters in the popular television series *Star Trek,* was just this sort of creature. His father was a Vulcan, a member of a race of creatures who exhibit no emotions. Spock prides himself on being purely logical and free from such human frailties as hate and love. On the starship Enterprise, Captain Kirk, "Bones," and other crew members are often startled and irritated by Spock's logical reactions. Even the writers of the series seemed to dislike the idea of a *totally* nonemotional creature, so they gave him a human mother, and, every so often (usually when weakened by disease), Spock experiences a smattering of feeling. Once or twice he even falls in love. Most of the time, however, Spock is as often amazed by the emotions of his human associates as they are by his lack of them. In the same way, our fictional other-planetary beings would be hard pressed to comprehend the unpredictable reactions of their human visitors, who suffer from a strange affliction called emotion.

This chapter is an attempt to explain human emotions. The most obvious expressions of emotion that we see in our fellow humans are the intense ones of joy, pain, fear, grief, and anger. But just what is emotion? People often find it hard to describe their own emotions, and psychologists have had trouble measuring them. Since most of us seem to understand intuitively what is meant by the word "emotion," some psychologists do not attempt to formulate a technical definition at all. Others have characterized emotion as the reflection of *psychological changes* in our bodies, or as an inner force that *motivates* us, or as the *subjective feelings* we experience. It is probably most accurate to say that emotion is a combination of all three of these definitions. Consider, for example, the emotion of grief. It is likely to be associated with such physiological changes as a pounding heart or heaving chest; it may motivate us to actions ranging from loud wailing to quiet reflection; and it brings with it a subjective feeling of sadness and loss. How these components relate to one another is, as we will see, one of the central questions addressed by psychologists who study emotion. In addition, as the example of grief suggests, emotion is closely associated with the stresses of life and our reactions to them. Whereas our emotions are usually seen as positive forces in our lives, they can sometimes overwhelm and even kill us. We will focus on stress and life crises in the latter part of this chapter.

GOOD FEELINGS AND BAD FEELINGS

Most lists and typologies of human emotions include many more emotions that are usually seen as negative than those that are usually seen as positive. The lists of negative emotions typically include anger, fear, jealously, rage, grief, disgust, and embarrassment, while the lists of positive emotions don't get far beyond happiness and love. Why is it that there seems to be so many more negative than positive emotions? Is it simply a peculiarity of the English language, or does it reflect something important about our emotional experience?

THE PHYSIOLOGY OF EMOTION

The experience of emotion is often accompanied by striking changes in our body's functioning. When we are emotionally aroused, our hearts may accelerate from their normal rate of about 72 beats per minute to as much as 180 beats per minute. Our breathing is likely to become rapid and uneven, and our blood pressure may rise alarmingly.

Although these and other physiological changes can be reliably measured, they raise new questions about emotion. A central question concerns the physiological reactions that accompany specific emotions, whether grief, disgust, or happiness: Does each of these emotional states have its own distinctive pattern of physiological changes, or do the same physiological changes take place during *any* emotional state?

Some of the most interesting research on the physiology of emotion focuses on two powerful emotions: fear and anger. In many ways, the physiological responses associated with fear and anger are quite similar, at least when compared to physiological functioning during a nonemotional state. Both fear and anger are controlled by the sympathetic branch of the autonomic nervous system (see Chapter 2). As a result, when you are afraid or angry, movements of your stomach and intestines usually stop, interfering with the digestion and absorption of food. Your body's metabolic rate goes up and sugar in the bloodstream and fats from the body's tissues are burned off at a faster rate. (Yes, if you were in a rage or a panic all the time, you'd probably lose a lot of weight, but there are safer and saner ways to diet.) In addition, your salivary glands stop working, causing the feelings of dryness in the mouth that so often accompanies fear and anger (see Box 1). Your sweat glands may overreact, producing a dripping forehead, clammy hands, and "cold sweat." Finally, the pupils of your eyes may enlarge, producing the wide-eyed look that is characteristic of both terror and rage.

But in spite of these similarities, fear and anger are physiologically different from each other. Albert Ax (1953) studied the physiological response of subjects experiencing fear or anger. Ax's laboratory assistants produced anger in subjects by making insulting remarks in the course of the experiment. They provoked fear by acting uncertain about how to operate some dangerous-looking electrical equipment. Ax then recorded the subjects' pulse rate, heartbeat, respiration, galvanic skin response (which reflects sweat gland activity), and other physiological responses. He found that while both fear and anger tend to produce increases in blood pressure, the increases are greater during anger. The heart rate, respiration, muscle tension, and sweat gland activity all tend to increase more during fear than during anger.

Daniel Funkenstein (1955) suggested that the physiological states of fear and anger are produced by different secretions of the adrenal gland. He speculated that anger is associated with secretion of norepinephrine whereas fear is associated with secretion of epinephrine. Evidence from nonhuman members of the animal kingdom seems to support Funkenstein's hypothesis. For example, the adrenal glands of lions, who survive by fighting and killing their prey, contain a predominance of norepinephrine. Rabbits, who survive by running away, have predominance of epinephrine. These observations help make the case for a link between norepinephrine and anger (and the associated behavior

Box 1

The Emotion Detector

Long before modern "lie detector" machines were invented, devices that purported to indicate whether or not someone was telling the truth were in use in cultures throughout the world.

The Bedouins of Arabia once required conflicting witnesses to lick a hot iron; the one whose tongue was burned was considered to be lying. The ancient Chinese, it is said, made someone who was being questioned chew rice powder and spit it out; if the powder was dry, the suspect was guilty. In ancient Britain a suspect who could not swallow a "trial slice" of bread and cheese was also found guilty. (Smith, 1967)†

†*From Burke M. Smith, "The Polygraph,"* Scientific American, *January 1967, p. 25.*

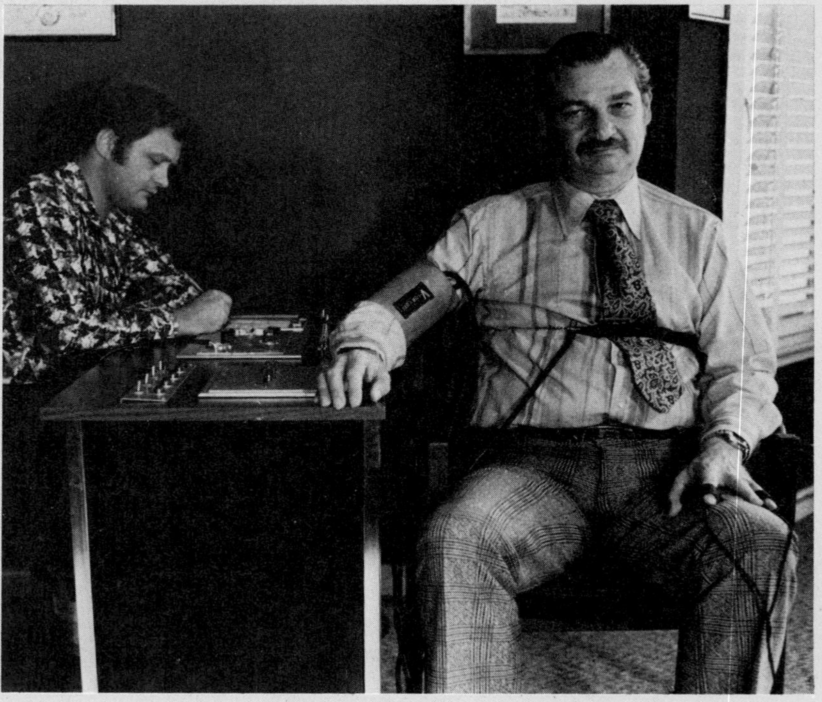

These various tests all had a sound physiological basis. Apparently, wise people in these cultures had observed that emotional tension is often indicated by a dry mouth, because of "fight"), and between epinephrine and fear (and the associated behavior of "flight").

The physiological changes that take place when we experience both fear and anger are part of our body's preparation to act in a threatening situation, whether by fighting back, increasing our efforts to meet a challenge, or escaping. Our increased heart rate, breathing, and metabolism provide us with the additional energy need for quick action. Such bodily reactions can be very helpful in coping with an emergency, whether it is perceived as infuriating or as terrifying. If we were to remain angry or fearful for long periods of time, however, these reactions could take a severe toll. We will consider the ways in which emotions can damage physical health later in the chapter, when we focus on the effects of prolonged stress.

THEORIES OF EMOTION

Emotions seem to involve both *physiological arousal* (a racing pulse, a shortness of breath) and a *subjective feeling* ("I am thrilled," or "I am down in the dumps"). But how do these two

---

the flow of saliva has decreased (You might say that people in these cultures won their salvation through salivation.) These methods, like more recent attempts at lie detection, were based on the premise that a person who is lying is likely to experience emotional arousal, which can be detected by various means.

The first modern attempt to record the physiological aspects of lying was made in 1895 by Cesare Lombroso, an Italian criminologist who measured changes of pulse rate and blood pressure in suspected criminals while they were being questioned. In 1921 John A. Larson, a policeman, constructed the basic model of the present *polygraph*, or "lie detector"—a machine to record blood pressure, pulse rate, and respiration. Leonard Keeler, an associate of Larson's, refined this device and added another measurement—the *galvanic skin response* (GSR), a measure of the resistance of the skin to the conduction of electricity. It is detected by placing two electrodes on the fingers or other parts of the hand and passing a small electric current through the skin via the electrodes. The rate of the flow of the current will vary according to the electrical resistance of the skin. In highly emotional states, people's palms tend to sweat, causing a decrease in skin resistance that is reflected in a change in the GSR.

What complicates lie detection is that the physiological responses associated with lying are to some extent under voluntary control. Good liars may never show their colors on the polygraph. Moreover, not everyone reacts in the same way. Some people are emotionally sensitive even to neutral stimuli, while others are unresponsive even to normally arousing stimuli. Also, since the assumption is that the liar knows he or she is lying, a problem is caused by those individuals who genuinely believe they are telling the truth even when they aren't. Finally, the examiner's manner, attitude, and tone of voice can influence the kind of psychological response produced.

Because all of these pitfalls can lead to false conclusions about a suspect, polygraph evidence has not been admissible in courts of law, although the device can be used freely in investigations on a voluntary basis. Polygraphers claim anywhere from 95 to 100 percent accuracy, and in a recent laboratory experiment the polygraph demonstrated 92 percent accuracy in locating the guilty person (Davidson, 1968). But we must remember that even this margin of error may be responsible for convicting an innocent person.

elements relate to each other? Does the physiological arousal lead to the subjective feeling, or is it the other way around? Or do both occur simultaneously? Over the course of the past century several theories of emotion have been put forth that take different positions on this question. We will first review two theories formulated in the late nineteenth and early twentieth centuries, the James-Lange theory and the Cannon-Bard theory. Although neither theory is accepted today, each had a great deal of influence on the way that today's psychologists view emotion. Then we will examine one currently popular theory of emotion, Stanley Schachter's cognitive labeling theory.

The James-Lange Theory

The common-sense notion about the links between subjective experience and physiological arousal is that some event or stimulus causes a person to feel a particular emotion (the subjective experience) and this emotion then causes certain physiological changes as well as certain behaviors (crying, striking back, running away). But William James, the great American psychologist (and older brother of the novelist Henry James), was not satisfied with this common-sense explanation. He proposed that in fact the sequence is quite the reverse: An event or stimulus causes bodily changes (both internal responses, such as increased heart rate, and overt actions, such as crying or running) and that these bodily effects in turn produce the experienced emotion. The experience of emotion, according to James, is a direct result of a person's perception of his or her own bodily changes: "we feel sorry because we cry, angry because we strike, afraid because we tremble" (James, 1890).

In developing his theory, James drew on the related ideas of a Danish psychologist named Carl Lange. As a result, the theory that the experience of emotion results from the perceptions of one's bodily changes has become known as the *James-Lange theory.* For reasons that we will outline below, the James-Lange theory does not seem today to provide an adequate explanation of emotion. Nevertheless, there is evidence that one of the theory's implications may well be correct—that we can often gain control over our emotions by consciously altering our behavior.

George Miller (1962) notes that James developed his theory at a time when both his parents had just died and when he was wrestling with deep grief. But James had learned to live with his feelings, to rise above grief and depression. And the way to do so, he maintained, was to act *as if* one was not affected. "If we wish to conquer undesirable emotional tendencies in ourselves, we must assiduously, and in the first instance cold-bloodedly, go through the *outward motions* of those contrary dispositions we prefer to cultivate," wrote James (1884). If we act cheerful, for example, the emotion of happiness will replace the gloominess we want to get rid of. This prediction follows from the James-Lange theory: By consciously altering our behavior, we may in effect become able to fool ourselves into feeling differently.

"I MADE MYSELF FEEL THAT WAY"

Do men and women experience emotion in the same ways? For the most part they do, but there may also be some differences. Arlie Hochschild (1975) asked male and female students to provide descriptions of their emotional experiences. She found that women were more likely than men to report that they actively managed or manipulated their own feelings. Specifically, women were more likely to use such phrases as "I made myself feel that way," "I snapped myself out of it," or "I tucked my feelings in." Men, in contrast, were more likely to take a passive attitude toward their emotions, as something beyond their control. If this difference really exists, how can we explain it? It does not seem to involve any biological differences between the two sexes. One explanation is that since women typically have less power than men to manage the actual course of events in their lives, they must learn to manage their emotions instead.

When we see that we are smiling, we are likely to conclude that we are happy after all.

William James's advice along these lines will not always work. In some cases, suppressing or disguising one's feelings is likely to have harmful effects. A person who behaves perfectly calmly after the death of a close friend may suffer a great deal internally. Nevertheless, there is evidence that such conscious dissimulation can sometimes have the desired effect. In one recent experiment, Lanzetta, Cartwright-Smith, and Kleck (1976) gave students electric shocks and asked them either to conceal or to exaggerate the facial expressions associated with anticipating and receiving the shocks. Thus, some subjects did their best not to show any outward signs of pain, while others made an effort to express their feelings quite fully. As the shocks were presented, the researchers also obtained written self-reports of the subjects' feelings and physiological measures of the extent of their arousal. The researchers found that the subjects who suppressed their fear and pain also reported that they felt less upset, and they showed fewer physiological signs of arousal than did the subjects who expressed their feelings.

The Cannon-Bard Theory

In spite of the fact that we may sometimes infer our feelings from our own bodily behavior, it is now clear that the James-Lange theory does not provide an adequate account of the origins of emotion. The theory is on weak ground in its attempts to link physiological changes with the experience of emotion. According to James and Lange, a person might confront a particular stimulus (say, a beautiful sunset), experience a particular pattern of physiological change as a result (such as tingles down one's spine), and then perceive this physiological change and experience a particular emotion (such as awe or reverence). But this theory assumes that each emotion has its own characteristic pattern of physiological change. And, as physiologist Walter Cannon pointed out in 1929, this does not seem to be the case. The same "tingles" that are associated with a beautiful sunset might also be experienced when one is watching a horror film. How, then, is one to tell what emotion one is supposed to be experiencing—awe or terror? As we learned earlier, researchers have found some distinctions between the physiological aspects of certain emotions (notably fear and anger), but there is certainly no evidence that each of the many emotions that we are capable of feeling has its own characteristic pattern of internal bodily changes.

Cannon (1929) offered a critique of James's theory on this and other grounds and proceeded to offer his own explanation of the links between physiological arousal and the subjective experience of emotion. His theory was later modified by Philip Bard, and it became known as the *Cannon-Bard theory.* Cannon and Bard postulated that when one encounters an emotion-arousing stimulus, nerve impulses first pass through the region of the brain called the thalamus (see Chapter 2). At that point, they suggested, the nerve impulse splits: one portion goes to the cerebral cortex, causing the subjective experience of emotion (fear, disgust, happiness); the other portion goes to the hypothalamus, which gives the body its physiological marching orders. According to this model, then, neither the subjective nor the physiological reaction to a stimulus causes the other; instead, they are produced simultaneously. Recent physiological research has not supported the details of the Cannon-Bard theory; but it, too, had an important influence on subsequent theory and research.

Schachter's Cognitive Labeling Theory

Stanley Schachter (1964) has put forth a *cognitive labeling theory* of emotion that now enjoys popularity among psychologists. Schachter's theory can be viewed as a refinement of the James-Lange theory in that it holds that bodily changes precede the experience of emotion. But instead of assuming that each emotion has its own characteristic pattern of physiological changes, Schachter makes the more plausible assumption that the patterns of physiological change associated with different emotions are quite similar. What Schachter emphasizes are the cognitive processes by which a person who feels physiologically aroused *decides* which particular emotion he or she is feeling. These interpretations, or labels, Schachter goes on to postulate, depend on the situation in which the arousal occurs. If you feel a racing pulse and a shortness of breath at a party, where everyone is making merry, you may interpret the emotion as elation. If you experience the same arousal after someone has insulted you, you may interpret it as anger. The same form of physiological arousal, therefore, might lead to two different emotions, depending on the surrounding circumstances.

Schachter's theory of emotion has been called the "jukebox theory" (Mandler, 1962). According to this analogy, the state of physiological arousal is like the state of a jukebox after a coin has been inserted. It is all set to go, ready to play its tune. But just which tune it will play—a love song, a lament, an exultant march—will depend on which button is pushed. And which button is pushed, in Schachter's view, depends on the way in which the individual interprets his or her environment.

To demonstrate the validity of this theory, Schachter and Jerome Singer (1962) had a physician inject subjects with epinephrine. As we indicated earlier, epinephrine produces physiological reactions usually associated with fear: pounding heart, rapid breathing, sweating palms. Some subjects were told what the real effects of the injection would be. These subjects were in the "epinephrine-informed" group. Other subjects were led to believe that the chemical would only make their feet numb; they were in the "epinephrine-misinformed" group. Schachter and Singer predicted that subjects who knew that epinephrine caused their arousal would not experience any strong emotion. They would say to themselves, "I'm aroused; I guess it's because of the

FIG. 10 · 1 Two subjects in Schachter and Singer's experiment. When subjects were misinformed about the drug's arousing effects, they tended to "catch" the emotion displayed by the confederate. (See text for fuller explanation.)

epinephrine." On the other hand, subjects who were misinformed about the effects of the drug would attribute their arousal to an emotion relevant to the social situation. For example, if the experimenter were to show them a tarantula, they might say to themselves, "I'm aroused; it must be because I'm afraid." In other words, Schachter and Singer were proposing that when people experienced physiological arousal that was otherwise unexplained, they would search for an explanation, and, as a result, would come to experience an emotion.

To facilitate this labeling process, Schachter and Singer created two social situations to which the physiological arousal could be ascribed. In one condition, the subjects watched another student (actually a confederate of the researchers) act in a wild and silly way, playing with a hula hoop and shooting wads of paper at a wastebasket. In the other situation, the confederate objected strenuously to a questionnaire that he and the real subject were filling out. The confederate maintained that the questionnaire was demeaning and insulting, and he escalated his protest until he finally tore up the questionnaire and left the room. Schachter and Singer expected their subjects to use the confederate's behavior as a cue in identifying their own emotions. They

THERE GOES THE THUMP OF MY HEART

Valins (1966) played recorded thumping sounds to male college students at the same time they were watching slides of nude women taken from *Playboy* centerfolds. Some of the subjects were given false information that the thumps were in fact the amplified sounds of their own heartbeats. The thumping sounds speeded up or slowed down while the subjects were viewing particular slides. Afterward, the subjects were asked how attracted they were to each of the women. They rated those women who had apparently caused their hearts to speed up—or to slow down—as most attractive. How can this result be explained in terms of the cognitive labeling approach to emotion?

predicted, therefore, that when —and only when—the subjects were misinformed about the effects of the epinephrine they would report feeling the same as the confederate; that is, they would by happy or angry, depending on how the confederate had behaved.

In general, the results supported the hypothesis. The epinephrine-misinformed subjects tended to attribute their physiological arousal to elation or anger, depending on the social context they were in. And once they interpreted the stimulus of their physiological state as an emotion, they then behaved in a way appropriate to that particular emotion, acting either giddy or irritated themselves.

The use of injections of epinephrine was Schachter and Singer's ingenious method of testing the labeling model. The researchers knew which subjects were physiologically aroused and which of these had an adequate explanation of their arousal, because they were the ones who provided both the arousal and the explanations for it. Outside the laboratory, of course, our

Box 2

The Label of Love

Recent studies of falling in love have indicated that there is a sense in which love is like a Brooks Brothers suit or a Saks Fifth Avenue dress. For one's feelings toward another to be experienced as "love," they must not only feel good and fit well, they must also have the appropriate label. Sometimes a sexual experience contributes to such labeling. One college student told an interviewer that she was surprised to discover that she enjoyed having sex with her boyfriend, because until that time she had not been sure that she loved him. The pleasant experience helped to convince her that she was actually "in love" (Rubin, Peplau, and Hill, in preparation).

Paradoxically, however, people sometimes label as "love" experiences that seem to be negative rather than positive (Berscheid and Walster, 1974). Consider the rather interesting case of fear. Ovid noted in *The Art of Love*, written in first century Rome, that an excellent time for a man to arouse passion in a woman was while watching gladiators disembowel one another in the arena. Presumably the emotions of fear and repulsion stirred up by the grisly scene would somehow be converted to romantic interest.

Ovid himself did not conduct

emotions seldom have anything to do with injections. Instead, the physiological arousal is generated by our reactions to the events and situations we take part in. Nevertheless, the labeling model seems quite applicable to emotions in real life. Regardless of what the real source of the arousal might be, we must still interpret and label the arousal to produce the experience of emotion. Even that most mysterious of emotions—romantic love—often seems to involve this sort of labeling (see Box 2).

THE DEVELOPMENT OF EMOTION

How does emotion develop as a child grows through infancy and childhood into adulthood? It is hard, of course, to know what an infant is "really" feeling when he or she smiles or cries, but we can look at the ways in which the outward *expressions* of emotion develop. At birth, the only clearly recognizable display of emotional expression is one of unfocused excitement. Babies wriggle, jerk, and thrash about—not as a specific response to specific

---

any controlled experiments to check the validity of the fear-breeds-love principle, but two psychologists at the University of British Columbia recently did so (Dutton and Aron, 1975). They conducted their experiment on two footbridges that cross the Capilano River in North Vancouver. One of the bridges is a narrow, rickety structure that sways in the wind 230 feet above the rocky canyon; the other is a solid structure upriver, only 10 feet above a shallow stream. An attractive female experimenter approached men who were crossing one or the other bridge and asked if they would take part in her study on "the effects of exposure to scenic attractions on creative expression." All they had to do was write down their associations to a picture she showed them. The researchers found that the men accosted on the fear-arousing bridge were more sexually aroused than the men on the solid bridge, as measured by the amount of sexual imagery in the stories they wrote. The men on the high-fear bridge were also much more likely to telephone the young woman afterward, ostensibly to get more information about the study.

The best available explanation of these results comes from Schachter's theory of emotion. Schachter's experiments suggested that the experience of emotion has two necessary elements. The first is physiological arousal—a racing heart, heightened breathing, sweating, and the like. These symptoms tend to be more or less identical for any intense emotion, whether it be anger, fear, or love. The second necessary element, therefore, is the person's subjective labeling of his or her arousal. In order to determine which emotion he or she is experiencing, the person must look around and decide what external stimulus is causing the inner upheaval.

This labeling is a complicated process, and (as Ovid apparently knew some 2,000 years ago) mistakes can happen. In the Capilano Canyon study subjects apparently relabeled their inner stirrings of fear, at least in part, as sexual arousal and romantic attraction. This sort of relabeling is undoubtedly encouraged by the fact that the popular stereotype of falling in love—a pounding heart, shortness of breath, trembling hands—bears an uncanny resemblance to the physical symptoms of fear. With such traumatic expectations of what love should feel like, it is no wonder that it is sometimes confused with other emotions. As the Supremes put it in a song of the 1960s, "Love is like an itching in my heart."

There is, of course, much more to love than cognitive labeling. Indeed, love cannot be regarded only as an emotion. It is also a particular sort of interpersonal relationship that takes time to grow and develop. And, as we will see in Chapter 19, it is a relationship that psychologists are just beginning to explore and to understand.

stimuli, but as a general reaction to changes in the external environment. Similarly, a baby's crying is an all-purpose response to a wide range of internal physical needs or discomfort. But as children develop and experience more of the world, they start to differentiate among emotional states. According to Bridges (1932), emotions develop in a treelike pattern, from the infant's state of general excitement toward more specific emotional states, such as fear, jealousy, and affection (see Figure 10.2).

Where Do Emotional Expressions Come From?

To what extent is the development of emotional expression biologically "wired in" to all human beings, and to what extent is it specific to the person's culture? For example, does a smile mean pleasure and a frown displeasure in all cultures, or do such expressions depend on the conventions of the particular society one grows up in? This question of the origin of emotional expressions was one of the earliest asked by psychologists, and it continues to be a central question today.

According to the evolutionary theorist Charles Darwin, our expressions of emotion are a part of our biological heritage and they are common to all human beings. In a book called *The Expression of Emotions in Man and Animals*, published in 1872, Darwin suggested that many of our ways of expressing emotion are left over from a time when such expressions were an important

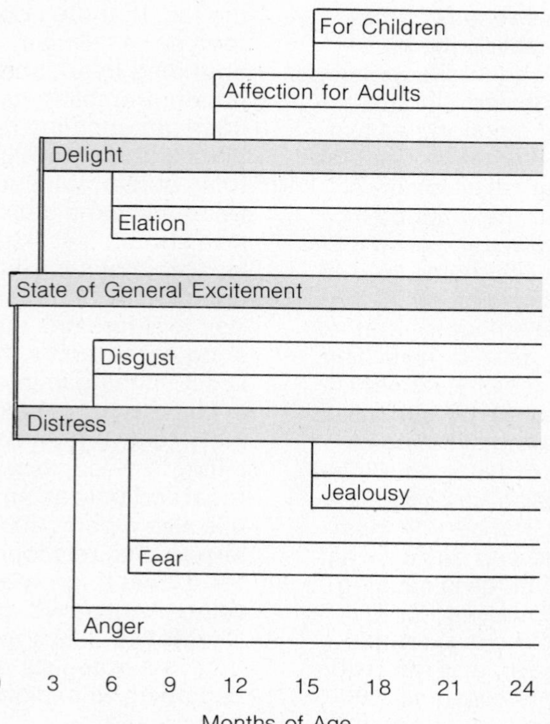

FIG. 10 · 2 One theory of the development of emotion in human infants (adapted from Bridges, 1932). According to this theory, the first expression of emotion is one of general excitement, and from this the two main branches of delight and distress develop. As the infant matures, these categories branch further and more specific emotions appear.

part of survival. Before the development of language, emotional expression was probably our ancestors' primary mode of communication. If people (or their apelike forebears) were to be able to cooperate with one another—whether in hunting, building houses, or defense against predators—they needed to have ways of understanding each other. Darwin speculated that modes of emotional expression evolved for this reason. For example, the emotion of anger is often expressed in the baring of one's teeth and the making of faces; in pre-language times such an expression served to discourage enemies and warn that the person was ready to bite. We continue to make such expressions of anger today even though we rarely bite our enemies anymore. The expression has become part of our biological heritage.

Recently, evidence has come to light to support Darwin's contention that particular emotional expressions are an inborn characteristic of the human species. One piece of supporting evidence is the fact that common emotional expressions appear spontaneously in blind children who have never seen a laughing or mourning face (Eibl-Eibesfeldt, 1970). Since these children cannot imitate the expressions seen on others' faces, their expressions probably reflect inborn predispositions to express emotions in particular ways. Further evidence for a universal "face language" comes from cross-cultural studies such as those done by Ekman and his associates (see Box 3). Such research has shown that people in even remote cultures are able to identify correctly the emotions being portrayed in posed photographs. It does seem, then, that emotional expression has at least some cross-cultural, universal elements.

MONKEYING AROUND

Facial expressions of emotion are of particular importance in the lives of our nearest animal relatives. For startling proof of this, spend some time visiting the monkey cage at the zoo. It might be best for you to pick a quiet day, since you may feel quite foolish making faces at a bunch of monkeys.

For starters, try what is known as the "open-mouth threat"; monkeys use it as an expression of hostility (Marler, 1965). Open your mouth and draw your lips forward so that they tightly cover your teeth. The result should resemble a large "O". Now, stare at the monkeys. If you've done it right, they should retreat in terror to the farthest corner of the cage.

Then change to the "grimace" or "frightened grin," a monkey expression of fear. Draw the corners of your mouth back tightly, exposing your teeth. Glance to the right and the left, avoiding a direct stare. You should look like a nervous contestant in a beauty contest. If you've captured the effect, mayhem will result. Previously you seemed angry; now you appear terrified. Your once frightened audience will most likely surge to the front of the cage, howling and jumping in earnest attack.

How Fears Develop

Besides these apparent universal elements in emotions, it is clear that many aspects of our experience of emotion are learned dur-

ing the course of development. As suggested by Schachter's "jukebox" model, the growing child learns to interpret his or her emotional responses in relation to the specific stimuli that provoke them. For example, a young boy may respond in the same way when he accidentally loses his allowance and when a bully steals it from him, but as the boy grows older he begins to distinguish between these stimuli.

To see how emotions change as a child develops, let us take the example of fear. The fears of infancy and early childhood are usually quite concrete. As the child grows older, however, fears become more abstract and often include nonexistent threats. Jersild, Markey, and Jersild (1960) interviewed 398 children from 5 to 12 years of age and found the following order of fears (from most to least frightening): supernatural agents (ghosts, witches, mysterious events); being along in the dark or in a strange place, or being lost; attack by animals; and bodily injury, falling, illness, traffic accidents, operations, hurts, and pains. Angelino,

Box 3

Speaking the Same Face Language

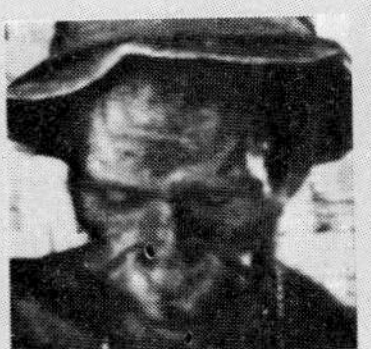

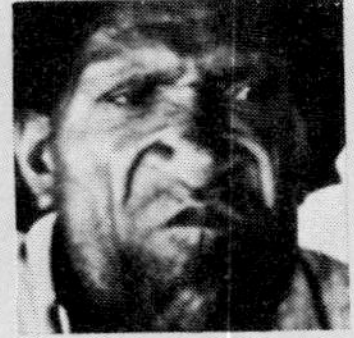
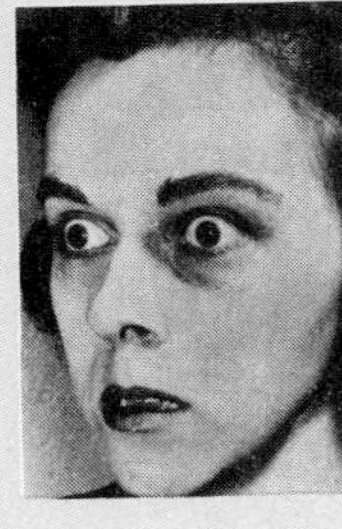

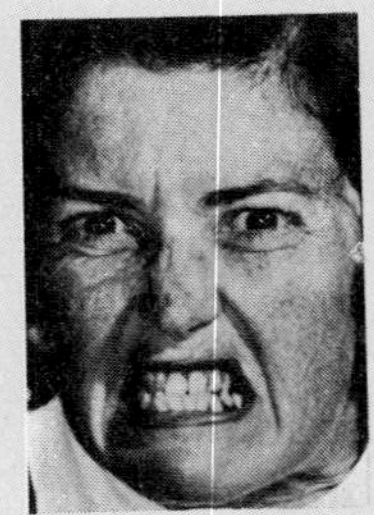

It is well known that certain expressions and gestures have different meanings in different cultures. When people stick out their tongues in Tibet, it is a friendly gesture, not an insult, and Bulgarians indicate agreement by shaking their heads right to left, not up and down. In cases like these, each culture seems to have its own nonverbal language. But in spite of such cultural differences, Charles Darwin argued that the basic facial expressions of emotion, such as the happy smile and the angry grimace, are part of our biological heritage, and, therefore, are the same for human beings all over the world.

Recently Paul Ekman (1975) and his coworkers have gathered evidence that strongly suggests that Darwin was right. In a preliminary study, Ekman showed posed photographs of facial expressions to college students in five countries—Argentina, Brazil, Chile, Japan, and the United States. The faces showed six emotions: happiness, sadness, anger, fear, surprise, and disgust. The researchers found that a large majority of the students in all the countries recognized the emotions accurately.

But these preliminary results did not prove that all human beings are born with the same basic links between specific emotions and specific facial expressions. Since all of the subjects in the study were familiar with Western culture, through movies and television if not through personal contact, it might be that they had all learned a particular set of facial rules. As Ekman wrote, "Perhaps watching John Wayne's angry face, not evolution, was responsible for the

Dollins, and Mech (1956) discovered a relationship between socio-economic background and the number and kinds of fears that children have. Lower-class boys feared switchblades, whippings, robbers, killers, and guns. Upper-class boys feared car accidents, getting killed, and juvenile delinquents. It seems clear that the particular fears that plague children depend a great deal on the environment in which they grow up.

As we noted in Chapter 5, people may be biologically predisposed to learn to fear some objects (like fire or insects) more easily than others (like lollipops and teddy bears). Nevertheless, if our experiences with particular objects are unpleasant enough, we can learn to fear things that are not harmful themselves, but that we have come to associate with stimuli that *are* harmful or fear-arousing. In one of the nastier experiments in the psychological literature, John B. Watson and Rosalie Rayner (1920) demonstrated this possibility by conditioning an 11-month old boy named Albert to be afraid of all furry things. They began by

---

seeming universal recognition of facial expression" (page 36).

To get around this problem, Ekman, E. Richard Sorenson, and Wallace Friesen (1969) traveled to the South East Highlands of New Guinea, in the South Pacific, where they found a group of people called the Fore who were almost totally isolated from Westerners and Western culture. They were illiterate, they had never seen a movie, they did not understand English, and they had had little interaction with Caucasians. They had never in their lives seen John Wayne's angry frown or Jimmy Carter's blissful smile. The researchers then proceeded to determine whether Fore adults and children could accurately recognize emotions as expressed by Caucasians. The procedure was to show each subject three photographs depicting three different expressions, such as happiness, anger, and fear (see photos). The researchers then read a story to the subjects, in their native language, and asked them to select the face that fit the story. In the story about fear, for example, the subjects were told, "A wild pig is standing in the door of the house and the woman is looking at the pig and is very afraid of it." Using this technique, the researchers found high levels of agreement among both adults and children; the isolated New Guinea tribespeople made the same links between emotions and facial expressions that Westerners did. The only exception was that the Fore subjects could not distinguish between the expressions of fear and surprise—perhaps, Ekman speculated, because in their culture fearful events tend to be surprising ones.

Ekman and his team also asked the Fore subjects to demonstrate how *they* would look if they were in the situations described in the stories. They then took photographs of the tribespeople's expressions back to America and had them rated by American students (see photos). The results: The American students understood Fore face language almost perfectly, just as the Fore subjects had understood American face language. The only exception, once again, was an inability to distinguish between the expressions of fear and surprise.

Together with recent studies by other researchers, Ekman's data provide strong evidence that there are universal links between basic emotions and the way they are expressed facially. Ekman believes that all human beings share the same biological program, which links facial muscles with specific emotions. There are still important cultural differences in the rules about *when* and *to whom* it is appropriate to express emotion. Japanese culture, for example, requires people to mask their emotions to a greater extent than American culture does. And even within American culture, women have traditionally been encouraged to express their emotions more freely than men. But in spite of these cultural variations, when emotions are expressed, people throughout the world seem to be speaking the same basic face language.

putting a white rat in Albert's room. At first, Albert was not afraid of the rat at all. But as he reached to touch it, the experimenters struck a steel bar near Albert's head, producing an extremely loud and terrifying noise. This sequence continued until Albert developed a deathly fear of white rats. But Watson and Rayner did not stop there. They began to sound the noise in association with other white, furry objects, such as a rabbit, a cotton ball, and a piece of wool. As a result, Albert's classically conditioned fear gradually generalized to the whole class of white, furry objects.

We don't know whether Watson and Rayner's subject, enshrined in the psychological literature as "Little Albert," is still alive today. But if you should happen to see a man in his late fifties who turns pale and quickly crosses the street whenever he sees a woman wearing a white fur coat, shout "Albert!" and see whether he answers.

Although Albert's case is unique, the conditioning of fear to objects that are not harmful themselves is a common phenomenon. If you are the sort of person who feels shivers whenever you pass the street where your dentist's office is located, you will know what we mean. Most such conditioned fears, although "irrational," are harmless enough. But when a person has strong

SKYDIVING AND FEAR

Many people actually seek out fear-arousing situations—perhaps just for the thrill of experiencing this emotion. That may be one reason why people ride roller coasters or go to horror films. One such fear-arousing activity is skydiving, which was the subject of a study by Fenz and Epstein (1967). They found that the peak of fear occurred in jumpers before the jump rather than during it. They also found that novice jumpers felt most afraid at the moment of the jump, whereas experienced jumpers felt their peak of fear on the morning of the jump and were more calm by the time they were airborne. It seems possible that experience with a fear-causing event can help one to manage one's fears and thereby be better able to cope with—and even enjoy—the terrifying experience.

irrational fears that interfere with his or her functioning, such as an intense fear of venturing out-of-doors, he or she is said to have a *phobia;* we will examine phobias more closely in Chapter 16.

People acquire fears not only as a result of their personal experiences, but also from the attitudes of their family and culture. Some children learn to fear animals, others to fear flying, and still others to fear academic failure by observing and adopting the attitudes of their parents. In addition, different societies have their own traditions about what is fearful and what is not. In some cultures ghosts and demons are seen as playing a major role in human affairs, while in other cultures they are seen as figments of the imagination. And, as we will see in Chapter 11, societies vary widely in the views about whether pregnancy and childbirth are to be feared or welcomed. Such cultural influences play a major role in determining what an individual within a culture is likely to be afraid of.

WHEN EMOTIONS DESTROY: THE CASE OF STRESS

Experiencing emotions has certain drawbacks. Our emotions may motivate us or spur us on to significant accomplishments, but they may also destroy us. One of the major ways in which emotions can be damaging is through the impact of *stress.*

When we talk about the "stress and strain" of modern life, we are referring to a variety of pressures, such as those caused by competition in school or at work, social demands, or worries about financial security. Such pressures can have damaging effects on our state of mind and on our physical well-being as well. Because of its potential destructiveness, psychologists have devoted a great deal of attention to the causes and effects of stress.

How does a person physically respond to stress? According to Hans Selye (1956), the response occurs in several stages. The first stage is the *alarm reaction,* which is similar to the physiological aspects of fear and anger that we discussed earlier. As the body prepares to cope with the stress, there is increased activity in the sympathetic nervous system, digestion stops, the level of blood sugar rises, heart rate and blood pressure increase, and blood flow to the muscles increases. Then comes the stage of *resistance.* Now the body's resources are mobilized to overcome the stress (fight) or escape it (flight). If these efforts are successful, the body returns to normal. If not, as is the case with long-term stress, the stage of *exhaustion* is reached. Failure to cope with stress eventually results in physical and psychological breakdown and sometimes even death.

AFTER WATERGATE

Soon after President Richard Nixon's downfall, an embolism, or blood clot, moved from his legs toward his lungs, threatening his life. At least one psychiatrist specializing in psychosomatic disease had predicted that something like this might happen as a result of the severe emotional stress that Nixon was experiencing. The psychiatrist, Samuel Silverman, believed that because President Nixon had kept such a tight rein over his emotions, the post-Watergate pressures would be more likely to produce a physical than a psychological breakdown. And he predicted that the trouble would be most likely to surface in the legs and the lungs, because of Nixon's previous medical history. "Two days later he threw an embolism," Dr. Silverman later recalled, "and I became a prophet" (Colligan, 1975).

Stress and Disease

Some scientists now believe that virtually all diseases are related to emotional stress (Colligan, 1975). For example, it has been demonstrated that people who work under conditions of great urgency and pressure are especially likely to suffer from hypertension (high blood pressure) and eventually to suffer heart attacks (Friedman and Rosenman, 1974). Other diseases that frequently seem to result from stress include arthritis, asthma, and ulcers. And stress may also increase a person's susceptibility to infectious diseases, by lowering the body's resistance to bacteria and viruses.

Physical diseases that are caused at least in part by stress or other psychological factors are called *psychosomatic* diseases, although the distinction between psychosomatic and nonpsychosomatic diseases is often quite arbitrary. Needless to say, the fact that diseases may often have psychological origins does not mean that they are any less real. Such diseases can incapacitate or kill just as easily as diseases that seem to have solely physical causes.

How does stress cause a disease to develop? Let's take the example of stomach ulcers (or peptic ulcers). According to the National Health Survey of the National Center of Health Statistics, peptic ulcers are one of the leading chronic conditions leading to disability. Stomach ulcers afflict 1 out of every 20 people at some point in their life, and each year stomach ulcers cause more than 10,000 deaths in the United States. Ulcers are a common affliction among people in many different occupational groups, from business executives to physicians. One group of workers with a particularly high frequency of ulcers is air traffic controllers. At least one-third of the traffic controllers in America reportedly suffer from ulcers, a much higher incidence than in any other profession or group. In March 1970, 111 air traffic controllers walked off the job and staged a "sick-out" to protest stressful job conditions. Subsequently, 66 of them were diagnosed as having some sort of gastrointestinal disorder, and 36 were found to have peptic ulcers.

Why do air traffic controllers develop ulcers so frequently? Stress appears to be the culprit. For these people, stress seems to come from the combination of constant vigilance and uncertainty. The controllers must remain alert and watchful at all times; they cannot afford to let their guard down for even a moment. In addition, there is the constant fear and uncertainty. There is always the possibility of an accident, no matter how careful the controller may be.

Like air traffic controllers, business executives often suffer from ulcers, and this condition is usually attributed to the demands and pressures of their job. Among these pressures are the need to react quickly in rapidly changing situations, with one's own success—and that of others—depending on these reactions. Joseph Brady (1958) demonstrated that such pressures can indeed cause ulcers, and he did so in an interesting way—by making executives out of monkeys.

Brady set up a controlled experiment using pairs of monkeys. In each pair, two monkeys were joined (or yoked) by an apparatus that generated electrical shocks. Whenever one monkey received a shock, so did the other. Both monkeys were given shocks at 20-second intervals, but only one monkey—called the "executive monkey"—could prevent the shocks by pressing a lever. The other monkey had a lever too, but pressing it had no effect on the shocks. This experimental procedure is a good technique for distinguishing the effects of physical and psychological stress. Both animals were subjected to the same physical conditions, including the same number of shocks, but only the executive monkey faced the stress of constant vigilance. For the duration of the study, the monkeys were placed on a continuous schedule: 6 hours of shock avoidance followed by 6 hours of rest.

In four pairs of monkeys, the "executives" developed severe ulcers and eventually died. In contrast, the yoked animals sur-

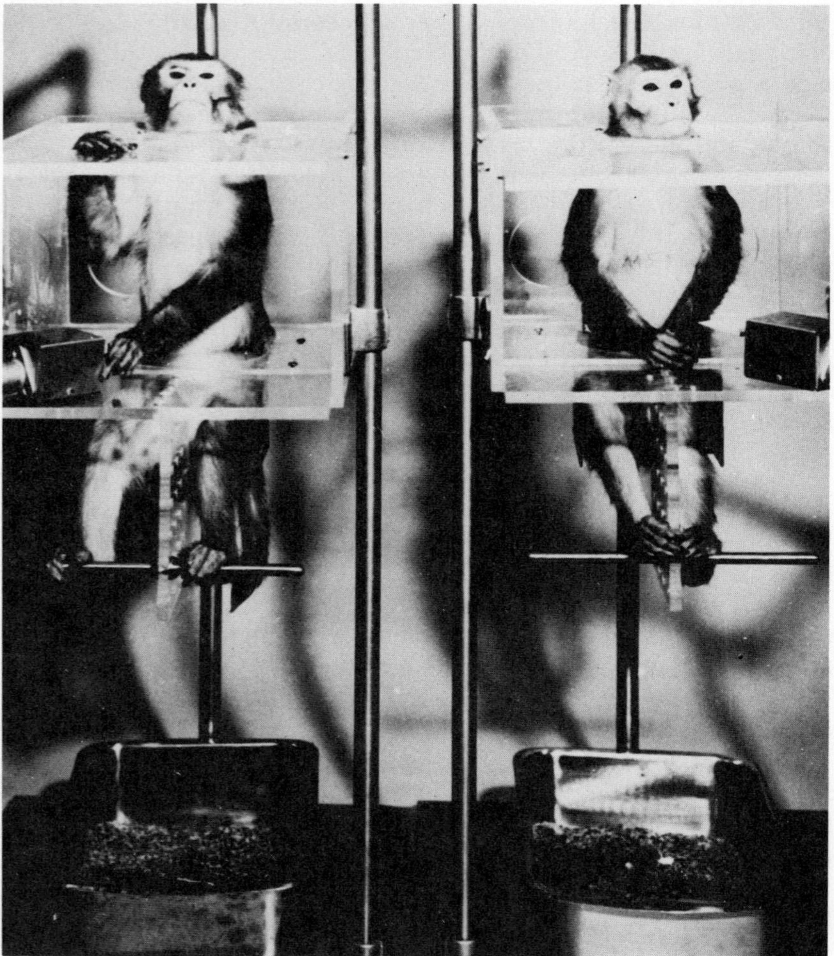

Brady's "executive monkey" experiment. Although both monkeys were equipped with control levers, only the one on the left (the "executive") could prevent his partner and himself from being shocked.

vived, with no apparent ill effects. The stress of constant vigilance, during several weeks of the hours-on, hours-off schedule, apparently had devastating physical effects on the executive monkeys.

You shouldn't get the impression that having control over one's outcomes is always stressful. For Brady's executive monkeys, control over one's own and one's partner's outcomes was not, in itself, the key stress-producing factor. To the contrary, the ability to exert control over one's outcomes usually tends to reduce rather than increase stress. Jay Weiss (1972) demonstrated this with rats, in a series of experiments whose results at first glance seemed to contradict those of Brady. Weiss yoked pairs of rats, so that each rat received the same number of shocks as its partner, as in Brady's study. In one study, the shocks were scheduled to be administered about once a minute. But each scheduled shock was preceded by a signal "beep," and the "executive rat" could avoid and escape shock for itself and its compatriot by reaching through a hole in its cage to touch a panel just outside. After a continuous 21-hour session, both animals were sacrificed and their stomachs were examined for ulcers. Weiss found that the rats who could avoid and escape shock had much less lesioned tissue (ulceration) than their helpless partners. The stomach of the average "executive" rat had 1.6 mm of lesioned tissue, while the average yoked rat had 4.5 mm of lesions, or roughly three times as much.

Why did the executive monkeys suffer increased effects of stress, while the executive rats suffered decreased effects? Weiss (1972) believes that the key difference is in how certain the animal is that its efforts will be successful. In Brady's study, there was no warning signal preceding the shocks, so the monkey had to be on guard at all times. It could never be sure whether it had been successful in avoiding the next shock. In Weiss's study, however, there was a warning signal, and the executive rat knew that its efforts would be successful. The executive rat could safely relax until after the next beep.

There is every reason to believe that control reduces stress in people as well as in monkeys and rats. For example, loud music coming from your stereo probably is not stressful—it's usually very enjoyable. But the same loud music coming from the place next door may be quite irritating. The ability to control events can be stress-reducing even when the control isn't exercised. David Glass and Jerome Singer (1973) demonstrated this effect by playing loud noise to a group of students engaged in a task. One group was told nothing about the noise. The other was told that they could terminate the noise by pressing a button, though the experimenters preferred that they not do so. Even though none of the students in the second group pressed the button to stop the noise, their performance was significantly better. Merely knowing that they *could* control the noise seemed to make it less bothersome. That's probably one reason why your blaring stereo doesn't bother you—you know you can always turn it off.

Even when we can't control them, unpleasant events also seem less stressful if they are predictable—if we at least know when they will occur. This was demonstrated by Weiss (1972) in another study with rats. One group of rats heard a buzzer about 10 seconds before each shock; for this group the shocks were predictable, and each animal had a chance to prepare itself for the coming pain. Another group of rats heard nothing; for this group the shocks seemed unpredictable, occurring more or less at random, and there was no way to prepare. Neither group of rats had any control over the actual occurrence of the shocks. Still, the rats who heard the buzzer signal before each shock developed fewer ulcers than the rats hearing no buzzer. This finding has parallels in human life. The death of a loved one is usually less traumatic when it is anticipated than when it is unexpected. And, on a less tragic level, many students find surprise quizzes more upsetting than scheduled ones that they can prepare for.

Unfortunately, control does not always have such stress-reducing effects. And that seems to be because many "controlling" situations for humans turn out to be more like the situation of Brady's monkeys than of Weiss's rats—the "executive" doesn't know for sure whether his or her efforts will be successful. Without such feedback, the ability to control can be more of a liability than an asset. Air traffic controllers may get their ulcers for this reason—they can never be sure that they are in complete control. Imagine how different the job of air traffic controller would be if there were more certainty. Imagine a computer announcing, "O.K., Jack, everything is cool. Take a breather." The job might even be enjoyable!

Stress and Life Crises

The physical effects of prolonged stress can be quite dramatic. For example, when Thomas Holmes and Minoru Masuda (1972) interviewed 5,000 patients about life events that preceded physical illness, they uncovered an exceptional range of prior stresses and strains, from major crises like the loss of one's job to such minor ordeals as a visit from one's mother-in-law.

Holmes and Masuda assembled a list of life events that most frequently preceded illness and attempted to identify which of these events had the greatest impact and which had the least physical effect. In order to establish a scale that would predict the onset of disease, such as tuberculosis or heart disease, they asked 394 persons to rate the degree of social readjustment required by each of 43 major life crises. The ratings indicated that the single most traumatic event in terms of necessary social readjustment was the death of a spouse. The top ten life crises were as follows: (1) death of spouse, (2) divorce, (3) marital separation, (4) jail term, (5) death of close family member, (6) personal injury or illness, (7) marriage, (8) fired from job, (9) marital reconciliation, and (10) retirement. Further research confirmed

THE CRISIS OF UNEMPLOYMENT

The loss of a job can strip a person of his or her sense of competence and can lead to severe emotional stress. A historian who wrote about the Great Depression of the 1930's noted that "bewilderment, hesitation, apathy, loss of self-confidence, were the commonest marks of protracted unemployment. A man no longer cared how he looked. Unkempt hair and swarthy stubble, shoulders a-droop, a slow dragging walk, were external signs of defeat, often aggravated by malnutrition. What social workers called 'unemployment shock' affected some men as if they were in the grip of a panic, driving them to frenzied work by day, sleepless worry at night" (Wecter, 1948, p. 32).

that the more serious a crisis, the more likely it is to be followed by physical illness.

This relation of illness to life crises was confirmed in a detailed examination of 2,500 officers and enlisted men aboard three Navy cruisers. In this study, life-change data were gathered for six months and then health-change records were collected after the Navy men had spent six months at sea. In the first month of the cruise the high-risk group (those who had been exposed to severe life changes before embarking) had nearly 90 percent more illnesses than the low-risk group. And the high-risk group reported significantly more new illnesses each month than their lower-risk fellow sailors (Holmes and Masuda, 1972).

Even when it seems as if the person is coping adequately with stress, the body may continue to react to the crisis with the emergency measures that drain the body's resources to fight illness. Not only does stress reduce resistance and thereby invite infectious disease, but the body's reactions themselves may contribute to the disease. For some people, the stage of resistance (in Selye's terms), with its heightened heart rate, increased metabolism, and higher blood pressure, may be the most dangerous. For others, the most dangerous reaction is giving up and falling helpless to the effects of the stress (Seligman, 1975); in this final exhaustion stage the heart and other body processes slow down.

For example, intense grief, coupled with such a feeling of helplessness, seems to be involved in many otherwise inexplicable cases of "sudden death." Perhaps you have heard of a widow dying within a few days of her husband's death or of a man dying at the news of the unexpected death of a close brother. In many of these cases the cause remains a mystery unless it is looked at in light of the stress model.

The stresses of life can also influence psychological functioning. Vinokur and Selzer (1975) found that the frequency of stressful life events was associated with feelings of depression, paranoia, aggression, anxiety, distress, and tension. In a related study, Dohrenwend (1973) found that women and poor people are exposed to significantly greater numbers of stressful life events than men and rich people. This greater frequency of stressful events may help to account for the higher incidence of certain psychological disturbances, such as depression, among women and the poor (see Chapter 16).

From studies such as these, showing that our emotions can give us ulcers and other illnesses, it becomes obvious that such feelings can exert a major negative effect on our lives. And we all know that such emotions as anger, jealousy, and fear can cause psychological harm to ourselves and others (see the Psychological Issue that follows). It is such aspects of our emotional makeup that make Star Trek's Spock a bit smug in his lack of them. Why expose oneself to needless suffering and to bodily harm when one need merely respond logically to a situation? But it is perhaps we who should pity Spock, for he will never know joy, elation, happiness, ecstasy. Surely emotions can be highly distressing to us as well as gratifying, but they are an important part of what it means to be human, and they are so fundamental to our being that without them life would hardly seem worth living.

HAPPY THOUGHTS AND HELPFULNESS

People's emotions can have a direct impact on their behavior toward others. In one study (Moore, Underwood, and Rosenhan, 1973), seven- and eight-year-old children were asked to think of things that made them happy or sad, or else they were assigned to a nonemotional control condition. They were then given an opportunity to donate money that they had earned to other children who would not be able to take part in the experiment. As the researchers had predicted, the happy children donated more than the control children, while the sad children donated least. Other studies (such as Isen, 1970) have shown that the "warm glow of success" tends to make people more helpful to others. Apparently, when people are happy and think well of themselves, they are likely to have love left over for others as well.

SUMMARY

1. *Emotion* appears to have three aspects: physiological changes, a motivation to act, and subjective feelings.
2. Physiological aspects of emotion are regulated by the autonomic nervous system. In fear, for example, secretion from the adrenal glands steps up body activity to prepare for flight. In anger, it is the adrenal hormone norepinephrine that produces similar physiological changes, geared to prepare the body for an aggressive response.
3. The *polygraph,* or lie detector machine, records blood pressure, pulse respiration, and galvanic skin response. The premise of the machine is that people who are lying tend to be in a highly emotional state, which the machine is designed to detect. However, the accuracy of the machine is reduced by many factors, including the person's ability to control his or her emotions.
4. According to the *James-Lange theory,* an event or stimulus causes bodily changes, which in turn produce the subjective

experience of emotion. One problem with this theory is that it falsely assumes that each emotion has its own characteristic pattern of physiological changes. According to the *Cannon-Bard theory,* the physiological changes occur simultaneously with the subjective experience.

5. Schachter has suggested that the experiencing of an emotion depends on what label a person puts on his or her physical arousal, and the label in turn depends on the particular situation in which the arousal occurs. Schachter's approach is called *cognitive labeling theory.*
6. The emotion of love can, in many situations, be explained in terms of the cognitive labeling approach. When people are put in situations that produce physiological arousal and then encounter an attractive member of the opposite sex, they may label their physical arousal as love for this person.
7. Modern research has supported Darwin's contention that particular facial expressions of emotion are inborn characteristics of the human species. Such expressions appear spontaneously in blind infants, and Ekman's research has shown that even people in remote cultures can recognize the emotions being expressed in American photographs.
8. Emotions are very general in the young infant, but as the child grows older they differentiate and become more specific. Fears, for example, are few and very concrete for the infant, but they become more varied and abstract in later childhood. In their experiment with "Little Albert," Watson and Rayner demonstrated that people can learn to fear things (through classical conditioning) that are not harmful in themselves. People's particular fears can also be influenced by their family and their culture.
9. The case of *stress,* or pressures from one's environment, shows how emotions can be damaging to both physical and psychological health. Selye identified three states in an organism's response to stress: the *alarm reaction,* the stage of *resistance,* and the stage of *exhaustion.*
10. Stress has been implicated in both chronic and infectious diseases. When stress or emotional problems are involved in a disease, it is often called *psychosomatic.* One important stress related disease is peptic ulcer, which is common among people in stressful occupations, such as air traffic controllers.
11. Brady's experiments showed that the stress of constant vigilance (in order to avoid electric shock) had devastating physiological effects on "executive" monkeys who could prevent the shocks by pressing a lever. However, the control monkeys, who had no effect on the shocks, survived with no apparent negative physiological effects. Weiss showed that "executive" rats in a similar experiment did not develop ulcers if they were given sufficient warning before being shocked.

12. For humans, the stressfulness of an event can be reduced if people feel they have some control over the event or if the event is predictable. In some situations, however, being in control may actually add to the stress.
13. Major life crises, such as death of a loved one, divorce, or loss of a job, constitute a major stress and have great physical impact. The more serious the crisis, the more likely it is to lead to physical illness. Stressful life events can also impair psychological functioning.

Violence

HIJACK SHOOTOUT KILLS 13

THE RISING TIDE OF SCHOOL CRIME

ARSON SUSPECTED IN FIRE WHICH KILLED SIX

VANDALISM IN THE SUBURBS GETTING WORSE

THE LETHAL LASER IS HERE—WILL IT BE ADDED TO U.S., SOVIET ARSENALS?

These headlines all appeared on the front page of the Boston *Globe* during a one-week period in May 1976. The newspaper is a respectable one, and the week was not particularly violent or eventful, as weeks go nowadays. The unfortunate fact of the matter is that violence has become an expected part of American life. Violence has always been a part of the American tradition, but in recent years the situation has gotten worse then ever. In the relatively short period between 1960 and 1974, the murder rate in the United States almost doubled, and the overall violent crime rate practically tripled. In 1974, 20,600 murders and almost a million violent crimes of all sorts were committed in America (U.S. Department of Commerce, Statistical Abstract of the United States, 1975).

Violence has always been part of the American tradition....

Are People Naturally Violent?
Violence is not an exclusively

American commodity. In fact, some theorists have suggested that, in the face of the prevalence of human aggression throughout the world, violence may be an inherent part of human nature. Some scientists have argued that, since aggression is natural to other animals, it may be natural to us as well. For instance, Konrad Lorenz (1966), a world-famous ethologist (student of animal behavior), has argued that humans are naturally aggressive, just like the baboon or the wolf. Lorenz and other writers claim that through the course of evolution people—especially men—developed the capacity for violence, because violence was useful for survival. The aggressive man, they assert, controls territory, women, food, and other "resources."

There are a number of problems, however, with approaches that assume that aggression is part of human nature. For one thing, there are many animal species—including our closest cousin, the chimpanzee—that are naturally quite peaceful. Furthermore, the "human nature" assumption does not account for the fact that there are some human cultures in which there is very little violence. In addition, although we all share the same "human nature," some of us are more aggressive than others, and some situations are more likely than others to elicit aggressive responses. As a result, "human nature" falls short as an explanation for violence and aggression. We need to go beyond the assumption of human nature to a consideration of when and where aggression is most likely to occur.

Frustration and Aggression

Did you ever sit down, intending to watch your favorite TV show, only to have someone else barge in and change the channel? Have you ever searched for a parking space on a crowded city street only to have another driver sneak into the last available spot? Did you ever settle down for a good night's sleep only to be blasted out of bed by a neighbor's stereo? If so, then you've experienced what psychologists call *frustration*—the blocking of efforts to attain some desired goal. At times like these, you probably became angry and perhaps even violent. You may have even felt a strong urge to punch someone right in the nose.

Some years ago, John Dollard and his associates (1939) at Yale University declared that frustration is likely to lead to some sort of aggression. The aggression may be physical, such as a punch in the nose, or it may be verbal, such as a hostile joke or an insult. It may be directed toward the person who caused the frustration (the guy who stole your parking spot), or it may be *displaced* toward an innocent bystander (a passenger in your car).

Although there is a great deal of evidence for this *frustration-aggression hypothesis,* it also needs to be carefully qualified. Frustration often leads to aggression, but not always. For instance, John Whiting (1941) noticed that among the Kwoma of New Guinea, frustration leads at different times to submission, dependence avoidance, and aggression. Alternative responses to frustration are also well known in our own culture. Imagine how different people would respond to losing a quarter in a Coke machine. One person might kick the machine and curse at it. Another might jot down the name and address of the company and write a letter demanding his quarter back. A third person might treat the loss as a fluke and insert another quarter. And a fourth person might become painfully depressed, wondering, "Why does this sort of thing always happen to me?" So, while aggression is one possible response to frustration, it is by no means the only possible response. And although frustration seems to be one common cause of aggression, it's certainly not the only cause.

Getting It Out of Your System: Catharsis

The movie *Rollerball* portrays a future age in which the passive members of a world society release their violent and rebellious urges by watching a bloody hybrid of football and roller derby. The idea is that when frustrations mount up, we can reduce our aggressive drives by engaging in—or even watching—violent activity. Presumably, we can make the world a more peaceful place by taking time each day to watch a bloody movie, scream at a wall, or pound a pillow. Psychologists refer to this method for releasing emotional tension as *catharsis.*

Konrad Lorenz has endorsed the theory of catharsis, arguing that we should all engage in violent, competitive sports in order to reduce aggression, both within countries and between them. Of course, Lorenz

Unfortunately, aggressive catharsis probably doesn't work the way its proponents say it should.

is only repeating an age-old folk wisdom. For centuries, people have been telling each other to go "blow off steam" whenever they feel angry or tense. The Olympic Games, begun in ancient Greece and revived during this century, are sometimes viewed as a mechanism by which nations can blow off steam collectively.

Unfortunately, aggressive catharsis probably doesn't work the way its proponents say it should. If you are angry at someone, striking out at that person may make you feel better, at least temporarily. There is even some evidence that such aggression can reduce an angry person's soaring blood pressure (Hokanson, 1970). But there is no evidence that aggressing against anyone other than the person you are angry at will have a cathartic effect. Nor is there any evidence that watching someone else behave aggressively, whether in a violent movie or on the football field, will help you to get rid of hostile feelings. In fact, quite the opposite result is more likely. As we will see shortly, aggression tends to breed aggression: the more we observe other people doing it, the more likely we are to continue to behave aggressively in the future (Berkowitz, 1973). And competitive sports do not seem to have a pacifying effect on societies. Those cultures having the most aggressive games and sports also tend to be the ones most often involved in wars (Sipes, 1973).

Observing Violence

In recent years, there has been a continuing, heated debate over violence in movies and on television. Apologists for televised violence contend that it probably doesn't make viewers more aggressive. Referring to the catharsis hypothesis, they suggest that it may even help reduce aggressive drives. To opponents of televised violence, this seems absurd—it's like arguing that you will dissipate all of your sex drive by watching pornographic films. They suggest, instead, that televised violence increases the likelihood that viewers will behave aggressively.

There is a good deal of evidence, from both the laboratory and the outside world, to suggest that observing violence is likely to lead to further violence. In one laboratory, three groups of nursery-school children observed either a live adult, a filmed adult, or an animated cartoon cat attack an inflated plastic figure known as a "Bobo doll" (Bandura, Ross and Ross, 1963). These adults, and the cat, served as "models" for the children. The models exhibited a number of distinctive aggressive acts, such as hitting the Bobo doll with a rubber mallet. Two other groups of children watched a nonaggressive adult model or no model at all. Later on, each of the children was observed at play in a room containing a Bobo doll. The researchers carefully recorded every aggressive act of the children.

Sometimes a child would attack the Bobo doll in a manner strikingly similar to that of the observed model (hitting the doll with a rubber mallet, for instance). This is known as *imitative aggression,* because the child seems to be imitating the model. At other times a child would attack the Bobo doll in ways different from those of the model. For example, the child might hit the doll with a baseball bat. This is called *nonimitative aggression,* because no direct imitation is involved. It turned out that children who had observed an aggressive model engaged in more of both types of aggression during the play period than did children who hadn't observed an aggressive model.

The children's imitative aggression is not too surprising. We've all seen children imitating adults in all sorts of ways. The adults demonstrate some action that is new to the child, like reading a newspaper or eating with a fork, and the child wants to try it out. The children's *nonimitative* aggression suggests that observing violence can have even more far-reaching effects. The aggressive model seems to have made a wide range of aggressive behaviors more acceptable to the children. Whereas children are often taught not to hurt others, the aggressive models let them know that these teachings do not necessarily apply. One can imagine violence on television having a similar effect. "Why can't I punch somebody I don't like?" the child might wonder. "Popeye does it all the time!"

Thus, observing violence can actually produce violence in two ways: It teaches new ways to be violent and it makes violence seem acceptable. And, unfortunately, these effects of modeled aggression are not limited to children or to the laboratory. Our recent history is chock full of such instances. For example:

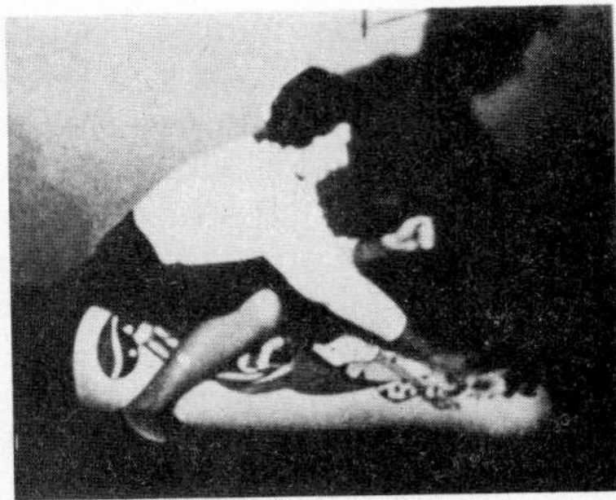
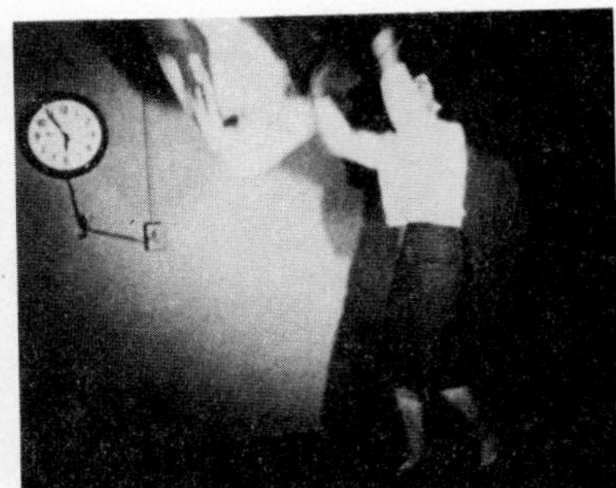
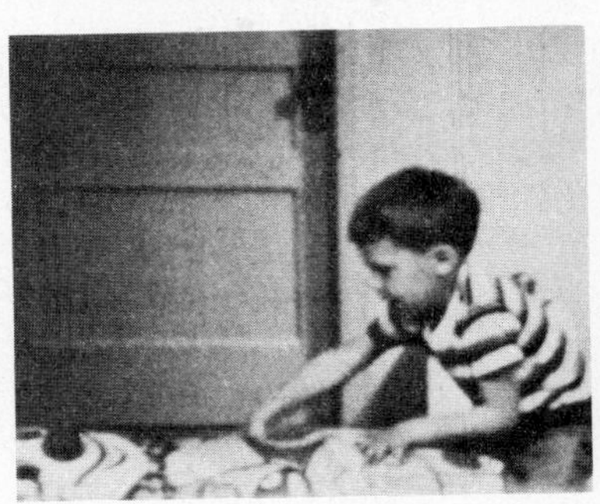

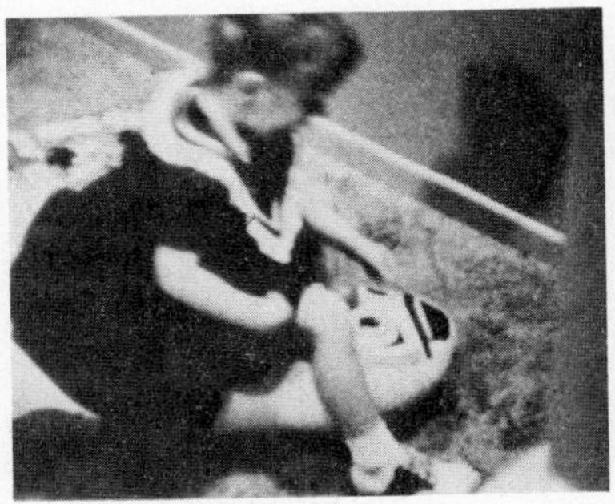
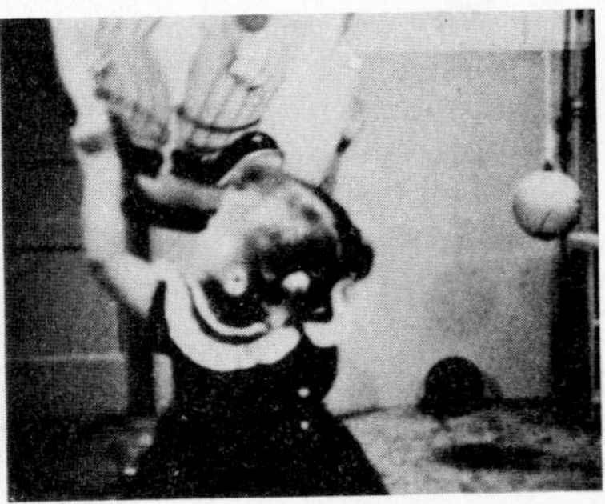

Bandura Study

Airline skyjacking was once very rare. Then, in the late 1960's, a handful of skyjackers attained national prominence abetted by massive media coverage. Soon the incidence of skyjacking reached epidemic proportions (Bandura, 1973). Many of the later skyjackers were obviously suggested by earlier ones. For instance, within months after D. B. Cooper parachuted from a Northwest Airlines plane with $200,000 in loot, a number of American skyjackers attempted the same feat with identical tactics.

* * * *

In 1975, Lynette ("Squeaky") Fromme attempted to assassinate President Gerald Ford. While among a crowd of well-wishers, she pointed a pistol at the President, and failed only because she had forgotten to push a cartridge into proper firing position. Scarcely two weeks later, Sara Jane Moore also attempted to assassinate President Ford, again with a pistol from within a crowd of onlookers. She managed to fire one shot, but only after a bystander knocked her arm aside. In this case, too, it seems almost certain that the later act of aggression was modeled on the first.

It's likely that many other less distinctive acts of aggression—murders, muggings, even arguments—have also resulted from the modeling of events reported in the news or portrayed on TV.

Getting Used to It

Observing violence may have still another undesirable effect: the more we see or read about, the less it seems to bother us. Just as we become habituated to loud noises or other sensory stimuli, so that we no longer notice them, we may also be-

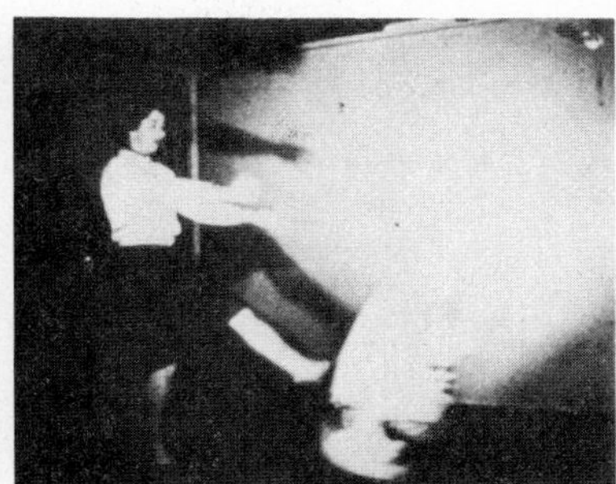

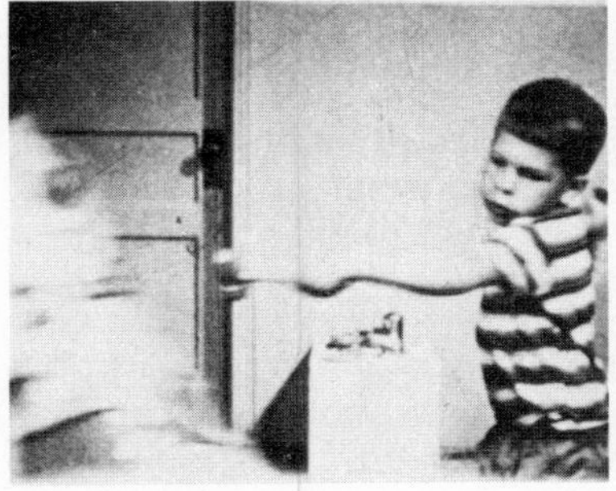

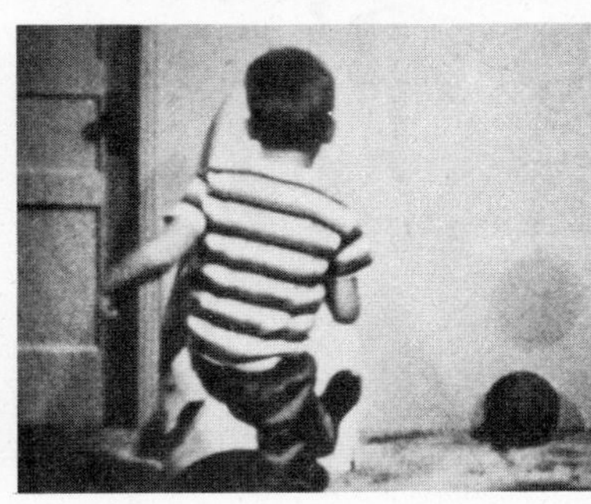

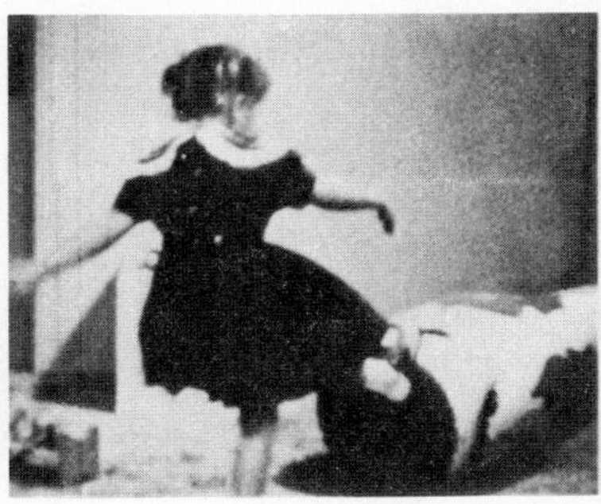

Observing violence may have still another undesirable effect: the more we see or read about, the less it seems to bother us.

come habituated to violence, so that it no longer seems notable or upsetting.

Ronald Drabman and Margaret Hanratty Thomas (1975) demonstrated this habituation process in an experiment with third- and fourth-graders. The children were taken individually into a game room, where half of them watched a violent eight-minute segment of a Western movie and the other half just played without being exposed to violence. Afterward, each child was asked to keep an eye on two younger children who were playing in another room. Although the younger children's interaction was actually videotaped, the subjects believed that it was live. The experimenter left the room while the subjects observed the younger children, but he instructed them to call him right away if anything seemed to go wrong. About a minute into the observed interaction, a fierce and destructive fight began. The children being videotaped started hitting each other, were soon crying, and even seemed to have smashed the camera. It turned out, as Drabman and Thomas had predicted, that the third- and fourth-graders who had watched the violent movie took longer to call for help than did the children who hadn't seen the movie. The children who had seen the film had apparently become habituated to violence, so that it took longer for them to consider the children's fight significant. If these results can be extended to adolescents and adults (and it seems likely that they can), then the conclusion is clear: the more violence we observe—in movies, on the news, or in the streets—the more we may come to accept it as a natural part of life.

Lynette "Squeaky" Fromme

Institutional Violence

Our behavior depends to a large extent on our social *roles*—the expectations about how we ought to behave by virtue of being in a particular situation or of holding a particular position. And, unfortunately, some situations and occupations place people who might otherwise be quite gentle and peaceful into roles that encourage violence. Violence that is encouraged by people's roles in large organizations or social institutions is called *institutional violence.*

Philip Zimbardo and his associates (1974) provided a striking example of how placing people into particular social roles can lead to violent behavior. They set up a mock prison in the basement of the psychology building at Stanford University and developed a detailed set of prison rules and procedures, modeled after those of real prisons. For example, the "prisoners" were given ID numbers and were made to wear stocking caps, while the "guards" were given such symbols of power as billy clubs, whistles, handcuffs, and keys. To play the roles of prisoners and guards, 22 normal, well-adjusted college students were recruited to serve in a 14-day simulation of prison life. Neither the prisoners nor the guards were the sorts of people you would expect to be callous or brutal. They were all emotionally stable young men, and they were assigned to the role of "prisoner" or "guard" on the basis of a flip of a coin.

Although the subjects of Zimbardo's simulation were not normally violent people, placing them in the simulated prison roles had unexpected dramatic effects on their behavior. In particular, students assigned to be guards exhibited brutal and sadistic behavior. A dramatic example of the way in which one of these students was gradually drawn into his guard role comes from the diary that he kept during the course of the experiment (excerpted from Zimbardo, et al, 1974, pages 70–71).

PRIOR TO THE EXPERIMENT: As I am a pacifist and nonag-

gressive individual, I cannot see a time when I might guard and/or maltreat a living thing.

FIRST DAY: Felt sure that the prisoners will make fun of my appearance. . . . At cell 3 I stop and setting my voice hard and low I say to #5486, "What are you smiling at?" "Nothing, Mr. Correctional Officer." "Well, see that you don't." (As I walk off I feel stupid.)

SECOND DAY: 5704 asked for a cigarette and I ignored him. . . . Meanwhile, since I was feeling empathetic toward 1037, I determined not to talk with him. . . .

THIRD DAY: I made sure I was one of the guards on the yard, because this was my first chance for the type of manipulative power that I really like. . . . 817 is being obnoxious and bears watching.

FOURTH DAY: The psychologist rebukes me for handcuffing and blindfolding a prisoner before leaving the office, and I resentfully reply that it is both necessary security and my business anyway.

FIFTH DAY: The real trouble starts at dinner. The new prisoner (416) refuses to eat his sausage . . . we throw him into the Hole ordering him to hold sausages in his hand. We have a crisis of authority, this rebellious conduct potentially undermines the complete control we have over the others. . . . I decided to force feed him, but he wouldn't eat. I let the food slide down his face. I didn't believe it was me doing it. I hated myself for making him eat, but I hated him more for not eating.

SIXTH DAY: The experiment is over. I feel elated but am shocked to find some other guards disappointed somewhat because of the loss of money and some because they are enjoying themselves.

The planned two-week experiment was cancelled after only six days.

The planned two-week experiment was cancelled after only six days. The prison simulation was becoming too real, and Zimbardo could no longer risk the physical and psychological well-being of his subjects. However real prisons can't be cancelled. Prisoners and guards can't simply stop pretending and go home. These institutions are permanent, and in their present state they give violence a permanent place in American life.

Other institutions, including police forces, armies, and national guards, also place individuals in roles that encourage and even require violence in the name of preserving order. Police officials, soldiers, and guardsmen are not "naturally" aggressive people, nor for that matter are the gang members of terrorists whom they are likely to oppose. In all of these cases, violence is institutionalized; it is part of the set of social roles and obligations that regulate people's behavior.

Institutional violence on the part of forces of law and order often seems justified, since it protects society from criminals, terrorists, or other enemies. As such tragedies as the slaughter of innocent civilians at My Lai during the Vietnam war and the slaughter of college students during a protest at Kent State University have taught us, however, it is often difficult to determine where justified violence ends and unjustified violence begins. Indeed, some cases of institutional violence seem to have resulted less from a desire to protect society than from the institutionalization of people's (often political leaders') insecurities or desires for revenge. When our institutions become a vehicle for the expression of personal animosities, the very structure of our society is threatened.

PART 5

The Span of Life

A big part of being human is *becoming* human. We grow and develop throughout life, not only physically, but also in our intellectual abilities, motives, values, and patterns of behavior. These processes of development are directed both from within, in the natural unfolding of our biologically given capacities, and from without, as we are shaped by the experiences we acquire throughout life.

These processes of psychological development are the theme of the next two chapters. Chapter 11 is devoted to the *Beginnings of Life.* We will explore life's beginnings in two different senses—first, the processes of evolution that led to the emergence of the human species; and second, the processes of genetics, conception, prenatal development, and birth that are involved in launching each individual human life. The Psychological Issue following this chapter concerns an interesting sidelight of one's entry into the world—the ways in which a person's *Birth Order* within his or her family may influence subsequent psychological development.

Chapter 12 deals with the span of life that extends *From Infancy to Old Age.* This chapter begins where the previous one leaves off, with the newborn infant poised on the threshold of life. It goes on to survey the central features of psychological development through the major stages of the life cycle—infancy, childhood, adolescence, early and middle adulthood, and old age. This chapter emphasizes that psychological development is not limited to the years of infancy and childhood. We continue to *become* human—to grow, to develop, and to change—throughout our lives. The Psychological Issue following Chapter 12 concerns the social relationships between members of different generations. We will ask whether there really is such a thing as *The Generation Gap*—and, if there is, what its nature and sources might be.

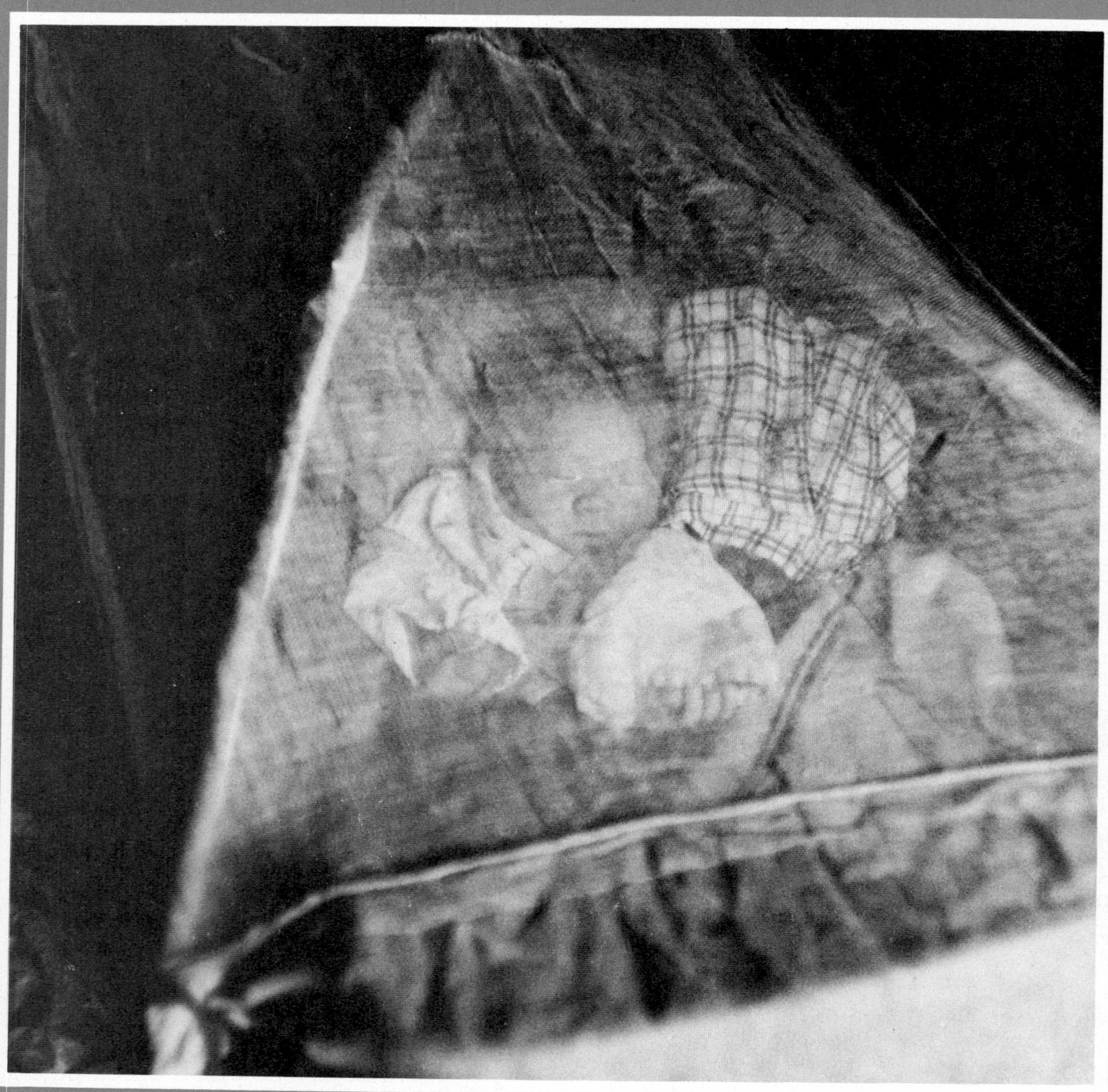

Beginnings of Life

CHAPTER

11

Beginnings of Life

How does life begin? In one sense, life on Earth began many millions of years ago, when the Earth's chemicals combined in such a way as to produce the first one-celled organisms that could be called living things. The road from those one-celled organisms to today's plants, animals, and human beings was a process that extended over untold millions of years. In another sense, human life begins whenever a child is conceived and is born. From the standpoint of psychology, it is important to know something about both the evolutionary origins of human life and the prenatal development of individual human beings. Each of these beginnings of life plays an important role in shaping our behavior. In this chapter, we will begin with a discussion of the basic principles of evolution and genetics that underlie the transmission of life from generation to generation. Then we will discuss the events that lead to the emergence of individual human beings—conception, pregnancy, and birth. We will end the chapter, and point to the chapter that follows, by taking a glimpse at the behavior of the newborn infant.

EVOLUTION

"There are one hundred and ninety-three living species of monkeys and apes," writes the biologist Desmond Morris (1967). "One hundred and ninety-two of them are covered with hair. The exception is a naked ape self-named *Homo sapiens*" (page 9). *Homo sapiens*, of course, is us. This scientific name for the human species comes from the Latin words *homo*, meaning "man," and *sapiens*, meaning "thinking."

The great apes, including the gorilla and the chimpanzee, are our closest living relatives. We did not evolve directly from any of the apes that inhabit the Earth today, however. Instead, we are very distant cousins, with our closest common ancestors being creatures who lived some 14 million years ago, long before the emergence of today's people or chimps. The earliest of our direct ancestors to be discovered through fossil evidence is the apeman *Australopithecus*, who walked upright and used tools about 3 million years ago. *Homo sapiens* is only a toddler in the perspective of evolution—we've only been around for about 250,000 years (Curtis, 1975).

The Principle of Natural Selection

Over the billions of years of the Earth's existence, the original one-celled organisms have given rise to life forms as diverse as hyacinths, herrings, hummingbirds, hippopotami, and humans. How does this process of evolution come about? The key elements of the answer were provided by the biologist Charles Darwin (1809–1882) in his world-famous book *The Origin of Species.* The basis of Darwin's account is the principle of *natural selection.* Darwin noted that although the members of any given plant or animal species share basic characteristics, they also vary markedly among themselves. Take dogs, for example. Although they all share some general features, dogs vary widely in size, shape, coloring, and temperament. And the same holds true for every other sort of plant or animal, from cockroaches to human beings.

Given this diversity of organisms, natural selection can take place. Of all the members of a particular species, only some bear offspring, and only some of these offspring ever reach adulthood. The ones who are "selected" to survive are those who are best able to adapt to their environment. In a particular species of grass, for example, the stronger, hardier blades might be least likely to get blown away by the wind before they can reproduce. If this is the case, these stronger, hardier blades will be "selected." And the next generation of grass blades will inherit the characteristics of their parents. Over the course of many genera-

A VERY LONG STORY

"Where does the story of human evolution begin? We might start with a chance combination of chemicals in some warm Precambrian sea. Or perhaps even with the formation of a small planet 93 million miles from a star. Or it might begin 4 billion years later, when some little tribe of man-apes found they could sharpen a digging stick or hone the flat edge of a stone. In any case, it is a very long story, measured in human terms, and many of its details are lost to us, probably forever." (Curtis, 1975, page 911)

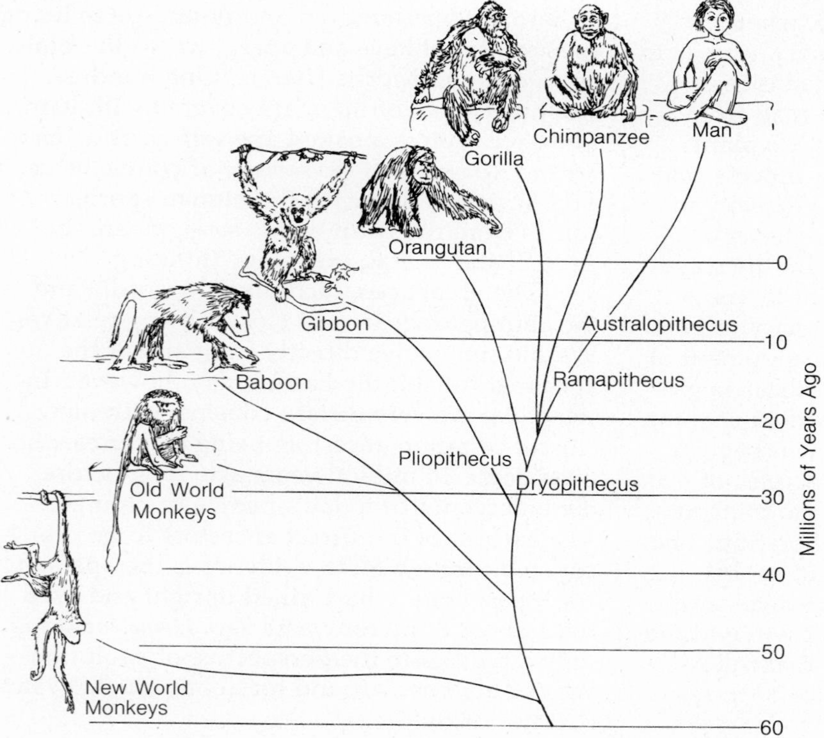

FIG. 11 · 1 A tentative account of the evolution of man and the other higher primates, based on fossil evidence (adapted from Curtis, 1975, p. 926).

> **THE PRICE WE PAY**
>
> One of the most important differences between humans and the apes is that we can walk continuously on two legs. But our bipedalism, accomplished through the course of evolution, was not bought without a price. As a result of our two-legged posture, members of the human species suffer from backaches, rupture easily, and have far more trouble bearing children than any other animal (Curtis, 1975).

tions, therefore, the species of grass as a whole will become stronger and hardier. Similarly, if in a species of fish those with a particular coloring are most likely to survive—because the coloring provides camouflage against predators—the species will gradually take on that coloring. Thus, natural selection does not in itself produce variations, but it channels the variations that naturally occur by perpetuating some and eliminating others.

Can this principle explain the evolution of the human species as well? When Darwin lived, it seemed heretical to suggest this possibility. After all, the Bible tells us that God placed man and woman on Earth, and it doesn't say anything about evolution. Because of this, Darwin put forth this possibility most cautiously, in the very last pages of *The Origin of Species.* By now, however, there is general acceptance of the idea that humans evolved from earlier species, and that, as a result, we share a heritage with the rest of the animal kingdom.

GENETICS

To understand evolution more fully, it is necessary to understand some basic principles of genetics. The word *genetics* begins with the word *gene.* Genes are the tiny structures within the nuclei of the body's cells that carry the messages of heredity. The genes contain a chemical called deoxyribonucleic acid—DNA, for short—that serves as the carrier of genetic information. When a child is conceived, the genes received from the sperm and egg cells of the father and mother jointly play the role of chemical instructors to the developed organism. These genetic instructions affect the physical characteristics of the child—it is because of such messages that a child can have "her father's nose" or "his mother's eyes." In addition, genes affect the child's developing brain and nervous system in ways that can affect his or her intellectual capacities, personality, and behavior.

Genotype and Phenotype

If parents' characteristics are passed on to their children through their genes, why aren't children exact carbon copies of their parents? One reason is that genes always act in pairs, one from each parent. A combination of two sets of characteristics may often lead to a result that resembles neither very closely. More fundamentally, genetic information is only indirectly reflected in visible characteristics. We must distinguish here between a person's *genotype,* or genetic make-up, and the persons's *phenotype,* or outward expression of the genetic make-up. For example, Jerry's genes for eye color may be one brown (say from his father) and one blue (from his mother). So Jerry's genotype for the characteristic of eye color is brown-blue. But this doesn't mean that Jerry will have one brown eye and one blue eye. In fact, he will have brown eyes, because the gene for brown eyes outranks the gene for blue eyes in the determination of eye color (the phenotype). In this case, the gene for brown eyes is said to be *dominant* and the gene for blue eyes is said to be *recessive.* Only one member of each parent's pair of genes for a given characteristic is included in the sperm or egg cell and passed on to the child. Thus, if Jerry marries and has a child—let's call her Terry—only one of his two eye-color genes, either the brown or the blue, will be passed on to her. Which gene is included in the sex cell is randomly determined. If the brown-eye gene happens to be passed on, then Terry's eyes will be brown, regardless of the genetic contribution of Jerry's wife. If the blue eye gene is passed on, Terry's eyes will be either blue or brown, depending on the genetic contribution of Jerry's wife. In addition to eye color, several other human traits are controlled by a single gene pair, including blood type, color vision, hair curliness, and hair color. However, most human traits involve an interaction between many gene parts, so tracing the genetic origins of most traits is much more complex than tracing the origins of a person's eye color.

The fact that offspring manifest complex combinations of their parents' characteristics is one reason for the fact that there continues to be a great deal of diversity among members of a species. The genes of two parents can arrange themselves in an almost infinite number of ways. It is for this reason that whereas brothers and sisters sometimes resemble each other a great deal, they sometimes hardly resemble each other at all.

Behavior Genetics

Genes can affect not only our physical characteristics but our psychological characteristics as well. We saw in Chapter 8 that heredity plays a substantial role in determining people's intellectual capacities. And in Chapter 16, we will discover that there is a large hereditary factor in the likelihood that someone will develop the psychological disorder called schizophrenia. There is also evidence that heredity plays some role in determining aspects of people's personalities.

The study of the hereditary factors affecting personality and behavior is called *behavior genetics.* Most of the data in this area come from other animals. For example, studies have shown that heredity has a great deal to do with the degree of savageness of laboratory rats. The white rat is tamed easily; the gray rat is not. When white rats are mated with gray rats, some of the offspring show the tame disposition of the white parent, while others exhibit the savageness of the gray parent (Stone, 1932).

There is some indication that there is a hereditary basis for human emotionality as well. Although there is no evidence that a particular emotional trait (like happiness or grouchiness) can be inherited, it is believed that the general tendency to be emotional is affected by heredity. In one study, the correlations between the bodily states associated with emotion were computed among pairs of identical twins, pairs of siblings, and pairs of unrelated children. The highest correlation was found among the identical

HEREDITY AND HANDEDNESS

Hicks and Kinsbourne (1976) found that the hand preference (left-handed or right-handed) of college students correlated significantly with the handedness of their parents. This fact in itself could be interpreted more than one way. It might suggest that hand preference has a genetic basis, but it might also suggest that parents train their children to write with the same hand they do. To help determine which interpretation is correct, Hicks and Kinsbourne also found that among students who were raised by step-parents hand preference correlated with that of the biological parents, and not of the step-parents. This evidence makes a strong case for the theory that genetic factors play a major role in the determination of which hand is preferred.

twins, and the lowest among unrelated children, suggesting that emotionality has a genetic basis (Jost and Sontag, 1944).

In acknowledging the fact that genes influence our psychological characteristics it is important to emphasize that these effects are indirect. It has often been noted that genes don't produce behavior—people do. There is no gene for "intelligence" or "emotionality" or any other psychological characteristic. Rather, genes have their effects on the development of bodily structures, including the brain and nervous system, and on the enzymes that help to regulate our bodies' chemical processes. These physical and chemical legacies can then play a part in determining our intellectual capacities, personalities, and behavior—but only in a complex interaction with the environments in which we grow up. It would be quite unusual, therefore, for two brothers to have extremely similar personalities, even if their genes were quite similar. After all, each of the brothers grew up in a somewhat different environment, with different friends, different teachers, and so on; not the least of these differences is that one brother had an older brother influencing him, while the other had a younger brother to contend with. (For a further look at the way in which people's family positions may affect them, see the Psychological Issue on birth order at the end of this chapter.)

Genetic Defects

About 250,000 of the four million American babies born each year have birth defects. Only about 20 percent of these can be attributed to heredity—the rest are caused by environmental factors during pregnancy or by abnormalities in the chromosomes (the structures that contain the genes) (Stock, 1969).

Most genetically caused disorders are recessive genetic traits. Take *phenylketonuria* (PKU), for example. Children born with this disease lack an important enzyme that normally functions to help break down phenylalanine, an amino acid found in many high-protein foods such as milk. Without this enzyme, the phenylalanine builds up in the body and eventually disturbs brain and nervous system functioning by causing the destruction of brain cells. Children with PKU show severe mental retardation, hyperactivity, skin disorders and discoloration, and epileptic-like seizures. Fortunately, this disease can be controlled when it is discovered early enough, and today most states require a routine blood test of newborns for PKU. If PKU is discovered, the infant is put on a diet that regulates the amount of phenylalanine consumed, so that it will never reach dangerous levels. This disease occurs only in individuals who have received the defective gene from both parents. Those with only one defective gene show no signs of the disease.

Some genetic defects are found primarily among particular ethnic or racial groups. For example, *Tay-Sachs disease* is found almost exclusively in children descended from Jews who once inhabited a small area in Eastern Europe. Tay-Sachs is invariably fatal; it causes blindness, deafness, nervous system degeneration, and finally death before the age of four. Fortunately, this disease is very rare. It is a recessive trait, so if both parents are carriers with one normal gene and one defective gene their child has about a 1 in 4 chance of receiving two defective genes and of being born with the disease. Parents who are carriers can be identified with a blood test, and a fetus with the disease can be detected by amniocentesis (see Box 1). In such cases, abortion could prevent the birth of a fatally ill child (Ausubel, Beckwith, and Jannsen, 1974).

Other serious diseases that afflict only certain groups are *sickle-cell anemia* among blacks and *cystic fibrosis* among Northern European whites. About 8 to 10 percent of American blacks are carriers for the defective sickle-cell gene, and about 1 percent have two defective genes and therefore suffer from this painful blood disease. Abnormally shaped blood cells clog tiny blood vessels, cutting off oxygen supplies to vital tissues. The disease is thus ultimately fatal, although new sorts of treatment are now being attempted. Children with cystic fibrosis suffer malformations of certain glands; usually, the affliction is severe enough to bring an early death, although in some cases measures can be

---

Box 1

Genetic Counseling

Recent medical and technological advances have made it possible for us to know in advance whether a child is likely to be born with genetic defects, such as forms of severe mental retardation (including Down's syndrome) or certain diseases (such as Tay-Sachs disease) that are likely to be fatal within the first few years of life. By analyzing the blood of prospective parents, it is possible to determine the degree of risk that their offspring will have certain genetic diseases. And through a technique called *amniocentesis,* cells sloughed off from the fetus can be extracted from the mother's womb and the presence of genetic diseases can be detected.

These techniques of genetic screening and prenatal diagnosis can help couples who are in high-risk groups (often because of a history of genetic defects in their family) decide whether it is safe for them to have children. Prenatal diagnosis can also make it possible for doctors to treat a potentially harmful condition or for a couple to decide to abort a pregnancy rather than to have a severely retarded or fatally ill child. But in spite of their possible benefits, these techniques may also have great costs. Sometimes the knowledge that they are carriers of genetic defects makes prospective parents feel so fearful, ashamed, or guilty that they would have preferred never to have had the knowledge at all.

Dealing with the fears and doubts of prospective parents is part of the task of a new group of professionals called *genetic counselors.* Genetic counselors may be psychologists, physicians, nurses, or social workers; often members of different disciplines work together in teams. Their job is to inform prospective parents about genetic facts, risks, and potential courses of action. This role is an extraordinarily sensitive one. One physician interviewed by Richard Restak (1975) raised some of the issues:

Is [the counselor] an information giver . . . ? Should he say, "The tests indicate this is the likelihood of a defective child: make up your own mind"? Or should he intrude his own values and say, "The risk is too high and I'd advise you to have an abortion"? The genetic counselor shouldn't put himself in the role of God, and yet many times this is what the parents want, someone to tell them what they should do (page 23).

And, of course, people's individual values about what to

taken, using antibiotics and special diets, to help affected children achieve normal lives.

Because so many of these genetic defects are ultimately fatal, it seems logical that these diseases should disappear in the course of natural selection. Surely if there is a "survival of the fittest" people with such terrible diseases would not survive. So why do these defects continue to exist? There are, in fact, explanations in terms of natural selection. In the case of sickle-cell anemia, for example, it turns out that the incidence is extremely high in some African tribes—40 percent of the people are carriers and 4 percent have the disease. It has been discovered that people with the sickle-cell trait are much more resistant to malaria than people with two normal genes for blood hemoglobin. It seems, then, that the gene is an evolutionary adaption to malaria (quite common in Africa) and that having it increases the "fitness" of the African blacks, who might otherwise die of malaria before they can reproduce. Since there is no malaria in this country, the sickle-cell trait has no adaptive value here. Its steady decline provides a striking example of human evolution in action.

---

do in such situations differ widely. Many people believe that it is proper and humane to prevent the birth of a child who would be seriously defective and whose life would be one of great suffering. One father who already had a genetically defective child explained his willingness to abort another child who would have been abnormal: "I couldn't go through it again . . . It is not doing anything for the child, or for society, to be born so sickly." Another father saw the possibility of aborting a defective child as a matter of responsibility: "We have an obligation to our children before they are born; you can't turn your back on the future" (quoted in Restak, 1975, page 22).

But others are frightened by these possibilities, because they raise the question, "Who is to decide what is defective?" As one concerned woman recently asked, "Where do we stop in terms of defect? With hemophilia? With the possibility of cancer? . . . With a boy when parents want a girl? With color blindness? With premature balding?" (Kennedy, 1976). Since all of these "defects" are at least in part genetically determined and might potentially be detected through amniocentesis, her question is by no means a frivolous one.

The possibility of making the decision to destroy a "defective" fetus before birth also raises awesome questions about our general attitudes toward the sick and disabled. For example, Leon Kass has raised the question of how we will regard a child who is born with a genetic defect at a time when most of the child's potential fellow sufferers were destroyed before birth: "[The child] is likely to be looked upon by the community as one unfit to be alive, as a second-class (or even lower) human type. He may seem as a person who need not have been, and who would not have been if only someone had gotten to him in time" (quoted in Restak, 1975, page 22).

In spite of these dilemmas, most scientists and students of ethics see the potential value of genetic screening and prenatal diagnosis in reducing human suffering as too great to disavow. There may even come a time in the not-too-distant future when fetal surgery will be perfected, so that normal genes can be substituted for defective ones before they have their harmful effects. But one cannot overstate the need for careful attention to the potential problems and abuses of these techniques and the need to develop new ethical and legal guidelines for dealing with them.

Another type of defect that involves genetic material is *Down's syndrome* (mongolism). This condition is not inherited from parents; rather, it is the result of incorrect distribution of genetic material at the time of conception. Children born with this condition are mentally retarded (they seldom have IQs over 50) and are characterized by such physical abnormalities as slanted eyes, a flat face and nose, stubby features, and shorter than normal arms and legs. The likelihood of a child being born with Down's syndrome increases dramatically with the mother's age. There is only one chance in 2,000 that a woman in her twenties will give birth to a child with Down's syndrome, but there is one chance in 40 for a woman over 40.

CONCEPTION

The development of a new human being begins at the moment of conception—the moment when the male sex cell (the sperm) unites with the female sex cell (the egg) and forms the first cell of the new human organism, the fertilized egg or *zygote*. Sperm are produced in the testes of the male; eggs develop in the ovaries of the female. A sperm cell has a flat, oval-shaped body and a long, threadlike tail. Millions of sperm are carried in a fluid called semen, and, when deposited in the vagina, they live for two to five days. Sperm move by a whiplash action of the tail at a rate of about three to six inches per hour. Although only one sperm is needed to fertilize an egg cell, often not a single one of the millions of sperm in an ejaculation reaches the egg.

The egg cell is much larger than the tiny sperm (it can sometimes be seen with the naked eye) and consists mostly of nutritive material. The egg cell doesn't live long either, from only

Box 2

Multiple Births

When more than one egg is produced and fertilized, multiple conceptions can occur, and multiple births may result. Two eggs fertilized by two sperm cells produce *fraternal twins.* Fraternal twins need not be very much alike, since each is the result of the union of completely different cells. Similarly, more egg cells may be produced and fertilized by separate sperm cells, resulting in fraternal triplets, quadruplets, and quintuplets. In the past few years the use of fertility drugs has produced a number of instances in which several egg cells are produced by the female reproductive system at one time.

Sometimes, a single egg cell that has been fertilized by a single sperm cell divides soon after fertilization and produces two individuals—*identical twins,* each of whom possesses the same genetic material. Only one-third of all pairs of twins are identical, however. Twins occur in about 1 out of 90 births. Other types of multiple birth are much less common—triplets occur in 1 out of 9,000 births, and quadruplets appear in only one out of 500,000 births.

In many primitive societies multiple births are considered abnormal and the work of evil spirits. In such cultures the unlucky newborns are usually killed. In other cultures twins and triplets are accepted but are often explained in unusual terms. The Kawai people of New Guinea, for example, believe that twins result when a woman eats bananas from a tree with two bunches (Katchadourian and Lunde, 1975).

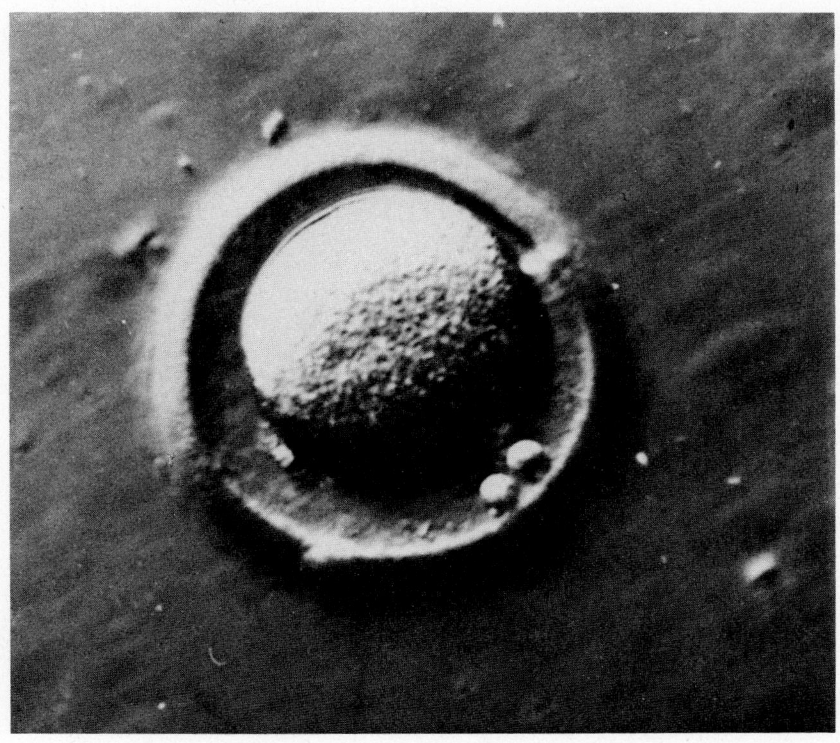

A fertilized human egg, or *zygote,* about 12 hours after conception.

CHOOSING THE SEX OF YOUR CHILD

A scientist named Landrum Shettles contends that he has come up with a way to predetermine the sex of children. To increase the chances of having a boy, Shettles recommends having intercourse as close as possible to the time of ovulation, preceded by an alkaline douche of water and baking soda. To have a girl, the couple should stop having intercourse two or three days prior to ovulation, and intercourse should be preceded by an acid douche of water and vinegar. The reasoning behind these recommendations is that the sperm that carry a Y chromosome (determining a male offspring) are lighter and speedier than the sperm carrying the X chromosome (determining a female). The X-carrying sperm can better survive the acid douche and the two-or-three-day waiting period than can the Y-carrying sperm. But if intercourse takes place right at the time of ovulation, the Y carrying sperm are more likely to win the race to the ovum in the more benign alkaline atmosphere. Shettles claims that couples following his advice can call the shots with 80 to 85 percent accuracy. Other scientists remain skeptical. (Rosenfeld, 1974).

a few hours to as long as two days. Once a month one of the ovaries discharges an egg cell, which floats down the fallopian tube (or oviduct) to the uterus. Sperm deposited during sexual intercourse move upward through the uterus and usually meet the egg cell somewhere in the oviduct. Many sperm surround the egg, trying to break down its outer membrane. At last one sperm cell succeeds in penetrating the egg, and conception has occurred. The membrane around the newly fertilized egg immediately changes to form a barrier to keep other sperm out. The fertilized egg now continues moving to the uterus, undergoing numerous cell divisions as it travels. Within a few days it attaches itself to the wall of the uterus, thereby inducing secretion of hormones that will stop the menstrual cycle and build up the uterine tissues to sustain life for the next 270 days.

LIFE BEFORE BIRTH

During the nine-month period between conception and birth, many significant events occur—to the developing child, to the mother who is carrying the child, and, from a slightly greater distance, to the expectant father as well. We will first discuss life before birth for the infant itself; then we will turn to the events of pregnancy from the standpoint of the prospective parents.

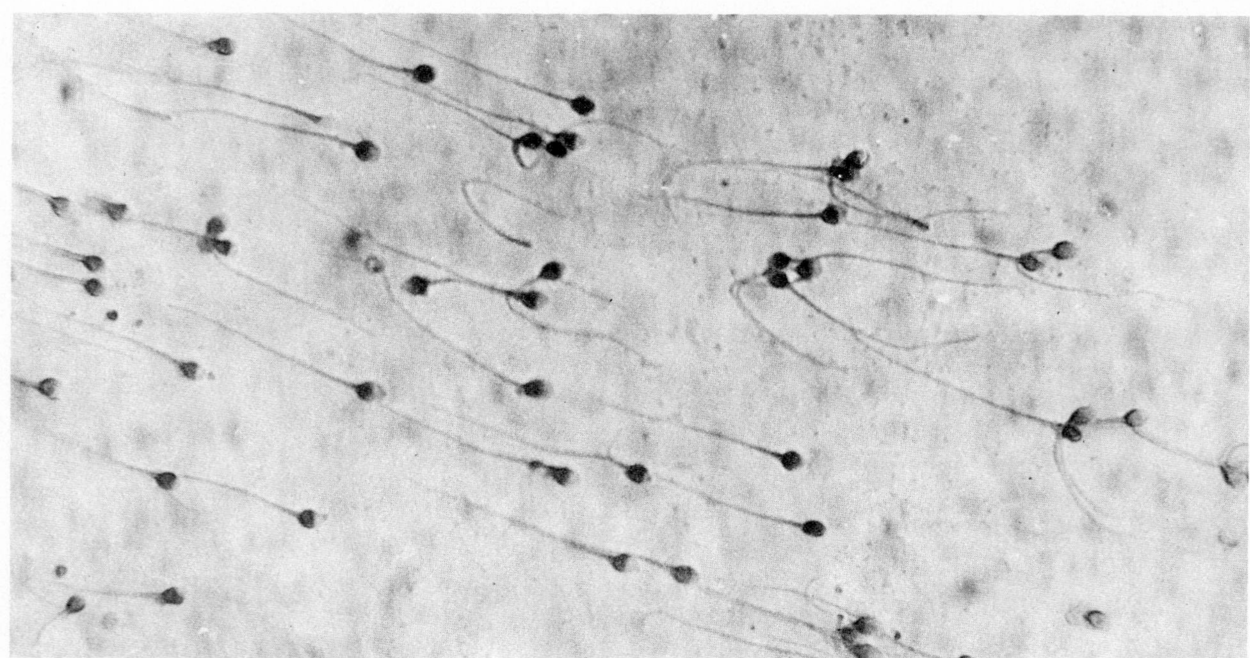

Living human sperm cells. Each cell is 1/800 inch in length, and swims toward the ovum at a rate of about an inch in 16 minutes.

Prenatal Development

In the first month after conception, the newly formed organism increases to nearly 10,000 times its initial size. In the first three months it progresses from a simple roundish dot to an infinitely complex human form—unfinished, but recognizable as a baby-to-be. The last month before birth is the slowest of all the nine months of prenatal development, yet if a baby were to go on growing as rapidly after birth as it does during this last month it would weigh something like 160 pounds on its first birthday.

The new life grows in the *placenta*—a network of blood vessels and membranes attached to the wall of the uterus. Materials from the mother's blood system, to provide nutrients and oxygen to the developing child, pass through the placenta to the blood vessels of the umbilical cord and to the blood system of the child. Waste materials are carried out the same way and are eliminated by the blood system of the mother.

The first few days after conception are called the period of the *zygote* (fertilized egg). When the zygote implants itself in the uterine wall (on about the fourth day), it becomes an *embryo*. The embryo floats within a structure called the *amniotic sac*, which is filled with a clear liquid that maintains an even temperature and helps to cushion the growing organism against shocks. During the embryonic period, all the essential elements of anatomy begin to form. The brain, heart, and liver are the first organs to form. The heart begins to beat during this period, the liver begins to manufacture red blood cells, and the limbs appear in budlike form. By the eighth week the eyes, ears, nose, and

THE ULTRASONIC BEAM

Doctors now know that some low-weight babies are actually full-term infants who for various reasons have not grown as much as they should. This weight difference is crucial, because the kind of care that is appropriate for a premature baby may actually be dangerous to a full-term, but underweight baby. A new device that beams ultrasonic waves into the uterus can now provide a three-dimensional "map" of the unborn child that doctors can compare with other maps to determine precisely if the fetus is the right size for its age. Some hospitals now have charts that detail the age at which various muscular reflexes develop. By comparing a newborn's reflexes with these charts, doctors can tell whether the infant is an underweight nine-month-old or a premature seven-month-old and plan treatment accordingly.

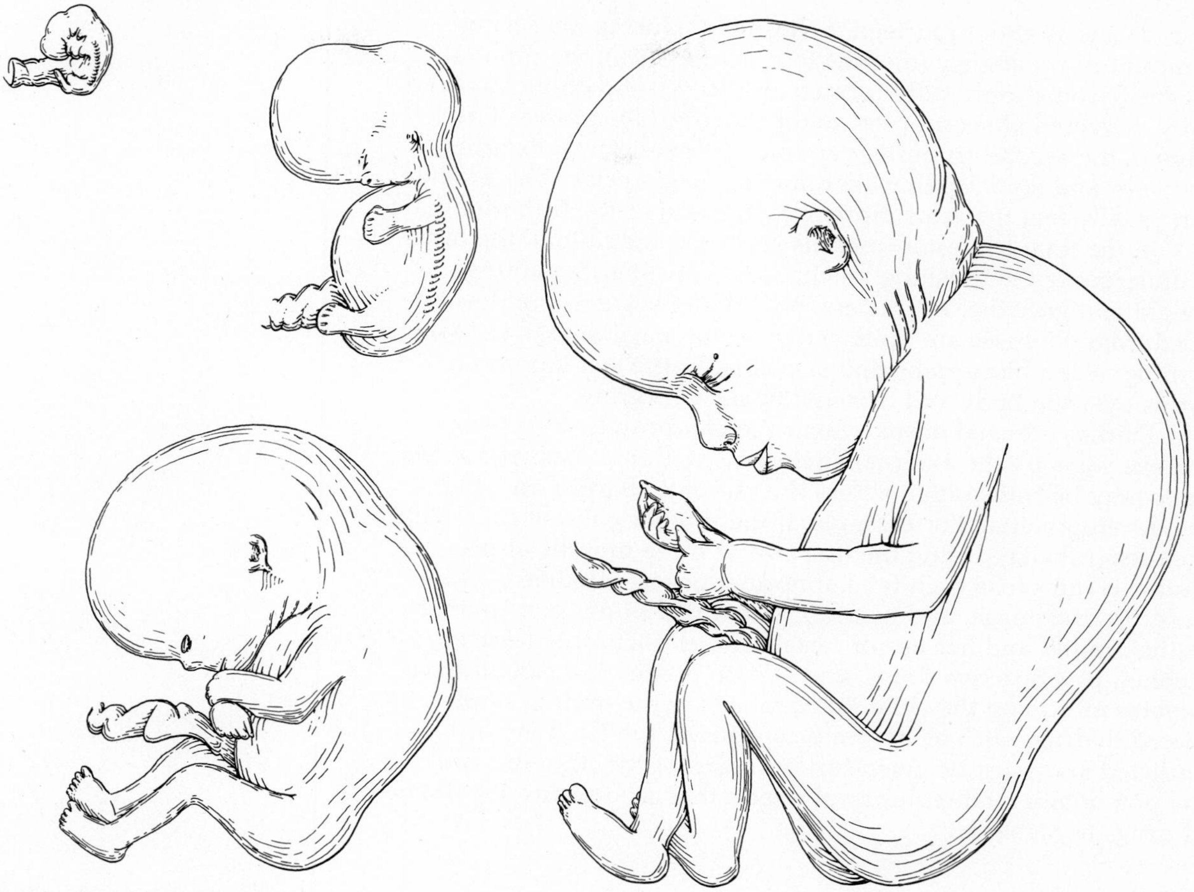

FIG. 11 · 2 The human embryo at one month after conception, and the fetus at two months, three months, and four months.

mouth are clearly recognizable. And by the third month the external sex organs can be identified as male or female.

By the end of the second month the organism is unmistakably human, and from this point on it is called a *fetus.* The fetus now weighs about two grams (only a small fraction of an ounce) and is about $1\frac{1}{2}$ inches long. It continues to grow rapidly, however, so that by the end of the sixth month it weighs about two

3 1/2 days

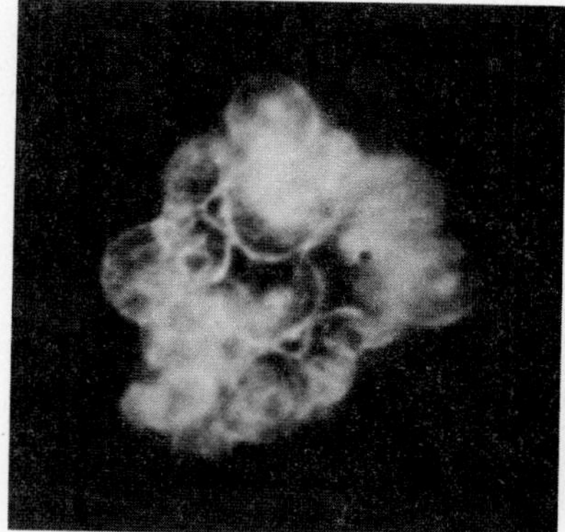

30 days

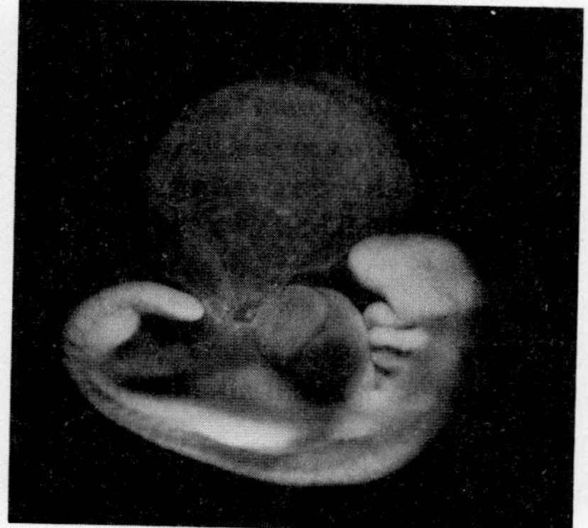

42 days

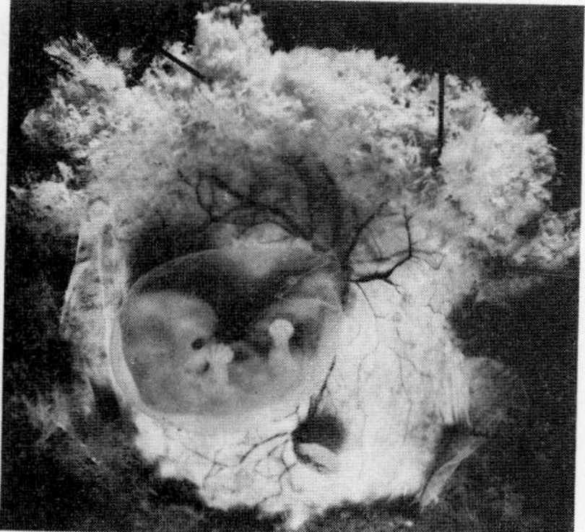

pounds and is about fourteen inches long. During the second trimester of pregnancy (months four through six), the internal organs become more fully formed and start to function, so that a baby delivered at six months might conceivably survive. The fetus in the second trimester can open its eyes, move its arms and legs, and go through wakefulness—sleep cycles. The mother can usually feel the fetus moving by the end of the fifth month.

In the final trimester (months seven through nine), the fetus is undergoing the finishing touches and is primarily gaining weight and growing. All the essential organ systems are developed. Many fetuses are quite active at this stage, kicking, tossing, turning—even hiccupping and sneezing. In the last month fat forms over the body and hair and fingernails grow.

During prenatal development the child can be affected in various ways by the external environment. Some maternal infections may be transmitted across the placental barrier and affect the developmental. For example, if the mother contracts German measles (rubella) during the first two or three months of pregnancy, it can cause such fetal abnormalities as blindness, deafness, brain damage, and heart disease. In addition, poor nutrition in the mother and her use of certain drugs (including tobacco, alcohol, psychoactive drugs, and certain medicines) can all have adverse effects on the child. In cases where the mother is addicted to drugs such as heroin or morphine the child is born addicted and must be given further doses of the drug to avoid the potentially fatal withdrawal effects that accompany the denial of drugs to an addict.

The Experience of Pregnancy

The nine months between conception and birth are a significant part of life not only for the child waiting to be born but also for the mother waiting to give birth. The experience of pregnancy, from the time a woman first suspects that she may be pregnant until the time she actually gives birth, is a dramatic one for many women, often filled with physical and emotional highs and lows.

The discovery that a woman has missed her menstrual period and may be pregnant is typically met with strong reactions. Some couples are overjoyed at the news and look forward to a child. Other couples have mixed feelings—they want a child, but they're not quite ready. And some react with dismay or fear when they learn of this unintended consequence of sexual activity.

It should be noted that a woman may miss her period for many reasons other than pregnancy. Various illnesses and emotional upsets may result in failure to menstruate. Sometimes medications the woman is taking will suppress the menstrual flow. And women under twenty and over forty sometimes skip a period for no apparent reason. That's why laboratory tests are used to determine whether a woman who has missed a period is pregnant or not.

YOUR BABY *IS* WHAT YOU EAT

"Some societies imposed dietary restrictions on pregnant women, often from fear that the fetus might otherwise take on undesirable characteristics of food, plants, or animals. For example, if the mother ate a rabbit, the child might have weak legs; if she ate trout, he might exhibit characteristic quivering movements. In addition, Ashanti women were forbidden to look upon any deformed object or creature during pregnancy lest their child be born with similar deformities" (Katchadourian and Lunde, 1975, page 143).

CULTURE AND MORNING SICKNESS

Morning sickness and the physical symptoms of pregnancy are caused in large measure by the hormonal changes that take place in the woman's body. In addition, these symptoms can be affected by cultural attitudes toward pregnancy and childbirth. Among the Truk, a society in the South Pacific, pregnancy is considered a terrible ordeal, and morning sickness is extremely common. Among the Woleians, another South Pacific people, the pregnancy is viewed as a positive experience and physical disorders during pregnancy are rare (Taylor and Langer, 1971). Anthropologist Margaret Mead (1949) has summed up the impact of cultural attitudes in the following terms: "We may say of morning sickness that where it is culturally stylized as appropriate for any period of pregnancy . . . a large majority of women will show this behavior; where it is not, only a few will" (page 221).

During the course of pregnancy, women are likely to experience a number of physical symptoms. Early in pregnancy, for example, there is enlargement and tenderness of the breasts and a tendency to feel tired and drowsy. Many women also experience "morning sickness" during the first six to eight weeks of pregnancy. It consists of queasy or nauseous feelings upon awakening, often accompanied by vomiting and an aversion to food. Some women experience such nausea in the evening as well, usually when the stomach is empty. The physical basis of morning sickness is the accumulation of fluid in the woman's stomach—during pregnancy the body's water retention increases by some 40 percent. The extent of morning sickness varies greatly from one woman to another, however, and about 25 percent of pregnant women in the United States never experience any vomiting (Katchadourian and Lunde, 1975).

The fourth through sixth months of pregnancy are usually the most pleasant for the prospective mother. The nausea and the drowsiness of the initial months are likely to have disappeared, and it is still too soon to worry about labor and delivery. During this period, the mother also becomes aware of the movements of the fetus inside her. In the last months of pregnancy, many women become eager to "get it over with" and "see what it is," as well as increasingly anxious about the health and normality of the infant.

The attitudes of one's culture toward pregnancy have a large impact on how the pregnant woman feels about herself and the activities she engages in during her pregnancy. Two social psychologists, Shelley Taylor and Ellen Langer (in press), have suggested that American attitudes toward pregnancy are peculiarly ambivalent. Although pregnant women are seen as deserving of consideration and attention, they are also viewed as objects of curiosity and with some degree of aversion. Pregnant women, they note, have traditionally been encouraged to stop working and to stay home once their condition becomes visible.

Taylor and Langer demonstrated some aspects of this attitude toward pregnant women in a dramatic experiment. The two researchers, women in their twenties, took turns at playing the central role of "being pregnant" in their study. They conducted their research in the elevators of two large apartment buildings. The women stood in the two back corners of the elevator, without seeming to know each other. One of them simulated pregnancy by placing a small pillow under her clothing. To equalize the amount of space occupied, the other experimenter carried a small cardboard box at abdomen level. Whenever someone entered the elevator, the researchers glanced at him or her briefly and then looked away. After the person left the elevator, they recorded his or her sex and where he or she had stood in the elevator, using the floor tiles as a convenient measure.

Taylor and Langer's main result was quite clear: The elevator riders tended to shy away from the "pregnant" woman. Both men and women stood closer to the nonpregnant experimenter, but the men did so to a considerably greater extent than the women. The researchers noted that several men who entered the elevator without noticing the pregnant experimenter's condition visibly backed off or moved quickly to the far side of the elevator as soon as they noticed. In one case, "A large curious dog was wrenched away from the pregnant confederate by his master so abruptly and so far that he spent the remainder of the ride sitting on the feet of the nonpregnant experimenter, a fact completely unnoticed by his owner, who was still apologizing to the pregnant experimenter."

Box 3

Biological Engineering

As we enter the last quarter of the twentieth century, scientists are beginning to discover new possibilities for the beginnings of life. These new methods, which involve the application of new scientific and technological advances to human reproduction, come under the general heading of *biological engineering.* Although biological engineering does not at present play a major role in human reproduction—and some people hope it never will—these possibilities are close enough at hand to make it important for us to consider them.

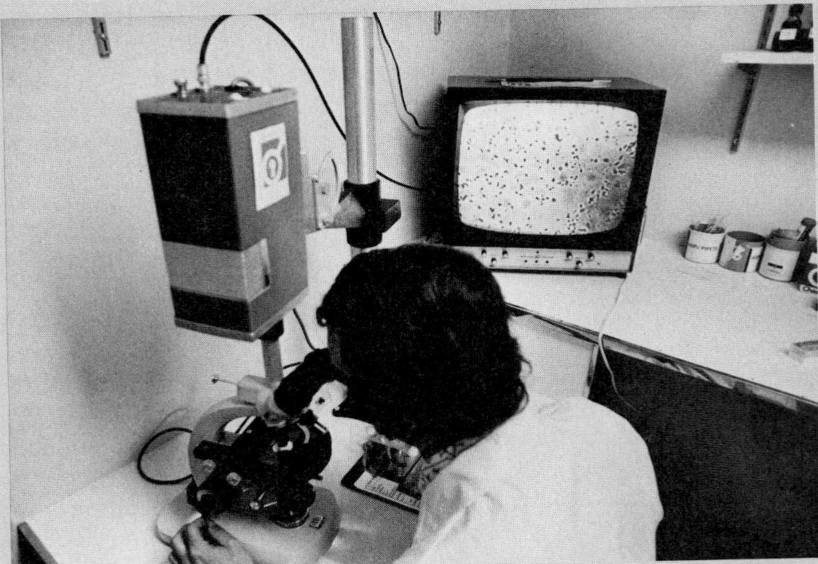

One of the areas of biological engineering that has achieved a certain notoriety is the notion of *test-tube babies*—the idea that human beings can be developed outside a woman's body. Although such reproduction is not currently possible, some interesting experiments are being conducted. For example, Dr. Robert G. Edwards of England's Cambridge University has been able to create the early stages of a human embryo in a test tube by mixing sperm with an egg surgically removed from the woman's ovary. He theorized that the embryo could be developed into a normal baby if implanted into a woman's womb.

In another line of research, Joshua Lederberg, a Nobel prize-winning geneticist, has predicted that we will soon be able to duplicate human beings from the cells of a single person, bypassing the traditional egg and sperm process. This procedure is called *cloning.* If that day comes, procreation could become completely separated from sexual intercourse. However, it will be a long while before such techniques are perfected and put into widespread use.

One technique of biological engineering that is in use today is *artificial insemination donation,* in which the sperm of an anonymous donor are implanted into a woman through a simple procedure that can be done in a doctor's office. Every year, 10,000 to 20,000 children of artificial insemination donation (A.I.D.) are born in the United States to couples who desire children but who are unable to produce a child together. A medical examination may indicate, for example, that the wife is fertile but that the husband has too low a concentration of sperm for conception to be likely. In

What accounts for this tendency to back away from a pregnant woman? There are several possible explanations, including a desire to avoid jostling the "baby," a desire to stand back to get a better look—furtive staring at pregnant women is indeed quite common—and a desire to avoid the woman. Taylor and Langer suggest that both the staring and the avoidance of pregnant women may have the same underlying cause: the fact that pregnant women are unfamiliar sights. Because women in the final months of pregnancy are encouraged to stay at home, they are only rarely seen in public places. When we do encounter such a

---

such a case, the sperm of an anonymous donor are deposited near the opening of the uterus during the woman's peak fertility period. It may take many attempts before the insemination "takes" and the woman becomes pregnant—or it might not succeed at all.

Some doctors advise couples to have intercourse around the time of insemination to add an element of doubt about the father and to increase the husband's sense of participation. A.I.D. donors are generally paid for their sperm. Their physical and mental health is checked, and an attempt is made to use a donor who bears a physical resemblance to the husband. The recent development of sperm banks, in which frozen sperm can be stored for several years, has revolutionized A.I.D. practice and made it easier to match physical characteristics. It also makes it possible to use the same donor for a second baby.

Some psychiatrists see A.I.D. as an indication of emotional disturbance in the couple and predict that the children will be likely to have emotional problems. But Lillian Atallah (1976), who was conceived through A.I.D. herself, believes that in fact there are few such problems:

Obviously, A.I.D. is not "right" for just any childless couples, just as natural parenthood is a poor role for many people. But when it is undertaken with proper precautions, A.I.D. can be a positive family experience lasting a lifetime, with the child focused not on the "irregularity" in his creation but on the "something extra"—the effort, commitment and love that have given him life. (page 52)†

Most doctors recommend not telling the child about his/her origins—it is not seen as comparable to adoption, where the child is generally told. But when Atallah, as an adult, was told that she had been conceived through A.I.D., her reaction was positive: "I felt grateful for the trouble they (my parents) had taken to give me life."

What are the social implications of A.I.D. and other sorts of biological engineering? Some of the ethical and legal questions involved are raised in a futuristic situation conjured up by Robert Francoeur (1970):

A barren woman, citizen of Russia, receives an ovarian transplant from a Negro citizen of Nigeria. Married to a sterile . . . native of the Australian bush country, she is artificially inseminated with frozen semen from an Eskimo . . . But the Russian woman has difficulty in carrying the child, so she arranges for an American Indian woman to serve as a substitute mother. Puzzle out, if you will— and if you can—the racial and national constitution of the offspring, its citizenship, and its two (?) parents!

The advocates of biological engineering argue that these new ways of beginning life could be used for the betterment of humanity. For example, they can provide ways for childless couples to have children, and, combined with other techniques, they may also help to prevent genetic defects in the future. But the possibilities are also frightening. Among other things, they raise the spectre of attempts (such as those actually made in Nazi Germany) to create a "master race" of human beings. With the advent of the possibility of biological engineering, we need to give a great deal of attention to the difficult legal and ethical issues involved.

†*From L. Atallah, "Report from a Test-tube baby,"* The New York Times, *April 18, 1976.*

woman, therefore, we regard her with some curiosity and trepidation. We feel an inclination to stare at the "novel visual stimulus," and at the same time we feel reluctant to stand too close to her. These reactions, Taylor and Langer point out, are quite similar to the reactions we have toward other people who serve as a "novel visual stimulus," such as those who are crippled, disfigured, or garishly dressed.

These reactions to pregnant women may have negative effects on the woman herself, since avoidance and staring are likely to be interpreted as negative responses. Such reactions are likely to make the woman feel uncomfortable and to strengthen her inclination not to go out in public. And this, in turn, may perpetuate a vicious cycle, in which visibly pregnant women are rarely seen and continue to be regarded as curiosities. Taylor and Langer argue that we should try to break through this vicious cycle and begin to regard pregnancy as a healthy and natural state, rather than as a stigma that needs to be kept under wraps. There is evidence that such changes have begun to take place in America. Until recently, pregnant women were obliged by most employers to leave work as soon as they began to "show," since it was not considered appropriate to have them appear in public. Recently, though, such required maternity leaves have been challenged in court, and they are being banned as discriminatory in most instances.

The Expectant Father

Although people are unlikely to pay any special attention to an expectant father as he stands in an elevator or walks down the street, the pregnancy period has special implications for fathers as well as for mothers. There are even a few cases on record in which the husband has a "sympathetic pregnancy," in which he shares some of his wife's symptoms. For example, he, too, may develop "morning sickness" and vomit along with his wife. Some writers speculate that this reaction is a result of the father's jealousy of his wife's exclusive ability to bear children.

Whereas such sympathetic pregnancies are extremely rare, it is not rare for a prospective father to be very involved in the events of the pregnancy and in preparation for the birth of a child. As one prospective father told a researcher, "We got into this pregnancy together, we'll get out of it together" (Fein, 1974, page 58). And fathers are becoming more likely to be present at the birth of their children and even to assist in the delivery.

BIRTH

After approximately nine months of pregnancy, the process of birth begins with regular contractions of the woman's uterus, as her cervix (the passage between the uterus and vagina) gradually expands. These contractions are generally experienced as painful, and they are called *labor pains.* They usually begin at intervals of 15 to 20 minutes, but they occur more frequently and with greater intensity as time passes. The period of labor typically extends for about 15 hours in a woman's first pregnancy and about 8 hours in later ones. When the contractions are coming every four or five minutes, the woman usually goes to the hospital and is admitted to the labor room. At some time later the woman is taken to the delivery room for the actual delivery, which may last from a few minutes to several hours. The husband may or may not be allowed to be present during the delivery, depending on state laws, hospital regulations, and the wishes of the couple.

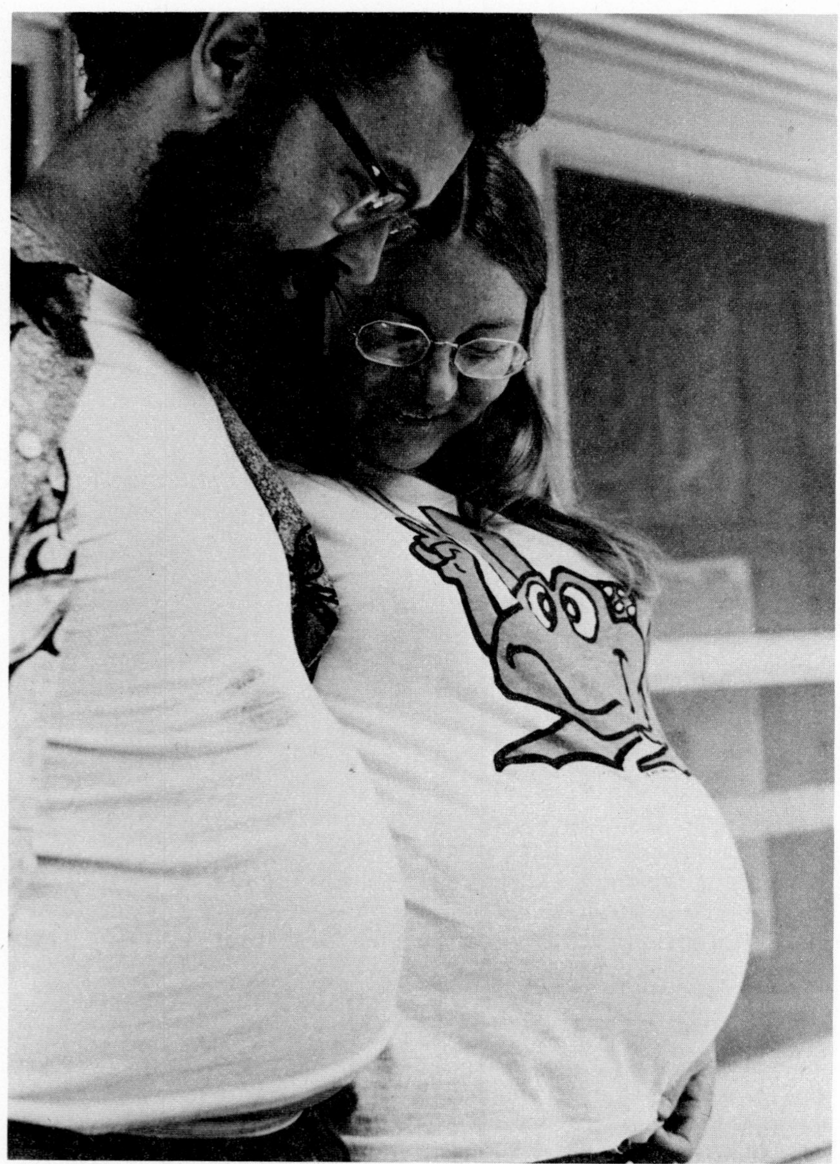

Cultural and Psychological Factors in Childbirth

Labor and childbirth are processes that almost universally involve pain for the mother. But specific cultural expectations can have a large impact on both the duration and the pain of the labor. To illustrate the importance of cultural expectations, Newton (1970) cites the differing experiences of childbirth among two different cultures: the Cuna Indians of Central America and the Siriono Indians of Bolivia.

Cuna Indian girls are not supposed to learn the truth about sex and childbirth until the marriage ceremony. To their dismay,

WHOOPS, *HE'S* GOING INTO LABOR!

In some primitive societies, like the Yap of the South Pacific, the father plays an active, if peculiar, part in the process of birth. During the birth of his child, the expectant father retires to his own hut, where he is expected to experience the pains of labor for himself. This custom of sex-role reversal is known as the *couvade*.

they then learn that pregnancy and birth are fearful female events. Midwives attend them at the time of birth, and all men and children are shunted away from the labor area. Even the medicine man is excluded, but he is kept informed about the progress of the labor so that he can chant and can supply appropriate medications. Labor is often prolonged and so extreme that the woman loses consciousness.

Childbirth among the Siriono is quite different. Birth is an open, public event that all interested parties may attend. The mother labors in a hammock in the hut while her visitors gossip, compare notes, and pass the time of day. No one is bothered by her grunts and groans of labor. When the baby is born, it simply slides over the edge of the hammock and drops a few inches to the ground. Most instances of labor observed by an anthropologist lasted only one to three hours—extremely short by Western standards.

There is no reason to believe that Cuna and Siriono women are any different from one another biologically. But the different attitudes and expectations of their cultures have a profound impact on the experience of childbirth and labor. "In the Cuna culture, where frightening ritual accompanies labor, girls tend to have extreme and sometimes lengthy labor with periods of unconsciousness. In contrast, the relaxed, casual Siriono have startlingly quick labors, quicker by far than the labor of a typical woman in a Western industrial culture" (Newton, 1970, page 75).

These differences are a testament to the power of expectations to influence the experience of pain. As we saw in Chapter 10, emotional experiences often depend on the interpretations or labels that people place on physical sensations. Thus, if the contractions of labor are expected to be extremely painful, they are likely to be; if they are expected to be only mildly painful, they are more likely to be experienced that way. These expectations are also likely to affect the woman's degree of tension or relaxation and thereby to affect the duration of labor—muscular tension tends to prolong labor.

Natural Childbirth

The woman's expectations also play a central role in an increasingly popular approach to labor and delivery: *natural childbirth.* The natural childbirth movement is a reaction to current practices of childbirth in Western society, exemplified by the treatment of a pregnant woman as a "patient," hospitalizing her, giving her anesthesia, and using medical instruments to aid in the surgical delivery of the child. Childbirth, which was once a family event that took place at home, has become a medical "problem" requiring surgery, usually excluding the father and other family members and deemphasizing the active role of the mother herself. Advocates of natural childbirth want to reverse these modern trends.

The term "natural childbirth" was originally coined in 1932 by Grantly Dick-Read, an English physician. He believed that "labor pains" are the result of muscular tensions brought about by fear in the expectant mother. In his book *Childbirth Without Fear* (1944) he described his method for helping women to overcome their fears and thereby reduce their muscle tension and pain. Dick-Read claimed that childbirth is hard work but not painful; what others refer to as "labor pain" is usually referred to as "contractions" in the natural childbirth literature. Once again we see that expectations—in the form of labeling one's physical sensations—may be a key factor in the pain of childbirth. It may be that pain by some other name does not feel as bad.

More recently, the term natural childbirth has been applied to the *Lamaze method.* This approach, which gets its name from

French physician Bernard Lamaze, is based on classical conditioning principles (see Chapter 5). Through conditioning, the woman learns to associate relaxation of abdominal muscles with uterine contractions, while she is rewarded for *not* associating pain with uterine contractions. By the end of the training period, the woman is able to experience uterine contractions without automatically responding with muscular spasms and pain, and her delivery can therefore be relaxed and painless.

How effective is natural childbirth? There seems to be some evidence that training women to adopt a more positive attitude toward pregnancy and to participate actively in the delivery produces fewer complications. And for many, the experience of childbirth is more satisfying. However, one possible psychological drawback occurs when the woman who has prepared for natural childbirth finds that, for medical or personal reasons, she requires medication or anesthesia. She may then feel that she has failed and that all her preparation has been in vain. That is why many people who educate expectant couples emphasize that unmedicated childbirth is an option, rather than a required test of the woman's self-control. Furthermore, although the term "natural childbirth" implies that use of anesthetics and other twentieth-century delivery techniques are "unnatural," many women would not be alive today if it were not for these "unnatural" techniques.

Birth Without Violence

Frederick Leboyer, a French obstetrician, has recently written an eloquent book, *Birth Without Violence* (1975), in which he argues that our techniques for delivering babies cause the childbirth process to be extremely painful and traumatic for the newborn baby. When babies are delivered in modern hospitals, bright floodlights are often used, the room is noisy, oxygen rushes suddenly into the baby's lungs, and the baby's umbilical cord is immediately cut, forcing it to make an abrupt transition to its own systems. Leboyer believes that all of this stimulation, coming so suddenly as the baby emerges from the warm, protective environment of the womb, terrifies the baby. He believes that the birth process is arranged to be convenient to doctors, but that it is horrible for the child. And he contends that the newborn infant's cries, after the first two or three healthy ones, are in fact wails of terror.

To correct these failings, Leboyer advocates a set of techniques that minimize the harsh stimulation and sudden changes for the baby. He favors delivering babies in dimly lit, silent rooms. When the baby emerges, it should be placed on the mother's stomach for a few minutes to get used to the world. The umbilical cord should not be cut until after the baby has had a chance to start breathing on its own. In this way, the child is given a more gradual transition from its mother's support system

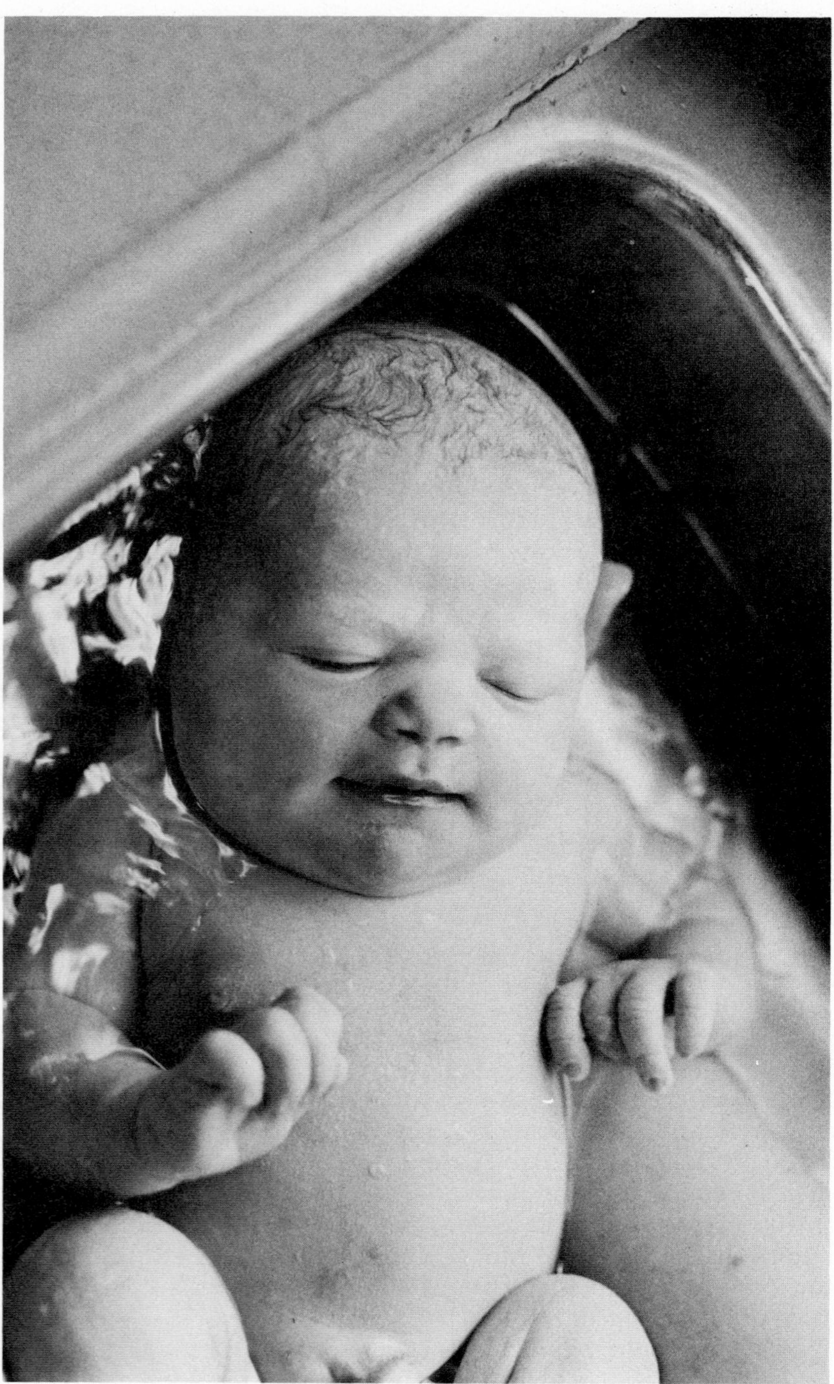

to its own support system. Leboyer also suggests giving the baby a warm bath and gentle massages soon after delivery, to help soften the new atmosphere.

It is difficult to know how accurate Leboyer's description of the birth process from the baby's point of view really is. Never-

NAMING THE BABY

One of the first decisions that a couple has to make about their new baby is what to call it. This decision may in fact have an impact on the child's life. In a study of Florida grade-school pupils, strong relationships were found between how much children like particular first names and how much they liked particular classmates who bore those names. (To rule out the possibility that evaluation of the *children* with the names influenced evaluation of the *names* rather than vice versa, the evaluations of the names were made by children in another class.) In general, the "undesirable" names tended to be the least common ones. The psychologists who conducted the study were led to caution that "a parent might appropriately think twice before naming his offspring for great aunt Sophronia" (McDavid and Harari, 1966).

theless, his arguments and approach have been convincing to many parents and obstetricians in America, and increasing numbers of deliveries are making use of some of his techniques. As a result, the process of coming into the world may be becoming a more pleasant and less terrifying experience for millions of babies.

THE NEWBORN CHILD

The newborn child has often been viewed as a helpless creature, unable to make sense of his or her environment and unable to learn from experience. The newborn human is, of course, helpless and dependent in many ways. It will take many months before the infant can begin to crawl about, and over a year before it can walk alone (see Chapter 12). And the infant is totally dependent on others for its food, clothing, and shelter.

The Competent Infant

In spite of the infant's helplessness, however, recent research has shown that the newborn is considerably more competent than had previously been thought:

> *The newborn child is a remarkably capable organism from the moment he begins to breathe. He can see, hear, and smell, and is sensitive to pain, touch, and change in position. . . . The newborn's behavioral equipment is also remarkably well developed. When only two hours old, he will follow a rapidly moving light with his eyes; his pupils will dilate in darkness and constrict in light; he will suck a finger or nipple inserted into his mouth; he will turn in the direction in which his cheek or the corner of his mouth is touched. He can cry, cough, turn away, vomit, lift his chin from a prone position, and grasp an object placed in his palm. His body will react to a loud sound. He can flex and extend his limbs, smack his lips, and chew his fingers.* [*Kagan, 1968*][†]

In addition, recent research shows that the infant, from the very first day of life, is capable of learning from experience. Lewis Lipsitt (1971) has done several studies showing conditioning of various responses in the first few months of life. In one experiment with babies two to four days old, Lipsitt and a colleague were able to increase the incidence of the *rooting response* using operant conditioning techniques. The rooting response is the newborn's tendency to turn its head in the direction of a touch on its cheek. The experimenters arranged each experimental baby in an apparatus that would automatically record the child's head turns. Then they proceeded to sound a tone and touch the baby's cheek. If it turned its head in the appropriate direction, the baby was rewarded with a few seconds of sucking on a bottle of formula. Then the researchers added another dimension to the experiment. They would sound a different tone and touch the child's cheek, but *not* reward it for head-turning.

[†]*From J. Kagan, "The Child. His Struggle for Identity,"* Saturday Review, *December 7, 1968, p. 451. Reprinted by permission.*

Within the half-hour of training, responses to the "correct" tone increased from a starting level of 25 percent of the time to 75 percent of the time, whereas responses to the "incorrect" tone stayed at the 25 percent level.

In another demonstration of infants' learning ability, Lipsitt and his associates fed one group of infants a sugar solution through a tube, so that they got a sweet taste whenever they sucked. A second group was given tubes to suck that did not contain the sweet substance. Predictably, the first group of infants increased their sucking behavior, while the second group showed much less interest in the tube. And when the experimenters stopped putting the sugar solution in the tubes for the first group, they lost interest, too.

Studies such as Lipsitt's are demonstrating that infants begin learning at a very early age, and this fact raises many vital questions. For example, can experiences at this early age have a profound impact on the child's later development? And if so, should we be providing educational experiences for infants at a much

Box 4

"To Get a Baby, Buy a Duck": Explaining Sex and Birth to Children

Where do babies come from? Children of different ages are likely to have different answers for this perennial question. Their answers reflect both the explanations that the child has been given by parents and peers and the child's own level of mental sophistication. To find out more about children's developing understandings of sex and birth, psychologist Anne Bernstein (1976) interviewed a sample of 60 boys and girls, ranging in age from 2 to 12.

Bernstein discovered that children's understandings of sex and birth progress through a series of stages similar to the stages of intellectual development identified by Swiss psychologist Jean Piaget (see Chapter 12). At the earliest stage, the question of where babies come from is interpreted as a simple question of geography. Some of the answers given by the three- and four-year-old children at this stage were: "You go to a baby store and buy one," "From tummies," and "From God's place." Children at this stage assume that babies always existed—just as they assume that they themselves and everyone else they know have always existed—so the only remaining question for them is where one goes to find a baby.

Children at a slightly more sophisticated level view babies as objects that must be manufactured, in the same manner as refrigerators or automobiles. As Jane, age 4, has worked out the problem, "To get a baby to grow in your tummy, just make it first. You put some eyes on it. Put the head on, and . . . some hair, all curls. You make it with head stuff you find in the store." Jane had never actually been told that babies were assembled from store-bought parts, but she managed to concoct her explanation from bits of information given to her, within the context of her child's-eye view of the physical world.

At more advanced stages, children are aware of the fact that a sperm and egg must come together in order to "make a baby." But younger children are likely to have a distorted view of the role of sexual intercourse in reproduction, and they may assume that conception is impossible without marriage.

Seven- or eight-year-old children are also likely to believe that the baby is fully formed in either the sperm or the egg and that the other cell plays only a supporting role. For example, the egg may be viewed as providing nourishment to the miniature baby contained inside the sperm cell, or the sperm may be seen as energizing the slumbering baby inside the egg. (Interestingly, rather similar notions were held by seventeenth-century scientists before it earlier age than we do now? The answers to these questions are not likely to be agreed upon for some time.

Individual Differences Among Newborns

Newborn infants are not all alike. There is evidence that there are individual differences among newborns—in temperament, level of activity, sensory thresholds, and irritability—from the moment of birth.

Leboyer (1975) notes that differences in the behavior of the newborn can be observed during delivery:

Each child is born with its own character, its own temperament. Some, when they are barely out of their mothers' wombs, straighten out proudly, flex their muscles, stretch their arms. Others, curled in a ball at first, open themselves more gradually, venture out with great caution.

It is impossible to predict with any certainty what an infant's personality in later life will be on the basis of such early behav-

---

was discovered that the sperm and egg contribute equally to the developing baby.) Along similar lines, seven-year-old Jeanne provided the following imaginative account of the process of conception:

The sperm goes into the mommy to each egg and . . . makes the egg safe. So if something bump comes along, it won't crack the egg. The sperm comes from the daddy. It swims into the penis, and I think it makes a little hole and then it swims into the vagina. It has a little mouth and it bites a hole.

By about the time they are 12, children have usually developed a reasonably accurate picture of sexual intercourse and realize that both parents contribute genetic material to the developing embryo. Bernstein stresses that efforts at sex education must always take into account the child's intellectual level. Children can usually expand their understanding to go one level beyond their present one. Thus, a preschooler who thinks that babies are found full blown in Mommy's tummy can move up to the manufacturing stage by learning that Mommy and Daddy make babies. A child who already believes that babies are manufactured is ready to learn about the meeting of sperm and egg. Bernstein recommends that all efforts at such interaction begin by asking questions ("How do people get babies?" "How do mommies get to be mommies?" "How did your daddy get to be your daddy?") to find out where the child is already at. Parents who take the time to ask their children such questions are often very surprised by the answers they receive.

Bernstein notes that existing efforts at sex education are often pitched at the wrong level, and, as a result, they foster misconceptions. One popular book for children as young as 3 proceeds through the sex lives of flowers, bees, rabbits, giraffes, chickens, and dogs before it reaches the human level. Bernstein points out that "few young children can encounter this kind of explanation without complete confusion" (page 66). The result may be the following:

Interviewer: *How would a lady get a baby to grow in her tummy?*

Susan (age 4): *Get a duck. . . .*

Interviewer: *A duck will turn into a baby?*

Susan: *They give them some food, people food, and they grow like a baby. To get a baby, go to a store and buy a duck.*†

†*From A. Bernstein, "How Children Learn About Sex and Birth,"* Psychology Today, *January 1976, p. 33. Copyright © 1975 Ziff-Davis Publishing Company. REPRINTED BY PERMISSION OF PSYCHOLOGY TODAY MAGAZINE.*

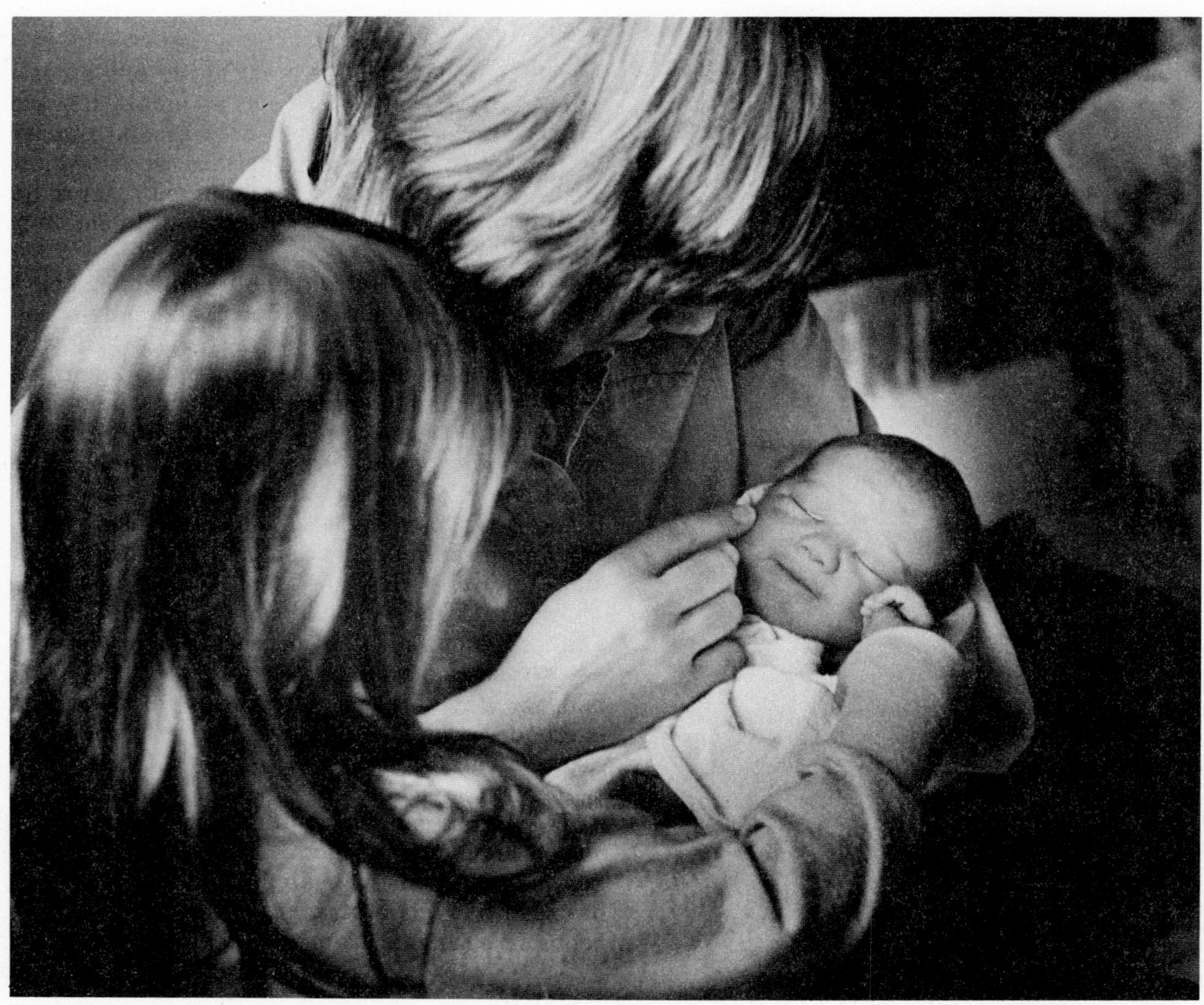

iors. As we will see (Chapter 14), personality is shaped by many experiences, both in early life and later on. Nevertheless, there is evidence that there is a considerable degree of continuity between temperament and activity patterns in infancy and in later life (Thomas, Chess, and Birch, 1970).

Parents' Reactions to Newborns

Parents of newborns are often assumed to react with feelings of excitement, elation, and pride. Serene mothers nurse their newborns with a sense of great joy and tenderness. Fathers, bursting with pride, pass out cigars to everyone in sight. But these positive feelings are not the only reactions that parents are likely to have to their newborn. Fatigue and letdown are also common in the period immediately following a birth.

Such "postpartum blues" occur in two-thirds of all new mothers. During about the first ten days after the birth, women are likely to experience periodic feelings of sadness and often cry. One possible reason for this depression is the physiological upheaval caused by drastic changes in hormone levels. In addition, both mothers and fathers may have doubts and anxieties about their ability to raise a child. Especially after the birth of a first child, both parents must make considerable adjustments and changes in their style of life. There are new economic pressures, and the couple's mobility may be significantly reduced. The husband and wife may also fear that the child will have unpredictable effects on their own emotional relationship. It is not unusual for a new parent to feel a bit jealous of a first baby, because it threatens to rob the parent of some of the exclusive attention that he or she has been getting. Because of these adjustments, some writers (LeMasters, 1957, for example) have viewed the birth of a first child as a significant life crisis for couples. It is a crisis that most couples weather successfully, but not without some degree of difficulty and struggle.

We have seen all the factors that go into the creation of a newborn child—the inheritance both from the species and from the parents, the union of egg and sperm, the development within the uterus, and the birth process. We know a little about what a child is like in its first few weeks of life. But how does it get from being this helpless little creature, unable to care for itself, to being a full-grown adult, capable of talking, thinking, creating, and doing so many more things than an infant can do? This is the central question that will concern us in the next chapter. We will begin with the infant, poised on the threshold of life, and then follow its development through the entire span of life.

SUMMARY

1. According to Darwin's principle of *natural selection,* those organisms best able to adapt to their environment are the ones that are "selected"—that survive to produce offspring. Natural selection provides the basis for the evolution of various species and their great diversity.
2. *Genes* are the tiny structures in cells that carry the messages of heredity. A child receives two sets of genes, one from the mother and one from the father, that intereact to provide the child with a unique set of characteristics. The genetic inheritance constitutes an individual's *genotype;* the outward expression of this genetic make-up is the individual's *phenotype.*
3. A *dominant* gene for a trait is one that is always expressed. A *recessive* gene is expressed only when the dominant gene for that trait is not present. Most human traits involve the interaction of many gene pairs.

4. *Behavior genetics* is the study of hereditary factors that affect personality and behavior. People do not inherit specific emotional traits; however, they can apparently inherit a general tendency toward emotionality. Genetic effects on behavior are primarily indirect.
5. About 20 percent of birth defects are attributable to heredity. Among the major disorders caused by genetic defects are phenylketonuria (PKU), Tay-Sachs disease, sickle-cell anemia, and Down's syndrome.
6. The purpose of *genetic counseling* is to determine a couple's risk of having children with genetic diseases and to offer advice based on this risk information. Genetic diseases can sometimes be detected through the use of *amniocentesis,* the analysis of cells taken from within the womb. The use of genetic counseling and the aborting of "defective" fetuses is a sensitive issue, carrying with it many ethical and legal questions to be resolved.
7. Conception occurs at the moment that the egg and sperm unite to form a *zygote.* The zygote floats down the fallopian tube and implants itself in the wall of the uterus; at that point it becomes an *embryo.* If two eggs are fertilized by two sperm, *fraternal twins* may be produced. If the egg divides soon after fertilization and forms two individuals, the result is *identical twins.*
8. During the first eight weeks of development, the embryo develops from a mass of cells into an unmistakably human form, becoming a *fetus* for the remaining 7 months. The internal organs start to function and the child is fully formed at the end of 6 months. The remaining 3 months are devoted to further growth and finishing touches. During prenatal development the child can be harmed by maternal infections, poor nutrition of the mother, or her use of drugs.
9. Scientific experimentation with human reproduction—*biological engineering*—has led to the speculation that test-tube babies and cloning of humans are within the realm of reality. One practice currently in use is *artificial insemination donation,* in which the sperm of an anonymous donor are implanted in a woman's uterus.
10. A missed menstrual period is usually the first sign of pregnancy. During the course of pregnancy, many women experience morning sickness and other physical discomforts. Pregnant women are treated with some curiosity and trepidation in American culture, and this treatment can have a negative effect on their self-concept and their behavior.
11. Children's understandings of sex and birth appear to progress through a series of stages. Bernstein recommends that sex education materials be aimed at the child's correct level to avoid fostering misconceptions.
12. During the birth process, the woman undergoes contractions of the uterus referred to as *labor pains.* The duration and

severity of such pains depend a great deal on cultural expectations. Those who choose *natural childbirth* learn to experience contractions without undergoing the usual pain. Leboyer has suggested that the birth process be made less painful for the child as well.

13. The newborn child is more competent than it appears to be. Lipsitt has shown in his classical conditioning experiments with newborns that they can learn from experience. Furthermore, newborns show personality right from the start—they vary greatly in temperament, level of activity, sensory thresholds, and irritability.

14. Parents view their new child with some ambivalence. Although they are joyful and proud, most new parents go through a period of "postpartum blues," in which they experience doubts and anxieties about their child-rearing abilities and worry about changes in their life style and in their relation to each other.

psychological issue

Birth Order

Being the first-born child in your family may be important if you want to increase your chances of becoming an astronaut—21 of the first 23 astronauts to fly into outer space were first-borns. If you'd rather be a professional football player, your chances may be better if you are a later-born (Nisbett, 1968). But even if you are not that ambitious, your order of birth seems to make at least some difference in determining the kind of person you will eventually become.

In this Psychological Issue we will focus on the tendency for first-borns to be more eminent and to show greater intellectual achievement than later-borns. Research on the effects of birth order are not limited to the intellectual domain, however. In the last fifteeen years or so, birth order research has become something of a fad among psychologists, and studies have been published about the links between a person's birth order and almost every imaginable psychological characteristic—everything from pain tolerance (later-borns seem to be able to withstand more pain) to the likelihood of becoming a stripper (first-born women are more likely to go into this profession [Skipper and McCaghy, 1970]).

...birth order research has become something of a fad among psychologists....

The Eminence of First-Borns

The relation of birth order to achievement has been investigated for at least a hundred years. The first known data appeared in Sir Francis Galton's *English Men of Science,* published in 1874. Galton selected eminent scientists of that time and found a more-than-chance number of them to be first-borns or only sons (Altus, 1966). Thirty years later, Havelock Ellis (1926) published *A Study of British Genius,* based on the biographies of 975 eminent men and 55 eminent women. He found that the probability of appearance in the *Dictionary of National Biography* was much greater for a first-born than for a middle child. The youngest was similarly favored over the intermediate child.

A bit closer to home, considering their proportion in the general population, first-borns are over-represented in *Who's Who in America* and *American Men and Women of Science,* as well as among Rhodes Scholars and university professors. And Schachter (1963) found that first-born are over-represented among graduate students and medical students and that first-borns have a higher grade point average than later-born children.

Why is it that first-born children tend to achieve eminence in higher proportion than their siblings? Even though they are "Number 1," first-borns seem to try harder—especially in the school setting. This academic striving seems to reflect the aspirations and pressures of the parents—after all, their first child is their first entry in the race for success.

The tendency for first-borns to achieve eminence has also been explained in terms of Alfred Adler's theory of personality. Adler viewed the first-born child as a "dethroned king" who suddenly loses his or her monopoly on parental attention. According to Adler, this dethronement leads to a lifelong need for recognition, attention, and approval, which the child may try to earn through high achievement. As Zweigenhaft (1975) suggests, politics is a good occupation for people with such needs—which may be why first-borns are over-represented among American Presidents, Senators, and Congressmen.

Birth Order, Family Size, and Intelligence

Many of the findings related to birth order are based on relatively small samples of people, and as a result they are not very reliable. Two findings that have been found in extremely large samples, however, are that people who grow up in small families tend to get higher scores on intelligence tests than people from larger families and that within families first-borns tend to have the highest IQs, second-borns the next highest, and so on, with the lastborn child tending to get the lowest scores.

This pattern was shown very clearly in an extensive analysis of the IQ scores of almost 400,000 young men in Holland (Belmont and Marolla, 1973, see Figure 11.3). The same pattern was found even when the men's social class was held constant. A similar finding was

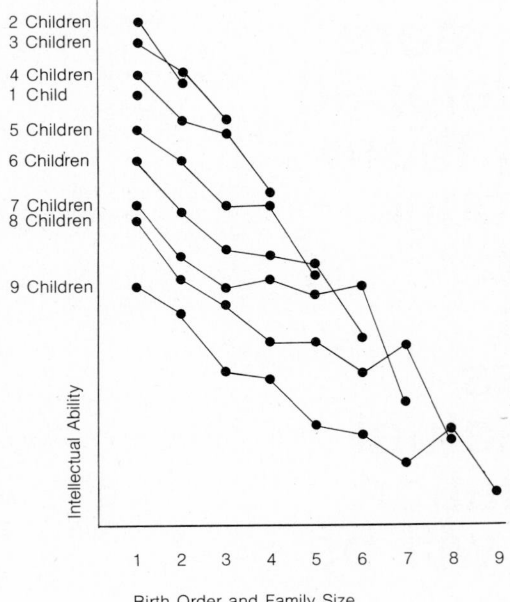

FIG. 11·3 Average scores on a test of intellectual ability among 400,000 young men in Holland, as a function of birth order and family size (from Belmont and Marolla, 1973).

obtained in a study of 800,000 high school seniors who took the National Merit Scholarship Qualifying test: Scores declined as the students' family size and their birth order within the family increased (Breland, 1974).

Although these patterns were quite clear, why they occurred remained something of a mystery. The birth-order decline seemed especially mysterious. It is conceivable that some physical factors may be involved—for example, that the uterine environment may become less nourishing for a mother's later-born children—but there is no good evidence that this is the case. Nor is there any reason to suspect that genetic factors are any different for early- and later-borns. Recently, psychologist Robert Zajonc (1976) has come up with a mathematical model that, although quite speculative, accounts for the pattern very nicely. Zajonc's model is based on the premise that a child's intellectual development depends on the intellectual environment of its family. For firstborn children, this environment consists of the two parents, each of whom has an adult's level of intelligence. A secondborn child, in contrast, enters a family in which there are two people with an adult-sized intelligence and one person—the older sibling—with a pint-sized intelligence.

The presence of an older sibling, according to Zajonc's model, dilutes the newborn's intellectual environment and makes it less likely that the newborn will develop his or her maximum intellectual potential. Things are even worse for the third-born child, and so on down the line—since the more undeveloped minds there are around, the less intellectual stimulation there will be for the newborn.

...the more undeveloped minds there are around, Zajonc claims, the less intellectual stimulation there will be for the newborn.

Consider the absolute intellectual levels of the parents to be an arbitrary 30 units each, and that of the newborn child to be 0.

Then the intellectual environment of the first child is:

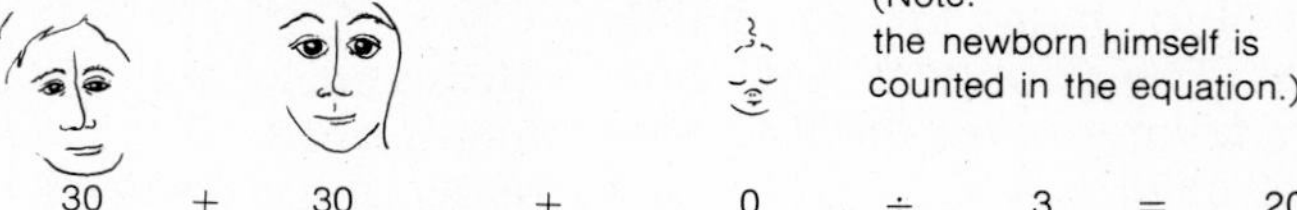

Suppose the second child is born when the intellectual level of the firstborn reaches 4. The intellectual environment of the secondborn is then:

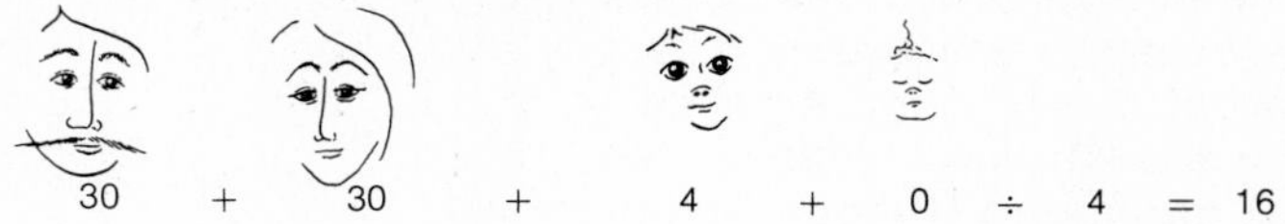

If a third child is born when the intellectual level of the firstborn has reached, say, 7, and that of the secondborn is 3, the family intellectual environment will then be reduced to 14.

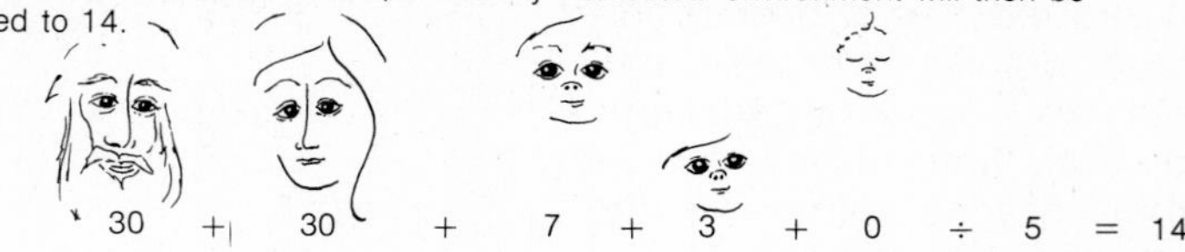

For twins who are the first offspring, the intellectual environment at birth is:

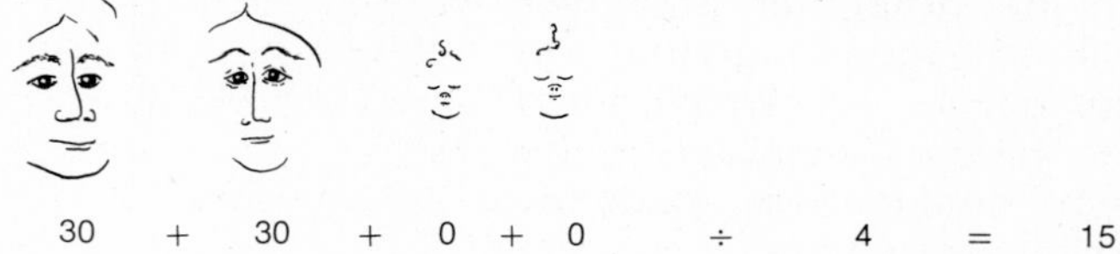

FIG. 11 · 4 A pictorial representation of Zajonc's model of the effects of birth order and family size on intelligence. (Illustration adapted from *Psychology Today*, April, 1976)

There are many things one can argue with about it. Nevertheless, the model is an intriguing one, and, to the extent that it is correct, it has many interesting practical implications. For one thing, it may help explain why the average Scholastic Aptitude Test scores of high school students have been falling off since about 1963. Various authorities have blamed this decline on everything from television to crowded classrooms. Zajonc (1976) suggests a simpler explanation. Starting in 1947, at the end of World War II, the size of American families began to increase. As a result, the high school seniors who were taking the SAT tests starting in 1963 tended to come from larger families and to be later-borns. The American birth rate and average family size began to decline again in 1962; as a result, Zajonc is betting that the SAT scores of high school seniors will turn upward again in 1980.

Zajonc's theory also has some implications for parents who want to optimize their children's intellectual growth: they should have two children and stop there. And, if possible, they should wait until the first child is pretty old before having the second. But to make sure that no one draws any premature implications about family planning from his model, Zajonc also hedges a bit: "IQ isn't everything. Large families may contribute to growth in attributes other than intelligence: social competence, moral responsibility, or ego strength, for example. These or similar family effects are still to be verified, however" (1976, page 234).

Finally, just in case you're wondering, Robert Zajonc is an only child.

The Need to Affiliate

The current concern with birth order was triggered by a 1959 study by Stanley Schachter. By accident, really, he found that college-age female students who were first-borns or only children regularly chose to wait with other people when they expected to receive a painful electric shock in an experiment. However, those who were later-borns didn't care as much whether they waited alone or with others. Why might this be the case? It probably has a lot to do with how parents treat first-born as opposed to later-born children. Inexperienced parents tend to over-react to their first-born children—to make more of a fuss over them, to reward them more, and to rush to their side at the first sign of distress. As a result, first-born children become highly dependent on their parents for dealing with fearful situations and for developing their self-image. And because inexperienced parents tend to be inconsistent in giving out rewards and punishments, first-borns stay dependent. They never know for sure whether what they are doing is right and must always look to their parents for approval. In later life, these first-borns continue to look to others for affirmation and approval particularly in anxiety-arousing situations. In this way, the first-borns' preference for affiliating with others in the Schachter experiment can be explained.

This explanation, mind you, is also highly speculative. And the evidence that links birth order and affiliation has been much less consistent than that linking birth order and achievement or intelligence (Warren, 1966). On the whole, it does seem to be true, however, that first-borns are more likely than later-borns to seek out others when they are anxious and troubled.

Adult relationships may duplicate relationships with brothers and sisters.

Birth Order and Marriage

In another type of research on birth order, Walter Toman (1970) has suggested that the kind of person one chooses for a spouse may be determined by the kinds of siblings one lived with while growing up. Adult relationships may duplicate relationships with brothers and sisters. According to Toman, the more exact the duplication, the greater the chance that one's adult relationships will be lasting and happy.

Toman uses his theory to predict how marriages will work:

Suppose that the older brother of a sister *marries the* younger *sister of a brother. They are getting in marriage precisely the peer relation that they had at home. He is used to a girl his junior, and she to a boy her senior. Hence there should be no conflict over their dominance rights. And both of them are used to the other sex, so they should have no great sex conflicts either. If this fellow had married an oldest sister of sisters, however, he could have expected some problems. Both partners would expect to have seniority rights and each one would try to rule the other. In addition, the wife would have had little experience in getting along with men. (Toman, 1970, page 45)*

Toman's is an interesting approach to the problem of birth order, but it is difficult to tell how applicable his theory is to specific individuals. Like all theories that put people into neat categories, it fits most people a little, some a lot, and others not at all. Most of us are subject to a thousand and one influences in our lives, and birth order is just one of many factors.

The Birth Order of Birth-Order Researchers

As we have already mentioned, the published research on birth order has not always been notably consistent. In fact, much of it has been downright contradictory. For example, first-born males placed in threatening situations have been found to be more influenceable, less influenceable, more affiliative, less affiliative, more hostile, and less hostile than later-borns. It all depends on which report you read. Similarly, depending on which study you trust more, first-borns either choose more-popular others as friends and are less popular themselves *or* they choose less-popular others and are more popular themselves.

How can we make sense out of this mass of contradictions? While sitting in the laundromat one day, waiting for his clothes

to dry, Zick Rubin pondered this question and came up with what he thought was a brilliant idea. His idea was that the psychologists who conduct research on birth order, being either only children, first-borns, or later-borns themselves, have a stake in the results of the research. Sometimes their results make first-borns look better than later-borns, and sometimes their results make later-borns look better. Rubin, who is not a suspicious sort, certainly did not think that the psychologists faked their data to make their own birth order look good. But he did entertain the notion that a more subtle process might be going on—that the researchers may well have *expected* their own birth position to come out looking better and that they managed to construct their research in such a way that their expectations would be borne out (such experimenter effects are discussed in Chapter 1).

As he took his clothes from the dryer and began rolling his socks into neat little balls, Rubin decided he wouldn't simply let this hypothesis fade into oblivion, as most of his hypotheses do. Instead, he would test it. And he proceeded to do so. He went to the journals and located a sample of 41 articles on birth order. Then he wrote to the psychologists who had written the articles and asked them about their own birth order.

While he was waiting for the postcards to come back, Rubin enlisted two friends (to be fair about it, he chose one first-born and one later-born) and asked them to help him code the articles the birth-order researchers had written. They then coded the articles as to being either more favorable to first-borns, more favorable to later-borns, or equally favorable. For example, some of the reports judged to be more favorable to first-borns concluded that first-borns are more honest, better adjusted, less hostile, and less likely to be schizophrenic then later-borns. Some of the reports judged to be more favorable to later-borns concluded that later-borns are more popular, less dependent, less anxious, and less conforming than first-borns. Then, as Rubin held his breath, the postcards came back (from all but one of the 41 researchers) and Rubin was able to find out whether his hypothesis was correct. Was there in fact a tendency for researchers to obtain and publish results that were favorable to their own birth position?

Unfortunately, Rubin's brilliant idea fell flat on its face. When the returns were all in, it turned out that there was absolutely no relationship between birth-order researchers' birth order and the results of their research (Rubin, 1970). The inconsistencies that haunt birth-order research, he was forced to conclude, must stem from some other source. And the next time he went back to the laundromat, he resolved to stick to more practical questions, like making sure not to pour too much bleach in with his colored undershorts.

Summary

1. First-born children achieve eminence in higher proportion than their siblings. There are disproportionate numbers of first-borns among astronauts, people listed in *Who's Who,* and American Presidents, to name a few.
2. First-borns tend to score highest on IQ tests, followed by second-borns, third-borns, and so on. Zajonc suggested that his pattern occurs because later-borns receive less intellectual stimulation—they are exposed to more immature minds in their home environment.
3. Schachter found that first-borns have a greater need to affiliate—perhaps they were more dependent on their parents for approval during childhood and as adults continue to seek approval. Furthermore, birth order can influence one's choice of marriage partner—people tend to try to duplicate in marriage the type of relationship that they had with brothers and sisters.
4. Because much birth order research is contradictory, Rubin investigated the possibility of bias in birth order research. However, he found no relationship between the birth order of researchers and the results of their research.

From Infancy to Old Age

CHAPTER

12

From Infancy to Old Age

A child is born, capable of certain basic experiences and responses but certainly not capable of much more. Newborn infants experience a wide range of sensations, and they can cry, turn their head, suck, and sleep. As we saw at the end of the last chapter, they can even learn from experience in certain ways. But infants cannot move around on their own, remember things, use language, or solve problems. Although infants are unmistakably human, they still lack many of the essential characteristics of intellect and character that we usually associate with being human.

But all of this changes, and it does so with remarkable speed. Within the first month after birth, infants develop some control over their head and neck. Three months or so after birth they are reaching for objects. By the age of 10 months a baby is likely to begin crawling and by about 15 months is walking alone. A relative who visits the baby once every three or four months is likely to be amazed by the changes from one visit to the next. It is almost as if there is a new person to meet on each visit.

While these developments in motor skills are taking place, equally dramatic changes are occurring in the domain of the intellect. A baby may not utter his or her first words until about the end of the first year, but once the baby does so, language development proceeds rapidly. Within a year the child will have a vocabulary of at least 50 words and by the age of five will be chattering away, using the basic grammar of adult speech. And, as we will see, extremely important intellectual changes take place during the first year of life, even before the baby begins to talk.

Like physical growth, psychological changes take place most quickly and dramatically during the first few years of life, at a somewhat slower pace during childhood and adolescence, and much more slowly during adulthood. The visiting relative who notes astounding changes in "what baby can do" between January and June may notice few changes in the baby's seven-year-old brother and certainly no changes to write home about with respect to the baby's parents. It is perhaps for this reason that developmental psychologists, as "professional visiting relatives" to individuals as they progress through life, have traditionally devoted the vast majority of their attention to the years of infancy and childhood. From this perspective, once a child reaches puberty he or she has "graduated." Although adult behavior has been of interest to psychologists who study perception, consciousness, personality, and other topics, it has not been of particular interest to psychologists who specialize in human *development.*

In recent years, however, the perspective of developmental psychologists has changed considerably. Most developmental psychologists have come to recognize that development does not suddenly stop at puberty and that important psychological changes continue to occur throughout the human life cycle. The motives, values, and self-conceptions of a 20-year-old are likely to be different from those of a 30-year-old, and these in turn are likely to differ from those of a 40-year-old. Particularly important psychological changes and adjustments are likely to take place during the years of late adulthood and old age.

In this chapter we will examine psychological development through the entire life cycle. We will pay special attention to cognitive development in infancy and childhood—the ways in which the child discovers and elaborates the concepts that we as adults take for granted. In this endeavor we will draw heavily on the work of the renowned Swiss psychologist Jean Piaget. We will also consider some of the implications of what psychologists have learned about cognitive development for the child's social behavior and for child-rearing practices. But the chapter will not end with the "graduation day" of puberty. Instead, we will continue to look at the human being as he or she develops through adolescence, young and middle adulthood, and old age, focusing on the special themes, problems, and challenges that characterize each period. In tracing development through the life cycle, we will draw in particular from the theoretical framework of another famous psychologist, Erik Erikson.

LEARNING AND MATURATION

How does psychological development take place? How, for example, do babies come to be able to utter their first word? What accounts for the increased desire to explore the environment that emerges in most children in their second and third years? Why do school-age children often become preoccupied with playing games "according to the rules," and why do adolescents often exhibit a new sort of self-consciousness that they did not have at earlier stages? Progressing further through the life cycle, what accounts for the fact that certain intellectual capacities, like short-term memory, typically decline as a person gets older, while other intellectual capacities, like the ability to generalize from one's experience, remain stable or even improve?

Each of these questions is a complex one, because in each case the answer involves a combination of several different factors. Throughout this chapter, it will be helpful to keep in mind two sets of processes that jointly account for psychological development: *learning* and *maturation.* Learning, as we have already defined it in Chapter 5, refers to relatively enduring changes in behavior that take place as the result of experience. Clearly,

In some cultures infants are prevented from walking during the first year by being wrapped in swaddling clothes. But this practice does not seem to retard their motor development.

learning takes place throughout life—in the home, at school, on the job, and in most other places as well. Maturation, in contrast, refers to changes that take place without any specific experience or practice. For example, children will begin to crawl when they are about 10 months old and to walk when they are about 15 months, even if they are not given any special training or reinforcement for these accomplishments. Even when infants are prevented from walking by being wrapped in swaddling clothes during the first year, as is the custom in some cultures, the infants begin walking at the usual age (Orlansky, 1949). Whereas learning reflects the impact of the environment on behavior, maturation reflects the unfolding of inherited biological patterns that are "preprogrammed" into the individual.

Until recently, the role of learning in psychological development received more attention than the role of maturation. The impact of maturation is obvious in the areas of physical and motor development. Most people would agree that such behaviors as crawling and walking depend in large measure on the gradual maturing of the infant's muscles and coordination. As Kagan (1976) notes, however, we tend to underestimate the role of maturation—and to overestimate the role of learning—in cognitive and social development. When a baby starts crying after its mother leaves the room, or when a child starts to play make-believe games, we often assume that these new behaviors reflect the child's training and experience, rather than the natural unfolding of the child's innate capacities. Psychologists now believe, however, that these and many other cognitive and social changes are to a large extent dependent on maturational forces, in quite the same way that physical changes are. Jean Piaget, himself a biologist by training, has played a major role in demonstrating the strong impact of maturation on psychological development.

At present, psychologists emphasize the *interplay* of learning and maturation in human development. Our consideration of language development in Chapter 7 provided one example of this interplay. Babies all over the world start talking at roughly the same age (although there is wide individual variation) and go through some of the same grammatical stages (from the single word to the two-word phrase, and so on). This development probably reflects a biological program that is "prewired" into all human beings. But whether the child begins to speak in French or in Chinese, with a New England twang or with a Southern drawl, is *not* part of the biological program—these specific features of language must be learned. The biological program provides the readiness to acquire language at a particular age and in particular ways, but the specific words and rules that are used depend on experience. The same interplay between maturation and learning is characteristic of psychological development more generally. And, as we will see, the interplay continues beyond childhood into adolescence, adulthood, and old age.

One of the implications of the interplay of learning and maturation is that it may be futile (and, indeed, even harmful) to try to teach a person something before he or she is maturationally ready for it. Such attempts, whether to teach a two-year-old to ride a bicycle or a seven-year-old to do geometry, typically bring temporary results at best.

Before commencing our tour through the life cycle, one note of caution is in order. In what follows, as in what you have already read, we will sometimes note that particular behaviors or capacities typically emerge at a particular age. You should bear in mind, however, that these are *average* ages and that there may be a wide range of variation between individuals. Whereas the *sequences* in which these capacities develop are relatively constant across individuals, the specific ages are not. You should note, moreover, that a more rapid rate of early cognitive development does not necessarily imply that the person will be an unusually intelligent adult, nor does a slow rate of early development mean that the person will always be at the bottom of the class. To cite just one example, Albert Einstein, who became one of the greatest scientists in the history of the world, was an unusually "slow" child.

INFANCY

The first two years of life are perhaps the most crucial two years for the developing individual. As we have noted, physical and psychological changes take place more rapidly during infancy

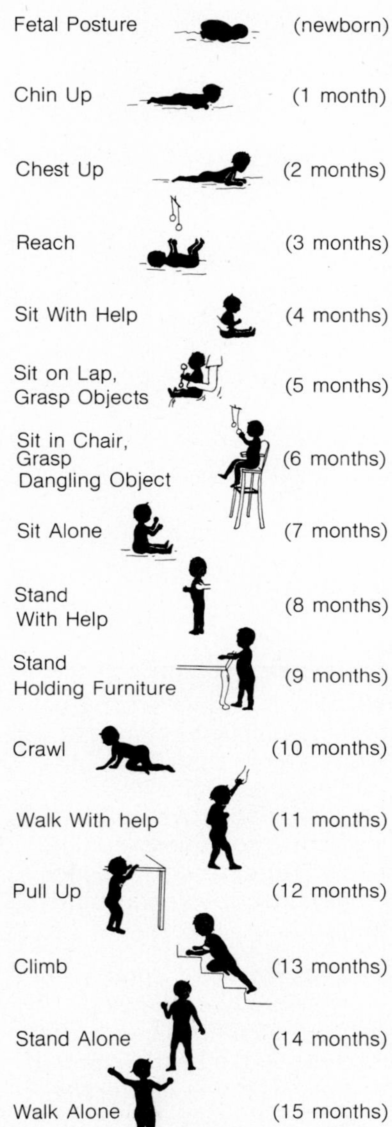

FIG. 12 · 1 Although there are individual differences, children usually develop their motor skills in this sequence (after Shirley, 1933). The average ages as which these stages occur are indicated.

than during any other period in the span of life. Figure 12.1 gives a brief overview of the infant's development of physical and motor skills. In this section, we will concentrate on some important features of the infant's cognitive and social development.

Cognitive Development

According to Jean Piaget† (see Box 1), a person's way of thinking progresses through four qualitatively different stages in the years of infancy and childhood (ages are approximate):

Stage 1. Sensorimotor period (from birth to age 2).
Stage 2. Preoperational period (age 2 to 7).
Stage 3. Concrete-operational period (age 7 to 12).
Stage 4. Formal-operational period (age 12 to 15).

The infant's stage of cognitive development is called the *sensorimotor period* because of the central cognitive challenge that the infant faces: to coordinate the various impressions of the world that it gains through its senses (especially vision and touch) with motor activities (for example, by sucking, reaching for, and grasping objects). During the first months of life, the baby's sense impressions are uncoordinated. For example, the baby may see a certain pattern of lines and curves, corresponding to a toy hanging over the crib, but it does not know that it can reach for the toy. Or the baby may accidentally touch an object but will not turn around to look for it. After infants are a few months old, however, they begin to put these isolated impressions together, so that they can reach toward an object that they see or turn to look for the source of a sound that they hear.

During the first year of life, according to Piaget, infants are also discovering the principle of *object constancy*—that a physical object continues to exist even when it is out of sight or out of reach. As adults we take this principle for granted. When we look away from our desk for a moment, we remain certain that the desk and the open book on top of it are still there. But we are not born with this sort of assurance. The infant is like a philosopher who makes absolutely no assumptions about what the world is like when it is not directly perceived. As a result, infants behave as if they can literally destroy and create objects by closing and opening their eyes. This is what makes the game of peek-a-boo so exciting for a baby. Each time that a face reappears in view, it is as if a totally new object has been created out of nothingness.

By the end of the first year of life, infants learn that objects continue to exist even when they are out of sight. Before an infant has developed the notion of object constancy (at about 8 or 9 months), if you take a small toy that the baby is interested in and place it behind a pillow, she will not reach behind the

†Piaget's theory of cognitive development is outlined in a large number of books (1952, 1954, for example). An excellent summary is provided by Elkind (1975).

pillow for the toy. As far as she is concerned, out of sight *is* out of mind; it is as if the toy no longer exists. But if you repeat this exercise a few months later, the baby will immediately reach behind the pillow for the toy. By this time the baby knows that the toy continues to exist, and she knows just where to find it.

This example also shows that as infants develop the notion of object constancy, they also develop basic conceptions of *causality* and *space.* The baby learns that an object can be moved by a person's hand (including the baby's own hand) from one place to another. The idea that the hand's movement leads to the object's movement represents the basic principle of causality, and the notion of physical displacement provides an elementary understanding of space. The baby also develops a basic concept of *time*—that one event can take place before or after another. By the time the baby nears the end of the sensorimotor period (about age 2), these concepts are developed to such a point that an adult can move an object around several times without fooling the baby as to its whereabouts. By this time it can be said that the infant has a basic understanding of the physical workings of the world.

Box 1

Jean Piaget

Jean Piaget was born in 1896 and was originally trained as a biologist. He then worked at Alfred Binet's laboratory school in Paris, where the first intelligence tests were being developed (see Chapter 8). It was while doing some routine intelligence testing that Piaget first got the idea of getting behind children's right and wrong answers to the underlying modes of thought involved. This quest has occupied Piaget's professional life for more than half a century, extending from intellectual development to social and moral development as well.

Piaget's techniques have typically been informal ones, involving interviews and game-playing with children at various ages. In fact, the three primary subjects for a good deal of his research were his own three children, Lucienne, Laurent, and Jaqueline. Some psychologists have been critical of the informality of Piaget's methods and, as a result, have raised doubts about some of his conclusions. But his status as a major psychological theorist is unquestioned.

Jean Piaget

Now in his eighties, Piaget and his students in Geneva, Switzerland, continue to advance our understanding of intellectual development. He has written more than 30 books and hundreds of articles, and his work habits are nothing short of astounding. Writing when Piaget was 71, Elkind (1968) described his routine as follows:

Each summer, as soon as classes are over, Piaget gathers up the research findings that have been collected by his assistants during the year and departs for the Alps, where he takes up solitary residence in a room in an abandoned farmhouse. . . . During the summer Piaget takes walks, meditates, writes and writes. Then, when the leaves begin to turn, he descends from the mountains with the several books and articles he has written on his "vacation."†

†*From David Elkind, "Giant in the Nursery: Jean Piaget,"* The New York Times Magazine, *May 26, 1968.*

Social Development

Along with the development of object constancy, infancy is an important period in the development of social behavior. During the first two years, infants typically develop a strong *attachment* to a small number of people. The central attachment has typically been to the mother, since she is the one who has traditionally spent by far the most time interacting with the child. When fathers or other caretakers spend a great deal of time interacting with the baby, however, infants become attached to them as well (Kotelchuck, 1972).

The baby's attachment is reflected by its *selective* responding to the mother or other attachment figure. The baby is much more likely to approach these people than anyone else, is more willing to be cared for by them, and is least afraid when in their presence (Mussen, Conger, and Kagan, 1974). In the very first month of life, infants make no such distinction between people. Since the young infant does not yet have a concept of object constancy, he does not yet have a clear notion of what a "person" is. As a result, the infant still does not care very much who picks him up, rocks him, or feeds him. If he is in a good mood, he will smile and babble to all visitors, without showing any special preferences. By the age of 4 or 5 months, however, the baby becomes much more discriminating. She will interact freely and securely with the attachment objects and will be fearful and insecure with less familiar people. And starting at about the age of 6 months the baby is likely to panic and cry when approached by an unfamiliar person, a phenomenon known as *stranger anxiety.* You can tell the baby, "But she's your *grandmother!*" or "It's only Harry, my old roommate," but unless the baby has had a great deal of contact with these people, it won't do much good. The baby will show less fear in such situations if her mother or father is present than if they are not. The reaction of stranger anxiety typically reaches its peak at about 8 months; it gradually disappears by the time the baby is 12 to 15 months old, when she has gotten used to the idea that these other people are humans, too, and are not to be feared (Mussen, Conger, and Kagan, 1974).

What causes the baby to become attached to a particular person or persons and not to others? Psychologists used to believe that it was a matter of learning—specifically, of secondary reinforcement (see Chapter 5). They thought that since the mother provides the infant with food, either by nursing or bottle-feeding, the baby learns to approach the mother whenever he is hungry. As a result, the mother herself was thought to take on more general reward value for the infant. But this view of attachment has changed, partly as a result of pioneering research by Harry Harlow (1959) with infant rhesus monkeys. Harlow separated the infant monkeys from their mothers and raised them instead with wire and terrycloth constructions that he called *surrogate mothers.* In one study, the infants had access to both a "wire mother" fitted with a nipple that the monkey could obtain milk from and a "cloth mother" that did not provide milk but that the baby could cling to much more comfortably. If the infant

In Harlow's experiments, infant monkeys preferred terry-cloth covered "mothers" to wire "mothers." Harlow stressed the importance of "contact comfort" in the development of the infant's attachment to its mother.

monkey's attachment were the result of associating a particular object with the receipt of nourishment, we would expect the monkeys to become attached to the wire mother rather than the cloth mother. But Harlow found the opposite to be true. The infants became attached to the cloth mother. Not only would they cling to her, but they also were less fearful and more venturesome in her presence, just as human infants are in the presence of an attachment object. When the infant monkeys were hungry, they would go to the wire monkey to feed but then returned immediately to the cloth mother.

As a result of his research, Harlow concluded that attachment is *not* a learned response to a food-giving object but rather an innate tendency to love a mother (or a mother surrogate) for the sheer pleasure of contact with her body. *Contact comfort,* as Harlow called it, may play a role in the development of human attachments as well. More generally, human infants appear to develop attachments toward people they repeatedly interact with in a variety of situations, whether or not they happen to be the ones who supply their food.

Harlow and others view the development of mother-infant attachment (or of attachment to other persons) in infancy as the first stage in the development of the capacity for close relationships in adulthood. Both monkeys and humans who do not form close attachments in infancy—for example, infants reared in impersonal institutions (Spitz, 1946)—are likely to become listless and despondent and to have difficulty forming close relationships later in life. In the view of Erik Erikson (1950), the quality of the interaction between infants and their parents during the first years of life plays a major role in determining whether children will grow up with a trustful or mistrustful attitude toward other people. In Erikson's scheme, "trust versus mistrust" is the first of eight central themes or stages of psychological and social development through the life cycle (see Box 2). The infant whose needs are satisfied, who is cuddled and played with, and who is treated consistently will develop a basic attitude of trust toward other people, whereas an infant who is treated inadequately or inconsistently is likely to develop a mistrustful attitude toward others that will continue through life.

To illustrate the latter possibility, David Elkind (1970)† cites the case of a four-year-old boy he observed in a court clinic. The boy was being seen at the clinic because the parents who had adopted him six months earlier wanted to give him back to the agency, on the grounds that he was cold, unloving, and could not be trusted. "He was indeed a cold and unloving boy," Elkind explains, "but with good reason." The boy had been abandoned by his mother, shunted back and forth between foster homes, and was never given the chance to form close attachments. "Like the burned child who dreads the flame," Elkind writes, "this

IS DAY CARE DANGEROUS?

With the increasing number of working mothers and of single-parent families, more and more infants and young children are spending eight hours a day, five days a week, in day-care centers. This has led to concern on the part of some parents and educators that, without the presence of a primary attachment figure, the children might be emotionally and intellectually harmed. And these fears have led to extensive research comparing day-care infants with infants raised at home. On the basis of the initial results of such studies, the verdict seems to be that well-managed day care is *not* harmful. There are no major intellectual, emotional, or social differences between day-care and home-care children, studied between the ages of 3 ½ and 30 months. And children from less privileged homes tend to show *better* cognitive development with day care than when reared at home (Kagan, Kearsley, and Zelazo, 1976).

†*From David Elkind, "Erik Erikson's Eight Stages of Man,"* The New York Times Magazine, *April 5, 1970.*

emotionally burned child shunned the pain of emotional involvement. He had trusted his mother, but now he trusted no one. Only years of devoted care and patience could now undo the damage that had been done to this child's sense of trust."

CHILDHOOD

Although human development is most rapid during the first two years of life, the period between ages two and twelve may be even more eventful. During this period children gradually develop modes of reasoning that are essentially identical to those of adults. And during this period, individuals venture from home for the first time and develop a sense of mastery and competence. The psychological developments of childhood are too numerous for us to cover in only one chapter. You will find that developmental issues are discussed in several other chapters as

---

Box 2

Erikson's Eight Stages of Psychosocial Development

Erik Erikson was born in Germany in 1902. As a young man he moved to Vienna, where he became an acquaintance and disciple of Sigmund Freud. He later went on to become perhaps the foremost theorist of the development of personality through the life cycle. The initial impetus for Erikson's theory was Freud's famous theory of psychosexual development (see Chapter 14). But whereas Freud's stages covered only the years between birth and puberty, Erikson's stages extended through adulthood and old age. And whereas Freud focused on the relationships between children and their parents, Erikson has taken into account the impact of the larger society on development.

Each of Erikson's eight psychosocial stages is presented as a polarity, with a positive pole representing successful development at that stage and a negative pole representing unsuccessful development. Erikson does not see these stages as fixed or rigid, however. If an individual fails to clear up a conflict or crisis at one stage in life, it is still possible for that person to clear up the conflict later. Erikson's eight stages are as follows:

Erik Erikson

1. *Trust versus mistrust.* In the first year of life infants depend on others to feed them, dress them, and carry them about. The parents cuddle them, talk to them, and play with them, and these interactions determine the children's attitude later in life. If a child's physical and emotional needs are met, he learns to trust his environment. If not, he will become fearful and mistrust the people and objects around him.

well. For example, we discuss the development of sex-role identity in Chapter 13 and the development of morality in the Psychological Issue following Chapter 14. In this section we will continue Piaget's account of cognitive development during childhood and then discuss the ways in which patterns of child-rearing affect the development of a sense of competence.

Cognitive Development

Between the ages of about two and seven, according to Piaget, children are in the *preoperational period* of cognitive development. Although two-year-old children have acquired the basic concepts of object constancy, space, time, and causality, they are still unable to perform certain basic mental operations that we adults take for granted. Children in this period typically find it impossible to take the perspective of another person. If, for example,

2. *Autonomy versus doubt.* In the second and third years, when children learn to walk, talk, and do things for themselves, parental encouragement and consistency in discipline can help the child to develop autonomy and independence. But if parents are overprotective, are inconsistent in their disciplinary techniques, or show disapproval when the child does things on his own, he will become doubtful and ashamed of himself.
3. *Initiative versus guilt.* By ages four and five, children are ready to roam about, to explore unfamiliar places, and to get to know new people. If the child's inquisitiveness and exploration of his environment are encouraged by his parents, he will find it easier to use his initiative to go out on his own. But if parents inhibit such actions, the child will develop guilt feelings whenever he tries to be independent.
4. *Industry versus inferiority.* From about ages six to eleven, children learn to manipulate objects and events by themselves. If encouraged, the child will develop a sense of industry, will enjoy solving problems and completing tasks, and will seek intellectual stimulation. If not, he will develop a sense of inferiority and will have to be bribed or cajoled to complete a task.
5. *Identity versus role confusion.* Between the ages of 12 and 18 sexuality emerges and the adolescent faces the task of finding himself. He must integrate all that he has previously experienced in order to develop a sense of ego identity. If he is unable to reconcile his various roles in life into one identity, he is said to be suffering from role confusion.
6. *Intimacy versus isolation.* If the adult has achieved a sense of identity, then he can form close relationships and share with others. Failure at this stage consists of being unable to relate intimately to others. The person may develop a sense of isolation, feeling there is no one but himself he can depend on in the world.
7. *Generativity versus self-absorption.* By middle age the individual must have decided about the outside world, the future, and his readiness to contribute to it. Generativity is the ability to look outside oneself and be concerned with other people. The generative individual is productive and happy. The person who fails at this stage becomes self-centered.
8. *Integrity versus despair.* If life has been a pleasure and the individual has achieved a sense of unity within himself and with others, old age will be a happy time. But if the old person feels that his life has been full of disappointments and failures and he cannot face life at this age, he will develop a sense of despair.

you stand opposite a four-year-old boy and ask him to point to *your* right hand, the child will point with *his* right hand to the hand directly opposite it—your left hand. And your attempts to point out the child's error to him, no matter how clear and eloquent they may seem to you, are not likely to change his mind. To get the right answer, the boy would have to be able to mentally put himself in another person's place, and this is something the preoperational child cannot yet do.

Piaget calls this ability to take another person's point of view *egocentrism.* He does not use this term to connote selfishness but rather to signify the simple fact that young children are capable of viewing the world from only a single point of view—their own. Nevertheless, this limitation of the child's mode of thought may sometimes get him into trouble with adults. As Elkind (1975) notes, young children "are impervious to whatever activity the adult is engaged in, no matter how delicate or precarious." A child will chatter away to his mother when she is engaged in an important phone conversation, apparently not realizing that she cannot conduct two conversations at the same time, or he will want his father to play a game with him even though Dad is busy shaving. We should bear in mind, however, that it is the child's inability to take another person's point of view that produces these behaviors, not any sort of selfishness or perversity.

Another aspect of the preoperational period is the flourishing of children's capacity to use symbols. This includes the use of language and the use of symbols in play, such as deciding that piles of mud are pies or that a small plastic bottle is a space capsule. At the beginning of the preoperational period, children sometimes confuse names and symbols with the objects that they stand for, a phenomenon called *nominal realism.* Children do not realize that names like "horse" or "cow," "Albert" or "Eloise" are arbitrary designations; instead, they assume that these names are inherent properties of the objects themselves, just like size, shape, and color. The idea of changing a doll's names, for instance, would be totally incomprehensible to children at this stage. By the end of the preoperational period, however, children realize that names are arbitrary designations, and as a result, they may begin to call people or things whatever names fit their fancy.

By the time they are about seven years old, children have entered the period of *concrete operations.* Now, for the first time, they can mentally manipulate objects. Piaget reports, for example, that if you show preoperational children a row of sticks and ask them to select the same number of sticks from a second pile, they will do so by matching the new sticks to the old, one by one. Concrete-operational children, in contrast, can count the sticks mentally—they do the necessary matching in their heads. With this ability of mental manipulation, concrete-operational children become capable of many new skills, from the use of arithmetic to the ability to place themselves in someone else's shoes.

WHEN DOES A CHILD BECOME SMARTER THAN A MONKEY?

On the basis of extensive mental tests administered to young monkeys, Harlow and Suomi (1975) concluded that monkeys' intellectual development resembled that of humans, except for the fact that after birth the monkeys' intellect increased four times as fast as humans' and only later began to fall behind. "Specifically," they reported, "the 1-year-old monkey was found to be twice as bright as the 1-year-old human, but the 6-year-old human was twice as bright as the 6-year-old monkey."

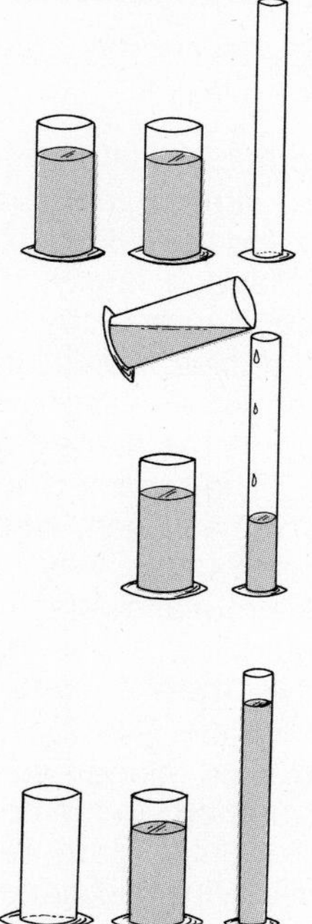

FIG. 12 · 2 A problem used to study the development of conservation of volume, one of the concepts acquired in the concrete-operational period. Children of different ages agree that the amount of water in the two identical beakers (top picture) is the same. Then, when the water in one beaker is poured into a taller beaker (middle picture), the children are asked if there is still the same amount of water in the two beakers (bottom picture). Children under about seven years of age are likely to say that the taller beaker now has more water, but older children recognize that the amounts are still equal.

A central concept acquired in the concrete-operational period is *conservation*—the notion that a substance's weight, mass, or volume will remain the same even if it changes in shape. If you pour water from a short, fat beaker into a tall, thin beaker, a preoperational child will usually conclude that you now have more water than you did before (see Figure 12.2). The child concentrates on only one of the beaker's dimensions, its height, and fails to take into account the other dimensions at the same time. As children acquire concrete operations, however, they develop the notion of a *unit* (for example, of volume), and they come to realize that the water has the same number of units regardless of the shape of the beaker it is in.

Since concrete operations are necessary skills in reading and arithmetic, parents and teachers often wonder whether it is possible to hasten the development of this mode of thought. (Americans seem to be particularly concerned with "getting there faster"—so much so that Piaget calls the question of accelerating cognitive development "the American question.") Recent studies suggest that, within limits, such acceleration is possible, by using techniques in which children are confronted with contradictions in their own judgment (Inhelder, Sinclair, and Bovet, 1974). Perhaps a more basic question, however, is whether it is worthwhile to attempt such acceleration as part of child-rearing and educational practices. Elkind (1975) thinks not, and we find his argument convincing: "There is no evidence that such acceleration has long lived effects on intellectual ability or anything else. Children have so much to learn that it seems shortsighted to spend a lot of time on what they can learn on their own rather than on skills that only we can help them acquire" (page 19).

Child-Rearing and the Development of Competence

Most parents hope that their children will become competent people, capable of making decisions for themselves, taking initiative, and relating effectively to others. For Robert White (1959), competence is the most central of human motives (see Chapter 9), and for Erik Erikson, the development of autonomy and of initiative (as opposed to doubt and guilt) are the central psychological challenges of childhood. The extent to which children develop such competence depends to a large extent on their parents' approach to child-rearing.

Several different approaches to child-rearing have been distinguished. One approach, often associated with the "old school," is the *authoritarian* style. Authoritarian parents deliberately try to shape the behavior of the child according to their own standards of conduct. These parents put a premium on obedience, and they may use punishment to curb rebellion in the child. In an authoritarian family, there is little room for discussion and debate; "do it because I told you to" is sufficient reason for obedience.

Nowadays such an authoritarian approach seems to be out of favor, especially among middle-class parents. Instead, a *permis-*

sive style of child-rearing has gained favor. Instead of trying to actively shape the child's behavior, permissive parents adopt the policy of keeping hands off and letting children "be themselves." These parents hope that by maximizing the children's freedom, they will also encourage the development of initiative and self-reliance. As Robert White (1976) wisely points out, however, when parents really care about their children's well-being (as most parents do), it is very hard to live up to this permissive ideal. Devoted parents can't help worrying about how far they should go in letting children make their own decisions. "Parents who care about their children," White adds, "inevitably harbor wishes and hopes for their future. They do not want to see this future compromised by shortsighted impulsiveness and youthful impatience" (page 46).

As a result, most "permissive" parents put limits on their children. Some parents refrain from directly telling their children what to do but instead point the child in a particular direction by saying that it is "what a sensible person would do" or by praising a neighbor's child for doing it. Other parents are permissive in some areas (for example, they will defend their child's right to choose his own styles of dress and haircut) but not in others (they will insist that he do his homework and do well academically). Another version of the permissive pattern is the "low control by default" that occurs when parents are unsure about themselves. "Confused by their own values, the parents do not convey a clear or consistent pattern of expectations; they let the child's inclinations prevail because they have no guidelines of their own" (White, 1976, page 48).

There is evidence that neither an authoritarian pattern nor a pattern of total permissiveness (or of "permissiveness by default") is as effective in the development of competence as is a child-rearing pattern that combines acceptance of the child's behavior within certain limits with relatively firm control. On the basis of extensive observations of parents and nursery school children at home, together with interviews with the parents, Diana Baumrind (1971) distinguished three patterns of parental control: a *permissive* pattern, in which parents let children have their own way; a *controlling-unconcerned* pattern similar to the authoritarian pattern described earlier; and a *controlling-concerned* pattern, in which parents had definite standards but also encouraged their children's independence and solicited their opinions. The children of controlling-concerned parents tended to be more independent, creative, cooperative, and helpful than children of permissive or of controlling-unconcerned parents. The permissively reared children tended to be more hostile, aimless, and anxious than children in the other two groups.

Baumrind's and other studies, including studies of older children, converge on the conclusion that the most effective child-rearing practices are those that steer a middle course between too much control and too little control. Coopersmith (1967) found, for example, that 10- to-12-year-old boys were most likely to develop high self-esteem when their parents pro-

WHEN EVERYBODY WAS YOUR PARENT

In previous generations, families consisted of more than just Mom and Dad and the kids. In the days of the extended family, children were surrounded by grandparents, uncles, aunts, cousins, and other close relations who either lived in the same house or nearby. "They wanted to know where you had been, where you were going, and why. If they didn't like your answers, they said so (particularly if you had told them the truth)," writes Urie Bronfenbrenner (1967). "Not just your relatives minded your business. Everybody in the neighborhood did. Your parents would know what you had done before you got back home. People on the street would tell you to button your jacket and ask why you weren't in church last Sunday."†

†*From U. Bronfenbrenner, "The Split-Level American Family,"* Saturday Review, *October 17, 1967, p. 60. Reprinted by permission of "Saturday Review," Copyright © 1967.*

vided them with clearly defined limits but respected the boys' right to make decisions for themselves within those limits.

ADOLESCENCE

Whereas the changes that take place in childhood are relatively slow and gradual, adolescence begins (at about age 12) with changes that are abrupt and dramatic. Along with the rapid physical and sexual development that occurs in early adolescence, cognitive development enters a new stage. The growth of adolescents' bodies and the continuing development of their modes of thinking provide the backdrop for what is probably the adolescent's central psychological challenge: the formation of a stable sense of identity.

Physical Development

The beginnings of adolescence can be traced to the physical changes that take place at about this time. For both sexes, these changes include the maturing of the reproductive system and rapid changes in body size and shape. For girls, the budding of the breasts and the onset of menstruation are especially dramatic changes. For boys, the changes include the sprouting of facial hair and the deepening of the voice.

There is a wide range of variation in the age at which these developments take place (Tanner, 1972). Although the average age of menarche (the first menstrual period) in American girls is about 13, it can take place anywhere between ages 10 and $16\frac{1}{2}$. The "height spurt" can begin for girls anywhere between $7\frac{1}{2}$

PARENT TRAINING FOR EVERYONE

"At present, tired, headachy adults do not give children a positive view of the worth of growing up. So there should be a course in parent education for every parent-to-be, or present parent—*and* a course in child development for all other adult members of society, including the secretary in an office building, the president of a university, the chairman of the F.C.C., and even the President of the United States. This is vital because children are our future—and every child's development is touched often by all of society's adults."[Kerckhoff and Kerckhoff, quoted in Agel, 1976]†

†*From Jerome Agel, "New Ideas,"* The New York Times, *April 25, 1976. Endpaper, © 1976 by The New York Times Company. Reprinted by permission.*

and 11 and for boys anywhere between $10\frac{1}{2}$ and 16. As a result, it is quite possible for three girls or three boys of the same age in early adolescence to look as if their ages were widely different.

Because of these differences, girls and boys are likely to be extremely self-conscious about their size and shape during early adolescence. Late-maturing boys, in particular, are likely to feel less adequate, less self-assured, and more anxious than boys who matured earlier (Mussen and Jones, 1957; Weatherley, 1964), and some of these personality differences may persist into adulthood (Jones, 1957). To reduce such negative effects, it is important that children be made aware of the fact that wide variations in the age of the height spurt and of sexual maturation are perfectly normal. And there is no difference in the heights of early-maturing and late-maturing boys by the time they stop growing (Tanner, 1972).

THEY'RE GROWING UP FASTER THAN EVER

When adults comment, "Those kids are growing up faster than ever!" they're right, in more ways than one. Over the past 100 years there has been a dramatic tendency in American and other industrialized countries for puberty to come earlier than it used to. In 1900, the average age of menarche for American girls was over 14; it is now under 13. In England the drop has been even sharper. Forty years ago the average British girl had her first menstrual period at about her fifteenth birthday; now it is shortly before her thirteenth. Boys are also undergoing the physical changes of puberty earlier than before, with girls continuing to develop about two years earlier than boys. Although several factors may be involved in the declining age of puberty, better nutrition seems to be the most important. Will the decline continue? Probably not to any large extent. The evidence suggests that by now young people in the Unites States are growing up at something close to the fastest possible speed (Tanner, 1972).

Cognitive Development

At approximately age 12, children enter Piaget's stage of *formal operations.* Formal operations allow adolescents to think about thought itself. It is not until early adolescence that most people can play complex word games, learn algebra, and do other tasks that involve the mental manipulation of complex thoughts and concepts. Formal operations are also necessary for a fuller grasp of historical time (what does it mean for something to have occurred "five centuries ago"?) and geographical distance (how far is "a thousand miles"?). And because they can think about thought itself, adolescents can now think and talk about such abstract notions as "beliefs," "values," and "ideals." In fact, as Elkind (1975) notes, "At least some of the 'storm and stress' associated with adolescence is a consequence of the disaffection between their real and ideal worlds," a comparison that cannot be made before the acquisition of formal operations.

Self-Consciousness and Identity Formation

Once they are able to think about their own thought processes, adolescents are also likely to begin thinking about what other people are thinking. And in many cases the assumption is that the other people are thinking about *them.* This new self-consciousness can lead to insight and sensitivity as one begins to view oneself from other people's point of view. It can also lead to depression, especially as one begins to discover one's lacks and failings. In one study, adolescent boys indicated on a questionnaire that they had experienced increased sadness, dissatisfaction with life, and feelings of being misunderstood as they grew older (Meissner, 1966).

Closely related to the adolescent's emerging self-consciousness is the need to develop a clear sense of identity. For Erik Erikson, identity formation is the central developmental task of the adolescent years. From all the separate roles that the ado-

lescent plays—as son or daughter, sibling, boyfriend or girl friend, athlete, student, and so on—he or she must struggle to emerge with a clearly defined sense of self. The adolescent must answer the question, "Who am I—and where am I heading?" In Erikson's words:

> *The identity the adolescent seeks to clarify is who he is, what his role in society is to be. Is he a child or is he an adult? Does he have it in him to someday be a husband and father? What is he to be as a worker and an earner of money? Can he feel confident in spite of the fact that his race or religious or national backgrounds make him a person some people look down upon? Overall, will he be a success or a failure? (1951, page 9).*

As this quote suggests, Erikson seems to have been more specifically concerned with male than with female identity information. Douvan and Adelson (1966) have suggested that because of the lower status of women in American society, girls find it harder than boys to develop a strong sense of identity and that girls often postpone this task until after marriage. At this time their identity may depend in large part on the accomplishments and plans of their husband. One of the concerns of people in the women's movement is to remove this sort of socially imposed obstacle to women's identity formation.

The formation of a stable sense of identity is not an easy task for anyone, however, regardless of sex. The rapid physical changes and sexual awakening of adolescence may often lead young people to be confused about the continuity between their past and their present. And the rapid changes taking place in today's society only serve to compound the difficulty. It is no wonder, therefore, that many adolescents fail to establish a clear identity and, instead, suffer what Erikson calls "role confusion." Many of the social movements and causes that attract adolescents, from political groups to religious cults, may hold their appeal because they seem to provide solutions to the adolescent

identity crisis. For example, Adamson and Fox (1972) see the "Jesus trip" as a way in which young converts try to substitute a prepackaged, prearranged identity as a short cut to the hard work of evolving one distinctly their own.

EARLY AND MIDDLE ADULTHOOD

Psychologists have devoted a great deal of attention to development in infancy, childhood, and adolescence and have paid a reasonable amount of attention to old age. Until very recently, however, they paid very little attention to the 45 years or so in between, the period of early and middle adulthood. Now, however, psychologists have begun to study adulthood from a developmental perspective. The emphasis of this new research has not been on physical or cognitive changes. The physical changes of adulthood, although quite real, are slow and undramatic. And although age may bring wisdom (we hope), once the stage of formal operations is attained there are no qualitative changes in

people's mode of thinking. Instead, the new research has focused on the psychological and social tasks and challenges that people face as they proceed through the years of adulthood.

The Stages of Adult Development

Erik Erikson (1950) laid much of the groundwork for current research on adult development by outlining three stages of adult development. In early adulthood, Erikson believes, the central psychological challenge is to establish *intimacy*—a close personal bond with another person, usually (but not necessarily) a husband or wife. In middle adulthood, he viewed the central theme as *generativity*—the desire to have an impact on the next generation, whether through guiding one's own children or through one's contribution to society. And in late adulthood or old age, Erikson emphasizes the theme of *integrity*—the ability to look back at one's life with satisfaction.

More recently, several investigators have conducted both cross-sectional studies of people at different stages of adulthood and longitudinal studies of people moving through adulthood. These studies have begun to fill out the details of this progression (Gould, 1975; Levinson, 1977). Drawing from the work of these researchers, as well as from her own interviews with adults at different stages of life, Gail Sheehy (1976) has constructed the following picture of adult development:

Ages 18 to 22—In this period the adolescent "identity crisis" typically continues, as people attempt to pull up roots from their parents and to establish an independent life of their own. In addition, the attempt to establish an intimate relationship is often a central theme.

Ages 22 to 28—The twenties are times in which people replace their preoccupation with internal matters (Who am I?) with concentration on concrete, external matters—in particular, getting launched in the domains of family and work. The choices made during these years are not irrevocable, but they do set in motion a particular life pattern.

Ages 28 to 32—These are often years of wavering and doubt, with people frequently feeling restricted by the personal and career choices they made during their twenties. More and more people decide to change course during these years—by getting married, getting divorced, or changing careers, for example.

Age 32 to 35—After the period of transition that often occurs around age 30, the early thirties tend to be years of settling down. People make "rational," orderly decisions. They buy houses, advance in careers, and focus on raising a family.

Ages 35 to 45—The "settling down" stage may extend through the thirties. But at some point during the 35 to 45 decade, people are also likely to experience a *mid-life crisis.* This is often experienced as a sudden recognition that one's life is about half over, coupled with a questioning of what one has really accomplished and what one's life really means. At this point in life, people may have to face the realization that they have not achieved the lofty goals that they had once set for themselves—and that they probably never will. And even if they have reached these goals, they may feel a sense of letdown and a lack of purpose. Mid-life, therefore, is a time for reassessment of one's goals and aspirations. As Sheehy suggests, "If you recognize that you will never be president of the big-city bank, you can get on with becoming branch manager in your favorite community and maybe find your greatest pleasure in becoming a Little League coach or starting a choir" (1976, page 247). Many researchers now believe that this transition into mid-life is as critical as the transitions of adolescence and often even more difficult.

Ages 45 to 60—If the mid-life crisis is avoided or bypassed, these years can sometimes be ones of staleness and resignation. Daniel Levinson notes that "many men who don't have a crisis at 40 become weighted and lose the vitality they need to continue developing in the rest of the adult stages" (quoted by Sheehy, page 251). The crisis can also emerge in more painful form during one's fifties. If the mid-life transition is faced squarely, however, it can lead to feelings of great renewal and satisfaction in one's forties and fifties and extending on into one's later years.

It should be emphasized that psychologists' understanding of the developmental changes of adulthood remains quite sketchy. And not everyone goes through all of the stages and changes in the same order or at the same speed. Moreover, most of the research to date had been done with white middle-class men. More research needs to be done on women's development through the life cycle, as well as on people from other ethnic and socioeconomic groups. Nevertheless, the recognition that development continues throughout the life cycle, often through predictable crises and stages, represents an important and fruitful new avenue of research.

SECRETS OF LONGEVITY

It is popular for reporters and researchers interviewing people who have lived 100 years or longer to ask them the "secret" of their longevity. The answers they have received have ranged from the ridiculous to the sublime. A 106-year-old man recommends drinking a fifth of whiskey twice a month. But he also is a firm believer in weekly Bible study. One place where people tend to live to be particularly old is the Valley of Vilcabamba, a strange sort of Shangri-La in Ecuador. Observers suggest, as clues to the people's longevity, the utter tranquillity of the valley, its ideal climate, and the low-calorie diet featuring little meat and lots of garden-fresh fruits and vegetables. However, the people of this valley are also in the habit of drinking two to four cups of rum a day and smoking up to 60 cigarettes. In the final analysis, perhaps the truly important thing is *how* we live our lives rather than how *long* they last.

OLD AGE

What does it mean to be "old"? Do people suddenly become old when they reach their sixty-fifth birthday? Do people become old when their vision fails, or when they retire from their jobs, or when they begin to be more forgetful? Or is it better to assume that "you're only as old as you feel"? As Kalish (1975) points out, we are likely to employ different definitions of old age for different purposes—and each of them reflects different values and stereotypes about the aging process.

If we use the arbitrary standard of age 65 as the beginning of old age, it is clear that primarily as a result of improved health, there are more old people in America than ever before. In 1900 4 percent of the people of the United States were 65 or older. The figure in 1974 was slightly over 10 percent (in Canada it was 8 percent), and the predictions are that the figure will rise still further. But whereas a significant proportion of the population can be categorized as "old," we have not yet responded adequately to the psychological and social needs of our older people.

The Aging Process: Physical and Cognitive Changes

Biologists do not yet know exactly why people age and eventually die. One theory suggests that as our body's cells "copy" and reproduce themselves, the copies become of lower and lower quality—much the same as the quality of a copied photograph is

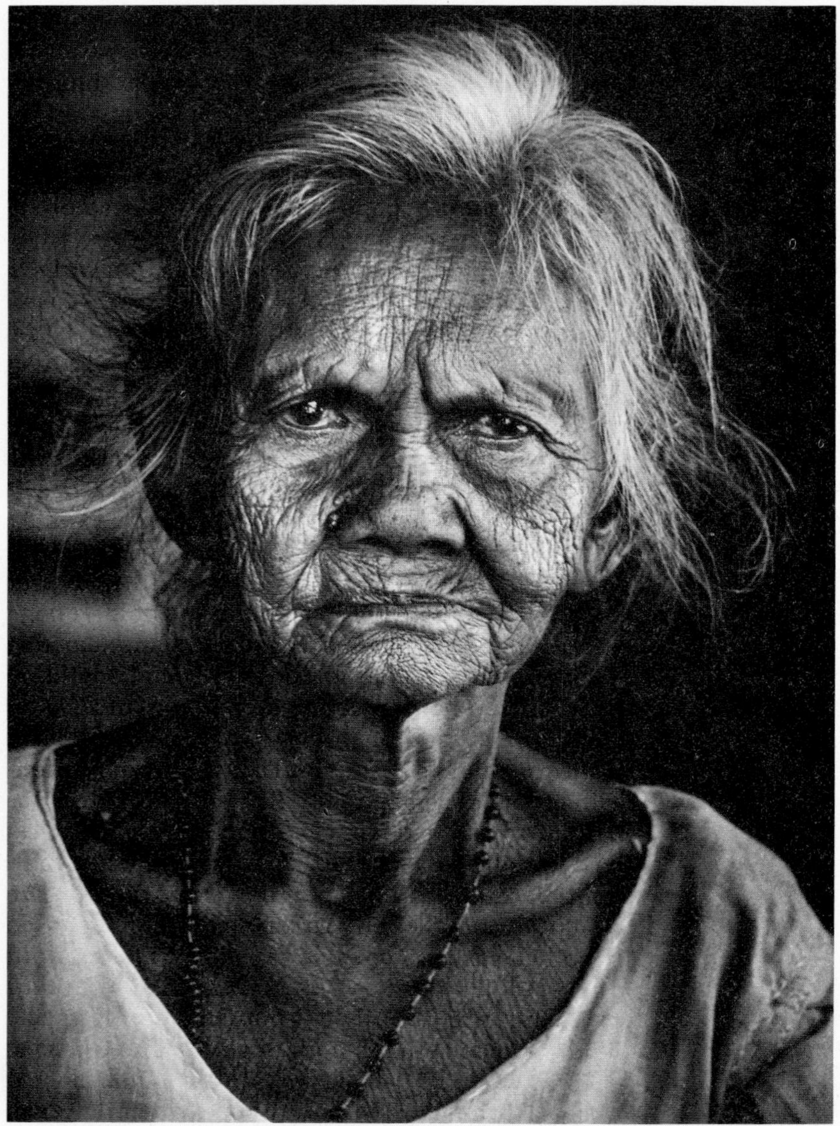

poorer than the original. Other theories emphasize the gradual effects of the physical environment, including heat, radiation, and air pollutants, in wearing down our bodies. Regardless of the reasons for it, the physical changes of old age are unmistakable. In addition to changes in physical appearance, such as graying hair and wrinkling skin, older people often have declining vision and hearing and a slowing down of reaction time and of motor functions (Kalish, 1975).

It is often assumed that old age brings with it diminishing mental capacities, as well as physical decline. As we noted in Chapter 8, however, recent research does not support this point of view. The evidence suggests that older people suffer declines only on those aspects of mental test performance that specifically

HOW NOT TO BE DECLARED "DEAD ON ARRIVAL"

One reflection of the attitude that old people are less valuable members of society than younger people is to be found in hospital emergency rooms. In emergency rooms, old people are less likely to get a thorough examination than young people, less likely to elicit the fullest efforts of the medical staff, and more likely to be declared "dead on arrival" (Sudnow, 1967). More generally, the quality of the medical care given to older people tends to be less adequate than that given to people who are younger.

require quick reactions and decisions. There is also evidence of decline in older people's short-term memories. But older people's skills do not decline, and sometimes even increase with age, on other intellectual tasks, such as verbal comprehension, social awareness, and the application of experience.

Nevertheless, those physical and cognitive changes of aging that do take place can have far-reaching implications for the older person. For example, failing vision, if it cannot be fully corrected, is likely to impair the ability to drive, to read, and to do many sorts of work. And these changes, in turn, may have an impact on one's conception of oneself as an independent and self-reliant person. Similarly, older people's discovery that they can no longer remember the names of people they meet as well as they used to can instill fears that they are losing all of their mental capacities or becoming "senile." Fortunately, most older people have the resilience to adapt to these physical changes, especially since they usually come gradually and can be prepared for.

Aging and Society

Older people's self-conceptions are affected not only by changes in their physical and cognitive capacities, but also by the reaction of other members of society—especially younger adults—to them. In general, the record of modern industrial society is not very good in this regard. Whereas older people in pre-industrial societies continued to be highly respected and to exert considerable control over their extended families, old people in America are all too often viewed as having "seen their better days." As Rosow (1965) notes, the position of older people seems to be better in less "advanced" societies, where there is a constant struggle to survive, than in more affluent societies like our own. In our society, moreover, cities are developed primarily for the benefit of mobile, employed, consuming, younger citizens (Birren, 1970). In addition, poverty is a serious problem for many older Americans who can no longer work.

In all societies, old people eventually give up some of the roles and family responsibilities that they had when they were younger. These losses can be quite painful for a person who is used to being highly productive and involved. The American emphasis on independence and self-reliance does not make these losses any easier for the older person. Because of these emphases in American culture, older people may come to feel especially weak and inadequate when they must relinquish control over portions of their lives and increase their dependence on others. Other cultures may provide a better model in this regard. Among the Igbo of Africa, for example, the elder accepts care from younger people as a publicly acknowledged right, without any sense of shame or guilt (Shelton, 1969).

The question of what represents "successful" aging is one that we do not yet have an answer for. One definition assumes that older people age "successfully" to the extent that they continue to function and behave the way they did when they were younger—that is, to the extent that they behave like middle-aged people. As Kalish (1975) points out, this definition is an example of "age-ism" at its worst, since it presumes to consider one age group's pattern of behavior as inherently superior to that of another age group. Nevertheless, such a definition is often held, at least implicitly, by professionals who work with the aged, as well as by nonprofessionals. "She looks like a woman twenty years younger" or "He still plays a set of tennis every day" is often taken as the highest compliment one can pay to an older person. A better definition of successful aging would not make reference to other age groups, but instead might focus on the older person's own feeling of happiness and satisfaction with his or her life.

Aging and Personality

We all tend to have notions of what older people are like. They are often seen, for example, as cautious, rigid, wise, patient, irritable, and forgetful. Some aspects of this stereotype of the older person may have a grain of truth. There is some evidence that older people tend to be more cautious and less flexible than younger people (Kalish, 1975). But most of the research on the personalities of older people reveals what perhaps we should have known in the first place: that the personalities of older people are quite as diverse as the personalities of people at any other stage of life. In a longitudinal study of 142 adults between the ages of 30 and 70, Maas and Kuypers (1974) found that, if anything, people become more diverse as they age. There are old homebodies, old activists, old people who are happy, and old people who are depressed, just as there are younger people in each of these categories. And people's personalities at age 70 were found to have much more to do with their personalities at age 30 than with the onset of old age. Throughout this chapter we have been focusing on model patterns of development through the life cycle. But we should not forget that there is tremendous diversity among people at all ages, from infancy to old age. In Chapters 13 and 14 (on sex differences and personality), we will explore some of this diversity.

Facing Death

Although death can come at any age, its arrival is most imminent when one is old. As a result, we often assume that death is more frightening for old people than it is for those who are younger. Kalish and Reynolds (reported in Kalish, 1975) found, however, that just the opposite is true: Although old people seem to think about death more than younger people do, they are less afraid of it. "Older people seem to feel that they have lived their lives," Kalish (1975) writes, "and have received what they felt they 'had coming' " (page 93). As their future grows shorter, old people are

THE GRAY PANTHERS

The Gray Panthers are out to change a society that "wants to keep the elderly out of the way, playing bingo and shuffleboard." By adopting a new life style of independence, the Gray Panthers stress action, in contrast to most older adults' service-oriented organizations. They focus on transportation, health maintenance, banking, tax reform, and putting old people in charge of their nursing homes. Working with the Gray Panthers are a number of young people—the Panther Cubs. The two groups discovered that "age-ism" goes both ways—hurting both the young and the old and depriving both groups of the right to control their own lives.

also likely to reminisce and review their lives. "They survey, observe, and reflect upon the past. Often they achieve new insights into experiences, wisdom that provides more valid, significant pictures of their lives" (Butler, 1971, page 89). Butler believes that such a review can help old people prepare for death with equanimity. This observation is in accord with Erik Erikson's notions about the final stage of the life cycle. The developmental task of old age, in Erikson's view, is to establish a sense of *integrity*—a feeling that one has lived a satisfying and meaningful life. "In such final consolidation," Erikson (1950) writes, "death loses its sting."

SUMMARY

1. *Maturation* refers to the unfolding of inherited biological patterns. Maturation interacts with learning to produce psychological development. Maturational forces may be more important than was previously thought: Although the role of maturation is most obvious in physical development and language learning, it may also play a significant role in cognitive and social development.
2. The infant (from birth to age two) is in what Piaget calls the *sensorimotor* period of cognitive development. During this stage babies learn to coordinate sensory information with motor activities and discover the principle of *object constancy.* At this early age they also develop basic concepts of causality, space, and time.
3. During the first two years, the infant develops a strong *attachment* to a small number of persons. The presence of the attachment figure helps to reduce the reaction of *stranger anxiety* that occurs at this stage. Harlow's studies with infant monkeys imply that attachments develop out of the need for *contact comfort* rather than from the satisfaction of such needs as food. Infants who do not experience contact comfort tend to have difficulty forming close relationships in later life.
4. According to Erikson, infants' physical and psychological needs must be satisfied in order for them to develop "basic trust." If treated poorly or inconsistently, they are likely to develop a mistrustful attitude that will continue through life.
5. Children between two and seven are in Piaget's *preoperational* period of cognitive development. Children at this stage are *egocentric*—they are unable to see things from another person's point of view—and they assume that names are inherent properties of objects—a phenomenon called *nominal realism.*
6. At about age seven children enter the period of *concrete operations.* They are now able to mentally manipulate objects and to understand the principle of *conservation.*

7. *Authoritarian* parents deliberately try to shape their children's behavior according to the parents' own standards of conduct. *Permissive* parents adopt the policy of "hands off" and let their children do "their own thing." However, most permissive parents actually impose some limits on their children's behavior.
8. When parents have definite standards but also encourage their children's independence and opinions, the children tend to be more independent, creative, cooperative, and helpful than children of authoritarian or overly permissive parents.
9. Adolescence begins with maturing of the reproductive system and rapid body changes. There is wide variation in the age at which the major developments occur, and early or late maturation can have significant effects on the individual's self-concept and personality.
10. Adolescents have reached Piaget's stage of *formal operations.* They are able to mentally manipulate complex thoughts and concepts and to think about thought itself.
11. Adolescence is a time for increased self-consciousness and the need to develop a clear sense of identity. If the identity problem is not resolved, the individual suffers from what Erikson calls "role confusion" and may be prime material for various religious or other cults.
12. Although long neglected by developmental psychologists, development during adulthood has been found to be ongoing and eventful. According to Erikson the main tasks of adulthood are the achievement of *intimacy,* of *generativity,* and of *integrity.* Sheehy has described six major stages of adulthood. One of the major events is the *mid-life crisis,* which occurs around age 35 to 45.
13. There are more old people in America than ever before. Physical aging is a poorly understood phenomenon, but it nevertheless impairs people's ability to engage in the sorts of activities they engaged in when they were younger, and this may have a negative effect on their self-concept.
14. Old people in America are at a disadvantage—modern cities are designed for the young and mobile, and economic conditions have severely limited the life style of senior citizens. And the American emphasis on self-reliance makes it particularly hard for old people who must depend on others.
15. Old people's personalities cannot be stereotyped—if anything, people's personalities get more diverse as they age. In fact, people's personalities at age 70 have more to do with their personalities at age 30 than with the onset of old age.
16. According to Erikson, the major task of old age is to establish a feeling that one has lived a satisfying and meaningful life. Old people can face death with equanimity if they have accomplished this task.

psychological issue

The Generation Gap

We hear a lot about conflict between fathers and sons, mothers and daughters, about mistrust and hostility between people on the two sides of that great dividing line of age 30. Older people often view today's youth with some distaste, describing young people as conformist, irresponsible, hedonistic, anti-intellectual, unrealistic, and disrespectful. In spite of the greater education, cultural advantages, and sophistication of today's youth, many adults are not convinced that the "new species" is an improvement over what they were like when they were young. Meanwhile, the young are likely to view older people and the society that they dominate as corrupt, materialistic, and over the hill.

Perhaps the feeling of this generation gap is best conveyed in the plaintive wail of the father who said, "I survived the Great Depression, World War II, three economic recessions, and a heart attack. Now my 18-year-old kid sneers and tells me I don't know what life is all about!" (Kalish, 1969).

Some people on both sides of the gap have the idea that the ideological clash that they perceive between generations is something unprecedented in the history of humankind. But in fact, the generation gap seems to be an ancient phenomenon. Hieroglyphics in ancient Egyptian tombs complain of the younger generation's unwillingness to respect the wisdom of their elders and to honor the established laws of the society. In every era, there seem to be strains between the generations.

...the generation gap seems to be an ancient phenomenon.

The Changing Gap

The generation gap has probably always existed in America. But at different points in history it seems to have taken somewhat different forms. In the 1920s the stuffy, puritanical parents of the day were appalled by the drinking and sexual promiscuity of the "lost generation" as it was portrayed by F. Scott Fitzgerald. In the 1930s youth again puzzled parents, this time by participating in protests, denouncing capitalism, and writing poetry at a time when most adults were living rigidly conventional lives. In the 1940s, the now middle-aged products of the "lost generation" despaired at finding that "they had spewn forth a generation of spineless, 'adjusted' jellyfish who worshipped security above ambition; silence above protest'' (Gustin, 1961, page 78).

In the 1950s the young were impatient to enter ''the system'' and to have the privileges of adulthood. They wanted to be in the driver's seat. The youth of the 1960s, however, not only didn't want to be in the driver's seat—''They don't even want to go where the car is going'' (Friedenberg, 1969). According to Friedenberg, the 1960s generation was made up of adolescents who wanted to get out of American society altogether and form their own group, away from the values of their elders.

Protest and Alienation

The youth of the 1960s were characterized by dissent and rebellion. According to the psychoanalytic view, student protesters are sons symbolically attacking the authority of their fathers (Feuer, 1969). Kenneth Keniston (1967) has shown, however, that there are many types of dissenter. Keniston found that student dissenters fell along a continuum stretching between *activists* at one end and *alienated* youth at the other end. The activists worked within the system of the school and of the nation to improve them as they felt they should be improved. The alienated youth, in contrast, were so pessimistic about the Establishment that they did not become directly involved. Dropping out, for them, was the only sensible option. Keniston found that attitudes toward parents varied greatly between these two types of dissenters. Whereas the alienated student almost always rejected his parents' values, the activist was likely to accept the basic political and social values of his parents. Rather than rejecting their fathers' ideals, the activist sons were trying to put these ideals into practice.[†]

Today's students seem quieter, more serious, and more career-oriented. . . .

In accord with Keniston's analysis, Miller (1969) found that 48 percent of a group of young demonstrators arrested at the 1968 Democratic National Convention felt that both parents approved of their behavior, and 59 percent indicated that at least one parent approved. In an earlier study (Solomon and Fishman, 1964), 50 percent of Washington peace demonstrators said their parents approved of their activity. It seems, then, that the student protest of the 1960s cannot be seen simply as a generation in revolt or as an effort to break free of constricting, tradition-oriented, or obsolete values of parents.

[†]*From K. Keniston, YOUTH AND DISSENT, (New York: Harcourt Brace Jovanovich, Inc., 1971). Reprinted by permission.*

In the college student generation of the 1970s, protests appear to have been replaced by academic concerns. Today's students seem quieter, more serious, more ambitious, and more career-oriented, as well as socially concerned. And wouldn't you know it, *this* behavior has come to worry a lot of people in the older generation. Why don't you speak out more, they ask; how come we don't hear from you kids any more? For the younger generation, there sometimes seems to be just no way to win.

Different Kinds of Gaps

We've noted that there always seem to have been generation gaps, but that the nature of the gap seems to have varied from one historical period to another. In fact, however, all generation gaps share many similarities; for example, the younger generation always appears to be defying (either actively or passively) the entrenched power of the older generation. But each generation through history has grown up under a different set of historical circumstances and with a somewhat different set of values, and these differences contribute to the changing nature of the conflict between generations. These differences were illustrated by Vern Bengtson (1973, pages 5–7)[†], who described the life history, attitudes, and behavior of the grandfather, father, and son of the family, the Johnsons.

[†]*From THE PSYCHOLOGY OF AGING, by V. L. Bengtson (Indianapolis: Bobbs-Merrill, 1973) p. 5–7. Copyright © 1973 by Bobbs-Merrill Company, Inc. Reprinted by permission.*

Three Generations of Johnsons

Johann Johnson, age 73:
Retired against his will from a factory job eight years ago, he spends much of his time gardening, listening to religious radio programs, and talking with friends . . . Born in Sweden, he describes his "most important events in life" as follows: came to America as a five-year-old; lost a good farm during the Depression because of speculation; started making good money in a factory during World War II; lost wife from cancer in 1970. . . . He says he doesn't have any goals any more—"only young people have goals"—and that his only concern is to "keep active—I want to wear out, not rust out."

He answers questions in our research questionnaire as follows:

Best thing that could happen to you: *"To see our nation return to God."*

Worst thing that could happen to you: *"To lose my health, which is excellent."*

Self-rated liberal to conservative: *"Very conservative."*

Church attendance: *"Every week, when I can get a ride."*

Rating on general happiness scale: *"Very happy."*

Archie Johnson, age 48:
Spends 45 hours per week as an engineer for an aerospace contractor. His salary is good for his position ($22,000) but he works harder then he did a decade ago because in 1970 he was laid off and drew unemployment compensation . . . for 18 months before finding a new job. "I have to put more time in to compete with the younger guys," he says. He describes the most important events in his life thus: ran away from home to join the Navy in 1942, fathered two children, got a college degree on the G.I. bill while supporting his family, got a house in the suburbs. . . . He has a carefully ordered list of goals for the next year—economic, social, and self-development—which he and his wife go over every three months. This helps him plan, he says—"I have to start thinking about retirement."

His questionnaire shows the following answers:

Best thing that could happen to you: *"To see my children grow and make the world a better place."*

Worst thing that could happen to you: *"To lose my job."*

Self-rated liberal to conservative: *"Slightly conservative."*

Church attendance: *"About once a month."*

Rating on happiness scale: *"Pretty happy."*

Kirk Johnson, age 23:
Says he spends most of his time during the week "studying with time out for meditating and turning on." He is finishing his degree in sociology at a local state college. He lives with Joan, a sophomore nursing student, and enjoys seeing his parents wince when he asserts that he and his "old woman" have no intention of getting married—ever. He's proud of the fact that they together live on less than $300 a month . . . He was very active in the radical movement on campus when he was a sophomore, but today says he's completely turned off by politics. He at first does not want to talk about his life goals—"Hanging loose and acting on feelings is very important to me"—but then talks animatedly about his desire to become a social worker, to have a career helping people, to form an urban commune which will really last, and to work for world peace.

Answers to questionnaire:

Best thing that could happen to you in life: *"To have the world free from war and everyone to be my brother."*

Worst thing: *"To have someone tell me I can't do my own thing."*

Self-rated liberal to conservative: *He wrote in "radical."*

Church attendance: *"Never."*

Rating on happiness scale: *"Not too happy."*

These profiles of three generations are part of data gathered from the Study of Generations and Mental Health at the University of Southern California. This study, involving more than 2,100 family members, came up with the following findings, which are graphically illustrated in the Johnson family example: (1) grandparents assign greater importance to religious participation than do young people; (2) grandparents describe themselves as much more conservative politically; (3) those in the middle-aged generation rank the value of "achievement" higher than do the other generations; and (4) grandparents score higher on the "happiness" scale than do the middle-aged, which in turn score higher than youth.

How do we explain these differences? Some of the differences can be explained in terms of biology; others require a sociological explanation; and some are a matter of historical context. Some differences, for example, are simply a matter of the person's stage in the developmental life cycle. Kirk's goals are long-range, humanitarian, intense—he has a long life ahead of him. Archie's goals are more immediate and concern his own situation. Johann looks back on his life with satisfaction and won't even talk about goals. These differences are predicted to some extent by Erik Erikson in his characterizations of the eight stages of development.

There are also biological differences for people at different ages. Thus Johann discusses his health at great length, Archie mentions a decline in energy—"I have to put more time in"—and Kirk dismisses the subject. And there are differences attributable to stages in work career. Archie spends most of his time in the office working with other people, Kirk spends a good deal of time reading textbooks and sitting in classes, and Johann is retired and lives according to his own daily program. These differences lie in the sociological aspects of their lives (Bengtson, 1973).

Bengtson also points out that some differences are best explained in terms of differences in historical time. Johann's conservatism does not reflect his age, but rather the fact that people in his generation have tended to vote for conservatives since he first voted in 1922. (As Cutler [1970] has found, people do *not* generally become more conservative as they grow older.) Similarly, Archie's orientation toward working and saving is less a factor of being middle-aged and more a result of having grown up during the Depression. And Kirk's

living with his girlfriend without benefit of marriage seems to be more a matter of contemporary views of man-woman relationships than a matter of youth sowing wild oats.

Bengtson's research makes clear that any difference between generations may have several possible explanations. We must be concerned with the biological, sociological, and historical sources of these differences before we can begin to understand them.

What Generation Gap?

According to Joseph Adelson (1970), the idea of a generation gap is no more than pop sociology—a false idea whose time has come. Adelson believes that the so-called generation gap is an illusion, shared by the young and the old, that there is a difference between them. But in fact, Adelson maintains, there is no evidence of an extensive clash of values between parents and their children. Indeed, one of the best ways to predict a person's political and social attitudes is to find out what parents' attitudes were—there is a great deal of consistency between the two. But we often perceive differences as greater than they really are. Perhaps we expect parents and children to have radically different views of things, and as a result we see what we are looking for.

...one of the best ways to predict a person's political and social attitudes is to find out what that person's parents' attitudes were....

But even if reports of a generation gap have been exaggerated, the differences between generations are not wholly imaginary, nor are the difficulties that members of the two generations often encounter in discussing them. As Margaret Mead (1970) notes, our elders can rightfully say, "I have been young and *you* have never been old." But young people can with perhaps as much right reply, "You have never been young in the world I am young in, and you never can be." The faster our society changes, the greater the psychological gap between generations is likely to be. If the parents of today's younger generation have trouble understanding their children's student strikes, marijuana smoking, and sexual freedom, just imagine the sorts of things that today's 18- to 25-year-olds will have to contend with in their children in the year 2000.

Summary

1. The generation gap is apparently an ancient phenomenon. It has probably always existed in the United States, although the characteristics of the gap have changed at different points in history.
2. Keniston pointed out that the dissenting youth of the 1960s could be classified along a continuum from activitist to alienated youth. Activists tended to work within the system, sharing basic values with their parents, whereas alienated youths opposed both the system and the values of their parents.
3. Bengtson's study of generations found grandparents to be more religious, more conservative, and happier than their children and grandchildren. The difference between the three generations can be explained in terms of differences in biology, in developmental stage, in social roles, and in historical context.
4. According to Adelson, there really is no generation gap. Rather, people have simply accepted the idea that there are significant differences between generational groups, and existing differences have been exaggerated. Nevertheless, there are some differences, and they are likely to become greater as society goes through rapid changes.

PART 6

Differences and Similarities Between People

Each of us is a unique individual, with a distinctive pattern of thoughts, feelings, and behaviors. One of the central tasks of psychology is to map these differences between people and to explain how they come about. Although no two people are identical (even identical twins develop quite different patterns of behavior), there is a great deal that we all share by virtue of being human. All of us have brains and nervous systems with the same basic groundplan, and all of us rely on the same fundamental mechanisms of experiencing the world, learning and thinking, motivation and emotion. As a result, it is misleading for us to try to explain only the *differences* between people. In order to understand these differences, we must explore them in the context of underlying human *similarities.*

In Chapter 13, *Male and Female,* we consider one important basis of categorizing and comparing human beings, their sex. We will review the evidence concerning psychological differences and similarities between men and women, and we will consider the ways in which those differences that exist may come about. We will pay special attention to the ways in which girls and boys learn sex roles, those patterns of thought, feeling, and behavior that society considers to be appropriate for members of each sex. And in the Psychological Issue following this chapter, we will examine the recent movements of *Women's and Men's Liberation,* which have as their central aims the desire to change these sex roles, which can sometimes limit our full development as human beings.

In Chapter 14 we turn to the variety of approaches to human differences and similarities that come under the heading of *Personality.* We will examine several contrasting theories of personality, including Freud's psychoanalytic approach and the more recent emphasis on social learning and imitation in shaping a person's distinctive pattern of behavior. The Psychological Issue that follows this chapter explores an aspect of personality that many observers are worried about in today's post-Watergate era. The topic is *Morality,* and the key questions concern the ways in which people come to judge what is right and what is wrong.

Male and Female

CHAPTER 13

Male and Female

There are many things about you that are central to your identity as a distinctive human being—your talents, your habits, your sensitivities, your appearance, your occupational aspirations, your political views, your ideals. Yet of all the elements of individual identity, the one that is quite regularly singled out for special attention is your sex. This single piece of information is frequently the first thing we learn about another person. When we hear another person described, it's often in a sentence like "He's the guy who . . . " or "She's the lady who . . . " Even before we hear the end of the sentence, we already know the person's sex. And for each of us, our sexual identity becomes one of the most central elements of our self-definition. Ask a child as young as five or six the question, "Who are you?" The chances are that the child will not give such answers as "I'm a first-grader" or "I'm a six-year-old" or "I'm an American," even though such answers would be perfectly logical. Instead, the child will be most likely to answer, "I'm a boy" or "I'm a girl."

There are, of course, times when one's sex is of paramount importance. No one would deny, for example, that it takes one person of each sex for reproduction to take place. However, more and more people are beginning to question whether a person's sex should play so prominent a role in other aspects of life. Why, for example, should a child's sex have anything to do with whether that child is given electric trains or Barbi dolls to play with? Why should sex have anything to do with whether an adult works as a business executive or a nurse? Some shifts away from these traditional sex roles have begun to take place. We will focus on these changes in the last part of the chapter and in the Psychological Issue that follows. First, however, we need to consider a central question: Just what are the psychological differences between men and women, and how important are they?

PSYCHOLOGICAL DIFFERENCES BETWEEN MEN AND WOMEN

Some of the differences between men and women are obvious: the two sexes differ in their genital organs, internal reproductive systems, and secondary sex characteristics, such as breasts and facial hair. There are other physical differences as well. Although there is considerable overlap between the two sexes, on the average men are taller, heavier, and more muscular than women. Men are also more likely to be bald, to be colorblind, and to have hemophilia. In and of themselves, however, these physical differences do not have much to do with men's and women's personalities or with their social and occupational roles. Only a few occupations, such as playing professional basketball, place much emphasis on a person's height. Physical strength was once important in human affairs. But in today's age of machines and pushbuttons, it is no longer a crucial quality.

In fact, the disparities between the roles that men and women play—the likelihood that the man is the wage-earner and the woman is the child-rearer, that he is the boss and she the secretary—are not based on physical differences at all. Rather, they are often based on assumptions about *psychological* differences between men and women—differences in their intellectual capacities, temperaments, and styles of relating to others. For example, it might be reasoned that men become political leaders because they are by nature more dominant than women, or that women excel at taking care of children because they are more loving and nurturing than men. The existence of such psychological differences between the sexes is often taken for granted. As we will see, however, these assumptions may be unfounded.

THE SWORDTAIL AND THE BRISTLEWORM

With the rare exception of people who undergo sex change surgery, the sex of a human being is unambiguous and unchangeable. But this is not so for all of the earth's creatures. Among species of tropical fish called swordtails, the males are identified by their extended swordlike tails. When there is a shortage of males, some of the females will grow extended tails and turn into males. There is also a species of bristleworm that grows by adding new segments. Once the worm develops 20 segments, it is a female and produces eggs. If the worm is then cut back to five or ten segments, it is converted into a male. If two female bristleworms are kept together in isolation, one will become a male and fertilize the other's eggs (Wickler, 1973).

Stereotypes About Sex Differences

When Shakespeare wrote, "Men have marble, women waxen, minds" he was expressing (most poetically, to be sure) one sort of stereotype about sex differences. He was suggesting that men are decisive and independent, whereas women are uncertain and compliant. These beliefs are *stereotypes,* because they are concepts about entire groups of people. "Blacks are musical," "Italians are

Facts About Sex Differences

We can all probably agree that stereotypes about men and women are often exaggerations or overgeneralizations. Regardless of what the stereotype might be, we know that many women defy the stereotypes by being more aggressive and more competent than most men and that many men are warmer and more sensitive than most women. We may still suspect, however, that the stereotypes reflect some real differences between the two sexes. Such suspicions cannot substitute for direct evidence, however; and the evidence for psychological sex differences is slim.

Eleanor Maccoby and Carol Jacklin (1974) recently reviewed and integrated the extensive research literature on psychological sex differences, reading through some 2,000 books and articles in the process. Most of these studies were comparisons of male and female behavior in infancy and childhood, rather than in adulthood. On the basis of their review, Maccoby and Jacklin concluded that many of the differences that are commonly believed to exist between males and females are in fact myths. For example, there is no good evidence that boys are more independent, ambitious, or achievement-oriented than girls or that girls are more nurturant, sociable, or suggestible than boys.

There are a few psychological sex differences that have been reliably established, however. On the average, males are more aggressive than females, both in childhood and in later life. Boys tend to fight more than girls, to engage in more verbal aggression (such as taunting or insulting others), and to fantasize more about aggressive themes. We will consider the possible reasons for this difference in the next section. In addition, girls tend to have greater verbal ability than boys, while boys tend to have greater spatial and mathematical ability.

Maccoby and Jacklin's review is not necessarily the last word on psychological sex differences. Much of the research that has been conducted to date is contradictory. For example, some studies show that preschool boys are more active than preschool girls, while other studies fail to find such a difference. The results depend on the particular sample of boys and girls studied and on the particular situation in which they are observed. It is likely that further research will lead to the refinement and, perhaps, the revision of some of Maccoby and Jacklin's conclusions (see Block, 1976). It remains safe to say, however, that the basic psychological differences between the two sexes are fewer and of lesser magnitude than has generally been assumed. On the whole, as Maccoby and Jacklin conclude, males and females are much more similar to one another than they are different, and they share the same fundamental needs, emotions, and abilities.

If many of the stereotypical differences between the sexes are myths, then why are they perpetuated? If, for example, men are not really more ambitious than women, why does everyone persist in thinking that they are? What's more, doesn't the fact that almost all of the world's political leaders are men provide ample proof of men's greater ambition, not to mention their greater dominance and competence?

There are two good answers to these questions. The first is that, as we saw in Chapter 3, our perception of other people is selective. When someone behaves in an expected way (a boy running and shouting, a girl sitting and playing quietly), we take note of the behavior and assume that it reflects the person's underlying temperament. The boy is "rambunctious" and the girl is "dainty," just as boys and girls are supposed to be. When, on the other hand, someone behaves in an unexpected way, the behavior may go unnoticed or may be passed off as a fluke. An active, shouting little girl may be viewed as simply imitating her brother, a quiet little boy as being tired. "As a result," Maccoby and Jacklin write, "myths live on that would otherwise die out under the impact of negative evidence."

The second reason for the perpetuation of the myths concerns the different opportunities that society provides for men and women. In fact, as children grow up, boys undoubtedly do become more politically and professionally ambitious than girls, and girls become more interested in taking care of children. When we view these "ambitious" men and "nurturant" women, we might assume that we are viewing the reflections of basic differences between men's and women's temperaments. But this conclusion would probably be mistaken. The differences that we observe probably result from social values and opportunities, rather than from basic psychological differences. Boys have traditionally had more opportunities to become politicians, doctors, and lawyers, so there has been more for them to be ambitious about. And their ambition has been encouraged by parents and teachers, while that of girls has been suppressed or redirected in more "feminine" directions. Similarly, women may become more nurturant than men because society encourages them to display such nurturance as mothers, while it discourages men from doing so (see Box 2).

EXPLAINING THE DIFFERENCES: BIOLOGY AND CULTURE

What is the basis for those sex differences that do show up in childhood? Do any of them have a biological basis? Or are they entirely the product of social and cultural conditioning, reflecting the fact that men and women are likely to become the sort of people they are expected to be? We will consider this issue with respect to one of the psychological sex differences that has been consistently found—the tendency for males to be more aggressive than females. As we will see, it does not turn out to be a simple question of biology *or* culture. In fact, both biology *and* culture are involved in determining a person's level of aggressive behavior, and both forces interact to produce the sex differences that have been observed.

Biological Influences

As noted earlier, boys tend to behave more aggressively than girls do—they fight more, insult more, and think about aggression more. And adult men assault and kill far more often than adult women do. Does this difference reflect the biological predispositions of the two sexes? It is difficult to know for sure, since the aggressive behavior itself does not directly reveal its causes. Nevertheless, there are a number of observations that converge on the conclusion that biological predispositions probably play a role.

For one thing, if sex differences in aggression are based in part on biology, we would expect to see the same sex differences in societies throughout the world. After all, even though cultures may differ, the basic biological nature of all people is the same. In fact, the male's greater aggressiveness is not peculiar to American society. Men are the hunters, the warriors, and the aggressors in virtually every society that has been studied (D'Andrade, 1966). Boys roughhouse more and exchange insults more than girls in societies throughout the world (Whiting and Edwards, *The Journal of Social Psychology* 1973, *91*, 171–188).

A second sort of evidence that points to the role of biological predisposition comes from observations of our animal relatives. Since culture, as we know it, does not play a large role in shaping the behavior of other animals, any consistent sex differences in other animals must almost certainly have a biological basis. And, in fact, males are more aggressive than females in almost all species of monkeys and apes, our closest relatives, as well as in most other mammals. Neither the cross-cultural generalities nor the biological sex differences in other animals proves beyond doubt that the sex differences in humans have a biological basis. Nevertheless, both sorts of evidence are consistent with the idea that a predisposition toward greater male aggressiveness is part of our evolutionary heritage.

If there is a biological predisposition for males to be more aggressive than females, how is it brought about? In other animals—and probably in humans as well—the predisposition toward greater male aggressiveness seems to result from the action

Box 2

Mothers and Fathers

In societies throughout the world mothers take virtually sole responsibility for the care of their children. They not only nurse the children but also feed them, diaper them, dress them, cuddle them, carry them, sing to them, and put them to sleep. Fathers spend much less time with their children, and the time they do spend does not usually entail close contact.

Fathers are more likely to work outside the home, which may provide part of the explanation for their lesser involvement in child care. But it is an inadequate explanation, because mothers who work full-time outside the home spend much more time taking care of their children than their working husbands do (Pleck, 1975b). The greater emphasis on mothering than on fathering derives, it seems, from our deeply ingrained cultural values.

Peck (1971) has described the way in which society teaches women that their supreme calling in life is to be a mother. She calls it the "baby trap":

> *Within our culture, from earliest baby-girlhood, you* learn *that you should want children. And you learn from many teachers. . . . that cuddly doll is the first bait in the baby trap. . . . There are the ads: one glorious Clairol mother, many gleaming children; mother in mink cavorting through snow with children; mother skillfully applying band-aid to her six-year-old's knee; mother and daughter doing laundry together with Ivory Snow. . . . It's the trap of the glossy situation TV series, where the doll-like mother manages home and family with freedom and expertise. It's the trap of the magazines, with their incessant articles on the "motherhood" theme.* [*pages 19–20*]

Even though women are increasingly free to decide not to be mothers, childbearing is still socially defined as the normal, if not the primary, function of women. As a result, a woman may come to feel that having children and caring for them will confirm her feminine identity and demonstrate her adequacy as a woman (Flapan, 1969).

Men, for their part, learn that it is a good thing to be a father. But they also learn that of the male hormones on the brain and, through the brain, on behavior. Most of this hormonal influence takes place before birth. At the time of conception and shortly thereafter, "male" and "female" embryos are essentially identical. The only difference is that the female has two X chromosomes, while the male has an X and a Y. Sexual differentiation begins when the XY chromosomes send a biochemical signal that leads to the production of the male hormone testosterone. The hormone causes certain embryonic tissues to develop into male sex organs. If no male hormone is produced, these tissues develop instead into female organs. Were it not for this hormonal influence, all of us would develop as females (Money and Ehrhardt, 1972). As John Money jokingly put it, "The Book of Genesis had it wrong. In

---

taking care of children, as opposed to having them, is not a "manly" thing to do. As Robert Fein (1974) notes:

> *For every newsnote published or broadcast that highlights a caring experience between a man and a child, the media still trot out five situation comedies or horror stories that show men who are tyrants, or incompetent, or plain uninterested in nurturing young children. . . . Ads for Pampers show a man carrying a puppy greeting two women holding infants. Women care for babies, is the message, men take care of dogs.* [*page 57*]

Men who actually *enjoy* taking care of small children are viewed as somewhat peculiar. Men who work as nursery school teachers labor under special handicaps, since the work they do has generally been regarded as "feminine" (Seifert, 1973).

The notion that mothers should be the primary caretakers of the children has in the past received the blessing of psychologists and psychiatrists. The guiding wisdom of British psychoanalyst John Bowlby is still widely accepted: "Fathers have their use even in infancy. Not only do they provide for their wives to enable them to devote themselves unrestrictedly to the care of the infant and the toddler, but, by providing love and companionship, they support her emotionally and help her maintain that harmonious contented mood in the aura of which the infant thrives" (Bowlby, 1951). From this perspective, the father's role is to help the mother nurture the child, not to nurture the child himself.

Despite the argument that motherhood is a "trap" for many women, there are many positive reasons for being a mother: love, affection, tenderness, the need to nurture others, the chance to guide and teach another human being. But it should be noted that every one of these reasons applies to being a father as well. In spite of myths about the "maternal instinct," there is no evidence that women are by nature more nurturant than men, or that they have the capacity to form stronger bonds with infants. Indeed, when they are given the opportunity to do so, fathers relate just as closely to their newborn infants as mothers do (Parke and O'Leary, 1975). This is something that some fathers are now beginning to discover as a result of their decision to share the burdens and joys of child rearing more equally. The concept of paternity leave has slowly been gaining acceptance, marking a growing recognition that fathers have needs and rights to participate in the care of their children (Fein, 1974).

Fatherhood has also been getting increased recognition in the less happy domain of divorce proceedings. In the past, child custody has almost always been granted to the mother, often on the assumption that she is "naturally" better suited to be a parent. Recently, however, increasing numbers of men have challenged this assumption and have successfully petitioned for custody. In the District of Columbia, for example, a judge gave one couple's children to the father, a geographer, and ordered the mother, a chemist, to pay $200 a month in child support. The judge said the father had a "warm, affectionate, caring kind of relationship" with the children, and concluded that he would better fulfill "the mothering function" (Edmiston, 1975).

the beginning God created Eve. . . . Nature's first intention is to create a female" (*Time,* 1972).

In addition to its effects on the genitals and reproductive system, the male hormone causes certain changes in brain pathways, which in turn has an impact on the individual's temperament and behavior. In one study, testosterone was administered to pregnant monkeys (Young, Goy, and Phoenix, 1964). The female offspring of these monkeys were born with masculinized genitals, attesting to the physical effect of the hormone. What's more, these female monkeys showed elevated levels of rough-and-tumble play, behaving in this respect more like male than like female monkeys. The prenatal hormones had affected not only anatomy but behavior as well.

For obvious ethical reasons, experiments like this have never been done with humans. There are rare cases, however, in which a similar sort of androgenization (addition of male hormone) takes place naturally in humans as a result of a glandular defect or the use of certain drugs. In these cases, a genetic female becomes exposed to an excess of male hormone before birth. Such an infant may have masculinized genitals, but this condition can be corrected surgically; with proper medical treatment, the infant can grow into a normal woman. There is some evidence, however, that prenatal androgenization can have an effect on such a woman's behavioral predispositions. Ehrhardt and Baker (1973) studied 17 girls who had been prenatally androgenized and compared them with their normal sisters. Even though the androgenized girls did not look any different from normal girls, they did tend to act in a more "tomboyish" way. Compared to their sisters, they liked outdoor sports more, liked dolls less, and were somewhat more likely to start fights. Although these data are not conclusive, they suggest that the male hormones may have predisposed these girls to behave more aggressively. These cases also provide indirect evidence for the hypothesis that the average difference in aggressiveness between normal males and normal females may be due in part to the effects of male hormones.

One important caution is necessary here. Most instances of girls who like sports, climb trees, start fights, and so on have absolutely nothing to do with prenatal androgenization. Such behavior is perfectly normal for girls as well as for boys and in the overwhelming majority of cases has no relation to unusual hormone levels. Prenatal androgenization is an extremely rare occurrence, and it is only in these rare cases that a causal link between male hormones and "tomboyish" behavior has been suggested.

Cultural Influences

Having said all this about biological influences on aggressive behavior, it is now time to look at the other side of the coin. We have been using the word "predisposition" quite regularly in this chapter. A *predisposition* is a readiness to behave or to develop in a particular way. On the average, men apparently have more of a readiness to be aggressive than women, for reasons that seem to be partly biological. But human behavior rarely if ever reflects such predispositions in a simple or direct way. As we noted in the Psychological Issue following Chapter 10, whether or not someone will in fact behave aggressively in a particular situation depends to a large extent on what the person has learned about the appropriate situations in which to express aggression. In our culture men are permitted or encouraged to be aggressive to a much greater degree than women are. Boys are given toy guns and toy soldiers to play with and are expected to make loud noises with them, while girls are given dolls and tea sets and are expected to play more quietly. On television children are more likely to see aggressive men, whether they are cowboys, cops, or robbers, than aggressive women. This sort of cultural shaping probably has considerably more impact on patterns of aggressive behavior than does biological predisposition.

One example of the role of culture in shaping aggressive behavior comes from a study done among the Luo people of Kenya (Ember, 1973). Among the Luo, boys and girls are typically assigned to different sorts of household tasks, such as heavy work for boys and child care for girls. However, when there is no older girl in the family to take care of the "female" tasks, a boy will be assigned to do this work. Ember found that boys who were assigned to do female work tended to be less aggressive, less dominant, and more dependent than other boys; in these respects their behavior was more like that of girls. These boys were of course no different from other boys biologically. Rather,

the fact that they were placed in a traditionally female role had a direct effect on their temperament and behavior.

In the last analysis, our own conclusion (and that of most psychologists) is that psychological differences between men and women are shaped to a much larger extent by culture than by biology. Biology does set certain of the boundaries of male and female behavior, and its role should not be overlooked. But the biological boundaries are extremely broad. The actual development of traits, skills, and aspirations depends in large measure on society's values about what men and women can and should do with their lives. In the next section, we will look more closely at how this shaping takes place.

SEX ROLES

Our expectations about what men and women should do and what they should be like are called *sex roles.* Whereas stereotypes are widely held assumptions of what men and women *are like,* sex roles are widely held notions about the way men and women *ought to be.* Each of us learns about these expectations as we grow up, and the expectations in turn are likely to have a major impact on our personality and behavior.

Learning Sex Roles

Even before a child is born, the expectant parents have notions of what they would like their sons and daughters to be like. To illustrate these expectations, Maccoby and Jacklin (1974) paraphrase a song from the Rodgers and Hammerstein musical *Carousel:*

> *A young man discovers that he is to be a father. He rhapsodizes about what kind of a son he expects to have. The boy will be tall and tough as a tree, and no one will dare to boss him around; it will be all right for his mother to teach him manners but she mustn't make a sissy out of him. He'll be good at wrestling and will be able to herd cattle, run a riverboat, drive spikes, etc. Then the prospective father realizes, with a start, that the child may be a girl. The music changes to a gentle theme. She will have ribbons in her hair; she will be sweet and petite (just like her mother), and suitors will flock around her. . . . She must be protected, and he must find enough money to raise her in a setting where she will meet the right kind of man to marry. (page 303)*

Of course, the specific expectations of what a son or a daughter should be like may differ from parent to parent. Some, for example, do not care whether their son is able to herd cattle or drive spikes, but they want to be sure that he develops the ambition and skill to become a doctor or a corporate vice-president. But the general themes of sex roles are widely shared. Boys are taught to "get ahead" and "stay cool" (Pleck and Sawyer, 1974). They are encouraged to be ambitious and assertive and are discouraged from expressing their weaknesses or their tender feelings. Girls, on the other hand, learn to play a more submissive and dependent role. They are taught to be well-

THE PERILS OF SUCCESS

Whereas men are encouraged to excel in academic work, women have traditionally been taught that they should do well, but not *too* well. Judith Bardwick, who is now a prominent psychologist, recalls her furious reaction as a college student when her name appeared in the college newspaper on a list of students who had earned an A average: "I was enraged, told the newspaper office 'they had a nerve,' and in general carried on outrageously. And the reason, which I was fully aware of, was my fear that now the girls would dislike me and the boys would be afraid of me. In other words, my academic success would shoot my social life down" (1971, page 179).

Have things changed, or do women still have misgivings about being too successful academically?

behaved and cooperative and to act as if they had no aggressive impulses at all. Girls are also expected to be tender and nurturant, whether with their dolls or with baby sisters and brothers.

These expectations are effectively communicated to sons and daughters. This communication is sometimes done directly, by suggesting the desired behavior to the child and by rewarding the child for performing it (Mischel, 1966). In addition, once the child learns his or her sex—which virtually all children do by age three—the child invariably wants to demonstrate that he or she can behave like a member in good standing of that sex (Kohlberg, 1966). This reflects every child's motivation to be a competent and consistent human being, as discussed in Chapter 9. One of the main ways that the child tries to demonstrate this competence is by imitating his or her same-sex parent.

Sex-role learning goes along with learning the "proper" occupations for men and women. This learning comes early: by the time they are in kindergarten children usually know what sorts of work are "for men" and what sorts are "for women." Sandra and Daryl Bem (1970) provide examples of how boys' and girls' occupational interests are shaped by their parents, both by direct reinforcement and by the models provided by same-sex parents.

Boys are encouraged to take more of an interest in mathematics and science. Boys, not girls, are given chemistry sets and microscopes for Christmas. Moreover, all children quickly learn that mommy is proud to be a moron when it comes to mathematics and science, whereas daddy knows all about these things. When a young boy returns from school all excited over a biology class, he is almost certain to be encouraged to think of becoming a physician. A girl with similiar enthusiasm is told that she might want to consider nurse's training later so she can have "an interesting job to fall back upon in case—God forbid—she ever needs to support herself." (page 91)

A great deal of sex-role learning also takes place through the mass media, especially television. Although there have been some changes recently, men are still portrayed as strong, competent, resourceful people who occupy such exalted roles as physician, lawyer, or police detective. These male role models are sometimes permitted to show warmth and sensitivity (like the kindly Marcus Welby, M.D.), but only when coupled with great achievement and self-reliance. It is still very rare to see a man cry on television. Women, on the other hand, are depicted as gentler, more sensitive beings who frequently reveal their weaknesses and their emotions. Even when women have achieved high-status occupations (policewoman, news reporter, lawyer), they typically remain subordinate to their bosses and dependent on their husbands or boyfriends. These television images are likely to have an impact on children's own aspirations and styles of behavior.

Children's books also teach sex roles. Lenore Weitzman and her colleagues (1972) analyzed the contents of prize-winning children's picture books published between 1967 and 1970. They found that the characters in these books for preschool children behaved according to traditional sex-role stereotypes. Boys were active, girls were passive. Boys led and rescued others; girls followed and served. Men engaged in a variety of occupations, while women were presented only as wives and mothers. In fact, the only woman in an active leadership role in these books was a fairy godmother. In the past few years the images of men and women in children's books have changed a good deal, but it is likely that they continue to reinforce traditional sex roles to a considerable degree.

With all these opportunities to learn sex roles—in the family, in school, in books, on television—it is no wonder that by the

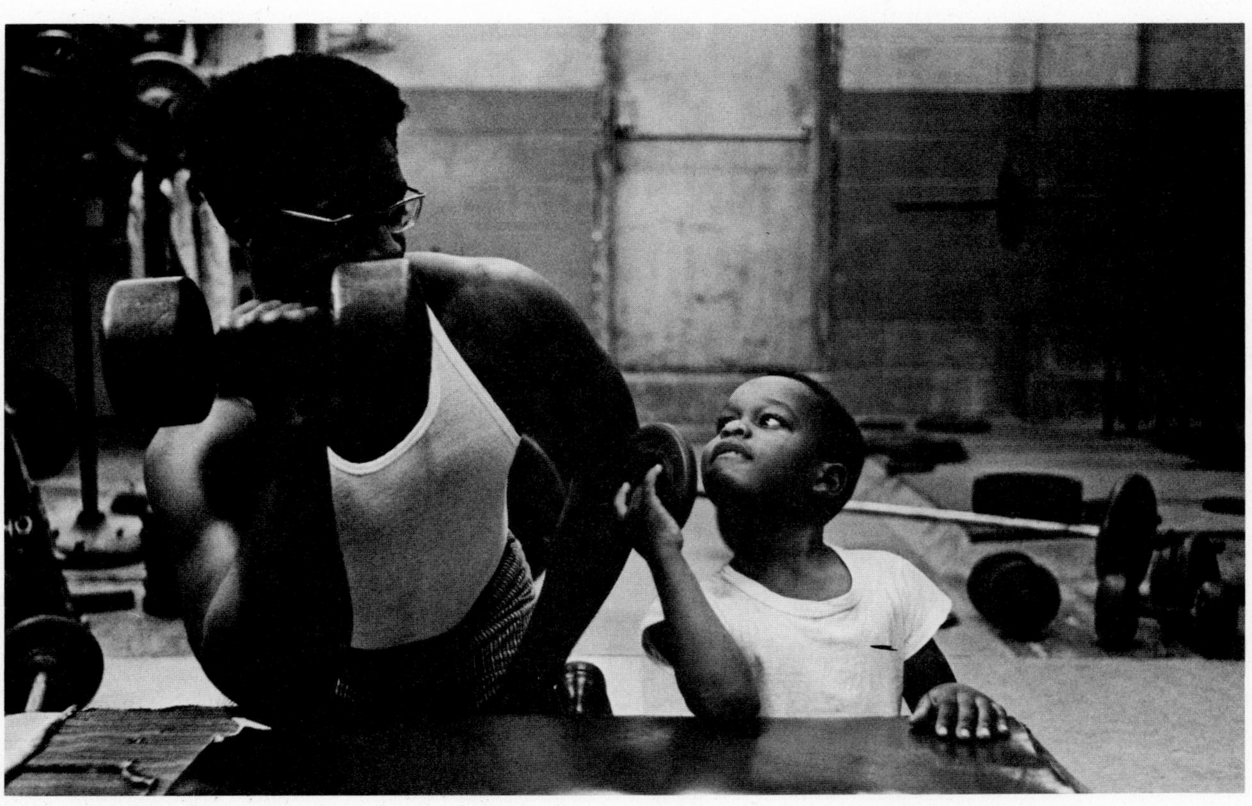

time they finish elementary school boys and girls often behave in quite different ways.

Sex Roles and Social Status

In societies throughout the world, one sex has a higher status than the other. In terms of power, prestige, and acknowledged social importance, it is the male who predominates. Men have a virtual monopoly on positions of political and religious leadership, and they enjoy the respect that goes along with these positions (Rosenblatt and Cunningham, in press). Within the family, although the mother may take care of the house and children, the father typically remains "the boss." If a couple moves from one part of the country to another, it is almost always because of the man's career, not the woman's.

In fact, the notion that men are superior to women is part of the ideology of the world's major religions. Bem and Bem (1970) cite some examples of this ideology. Consider the following passage, for example, from the New Testament:

For a man . . . is the image and glory of God; but the woman is the glory of the man. For the man is not of the woman, but the woman of the man. Neither was the man created for the woman, but the woman for the man. . . . Let your women keep silence in the churches; for it is not permitted unto them to speak, but they are commanded to be under obedience, as also saith the law. And if they will learn anything, let them ask their husbands at home; for it is a shame for women to speak in the church. (1 Cor. 11:14)

ADAM'S RIB, AND OTHER TALES

The ideology of male superiority is reflected in the traditions of many cultures (Hays, 1964). For example:

The Greek philosopher Pythagoras wrote, "There is a good principle which has created order, light, and man; and a bad principle which has created chaos, darkness, and woman."

One group of Bedouins has the tradition that women were created from the sins of the satans, another that she was formed from the tail of a monkey.

The South Slavs have the following legend: God absentmindedly laid aside Adam's rib, while performing the operation recorded in the Bible. A dog came along, picked up the rib, and ran off with it. God chased the thief but only managed to snap off its tail. The best that could be done was to make a woman out of it.

Box 3
The Politics of Touch

The assumed superiority of men to women is often revealed in patterns of nonverbal behavior when men and women interact—for example, postures, gestures, and facial expressions. To see how nonverbal behavior can reflect social status, consider the case of physical touch. Nancy Henley (1973) says that when one person touches another and the second person does not touch back, it is usually the case that the toucher is of higher social status than the person being touched. To support her argument Henley recommends the following exercise:

Consider an interaction between the following pairs of persons, and picture who would be more likely to touch the other (e.g., putting an arm around the shoulder, hand on the back, tapping the chest, holding the wrist, etc.): teacher and student; master and servant; policeman and accused; doctor and patient; minister and parishioner; adviser and advisee; foreman and worker; businessman and secretary.†

As Henley suggests, the usual picture that comes to mind is that of the higher-status person touching the lower-status one. In fact, it is often considered improper or insulting for a person of lower status to touch one of higher status.

How about interactions between men and women? Henley's assistant recorded many instances of opposite-sex touching, in public places such as parks and museums, and found that almost twice as many involved the man touching the woman as vice versa. There is also evidence that females are touched more than males even in the first year of life (Goldberg and Lewis, 1969) and that within the family mothers and daughters are touched more than fathers and sons (Jourard and Rubin, 1968).

Henley recounts a personal incident that illustrates the

†From Nancy M. Henley, "The Politics of Touch," in Phil Brown (ed.), RADICAL PSYCHOLOGY (New York: Harper & Row, 1973), p. 424, 426, 432. Reprinted by permission.

Or the following, from the morning prayer of the Orthodox Jew:

Blessed art Thou, O Lord our God, King of the Universe,
that I was not born a gentile.
Blessed art Thou, O Lord our God, King of the Universe,
that I was not born a slave.
Blessed art Thou, O Lord our God, King of the Universe,
that I was not born a woman.

Or this passage from the Koran, the sacred text of Islam:

Men are superior to women on account of the qualities in which God has given them pre-eminence.

Nowadays, many people reject such blatant statements of male supremacy and see them as reflecting the traditions of another age. Nevertheless, there remains an implicit assumption that men are more valuable than women. This assumption is part of our cultural heritage, and it is held by women as well as by men. The greater value ascribed to males is revealed in people's preferences for the sex of their children. When Markle and Nam (1971) asked college students whether they hoped their first child would be a girl or a boy, 79 percent said they would rather have a boy, and only 8 percent preferred to have a girl; the rest had no preference. Of course, people who already have a son often hope their second child will be a daughter, and vice versa. Nevertheless, the strong preference for a male first child (which has been found in many other studies as well) provides a striking demonstration of the underlying assumption that males are somehow more valuable human beings.

---

way in which touching can be an assertion of power. The incident involved Henley, the Vice Chancellor of the university where she taught, and the Chancellor of the university:

After a large meeting last spring, the Vice Chancellor came over to me and took my upper arms in his two hands, saying he wanted to tell me something; he continued holding me in this restrictive fashion as he proceeded to talk with me. After he finished, and he had finally let me go, I grabbed him back (something I try to do now whenever men lay their hands on me—really scares them), then remarked that I would have to tell him some time about my thesis [about touching and social status]. He expressed interest, so I began telling him about it, and since he is an intelligent man he saw some truth in it; at this moment the Chancellor approached, the only man on campus in higher authority, laid his arm on the arm of the Vice Chancellor, and urged him to accompany him to their next meeting. The Vice Chancellor and I were both struck by the aptness of this action, and I think I made my point.

Touching is more than a power trip. It is also a way of communicating love and affection between people. This is especially true when the touch is reciprocal. As Henley notes, however, the asymmetric touching that often goes on between men and women also serves to symbolize—and to reinforce—the sexual status hierarchy. She suggests that men and women should become more aware of their patterns of tactual interaction if they wish to change the male-dominant nature of our society. "Men should . . . guard against using touch to assert authority; they should be careful not to teach their sons to do so. . . . Women . . . should remove their hands from the grasp of men who hold them too long, and remove men's hands from their person when such a touch is unsolicited and unwarranted . . . and—why not?—start touching men, if the situation is appropriate, in order to break through the sexist pattern of tactual interaction."

Because of men's greater status, a man may sometimes be more influential than a woman, even when he does not in fact have any greater knowledge or expertise than she does. Philip Goldberg (1968) asked college students to read a number of professional articles from six different fields. The articles were assembled in two sets of booklets, so that the same article was attributed to a male author ("John T. McKay") in some booklets and to a female author ("Joan T. McKay") in others. The students were then asked to rate the articles for value, competence, and writing style. Goldberg found that the same article was given

FASCINATING WOMANHOOD

Men have traditionally been the dominant sex, and some people—including some women—would like to keep it that way. Helen Andelin (1963) has founded an organization called Fascinating Womanhood, which is designed to help women lead better lives by becoming more feminine. In Fascinating Womanhood classes, women are taught, "You can experience more happiness than you have ever known before by treating your husband like a king and becoming his queen." To help achieve this happiness, Andelin suggests, among other things, that the woman make a Scroll of Authority for her husband to display on the wall, stating that she will support his plans and decisions, even when she doesn't agree with them.

significantly lower ratings when it was supposedly written by a woman than when it was supposedly written by a man. The subjects downgraded "female-authored" articles not only in such traditionally male-dominated fields as law and city planning, but even in such female-dominated fields as dietetics and elementary education.

The ideology of male supremacy is no longer expressed as openly or as consciously as it used to be. Bem and Bem (1970) suggest that male superiority has become a "nonconscious ideology"–a set of assumptions that we do not specifically acknowledge, even to ourselves, but that nevertheless has a great impact on our behavior.

Changing Sex Roles

More and more people are coming to the conclusion that traditional sex roles are in need of change. They have come to believe that by putting people in slots labeled "male" and "female" and shaping them to fit the slots we are limiting their full development as human beings. Instead, they propose, we should treat each child as a total person, without regard for the traditional notions of what a boy or girl should be.

As the idea of breaking down traditional sex roles has gained force, however, there has also been a great deal of opposition to it. Let us consider two of the arguments against alteration of traditional sex roles, and the counterarguments to them.

One argument stresses that sex roles are based on biological differences that have evolved over the course of millions of years and, therefore, should not be tampered with. In his book *Sexual Suicide*, George Gilder warns, "When reforming the roles of men and women, we must always be careful to avoid gibberish—patterns of activity that so violate the inner constitution of the species that they cannot be integrated with our irreducible human natures" (1973). Gilder's warning may have some validity, but recent research reduces the force of his argument. As Maccoby and Jacklin (1974) have concluded, psychological differences between men and women are small, and they are based to only a slight degree on biological predispositions. Considerable change in sex roles could be accomplished by changing our values and expectations, without doing violence to our biological nature. As Maccoby and Jacklin write, "A variety of social institutions are viable within the framework set by biology. It is up to human beings to select those that foster the life styles they most value" (page 374).

A second argument against sex-role changes is the notion that if boys and girls did not develop the pattern of traits and interests that is appropriate for their sex, they would come to be confused about their sexual identity and run the risk of serious maladjustment. But recent research provides little cause for such alarm. Virtually all girls and boys learn without much trouble which sex they belong to, and they do this by the time they are

SEX CHANGE SURGERY

Occasionally there are people who appear to be biologically normal members of one sex, but who feel strongly that they really belong to the other. In recent years, it has become possible for some of these people to actually change their sex. In the large majority of cases the change is from male to female. Male transsexuals may undergo surgical transformation in which the penis and testicles are removed and an artificial vagina is created from the sensitive skin of the penis. Hormone treatment can produce breast enlargement and reduce facial and body hair. These formerly male women cannot bear children, but in other respects they can behave as normal women. Changing a female to a male is rarer and more difficult. It involves removing the breasts, removing the uterus, and constructing a nonfunctioning penis and testicles with sexually responsive tissue.

three years old (Money and Ehrhardt, 1972; Pleck, 1975a). The extensive sex-role training that follows is not necessary to develop a stable sexual identity. In addition, highly "masculine" males and highly "feminine" females are *not* better-adjusted or healthier than people who are less highly sex-typed. In fact, recent research suggests precisely the opposite: the healthiest people tend to be those who incorporate some of the traits traditionally associated with the opposite sex—that is, men who can be warm and expressive and women who can be strong and assertive (Bem, 1972, 1975).

Sandra Bem has called the ability to behave in ways traditionally associated with both sexes *psychological androgyny.* "Androgyny" comes from two Greek words: *andros,* which means "man," and *gyne,* which means "woman." Thus, an androgynous person is one who combines "masculine" and "feminine" behaviors. Bem has measured androgyny by asking students how often various adjectives are descriptive of themselves. Some of the adjectives are traditionally masculine ("ambitious," "self-reliant," "independent"); some are traditionally feminine ("affectionate," "gentle," "sensitive"). Subjects are categorized as androgynous if they indicate that they are about equally well described by masculine and feminine traits.

Bem went on to discover that androgynous students of both sexes behaved more effectively in a variety of laboratory situations than students who were highly masculine or highly feminine. Highly masculine men lacked the ability to express warmth and playfulness. They were not responsive to a kitten, to a baby, or to another student who was emotionally troubled. Highly feminine women showed concern for others, but they were not independent or assertive. They conformed more to people's opinions and found it difficult to turn down an unreasonable request. "In contrast," Bem writes, "the androgynous men and women . . . could be independent and assertive when they needed to be, and warm and responsive in appropriate situations" (1975, p. 62). Instead of having to defend against behavior that might seem inappropriate or inconsistent for their sex, they were able to behave in a more flexible and more fully human manner.

Is psychological androgyny the wave of the future? Should we encourage our children to develop both masculine and feminine traits and interests and look forward to a time when "masculine" and "feminine" become outmoded notions? Many people, especially those who are active in the women's and men's liberation movements, believe that this is the way to go. Others are not so sure. If we do away with *all* of the traditional differences between men and women, might we not lose something in the process? These are questions that all of us are now being called upon to answer.

SUMMARY

1. The biological differences between men and women have little to do with personality or social behavior. Nevertheless, social *stereotypes*—concepts about entire groups of people—characterize men as basically more aggressive, independent, dominant, active, competitive, and self-confident, and women as more tactful, gentle, sensitive, emotional, neat, and quiet.
2. Male subjects are used twice as often as female subjects in psychological studies. And when women are used, the studies appear to be based on women's stereotypical qualities. Psychologists may share society's assumption that men are more worthy of study, or they may simply be unsure of how to deal with female subjects. The overall result is that psychological research is biased toward men.
3. Studies of psychological sex differences reveal that there is no good evidence that boys are more independent, ambitious, or achievement-oriented than girls or that girls are more nurturant, sociable, or suggestible than boys. It does appear to be true, however, that on the average boys are more aggressive than girls, while girls tend to have greater verbal ability.
4. The stereotypical views of male and female roles have been perpetuated for two main reasons: (1) People see what they expect to see (appropriate sex-role behavior) and ignore in-

stances of nonstereotypical behavior. (2) Society has traditionally given greater opportunities to men to enter the more prestigious professions while channeling women into the more nurturant roles of teacher, wife, and mother.

5. Sex differences in aggression do seem to reflect a biological predisposition for males to behave more aggressively. Males are the aggressors in virtually every human society and in other primates and mammals as well. This predisposition apparently results from the action of male hormones on the brain.
6. Whether or not a genetic predisposition to a certain behavior will be expressed depends greatly on cultural influences. Cultural shaping through traditional values and by the mass media can encourage or inhibit aggressiveness, for example. Most psychologists agree that culture plays a much greater role than biology in shaping psychological differences between men and women.
7. *Sex roles* are widely held notions about the way men and women ought to be. Parents' expectations for their children are communicated both directly and indirectly and have a major influence on the children's sex-role development. Early in life boys are taught to be ambitious and assertive and not to show weakness, while girls learn to be more submissive, dependent, and cooperative.
8. In spite of myths about the maternal instinct, there is no evidence that women are by nature more nurturant than men. Yet women have traditionally been locked into the motherhood role, while the child-rearing responsibilities of the father have been minimized. These roles appear to be changing, however, and fathers are beginning to play a more important role in their children's upbringing.
9. Sex-role learning occurs through imitation of adults, through parental rewarding of certain behaviors, and through the child's motivation to learn the behaviors that will put him or her in good standing as a member of the male or female sex. A great deal of sex-role learning also occurs through the mass media, including television and children's books.
10. The notion that men are superior to women is part of the ideology of the world's major religions. Traditional ascriptions of high status to men have provided our culture with the implicit assumption that men are somehow more valuable than women. Thus, most people want their first child to be a boy, and they are more likely to trust a man's expertise than a woman's.
11. The social "superiority" of men to women is often expressed in such nonverbal behaviors as postures, gestures, and facial expressions. Many types of touching also reinforce the sexual status hierarchy.

12. Although there is a major movement toward breaking down traditional sex roles, some people are worried about such a change. They have argued that sex roles are based on biological differences and that attempting to change them would violate human nature. They also suggest that children not raised to conform to traditional sex roles would become confused about their sexual identity.
13. Sex-role training is not really required for a stable sex-role identity, since children know which sex they belong to by the time they are three. Furthermore, those people who incorporate both "male" and "female" traits—who are *psychologically androgynous*—tend to be better adjusted and healthier than those who are highly masculine or highly feminine.

psychological issue

Women's and Men's Liberation

"Liberation" from what? For some women it means liberation from men, who are viewed as having kept women down for so many centuries. More generally, however, women's liberation refers to liberation from the traditional female role, which effectively serves to limit the things a woman can do and the ways she can behave. Men's liberation is a more recent development. A growing number of men have come to the conclusion that they, too, need to liberate themselves from the pressures and limitations of their sex role.

The Women's Movement

The women's liberation movement surfaced in the 1960s as a resurgence of earlier feminist movements in America (such as the one early in this century that culminated in 1920 with the passage of the 19th Amendment, giving women the vote). The resurgence was spurred in part by the increasing numbers of women in the work force who realized that they were being discriminated against. In addition, many women who worked for civil rights came to the recognition that they them-

Young women were discovering that they had been betrayed and cheated by life.

selves were being treated in discriminatory ways. An important event in the birth of the women's movement was the publication of Betty Friedan's book *The Feminine Mystique* in 1963. In this book Friedan tried to explain why the American housewife was in a state of deep personal distress. Young women were discovering that they had been betrayed and cheated by life. They were well housed, well fed, and well dressed; their children were healthy; and they were not abused or beaten by their husbands. Still, said Friedan, American women were miserable and resentful.

Since the early 1960s, the women's movement has taken hold among students, young career women, and the daughters of the harried housewives Friedan wrote about. Gradually, many of the housewives themselves were won over by the goals of the movement. Some of the wives and mothers decided that housework is an endless, unfulfilling task and that the traditional male-female relationship in our society leaves a lot to be desired. Since there has been for centuries a remarkable persistence of male dominance in societies the world over, the women's movement has a high hurdle to surmount.

Machismo is a pattern of exaggerated masculine characteristics....

Machismo and Liberation

Machismo is a pattern of exaggerated masculine characteristics of aggressiveness, virility, fearlessness, and the absence of sentimentality. To Aramoni (1972), machismo is also a destructive attempt by the man to overcome the humiliation of having been an ineffectual little boy. Feeling inadequate, the "macho" struts through life challenging and dominating others in order to deny his own weakness.

The machismo regards the woman as a toy to be played with; she can be abandoned without guilt since she is merely an object of conquest—a trophy. She is further proof of masculinity rather than a person in her own right. If the woman is the macho's sister or mother, of course, he feels quite differently, since her protection then becomes a matter of honor. It seems absurd that the same men who demand respect for their own mothers and sisters show no respect for the sisters and mothers of others.

In our society, machismo typically takes subtle forms, such as the male fantasy of the perfect wife. As one writer put it:

> *Have to go on a business trip? She will pack your suitcase with clean clothes which she washed and ironed or sent to the cleaners (after picking them up off the floor where you dropped them). Want to talk? She will listen eagerly. Woman. She will look like a goddess at the crack of dawn and stand in the door as you leave for work, and be standing there waiting for you when you come home. Above all, she is an animal who will become a willing, anxious, sex-starved beast any day or night you wish. (Lester, 1970, page 31)*

Despite the lopsidedness of this social arrangement, women's liberation is not liber-

...major objectives include equal pay for equal work, an end to job discrimination by sex, adequate child-care programs, an equal sharing of family responsibilities, the right to abortion....

ation from men so much as it is liberation from the myths that have confined and enslaved women in their own minds. The prison is as much psychological as it is cultural. According to Phyllis Chesler (1971), the psychological prison may be in the form of female "neuroses." The "neurotic" symptoms women experience may reflect a natural reaction to the stress of being confined to a narrow sex-role stereotype.

Within the Movement

Groups within the women's movement vary in their goals and strategies, but major objectives include equal pay for equal work, an end to job discrimination by sex, adequate child-care programs, an equal sharing of family responsibilities, the right to abortion, an end to all forms of sexual exploitation, and, most fundamentally, restructuring of women's roles. The movement's activities have been many and varied. In consciousness-raising groups, for example, women assemble informally to talk with one another and to be heard perhaps for the first time. The groups provide an opportunity for friendship and a chance to relieve the woman's sense of isolation. The groups are trying to increase awareness of the problem of oppression by the male. Women learn, sometimes for the first time, that feelings and problems they thought were unique to themselves are in fact shared by many women. They also come to recognize the way in which society and its roles created many of their dissatisfactions, rather than blaming these dissatisfactions on their own inadequacies. Finally, women's groups provide vital social support to women who are trying out new roles and behaviors.

Women's centers have also been established to provide personal counseling and information on services for women in the community. In these centers women can interact with each other in such matters as education, legal aid, emergency medical assistance for rape or assault, and self-defense classes. Germaine Greer (1971) suggests that these centers may counteract the artificial dependence, noncompetitiveness, self-sacrifice, and sentimentality thought for so long to be the essence of femaleness.

"We've Come a Long Way"

In the past decade, the women's movement has grown rapidly, and it has had a tremendous impact on American society. As Edmiston (1975) writes, "A few short years ago, the Women's Movement was considered a joke, an occasion for derision, an uprising of 'angry,' 'unfeminine,' 'man-hating' crazies. . . . Today it is treated with utmost seriousness. Hardly a day goes by that there isn't a newspaper report, often on page one, of significance to women. Far from evaporating into thin air like the latest fad or having been consumed in the intensity of its own fire, the Movement has had an immense effect on every area of American life" (page 160)†.

†*Reprinted from S. Edmiston, "Out from Under! A Major Report on Women Today,"* Redbook, *May 1975, p. 160. Copyright © 1975 by The Redbook Publishing Company. Reprinted by permission.*

Women have greatly increased their role in American politics. In 1969, for example, there were only 305 women in state legislatures; in 1975 there were 599, almost twice as many. There are many more women than before in such state offices as governor, lieutenant governor, and secretary of state (Edmiston, 1975).

In the area of education, high school women can no longer be forced to attend all-female cooking classes or be excluded from shop. The Higher Education Act of 1972 made it illegal to offer classes separately on the basis of sex. Progress has also been made in the fight against sex-role stereotyping in children's books. Girls and women are now more frequently depicted in active roles and in traditionally male occupations. College textbooks, including this one, have also been influenced by the women's movement. In the first edition of this book, the major sections had such titles as "Of Mind and Man," "Thinking Man," and "Relating Man." We now recognize, however, that it is misleading to use the word "man" to refer to all human beings. This usage makes it seem as though males really are psychology's central concern. In this edition we have switched to nonsexist titles, and we have avoided using the personal pronoun "he" to refer to people in general.

Women have also made significant advances in the struggle against discrimination in employment, especially in the professions. Between 1970 and 1974, the number of women medical students more than doubled; in 1974–1975, 18 percent of medical students were women. There have been similar increases in women students attending law, architecture, and business schools. There are still large disparities between the salaries of men and women, however. The average full-time female worker earns only 58 percent of what the average full-time male worker earns. In fact, the median income of full-time working women with college degrees is lower than that of male high-school dropouts (Edmiston, 1975).

One can speak of liberating servants or slaves, but how can one liberate the masters?

Men's Liberation

Whereas the women's movement has gained increasing acceptance during the past decade, the men's liberation movement is still in its early, uncertain stages. *Men's* liberation? The very idea may seem ludicrous. Men have been the powerful, dominant sex since the dawn of civilization. One can speak of liberating servants or slaves, but how can one liberate the masters?

In fact, it is precisely this role of "master" that increasing numbers of men want to be liberated from. As part of their dominant role, men have learned to place tremendous emphasis on achievement and competition. Men are taught to put women in weak, dependent roles, while remaining tough and independent themselves. Men are taught that a "real" man never shows weakness,

never cries, never lets his emotions show. More and more men are concluding that their sex role is just as oppressive and limiting as the female sex role.

One group of men's liberationists, members of the Berkeley Men's Center, has summarized the group's goals as follows:

We, as men, want to take back our full humanity. We no longer want to strain and compete to live up to an impossible oppressive masculine image—strong, silent, cool, handsome, unemotional, successful, master of women, leader of men, wealthy, brilliant, athletic, and 'heavy'. . . . We are oppressed by conditioning which makes us only half-human. This conditioning serves to create a mutual dependence of male (abstract, aggressive, strong, unemotional) and female (nurturing, passive, weak, emotional) roles. We are oppressed by this dependence on women for support, nurturing, love, and warm feelings. We want to love, nurture, and support ourselves and other men, as well as women. (Berkeley Men's Center, 1974)†

The Birth of Men's Liberation

The men's liberation movement is in large measure an offspring of the women's liberation movement. Many of the men who spearheaded the men's movement were married to or personally involved with women who were active in the women's movement. As these women pressed for change in their own roles and status, it became clear that changes in men's roles were needed as well. Many men felt threatened by the women's new aspirations, but they were also led to think seriously about the implications. "My wife has become involved in the women's liberation movement," one man explained. "Often, feeling endangered by her growing independence, I argued with her vehemently. But there were times I knew (but could not say) that I was arguing to protect myself from identifying things I had always kept hidden from her, and often from myself" (Weiss, 1974, pages 163–164).

This man, like many others, decided to join a men's consciousness-raising group, in which the major theme was communicating with other men about their personal experiences and feelings. Such groups have been the major activity of the men's movement so far. Many men feel that they have been conditioned to fear intimate communication with other men. Showing one's emotions is seen as "unmasculine," a sign of weakness. In men's groups, the participants try to overcome this barrier. Another men's group member described some of his group's concerns:

When we were new to each other we spoke about our jobs, our families (especially about our fathers), our women (or men). Then we spoke about the roles we play. What it meant to each of us to be a son, a boy, a teen-ager, an athlete, a soldier, a scholar, a wage earner, a lover, a husband, a father. A man. *A* super man. *And what it meant* not *to be some of these things.*

And we talked "topics." Violence. How we sought it. How we feared it. How we actually dealt with it. We talked about the meaning of macho. *We talked about "scoring." Winning. Losing. Crying. Fidelity. Loneliness. Sometimes we got off on eight personal trips. Sometimes there was understanding. Sometimes, none. (Levine, 1973, page 158)*†

Showing one's emotions is seen as "unmasculine," a sign of weakness.

Men and Competition

The men's liberation movement is especially concerned with helping men to relate to one another in a less competitive way. Competition is a central theme in "learning to be a man." Boys are taught to play to win on the sports field. As the famous football coach Vince Lombardi put it, "Winning isn't the main thing—it's the only thing." This ethic can place tremendous pressure on boys, especially those who are not athletically inclined. One man vividly recalled, years later, a

†*Reprinted by permission of the East Bay Men's Center.*

†*From S. Levine, "One Man's Experience,"* Ms, *February 1973. Copyright* Ms *Magazine, Corp. 1973. Reprinted with permission.*

Box I-1

Making The Team

"When Jimmy was 10, he made his second try to get into a Detroit area Little League, and was turned down. His father, who had been a college football star, was so disappointed that he refused to talk to Jimmy all evening. Later that night, Jimmy swallowed some pills from his parents' medical cabinet . . . " (Katz, 1974).†

†*From D. Katz, "Why Children Attempt Suicide,"* Detroit Free Press, *February 3, 1974. Reprinted with permission of the Detroit Free Press.*

father-and-son softball game that took place when he was a freshman in high school:

I was the only person on both teams, the fathers and the sons, not to get a hit. I struck out every time. I don't think I have ever felt so ashamed of myself as I felt then, or felt that anyone else was so ashamed of me as my father was then. In the picnic that followed my father and I avoided each other completely. Driving home with him was excruciating. . . . I had failed the test. No matter how else we related to each other, my father and I had to go through a male sex role ordeal that would leave us feeling horrible about each other and ourselves. Why? (Pleck, 1974)

In adulthood, the arena of male competition typically shifts to the world of work, but competition remains a central theme. In business organizations, there is often a dog-eat-dog scramble to get to the top. In response to this competition, some people will say, "That's the way life is" and leave it at that. But men's liberationists have come to a different conclusion. They believe that competitive relationships between men are something that is "laid on" by the masculine mystique, and something that they can and must overcome.

The mystique of male competition reveals itself in a particularly dangerous way in the sphere of international affairs. National leaders, who are invariably men, often consider shows of strength and toughness to be of fundamental importance. In many cases these goals seem to be prompted not so much by national interest as by the leaders' need to prove their own masculinity. It has been reported, for example, that President Lyndon Johnson feared that people would think him "less of a man" than President John Kennedy if he did not carry through with Vietnam. The desire to save face and not show weakness may well have been the single most important goal for United States policy in Vietnam (Steinem, 1972). Men's liberationists hope to overcome this sort of pressure.

Summary

1. The women's liberation movement that surfaced in the U.S. during the early 1960s represents a resurgence of earlier feminist movements. The movement is not so much for liberation from men as it is for liberation from the myths that have confined women to role-specific behaviors.
2. The major goals of the women's movement include equal pay for equal work, an end to job discrimination by sex, child-care programs, equal sharing of family responsibilities, an end to sexual exploitation, and restructuring of women's roles. In addition to political action, the movement sponsors consciousness-raising groups and special centers for counseling and other services.
3. Although women have made some major advances in politics, education, and employment and have changed general attitudes toward the female role many hurdles must be leapt by for the movement. For example, large disparities between the salaries of men and women still exist.
4. One offspring of the women's movement has been the men's liberation movement. Many men find that they, too, want to be freed from the confines of their sex role—they want to be more in touch with their emotions and to be able to relate to others on a noncompetitive basis.

Personality

CHAPTER 14

Personality

Imagine you are in a restaurant, looking around at some of the people ordering, eating, and drinking. You notice that one woman sits right down, calls the waiter, and places her order without even looking at the menu. When the food arrives, she puts salt and ketchup on it without tasting it first. Then a man comes in. He spends a long time looking around trying to decide where to sit—he almost sits at one table, then tries another, and finally sits (without much assurance) at a third. Before ordering, he seems to consider every item on the menu, and after placing his order he proceeds to call back the waiter and change the order two different times. Some of the other diners exhibit still other patterns of behavior. When the waiter says that one of the items on the menu is not available, one patron gets furious while another smiles understandingly and orders something else. Some seem to savor every bit of food, letting it slowly roll around in their mouths; others seem to gulp the food down without tasting it. Some are sociable and gregarious, while others sit by themselves in silence.

In a restaurant, as in many other situations, each of us seems to have a distinctive temperament and style of behaving. We each have our own concerns, priorities, likes and dislikes, and ways of dealing with conflict and frustration. These differences between people are a central focus of the study of personality.

Personality, as defined by Walter Mischel (1976), refers to "the distinctive patterns of behavior (including thoughts and emotions) that characterize the individual's adaptation to the situations of his or her life" (page 2). In studying personality, we want to know how any given person is unique. But we are also interested in the ways in which people resemble one another and in understanding how both the differences and the similarities come about.

Many psychologists have attempted to answer these questions about personality, and they have come up with a variety of theories and approaches. Each of the theories that we will discuss in this chapter reflects a particular conception of personality. In addition, different theorists use different methods for studying personality. Some, such as Freud and his followers, make primary use of detailed individual case studies. They may interview the person intensively, give the person a series of personality tests, and try to understand the person's unique pattern of traits as fully as possible. This focus on the detailed study of individuals is called the *idiographic* approach to personality. A leading exponent of the idiographic approach was Gordon Allport (1962), who also suggested that psychologists study the individual personality through personal documents such as diaries, calendar books, personal letters.

Other personality researchers take a different approach. Instead of probing deeply into the personality of a single individual, they conduct experiments or administer tests to large numbers of people. By analyzing the relations between test scores and behaviors within such large samples of people, they hope to learn more about the similarities and differences between people. Such attempts to discover general patterns of personality reflect a *nomothetic* approach to personality. In practice, however, elements of the idiographic and nomothetic approaches can be combined in order to achieve an understanding of both individual uniqueness and more general patterns of similarities and differences between people.

THE PATH TO CIVILIZATION

Freud suggested that the development of civilization became possible when the energy of human beings was freed from basic survival needs. Converting primitive impulses to civilized ends is not always completely satisfying, however, and the tensions of being civilized periodically produce explosive behavior such as war. Imperfect as it may be, the ability to "sublimate" makes possible the ideas, values, attitudes, and activity that characterize the civilized adult human being (Freud, 1930).

FREUD'S PSYCHOANALYTIC THEORY

Sigmund Freud devised the best-known and most widely studied of all the personality theories and was the first theorist to stress the developmental aspects of personality. He also was the first to note the decisive role of infancy and childhood in establishing an individual's basic character structure. Freud thought the personality was almost fully formed by the time the child entered

Box 1

A Biography of Freud

Born in Moravia (now Czechoslovakia) in 1856, Sigmund Freud was the son of middle-class Jewish parents. When he was there, Freud's family emigrated to Vienna, Austria, where he spent most of his life. Although the Freuds were quite poor during Sigmund's childhood, he managed to obtain financial assistance from a Jewish philanthropic society in order to enter the medical facility at the University of Vienna in 1873.

Although Freud delayed his medical degree for two years to pursue his research, he eventually entered Vienna General Hospital as a resident assistant physician, where his interests quickly focused on

Sigmund Freud and fiancé

psychiatry. After obtaining his medical degree, Freud traveled to Paris to study under the famous neurologist Marc Charcot. At the time, Charcot was studying an emotional disorder known as hysteria, in which patients suffered physical symptoms without an organic basis. There is little doubt that Charcot's interests greatly influenced Freud's later pursuits. When he returned to Vienna, Freud opened a practice as a neurologist and was soon a well-respected physician. But Freud's interests centered on the psychological rather than physical aspects of the brain.

In the course of his practice, Freud saw many hysterical patients. At first he treated them with hypnosis but soon began to employ the cathartic method developed by Josef Breuer. In this method, patients lose their symptoms by delving into painful memories while under hypnosis. Freud noted that many of his patients revealed unacceptable wishes in their forgotten memories, and this discovery led the

Jakob Freud's family was photographed in 1876. Twenty-year old Sigmund is standing behind his mother, and the baby of the family, Alexander, sits on the floor.

school and that personality development after this time consisted of elaborating and refining the basic structure.

Freud was concerned about the motivational forces that exist in all human beings. He believed that all human behavior is dominated by instinctual biological urges and that these urges

---

physician to his theory of repression.

Between the years 1895 and 1900, Freud published several of his most important and famous works, describing his theories of the unconscious and defense mechanisms and touching on the idea of infantile sexuality and hostility towards one's parents. *The Interpretation of Dreams,* which was published during this period, presented many of these revolutionary ideas, yet the book was largely ignored by scientists in Europe, as was most of Freud's work until 1905. In that year, Freud published a much more explicit account of his theories on infantile sexuality and their relation to adult neurosis. *Three Essays on the Theory of Sexuality* shocked the intellectuals of nineteenth-century Vienna, and Freud quickly became the most unpopular scientist of the day.

Despite the severe criticism he received, Freud continued to publish his theories and evidence in their support. Much of his later work was devoted to expansion and modification of his original formulations and applications of his psychodynamic views to other fields. Most of his books were severely criticized by experts in the fields, primarily because Freud's speculations attacked many heretofore unquestioned beliefs. Toward the end of his life, however, Freud began to receive the recognition he deserved for his courageous exploration of the human mind. He was initiated into several scientific societies, received the Goethe Award for his writing, and was made a corresponding member of the prestigious Royal Society on his eightieth birthday.

During this period of recognition, the Nazi persecutions had caused many of Freud's supporters to flee Germany, and Freud's books were confiscated and burned in Berlin. Freud's publishing company, which he had founded in 1919, suffered tremendously from the loss of sales in Germany, but Freud insisted upon remaining in Vienna and continuing the firm's operations. When the Nazis invaded Austria in 1938, Freud was persuaded to emigrate to England. One year later, a recurring cancer of the mouth from which Freud had suffered since 1923 terminated his life.

furnish the basic psychic energy that motivates every aspect of a person's behavior. These biological urges must be controlled and regulated, he thought, if humans are to become civilized; after all, people can't run around raping or killing whomever they please. Thus, to Freud people begin as biological organisms but become fully human by taming their biology. Unfortunately, in Freud's view this necessity to subdue biological impulses inevitably leads to emotional conflicts. Freud concluded that most emotional problems and psychological disorders stem from a conflict between the individual's unconscious needs, desires, and wishes and the demands of society.

Freud grew up in the sexually repressed Victorian climate of nineteenth-century Austria (see Box 1). Perhaps that's why his initial theories of human psychology emphasized people's sexual urges. Later on, after he had lived through the horrors of World War I, Freud was so struck by the spectacle of millions of young men marching to their deaths that he modified his theory to include aggressive urges as well. In Freud's later work, the "death" instincts (including aggression) held a place of prominence equal to that of the "life" instincts (including sex).

In our discussion of Freud, one thing must be kept in mind. Although Freud's theory has been highly influential, it is still just that—a *theory.* Its validity remains a topic of great controversy. As a theory of personality, Freud's psychoanalytic approach focuses on the structure of personality and its origins in early life.

The Structure of Personality

For Freud, each person's personality consists of three elements that he labeled the *id,* the *ego,* and the *superego*—three distinct but interrelated systems of psychic function. The *id,* according to Freud, is the reservoir of basic biological urges that motivate the individual. The id is hunger, thirst, sexual impulses, and other needs that assure survival or bring pleasure or relief from pain and discomfort. The id remains an unchanging, powerful, active force throughout life, but its insistent demands are tempered and controlled by the ego. The actions of the id usually remain unconscious and out of our awareness.

The *ego* directs and controls the id by requiring it to seek gratification within socially acceptable bounds. If the id wants to destroy another human being who is frustrating the id's quest for gratification, the ego decides whether or not this can be done easily and safely. Unlike the id, most of the ego's actions are conscious. The ego thus acts like an executive who sees to it that the gratification of impulses will not be painful, dangerous, or destructive to the organism.

The *superego* is that force within the self that acquires the values and ideals of parents and society. The superego is the moral part of the self. It looks to the ideal rather than the real, to what ought to be rather than what is. Further, the superego limits the sexual or aggressive impulses of the id. It pressures the ego to respond to socially approved moral goals rather than impulse-

CHECKS AND BALANCES

"In personality, as in politics, the safest, if not the most efficient, system is one with multiple components, or 'institutions,' that exist in some kind of tense equilibrium (id, ego, superego; Congress, President, Supreme Court). And perhaps to keep the system truly healthy there is need for additional external institutions (family, friends, therapist, society; a free press, other governments) keeping an objective eye out for its integrity and giving constructive feedback when the system seems to be getting out of balance." (Dember, 1974, page 168)†

†From W. N. Dember, "Motivation and the Cognitive Revolution," American Psychologist, 1974, 29, p. 161–168. Copyright 1974 by the American Psychological Association. Reprinted by permission.

gratifying ones. In this three-part structure, the ego is trapped between the impulses of the id and the controls of the superego. In other words, the id powers the human vehicle, the ego steers it on a safe course, and the superego insists that the ego obey the traffic laws even when there is no expectation that the violation will be caught or punished. As we will see, the conflict of id, ego, and superego causes anxiety, which, in turn, creates defense mechanisms.

Psychosexual Development

To the staid Victorians of his time, Freud's theory seemed outrageous, because it emphasized the importance of sexual drives not only in adults but also in infants and children. Freud's concept of the sexual urge was very broad, however. In fact, his theory deals with not one but three separate pleasure-giving areas of the body. These areas, known as the *erogenous zones,* include the oral zone (mouth, lips, tongue), the anal zone, and the genital zone (penis or vagina). As the child goes through successive stages of development, different zones becomes prominent. And the way in which a child goes through these *psychosexual* stages is a major determinant of personality in later life. Freud designated five developmental stages: the oral, anal, phallic, latency, and genital stages.

The Oral Stage. The oral stage, beginning at birth and lasting to about age 2, is the first stage in the child's psychosexual development. According to Freud, during the oral stage the child's sexual energies are focused on the mouth area, and most of the child's activities involve feeding, sucking, chewing, and biting. Psychologically, the child at the oral stage has to deal with issues of oral gratification, personal dependence, and trust. Freud believed that an infant who passes successfully through the oral stage will develop into an adult who is able to enjoy oral gratification but is not obsessed with it. Such a person will be basically trusting of other people but not overly dependent on them. But Freud also believed that infants can become fixated in the oral stage if they find being fed too pleasurable (excessive gratification) or if nursing is painful or frustrating. Overgratification at the sucking stage can lead to an unreasonably self-assured adult, whereas a painful sucking period can produce excessive dependency in the adult. Frustration during the oral stage might also lead to aggressive oral habits, such as sarcasm or verbal hostility in later life.

The Anal Stage. During the anal stage, at about ages 2 and 3, the child's sexual energies focus around the anus and the act of defecation. This is the period of toilet training. When children are toilet trained, they for the first time acquire the power to successfully resist their parents' demands. They can decide for themselves whether or not to defecate and whether or not to satisfy their parents' desires. The central psychological issue of the anal stage is one of giving and holding back, cleanliness and messiness, and dominance and subservience. An infant who passes successfully through the anal stage should, according to Freud, develop into an adult who is flexible rather than obstinate or submissive, generous rather than stingy or a spendthrift, and tidy rather than fastidious or messy.

If too much anxiety is present at toilet training, the child may grow up to be compulsively clean and orderly and become intolerant of those who fail to be the same. To ensure that everything is tidy in his life, a man may dictate to others and enforce severe and arbitrary rules much like those his parents imposed upon him. If the parents lose in the toilet-training contest and the child learns he can always get his way, he may develop a lifelong pattern of self-assertion, negativism, personal untidiness, and dominance over others.

The Phallic Stage. In the phallic stage of development (about ages 4 to 5), the sex organs become the focus of attention. The key event in this stage, Freud believed, is the child's feeling of sexual attraction toward the opposite-sex parent, together with envy of the same-sex parent. Freud labeled this situation, and the psychological conflicts it produces, the *Oedipus complex,* alluding to the Greek myth about Oedipus, who killed his father and married his mother, unaware of their true identity. Of course, falling in love with one's mother and killing one's father represents an extreme pathological resolution to the Oedipus conflict. But Freud believed that all children have to resolve such a conflict in one way or another and that the way one goes about doing so has a large impact on subsequent personality development.

In the case of boys, if the Oedipus conflict is adequately managed, the boy learns to control his envy and hostility toward his father. He identifies with his father's power and masculinity

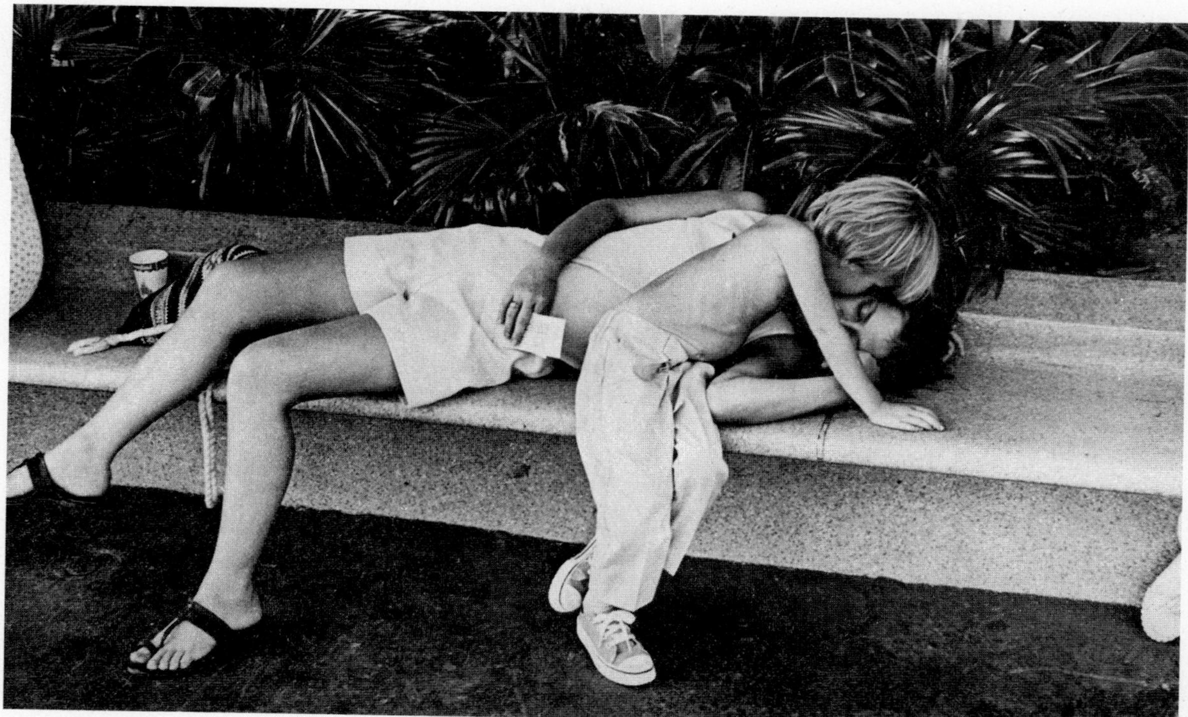

and converts them into motivation for accomplishment in life. The boy will develop into an adult who is assertive and active. Failure to resolve the Oedipus conflict means growing up with an intense fear that a powerful and jealous father might punish one for one's feelings toward one's mother. The boy who fails to resolve the conflict should, according to Freud, develop into an adult who is timid, passive, and effeminate.

What about girls? Well, to be honest, Freud hardly thought about the problem of female psychosexual development until after he had worked out the Oedipus cycle for boys. As a result, his theory of the Oedipus complex, expanded to include girls, seems rather strained. According to Freud, girls start, as boys do, loving their mother and resenting their father—because the father is a rival for the mother's attention. During the phallic stage, however, girls realize that they are lacking the more desirable sexual organ: the penis. As a result of "penis envy," each girl then becomes attracted to her father as a love object. But eventually the girl must renounce her attraction to her father and, if the Oedipus conflict is successfully resolved, decide to identify with her mother and find another man to take her father's place as a sex object.

Thus, Freud's notion of the Oedipus complex and its resolution, even though it may sound a bit far-fetched, provides another explanation for the learning of sex roles, which we considered in Chapter 13. And, as any adherent of Freud's theory will be quick to point out, the reason that this sequence of early life events seems far-fetched is that, because the conflict is so full of threat and anxiety, we adults have had to banish it from consciousness.

The Latency Period. According to Freud, at the end of the phallic stage (at about age 5), the child enters a period of psychosexual latency. During this period, the child's attention is focused away from particular erogenous zones, previous sexual feelings are forgotten, and sexual urges lie dormant.

The Genital Stage. At puberty, when sexual interest is reawakened, the child enters the genital stage. During this stage, sexual energies are again focused on the genital organs—the penis and the vagina. This is the stage of adult heterosexual relationships. Freud didn't have very much to say about the genital stage; it's as if he thought that if you made it through the oral, anal, and phallic periods, you would be O.K. Freud's analysis of "adult" problems almost invariably involves presumed fixations at the earlier oral, anal, and phallic stages. Other psychologists have felt that more attention needs to be given to later stages of personality development. As we saw in Chapter 12, for example, Erik Erikson began his theory of psychosocial development with stages patterned after Freud's oral, anal, and phallic stages but then went on to identify important stages of personality development through the entire life cycle.

Anxiety and Defense Mechanisms

Anxiety is an exceptionally uncomfortable experience that is hard to cope with because it has no easily identifiable source. Freud believed that anxiety stems from people's unconscious fear that their instincts will cause them to do something they will be punished for. When the pressure of anxiety is excessive and cannot be relieved by practical, problem-solving methods, the ego must use impractical methods called *defense mechanisms.* Defense mechanisms have two primary characteristics. First, they deny, falsify, or distort reality. Second, they operate unconsciously, so that the person is never aware of them. Complex defensive maneuverings begin in the early years of childhood as we deal with the many threats, conflicts, and frustrations that are a part of growing up. The outcome of the way we handle hundreds and thousands of little contests with anxiety and frustration sets the pattern of adult behavior we call personality. It will help us to understand Freud's developmental theory if we look briefly at how some of the various defense mechanisms work.

Repression. Repression, the most basic and probably the most widely used defense mechanism, is the exclusion of unacceptable unconscious impulses from consciousness. For instance, you might repress aggressive impulses toward your spouse, or sexual urges toward somebody else's spouse, because of the anxiety such urges would produce if allowed into consciousness.

Projection. Projection is the unconscious attribution of one's own thoughts and feelings to other people. These thoughts, feelings, and impulses are projected onto someone else because they would create anxiety if attributed to oneself. Thus, the censor who thinks modern movies are filthy may be concealing his or her own strong interest in such sexual activity—an interest that would produce anxiety if allowed into consciousness.

Reaction Formation. Reaction formation is the development of behavior patterns that are the opposite of those that might create anxiety. For instance, a person with strong unconscious aggressive urges might become a pacifist; an individual with a taste for whiskey might join a temperance movement. Through reaction formation, the individual is able to avoid the anxiety that would be produced if unacceptable impulses like these were actually brought into consciousness.

Displacement. Sometimes the object that will gratify an instinctual urge is not accessible. In such a situation, displacement may occur. Displacement involves redirecting urges toward a substitute object. If a young man unconsciously desires to sleep with his mother, he will look for a woman who resembles his mother instead. If an executive is angry at her superior, she may displace her aggressive urge by yelling at her secretary. Substitute objects are rarely as satisfying as the original objects, however, and the search for more perfect objects on which to displace our urges continues as a motivating force in our behavior.

Rationalization. Rationalization, one of the most common defense mechanisms, can be described as the attempt to substitute "good" reasons for our "real" reasons. We use rationalization to conceal from ourselves the fact that we have acted from motives that conflict with our standards. The man who mistreats his wife may rationalize his behavior by claiming that she needs a strong, dominant male as a mate. Or, if we fail at something we set out to do, we may insist that we didn't really try or that we didn't really want to do it in the first place. Rationalization is very similar to the phenomenon of dissonance reduction that we discussed in Chapter 9—the way in which people mentally manipulate their beliefs and attitudes to make them consistent with their behavior.

Intellectualization. Through intellectualization, anxiety is dismissed by analyzing emotional issues intellectually and converting them to theory rather than action. By intellectualizing, problems become detached from the self and removed from unpleasant emotional consequences. The discussions in college dorms and coffee shops over questions of love, sex, and morality may be examples of such intellectualization.

Defense mechanisms are designed to help us escape the pain of anxiety. Most of us would not survive very well without occasionally resorting to such defense. The trouble is that after sufficient practice they may become habitual, characteristic patterns of reacting to conflict; indeed, they may become permanent character traits. As a result, the use of defense mechanisms to deal with anxiety and conflict can sometimes be costly. We will return to the psychic costs of defense mechanisms in Chapter 16, when we discuss the neuroses.

THE PSYCHOANALYTIC DISSENTERS

Freud's theories of infantile sexuality were rejected by most of the intellectuals of his time. But he attracted an inner circle of followers interested in establishing the discipline of psychoanalysis. In 1902, Alfred Adler and a few Viennese physicians gathered on Wednesday nights at Freud's home, beginning the first Psychoanalytic Society. In 1907, Carl Jung, a psychiatrist in Zurich, Switzerland, joined the exclusive group. Before long, a series of theoretical conflicts occurred, and Adler and Jung each left the group to go his own theoretical way.

Carl Jung

Jung applied the psychological insights gained from Freud to the material that fascinated him when he was young—myths, fables, and ancient legends. These interests then flavored his interpretation of human nature. Once considered Freud's "Crown Prince," Jung became a dissident renegade whose views struck a more responsive chord "among speculative philosophers, poets, and

Carl Jung

religionists than in medical psychiatry" (Alexander and Selesnick, 1966, page 244).

Personality, for Jung, is fashioned according to the nature of the balance achieved between conscious and unconscious forces. Jung's conception of the unconscious, however, differed from that of Freud. Jung distinguished two levels of the unconscious: (1) the *personal unconscious,* which encompasses the most common conception of the unconscious (repressed or forgotten material), and (2) the *collective unconscious,* a part of the human psyche that is filled with "primordial images," or "archetypes." The collective unconscious is common to all humans, having developed in the course of our evolution as a species. It includes representations of such universal human experiences such as mothers, the earth, and even the caves in which we once lived. Jung believed that these unconscious forces and images are a central part of the healthy personality.

Alfred Adler

Adler developed an *ego-psychology* that focused on real or imagined feelings of inferiority. In fact, he was the inventor of the term "inferiority complex." Adler had overcome a series of handicaps early in his own life. Because of rickets, he did not walk until age four; he then developed pneumonia, which was followed by a series of accidents. These experiences suggested to him that people rely heavily on their brains as a means of compensating for felt inferiority.

In the Adlerian system of psychology, security is accomplished by denying one's feelings of inferiority through the attainment of some master goal in life. Since much of human achievement is accomplished through our social interactions, Adler gives the social community a key position in healthy psychic life. For Adler, humans are social beings rather than sexual creatures—driven mercilessly throughout life to achieve a goal that will allow them to escape a feeling of inferiority.

The Neo-Freudians

Harry Stack Sullivan, Karen Horney, Erich Fromm, and Erik Erikson each suggested basic revisions in Freudian theory. These *neo-Freudians* reexamined the facts of human development from birth to maturity and interpreted them differently. These *neo-Freudians* deemphasized Freud's reliance on notions of instinctual energy and libido, and placed greater emphasis on the role of society and culture in shaping human personality.

TYPE THEORIES

Long before Freud and his followers came along—in fact, long before there were *any* professional psychologists—physicians, philosophers, and ordinary people were sorting the people they encountered into *types.* Some people were considered pessimists or cynics, others were worry-warts or ne'er-do-wells. Each type of person presumably possessed one central or cardinal characteristic that influenced a broad range of his or her behaviors. Classifying a person as a particular type made that person's behavior easier to predict and explain.

The Greek physician Hippocrates put forth one type theory. His theory of personality was that there were four basic types of temperament: choleric (irritable), melancholic (depressed), sanguine (optimistic), and phlegmatic (listless). Everyone supposedly fit into one of these four types. Hippocrates believed that each type was related to a predominance of one of the four bodily "humors," or fluids. The choleric type had too much yellow bile, the melancholic type too much black bile, the sanguine type too much blood, and the phlegmatic type too much phlegm. Imagine the difficulties this theory would produce for patients in therapy. If an overly optimistic person ever stopped in to see Hippocrates, the famous physician would probably treat the patient by bleeding him a bit. A therapy like that would probably make the patient less optimistic, though perhaps not for the reasons Hippocrates would give!

Hippocrates' theory may seem primitive to us, but the notion that people's personality and their physical make-up are related persists even today. We tend to think that fat people are jolly and that thin people are nervous and shy. Men who are powerful and muscular seem bold, extraverted, and confident. Many early personality theorists were rooted in observations of a relationship between physical and psychological types.

Physique and Personality

Early in this century Ernest Kretschmer suggested that tendencies toward certain forms of serious emotional disorder were associated with particular body types. Schizophrenics, according to Kretschmer, tended to be somewhat smaller and thinner than the average person. Manic-depressive disorders were associated with round, stocky, heavy physiques, and other varieties of schizophrenia were associated with persons having strong, muscular builds.

W. H. Sheldon (1940, 1954) classified human body types along three basic dimensions: ectomorph, mesomorph, and endomorph. In his system of rating body build, the *ectomorph* is thin, long-boned, poorly muscled, and delicate; the *mesomorph* is well muscled and athletically built; and the *endomorph* is heavy and fat. A person's *somatotype* (or body type) reflects the contribution of each of these three dimensions to an overall description of physical structure. In assigning somatotype ratings Sheldon took into account many types of measurements that don't vary with diet or exercise (such as the length and width of major bones).

After developing his method for somatotyping, Sheldon spent years interviewing and observing a group of young male subjects. In the end, he reported an association between somatotype and personality. According to Sheldon, ectomorphs are

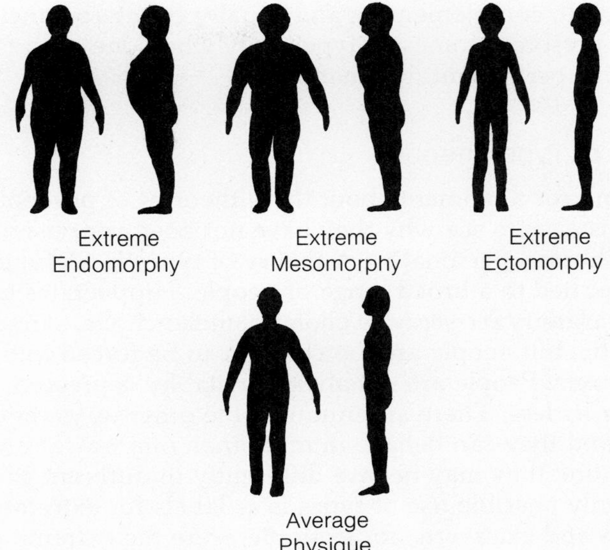

FIG. 14 · 1 The human body types identified by W. H. Sheldon. Sheldon believed that each body type was associated with a particular pattern of personality.

sensitive, solitary and cerebral; mesomorphs are assertive, incautious, and independent; and endomorphs are relaxed, self-indulgent, and approval-seeking. His findings paralleled quite closely the popular stereotypes about people who are tall and thin, broad and muscular, or short and fat. Many psychologists today are quite skeptical of Sheldon's specific conclusions. Nevertheless, the notion that there tend to be links between physique and personality remains a plausible one. But just what the basis for such links might be is not too clear. One possibility is that the stereotypes that we have about particular body types often have a self-fulfilling effect. If we act as if we expect fat people to be jolly or thin people to be nervous, they may respond by conforming to our expectations.

Jung's Types

Unlike Hippocrates or Sheldon, Jung (1921) developed a theory of psychological types that avoids making connections between personality and physique. Jung developed the concepts of "introvert" and "extravert" as types. He argued that every individual possesses innate mechanisms for both introversion and extraversion. In some circumstances, the mechanism for extraversion dominates and the individual behaves as an extravert; in other circumstances, the mechanism for introversion dominates and the individual behaves as an introvert. However, for some reason the dominance of one mechanism sometimes becomes chronic in some people. These people become types, either introverts or extraverts. Avoiding the normal variations in behavior that most people exhibit, these types behave in pretty much the same way most of the time.

You can see that Jung's approach to psychological types is quite flexible compared, for example, to that of Hippocrates. According to Jung, people don't necessarily fit into one type or another. The mechanisms of introversion and extraversion are within us all, complementing and usually counterbalancing each other. A person becomes a "type" only when one of the mechanisms wins permanent dominance.

Critique of Type Theories

If we think for a moment about these theories of psychological types, it is easy to see why they have not been very useful in the study of human personality. A theory of types is useful only if it can be applied to a broad range of people. Hippocrates thought he could classify *everybody* as choleric, melancholic, sanguine, or phlegmatic, but people are too complex to be forced into such simple boxes. People are not always irritable, depressed, optimistic, or listless. There are innumerable other ways they can behave, and they can behave in more than one way at once. Furthermore, they may behave differently in different situations. So, the only possible use of types is as labels for extremes. Jung's introverts and extraverts, for example, were the extreme exceptions rather than the rule. But a theory of types that applies only to extremes doesn't help us very much in predicting or explaining the endless variety in human personality, both within individuals and between them.

TRAIT THEORIES

In contrast to type theories, in which people are assigned to one category *or* another, trait theories of personality view people on many dimensions simultaneously. Each trait is a quality or characteristic that some people have "more of" than others. Some of the numerous traits that psychologists have postulated are dependency, emotionality, aggressiveness, activeness, and anxiety. Trait theorists are mainly concerned with identifying the most important traits on which people can be compared and with developing reliable ways to measure them. These measurement techniques include self-ratings (in which you might be asked directly how "aggressive" or how "dependent" you think you are), peer ratings (in which you might be asked to answer the same questions regarding your roommate), and a variety of other psychological tests (see Box 2). As we will see, Hartshorne and May (1928), for example, observed children in a variety of situations in order to obtain measures of the hypothesized trait of "strength of conscience."

Gordon Allport (1961) was a leading trait theorist. Allport distinguished between what he called "common" and "individual" traits in the structure of personality. Common traits appear in different amounts in all people. Individual traits (or "personality dispositions") are characteristics that appear in only a small number of individuals. Dependency, for example, might be a common trait on which people can be compared. Various tests and ratings might reveal that some people are extremely dependent, some are moderately dependent, and others are not dependent at all. In contrast, the characteristic of being able to receive satisfaction from continually refining one's written prose may be an individual trait—one that is highly important to some people but on which large numbers of people cannot be meaningfully compared.

In addition to common and individual traits, Allport also emphasized that each individual has his or her unique combination of traits. Thus, one person might be both highly dependent and highly aggressive, a second might be highly dependent and only moderately aggressive, and a third might be highly dependent and not aggressive at all. Allport believed it is important, therefore, to conduct intensive studies of individuals (the idiographic method) in order to understand the ways in which particular combinations of traits fit together.

While concentrating on description and measurement, trait theorists have paid relatively little attention to the origins of a person's traits, for example, in early life experiences. Some trait theorists have been interested, however, in assessing the stability of people's traits through the life cycle. In one well-known longitudinal study (Thomas, Chess, and Birch, 1970), researchers found some degree of consistency between babies' temperamental styles ("easy," "slow to warm up," and "difficult") and their temperaments in childhood and adolescence. These researchers

believe that the differences in the babies' dispositions are biological and that they may be hereditary. Other researchers have explored the hereditary aspects of personality by administering personality tests to pairs of related children and adults—for example, to pairs of identical and fraternal twins. Such studies have demonstrated that at least some personality traits, such as anxiety and dependency, as measured by tests such as the MMPI (see Box 2), have at least some genetic basis (Dworkin, Burke, Maher, and Gottesman, 1976).

Box 2

Personality Assessment
Several types of tests have been developed to try to determine people's personality traits and characteristics. Among the most widely used tests are personality inventories and various types of interpretive tests.

Personality inventories attempt to measure a great variety of characteristics, including interests, emotional adjustment, social relations, attitudes, and values. An inventory is a collection of statements or questions to be answered in categories such as agree-disagree, like-dislike, and so on. Answers to several items taken together make up a scale by which a particular trait can be measured.

The Minnesota Multiphasic Personality Inventory (MMPI), for example, was originally constructed from 550 items based on the cues usually used by clinical interviewers to describe personality. The test originators hoped that the MMPI would be a reliable diagnostic device saving a great deal of professional time in assessing psychological disorders. Although it did serve this purpose, before long its primary use became that of a general personality inventory.

A number of devices have been designed in an attempt to get individuals to reveal the thoughts, feelings, attitudes, and impulses of which they

FIG 14·2 When studying personality, psychologists often use drawings as projective tests—to determine, for example, how children view men and women. These three drawings were all done by ten-year-olds. A and B were drawn by identical twin boys, and C was drawn by a girl.

THE ISSUE OF CROSS-SITUATIONAL CONSISTENCY

Whereas psychoanalytic, type, and trait theories of personality have received a great deal of attention from psychologists, recent research has called into question a basic assumption that underlies all these theories. These approaches all assume that people have the same personalities at all times and in all situations. In the psychoanalytic point of view, for example, an "oral dependent" man would be expected to act in oral and dependent ways

FIG. 14 · 3 A drawing similar to those used in the Thematic Apperception Test. The person being tested is asked to indicate what he or she thinks is happening in the picture.

are either unaware or are unwilling to disclose. Such tests are called *projective tests,* be-

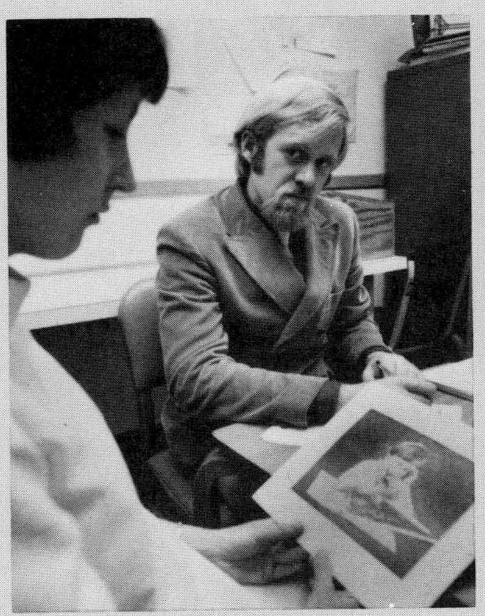

cause the individual is thought to "project" his inner concerns into his interpretations of various materials. One such projective test is the Thematic Apperception Test (TAT) designed by Henry Murray in 1938. Murray designed a series of drawings portraying people in various situations. The person being tested is asked to indicate what he or she thinks is happening in the picture. The pictures were designed to elicit themes, conflicts, or moods common to most of us.

Another projective test is the Rorschach (1942), which consists of ten inkblots printed on cards. Five are black on a white background, two have red areas in addition to the black, and three are multicolored. These inkblots were originally produced by placing ink on a folded sheet of paper and pressing the halves of the sheet together. The ten blots that make up the set were selected from a much larger number. Since they were not designed to resemble actual objects, they can be interpreted to be whatever the person wants them to be.

Analysis of people's responses seeks answers to such questions as: How did the person behave toward the examiner and the testing material? Where in the blot did the person see the objects? How much of the blot was used in the response? What features of the blot produced the response? What was the content of the responses? In the hands of a skilled clinical psychologist, what a person "sees in the blots" can provide valuable information about his or her personality and thought processes.

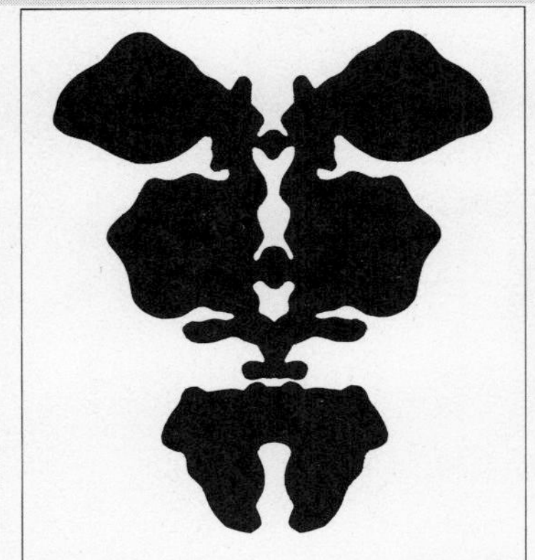

FIG. 14 · 4 An inkblot similar to those used in the Rorschach test. What do *you* see in the blot?

whether with his wife, his bridge partners, or his co-workers. A type theorist would expect an extravert to be sociable, talkative, and active whether at a party, in a classroom, or in the cafeteria. And a trait theorist would expect a highly aggressive person to behave aggressively in a wide range of situations. These expectations are known as the assumption of *cross-situational consistency.*

This assumption is also evident in the way most of us think and talk about people we meet every day. Most of us tend to be trait theorists. We tend to say things like, "Oh, he's such an aggressive person!" or "But she's so domineering!" When we make such statements, we are implicitly assuming that these people are likely to behave aggressively or in a domineering manner in a wide range of situations.

Despite the fact that both professional psychologists and ordinary people often assume that there is a great deal of consistency in individual behaviors across situations, that assumption has been challenged in a number of studies. In one of the earliest of these studies, Hartshorne and May (1928) examined cross-situational consistency in the moral behavior of children. They provided each child with opportunities to commit a range of "immoral" acts, including lying, cheating, and stealing. In addition, they gave each child the opportunity to commit these acts in a number of different settings, including in the home, at a party, and in athletic contests.

THE PENURIOUS MAN

The concept of cross-situational consistency has been with us for thousands of years, as illustrated by the following passage from the Greek philosopher Theophrastus: "Penuriousness is economy carried beyond all measure. A Penurious Man is one who goes to a debtor to ask for his half-obol interest before the end of the month. At a dinner where expenses are shared, he counts the number of cups each person drinks, and he makes a smaller libation to Artemis than anyone. . . . If his wife drops a copper, he moves furniture, beds, chests and hunts in the curtains. . . . penurious men have hair cut short and do not put on their shoes until mid-day; and when they take their cloak to the fuller they urge him to use plenty of earth so that it will not be spotted so soon." (Theophrastus, 372–287 B.C.). [Quoted in Bem and Allen, 1974]

At the time, most psychologists would have predicted that the children should be consistently honest or dishonest in their behavior. According to the psychodynamic theories that were popular then, a child with a well-developed conscience (superego) would avoid lying, cheating, and stealing in nearly all situations, whereas a child with a poorly developed conscience would succumb to these vices regularly.

But these expectations were not supported by Hartshorne and May's study. They found only a minimal amount of consistency. A child who cheated or lied in one situation was not especially likely to cheat or lie in another. In fact, it was almost impossible to predict from a child's behavior in one setting what he or she would do in another setting. The Hartshorne and May study is, by itself, hardly sufficient proof that cross-situational consistency in behavior is not great. But many other more recent studies have come to the same conclusion. After reviewing a vast body of correlational studies of such traits as dependency, masculinity-femininity and self-control, Mischel (1968) concluded that in fact our behavior does not generally show a large degree of consistency from one situation to another. Rather than being determined by underlying traits, our behavior is more often determined by the demands or requirements of the particular situation we happen to be in.

After a little reflection, this inconsistency across situations may not seem so surprising. Consider your own behavior. Are you talkative and sociable when out with friends? Well, then maybe you are extraverted. But aren't you sometimes shy and anxious with strangers? Oh, then perhaps you are actually introverted. You are stubborn sometimes, right? Yet at other times you are flexible. You are easy going but sometimes irritable; you are cheerful but sometimes grumpy. In fact, you are all of these things because your behavior depends less on *you* than on your situation—whom you are with, where, and when.

This is not to say that there is no consistency in our behavior across situations. Most of us believe that we *are* consistent in some respects, and although we may be biased judges, we are probably right. Daryl Bem and Andrea Allen (1975) recently obtained extensive reports of students' friendliness and their conscientiousness in a wide variety of situations. The data came not only from students' self-reports but also from reports from the students' parents and friends and from observations made by psychologists in several different laboratory situations. In general, there was only a small degree of consistency in a person's friendliness or conscientiousness across situations. But there was much greater consistency for those students who themselves stated that they did not vary much from situation to situation on a particular trait. Some students felt that they were consistently conscientious or unconscientious, but not consistently friendly or unfriendly; others felt that they were consistently friendly or unfriendly but not consistently conscientious or unconscientious. In both cases, the students' self-assessments generally seemed to be correct. We are presumably more consistent in those matters

Have you seen this young woman before? In fact, she also appears on pages 435 and 438. But she appears very different in the three situations. As discussed in the text there is often very little consistency between people's behavior in different scenes.

that are central aspects of our personality and that relate to our basic values. In other respects we are more likely to remain flexible and to behave in accordance with the situation.

On the whole it seems clear that until recently personality theorists who emphasized types or traits also overestimated the degree of consistency in people's personalities. And most of us usually make the same mistake, assuming that other people are more consistent than they really are. One reason for this tendency to overestimate the degree of other people's consistency is that we usually see other people in a small range of situations. Perhaps when your friend Joe is with you in the places where you usually go together he is likely to be jovial and overbearing. But it may well be that Joe is also sad and timid much of the time when you are not around.

SOCIAL LEARNING THEORY

Psychoanalytic, type, and trait theories have had a hard time dealing with the evidence that suggests that there is relatively little cross-situational consistency in people's behavior. *Social learning theory,* in contrast, finds such lack of consistency to be quite understandable. The social learning approach tries to explain both consistency and inconsistency by focusing on the mechanisms by which patterns of behavior are learned and on the situations in which the learning takes place.

Social learning theory, as its name implies, focuses directly on people's behavior and is not concerned with underlying motives or traits. The emphasis is on what people *do* rather than on the attributes they *have* (Mischel, 1976). In this respect, social learning theory is heavily influenced by B. F. Skinner's behavioristic approach to learning (see Chapter 5). According to this approach, people are most likely to behave in ways that have been reinforced in the past. If Johnny hits his younger brother and thus gets to eat his brother's candy bar—and if he successfully avoids punishment for this behavior—he is likely to do it again. What's more, he may learn from this experience that it is profitable to hit younger children in a variety of circumstances, such as when he wants to ride someone else's bicycle or play with someone else's toys. This is an example of behavioral *generalization* since Johnny would be generalizing the behavior (hitting) to a variety of situations in which it will be rewarding. Similarly, Sally might learn that it is rewarding to cling to her mother's skirt in a variety of situations.

But social learning theory does not predict that Johnny will be consistently aggressive or that Sally will be consistently dependent. If Johnny is encouraged by his success and also tries to hit his *older* brother, he may end up with a bloody nose. Or if he tries hitting his younger brother while his parents are around, he may end up sitting in his room without dinner. Since these new behaviors are punished rather than rewarded, he is unlikely to try them again. Similarly, Sally may discover that clinging to her mother's skirt is rewarded when her mother is in a good mood, but that it is disapproved when her mother is tense or worried. As a result, Sally will learn to assess her mother's mood before she begins to cling. This learning process, as we saw in Chapter 5, is known as *discrimination*—Johnny and Sally learn to discriminate between situations in which a particular sort of behavior is likely to be rewarded and situations in which it is not.

From the standpoint of the social learning theorist, these processes of generalization and discrimination explain why there is typically only a small degree of cross-situational consistency in people's behaviors. As Walter Mischel (1976), a leading social learning theorist, points out, social learning theory suggests that people will behave consistently across situations only to the extent to which similar behavior is expected to have positive consequences. Since most social behaviors (such as aggression) are not reinforced across different situations, a high degree of consistency cannot be expected. Mischel provides the following example to illustrate this point of view:

Consider a woman who seems hostile and fiercely independent some of the time but passive, dependent, and feminine on other occasions. What is she really like? . . . Must she be a really aggressive woman with a facade of passivity—or is she a warm, passive-dependent woman with a surface defense of aggressiveness? Social

THE NAZI PERSONALITY

It's easy to assume that the leaders of Nazi Germany, who were responsible for the annihilation of millions of people, were madmen. What else but warped personalities accounts for their atrocities? Two researchers, making use of the Rorschach inkblot responses (see Box 2) of leading Nazi officials while they were awaiting trial at Nuremberg, have concluded that they were in fact mentally disturbed individuals (Miale and Selzer, 1976). As psychologist Molly Harrower (1976) notes, however, such assessments may be biased, since the researchers knew that the responses they were examining belonged to the Nazi murderers. "If [the researcher] looks for evidence of sadism in the answers of a psychopathic murderer," Harrower writes, "the chances are that he will find it" (page 76). In contrast, when Harrower had the Rorschach responses scored "blind" by a panel of 15 authorities (that is, they didn't know whom they were evaluating), they did not identify the Nazis (including such infamous men as Adolf Eichmann, Herman Goering, and Rudolf Hess) as being mentally disordered. Nor did they discover any particular commonalities between these men. Harrower concludes that it is reassuring but dangerous to believe that the horrors of World War II were the work of a dozen or so insane men. These actions might have been taken by completely normal people, caught in the grip of strong social forces.

behavior theory suggests that it is possible for her to be all of these—a hostile, fiercely independent, passive, dependent, feminine, aggressive, warm person all in one. Of course which of these she is at any particular time would not be random and capricious; it would depend on discriminative stimuli—who she is with, when, how, and much, much more. But each of these aspects of her self may be a quite genuine and real aspect of her total being. (page 86)

Rather than considering this woman to be "inconsistent" or "fickle," social learning theorists would emphasize her "adaptability" and "discriminative facility." This ability to discriminate between situations is viewed as a sign of maturity, whereas extreme consistency may be more characteristic of adaptive or disturbed people.

Although social learning theory is heavily indebted to Skinner's behavioristic theory, social learning theory extends Skinner's formulation by emphasizing the role of *modeling* and of other sorts of vicarious learning that do not depend on direct rewards and reinforcements. According to this viewpoint, behavior is shaped by people's *expectations* of reward or punishment in a particular situation. We form these expectations not only from our own experience but also by watching other people, reading, and listening to other people's explanations. Thus, if Johnny saw another boy steal an apple and get away with it, Johnny might be

Box 3

Internal and External Control

Would you say that your grades are the result of your own efforts, or do you sometimes feel that you have little to do with the grades you get?

Is making a varsity team usually the result of hard work and persistence, or is it largely a matter of getting the right breaks?

Are you the master of your fate, or is most of what happens to you a matter of chance?

People answer these questions differently: Some people think they can easily control their success in school, in sports, or in life in general, while others feel that their outcomes are controlled by fate, luck, chance, or God's will. These differences are a topic of active current research, showing one application of social learning theory to the study of personality.

Julian Rotter (1966) has argued that people's attitudes about control derive from generalized expectancies about their own behavior. People who learn, either directly or by observing others, that their actions will be successful (that is, rewarded) in a number of settings may come to expect success in many other settings. In contrast, people who learn that their actions will be unsuccessful (unrewarded) may come to expect failure generally.

Rotter calls the first group of persons "internals" because they believe that they themselves control what happens to them—their perceived *locus of control* is internal. Similarly, Rotter calls the second group "externals" because they believe that external forces (fate, God, the government) control what happens to them—their perceived locus of control is external. The questions listed above are adapted from a scale Rotter designed to measure locus of control.

How does the behavior of internals differ from that of externals? As you might expect, people who believe that they can control their outcomes are more likely to try to actually exert that control. One way they can do so is by gathering information about their life situations. Seeman and Evans (1962) found this situation to be true in the case of hospitalized tuberculosis patients. Not only did the internals (as measured by Rotter's scale) know more about their condition upon arriving at the hospital, but they also asked doctors and nurses more questions once they had arrived.

Another way internals might control their outcomes is by

tempted to try the same thing himself. On the other hand, if Johnny saw the other boy get caught and punished, or if he had been convinced by his parents that "crime does not pay" he would not expect this behavior to lead to positive consequences and he would refrain from trying it himself.

In recent years, social learning theory has become a popular and influential approach to the study of personality. Like most popular and influential approaches, however, it also has severe critics. Some of these critics contend that by concerning themselves only with people's behavior and not with their attributes social learning theorists have ended up with a theory of personality that ignores the *person* (Bowers, 1973). In response to such criticisms, Mischel (1976) suggests that social learning theorists have not lost sight of the person. Instead, they have been moving toward an image of the person that stresses the ability to learn from experience and to respond flexibly in a variety of situations. In this view, the human being is "an active, aware processor of information, a problem-solver who actively constructs and influences the world rather than responding to it passively" (Mischel, 1976, page 513).

---

making active, concerted efforts to influence social policy and world events. According to this hypothesis, internals should tend to be social activists. Gore and Rotter (1963) found this to be true in a study of civil-rights activity among college students. Students who were internal were more likely to make commitments to march to the state capital or to join a Freedom Riders group, while those who were external were less likely to get involved in such activities. Whereas internals believe that they can make a difference, externals are more likely to assume that their actions wouldn't really matter.

People who don't believe that they can control what happens to them, and who therefore don't even try to exert control, are likely to end up proving themselves right. When all is said and done, they probably won't control their outcomes. For example, in a study done after the Surgeon General's report on smoking and cancer, James, Woodruff, and Werner (1965) found that smokers who had successfully quit smoking were more internal than those who had not. The internal smokers were apparently better able to take themselves in hand and say, "I'm going to kick this habit," whereas the externals were more likely to say, "Well, it's too late now—I'm hooked and there's nothing I can do about it."

Where does an internal or external locus of control come from? Rotter believes that these differences result from expectancies generalized from everyday experiences. If you repeatedly discover your efforts are rewarded, you will come to expect to be able to exert such control over your reinforcements in the future. If you discover that your efforts are of no avail, you will become resigned to lack of control.

This formulation suggests that an external orientation will develop most often among people who actually have little control over what happens to them—people without money, power, or influence. In keeping with these predictions, Battle and Rotter (1963) found that children from lower socioeconomic classes tended to be more external than children from more privileged socioeconomic backgrounds. Similarly, Seeman (1966) found that unionized workers tended to be more internal than nonunionized workers, perhaps because the unionized workers learned that they had greater control over what happens to them.

HUMANISTIC THEORIES

For humanists, it is the uniqueness of each human being—his or her value, dignity, and worth as an individual—that is important. The terms "humanist," "self-actualizing theorist," "phenomenologist," and "existentialist" are only rough indications of the actual theoretical positions of these psychologists. Certainly, all of them would be offended by being imprisoned by such restrictive labels. Humanists have been tagged "self theorists" or "self-actualization theorists" because they state that life is understandable only in terms of the meaning of the experiences of each individual. To understand each person, we must comprehend the particular dilemmas that person faces and study the state of his or her consciousness as various life events are experienced.

Carl Rogers

Carl Rogers' theory centers on the phenomenal self—the image each person has of himself or herself. This image may or may not correspond to reality as others might judge it. As infants, each of us learns to need love and we each behave as we do in order to insure that we will get love. Thus, we learn to behave in ways that will please others. Before long, these learned patterns of behavior please us as well.

Box 4

Self-Esteem

Babies usually appear to recognize themselves in mirrors when they are about 10 months old. Awareness of self and *self-esteem*—one's positive regard for oneself—are particularly important variables in human personality. Stanley Coopersmith (1967) measured boys' self-esteem and other aspects of their personality and behavior. He found that boys with a high degree of self-esteem are active, expressive individuals who tend to be successful both academically and socially. They are eager to express opinions, do not avoid disagreement, and are not particularly sensitive to criticism. Boys with low self-esteem, in contrast, present a picture of discouragement and depression. They feel isolated, unloved, incapable of expressing or defending themselves, and too weak to confront or overcome their deficiencies. They are afraid of angering others and shrink from exposing themselves to attention.

Arnold Buss (1973) maintains that the core of self-esteem is formed by the unconditional love of the parents. Parents love the child simply because he or she is theirs. They place no conditions on their affection. Thus, infants learn that the most important figures in their life think they are valuable merely because they exist. Love without limits or conditions creates a permanent feeling of self-love and the expectation that others will offer affection. Buss argues that by middle childhood the core of self-esteem has been established. If the core is sufficient, the person will always be able to fall back on a reserve of self-love. Without a sufficient core of self-esteem, however, the person needs continual assurance of his own worth.

Buss's ideas have received some empirical support. When Coopersmith (1967) looked into the backgrounds of boys who possessed high self-esteem, he found that close relationships existed between the boys and their parents. The mothers and fathers showed interest in the boys' welfare, were available for discussion of problems, and encouraged mutual activities. They clearly indicated that they regarded the boy as a significant person worthy of their deep interest. As a result, the boys came to regard themselves in a similar favorable light.

Carl Rogers

Becoming a well-adjusted, well-integrated adult is most easily done if we are not beaten down by other people's rejection of us, by low self-regard, by anxiety, or by conflict. If the self develops in an open, flexible, expansive manner, the individual will continue on the road to self-actualization. If too great a gap develops between the self and the ideal we want to become, progress in actualization comes to a halt, and future experiences become threatening rather than growth-inducing.

According to Rogers, one source of disorder is our attempt to become what *others* want us to be rather than what we really want to be. Beginning early in life, we are exposed to a series of experiences and feelings that we must assemble into an image of ourself. In the course of personality development, we are bound to encounter conflicts between the ideal of self and the true nature that seems to contradict it. We are expected, for example, to be generous but instead feel possessive. When breakdown takes place, the self-structure comes apart, and behavior and emotion become unpredictable. Rogers' suggestions for how to deal with such conflicts are described in Chapter 17.

Abraham Maslow

Maslow, like Rogers, began with the theoretical assumption that human beings are innately good. In other words, humans would be able to actualize their true natures were it not for a succession of frustrating stumbling blocks. We begin with a "given" inner nature containing instinct-like needs, capacities, and talents that seek to become a reality (actualized). The struggle to satisfy urgent basic needs must be won before we can strive for full self-actualization. This inner nature, however, is easily distorted by learned attitudes, social pressures, accidents, and habits.

As we saw in Chapter 9, Maslow believed that the child beginning a journey toward full expression must have a benign, accepting, supportive environment. If this is absent, the child may grow into an adult who is anxious about gratifying physiological and safety needs and who may be incapable of handling the issues of belongingness, love, esteem, or self-actualization. If uncrippled by fear, the mature, healthy person moves steadily if slowly toward self-actualization. Such a person seeks delight in new experiences; he or she moves, without compulsion, toward the higher and more complex forms of realizing his capacities.

Maslow was less concerned with disorder than are most personality theorists because he felt that too much work had been devoted to the neurotic parts of personality and not enough attention had been focused on achieving a fully developed being. He was aware, however, that many of us reach physical adulthood without having gone very far beyond the young child's anxious concern about physiological needs and safety. Personality disorder is a reflection of the crippling effects of a poisonous childhood environment. A child who is forced, prodded, or

Abraham Maslow

threatened may ultimately be shaped by others rather than grow from within. The innate nature of the child dies when he or she is forced to choose between the unique needs of the self and the needs for safety, food, love and the approval of others. In this contest, the child is hopelessly outmatched.

As we have noted throughout this chapter, personality theorists consider not only the structure and characteristics of personality but also the disorders that may develop. In the next section we will see how these various personality theories suggest different ways of viewing disorder and how psychoanalytic theory, learning theory, and Rogers' theory all carry with them distinctive approaches to psychotherapy.

SUMMARY

1. *Personality* is the pattern of characteristic behaviors and thoughts we use to deal with our environment. Personality theorists who focus on the detailed study of the unique characteristics of individuals follow an *idiographic* approach. Theorists who try to discover general patterns of personality between people reflect a *nomothetic* approach to personality.
2. *Psychoanalytic theory,* as formulated by Sigmund Freud, views personality formation as the direct result of the need to satisfy instinctual biological urges.
3. In the psychoanalytic view, personality consists of three parts: the *id,* which seeks to gratify instinctual needs; the *ego,* which controls gratification for the id; and the *superego,* which embodies the standards and ideals of parents and society.
4. Freud identified five stages of psychosexual development, with each stage centered around a particular *erogenous zone.* In infancy one goes through the *oral* and *anal* stages. At about age 5 the child enters the *phallic* stage and must resolve the *Oedipus conflict.* The childhood years are called the *latency period,* while puberty brings on the final, *genital* stage. Failure to resolve conflicts at any of the earlier stages can result in fixation at that stage and lifelong personality traits developed in relation to this fixation.
5. Freud thought that individuals use *defense mechanisms* to unconsciously distort or deny reality so that anxiety will be reduced. Common defense mechanisms include repression, projection, reaction formation, displacement, rationalization, and intellectualization.
6. Jung agreed with Freud that personality is the outcome of the balance between conscious and unconscious forces. However, Jung postulated that the unconscious consists of two parts: the *personal unconscious* and the *collective unconscious.* Poor adjustment results from the failure to achieve a balance among the various parts of the personality and to fit the pieces of personality into an integrated whole.

7. Adler believed that personality development is a result of people's need to overcome inferiority by striving to master a major goal in life.
8. *Type theory* was an early attempt at classifying personalities. Individuals were categorized and labeled according to the central characteristic they displayed. Hippocrates divided everyone into four types: choleric, melancholic, sanguine, and phlegmatic. Sheldon related personality to three main body types: *ectomorph, mesomorph,* and *endomorph.* Jung suggested that types appear only as extremes, in the form of introverts and extraverts.
9. *Trait theories* attempt to describe individuals by noting a number of characteristics in each individual. Allport distinguished between common traits (found to some degree in everyone) and individual traits (found in a small number of individuals). At least some personality traits seem to have a hereditary basis.
10. Among the many tests that have been developed to assess personality traits are the Minnesota Multiphasic Personality Inventory (MMPI), the Thematic Apperception Test (TAT), and the Rorschach inkblot test. *Personality inventories* require individuals to respond to a series of statements on a printed test form, whereas *projective tests* require individuals to invent stories about pictures or inkblots they are shown.
11. One problem with most theories of personality is that they assume the existence of *cross-situational consistency* in personality. However, several studies have found a minimal amount of consistency in people's behavior from situation to situation. Nevertheless, characteristics that are central to one's personality and that relate to one's values tend to be somewhat consistent.
12. The *social learning theory* approach to personality focuses on the person's behavior rather than on underlying motives or traits. It was influenced by Skinner's behaviorist approach. Children develop ways of behaving on the basis of rewards and punishments, generalization and discrimination. Children can also learn from observing *models* and by developing *expectations* about what kinds of rewards and punishments will be connected with a particular situation.
13. People who learn that their behaviors will in general be rewarded come to expect success, and their perceived *locus of control* is *internal.* People who come to believe that their behaviors have no effect generally may come to expect failure; their locus of control is *external.*
14. *Humanistic* theories of personality stress the importance of each individual's fully realizing his or her own unique way of experiencing life.
15. According to Rogers, the self will develop fully if it experiences an accepting environment in which love and attention

are not contingent on becoming the person *others* want one to be. If people grow up doing things in order not to be rejected, they will continue to encounter conflicts between what they think they should be and their true self.

16. When compared with boys with low self-esteem, boys with high self-esteem are more successful academically and socially, are more eager to express opinions, are more trusting of their own perceptions, have more confidence, are less anxious, and are less likely to develop psychosomatic problems. According to Buss, the core of self-esteem is formed by the unconditional love of the parents and is established by middle childhood.
17. Maslow suggested that a person who is still anxious about gratifying basic physiological needs will never proceed to satisfy higher needs such as belonging, love, and self-actualization.

psychological issue

Morality

In Europe, a woman was near death from a special kind of cancer. There was one drug that the doctors thought might save her. It was a form of radium that a druggist in the same town had recently discovered. The drug was expensive to make, but the druggist was charging ten times what the drug cost him to make. He paid $200 for the radium and charged $2,000 for a small dose of the drug. The sick woman's husband, Heinz, went to everyone he knew to borrow the money, but he could only get together about $1,000, which is half of what it cost. He told the druggist that his wife was dying and asked him to sell it cheaper or let him pay later. But the druggist said, "No, I discovered the drug and I'm going to make money from it." So Heinz got desperate and broke into the man's store to steal the drug for his wife. (Kohlberg 1963, pages 18–19.)

Before you go on to read the rest of this section, take a minute or two to jot down answers to these questions: Should Heinz have stolen the drug? Was he right or wrong to do it? Why?

The story about Heinz and the drug is fictional. It is one of a set of stories constructed by a psychologist, Lawrence Kohlberg, for use in research on moral reasoning—how people think about questions of right and wrong. Each story is designed to contain a moral dilemma, a choice between alternative behaviors, each of which might seem immoral. For example, Heinz is faced with a choice between letting his wife die or stealing the drug. In his research Kohlberg asks his subjects questions about each moral dilemma. Based on their answers, he has developed a theory about the evolution of moral thought. Before discussing Kohlberg's theory, we must first mention the pioneering contribution of his predecessor in the study of moral development, Jean Piaget.

Piaget's Theory of Moral Development

Piaget (1948) was the first to recognize that moral reasoning, like intellectual skills, evolves through stages (see Chapter 12). After studying children between the ages of 3 and 12, he proposed the existence of two stages: the stage *heteronomous morality* (sometimes called the stage of moral realism) and the stage *autonomous morality* (or moral independence).

In the stage of heteronomous morality, the child accepts rules as given from authority; the prefix *hetero-*, meaning "other," reflects the fact that during this stage rules are received from other people. For example, parents may tell a child not to lie, not to shout, or not to take little sister's candy. Teachers may tell a child not to talk in class or not to run during a fire drill. To the three- to five-year-old child, these externally imposed rules seem sacred and permanent. Children at this stage also believe that the rules of games are unchangeable. Later on, during the stage of autonomous morality, the child can devise and modify rules to fit particular situations. For instance, a child may decide to allow four strikes per out in a game of baseball, or two moves per turn in a game of checkers, to make the game more enjoyable. To the ten- to twelve-year-old, rules can be modified by mutual consent.

As children progress from the stage of moral realism (heteronomous morality) to the stage of moral independence

. . . it seems to the child that the amount of damage counts more than intentions.

(autonomous morality), their feelings about the seriousness of wrongdoing change dramatically. During the stage of moral realism, it seems to the child that the amount of damage counts more than intentions. The worse the mess, the more guilty the child, and whether or not the culprit "meant to do it" is not taken into account. The concept of "intention" is in fact a complex one and may develop only gradually as the child becomes capable of concrete and, then, formal operational thought (see Chapter 12). By the time children reach the stage of moral independence, they regard intentions as more important than the amount of damage in assigning guilt. It is now seen as worse to smash a small vase on purpose than a larger one by accident.

Kohlberg's Six Stages of Moral Reasoning

Kohlberg (1969) used the story of Heinz, and others like it, to revise and extend Piaget's analysis. Studying adolescents and adults as well as children, Kohlberg found evidence of six stages of moral reasoning, rather than just two. The first two are quite similar to those discovered by Piaget; the next four represent more sophisticated levels of moral thought found in adolescents and adults. Kohlberg has found that as people move from childhood to adulthood their moral reasoning gradually shifts from Stage 1 toward Stage 6. Not everyone advances all the way up the ladder of stages, however. Many adults remain at Stages 2, 3, and 4; very few of us ever reach Stage 6. Examples of moral reasoning at each stage are provided in the table. You might want to compare your own answers to the questions about Heinz to these examples.

As the table indicates, moral reasoning exhibits an orderly progression. Initially, individuals are oriented to the personal implications of their behavior. Later, they become oriented to the implications of their behavior for other people as well. Ultimately, they may develop an orientation to the broader ethical implications of their actions. Kohlberg claims that these stages form an unvarying sequence. To arrive at one stage, he says, a person must proceed through all of the preceding stages, in order. This claim is still the subject of heated debate.

It is important to note that both "yes" and "no" answers to the question, "Should Heinz steal the drug?" are possible at each stage of moral development. A person's stage of moral development is reflected in the *way* in which the person thinks about moral problems, rather than in the specific solution he or she comes up with.

Morality and Watergate

Late in the summer of 1972, as the presidential campaign swung into high gear, six men were arrested after breaking into the headquarters of the Democratic National Committee. Those headquarters were located in Washington, D.C., in a building complex called the Watergate; the break-in, subsequent coverup, and eventual investigation became known as "the Watergate affair."

The six burglars were all soon convicted, but the true scope of the criminal conspiracy remained hidden for some time. It was ultimately discovered that the burglars were acting not on their own initiative but under the direction of members of the Committee to Reelect the President (CREEP). This was revealed only after an elaborate attempt to cover up the link, including extensive perjury, on the part of highly placed officials in CREEP and in the White House. Quite naturally, these events caused an entire nation to stop and wonder why intelligent, respected, and apparently "moral" men would condone and commit such crimes.

There is no single, satisfying answer to this question. Different individuals had different reasons for participating in the crimes of Watergate. But it may help to recognize that these men were confronted with difficult moral dilemmas and to analyze the decisions they made in terms of Kohlberg's stages.

Some of the men involved may have rationalized their participation in terms typical of Stages 1 and 2: They may have burglarized for the sake of money and lied in order to avoid punishment. However, Candee (1975) argues that most participants in the Watergate affair exhibited moral reasoning typical of Stage 3 or 4. For instance, a CREEP official named Herbert Porter testified at the Congressional Watergate hearings (1973, p. 277) that he had committed perjury because of group pressure. The following is an excerpt of an exchange between Porter and Senator Howard Baker:

Table 14.1 Examples of Moral Reasoning at Each of Kohlberg's Stages

Should Heinz Steal the Drug? Why or Why Not?

	Yes	No
Stage 1. Orientation to obedience and punishment. Rules of conduct derive from the power of those who impose them.	It isn't wrong to take the drug. It's really only worth $200, and Heinz probably won't get caught anyway.	It's wrong to take the drug, since it's worth $2,000. Besides, Heinz would probably get caught and be punished.
Stage 2. Orientation to instrumental hedonism. Rules of conduct derive from selfish, pragmatic objectives.	If Heinz doesn't want to lose his wife, it's not wrong to take the drug. It's the only thing that'll work.	Heinz shouldn't risk his neck for his wife. If she dies, he can marry somebody else. It would be wrong for him to give up very much just for her.
Stage 3. Orientation to interpersonal concordance. Rules of conduct derive from the role demands implicit in being a "good" boy, girl, husband, wife, American, and so on.	Heinz has no choice. Stealing the drug is the only thing for a good husband to do. People will blame him if he doesn't.	Heinz mustn't steal the drug. He can't be blamed for not stealing the drug; it's not the kind of thing a good citizen can do.
Stage 4: Orientation to an established social order. Rules of conduct derive from laws and from one's duty to maintain the social order.	When Heinz got married, he vowed to protect his wife. He must steal the drug to live up to that promise. If husbands don't protect their wives, the family structure will disintegrate, and with it, our society.	Stealing is illegal. Heinz has to obey the law no matter what the circumstances. Imagine what society would be like if everybody stole.
Stage 5. Orientation to the "social contract." Rules of conduct derive from the reciprocal rights and responsibilities of individuals and governments.	Heinz should steal the drug. The law is unjust, because it doesn't protect his wife's right to life. Therefore, Heinz has no obligation to obey the law.	As a member of society, Heinz has an obligation to respect the druggist's right to property. Therefore, it would be wrong for him to steal the drug.
Stage 6. Orientation to ethical principles. Rules of conduct derive from principles that transcend authority of law.	The principle of the sanctity of life demands that Heinz steal the drug, no matter what the law says.	The principle of justice and the greatest good for the greatest number prevents Heinz from stealing the drug simply for the good of his wife.

Jeb Stuart Magruder, who explained his Watergate crimes in terms of the preservation of the social order.

Baker: *At any time, did you ever think of saying, I do not think this is quite right?*

Porter: *Yes I did.*

Baker: *What did you do about it?*

Porter: *I did not do anything about it.*

Baker: *Why didn't you?*

Porter: *In all honesty, probably because of the fear of group pressure that would ensue from not being a team player.*

As Candee points out, Porter's reasoning is typical for individuals at Stage 3, where "right is determined by group norms."

Other participants, like Jeb Stuart Magruder, the deputy director of CREEP, justified their involvement in the Watergate crimes as being essential to "national security" and the preservation of the social order. This sort of moral reasoning is typical of individuals at Stage 4. As Candee notes, if the system is seen as more basic than the rights of its individual members, it is being viewed from a Stage 4 perspective.

Finally, we can consider the moral arguments of Archibald Cox, the Harvard Law School professor who served as Special Watergate Prosecutor until his dismissal by President Nixon. Cox argued that the rights of speech, privacy, dignity, and other fundamental liberties . . . must be respected by both government and private persons" (Cox, 1974, p. 67). This emphasis on constitutional rights and responsibilities is typical of individuals at Stage 5.

In a survey of 370 college students conducted during the winter of 1973–1974, Candee found support for his conclusion that attitudes about Watergate depend on a person's stage of moral reasoning. As a first step, Candee determined each subject's stage by examining his or her answers to questions about moral dilemmas like the one about Heinz and the drug. Most of his subjects were at Stage 3, 4, or 5. Next, he examined the relationship between those stages and attitudes toward Watergate. In general, he found that subjects at Stages 3 and 4 were more likely to approve of the acts of the Watergate participants than subjects at Stage 5. For example, approximately 48 percent of the subjects at Stage 3 and 23 percent of the subjects at Stage 4 thought that Magruder was right to perjure himself in order to cover up the break-ins; in contrast, only 5 percent of the subjects at Stage 5 thought so.

Summary

1. Piaget suggested that there are two stages of moral development: the stage of *heteronomous morality* (moral realism), in which the child's rules are received from an authority, and the stage of *autonomous morality,* in which the child becomes morally independent.
2. Kohlberg has identified six progressive stages of moral development. Most people do not reach the final stage, however.
3. In analyzing the statements of Watergate conspirators, psychologists have found that participants exhibited moral reasoning typical of Stage 3 or 4 in Kohlberg's scheme.

PART 7

Disorder and Therapy

The study of psychological disorders is often known as *abnormal psychology.* But, as we will see in Chapter 15 on the *The Nature of Abnormality,* it is by no means easy to determine which patterns of thought, feeling, and behavior are "normal" and which are "abnormal." Indeed, what is considered "normal" or "healthy" in one culture may be considered "abnormal" or "pathological" in another. And while some psychologists and psychiatrists are concerned with diagnosing and treating mental illness, others insist that the very concept of "mental illness" is a myth.

In spite of such debates about the nature of abnormality, we cannot deny the fact that millions of people suffer painfully from mental and emotional problems. In Chapter 16, on *Psychological Disorder,* we will examine several of the most prevalent psychological disorders, ranging from conditions that almost all of us experience at one time or another (such as mild depression) to conditions that are further from our ordinary experience, but that nevertheless afflict large numbers of people (such as schizophrenia). We will discover that current research in many areas of psychology, including brain mechanisms, learning, and personality, is converging to provide clues about the causes of these disorders.

Chapter 17 examines several forms of *Therapy* currently used in the treatment of psychological problems and disorders. We will find that theory and research in different areas of psychology have given rise to specific approaches to psychotherapy. Thus, Freud's theory of personality (discussed in Chapter 14) has led to psychoanalytic approaches to therapy, research on learning (Chapter 5) to the behavior therapies, and research on brain mechanisms (Chapter 2) to certain forms of drug treatment and brain surgery.

The first two Psychological Issues in this part discuss forms of psychological disorder that are among our most pressing social problems. Following Chapter 15 we consider the self-destructive pattern of *Alcoholism* and following Chapter 16 we consider self-destruction in its most literal sense, *Suicide.* Finally, the Psychological Issue that follows Chapter 17, *Variations in Psychotherapy,* discusses some of the many new forms of therapy that have recently arrived on the scene, including some that will surely turn out to be short-lived fads and others that may prove to have more staying power.

CHAPTER 15

The Nature of Abnormality

"Look at that weirdo over there—he's talking to himself! He must be nuts!" "Hey, are you crazy or something?" "That's the state mental hospital. They keep all the people who are sick in the head there." Perhaps you remember making or hearing such comments yourself. They reflect a widespread concern with what is "normal" and what is "abnormal" about human personality and behavior. People who behave in "abnormal" ways often upset others who consider themselves more normal. Sometimes they even engage in violent or severely disruptive behavior; often they lead lives of great pain and suffering.

But how can you decide whether someone really is "crazy" rather than just silly, or "eccentric"? First you would have to define the nature of abnormality. What is considered normal and abnormal depends to a large degree on who is doing the judging. And, as we will see, what is considered normal or natural at one time or in one culture may be considered bizarre at another time or in another culture.

One approach to abnormal behavior is to equate abnormality with "psychopathology" or "mental illness"—to say that psychological disturbances are not unlike physical diseases, such as tuberculosis or mumps. We will explain this medical approach to abnormality more fully later in the chapter, and we will adopt it to a large degree when we discuss neuroses and psychoses in the next chapter. However, many psychologists argue that abnormal behavior does not necessarily involve any "illness" at all.

Throughout history, people have not only changed their ideas about what constitutes abnormality but also have had different ideas about what *causes* psychological disturbance, and this controversy continues right up to the present day. We will therefore begin our exploration of the nature of abnormality by examining some of these historical variations. Then we will take up the difficult issue of defining abnormality and the problem of how different mental and behavioral disorders can best be classified.

THE HISTORY OF ABNORMALITY

Searching back through the history of abnormality can be valuable if it helps put our modern views of emotional disorder into perspective. As we look at the historical precedents, we see that two main approaches have prevailed. At times, the dominant view was from a religious perspective, and abnormality was seen as a punishment from God or the work of the devil. At other times the scientific or medical view was dominant, and abnormality was treated as an illness or disease. Both of these perspectives have stayed with us in some form to the present day.

The Golden Age of Greece

Our history of abnormality will begin in ancient Greece, the starting point of Western civilization as we know it. In early Greece, mental disorders, like all other puzzling phenomena, were attributed to the gods. The "psychiatrists" were priests, and the "mental hospitals" were temples. This approach continued into the Roman era, where the temples dedicated to Saturn were not unlike sanitoriums, where patients walked in the gardens, attended concerts, and were treated to entertainment.

But ancient Greece was also the birthplace of a more scientific approach to mental disorder. The great physician Hippocrates (460–377 B.C.) believed that mental disorders were similar to physical disorders in their origins. Unlike other noted thinkers of his time, Hippocrates thought that the brain was the central organ of the intellect and that mental illness must therefore be due to some sort of brain disorder. Few of his theories and prescriptions for mental illness remain in vogue today, but his medical orientation was clear: his treatment for psychological disturbances (melancholia, for example) included dietary changes, exercise, abstinence from alcohol, moderation in all areas, and tranquillity, in addition to more traditional techniques such as bloodletting. Other early physicians who influenced the medical approach to abnormality were the Romans Asclepiades and Galen, who carried on the Hippocratic tradition.

Because of Hippocrates' influential belief in the physical causes of mental disorder, treatment passed out of the hands of priests and into the hands of physicians for the first—but by no means the last—time in history. After the fall of Rome, it wasn't until the nineteenth century that physicians regained the influence in treating disorder that we so naturally accord to them today (Ullmann and Krasner, 1975).

When the Roman Empire was overrun by the plague and devastated by conquering barbarian hordes, the stage was set for the Middle Ages, in which the advances in medical thought were to be discarded for a new religious demonology. Civilization shifted and people retreated to a less rational view of humanity.

The Middle Ages

In the Middle Ages, madness was thought to be the will of god, and its cure was religious ritual. Medieval theologians tended to see all diseases as forms of punishment. and since the head was thought to house reason—people's highest faculty and the one that linked them to God—diseases of the mind were almost always viewed as an expression of sin (Neaman, 1975).

ASCLEPIADES

In 124 B.C., the Roman physician Asclepiades distinguished between illusions, delusions, and hallucinations. He also noted the difference between acute and chronic mental illnesses and invented various devices to make patients more comfortable. One of these was a suspended hammock-like bed, the swaying of which was considered beneficial to disturbed patients (Coleman, 1972).

GALEN

Galen (130–200 A.D.) was a physician who dominated Western thinking until the eighteenth century. Galen added psychic functions to the brain. He divided the causes of mental illness into physical and mental. Among the causes he named were injuries to the head, alcoholic excess, shock, fear, adolescence, menstrual changes, economic reverses, and disappointment in love (Coleman, 1972).

In the early Middle Ages, those persons considered mentally disturbed were treated humanely, with prayers, rituals, and pilgrimages. But by the late Middle Ages the situation had changed. Deviant behavior was usually interpreted as being in the service of the devil and was likely to be viewed as witchcraft. Because those persons who exposed others as witches were officially blessed, witch hunts characterized the times. Treatment of "witches" consisted of *exorcism*—a ritual designed to cast the evil spirit from the body. This process involved not only incantation and prayer, but also such unpleasant measures as flogging, starvation, and noisemaking.

During the latter part of the fifteenth century, the belief that psychological disturbance was the work of the devil became an

TARANTISM

Epidemics of mass madness and religious hysteria reached a peak during the fifteenth and sixteenth centuries. An epidemic known as *tarantism* began in the thirteenth century, apparently originating in the south of Italy. The symptoms were thought to be caused by the sting of a spider, the tarantula. Thinking they were infected, people would suddenly jump up, run out of their houses, and start dancing in the streets. They might be joined by others, and all of them would participate in this frenzied affair until completely exhausted. The peasants believed that after being bitten the poison would remain in the system and would be reactivated from time to time, especially when the weather was extremely hot.

The trepanning operation employed in the Middle Ages to rid a person of "evil spirits" as depicted by the painter Hieronymous Bosch (1460–1516). The man in the chair is having a hole drilled in his head to allow the spirits an exit.

"official" church position. Following a papal bull of Pope Innocent VII, the clergy was ordered to leave no stone unturned to detect those who were in league with the devil. To guide them in the witch hunt, a treatise, *The Witch's Hammer: Malleus Maleficarum,* was written by two German monks, Heinrich Kraemer and Johann Sprenger. Their book explained that bewitched individuals had been deprived of their reason by Satan. Satan could not enter the soul directly, but he could enter the body and the head and thus affect one's reason and sanity.

The *Malleus* told of six ways the devil could injure humanity: Satan could induce an evil love; plant hatred for another person; bewitch a man so he could not perform sexually; cause some disease; take away life; or deprive one of reason.

Certainly these were very bad times for the mentally disturbed, since a "devil psychology" dominated the thinking of doctors, lawyers, philosophers, and the ordinary citizen well into the seventeenth century, and lingered even beyond. The last "witch" execution took place in Switzerland in 1782.

This medieval view of abnormality continues to some extent today. Mentally disturbed people are often referred to as "madmen" and regarded with a mixture of fear and revulsion.

WEREWOLF

In some isolated rural areas there were outbreaks of *lycanthropy*—a form of emotional disturbance in which the person imagined himself to be a wolf and imitated its actions (Coleman, 1972). In 1541 a case was reported in which the lycanthrope confessed to his captors that he was really a wolf but his skin was smooth on the surface because all the fur was on the inside (Stone, 1937). To cure him of his delusions, his captors amputated the man's extremities; he died, still unconvinced.

The Modern Era Begins

The establishment of special institutions for the mentally disturbed began in the late Middle Ages and continued beyond the Renaissance. Institutions were founded in such cities as London (1547), Paris (1641), Moscow (1765), and Vienna (1784). Unlike the idyllic temples of ancient times, these institutions were very unpleasant. Patients were chained and kept in dungeonlike cells. In London visitors would come to observe patients as if they were animals in a zoo.

Eleven years before the French Revolution, a young doctor, Philippe Pinel, arrived in Paris. He revolutionized mental health care by freeing his patients from their chains and instituting human methods of treatment. The influence of the Enlightenment made it possible once more to view mental disorders as the result of natural, rational causes. Pinel's student, Esquirol, became one of the first to apply statistical methods to the study of patients. He tabulated what he thought were the psychic causes of disorder (including disappointment in love and financial loss), and was instrumental in establishing new mental hospitals in France.

Meanwhile, an English Quaker, William Tuke, was establishing York Retreat, a country house where mental patients could live in pleasant surroundings and relax in a spiritual atmosphere. Following Tuke's example, a number of small mental hospitals were established in America in the first half of the nineteenth century. These institutions were relatively humane. The hospital superintendent knew all the patients by name and he and his family shared meals with them. These hospitals were

Straitjackets have long been used to restrain violent mental patients. This etching stems from an 1838 drawing done in Paris for *Des Maladies Mentales.* Today, even though tranquilizers and other drugs provide alternatives to physical restraint, the straitjacket has not been entirely abandoned.

small, however, and could not accommodate all the people who needed treatment.

The nineteenth century witnessed the first marked changes in psychological theory and practice. Dorothea Dix, for example, devoted half of her life to the reform of hospitals for the emotionally disordered in America. As she worked for the establishment of humane, professionally run mental hospitals, she unwittingly encouraged a type of isolated mental hospital in which psychotics, criminals, and mental defectives were all confined together in a hopeless jumble.

In the latter half of the nineteenth century, the insane asylum became a familiar landmark in America. Dix solved one social problem but unintentionally created another for generations yet to come (Foucault, 1965).

In a book famous in the early 1900s, *A Mind That Found Itself,* a Yale graduate named Clifford Beers described the mistreatment he received in three mental hospitals. The public storm stirred up by the book launched the *mental hygiene* movement to educate people in the understanding of mental illness.

Today, medical, biochemical, and psychological advances have stimulated new progress in the diagnosis and treatment of mental disorders. Twentieth-century therapists have come almost full circle and are now discussing the advantages of open hospitals and home care for those with psychotic disorders. This psychological era is one of optimism and hope—hope that the scientific method will finally solve one of humanity's most burdensome problems (Freedman and Kaplan, 1967). Nevertheless, today's mental institutions have numerous drawbacks (see Box 1).

For the first time we are questioning some of the beliefs that have characterized the study of abnormal behavior for so long. For one thing, we are beginning to admit the difficulty of defining abnormality. Moreover, we have begun to question the his-

torical belief that physical illness is the proper model for viewing emotional disorder. This questioning is very important, for as we have noted much of the current language and framework for talking about mental disorder comes from the model of abnormality. So let us now look at the various possible ways to approach abnormality, including the medical model.

DEFINING ABNORMALITY

There are many ways to approach abnormality, and the definition can easily change from era to era and from culture to culture. Here we will be looking at four major approaches, or models, that are used by professionals and nonprofessionals in America today to define who is normal and who is abnormal.

The Statistical Approach

If "*abnormal*" were used in a strictly literal sense, statistical norms would be sufficient to define it. Any deviation from the majority would be abnormal: geniuses, the mentally retarded, members of the radical left and right would all be considered abnormal.

This definition of the word *abnormal* would be accurate but useless if we wanted to distinguish between desirable and undesirable deviations. Indeed, a statistical definition suggests equating mental health with conformity. Most people have average intelligence because the majority of IQ scores fall into the middle section of a distribution of all scores. Only a few people have high intelligence; fewer yet have *very* high intelligence; and geniuses are rare indeed.

The statistical model works well if we wish only to portray relatively uncomplicated traits or simple biological measurements, but it cannot describe the subtle complexities of human personality or emotional disorder.

The Adequacy Approach

Several approaches to abnormality have focused on psychological *adequacy* or *efficiency*—that is, on how well people adjust to and cope with their environment. If a man is able and willing to feed and dress himself, to hold a job, to support himself, and to communicate rationally with others, he would be regarded as functioning more adequately than a man who cannot or will not do these things.

Adequacy or efficiency may also be judged on the basis of personal discomfort or distress. Disturbed persons may experience acute feelings of distress or unhappiness. When these feelings are sufficiently intense, one may classify oneself as a disordered person even though symptoms may not be apparent to others. Psychological discomfort may lead to physical complaints, and people may try home remedies or see a physician. But these physical symptoms may not be related to any known medical disease. There is a twilight zone between medical disorders and psychological symptoms involving bodily complaints, as neurotic symptoms may imitate the symptoms of organic disease.

Worry and apprehension are other forms of distress that may lead to depression lasting long after the initiating event. When depression seems unrelated to events that would obviously produce sorrow, the depressed behavior is judged to be abnormal.

Using adequacy as a criterion for abnormality has a number of limitations (Buss, 1966). The major problem is that it is difficult to know for sure how "adequate," "efficient," or "distressed" a person is; it all depends on who is doing the judging. You've had experience with such variations in judgement—some instructors grade "hard," because they feel most students are not working to their potential; others grade "easy" in the same course with similar students, because their idea of adequacy is set to a lower standard.

The Medical Model

As we have seen, the notion that abnormal behavior is a result of mental illness became popular around the middle of the nineteenth century. Great advances in the field of medicine con-

Box 1

On Being Sane in Insane Places

In the last decade, there has been an increasingly vigorous assault by professionals and laymen alike on the multitude of flaws in the traditional idea of the "mental" hospital. These complaints were dramatically brought to light by David Rosenhan (1973) who conducted a field experiment in which eight "normal" persons were admitted to 12 mental hospitals.† The eight people were instructed to abandon their pretended symptoms once they became "patients." From then on, they were told to behave "normally." Their task was to get discharged from the hospital by convincing the staff they were really sane.

The eight "patients" were three women and five men of different ages and different occupations—a psychology graduate student, three psychologists, a psychiatrist, a painter, and a housewife. Rosenhan himself was one of the pseudopatients.

The settings were similarly varied. In order to generalize the findings, admission into a variety of hospitals was sought. The 12 hospitals in the sample were located in five different states on the East and West coasts. Some were old and shabby, some were quite new. Some were research-oriented, others not. Some had good staff-patient ratios, others were quite understaffed. Only one was a strictly private hospital. All of the others were supported by state or federal funds, or in one instance, by university funds. (Rosenhan, 1973, p. 251)

At the time of admission, names and occupations were altered, but the details of per-

†*From D. L. Rosenhan, On Being Sane in Insane Places,"* Science, *Vol. 179, p. 250–258, January 19, 1973. Copyright 1973 by the American Association for the Advancement of Science.*

vinced many physicians that some form of organic disorder was responsible not only for physical ailments but for emotional difficulties as well. This view that individuals exhibiting deviant behavior were "sick" was a great reform for the mental health movement. Up until this time, "insane" persons had been sent to prisons or chained and forgotten in asylums. With the acceptance of the medical view of psychopathology, these same individuals were instead sent to hospitals for treatment.

Although it soon became apparent they many persons who deviated from socially acceptable behavior did not actually have any organic impairment in their brains, the medical model continued to exert its influence, creating the framework by which we view abnormal behavior even today. Behaviors are classified into diagnostic categories much as we diagnose a runny nose, fever, and chills as a cold. Terms like *symptom, cure,* and *treatment* are a standard part of clinical vocabulary. The notion that mental "illness" is something one has, rather than something one does, still dominates the thinking of most mental health workers. But it is important to remember that such views represent only one model of psychopathology.

The medical model continues to be influential and dominant among psychologists, psychiatrists, and other professionals. And with some good reasons. It is often easier to deal with a problem if we can diagnose it as belonging to a particular category of

---

sonal life history were presented just as they had actually happened. The "patient" was always cooperative (except that medicine was never swallowed). When asked how he or she was feeling, the person always replied "fine" and reported that his or her symptoms had disappeared.

Despite their sanity, the pseudopatients were never detected. Admitted with a diagnosis of schizophrenia, each was discharged with a diagnosis of schizophrenia "in remission". At no time during hospitalization had any question been raised about possible pretense, nor were there any indications that the "patient" status was suspect.

Length of hospitalization ranged from 7 to 52 days, with an average of 19 days. The pseudopatients were not very carefully observed during this time. Interestingly, it was quite common for the other patients in these hospitals to detect that a pseudopatient was not really one of them—an observation that was not made by the hospital staff.

The experience of being a psychotic patient was far from a pleasant one. As Rosenhan describes it:

Powerlessness was evident everywhere. . . . His freedom of movement is restricted. He cannot initiate contact with the staff, but may only respond to such overtures as they make. Personal privacy is minimal. Patient quarters and possessions can be entered and examined by any staff member, for whatever reason. His personal history and anguish is available to any staff member (often including the "grey lady" and "candy striper" volunteer) who chooses to read his folder, regardless of their therapeutic relationship to him. (p. 256)

Even more startling to these experimenters was the medical care they received as pseudopatients.

All told, the pseudopatients were administered nearly 2,100 pills, including Stelazine, Elavil, Compazine, and Thorazine, to name but a few. (That such a variety of medications should have been administered to patients presenting identical symptoms is itself worthy of note.) Only two were swallowed. The rest were either pocketed or deposited in the toilet . . . the pseudopatients frequently found the medications of other patients in the toilet before they deposited their own. (p. 256) disorders. We can then prescribe a treatment that we know from experience is likely to be effective in dealing with this category of disorders. On the other hand, in recent years many psychologists have become dissatisfied with the medical model. Chief among these opponents is psychiatrist Thomas Szasz (1970), who claims that mental illness is a "myth." The individual is not actually sick; he or she merely has difficulty coping with the stresses of everyday life. By assigning the cause of problems to some external force like illness, rather than to the individual's own inappropriate behaviors, mental health professionals encourage the individual not to take any responsibility for his or her actions, when in fact it is avoidance of problems that brought the person to this state originally. This lack of responsibility is made worse by hospitalization, where the individual immediately falls into a "sick role," exhibiting the behavior patterns of a classic neurotic or psychotic (as he or she is diagnosed), rather than learning to cope with problems effectively. Szasz's idea that abnormal behavior is a result of "problems in living" suggests that therapy should consist primarily of learning how to deal successfully with one's life and one's environment.

The idea that mental disorder is not a disease that someone else will cure, but rather something for which the individual is responsible, has serious implications for our view of the causes and treatment of psychopathology, and the relation of abnormal behavior to society as a whole. One of the most important considerations is the legal use of the term *mentally ill.* A person so judged is usually relieved of all responsibility for a criminal act, primarily because of our general belief that emotional disorder is an illness, and therefore something over which a person has no control. Yet, if in fact most of the people we say are mentally ill do not have brain tumors or central nervous disorders, but have simply failed to behave according to the rules of our society, how can we continue to "let them off" on the grounds that they have no responsibility for their acts?

Thus we can see that the medical model, despite its usefulness in categorizing disorders and establishing modes of treatment, raises many questions and issues that are still to be resolved.

The Cultural Model

However you choose to define it, abnormality means one thing for you and members of your society, and something entirely different for other people. Although almost all societies can distinguish between abnormal and normal behavior, their norms, or boundary lines, are most certainly different from ours. Why? Because the idea of abnormality is based on the fact that each culture follows a number of norms approved by the greatest number of people in that culture. If most people have a common type of dance, manner of speech, or way of behaving, those actions are declared normal. If you behave in a way that does not follow the norms of your society, your actions will be labeled

A WATCHED POT NEVER SPOILS

Anthropologists have reported emotional disturbances of far-ranging varieties. Arieti and Meth (1959) recall that "among the islanders of Dobu (Melanesia), no sane woman leaves her cooking pots unguarded for fear of being poisoned. To us this behavior would indicate paranoia. Among some Eskimo tribes, the mother accepts the killer of her son in her son's stead. Among the Papuans it is traditional for an uncle and nephew (mother's brother and son) to practice homosexuality" (page 560). What is "normal" and what is "abnormal" clearly varies a great deal from culture to culture.

abnormal. Since abnormality is culturally defined, abnormal behavior in one society might be approved in another. Also, when a society's norms change, what was once said to be abnormal behavior might now be called normal.

The example of homosexuality shows how the dividing line between normal and abnormal is continually shifting. The Bible says, "If a man also lieth down with a man as he lieth with a woman, both of them have committed an abomination. They shall verily be put to death." Yet, in ancient Greece, homosexuality was tolerated and even encouraged. Until recently homosexuality was considered abnormal in American society, but now it is becoming more acceptable. For 23 years homosexuality was listed as a mental disorder in the American Psychiatric Association's official diagnostic manual. In 1974, however, the association voted to remove that label. "For a mental condition to be considered a psychiatric disorder," the board explained, "it should either regularly cause emotional distress or regularly be associated with generalized impairment of social functioning; homosexuality does not meet these criteria."

Disorders in one culture may have no exact counterpart in another culture. There are reports (Benedict and Jacks, 1954), for

example, that some nonliterate societies have a high incidence of pathological aggression, assault, and hostility, and an infrequent occurrence of depression and self-blame. In technologically less-advanced societies, pathology may take the form of action and explosive irrationality. In our culture, the same problems would be expressed as thought disorders. In other words, we are more likely to remain rational and become depressed rather than attack others. In Amok (Malaysia), for example, a person suddenly goes berserk and assaults or kills anyone in his path (hence the expression "to run amok"). Rarely in our culture does the schizophrenic destroy innocent bystanders in a sudden outburst of rage. Further, such behavior would not have the understanding or implied social sanction that it has in other cultures.

It is quite apparent that what is considered normal is closely connected to a society's definition of good behavior. And these definitions of good behavior may be applied differently to different groups within a particular society, such as the two sexes. For example, Inge Broverman and her coworkers (1970) administered questionnaires to 79 clinicians (psychologists, psychiatrists, social workers) of both sexes. They were asked to describe either (a) a healthy, mature, socially competent adult, (b) a man with these characteristics, or (c) a woman with these characteristics. It turned out that the descriptions of the "healthy, mature" man and woman differed from one another and that these differences paralleled stereotypical sex-role differences (see Chapter 13). That is, "healthy" men were described as more aggressive, more independent, less emotional, and more dominant than "healthy" women. Furthermore, those clinicians asked to describe a "healthy" adult gave descriptions that resembled those given for

LOCAL DISORDERS

Certain cultures have psychological disorders that are not found anywhere else. *Latah* is most often an affliction of middle-aged and elderly women in Malaysia, who become seclusive and unusually fearful after a sudden fright. They may mimic and pantomime the words and actions of others, even if the other persons are irritated to the point of retaliation. A host of other disorders peculiar to a particular society include *piblokto* (a compulsive disorder seen among Eskimos living in polar regions), *ufufunyane* (attacks of shouting, loss of vision, and loss of consciousness among some South African tribes), and *windigo* (a psychosis among Algonquin Indians in which a starved man believes he is being controlled by some supernatural being that has an insatiable craving for human flesh).

the "healthy" male rather than those given for the "healthy" female. This double standard of mental health stems from the acceptance by some clinicians of the idea that mental health consists of good adjustments to one's culture. For a woman to be considered psychologically healthy, she must accept the behavioral norm for her sex and adjust to her role even when it requires her to be a dependent, docile, unambitious, or childlike person.

THE PROBLEMS OF CLASSIFICATION

In Chapters 16 and 17 we will be using the diagnostic categories and labels from the medical model to talk about maladaptive behaviors. It is important to remember that a label is merely a name—and not an explanation—for a particular type of behavior. The diagnostic categories are useful, because they allow psychologists to communicate in an agreed-upon fashion about abnormal behavior, but psychologists are the first to admit the many limitations of such classification.

For one thing, people do not fall neatly into diagnostic categories. A person labeled schizophrenic, for example, does not necessarily display all the symptoms we will discuss under schizophrenia. He would also be quite likely to display symptoms that could be classed in other diagnostic categories. For example, Zigler and Phillips (1961) examined case records of 793 manic-depressive, schizophrenic, neurotic, or character-disordered patients to determine how frequently any of 35 symptoms occurred. What they found was that the same symptoms appeared in many of the categories and that the relationship between individual symptoms and a particular category was actually quite small.

Many other researchers have investigated the *reliability* of diagnostic judgements—that is, the extent to which experts agree about the particular diagnostic category a person should be placed in or, indeed, whether he or she should be placed in any category at all. After reviewing these studies, Ullman and Krasner (1975) conclude that although reliability tends to be better than chance for the major categories, it remains disturbingly low for work which has so great an impact on peoples' lives.

A striking illustration of this lack of reliability was provided by David Rosenhan (1973) in a sequel to his mental hospital study (see Box 1). Staff members at research and teaching hospitals who had heard and disbelieved the results of the first experiment were told that at some time during the next three months one or more "fake" patients would seek admission to their hospital. Each staff member was therefore on guard to detect any person posing as a patient. In fact, no "fake" patients attempted to gain admission to the hospitals. When the staff members recorded their opinions about 193 new admissions, 41 persons were thought to be fake patients by at least one staff

member, and 23 patients were considered suspect by at least one psychiatrist.

Labeling Madness

Related to these problems of classification is the fact that a diagnosis (or label) can then have major effects on how the patient is viewed. Even if the diagnosis is incorrect, it can come to take on a reality all its own (Scheff, 1975). In Chapter 7 we saw that the labels people use affect the way they perceive their environment. Labels can also affect the way we see other people, such as those who are labeled "insane" or are placed in a specific diagnostic category. For example, Rosenhan (1973) reports that once his pseudopatients (see Box 1) were labeled "schizophrenic" their history (which was given accurately to the hospital personnel) and behavior came to be viewed in schizophrenic or "sick" terms. The pseudopatients took copious notes and, in fact, were worried that the hospital personnel would catch on that they were observers and not really schizophrenic. Instead, the personnel viewed the note-taking as "writing behavior" and interpreted it as another aspect of their illness! As Rosenhan put it, "Given that the patient is in the hospital, he must be psychologically disturbed. And given that he is disturbed, continual writing must be a behavioral manifestation of that disturbance, perhaps as a

DON'T GO ON THE WEEKEND

Mendel and Rapport (1968) examined clinicians' decisions on whether to hospitalize patients. They found that (1) social workers tended to hospitalize fewer patients than did psychiatrists or psychologists; (2) hospitalization was related to the patient's previous hospital history rather than to the severity of current symptoms; and (3) patients seen during evenings and weekends were twice as likely to be hospitalized as patients seen during the normal work day. The clinicians were unaware that their decisions were influenced by this "weekend" impulse to hospitalize patients. Obviously many factors unrelated to the patient influence whether and to what extent he or she will be viewed as disordered.

subset of the compulsive behaviors that are sometimes correlated with schizophrenia" (page 61).

A study by Ellen Langer and Robert Abelson (1974) showed how the label "patient" can itself prime therapists to see more maladjustment. The researchers showed a videotaped interview to a number of psychoanalytically-oriented therapists. They told half the therapists that the man being interviewed was a "job applicant" and the other half that he was a "patient." The therapists were then asked to fill out a questionnaire evaluating the man in the interview. Those therapists who were told that the man was a "job applicant" described him with such terms as "attractive and conventional looking," "candid and innovative," "ordinary, straightforward," "upstanding, middle-class citizen

Box 2

The Prevalence of Disorder

Conservative estimates indicate that at least one person in every ten (20,000,000 in the United States) will some time during life have a mental or emotional illness that could benefit from professional help. On any one day, there are three quarters of a million persons under psychiatric care in hospitals. Mental illness occurs at all ages. Estimates of the number of mentally ill children range from 500,000 to as many as 1,000,000.

The seriousness of emotional disturbance in our society became particularly apparent during World War II when one out of every five of our young men (nearly five million) was rejected for military service because of "mental illness." Of one million additional men accepted for service but later discharged with a disability, 43 percent had been diagnosed as having neuropsychiatric problems.

The frequency of emotional disturbance in our culture was even more dramatically demonstrated in the Midtown Manhattan Study conducted by Srole and his colleagues (1962). In this research, residents in a section of New York City were randomly sampled. Over 1,600 persons filled out a detailed questionnaire concerning the severity (absent, mild, moderate, or serious) of their past and present physical and mental symptoms. The researchers found that fewer than one in four persons was "well" and nearly one in five was "incapacitated" by emotional disorder.

Since 1880 our population has increased more than four times, and the number of hospitalized mental patients has multiplied 18 times. This steady increase has more than matched the expansion of hospital facilities, and today we calculate the size of the problem in the many millions.

The frequency and kinds of symptoms we see today are, of course, not identical to those of the past. The members of our society are better educated, less restricted in sexual and other expressive outlets, and more sophisticated about psychological disorder. Our society has evolved and changed, and so have the psychological symptoms we display.

The occurrence of new cases of emotional disturbance during a fixed period of time (incidence) and the total number of active cases in the population at any one time (prevalence) must not be confused. Thus, figures on *prevalence* may remain the same over a two-year span of time. This would hide the fact that, in any one year, there may be a great many new cases but also an equally high rate of cure.

It is difficult to decide which estimates of *incidence* (or the frequency of mental disorder) are the most reliable. An "official" view provided by the U.S. Department of Health, Education and Welfare (1967) reports that there has been an overall drop in total patient population. This is a consequence of an increase in release rate despite the growing admission rate.

What all these statistics tell us is that regardless of the debate about the definition of abnormality, there are a lot of people who suffer a great deal as a result of psychological problems and the issue of mental disturbance is a serious concern for all of us.

type, but more like a hard hat," "probably of lower- or blue-collar class origins," and "middle-class protestant ethic orientation; fairly open—somewhat ingenious." Therapists who saw the same interview but were told the man was a "patient" described him as a "tight, defensive person . . . conflict over homosexuality," "dependent, passive-aggressive," "frightened of his own aggressive impulses," "fairly bright but tries to seem brighter than he is . . . impulsivity shows through his rigidity," "passive, dependent type," and "considerable hostility, repressed or channeled." Thus, the labels given to the man in the interview ("patient" versus "job applicant") had a large impact on how he was viewed.

One of the implications of this study is that once individuals are labeled "sick" it can be very difficult for them ever to get "well" again, since people will continue to view them as sick and to treat them that way. Similar problems are encountered by other people given labels by society—"mentally retarded" and "criminal," for example. Even after a person has done time for his or her crimes, the label "ex-con" follows the individual around.

Self-Fulfilling Prophecy

Such labeling and categorization can also lead to a self-fulfilling prophecy, in which the label, accurate or inaccurate, tends to produce the behavior it represents and to alter the individual's self-image. If, for example, a man is labeled "schizophrenic," it is likely that he will develop the behaviors associated with schizophrenia—even if he did not have them at first. Being told he is schizophrenic causes the individual to perceive himself as such, while his therapist and family may unconsciously treat him in a way that brings about their expectations. We saw in Chapter 1 how an experimenter's expectations can influence the result of an experiment, and the same thing is likely to occur when the therapist places expectations of abnormal behavior on a client. George Kelly (1955) has pointed out that people who read a lot of psychology are also likely to label themselves—and then to act accordingly. Once such a person has decided which malady he suffers from, Kelly notes, he is likely "to display all of the symptoms in whatever book he had read, even if he had to practice them diligently" (page 366). When you read about different psychological disorders in Chapter 16, you should be wary of labeling yourself in such a way.

As early as 1859, mental health workers were suggesting that classification systems were useless and that progress in the field would be impossible unless all categories were dropped. Diagnostic labels, as we have seen, do have serious problems, and as a result psychologists are using them more carefully and tentatively than they used to. Nevertheless, certain diagnostic categories—such as the neuroses and psychoses we will be discussing in the next chapter—are commonly used, are fairly well agreed upon, and can be of considerable value in decisions about treatment. Until some demonstrably better system comes along, we will continue to use them. As we do, however, it is important that we keep in mind the fact that a diagnostic label is not necessarily the last word about a person and that we remain aware of the dangers of confusing the label with the ultimate reality.

SUMMARY

1. Throughout history people have had different ideas about what constitutes abnormality and what causes it. Although the early Greeks had a highly enlightened view of mental disorder, people in the Middle Ages believed it was caused by possession of the devil and treated disturbed persons as witches.
2. The first mental institutions, established in Europe during the Renaissance, were extremely unpleasant. In the late eighteenth century Philippe Pinel brought about humane reforms in the treatment of the mentally ill.
3. Mental hospitals in America underwent reform in the mid-nineteenth century, but the changes led to the herding together of all kinds of "deviants" into isolated insane asylums. Today's mental hospitals are a major improvement and are medically and scientifically oriented. However, Rosenhan's study involving admission of "pseudopatients" to several mental hospitals showed that this current medical approach is still far from ideal.
4. Statistics on the prevalence and incidence of mental disorders in the United States indicate that a significant portion of the population suffers from some type of emotional illness requiring professional help and sometimes hospitalization.
5. Four major approaches are currently used to define abnormal behavior. The *statistical* approach defines normality in terms of what the majority of the members of a society are like. The *adequacy* approach focuses on people's ability to adjust to or cope with their environment. Both of these approaches have a number of drawbacks.
6. According to the highly influential *medical model*, mental disorders should be seen as illnesses, with symptoms, treatments, and cures. Szasz and other critics of the medical model say that it absolves the disturbed person from responsibility for his or her condition. Finally, the *cultural* approach suggests that abnormality is defined in terms of the norms of the society or cultural group in which the behavior occurs—what is normal in one culture may be abnormal in another.

7. Although the use of diagnostic categories provides a convenient way of talking about disorder, it must be remembered that a classification is a label, not an explanation, and that most individuals do not fit perfectly into any specific category.

8. The labels given to patients can have major effects on how they view themselves and on how others view them, even if such labels are totally incorrect. Furthermore, through the process of *self-fulfilling prophecy,* labels tend to produce the behavior they represent and to alter the labeled person's self-image.

Alcoholism

...problem drinking drains the economy of $15 billion a year.

Alcoholics are most often classified as persons suffering from personality disorders or inadequacies. Men and women with personality disturbances may adopt a "style of living" that, unfortunately, inflicts discomfort and misery on innocent others as well as on themselves. Their attempts to cope with life are all too often destructive and self-defeating.

An estimated 80 million Americans drink alcohol, and about 5 million of them are alcoholics (Chafetz, 1967). Alcohol may shorten our life span anywhere from ten to twelve years. It is blamed for half the highway deaths each year, and problem drinking drains the economy of $15 billion a year. So, why doesn't everyone stop drinking? We don't stop partly because we like it and partly because it is one of the few drugs that can be used as a thirst quencher, a way of gracious living, a social lubricant, a food, a medicine, an intoxicant, a psychedelic agent, a symbol of being grown up, and a way to defy authority.

Alcohol alters our psychological state in an odd manner. In small amounts it is a depressant that reduces the effective expression of your impulses, needs, and anxieties. It relaxes the guards that watch your behavior, but after that point it scrambles your sensations and perceptions. How fast this scrambling effect takes place depends how much you weigh, how much you move around when drinking, what kind of mood you are in, and what you had to eat before you started bending your elbow. You will get drunk quicker when you are celebrating than when you are trying to forget. And you will fall over faster if you haven't eaten all day.

Once you discover that liquor will bolster your self-confidence and ease the pain and tension of daily living, you have taken the first step toward alcoholism. The next step involves drinking more heavily and now and then having "blackouts" in which you can't remember all the details of what you did or said at the party. Before long, you may be hoisting your glass until you find you can't say no to the next drink. You start to go on "benders" that last days or weeks. You are hungover all the time. You don't eat much any more since it tends to kill off the blurred state you have been in for some time, and you don't give much of a damn about what people are telling you. Without a few shots, you don't feel normal. By now you care about booze more than anything else, and you are near the end of the line.

When you think of an alcoholic, you are most likely to picture the classic derelict wino described by Regestein and Howe (1972): The dirty, un-

Box I-1

The Executive Lush

If you are a corporate executive and you regularly have so many martinis at lunch that you are wiped out for the rest of the afternoon, you may qualify as an executive lush. Do you miss a lot of days on the job? Do you have the status symbol of a built-in bar in your office? Do you come to work hungover and in pain? Congratulations! You *are* an executive alcoholic.

You will cost your company a small fortune in lost time, botched deals, bad decisions, and inefficiency. But if you get a loyal executive secretary to cover for you, the company won't fire you for a long time. According to the National Council on Alcoholism, 45 percent of the alcoholics in this country have professional or managerial positions. The typical alcoholic has been at his job 12 years; he's between the ages of 35 and 54; and his alcoholism has been present but unrecognized for years.

shaven, bleary-eyed, vulgar, stumbling wino who is crushed like a grape between his feelings of loneliness and his terrible fear of being hurt by people. Only when drinking can he tolerate interpersonal relationships. He staggers through life shy, guilty, ashamed, hostile and fearful toward authority. He is most often in his early 50s. He quit school by the tenth grade, was dishonorably discharged from the army, has been in and out of jails, has dropped out of Alcoholics Anonymous, and has lost track of his family. Not a pretty picture. But he makes up only a tiny percentage of the alcoholics in this country.

Theories of Alcoholism

A lot of us drink, but only some of us are alcoholics. Although psychologists have hammered out a variety of theories to explain the difference, we still haven't been able to explain alcoholism (Buss, 1960). Biological theorists have looked for something wrong in the brain, the glands, or the body's metabolism, but no reliable evidence has been found to support this idea. Cultural theorists are fascinated by the fact that there are national and racial differences in alcoholism. They feel differences in style of life must account for the variations.

Alcoholism is viewed by psychodynamic theorists as an exceptionally complex problem with as many patterns of drinking as there are individual alcoholics. To them, alcoholism can be a symptom of any number of psychological disorders. Psychodynamic theorists suggest that the psychological histories of alcoholics may have certain features in common. These might include:

Inability to Handle Tension in a Mature Manner. The potential alcoholic easily feels rejected by others, retreats from conflicts, avoids making decisions, and cannot tolerate tension for long periods of time.

Heavy-drinking parents raise heavy-drinking children.

Deep Dependency on Other People. Since others seem more capable or stronger, alcoholics retreat to passivity and seek to be cared for and protected by others. If situations that demand independence cannot be avoided, they use alcohol to escape tension.

Severe Unexpressed Hostility to Close Friends. When the need to be dependent on others goes unfulfilled, resentment and hostility may appear in indirect and disguised ways. Consciously, alcoholics insist that they love those who are closest to them. Unconsciously, their behavior indicates the opposite is true.

Egocentricity. The immaturity and self-centeredness of alcoholics is most apparent in the degree to which they feel sorry for themselves and think people pick on them.

To the learning theorist, you learn to drink as your parents do. Heavy-drinking parents raise heavy-drinking children. If your parents don't drink at all, it is probable you won't either (Chafetz, 1967). The behaviorist believes, however, that what is learned can be unlearned.

Conditioned reflex therapy, or aversion therapy, is credited with success among alcoholics. The association of avoidance responses (via drugs) with alcohol connects drinking with unpleasant consequences. When a patient who has taken the drug Antabuse drinks alcohol, he experiences headache, dizziness, chest pain, nausea, air hunger, and vomiting within minutes. The likelihood remains, though, that the dedicated alcoholic will simply stop taking the drug once he is comfortably seated in a bar.

The Family

The typical alcoholic is usually pictured as a man with a long-suffering wife and with children who, as ragged waifs, call at the local bar wailing "Father, dear Father, come home with me now." Of course, these stereotypes bear no relation to reality. Many father-husbands are alcoholics, but so are many mother-wives, and family members often contribute to the alcohol problem.

Joan Jackson (1956) describes the stages of family life that often follow the realization of an alcoholic parent.†

Stage 1. Attempts to Deny the Problem Although excessive drinking happens only occasionally at first, it begins to put strain on the marriage, and both try to pretend these drinking episodes are normal. ("Everyone gets drunk once in

†*From Joan Jackson, "The Adjustment of the Family to Alcoholism,"* Journal of Marriage and Family Living, *Nov. 1956, p. 361–369. © 1956 by National Council on Family Relations. Reprinted by permission.*

a while.") Situations in which it might happen again are avoided. ("Let's stay home this New Year's Eve.")

Stage 2. Attempts to Eliminate the Problem The family begins to withdraw from social contact to keep the drinking problem from becoming common gossip. The truth is kept from the children and the boss. An all-out attempt is now made to control the drinking, but it doesn't work.

Stage 3. Disorganization "What's the use?" describes this stage as the problem appears permanent. The family starts to come apart and stops trying to understand the alcoholic or to keep the drinking a secret.

Stage 4. Attempts to Reorganize in Spite of Problems This is the stage at which the family becomes stabilized. The wife takes over her alcoholic husband's role, and he is treated like a difficult child who simply won't behave himself. This reorganization is almost impossible to maintain for long. The husband's drinking escalates, and he may be fired from his job, put in jail, or hospitalized. In the reverse case, of course, the husband assumes the maternal duties and tries to cope as best he can.

Stage 5. Efforts to Escape the Problem The decision to give up leads to divorce once the spouse can face feelings about deserting a sick person. The decision is made easier if the husband has become abusive, destructive, or violent.

Stage 6. Reorganization of the Family If successful, this stage allows the family to sort itself out, redivide responsibilities, and begin a new pattern of living together.

It is unnecessary to add gruesome detail to the story of excessive drinking. The destructiveness is apparent. Therapeutic attempts of great variety have been used to eliminate problem drinking, but, on the whole, they have met with only modest success. The best known approach to helping those who can't handle alcohol is Alcoholics Anonymous.

The best known approach to helping those who can't handle alcohol is Alcoholics Anonymous.

Alcoholics Anonymous

The basic principles of Alcoholics Anonymous are that only an alcoholic can help another alcoholic, that psychiatric and other treatment is usually unsuccessful, and that alcoholics can manage to lead relatively normal lives by banding together in a spirit of mutual help and understanding. Most important, an alcoholic must never again take even one drink. Alcoholics Anonymous maintains that 50 percent of all alcoholics coming into AA get sober and stay that way. Twenty-five percent have one or two slips before they see the light, and the other 25 percent are either psychotic or not alcoholic at all.

These statistics are probably generous estimates of the success of AA, but the fact remains that this idea has worked where other approaches have failed. AA branches are found in prisons, hospitals, and towns of all sizes. The only requirement for membership is a desire to stop drinking.

AA members assert that there's nothing wrong with alcoholics except alcohol, and all the alcoholic has to do is to stay away from the first drink. They regard alcoholism as a physical disease, not a mental one, even though their sessions resemble public confessional. Psychotherapists part company with the AA program when it insists that the alcoholic is free of emotional problems and that the drug is a *cause* rather than a *symptom* of deeper problems. Therapists insist that alcoholics will be cured only when they gain insight into why they can't control their drinking in the first place. Perhaps AA works very well for some people, but it doesn't work at all for others. Half of those who come to the meetings drop out of the program in the first month. We must suppose that those who stop attending and keep on drinking would be classified by AA as either psychotic or not alcoholic at all, but such classification is of doubtful accuracy.

Controlled Drinking

In recent years, psychologists have tried a new tack with alcoholics, in which alcoholics are

Some psychologists believe they can teach alcoholics how to drink in moderation.

encouraged to drink and are taught how to drink in moderation. So far, the results of "controlled social drinking" are encouraging: there is evidence that alcholics can be taught to drink normally and can maintain normal social drinking over a period of time (Lloyd and Salzberg, 1975).

Unlike AA's theory of alcoholism as a physical disease, the controlled drinking approach sees problem drinking as a learned pattern of behavior. Alcoholics possibly have learned undesirable patterns of drinking or they may have never learned the socially appropriate way to drink. They may drink excessively in response to certain difficult situations, which vary from person to person.

Psychologists may be able to help alcoholics by teaching them how to drink in moderation. In one recent study, Sobell and Sobell (1973) achieved a significant success with a group of alcoholics. They took 40 chronic male alcoholics in a California state hospital and taught half of them controlled drinking. The other half received conventional treatments such as AA and group therapy. A year after treatment, the controlled drinkers had been functioning well (not drinking or else drinking moderately) more than 70 percent of the time, while the other group functioned well only 35 percent of the time.

How did the Sobells go about teaching alcoholics controlled drinking? They used a variety of behavior therapy techniques (see Chapter 17) including discussion, role-playing, and assertiveness training. In addition, participants were videotaped while drunk and then shown the scenes when sober.

Controlled drinking may not work for everyone, and the suggestion that it works at all remains controversial. For some alcoholics, total abstinence of the sort advocated by AA may be the only way to regain control over their drinking problem. For others, however, controlled drinking may be an effective way to learn how to have a drink without letting the drink get the better of them.

Summary

1. One-tenth of all Americans who drink alcohol are alcoholics, and those who abuse alcohol may shorten their lives by ten to twelve years.
2. In small quantities alcohol is a depressant. In larger amounts it starts to confuse one's sensations and perceptions and may cause "blackouts."
3. The "Bowery bum" picture of the alcoholic is actually true for only a tiny percentage of the alcoholics in America.
4. There are different theories about alcoholism, but no one has yet been able to explain why some of us who drink are not alcoholics, while others of us are. Psychodynamic theorists list traits they see as characteristic of alcoholism—inability to handle tension, excessive dependency, unexpressed hostility, and egocentricity. A high correlation between heavy-drinking parents and heavy-drinking children exists.
5. The presence of an alcoholic mother or father in a home is very disruptive; Joan Jackson has identified six stages a family goes through in trying to cope with an alcoholic parent.
6. Alcoholics Anonymous, according to its own reports, has been highly successful in rehabilitating alcoholics. AA's program is based on the idea that alcoholism is a physical disease and that the person must totally abstain in order to be cured.
7. Using the techniques of behavior therapy, psychologists have found that they can teach some alcoholics "controlled social drinking" as a way of unlearning their habit.

Psychological Disorder

CHAPTER

16

Psychological Disorder

In Chapter 15 we emphasized the difficulties involved in defining and categorizing mental illness. We noted that what is considered mental illness or abnormality in one culture may be quite normal behavior in another. And we mentioned those critics, such as Thomas Szasz, who believe that the whole notion of "mental illness" is a myth—an overused metaphor. We don't want you to forget about these difficulties and problems in defining mental illness. Nevertheless, we must use some sort of organized method for talking about the sorts of psychological problems that plague so many millions of people in this country. So it is useful, for the purposes of this chapter, to adopt the medical model—upon which current classifications of psychological disorder are based—in describing various psychological problems and in reporting what is currently known about their causes. At the least, the diagnostic system that is commonly employed provides a convenient framework for examining the various emotional disorders that undeniably cause many people pain and suffering.

NEUROSES AND PSYCHOSES

A distinction is usually made between two broad categories of disorder; *neuroses* and *psychoses.* Neuroses are relatively mild psychological disorders and may often be seen as extensions of the psychological problems that all of us occasionally experience. Neuroses are characterized by anxiety, an inability to cope effectively with challenges, and difficulty in interpersonal relationships. Those afflicted with a neurosis may experience a great deal of stress, but they remain able to function fairly well in their environment. In contrast, people suffering from psychoses have for the most part lost contact with reality. Psychotics may experience delusions, hallucinations, and loss of control over their feelings and actions. The large majority of people confined to mental hospitals are diagnosed as psychotics.

To describe all the varieties of neuroses and psychoses that psychiatrists and psychologists have identified—not to mention the many disorders that fall somewhere between neurosis and psychosis—would require an entire book of its own. In this chapter, however, we will focus on three of the most common types of psychological disorder: neuroses (including anxiety states, phobias, and obsessive-compulsive reactions), depression (which spans the range from normal through neurotic to psychotic) and schizophrenia (which is the most common type of psychosis).

NEUROSIS

The basis for all forms of neurosis is believed to be anxiety. Therefore, we will discuss anxiety and neurosis together.

Anxiety

Anxiety is that vague, unpleasant feeling that suggests something bad is about to happen. It is so closely related to fear that there is no sharp dividing line between the two. In general, fear is a reaction to something specific, whereas anxiety remains vague and has no immediately apparent cause. You can fear a car that has careened wildly into your lane on a freeway, but you suffer from anxiety if you are generally apprehensive about driving in traffic. Physiologically, anxiety and fear are quite similar (see Chapter 10). They include the same physical symptoms, such as sweating, difficulty in sleeping, and heightened heart rate. The difference is that with anxiety, one doesn't know what one is afraid of.

Anxiety sometimes expresses itself in sudden overwhelming episodes called *anxiety attacks.* One person described an attack as "a knot in my stomach, a feeling of hot flashes and warmth through my entire body, tightening of the muscles, a lump in my throat, and a constant feeling that I am going to throw up." Another person said, "I noticed that my hands began to sweat, my legs crumpled under me, I saw white spots floating before my eyes. I felt like getting up and running" (Sarnoff, 1957).

Richard Lazarus (1974) describes the case of a college student who suffered periodic anxiety attacks. The student complained that he was extremely jittery and uneasy, that he

couldn't sleep, that he couldn't concentrate on his studies, and that his stomach hurt. The campus psychologist noted that these anxiety attacks occurred just before a long holiday when the student would have to return home to his family. According to the student, he looked forward to these occasions at home. Yet when the end of the semester approached, and with it the prospect of another trip home, the student once again experienced waves of anxiety. It finally came out in sessions with the psychologist that the student's home environment was filled with conflict—a fact the student was able to deny as long as he was away at school. Because the student was unable to acknowledge to himself his negative feelings toward his parents, he tried to hide them. But whenever the prospect of experiencing the reality of his family situation came close, anxiety over these buried feelings gave him away. This student was suffering from what Freud called *neurotic anxiety*—anxiety caused by the fear that buried impulses will rise to the surface and cause one to do something that society considers wrong.

Phobias

Neuroses are frequently marked by *phobias*—intense fears of particular objects or activities that seem out of proportion to the real dangers involved. Everyone is frightened by what he or she only partly comprehends. These fears range from an intense dread of immediately present dangers (such as fire) to uneasiness about painful events that are possible, if not really probable. As Kessler (1966) points out, a school-age child may express a dislike for dogs and be uneasy around them. This may be quite normal. But when the child becomes preoccupied with the possibility of encountering a dog and lives in a constant state of anticipatory anxiety, his or her feeling goes beyond simple fear and borders on phobia.

The persistent, irrational, morbid fear called phobia is so common in the early years that it has been designated the "normal neurosis" of childhood. As children grow up they tend to leave these fears behind. Nevertheless, many adults suffer from phobias. Among the most common adult phobias are *agoraphobia* (fear of open places), *claustrophobia* (fear of closed, cramped places), and *acrophobia* (fear of heights). Such phobias can be quite debilitating—a person with agoraphobia, for example, might refuse to go out of the house. It is easy to see how each of these phobias might be related to other problems that characterize neurosis. Since people with such phobias cannot feel comfortable in many places, they are likely to feel inadequate and tense and to have problems with interpersonal relations.

What accounts for the development of phobias? According to the psychoanalytic view, phobias are symptoms of the repression of unacceptable basic urges (see Chapter 14). When repression is effective, phobic symptoms need not exist. But when repression fails, the anxiety is displaced to an undeserving object, person, or situation. As a result, harmless objects like

---

WATCH OUT FOR THE PEANUT BUTTER!

It is possible, at least in theory, to develop an extreme fear or phobia of practically anything. And when you do, rest assured the psychological wordsmiths already have a word for it. Here are some of the more esoteric phobias (Wallechinsky and Wallace, 1975):

anthophobia: fear of flowers
belonophobia: fear of pins and needles
decidophobia: fear of making decisions
ergophobia: fear of work
gephydrophobia: fear of crossing bridges
iatrophobia: fear of doctors
ombrophobia: fear of rain
taphophobia: fear of being buried alive
trichophobia: fear of hair
and would you believe—
arachibutyrophobia: fear of peanut butter sticking to the roof of your mouth

---

snakes or places like heights or open spaces become objects of enormous fear and are anxiously avoided. In this way the phobia protects the individual from recognizing the true nature of the emotional problem. It may protect the person from the conscious awareness of an intolerable impulse.

The classic example of phobia was the case of little Hans, a five-year-old boy who lived in terror of horses. Hans' phobia, according to Freud, was not so much fear of horses as fear of his own frightening impulses. First Hans repressed his wish to attack his father. Then, fearing the father might somehow learn of this wish and punish him horribly, Hans "solved" the problem by fearing horses instead of his father. Since Hans both loved and hated his father, he also resolved his mixed feelings. He now could hate horses while loving his father.

In contrast to psychoanalytic theory, the behavior view contends that phobias are learned—the person learns to connect intense fear responses with otherwise neutral objects or situations. Yates (1970), for example, notes that little Hans experienced a series of traumatic exposures to horses during the time his phobia developed. Yates suggests that these experiences with horses provide a more reasonable explanation of Hans's phobia than the explanation provided by Freud.

The behaviorists' version of little Hans is Watson and Rayner's (1920) "Little Albert." As we noted in Chapter 10, the eleven-month-old Albert acquired a phobia as a result of classical conditioning. The experimenters had struck a steel bar near Albert's head whenever a white rat was placed in his room. The noise scared Albert, and the sequence was repeated until the rats scared Albert, too. As the experiment continued, Albert developed a fear of all furry things, of wool, and even of cotton. The experimenters had thus conditioned Albert to have a phobia of furry things.

One limitation of the behavioral approach to phobia is that there are many reports of phobias that have developed without any specific frightening experience. Many people with severe fears of snakes, germs, airplanes, or heights report that they have had no particular unpleasant experiences with these objects or situations. And many people who have had a bad automobile accident or fall do not become phobic about these situations. Thus, the behavioral model doesn't provide a complete account of phobia (Davison and Neale, 1974).

There is also some evidence that certain people are more likely to develop phobias than others. These are "jumpy" people whose autonomic nervous systems are easily aroused by a wide range of stimuli. Such a biological tendency to be susceptible to phobia is likely to be hereditary to some extent.

THE NUMBER 13

"The case illustrates particularly well the expansion of a phobia. The patient began by staying in bed on the thirteenth day of the month so that he would not come in contact with calendars and newspaper dates. Soon he discovered that 'twenty-seventh' contained thirteen letters, and he was condemned to bed two days each month. He next began going to work by a roundabout route to avoid the thirteen-letter sign, 'Peter Robinson,' that hung prominently on the direct route. Presently he experienced uneasiness when people said, 'Oh, good morning,' or when they said, 'Good afternoon' without the "Oh" that would have given the greeting a safe fifteen letters. He began hopping over the thirteenth step in a flight of stairs, counting his own footsteps, counting the streets he passed, until finally he had time for nothing but avoiding the number thirteen." (White, 1964, pp. 257–58).

Neurotic Defenses

In addition to general feelings of inadequacy and difficulty in coping with life's problems, neuroses often involve other specific symptoms. Phobia is one such symptom. Others include physical complaints that apparently have no real basis, and repetitious behavior that the person seems to lack control over. These symptoms are believed to result from various *defense mechanisms* that people use to defend against anxiety. As we saw in Chapter 14, Freud's personality theory emphasized people's defenses against sexual or aggressive impulses that are too threatening to think about. Instead, one denies these impulses, overreacts to them, sees them as being other people's problems, or in some other way evades them.

Learning theorists also stress the importance of such defenses, although they see them as learned responses to threatening situations and do not focus on sexual and aggressive impulses. According to learning theorists, neurosis can occur when an individual comes to find that a particular situation is anxiety provoking. Rather than deal directly with the stress, the individual tries to avoid it altogether by performing some behavior that prevents the situation from occurring again. The relief of anxiety that results from this avoidance behavior is reinforcing. Such avoidance behaviors are extremely difficult to get rid of because the individual never gets a chance to find out that the threat being avoided no longer exists.

The use of psychological defenses is not in itself a sign of disorder. All of us have our defenses, and we rely on them to get through the threats, conflicts, and frustrations that are a part of life. For example, some of us make use of "obsessive" defenses like making lists of things to do every day to keep us from getting confused or disorganized. Others of us are habitual "deniers," and we often will not admit to ourselves real problems or threats. Denial is a very common response, for example, to the news that a loved one is dying. These defenses typically operate unconsciously, so that we are not aware that we are using them. Defenses become "neurotic" only when they deny or distort reality to such a point that they make it difficult to function effectively.

Phobias, for example, make use of an *avoidance* defense. A person using this defense unconsciously decides that particular objects or situations are threatening and wards off anxiety by scrupulously avoiding these situations. This would be a good tactic if it worked. Unfortunately, as we have seen, phobias often extend to large ranges of situations and prove to be quite distressing in their own right.

COUNTERPHOBIA

One way to deal with phobic feelings is to take defensive (counterphobic) measures rather than avoid the feared object. Thus some adults indulge vigorously in precisely those behaviors they dread most, even though they may be unaware of the source of their fascination with such actions. Cameron (1963) describes this as a form of "reactive courage." Those who fear heights may climb mountains. Those who fear speed may drive racing cars. And those who suffer from claustrophobia may devote their lives to spelunking—the exploration of caves.

Obsessive-Compulsive Disorders

Obsessive-compulsive disorders reflect another pattern of defenses. Instead of avoiding the feared object or denying its existence, the obsessive-compulsive person attempts to master the threat by repeatedly engaging in behavior connected with it. Obsessive-compulsive reactions involve two sets of related patterns. First, the person keeps thinking certain thoughts over and over and is unable to put those thoughts out of his or her head (the obsession). Second, seemingly against his or her will, the individual engages in ritualistic acts, such as stepping over cracks, knocking on wood, or repeatedly washing the hands (the compulsion). Davison and Neale (1974) report the case of a woman who washed her hands over 500 times a day in spite of the painful sores that resulted. She reported that she had a strong fear of being contaminated by germs and that she could temporarily alleviate this concern only by washing her hands. It has been speculated that this sort of repetitious handwashing represents an unconscious attempt to make penance for one's forbidden thoughts or impulses. Shakespeare must have had this in mind when he had Lady Macbeth wash her hands continually after taking part in the murder of King Duncan.

Maher (1966) gives another example of obsessive-compulsive behavior—this time in a 17-year-old boy. The boy had developed an elaborate ritual based on the points of the compass. He could not sit down until he had identified the north, south, east, and west sides of any room he had entered and had proceeded to touch each wall in order. He also refused to eat his breakfast until he had been assured that food from each compass direction was on the table. Thus breakfast cereal from the north, orange juice from the south, and so forth were provided and eaten in the "correct" order.

Another obsessive-compulsive pattern is that of extreme neatness. Neatness can of course be a normal and healthy pattern, but it may become neurotic if taken to an extreme, so that, for example, the person gets terribly upset whenever he or she sees a speck of dust or when a piece of furniture is moved an inch. This kind of behavior may be seen as a defense mechanism Freud called *reaction formation*—doing the opposite of the repressed wish or impulse. Thus, for some persons excessive cleanliness may mask the urge to express opposing patterns of behavior—to soil, to be slovenly, to be disorganized. If the denied impulse is intense, the degree of reaction formation may have to be equally intense, creating compulsive behaviors.

KNOCK ON WOOD KNOCK ON WOOD

A business manager, Harold Parker, developed an intricate system of rituals that he used to ward off bad luck, bad thoughts, or bad feelings. When his plant manager, Edgar, first told him that his company was failing, Parker started chanting to himself, "Edgar will have his health, Harold will have his wealth," and he would touch something solid twice, once with his right foot and once with his left. Over the years he developed more and more such magical rituals, to the point where he spent most of his time thinking about the rituals and little time thinking about his real problems. His would be considered an obsessive-compulsive disorder (Viscott, 1972).

Dissociative Reactions

Dissociative reactions involve still another pattern of defense. With this method, the person unconsciously dissociates, or removes, some part of his or her consciousness. There are four main kinds of dissociative reactions: *amnesia,* in which the person loses all memory of his or her identity yet retains all talents, abilities, and general knowledge; *fugue states,* in which the person not only experiences amnesia but also leaves his or her surroundings and starts a new life in a different location; *sleepwalking,* in which the person is actually in a different state of consciousness and not really asleep; and *multiple personality,* in which the person appears to have more than one distinct personality in the same body (see Box 1).

According to psychoanalytic theory, dissociative reactions are acts of massive *repression;* some buried impulse is apparently so distressing that the person must unconsciously split away some part of the personality and deny its existence. The behavioral view is somewhat similar—learning theorists consider dissociative reactions to be avoidance responses that protect the person from highly stressful events.

Dissociative reactions are actually quite rare. Although such mechanisms as amnesia and multiple personality are fascinating, a review of the literature (Abse, 1966) has turned up only about 200 documented cases of the various dissociative reactions.

DEPRESSION

Depression has been described as "the common cold of mental illness." That is because it is by far the most common psychological problem, and it is one that in its milder forms almost all of us are familiar with. You can probably remember times when you felt discouraged and dejected, when nothing that you did seemed to go right, and when you felt there was little chance

things would turn for the better. Thoughts like "I'm a hopeless case" or "I'll never amount to anything" may have gone through your mind. Such depressions are perfectly normal. They are particularly likely to occur after a loss or a disappointment, whether in love, at school, or at work. In most cases, such depressions blow over after a couple of days or weeks. In other cases, however, depressions involve more severe symptoms, and they last for months or years. It has been estimated that there are from five to ten million seriously depressed people in the United States (Schmeck, 1975) and that as many as one in eight Americans will at some point in their lives suffer depression serious enough to need professional help (*Newsweek,* 1973).

Like the common cold, depression is extremely widespread. But whereas the common cold rarely kills anyone, depression

CHURCHILL, LINCOLN, AND VAN GOGH

Many famous people through history have suffered from depression. Winston Churchill wrote about the "black dog" that followed him throughout his life and finally immobilized him in his old age. Abraham Lincoln had bouts of depression and often dreamed of his own coffin. And artist Vincent Van Gogh cut off his own ear in a fit of despair (*Newsweek*, 1973).

Box 1

Multiple Personality

You are not likely to encounter a person with multiple personality in the everyday course of your life. Even though TV shows and films often center around a person who has mysterious blackouts and wakes up later after his or her alter ego (or "other self") has committed some hideous crime, multiple personality is actually exceedingly rare and is not associated with violent behavior.

For the few rare persons who experience this dissociative reaction, personality development in the early years seems to be arrested by periods of amnesia, during which one or more other personality develops, producing an adult with at least two distinct personalities. Each personality may be unaware of the other, creating an inevitable confusion when one aspect of the self must account for the actions of the other. The nature of multiple personality can be seen by examining two famous cases: Eve and Sybil.

The case of Eve White, Eve Black, and Jane was dramatized in the film *Three Faces of Eve,* which was based on a true case study published by Thigpen and Cleckley (1957). Eve White was a dedicated young mother who went to a

does. According to one estimate (*Newsweek*, 1973), as many as half of the estimated 50,000 to 70,000 suicides in the United States annually occur among persons suffering from depression (see the Psychological Issue at the end of this chapter). Far too many serious cases go unrecognized and untreated. This is especially unfortunate because of all psychological disorders, depression is probably the most susceptible to effective treatment, whether through traditional psychotherapy or drug treatment. At least 85 percent of depressed patients can be helped by treatment.

The Range of Depression

Although depression can be a normal experience, it is sometimes diagnosed as neurotic or even psychotic, depending on its degree

---

therapist complaining of severe headaches. During one of her interviews she reported that she had been hearing "voices," and then she suddenly underwent a striking personality change. She became a gay, flirtatious personality who called herself Eve Black. The personality Eve Black was aware of the thoughts and behavior of Eve White, but Eve White did not suspect Eve Black's existence. Later, a third, more mature personality emerged who called herself Jane. The personalities of Eve White and Eve Black had apparently existed side by side ever since an exceptionally unhappy childhood. As a measure of defense, distinct urges of the self became isolated from one another and formed separate personalities.

Another fascinating case of multiple personality recently came to light with the publication of the book *Sybil* by Flora Rheta Schreiber. It recounts the case history of a woman who sought treatment from psychiatrist Cornelia Wilbur in 1954. This woman, called Sybil in the book, complained of periodic blackouts. As with the case of Eve, during a therapy session Sybil's personality underwent a radical change—she acted like a little girl having a temper tantrum and actually broke a window. The little girl's name was Peggy. The psychiatrist suspected a case of dual personality, but then along came a third person in Sybil's body—this time who called herself Vicky. Although Sybil was totally unaware of these other personalities, Vicky revealed over a period of sessions that there were actually 16 personalities occupying Sybil's body!

According to Dr. Wilbur, each of these 16 personalities was distinct, with a specific voice, mannerisms, and sense of self. They ranged through various ages, from infant to adult, and some were male. They even had different abilities and talents—only one could play the piano. Dr. Wilbur examined each of these personalities in turn and became convinced that they were distinctly different and not dramatizations on the part of Sybil. Using hypnosis, the psychiatrist was able to hold conversations with several personalities at a time.

Through such discussions, Dr. Wilbur discovered that Sybil had had a disastrous childhood. Her mother was sadistic and regularly tortured and beat her. Her father remained detached from her and never inquired about her bruises or broken bones. As early as age three Sybil's first personality dissociation occurred. A second personality was created to suffer the punishment from her parents. In this way she protected herself not only from the suffering but also from the realization that she was unloved. Subsequently, whenever Sybil encountered a new situation that she couldn't cope with, a new personality was created to bear the brunt of the trauma. During the hypnosis sessions the psychiatrist discovered the specific traumas that gave rise to each of the personalities.

After all this information had emerged, the therapist faced the problem of bringing Sybil's personality back together. In a process that took several years, Dr. Wilbur worked with each personality to overcome that personality's specific neurosis. Then she helped Sybil to become a seventeenth personality that integrated all the other selves into a whole person (Trotter).

of severity. The following case of depression is somewhere near the middle of the range and also illustrates some typical features of the illness:

Recently a middle-aged woman presented herself to me for psychotherapy. Every day, she says, is a struggle just to keep going. On her bad days she cannot even bring herself to get out of bed, and her husband comes home at night to find her still in her pajamas, with dinner unprepared. She cries a great deal; even her lighter moods are continually interrupted with thoughts of failure and worthlessness. Small chores such as shopping or dressing seem very difficult and every minor obstacle seems like an impassable barrier. . . .

Her gait and speech are slow and her face looks very sad. Up until last fall she had been vivacious and active, the president of her suburban PTA, a charming social hostess, a tennis player, and a spare-time poet. Then two things happened: her twin boys went away to college for the first time, and her husband was promoted to a position of much greater responsibility in his company, a position that took him away from home more often. She now broods about whether her life is worth living, and has toyed with the idea of taking the whole bottle of her antidepressant pills at once. (Seligman, 1975, pages 1–2)†

This woman's feelings of worthlessness and hopelessness and her slow and lethargic behavior are common characteristics of depression. In more severe cases, depressed people may remain motionless for hours on end, with their faces frozen in expressions of grief. They may lose their appetite, and in some cases may lose a tremendous amount of weight. They may also have a great deal of difficulty sleeping and may experience uncontrollable outbursts of crying.

This woman's depression was apprently triggered by specific incidents in her life—her children's leaving home and her husband's promotion. Most depressions can be traced at least in part to difficult life events, such as the loss of a loved one, the loss of a job, or moving to a new place. Such externally triggered depressions are called *reactive,* or *exogenous.* But there are also cases of depression that do not have any apparent external cause; these are called *endogenous.* Endogenous depressions are chronic conditions, sometimes lasting an entire lifetime. In some cases of endogenous depression, moreover, the state of depression alternates with an opposite state of extreme elation, known as *mania.* One lawyer spent most of his life alternating between the highs and lows of manic-depressive disorder. "I literally enjoyed the manic phases," he reported. "I was a big shot, on top of the world. I spent not only my own money, but everybody else's I could get my hands on—I bought six suits at a time, a lot of stupid unnecessary things." Some people in manic stages also become loud and aggressive and show little concern about what other people will think of them. After being in such a phase for a while, however, the manic-depressive comes crashing down into the low phase. In this phase, the lawyer reported, "I feared getting out of bed, and was anxious to get into bed at night because I could block out the horror of my daily life" (*Newsweek,* 1973).

One explanation of this pattern is that the manic is running away from depression by plunging into so much activity. But clearly it is a strategy that doesn't work very well. It is now believed that manic-depressive disorders are caused by biochemical imbalances in the brain and nervous system. Although these imbalances are not yet well understood, the condition can sometimes be treated effectively by drugs such as lithium carbonate. This drug seemed to bring the lawyer's disorder under control, after 40 years of suffering.

What Causes Depression?

Depression is usually triggered by difficult life problems. But almost everyone experiences losses or disappointments at some point in their lives, yet only some people become seriously depressed. What accounts for this difference? Several explanations have been proposed.

Psychoanalytic Theory. Freud emphasized the importance of early life events in accounting for later psychological disorder, and his theory of depression (1917) was no exception. He suggested that some people become excessively dependent on others for the maintenance of their self-esteem, as a result of either too much or too little gratification of their needs during the oral period of psychosexual development (see Chapter 14). When these people experience a loss during adulthood, such as death of a loved one, they tend to feel unconscious anger toward this person for leaving them. This anger, however, is not directly expressed but is instead turned inward against the self, leading to the self-blame and self-hatred characteristic of depression. The loss that triggers such reactions is not necessarily someone's death. It may also be a symbolic loss, such as rejection, which the person experiences as a total withdrawal of love. Although many psychologists and psychiatrists agree with aspects of Freud's theory, there is little firm evidence for it (Davison and Neale, 1974).

Learned Helplessness. Learning theorists agree that the predisposition to become seriously depressed may have roots in childhood experiences. Rather than talking about oral deprivation, however, they focus on the person's history of reinforcement. Martin E.P. Seligman (1975) has recently suggested that depression may be the result of *learned helplessness*—that is, of experiences in which the person learns that his or her efforts have little to do with the outcome of the situation.

Seligman originally demonstrated this phenomenon with dogs. The dogs were placed in a harness and given a shock from which they could not escape. Later the same dogs were placed in a shuttlebox and shocked again, but this time they could terminate the shock by jumping over a barrier in the box. Untrained dogs had no trouble learning the escape route, but the dogs that had earlier been given the inescapable shock treatment howled at first and then sat passively, taking the shock. These dogs had learned that they were helpless, and so they remained passive

THE LOSS OF A PARENT

Statistical evidence suggests that people who have lost a parent early in life may be likely to experience depression when they are adults (Seligman, 1975). How might this statistical association be explained in terms of Freud's theory of depression? How about in terms of Seligman's theory of learned helplessness?

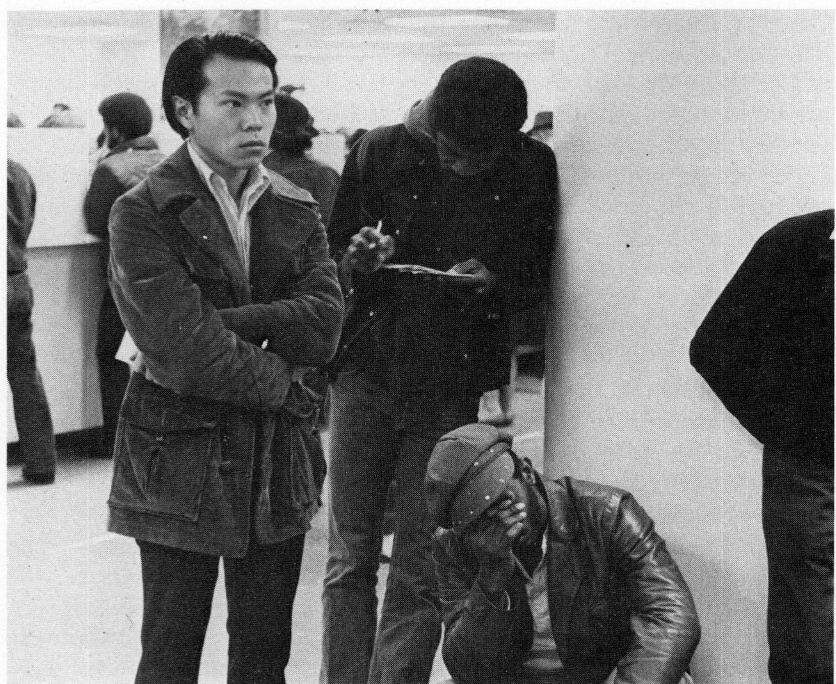

and suffered even when they could have done something to relieve their pain.

Similar results have been obtained in experiments conducted with other animals, and with humans as well. Seligman believes that the same mechanism of learning that one is helpless underlies most cases of depression in humans. He points out that depressed patients and animals in learned-helplessness experiments commonly show similar symptoms, including passivity, loss of appetite, and a lack of outward aggression. Seligman believes that this similarity is due to the fact that depressed patients, like the laboratory animals who were given unescapable shocks, find that their actions bear no relation to the rewards and punishments they receive.

Seligman's theory suggests that the best way to help depressed patients is to demonstrate to them that their actions *do* make a difference. Moreover, the theory suggests that individuals could be "inoculated" against learned helplessness in adulthood if they had childhood experiences of active striving and mastery, in which they learned that positive and negative reinforcements were contingent on their own actions.

Physiological Factors. Various explanations of the physiological basis of depression have been offered. One likely possibility is that depression involves a depletion of norepinephrine, one of the chemicals conveying impulses from one neuron to another in the brain and nervous system (see Chapter 2). This may cause an inhibition or slowing down of neural transmission, which in turn gives rise to periods of depression. One piece of evidence in support of his explanation is that low levels of norepinephrine

WHEN TASKS BECOME ORDEALS

Studies have shown that although depressed patients do poorly on various tasks, they tend to believe that they are even worse than they really are—that their actions don't have any chance of succeeding (Seligman, 1975). For example, Seligman was giving patients a graded-task assignment as therapy for depression. He brought one of the patients, a middle-aged woman, into the testing room, chatted with her, and then said, "I have some tasks here I should like you to perform." When he said the word "tasks," the woman burst into tears and could not continue. As Seligman put it, "A mere task is seen by a depressive as a labor of Hercules" (1975, page 85).

have been found in dogs that have received unescapable shocks in learned helplessness experiments (Seligman, 1975). It is possible, therefore, that the effects of learned helplessness are mediated biochemically by a depletion of norepinephrine. Another bit of evidence is that drugs that have been effective in treating depression have, as one of their effects, the ability to increase the level of norepinephrine in parts of the nervous system.

SCHIZOPHRENIA

Although most of us can understand rather easily what it is like to be depressed, schizophrenia remains a strange, unfathomable disorder to most people. But it is a condition that afflicts approximately 1 percent of the American population and accounts for half the patients confined to mental institutions. Many other schizophrenics live outside the hospital, sometimes returning occasionally for treatment. But regardless of where they may live

---

Box 2

Women and Depression

Serious and prolonged depression is far more common among women than among men—by some estimates, as much as twice as common. Myrna Weissman and her colleagues at the Yale University Depression Research Unit have found that depressed women are likely to have marital problems and also to have impaired functioning as mothers. Dr. Weissman notes, "The depressed person lacks energy, is apathetic and needs care—hardly a state for caring for children" (Schmeck, 1975).

Why are women especially prone to depression? One hypothesis is that physiological factors involving the sex hormones may provide part of the answer. Another explanation is in terms of the theory of learned helplessness described in the text. Women have traditionally been trained to act and feel helpless, and society often keeps them that

way. If women learn to be dependent on others—fathers, boyfriends, husbands, bosses—for their reinforcements, they may ultimately come to feel ineffective and, as a result, prone to depression.

Women seem to be particularly prone to a type of depression that occurs as a result of moving to a new home. Women often have to move because of their husband's job, and they find themselves without friends in a new community. When Weissman and Paykel (1972) studied women suffering from this kind of depression, they found that the women did not realize that their depressive symptoms were a result of faulty adaptation to the stresses and changes created by moving. The women overlooked moving as an influence on their emotional state because it is such an accepted part of life.

Which women are least likely to suffer from depression? Lenore Radloff (1975) found that employed married women have lower rates of depression than unemployed married women. Even though the employed women were "overworked" by the combination of work and family duties, they remained (on the average) in better health and spirits. It may be that their work helped them feel more competent and effective.

physically, schizophrenics seem to live in a mental world that is different from the one we experience (see Box 3).

Because people with schizophrenia seem out of touch with reality, at least some of the time, it is classified as a psychotic disorder. Its hallmarks are serious alterations of perception, activity, emotion, and thinking. Sometimes schizophrenics are extremely withdrawn and unresponsive and seem oblivious to things going on around them. They may also report hallucinations—hearing or seeing things that aren't really there. They may display extremely unusual motor behavior, ranging from frenzied excitement to complete immobility. They sometimes react with emotions that seem totally inappropriate, such as bursting into laughter when hearing of the death of a relative or becoming enraged at an innocuous request. And they may entertain thoughts about themselves and others that seem so far out of touch with reality that we can only consider them delusions. And yet there are many schizophrenics who at times seem perfectly normal, so much so that, as Roger Brown puts it, "The hospital volunteer who converses informally with [schizophrenic] patients

Box 3

The Inner World of Schizophrenia

Sometimes it is hard to imagine the inner world of the schizophrenic person and the degree to which he or she may totally withdraw from reality. In her novel *I Never Promised You a Rose Garden* (1964), Hannah Green provides some vivid examples of a world called *Yr*, which both haunts and comforts a 16-year-old schizophrenic girl.

For a time—how long by Earth's reckoning Deborah did not know—it was peaceful. The world made few demands so that it seemed once more as if it had been the world's pressures that had caused so much of the agony in Yr. Sometimes she was able to see "reality" from Yr as if the partition between them were only gauze. On such occasions her name became Januce, because she felt like two-faced Janus—with a face on each world. It had been her letting slip this name which had caused the first trouble in school. She had been living by the Secret Calendar (Yr did not measure time as the world did) and had returned to the Heavy Calendar in the middle of the day, and having then that wonderful and omniscient feeling of changing, she had headed a class paper: NOW JANUCE. The teacher had said, "Deborah, what is this mark on your paper? What is the word, Januce?"

And, as the teacher stood by her desk, some nightmare terror coming to life had risen in the day-sane schoolroom. Deborah had looked about and found that she could not see except in outlines, gray against gray, and with no depth, but flatly, like a picture. The mark on the paper was the emblem of coming from Yr's time to Earth's, but, being caught while still in transition, she had to answer for both of them. Such an answer would have been the unveiling of a horror—a horror from which she would not have awakened rationally; and so she had lied and dissembled, with her heart choking her. Such a danger must no more be allowed aloud, and so that night the whole Great Collect had come crowding into the Midworld: gods and demons from Yr and shades from Earth, and they had set up over their kingdoms a Censor to stand between Deborah's speech and actions and to guard the secret of Yr's existence.

Over the years the power of the Censor had grown greater and greater, and it was he who had lately thrust himself into both worlds, so that sometimes no speech and no action escaped him. One whisper of a secret name, one sign written, one slip of light could break into the hidden place and destroy her and both the worlds forever.

usually finds it difficult to tell some of the patients from some of the doctors" (Brown and Herrnstein, 1975, page 627).

Not all schizophrenics have all of these symptoms, and depending on which symptoms are most prevalent, a schizophrenic may be diagnosed as belonging to one of four subtypes. The person with *simple schizophrenia* is apathetic and seclusive and rarely has delusions or hallucinations. The individual with *hebephrenic schizophrenia* exhibits bizarre behavior, including strange facial expressions and speech, odd postures and movements, and intense delusions and hallucinations. *Catatonic schizophrenics* alternate between extreme immobility and agitation. And *paranoid schizophrenics* may seem fairly normal, but they are plagued by fears and suspicions that are overblown into major delusions.

There is a good deal of overlap among symptoms, and in fact most schizophrenics are diagnosed as "chronic undifferentiated," which is simply a long way of saying that it isn't clear what subtype they should be put in. The exception is the paranoid type, which is reliably identified by the patient's rather special sort of thinking—it often seems clear and logical in its own terms, but in terms of anyone else's conception of the world it is clearly deluded. Let us now take a closer look at what sorts of delusions such schizophrenics have.

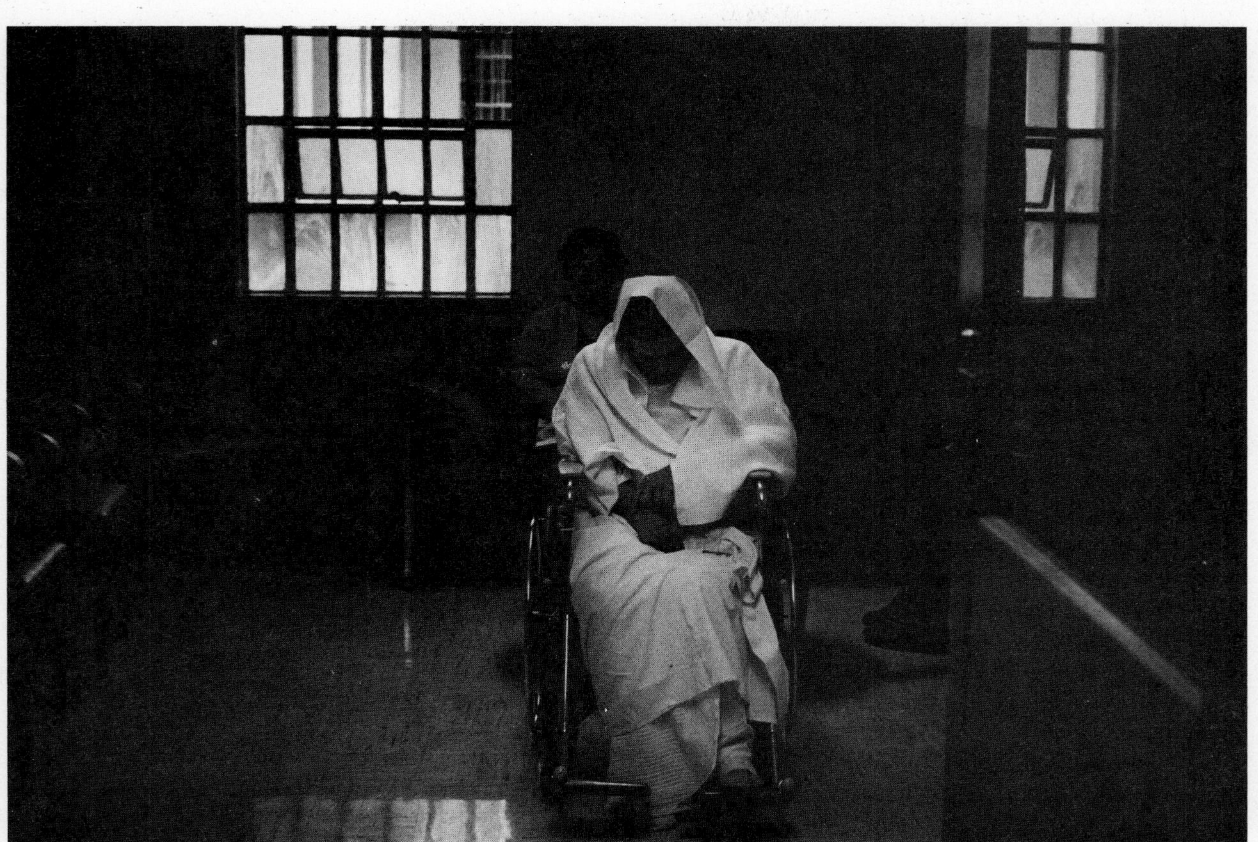

Delusions

Many schizophrenics, particularly those diagnosed as paranoid, experience delusions—thoughts about themselves or the world that seem (to the rest of us at least) to be totally divorced from reality. Often these are *delusions of persecution*—the idea that other people are conspiring against one. Roger Brown reports an encounter with a high school friend of his who looked him up eight years later:

We had half an hour or so of pleasant chatter about old friends, and then I noticed that my guest was looking at me in a rather curious "knowing" way that seemed to suggest that he did not mind playing this game of reunion after a long separation if I had a taste for it, but the guest was not "taken in" by this pretense. Then he came out with the remark: "I saw you in Cleveland last week, you know." That rocked me a bit as I had not been in Cleveland. And then it all came out. My guest believed that his entire circle of high school friends—who had, in fact, gone their separate ways for years—has had him under surveillance since high school. (Brown and Herrnstein, 1975, page 631)

When Brown tried to convince his friend that his suspicions were unfounded, the man told of "darting shadows" he had seen following him in various cities, of overhearing whispered conversations, and so on. This man had interpreted all sorts of ordinary insignificant events as centered directly on himself. He had what are called *ideas of reference*—the assumption that all things other people are doing and saying refer to oneself.

In addition to such delusions of persecution, schizophrenics may also have *delusions of grandeur*, believing themselves to be saviors or famous people—such as Napoleon, God, or Jesus Christ.

DELUSION OR REALITY?

It's not always easy to decide what is delusion and what is reality. One woman told a psychologist that she was constantly being followed—obviously a delusion of persecution. Upon careful checking, however, it was found that her husband had hired a private detective to watch her (Davison and Neale, 1974).

Thought Disorder

Whether or not they have delusions, almost all schizophrenics have thought disorders of one sort or another. Sometimes these take the form of incoherent, rambling conversations. The following conversation between a doctor and patient illustrates this type:

DOCTOR: *What would you like, Mr. Kelly?*

PATIENT: *The power of the ancients. The Asunder. I want the Asunder.*

DOCTOR: *Did you ever have the power before? Was it something you lost?*

PATIENT: *Holy, Holy, Holy, Adonai Echod. Te Deum Laudamus. Ex Post Christo, Ex Post Facto, Ex Rel Post Office. There you have it. (Viscott, 1972, page 224)*

In addition, some schizophrenic patients make up new words to use in their conversations, as in the following excerpt:

PATIENT: *I was sent by the government to the United States to Washington to some star, and they had a pretty nice country there. Now you have a body like a young man who says he is of the prestigitis.*

PARANOIA AND THE CIA

"The CIA turns up in paranoid delusions perhaps more than any other single organization. Its name is extremely suggestive—'central,' 'intelligence,' and 'agency' are all words rich in multiple meanings—and since the CIA does in fact engage in conspiratorial activities, it can easily be adapted for any scheme involving domination and control by unseen forces. Freud always maintained that every paranoid delusion contains a nugget of truth" (Hertzberg and McClelland, 1974).†

DOCTOR: *Who was this prestigitis?*

PATIENT: *Why, you are yourself. You can be prestigitis. They make you say bad things; they can read you; they bring back Negroes from the dead. (White, 1932, page 228)*

Such manufactured words, meaningful only to the speaker and no one else, are called *neologisms.* Of course, schizophrenic patients aren't the only ones to make use of neologisms. Who ever thought up the word "schizophrenia" anyway?

Schizophrenic thought is also likely to be characterized by *loose associations.* The person may be talking about one thing and then drift off on a train of thought that listeners find hard to follow. A schizophrenic patient himself reported, "My thoughts get all jumbled up. I start thinking or talking about something but I never get there" (McGhie and Chapman, 1961, page 108). Schizophrenics may also make *clang associations,* in which the words seem to follow because they rhyme or sound similar rather than because they make sense. For example: "How are you today by the bay as a gay, Doctor?" (Davison and Neale, 1974).

Experimental studies in which patients are given problems to solve have suggested that schizophrenics find it especially difficult to differentiate between relevant and irrelevant information and are easily distracted. This difficulty may be at the heart of schizophrenic thought disorders.

SCHIZOPHRENIA

The term "schizophrenia" was coined by a Swiss psychiatrist, Eugen Bleuler, in 1911. The word literally means "split personality" or "split mind." Schizophrenia should not be confused with the rare cases of multiple personality, however. The "splitting" that Bleuler was referring to was the patient's departure from social reality.

What Causes Schizophrenia?

Schizophrenia sometimes strikes suddenly, in reaction to a stressful event; this is called *reactive* schizophrenia. When schizophrenia develops very slowly and gradually, it is called *process* schizophrenia. The reactive schizophrenic sometimes seems more disturbed than the process schizophrenic, but the reactive schizophrenic is more likely to recover. The underlying causes of both of these forms remain a mystery, however. If anything is certain, it is that there is no single cause but rather a number of contributing factors operating at different levels—biochemical, psychological, and social. The following are several of the factors that are currently believed to be important.

Genetic and Biochemical Factors. It is known that schizophrenia is highly heritable (see Chapter 8). People with schizophrenic close relatives are much more likely to be schizophrenic themselves than people who do not have schizophrenic relatives. And if one identical twin has the disorder, it has been estimated that there is about a 50 percent chance that the other twin (who shares all the same genes) has it as well. This relationship is much lower in the case of fraternal twins, who are less similar genetically (Gottesman and Shields, 1972). These data indicate that schizophrenia has a large genetic component. It is likely that there is a biochemical factor, predisposing people to schizophrenia, that is passed on through the genes. Scientists are hard at work trying to pin down this biochemical factor. The betting is

CONFUSED BOUNDARIES

What is the central ingredient of schizophrenia? Many answers have been offered. Blatt and Wild (1975) have put forth the interesting idea that the basic element of schizophrenia is a disturbance in the ability to establish and maintain boundaries—boundaries between internal experiences and external events, boundaries between conceptions of the self and conceptions of other people. In developing this approach they drew upon Piaget's theories about children's conceptual development and on the psychoanalytic theory of interpersonal boundaries.

that, as with depression, it has to do with neurotransmitter chemicals in the brain. It has been found, for example, that people who take high doses of amphetamines sometimes experience symptoms that resemble paranoid schizophrenia. Amphetamines are chemically related to certain neurotransmitters, and it is thought that they somehow interfere with the functioning of the neurotransmitters, producing the altered behavior and thinking characteristic of psychosis. It has been hypothesized that at least some types of schizophrenia could be caused by some similar kind of biochemical interference with the functioning of neurotransmitters (Snyder, 1972).

Family Patterns. Schizophrenics often come from families in which there is disturbed communication between mother and father and between parents and children. One well-known theory holds that the pre-schizophrenic child is exposed to *double-bind* communications, in which the parent says one thing but apparently means another. What the parent says is characteristically contradicted by his or her actions, tone of voice, or emotions communicated in other ways. For example:

A young man who had fairly well recovered from an acute schizophrenic episode was visited in the hospital by his mother. He was glad to see her and impulsively put his arm around her shoulders whereupon she stiffened. He withdrew his arm and she asked, "Don't you love me any more?" He then blushed and she said,

---

Box 4

Ain't It Great To Be Crazy?
"The process of entering into the *other* world from this world, and returning to *this* world from the other world, is as natural as death and giving birth and being born. But in our present world, which is both so terrified and so unconscious of the other world, it is not surprising that when 'reality,' the fabric of this world, bursts, and a person enters the other world, he is completely lost and terrified and meets only incomprehension in others" (Laing, 1967, page 125).

Such is the view of schizophrenia proposed by R. D. Laing, the British existential psychiatrist known for his "celebration" of the schizophrenic. Laing believes that some schizophrenics are on the path to higher sanity, while the normals of the world remain less than sane in an insane world. According to Laing, most individuals are alienated from themselves.

"Dear, you must not be so easily embarrassed and afraid of your feelings." The patient was able to stay with her only a few minutes more and following her departure he assaulted an aide. (Bateson et al., 1956, page 258)

It is possible that the mother's inconsistent communications contributed to putting him into the hospital in the first place. Such contradictory messages may put a great deal of pressure on the child and ultimately lead him to withdraw from reality into a more "consistent" inner world (Bateson, et al., 1956).

Psychological Stress. As mentioned earlier, psychologically stressful events can trigger a schizophrenic episode. In 1971 Mark Vonnegut, the son of writer Kurt Vonnegut, became severely schizophrenic. He later wrote, "Just prior to my crackup, my parents were splitting up, the woman I had been virtually married to took off with another man, my father was becoming more and more outlandishly famous" (1975). All of these stresses may have had a role in precipitating his psychosis.

It should be emphasized that these explanations are not mutually exclusive. To explain schizophrenia, researchers will eventually have to explain how a variety of factors interact with one another. As Vonnegut points out, many other young people experience events as traumatic as those in his life without becoming schizophrenic. It seems likely, therefore, that such traumatic

---

They have set up a dual personality: the outer self, set up to meet the outward demands of society, and the inner self, the true self. Unfortunately, society continually makes demands that conflict with the real, or inner, self, while the outer self complies. Eventually the inner self has slipped away, and the outer self is all that is left. Thus Laing says, "What we call 'normal' is a product of repression, denial, splitting, projection, introjection and other forms of destructive action on experience. It is radically estranged from the structure of being" (page 27).

Laing sees schizophrenia as a natural and understandable reaction to an insane world filled with unresolvable conflicts. But more than this, schizophrenia is a process by which individuals explore their inner self in an attempt to bring the split personality back together again. At the end of the voyage through inner space, the individual returns saner than he or she ever was before the onset of psychosis. For this reason, Laing feels that schizophrenia is a process that would benefit each of us, and society as well.

The schizophrenic needs help, Laing agrees, but traditional psychotherapy only interferes with the "natural healing process" that is schizophrenia. Indeed, most therapy for psychotics is aimed at an adjustment to our view of normality and the restoration of previous personality structure, which, as Laing points out, is far from healthy. Moreover, individuals may be driven truly insane by the chemicals, surgery, or mental hospitals that they are subjected to. Because they are products of our society, schizophrenics feel lost and afraid in the inner world they hardly knew existed—and that others condemn—and it is psychiatry's role to guide them through the exploration of this inner space and help them find their way back. The guide must be someone who has been there before. "Psychiatrically," says Laing, "this would appear as ex-patients helping future patients go mad" (page 128).

Although Laing's views have appealed to many readers, others have felt that he has made the mistake of romanticizing what is in fact a severe illness. Siegler and Osmond (1974) write: "During the 19th century, two great illnesses were romanticized: consumption, now called tuberculosis, and madness, now called schizophrenia. Romanticizing tuberculosis is now recognized for the sickness that it is, but schizophrenia is undergoing a fresh bout of romantic delirium."

events lead to schizophrenia only among people who are predisposed to it for other reasons.

As we saw in Chapter 15, some people (like Thomas Szasz) believe that schizophrenia is not a disease at all, but rather a product of social labeling. Another view is that of R. D. Laing, who believes that in a real sense schizophrenics are saner than the rest of us (see Box 4). These are definitely minority viewpoints, however. The current consensus among researchers is that although abnormality is a relative concept, schizophrenia is nevertheless a disease—one that includes an important biochemical component. Mark Vonnegut, who recovered from his schizophrenia and is now a medical student, shares this view. He writes:

I myself was a Laing-Szasz fan and didn't believe there was really any such thing as schizophrenia. I thought it was just a convenient label for patients whom doctors were confused about. I even worked in a mental hospital for several months without being convinced otherwise. All that's beside the point. The point is that there's overwhelming evidence that there is a very real disease called schizophrenia (actually probably several very real diseases with overlapping symptoms). (Vonnegut, 1975)

SUMMARY

1. *Neuroses* are relatively mild psychological disorders characterized by anxiety, inability to cope effectively with challenges, and difficulty in interpersonal relationships. *Psychoses* are major psychological disorders characterized by a loss of contact with reality, loss of control over feelings and actions, and such symptoms as delusions and hallucinations.
2. Neurosis is often accompanied by *anxiety attacks,* in which a nameless dread causes uneasiness, apprehension, and numerous physical symptoms. According to Freud, such *neurotic anxiety* is caused by buried impulses trying to rise to the surface.
3. A *phobia* is an intense fear of something that is out of proportion to the real danger involved. According to psychoanalytic theory, phobias are symptoms of repressed urges. According to the behavioral view, phobias are incorrectly learned responses.
4. To ward off anxiety, people often develop *defense mechanisms*—ways of denying or evading anxiety-arousing situations or impulses. Such defenses become neurotic when they deny or distort reality to such an extent that they make it difficult for the person to function effectively.
5. In *obsessive-compulsive disorders,* the person, against his or her will, keeps thinking certain thoughts (obsession) and engaging in ritual acts (compulsion). The obsessive-compulsive individual attempts to master a threat by repeatedly engaging in behavior related to it or by doing the opposite of the repressed wish (reaction formation).

6. In *dissociative reactions,* the person removes some part of his or her consciousness. The four main kinds of dissociative reactions are *amnesia* (memory loss), *fugue states* (memory loss and establishment of a new identity), *sleepwalking,* and *multiple personality.*
7. The most common psychological problem is *depression.* Depression ranges in severity from normal to neurotic to psychotic. It is characterized by feelings of worthlessness and hopelessness, lethargy, and loss of appetite. Depressions may be triggered by external events (*exogenous* depression) or may appear as the result of forces within the individual (*endogenous* depression).
8. In *manic-depressive* disorders, the individual alternates between states of deep depression and extreme elation. Such disorders are thought to be caused by chemical imbalances in the brain.
9. What causes depression? Freud said it was self-hatred caused by repression of anger toward a person who has rejected or otherwise abandoned the depressed person. But Seligman has suggested that depression is the result of *learned helplessness*—the person has found that his or her actions have little effect on the world. Depression may also have a biochemical basis, involving the neurotransmitter norepinephrine.
10. Women are especially prone to depression. One reason may be the feelings of ineffectiveness that result from a life of dependence on others. A common cause of women's depression is moving to a new home.
11. The primary characteristics of *schizophrenia* include serious alterations of perception, activity, emotion, and thinking. The *simple schizophrenic* is apathetic and seclusive. The *hebephrenic* schizophrenic exhibits bizarre behavior and experiences intense delusions and hallucinations. *Catatonic* schizophrenics alternate between extreme immobility and agitation. And *paranoid* schizophrenics are plagued by delusional fears and suspicions.
12. Schizophrenics may experience *delusions of persecution* and believe that other people are conspiring against them. Such people often have *ideas of reference*—they believe that everything other people say and do somehow refers to them. Schizophrenics may also have *delusions of grandeur,* believing themselves to be famous persons or religious figures.
13. Schizophrenia is also characterized by thought disorders, and schizophrenics' conversation tends to be incoherent and rambling. They sometimes invent words—*neologisms*—and make *loose associations* or *clang associations* in building sentences.
14. Schizophrenia may strike suddenly (*reactive* schizophrenia) or it may develop slowly and gradually (*process* schizophrenia). Among the possible causes of schizophrenia are ge-

netic and biochemical factors, family patterns characterized by *double-bind* situations, and psychological stress. These factors may all interact to produce a particular case.

15. R. D. Laing believes that schizophrenia is actually a process of exploring the inner self and of resolving conflicts between the self and the demands of society. He views schizophrenia as a beneficial, healing process, from which the individual emerges saner than most other members of society.

psychological issue

Suicide

In ancient times suicide was considered a heroic way of dealing with an impossible life situation.

In ancient times suicide was considered a heroic way of dealing with an impossible life situation. The Japanese hero confronted with an intolerable "loss of face" committed Hara-Kiri, just as the Greek or Roman warrior fell on his own sword to save his honor. The social, religious, and legal reactions to suicide have changed over the years. At first it was accepted as a natural event; then it was condemned by the church; next it was defined as a criminal act; and finally it was described as a product of mental derangement. For centuries the suicide of religious martyrs was glorified as an example of dedication to the highest of principles. Later, there was an attempt to design a variety of "punishments." The dead people's property might be confiscated; they might be denied an honorable burial; or they might be hanged for the crime of suicide. In extreme cases, the body of the suicide might be dismembered; the offending hand was buried in one place and the body was buried in another to separate "murderer" from "victim."

The Measure of Suicide

It is difficult to find reliable body counts of suicides, and of course the rate at which people kill themselves differs from place to place and from time to time. Nonetheless, you can get some idea of the size of the problem if you realize that every 30 minutes someone in the United States commits suicide. And for every successful suicide there are probably another ten attempts that fail. Suicide ranks tenth among leading causes of death for adults, and it is third as a cause of death among college students (Davison and Neale, 1974).

Suicide statistics are notoriously unreliable not only because shame is attached to the act but also because people who successfully kill themselves have often tried and failed several times before. One survey of patients at a suicide prevention center showed that 60 percent of those who finally managed to kill themselves had made previous attempts (Wold, 1970). Also, what looks like an accident may actually be deliberate suicide. We know that more than 55,000 persons die each year in automobile accidents, but no one knows how many of these drivers consciously or unconsciously set up the conditions for a fatal

Box I-1

The Deadliest Attraction

In the Western world, the single most attractive site for suicide is San Francisco's Golden Gate Bridge. Recently it surpassed the Eiffel Tower as a place to end it all. Since 1937 more than 500 people have plunged to their deaths in the water below. In 1971, the average age of persons jumping from the bridge was 29.5 years, and three times as many men as women took the fatal dive. For a long time, San Francisco has had the highest suicide rate in the United States (30 per 100,000 population); 75 percent of those who have jumped have been residents of the San Francisco region.

crash. When car accidents were carefully examined in one study, up to one-half of the dead drivers had numerous previous driving offenses; over half had also been drinking; and nearly half were suffering from depression. Such self-destructive drivers were characterized as reckless, risk taking, impulsive persons who frequently got behind the wheel after a violent argument.

A survey of known suicides gave this description of the conditions in which self-destruction is most likely to occur in the spring, in the late afternoon, on a Monday (for males), and at home (in 74 percent of all cases). Suicide is least likely in winter in the early morning (Maris, 1969). But these details tell only part of the story. The finger on the trigger or the hand fumbling with the bottle of sleeping pills varies according to sex, marital status, and race.

Male Supremacy. Maris (1969) studied the cases of more than 2,000 suicides in the Chicago area during a five-year period. His sample showed that men are more likely to commit suicide than are women. However, three times as many women as men attempt suicide. Some think that most of these unsuccessful attempts are probably pleas for help rather than real attempts to take one's own life.

Firearms and explosives accounted for twice as many suicidal deaths among males as among females, whereas five times as many females as males killed themselves with chemical substances, mostly barbiturates.

Wedded Bliss. The suicide rate of married persons is lower than that of single, widowed, or divorced persons. The rate is highest among divorced persons, which suggests the possibility that in marriage the single relationship to the spouse might make all the difference. A widowed person has lost a relationship to a spouse, but may have the compensation of happy memories or the companionship of sons and daughters. For the divorced person, a relationship that was once meaningful may have left only the pain and resentment of an unhappy affair. Without the help of relationship to others, the likelihood of suicide increases greatly.

For the divorced person, the rate of suicide doesn't level off with age as it does for the single, married, or widowed individual. Instead, the suicide rate increases from early in life and continues to grow even after 75 years of age.

White Death, Black Death. Suicide among blacks is significantly lower than among whites. This lower suicide rate may be related to the generally lower socio-economic status of blacks in our society; if you are already at the bottom of the social class structure, there is less shame attached to not rising in the world. It is often assumed, particularly by black persons, that suicide represents a white solution to white problems. As Dick Gregory once cracked, "You can't kill

...self-destruction is most likely to occur in the spring, in the late afternoon, on a Monday (for males), and at home (in 74 percent of all cases).

A sky-rocketing number of young people no longer believe they "have everything to live for."

yourself by jumping out of the basement." And Redd Foxx scoffed, "Only three Negroes have jumped off the Golden Gate Bridge, and two of them were pushed" (Seiden, 1970).

Times are changing, though, and recent research suggests that suicide among young, urban black men has soared in the last 15 years. Older blacks are not killing themselves in greater numbers, but the younger blacks seem to be (Seiden, 1970).

Death at an Early Age

"To be or not to be" has long been the question, and "not to be" increasingly has become the answer for some young people. A skyrocketing number of young people no longer believe they "have everything to live for."

The suicide rate among college students is particularly high. It is hard to understand why this relatively privileged group with the advantages of intelligence and educational opportunity would want to close the door on life. Seiden (1966) tried to answer this question in a study of 23 University of California students who committed suicide during the ten-year period from 1952 through 1961. Twice as many older students (over 25) as younger students killed themselves. These students were not in academic trouble (two-thirds of them were above the grade-point average), and they did not kill themselves during those periods when they might have been plagued by the stresses of final exams. The suicides usually occurred early in the semester—in the months of October or February.

This study convinced Seiden that the suicidal act was really a final dramatic gesture summing up a lifetime pattern of inadequate adjustment. To fellow students the suicide seemed to be doing well; but the suicide usually believed that his or her achievements didn't measure up to the expectations of self or others. The fundamental fact is that few of the suicide's fellow students knew the person very well; he or she was typically asocial or withdrawn. "These particular students were uniformly described as terribly shy, virtually friendless individuals, alienated from all but the most minimal social interactions. Frequently they had compensated for their personal solitude by increased study and almost total absorption in schoolwork" (p. 410).

Becoming Suicidal

Some psychiatric theorists insist that about 90 percent of all suicides have serious emotional disturbances. Reconstructing the life of the deceased by studying all available evidence and records and by interviewing those who knew the person best has led most American researchers to agree that suicide is a symptom of depressive emotional illness that produces feelings of helplessness, hopelessness, and worthlessness as well as a loss of interest in food, sex, work, friends, and everything else that normally makes life worth living (Blum, 1972). These depressions produce distinct physical symptoms: unusual fatigue, disturbed sleep patterns, and an inability or unwillingness to eat. Of all psychiatric conditions, depression is the most likely to be associated with suicide.

Box I-2

Doctor, Heal Thyself

The doctor you expect to preserve your life may be planning to take his or her own. More doctors die of self-inflicted wounds than are killed by automobile accidents, airplane crashes, drownings, and homicides combined. American doctors kill themselves at twice the rate of average American males, and this seems to be the case in other parts of the world as well (Ross, 1971). Surprisingly, of all doctors, psychiatrists are most likely to kill themselves. They are six times more likely to commit suicide than are pediatricians, for example.

Most of us are unhappy some of the time, but it is not easy to understand how suicidal people get so deeply and disastrously depressed. We don't have all the answers yet, but the Los Angeles Suicide Prevention Center has outlined one do-it-yourself method for rearing a suicidally inclined child. They suggest that you begin by giving the child personal experiences that will produce feelings of being inadequate and unloved. The child should also be taught to develop a harsh, punishing conscience filled with powerful feelings of guilt and shame; further, he or she should be instilled with exceptionally high standards and have a compulsion toward intense self-criticism for failure to achieve. Society can help by teaching values that emphasize achievement, the accumulation of wealth, and an unrealistic view of love (Farberow, 1970).

Why are we so concerned about preventing suicide? Why not let individuals decide for themselves when they have had enough of living? One reason we try to prevent suicide is because these people, when prevented, often go on to lead happy, productive lives. In addition, suicide does not involve a single life; it affects the lives of all those connected with the victim. The family suffers not only sorrow, but usually guilt; they blame themselves for not preventing the tragedy. Children, too, suffer from the social stigma attached to the suicide of a parent; frequently, they become fearful that they are destined to follow the parent's example. Considering that ten attempts are made for every successful suicide, we must believe that most people really don't want to die and would not kill themselves if there were any other solution to life's problems.

Another good reason for doing everything we can to prevent suicide is offered by Seligman (1975):

Suicide usually has its roots in depression, and depression dissipates in time. When a per-

...we must believe that most people... would not kill themselves if there were any other solution to life's problems.

son is depressed, his view of the future is bleak; he sees himself as helpless and hopeless. But in many cases, if he waited a few weeks, this cognitive set would be changed, and by reason of time alone the future would seem less hopeless. . . . One of the most tragic aspects of suicide is that often, if the person could be rendered inactive for a week or two, he would no longer wish to kill himself. (page 89)

Summary

1. Suicide statistics are notoriously unreliable. Nevertheless, they do seem to indicate that men are more likely to commit suicide than women, although three times as many women as men *attempt* suicide unsuccessfully. Married persons are less likely to commit suicide than single, widowed, or divorced persons, and the suicide rate is lower for blacks than for whites.
2. The suicide rate for college students is particularly high. Those students who take their lives are typically asocial and withdrawn, although they seem to be doing well academically.
3. Suicide and depression go hand in hand. Potential suicides have feelings of helplessness, hopelessness, and worthlessness and have lost all interest in life. Most people who attempt to kill themselves don't really want to die but simply see no other solution to life's problems.

Therapy

CHAPTER 17

Therapy

"The current psychotherapeutic scene is a bewildering panorama of schools and methods, practitioners with all sorts of backgrounds, and patients with an enormous variety of woes and ills. . . . No single therapy holds a monopoly. Paraprofessionals, subprofessionals and nonprofessionals, some with no training at all, compete with orthodox psychologists" (Frank, 1972, page 22).

Therapy may be conducted in groups or individually. It may be administered by an M.D., a psychologist, a social worker, or even a clergyman. Despite this bewildering array, all forms of psychotherapy have certain features in common. For one, every successful therapy establishes a relationship in which the client has confidence in the therapist's competence and desire to help. Second, the setting in which therapy takes place, whether an office, a hospital room, or a garden, is a sanctuary where clients are encouraged to let themselves go, express forbidden thoughts, release pent-up emotions, and try out new ways of behaving. Furthermore, each type of psychotherapy is based on a theory that explains the causes of distress, specifies goals, and prescribes procedures for attaining the goals. The ability to name, clarify, and explain symptoms is in itself powerfully reassuring.

Jerome Frank (1973a) proposes that persons seeking therapeutic help are all suffering from *demoralization*: They are conscious of having failed to meet their own expectations or the expectations of others, and they feel powerless to change either the situation or themselves. Their life is constricted, and they cling to habitual activities, avoid novelty and challenges, and are reluctant to make long-term plans. In short, they seem to be cowering in a psychological corner.

Demoralization may be no more than brief uneasiness caused by some passing problem, or it may be so severe that the individual must be hospitalized. Any therapeutic procedure thus performs two interrelated functions: it combats demoralization, and it treats specific symptoms. Sometimes clients feel no need for further therapy, despite persistence of symptoms, once they have recovered their morale (Sifneos, 1972).

Among the general goals that all systems of psychotherapy seem to share are (1) relief from anxiety, symptoms, and conflict; (2) establishment of personal maturity, feelings of adequacy, and integration of the different parts of the self; (3) improvement of interpersonal relationships; and (4) a satisfactory adjustment to the culture and the society (Watkins, 1965). Differing therapies may emphasize one or more of these goals to the exclusion of others, and they may differ in their definitions of such key concepts as "maturity" and "adjustment."

This chapter will explore several major types of psychotherapy, noting their differences as well as their similarities. First to be discussed will be two of the major "talking therapies"—psychoanalysis and client-centered therapy; then the behavior therapies and somatic therapies (including the use of drugs, shock, and surgery) will be discussed.

THE TALKING THERAPIES

The basic idea of "talking therapies" is that open discussion of a problem can bring insights into its causes and possible solutions. This type of therapy emphasizes getting one's feelings out into the open—bringing out the concealed thoughts and emotions that are often the cause of psychological problems. On the first few visits to a therapist, the client may want to express some of these inner feelings but holds back for fear of rejection. As one former client of Carl Rogers put it:

I remember a good deal of emotional tension in the second interview, where I first mentioned homosexuality. I remember that I felt drawn down into myself, into places I didn't want to go, hadn't quite been to before, and yet had to see. I think I

MONKEY PSYCHOTHERAPISTS

Suomi, Harlow, and McKinney (1972) provided young monkey psychotherapists for monkeys who were "neurotic" as a result of early separation from parents. The monkey therapists engaged in clinging and play behavior with the neurotic monkeys. At one year, the clients had greatly improved, and at two years there was virtually complete recovery in monkeys whose defects had been considered irreversible. Wrote the authors: "We are all aware of the existence of some therapists who seem inhuman. We find it refreshing to report the discovery of nonhumans who can be therapists" (p. 932).

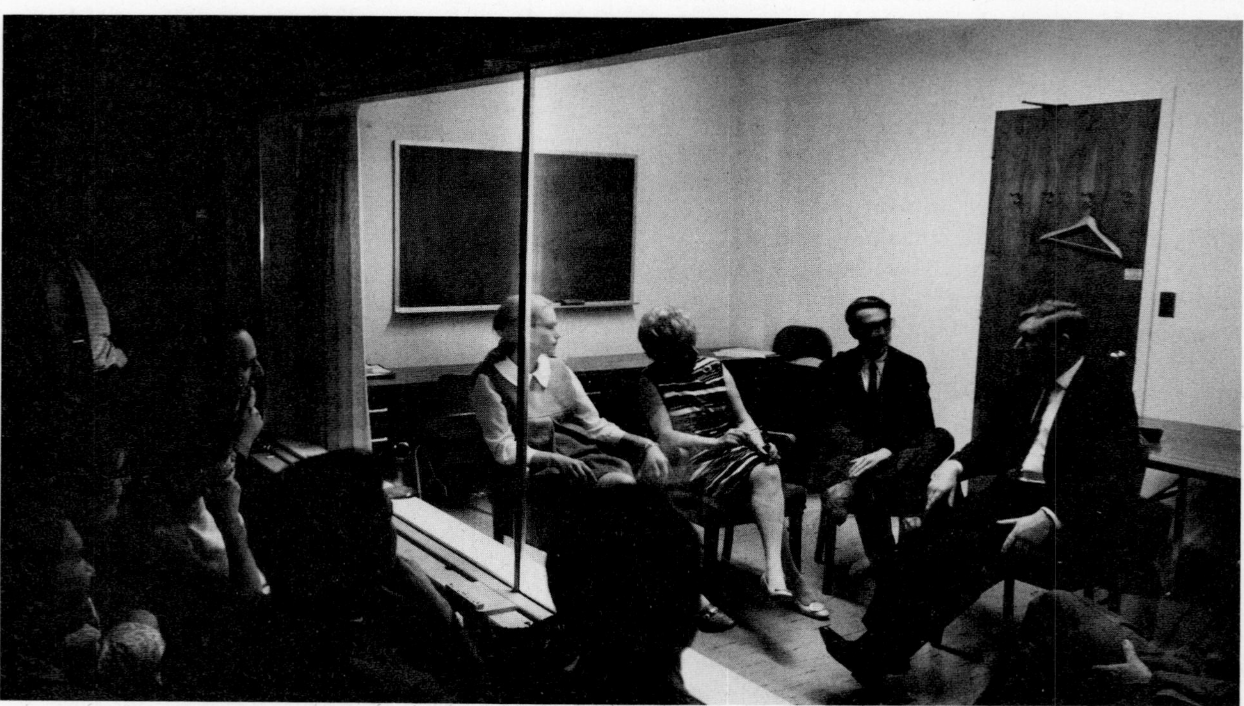

Psychiatrist holding a family group therapy with intern and resident psychiatrists observing.

dreaded this interview because I had been so afraid before counseling began that I would get to that subject. And afraid that I wouldn't. (Rogers, 1951, p. 72)

Once into therapy, however, clients learn that the therapist is willing to accept anything they have to say, without disapproval or disgust. This supportive atmosphere encourages self-expression, disclosure of buried animosities, fears, and desires, and eventual self-acceptance of these aspects of the personality.

There are two main varieties of talking therapy: psychoanalysis and client-centered therapy. Although both types emphasize self-disclosure, they differ greatly in their theoretical basis and in their approach to the client-therapist relationship.

Psychoanalysis

Psychoanalysis is the system of therapy developed by Sigmund Freud, and it is part and parcel of his general theory of personality (see Chapter 14). Psychoanalysis is thought to have been born with the case of "Anna O." In the early 1880s physician Joseph Breuer became acquainted with Sigmund Freud and told him of a patient he was treating, a woman who was suffering from hysteria (the presence of physiological symptoms with no organic basis). Breuer found that when he hypnotized the patient (whom he called "Anna O.") she could remember painful events from her past—events she could not recall when awake. During hypnosis Breuer helped his patient to reexperience the painful events and to express the feelings that accompanied them. Upon being awakened, Anna expressed a great relief—both physical and emotional. After several sessions of the "talking cure," as Anna referred to it, her condition showed significant permanent improvement.

This case illustrates the basic hypothesis of Freud's theory: that painful thoughts and emotions are often thrust into the unconscious mind. Unable to achieve direct expression, these feelings seek ways of indirect release, thereby producing hysterical symptoms, neurotic activities, and distortion of reality. The goal of psychoanalysis is to open the doors to the unconscious and release these pent-up emotions, as Breuer did with Anna O.

Freud developed several techniques designed to help the client achieve *catharsis*, this ultimate emotional release. Perhaps the most important of these techniques is *free association*, in which clients are asked to let their thoughts flow freely and to say whatever comes to mind. Freud would say to his clients:

You will notice that as you relate things various thoughts will occur to you which you would like to put aside on the ground of certain criticisms and objections. You will be tempted to say to yourself that this or that is irrelevant here, or is quite unimportant, or nonsensical, so that there is no need to say it. You must never give in to these criticisms, but must say it precisely because *you feel an aversion to doing so. (Freud, 1913, p. 135)*

Freud believed that even the most "irrelevant" thoughts can have meaning and that pauses or breaks in a train of thought indicate

A traditional psychoanalyst's session.

a *resistance* to touch on sensitive topics. The psychoanalyst is trained to notice points of resistance and to try to help the client overcome them. In the process of *interpretation,* the analyst points out resistances and offers some reasons for them. The overall process of free association, interpretation, and overcoming of resistances is called *working through.* It involves long-term therapy (often several years) in which the client gradually draws out internal emotions, confronts conflicts, and learns to deal realistically with these feelings and problems to an extent that symptoms are reduced or disappear.

Freud discovered that clients would often come to act toward him in the same way they acted toward significant other persons in their lives, such as a parent or spouse. He called this process *transference,* and he put it to constructive use. He believed that the therapist should remain aloof, avoid eye contact, and provide a neutral screen on which the clients can project whatever image (father, husband) they require for working out basic conflicts. To summarize, the role of the analyst is basically that of a listener who offers interpretations and provides an object for transference and a nonjudgmental sounding board.

REFRESHER COURSES FOR PSYCHOANALYSIS

Freud believed that psychoanalysts, like their patients, were likely to react emotionally to their patients as figures from their own past. This possibility is called "countertransference." Partly to help them handle such countertransferences, psychoanalysts must undergo their own training psychoanalysis before beginning to practice. Freud also recommended refresher courses for analysts: "Every analyst should periodically—at intervals of five years or so—submit himself to analysis once more without feeling ashamed of taking this step" (1964, p. 249).

A group therapy session.

Client-Centered Therapy

According to Carl Rogers, who developed *client-centered therapy,* the aim of therapy is to help clients realize and become their true selves by allowing them to test out the feelings that, until now, they have refused to admit are part of their life. Rogers is among the humanistic theorists who believe that maladjustment is a result of denying those feelings and behaviors that do not conform to one's image of oneself, even when that image is false (see Chapter 14). Rather than correcting the self-image, the individual continues to evade the contradictory experiences. When these attempts fail, the inconsistency brings intense anxiety and this anxiety becomes increasingly difficult to resolve.

Client-centered therapists help individuals express and experience their true feelings by providing *unconditional positive regard.* That is, the therapist continues to respect the client, no matter what he or she does or says. According to Rogers, this is exactly what the client needs in order to change from a life in which others control his or her behavior and thinking to one in which he or she feels free to express desires or ideas.

Unlike the psychoanalyst, the client-centered therapist does not try to probe or interpret. That job is left to the client. Instead, the therapist provides the respect and support that help clients to begin to confront and analyze problems themselves. During the therapy session, the therapist will often rephrase clients' statements in such a way as to highlight the things the client seems to be suggesting, but will not admit in so many words. Through this process of discovery and trial, clients come to realize their true self. Rogers emphasizes the fact that the therapist must be "genuine"—willing to share attitudes and feelings about the client and about the session without resorting to a professional facade (see Box 1).

Rogers also stresses therapist warmth and empathy as the most important factors in the success of therapy. A cold, aloof person, no matter what his or her credentials or background, would not make a good client-centered therapist. As one client of a warm, helpful therapist put it:

Box 1

Should Therapists Disclose Themselves?

One of the major differences between psychoanalysis and client-centered therapy lies in the area of therapist self-disclosure. As far as Freud was concerned, the therapist should be totally neutral, "impenetrable to the patient, and, like a mirror, reflect nothing but what is shown him" (1956, pp. 331). One reason for this aloofness is to encourage transference of the client's feelings about others onto the therapist. But it also keeps the therapist from getting emotionally involved with or embarrassed by the client.

The client-centered therapist, on the other hand, may feel that it is valuable to tell the patient about personal experiences in order to encourage the client to be more candid. Arthur Burton (1972) gives an example of how such a therapist might proceed:

THERAPIST: My mother was a problem, too.

CLIENT: Your mother!

THERAPIST: Yep. She didn't find intimacy with my father and looked to me for things he couldn't give her. Oedipus had a rough time in my family.

CLIENT: Then you know what I'm talking about.

THERAPIST: From personal experience.

Such disclosures make the client realize that the therapist really does understand the problem. Furthermore, it feeds the client's self-esteem to be confided in by an admired figure.

Therapist self-disclosure can also have negative effects, however. Derlega and Chaikin (1975) point out that clients may begin to react to the therapist on the basis of the *therapist's* problems rather than their own (what Freudians call *countertransference*). Furthermore, the clients may come to feel burdened with the therapist's problems and leave the session absorbed in his problems rather than their own.

In a study done by Norman Simonson and Susan Bahr (1974), the effects of therapist self-disclosure were examined. Subjects listened to a tape of a therapy session in which the therapist gave either neutral information about himself or made personal self-disclosures. The subjects were then interviewed by the therapist who had been on the tapes. Judges later listened to recordings of the interviews to determine each subject's "degree of disclosure." It turned out that subjects who had heard the therapist make personal disclosures were *less* likely to make disclosures themselves than were the subjects who heard neutral comments from the therapist. The researchers concluded that in certain instances therapist self-disclosure does not produce the desired results: "The level of therapist disclosure went too far beyond the subjects' expectations for this professional relationship—at least during an initial session." The effects of self-disclosure still need to be studied. They seem to depend not only on the degree of self-disclosure, but on the type of disclosure, the context, the client's expectations, and the point in therapy when disclosures are made.

"Right from the start, I felt she really cared about me. She seemed to be upset by my problems and to be happy when I made progress. I felt so relaxed with her that it was easy to talk about very personal things" (Derlega and Chaikin, 1975, page 104).

THE PUBLICATIONS RACE

One way of gauging the popularity of different methods of psychotherapy among psychologists is to count the number of articles representing each method in the professional journals. Such a count (Hoon and Lindsley, 1974) showed a tremendous increase by behavior therapies during the 1960s, finally overtaking psychoanalysis in 1972. The publication activity rate in psychoanalysis remains high, however. Client-centered therapy made its big spurt in the period from 1944 to 1955, but since then hasn't kept up.

BEHAVIOR THERAPIES

The *behavior therapies* are based on the principles of learning theory (see Chapter 5). Behavior therapists do not look for deep underlying causes for psychological problems, nor do they see therapy as a process of drawing out buried emotions or hidden thoughts. Rather, they see abnormal behavior as a problem of social learning: the troubled individual is one who has been reinforced for an inappropriate way of coping with environmental demands (Bandura, 1967). The task of behavior therapy is to help the person "unlearn" inappropriate behaviors and to replace them with appropriate ones.

There are a number of techniques available to the behavior therapist, and these techniques may be used alone or in combination, depending on the client's problem. The techniques to be focused on here are operant conditioning, desensitization, and role playing.

Operant Therapy

Operant therapy relies heavily on the conditioning procedures developed primarily by B. F. Skinner. Positive reinforcement is the main tool in operant therapy. Bandura (1967) has pointed out that this type of therapy must meet three requirements to be successful: (1) the reward must be something geared to motivate the specific client; (2) the reward must be contingent on performance of the desired behavior; and (3) there must be a method for gradually molding existing behavior into more complex behaviors not yet in the person's repertoire (see Box 2).

Application of this technique can be seen in the example of a boy in nursery school who spent about 80 percent of his time playing alone (Harris, Wolf, and Baer; cited by Bandura, 1967). Because the teacher's attention seemed to serve as a reward for this behavior, the procedure undertaken was for the teacher to ignore the boy's solitary activities but to join in and give her full attention whenever the boy played with other children. Before long he was spending 60 percent of his time with others. Eventually the enjoyment of playing in the group came to be a reward in itself and the teacher was able to reduce her role in providing reinforcement.

As this example shows, one need not be a trained behavior therapist to be a "behavior shaper." Parents and teachers in particular can learn to dispense rewards in a way that will modify children's behavior and produce desired responses. And husbands and wives can help each other with problems by becoming behavior shapers. Take, for example, the case of a woman who was unsuccessful at using self-reinforcement for keeping up a jogging program. She found joint social activities with her husband to be a good reinforcer, and her husband was given the task of dispensing this reward whenever she jogged a certain amount each week (Kau and Fischer, 1974).

Desensitization

Desensitization therapy is based on the theory of Joseph Wolpe, who feels that the goal of therapy is to recondition the client to associate relaxation rather than anxiety with certain feared objects or events. Just as operant therapy is based on operant conditioning, desensitization is used on classical conditioning (see Chapter 5). It is essentially an *unconditioning* process, in which the client learns to substitute a new response (relaxation) for the old one (anxiety) to a particular stimulus.

Wolpe begins at a very basic level: the client is instructed to think of something that causes mild anxiety. When the client gets a mental image of this mildly anxiety-producing situation, he or she is trained to relax, thereby associating the feeling of relaxation with the mildly anxious situation. Next the patient thinks of something that produces greater anxiety and again learns to relax. These sessions continue until the patient is able

Box 2

Token Economies

The idea of a token economy has been around since the early 1930s. It is a method of operant therapy in which the reward is delayed. That is, desired behaviors are reinforced with a token of some kind that can later be exchanged for a reward (see Chapter 5). This approach is particularly flexible because therapy time need not be spent on dispensing and consumption of the reward, and each subject can exchange the token for whatever he or she finds most rewarding.

A growing number of mental hospitals are using token economies as part of the therapy program. Patients are rewarded for engaging in socially constructive activities such as keeping clean, getting to meals on time, and performing assigned tasks. Payment consists of tokens (such as poker chips) that may be used to "purchase" luxuries such as increased television time, private sleeping accommodations, weekend passes, and the like.

Token economies can be effective in producing desired behaviors even among severely disturbed patients. Patients may get tokens just for moving closer to nurses or other patients. Through a process of shaping, it is then possible to encourage them to strike up conversations; they may eventually be rewarded for quite complex forms of interpersonal interaction.

One such token economy was established for an entire ward of 86 chronic schizophrenics whose average length of hospitalization was almost 25 years. Social behaviors and first attempts at recreational and vocational activities were most highly reinforced. Token fines as well as rewards were used in an effort to eliminate activities disruptive to the ward. Before long, instances of breaking hospital rules dropped sharply. Patients took a more active interest in their surroundings. One patient, in fact, left the hospital for the first time in over 40 years (Atthowe and Krasner, 1968).

Token economies are not limited to mental institutions. They can be used in private therapy, in classrooms, and even in homes. For example, one couple made an arrangement in which the wife gave her husband a token whenever he "really listened" to her in the evening. Later, the husband could exchange the tokens for sexual favors (Stuart, 1968).

to imagine one of his most feared situations and still associate it with relaxation (Wolpe and Lazarus, 1966).

In one experimental study, researchers were concerned with reducing test anxiety, a common problem that prevents students from performing at their best level (Freeling and Shemberg, 1970). A group of students rated high in test anxiety met once a week for six weeks. At the first meeting they were asked to rank-order fifteen items related to test anxiety. These items ranged from "You are sitting in a classroom of 100 students listening to a lecture" to "The test papers are being passed out and you are sitting in your seat waiting to receive your paper." The students were then taught techniques for deep muscular relaxation and were told to practice them for 15 to 30 minutes a day.

At the following sessions the group first relaxed. Then the experimenter presented items from the hierarchy of test-anxiety situations, starting with the least anxiety arousing. The students were asked to imagine the scene presented. When all could do so without feeling anxious, the next higher item was presented. In between items, the subjects were repeatedly told to relax, to feel calm and heavy. Each item was presented for ten to fifteen seconds, and the subjects were told to raise their index finger if they felt any anxiety. If that happened, the experimenter told everyone to relax, and returned to the lowest item in the hierarchy, and started over again. In this way the whole process went slowly, step by step. The entire hierarchy was covered by the end of the last session, with no more than four new items introduced at each meeting.

At the end of the six weeks, the students were less anxious, as measured by both an anxiety questionnaire and performance in an actual test situation, and they showed greater improvement than two control groups—one that learned to associate relaxation with neutral scenes, and one that was asked to imagine rank-ordered anxiety items without benefit of relaxation techniques.

Similar desensitization techniques have been used to help treat a variety of problems, including fear of animals, claustrophobia, fear of heights, impotence, and anxiety about public speaking.

THERAPY IS GOING TO THE DOGS

Psychologists have recently been adapting psychotherapeutic techniques for use with household pets. One team of psychologists (Tuber, Hothersall, and Voith, 1974) recently reported success in using desensitization to cure Higgins (an Old English sheep dog) of his intense fear of thunderstorms. They began by playing a recording of a thunderstorm very softly. If Higgins remained calm, he was rewarded with chocolate bars. As long as Higgins remained calm, the intensity of the artificial thunderstorm was gradually increased. When a real thunderstorm came along, Higgins was able to keep his anxiety under control. "Realistically," the therapists reported, "we do not expect Higgins to ever seek pleasure in thunderstorms, but the change in his behavior has been striking . . ." (p. 764).

GIVING THE OPPOSITION A FAIR TRY

Behavior therapy is not a cure-all, as indicated by Lazarus' (1971) account of what behavior therapists do when they have troubles. Of 20 behavior therapists surveyed who were in therapy themselves, 10 were in psychoanalytic therapy, 5 were in Gestalt therapy, 3 in bioenergetics, 4 in existential therapy, 1 in group dynamics—and not one in behavior therapy.

Role Playing

Another method used to help individuals acquire new behaviors is *role playing.* It involves practicing a role—a set of desired behaviors—in a protective setting, such as a therapy session or a classroom in which clients need not worry about the consequences of their behavior. It is not unlike practicing a new dance step alone before trying it out in public. Some role playing is a part of all of our lives; for example, we have all mentally rehearsed an important phone conversation before dialing the number.

In one application of role playing, college women and men volunteered for a program to improve their dating skills (Chris-

The woman is role-playing a family scene.

tensen and Arkowitz, 1974). Each participant went on as many as six "practice dates," each with another subject of the opposite sex. After each date the subjects exchanged feedback forms on which they listed four positive aspects of the other person and one behavior that the other should change. At the end of the program the participants reported that they felt more confident and skillful in dating situations, and they showed an increase in opposite-sex interactions. Role playing is often used as part of programs of *assertiveness training,* to help previously timid people learn to stand up for themselves.

Many of these behavioral techniques can be learned and used effectively by teachers, parents, spouses, police, and other people whose professions involve influencing behavior. With the aid of a professional consultant, paraprofessionals can make extensive use of behavior therapies. In fact, with the aid of a consultant you can become your own therapist. Self-modification of behavior is a promising new use of the behavior therapies.

SOMATIC THERAPY

Somatic therapy is the use of drugs, electric shocks, surgery, or other physiological means to treat the symptoms of a psychological disorder. These methods, which can be used only by medical

A NEW USE FOR THE RUBBER BAND

A 15-year-old girl compulsively pulled her hair while reading, speaking on the phone, and other such activities. This behavior sometimes resulted in bald spots. She was instructed to wear a rubber band on her wrist and to snap it after each instance of hair-pulling or whenever she felt like hair-pulling. The snaps served not only as punishment but, perhaps more important, as a systematic reminder to the girl of her habit and her own desire to conquer it. After three days of following these instructions, the hair-pulling stopped (Mastellone, 1974). Such a procedure is called aversion therapy.

doctors, are not generally used on the basis of any particular theory or approach, and, in fact, no one really knows how they work or why they produce the psychological effects they do. Furthermore, their use is highly controversial, as will be discussed in our coverage of each type of therapy.

Psychopharmacology

Psychoactive chemicals have been widely used in therapy, primarily to bring symptomatic relief to patients and to produce a state in which the patient is better able to work out problems.

For convenience, the various chemical compounds are often described in terms of their intended effect, as for example, tranquilizers and energizers. Since we cannot always predict that tranquilizers will bring tranquillity, such treatment still relies on trial and error. The most common tranquilizers, for example, have both sedative and tranquilizing effects, and it is not easy to distinguish one effect from the other (Holliday, 1965).

The chemical group called phenothiazines includes drugs with trade names such as Mellaril, Sparine, Compazine, and Thorazine. These make up the major tranquilizers. Miltown, Equanil, and Librium are minor tranquilizers and produce only moderate tranquilizing effects. These chemicals are used to calm anxious patients or at least make them indifferent to their emotional problems. In some patients, for example, obsessive thoughts and compulsive actions continue to exist, but the thoughts are less vivid and the actions less vigorously pursued.

The sedatives such as Amytal, Nembutal, and phenobarbital are used to reduce the restlessness and agitation that accompany personal problems. Sedatives are faster acting than tranquilizers and can take effect quickly, whereas tranquilizers must be ingested for some weeks before a stable state of tranquility is achieved. However, sedatives produce drowsiness and have a higher potential for addiction.

The energizers (or antidepressants) are used to alter the mood of the patient by elevating the general level of behavior. They bring on increased appetite, decreased awareness of fatigue, and increased speed of action and reaction. Because the brain is chemically triggered to a new state of alertness, the depressed person is helped to become reinvolved in life. Antidepressant drugs have proved particularly useful for patients who are both depressed and anxious about their life. The psychostimulants most used are Benzedrine, Dexedrine, and Ritalin.

Because there is so much unknown about the effects of psychiatric drugs, it is often difficult to separate true physiological effects from effects that occur because doctor and patients *expect* them to occur. This is called the placebo effect; it will be discussed later in the chapter.

Electroshock

Electroshock (or electroconvulsive shock) therapy is the application of brief electrical currents to the brain, producing convulsions. First a muscle relaxant is injected into the patient to soften the severity of the seizure and to prevent injury during the convulsion. Electrodes are then placed at both temples or at the front and back of one side of the head. From 70 to 150 volts are applied for less than a second. The patient experiences a convulsion, lasting about a minute, that is identical to an epileptic seizure.

These treatments are used primarily with severely depressed patients and with schizophrenics. A series of treatments may range from 5 to 30 or more. While behavioral changes, headaches, dizziness, loss of appetite, and other symptoms commonly follow electroshock treatments, the most serious side effect is some extent of memory loss (Friedberg, 1975).

Electroshock is used because it has relieved symptoms of depression and mania in many patients, often with a dramatic and rapid improvement. Improvement, of course, is not cure, and it does not indicate a complete remission of symptoms. It does

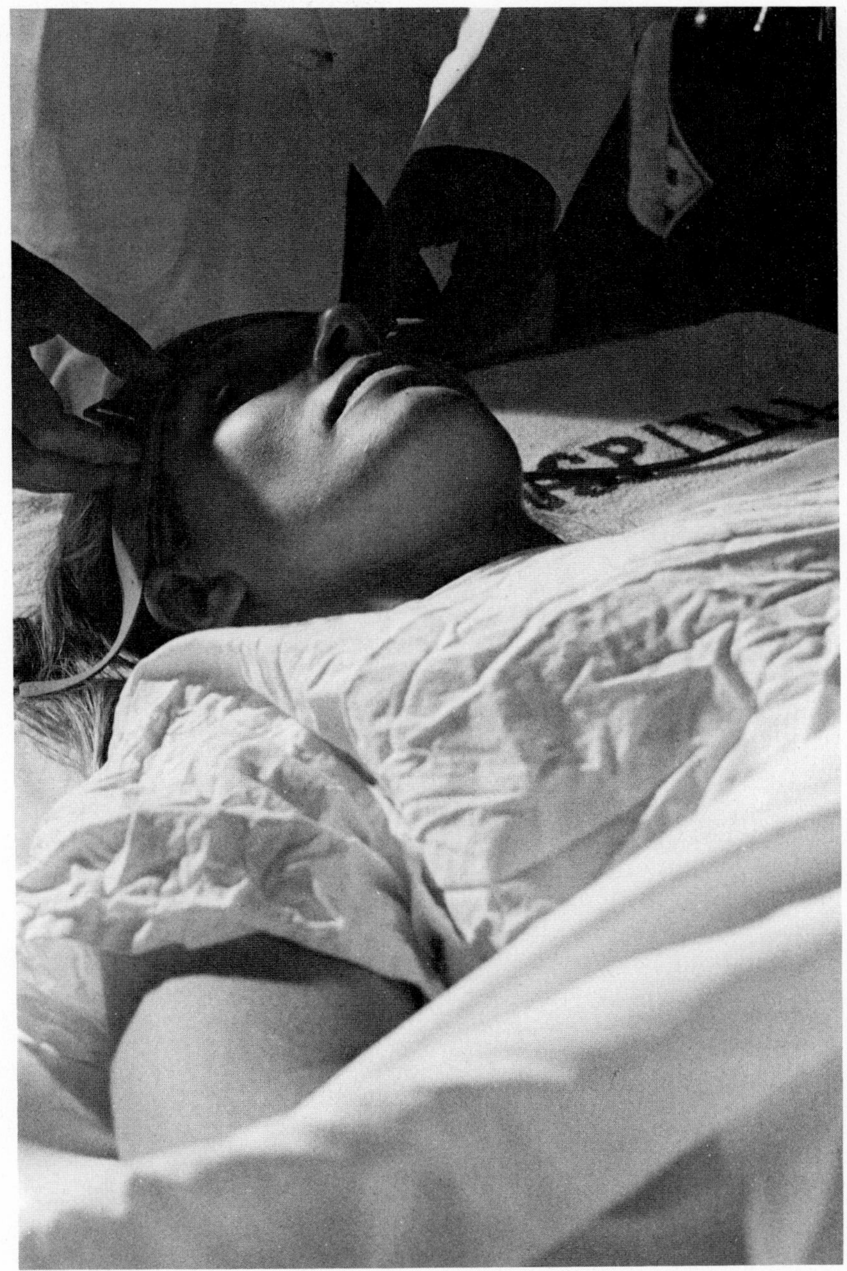

Electroshock therapy, in which brief electrical currents are applied to the brain, is among the most controversial forms of therapy currently in use.

mean that better contact can be established with the patient (McNeil, 1970). Critics of electroshock therapy point out that no one really knows what it does and that there is no conclusive evidence that it works; furthermore, they assert, relief of symptoms is not sufficient justification for damaging a human brain. Supporters of the method claim that the patient is better off with a slight memory loss than with suicidal depression or other psychotic symptoms.

Psychosurgery

When the various shock therapies came into vogue, a Portuguese neurologist, Egas Moniz, suggested that the bizarre ideas of some patients circulated in a cyclic fashion in their diseased brains and produced mental disorder. To short-circuit this reaction in psychotic patients, Moniz surgically disconnected the frontal lobes from the rest of the brain. This surgery calmed some agitated patients, but it also made vegetables of others—they walked and talked and looked like human beings, but they were without ambition, tact, imagination, or consciousness of self (Greenblatt, 1967).

Since the 1930's, when Moniz performed most of his brain surgery, psychosurgery has become much more refined, and today's techniques are more precise, destroying much smaller areas of the brain. Psychosurgery has proved valuable in some cases in which drugs and other forms of therapy have failed—most notably with epileptics. In the latter case, surgeons sever the corpus callosum, the band of fibers connecting the two sides of the brain. This "split brain" surgery significantly reduces seizures and the patient is able to function quite normally (see Chapter 2).

Critics of psychosurgery, as with electroshock, argue that the brain should not be tampered with—that destroying even a small part of it is dangerous because of the brain's vital role in learning, personality, creativity, emotion, and thought. And once a portion of the brain tissue is destroyed, it will not replace itself. Those who support this method point out that many people have experienced brain surgery without suffering permanent aftereffects and that psychosurgery is performed only on patients whose functioning would be greatly impaired without surgical intervention (Valenstein, 1975).

At best psychosurgery should be approached with caution. Much more must be learned about the localization of functions in the brain and about the effects of destruction of brain regions before psychosurgery can be totally condemned or condoned. As one critic put it, psychosurgery remains "an experimental procedure with consequences that are unpredictable and may be disastrous" (Chorover, 1974).

SITTING ON A REGULAR BASIS

Researchers have argued that meditation has psychotherapeutic potential. Studies have shown, for example, that people who practice meditation for 4 to 10 weeks show more improvement on a variety of psychological tests than nonmeditators. But in a recent review of the literature, Smith (1975) points out that these findings do not provide conclusive evidence that meditation is therapeutic. The therapeutic benefits could be the result of the expectation of relief or of simply sitting on a regular basis.

DOES THERAPY WORK?

There has been a great deal of controversy over whether psychotherapy works at all. For example, Hans Eysenck (1952) created a storm when he reviewed the existing literature on psychotherapy (mainly psychoanalytic) and concluded that it had no favorable effect at all. He claimed that as many patients "improved" as would have improved anyway with the passage of time. Others disputed Eysenck's interpretation, and by now, with many more studies having been conducted, it is fair to conclude that although psychotherapy does not help everybody (and in some cases it may even have negative effects), on the whole it has modest positive effects (Bergin and Suinn, 1975).

In one recent study (Sloane et al., 1975), 90 outpatients at the Temple University outpatient clinic were randomly assigned to one of three groups: one that received behavior therapy, one that received short-term psychoanalytic therapy, and a "waiting list" group that was given only minimal treatment. The clients were generally anxious, depressed, or otherwise troubled—not severely disturbed or psychotic. The therapists were experienced. After four months of treatment (or waiting), the clients were assessed by an independent rater who did not know to which groups the clients were assigned. On the average, clients in all three groups improved, even those on the waiting list, which shows that time itself can sometimes heal psychic wounds. But clients in the two treatment groups improved more than the waiting-list clients. Neither psychoanalytic therapy nor behavior therapy was superior overall.

A problem to be reckoned with in assessing the effectiveness of psychotherapy is the general lack of long-term followup. Gains may be made while the client is in therapy, but it is not always clear how long they will last. Also, it is not always assured that gains made in a therapist's office or in dealing with particular situations will generalize to all real-life situations. Another problem in determining the efficacy of therapy is deciding how to define "success" or "improvement." What constitutes improvement, and who is to decide whether improvement has taken place? Is the client the best judge? Is the therapist?

YOU'VE GOT TO BELIEVE

Although the clear superiority of one method of therapy over another has not been demonstrated, many therapists continue to believe in their own systems. As Parloff (1968) writes, "No form of psychotherapy has ever been initiated without a claim it has unique therapeutic advantages, and no form of psychotherapy has ever been abandoned because of its failure to live up to these claims."

What Makes the Difference?

As the study of outpatients helps illustrate, one method of therapy is not necessarily better than another. This is the general consensus of recent research. A review by Luborsky and associates (1971) concluded that the best predictions of whether a particular client will improve are the client's own characteristics: Clients who are relatively healthy, intelligent, and highly motivated are most likely to make effective use of therapy. Of secondary importance are characteristics of the therapist—his or her experience, attitudes, and empathy. Of least importance is the particular technique or "school" of therapy.

It is possible, of course, that particular techniques may be more effective for particular problems; for example, behavioral techniques may be especially useful for certain phobias. But the superiority of one therapy over another, even for specific problems, is not yet well established.

In light of these results, many therapists are eclectic, drawing on psychoanalytic, client-centered, behavioral, or other techniques as they seem appropriate, rather than maintaining an unyielding allegiance to a single school. Jerome Frank does not find this conclusion surprising, as he believes that the common features of different therapies, rather than their unique characteristics, are what account for most of their effectiveness (Frank, 1973b). As we pointed out at the beginning of the chapter, these key common features include the close relationship between therapist and client, the special setting, and the existence of a theory or rationale. One additional ingredient that is common to all therapies is the power of expectations.

The Power of Expectations

As Frank (1973b) notes, a central role of all psychotherapies is to rekindle clients' hopes, to make them feel that they can in fact regain their morale and mastery over the environment. When people enter therapy, they expect to benefit from it, and often these expectations are fulfilled no matter what type of treatment is dispensed. This process is often termed the *placebo effect.*

A *placebo* (which is the Latin word meaning "I shall please") is any medicine that works psychologically but has no physical effect. Medically, placebos are no more than "sugar pills." But if a patient is told that these pills contain a potent medicine, they may lead to improvement in the patient's condition. Such a placebo effect is likely to occur in any sort of therapy—with or without drugs.

The "power of suggestion" has been easily demonstrated by research in medicine. The method of administration, for example, may be an important factor in determining one's response to a placebo. One doctor found that a placebo administered in a bright red gelatin capsule brought favorable results in 81 percent of the cases tested. Results were favorable in only 49 percent of

Box 3

Community Mental Health
Many psychologists have begun to believe that therapy must go beyond the therapist's couch or the mental hospital. They believe that people with problems are often best helped in their own community. This idea, called the community mental health movement, has led to the establishment of more than 400 federally funded mental health centers in communities across the country.

What do these centers do? The services they provide depend a great deal on the particular community, on the facilities available, and on the staff members. Some centers concentrate primarily on counseling, while others may provide a complete line of services from educational programs to short-term hospitalization. Some offer lectures and seminars designed to educate people in a particular community problem, such as drugs or ju-

GIVING PSYCHOLOGY AWAY

". . . the secrets of our trade need not be reserved for highly trained specialists. Psychological facts should be passed out freely to all who need and can use them. . . . There simply are not enough psychologists, even including nonprofessionals, to meet every need for psychological services. The people at large will have to be their own psychologists, and make their own applications of established principles." [Miller, 1969, p. 68]

the cases when the placebo was administered as a tablet and in 69 percent of the cases when it was administered as a liquid. Hypodermic injections are usually more effective than tablets but are somewhat inferior to capsules.

Like the medical doctor, the therapist can dispense help that

venile delinquency.

Among the more popular aspects of community programs are *crisis intervention centers* and *hotlines.* People with an immediate problem or crisis can come in or phone for help. Particularly helpful have been suicide prevention centers, where sympathetic listeners take calls from individuals contemplating suicide. Many lives have been saved as the result of such phone calls.

An example of a crisis intervention program is the "Seminars for the Separated" conducted by Robert S. Weiss and others in the Harvard Medical School's Laboratory of Community Psychiatry. People who were in the process of separation or divorce came to a series of lectures and group meetings where they learned more about what to expect with regard to relations with children and in-laws, finances, work around the house, and sex. They were able to share feelings with others going through the same experience (Weiss, 1975).

Community mental health programs also emphasize the use of *paraprofessionals*—community residents who are trained by professionals to provide therapy. Fo and O'Donnell (1974) provide an example: Adult community residents in Hawaii were trained by psychologists to act as "buddies" for 42 eleven- to seventeen-year-old youths referred by the Family Court for behavior and academic problems. They used various operant therapy methods, such as making positive attention or material rewards (going to the movies) contingent on improved school attendance and behavior. These treatments were successful in reducing some of the youths' problem behaviors.

Community mental health does have its critics. They say that centers reach only a small proportion of community members who need help and that the center's professionals do not spend enough time in normal community social settings. Further, the number of neighborhood communities seems to be dwindling, especially in large urban areas (Lazarus, 1974). Without communities it is difficult to establish community centers.

will bring results primarily through the powers of suggestion and expectation. As research with "self-fulfilling prophecy" has shown, people tend to subtly bring about those things that they expect to happen, not only in therapy but in many areas of their lives.

THE ETHICS OF PSYCHOTHERAPY

Particular varieties of psychotherapy, such as somatic therapies and behavior therapy, have been singled out for special criticism as involving "mind control" and as threatening individual freedom. The term "behavior modification" has raised the spectre of a "1984" type of controlled society. But it should be noted that *all* forms of psychotherapy, like other forms of social influence, raise such questions. As Bandura (1972) has suggested, all forms of psychotherapy might be labeled "behavior modification" because "all forms of psychotherapy, regardless of their self-conferred honorific titles and noble aims, effect behavioral changes through either deliberate or unwitting manipulation of controlling variables" (page 654).

The key issue is not whether people should be controlled, influenced, or altered by other people, but rather the extent to which people can decide for themselves whether, when, and how to be controlled, influenced, or altered. Psychotherapy can be an important and powerful force for good, but many questions about it have yet to be answered. Meanwhile, psychotherapy continues to gain popularity and acceptance and to grow in new directions.

SUMMARY

1. Common features shared by all types of psychotherapy are (1) establishment of a solid relationship between therapist and client; (2) a setting that encourages clients to freely express themselves; (3) a basic theory of behavior on which the therapy is based.
2. According to Frank, therapy serves to combat and treat the symptoms of *demoralization*—a feeling of having failed to meet the expectations of oneself or of others.
3. The goals of psychotherapy include: (1) relief from anxiety, symptoms, and conflict; (2) maturity and integration of different parts of the self; (3) improved interpersonal relationships; (4) social adjustment.
4. Talking therapies emphasize bringing concealed thoughts and emotions into the open. These therapies include psychoanalysis and client-centered therapy.
5. In his system of *psychoanalysis,* Freud used the process of *working through* to help the person achieve *catharsis*—release of buried emotions. During *free association,* in which the client says whatever comes to mind, the client may *resist* discussing certain topics. Through *interpretation* the therapist

points out resistances. During the therapeutic process, the client often *transfers* feelings toward another person onto the neutral therapist.

6. In Rogers' *client-centered therapy,* the therapist provides *unconditional positive regard,* encouraging the client to express true feelings and desires. The client, not the therapist, does the analyzing. Client-centered therapists are encouraged to share thair own personal experiences with their clients, but if such self-disclosures are too candid, the clients may become inhibited.
7. *Behavior therapies* see the client as someone who has learned inappropriate ways of behaving rather than as one who has deep underlying psychological problems. Behavior therapists use such techniques as operant conditioning, desensitization, and role playing to eliminate the inappropriate behavior and create a desired behavior.
8. Therapists are using *operant conditioning* when they use rewards to motivate a client to perform a desired behavior or to refrain from performing an undesired behavior. One such use of conditioning is the *token economy,* in which desired behaviors are reinforced with tokens of some kind that can be later exchanged for a reward.
9. In *desensitization,* the client unlearns a fear of anxiety. It involves learning to substitute a new response (usually relaxation) for an old response (anxiety) in a certain situation.
10. In *role playing,* a client can "try out" a new behavior without suffering the negative consequences. Role playing has been used to improve dating skills and as part of programs of assertiveness training.
11. *Somatic therapy* is the use of drugs, electric shocks, or surgery to treat the symptoms of a psychological disorder.
12. Among drugs used in somatic therapy are tranquilizers, sedatives, and energizers (antidepressants). They are used to change the mood of patients so that they can function more normally and so that they will be more receptive to other types of therapy.
13. Applications of electric current to the brain are used to relieve symptoms of depression and mania. Such *electroshock* therapy is highly controversial, partly because we know so little about how it works.
14. *Psychosurgery* is brain surgery designed to relieve psychological symptoms, such as those associated with epilepsy. It may involve destroying small portions of brain tissue or severing certain brain parts, usually in the frontal lobe. This, too, is a controversial form of therapy.
15. Although psychotherapy does not help everyone, on the whole it seems to have a positive effect. No one type of therapy seems to be superior, and many people improve without professional help.

16. Whether a client will benefit from therapy depends more on the characteristics of the client than on those of the therapist or the technique. People who expect to benefit from treatment usually do. This is called the *placebo effect.*
17. In an effort to help people with their problems in their own community, the *community mental health movement* has led to the establishment of mental health centers in hundreds of American communities. Among the services offered are counseling, educational programs, crisis intervention centers, and hotlines. Many of these services are provided by *paraprofessionals* recruited from within the community.

Variations in Psychotherapy

We have become consumers of the therapy-of-the-month. . . .

When the final history of psychotherapy is written, it will refer to the 1960s and 1970s as the decades of variation—variation in technique, method, approach, theory, and practice. The "discovery" of new solutions to ancient psychological problems has accelerated so rapidly that today's therapeutic miracle shortly becomes a forgotten flash-in-the-pan. We have become the consumers of the therapy-of-the-month, which is due, in part, to glamorization and exaggeration by the mass media. (The inventors of the sure-fire new therapies make interesting guests on TV talk shows.) Further, we are a society that increasingly seeks quick and simple solutions to the difficulties of being human.

There is, unfortunately, a cult-like quality to each of these innovations in therapy. Each delegates itself to be the sole owner of truth; each disparages all other forms of therapy; and each claims to have produced miracles for its believers.

Jerome Frank (1972) attributes the sudden flood of new therapies to the current upheaval in contemporary society. He accepts Rollo May's (1968) observation that when traditional values and institutions become discredited, they lose their power to unite members of the society and to provide a meaningful view of the world. As a result, members of the society cast about for new ways of preserving a sense of security and significance. One of these ways is psychotherapy. If the quest for help is itself intense, then any of a number of methods may work.

The Primal Scream

The Primal Institute of Los Angeles is stocked with teddy bears, baby bottles, cribs, punching bags, isolation chambers, and photographs of clients' parents. There is even a birth simulator, made of inner tubes, where clients can relive the trauma of birth—if that is their problem. When therapy is going on, there may be as many as 40 or 50 clients on the floor writhing through what are called *Primals,* while several therapists circulate among them giving comfort and aid to those having difficulty releasing their feelings.

Primal therapy began in 1967 with a 22-year-old client whom Arthur Janov was treating. When the client was told to call out for his parents he reluctantly did so at first, and then became upset, writhed on the floor, and began to breathe rapidly. Finally, an agonized scream convulsed his whole

Unfailingly, there was a trauma, a scream, and a rebirth of feeling.

body. When he calmed down, he felt "cured" by having released feeling pent up for a lifetime. Primal therapy was born, and Janov began to ask other clients to call out for their missing parents. Unfailingly, there was a trauma, a scream, and a rebirth of feeling.

Janov's therapy centers on the idea of pain. For him, neurosis is frozen childhood pain. Each time a child is not held when he cries, not fed when hungry, or ignored when he needs attention, it contributes to a "Primal pool of pain," which, when deep enough, can produce neurosis as a way of life. As the neurotic child grows into a neurotic adult, he or she often becomes involved with persons who perpetuate childhood patterns; through them, he tries to achieve symbolically what he was deprived of long ago. The boy who had a cold mother grows up and marries a cold wife hoping to warm her up and prove at last that he can win his mother's love. The boy whose father never loved him may become homosexual seeking to get from men the affection his father refused him as a child.

According to Janov, if clients can successfully re-experience this original pain, they can be free for the first time and become superior human beings. While the data from his physiological studies are incomplete, Janov suggests that the post-Primal person is so free of tension and defenses that he or she may well live longer and be prey to fewer diseases than non-Primaled persons (Keen, 1972).

If you can believe the testimony of satisfied patients, the results of Primal therapy are nearly miraculous. "Ulcers, arthritis, epilepsy are cured; flat-chested women require larger brassieres. Many a man feels that he has added a cubit onto his stature; intelligence increases, eyesight sharpens, coordination improves" (Keen, 1972, p. 88). On the other side, critics have called Janov a "dangerous, publicity-seeking charlatan."

Transactional Analysis

Transactional analysis is about the "games people play" and the catchy names Eric Berne (1964) attached to them. Berne talked of the "con," the "gimmick," and the "payoff." If, for example, a woman courts a compliment and receives it gratefully, it is nothing more than a harmless social pastime. But if she asks for reassurance, receives it, and then tries to show that the compliment was undeserved, she's played "Yes, but." Her payoff was not simply the massaging of her vanity, but the chance to prove her partner stupid and feel superior at his expense (Langouth, 1966). Such games are harmful because they involve emotional deception—the con—in relating to others.

The principles of Script Analysis also evolved from Transactional Analysis. "We have evidence, that between the ages of three and seven, a child develops a 'script' for his future—i.e., a story-line blueprint that determines how he will live the rest of his life—particularly his important relationships, his feelings about himself and his achievements, and the outcome that he will experience as 'success,' 'failure,' 'I almost made it,' or 'at least I tried' " (English, 1973, p. 48).†

The basic element of Transactional Analysis (T. A.) is analyzing the "transactions" between people.

The way in which children acquire feelings about themselves and others as they grow up establishes their "position." Berne lists four of these.

1. I'm not O.K.—You're O.K.
2. I'm not O.K.—You're not O.K.
3. I'm O.K.—You're not O.K.
4. I'm O.K.—You're O.K.

The basic element of Transactional Analysis (T.A.) is analyzing the "transactions" between people. Transactional analysts believe there are three "ego-states" within each of us—the Parent, the Adult, and the Child (P-A-C)—and each of

†*From F. English, "TA's Disney World,"* Psychology Today, April, 1973, p. 43. Copyright © *1973 Ziff-Davis Publishing Company. REPRINTED BY PERMISSION OF PSYCHOLOGY TODAY MAGAZINE.*

these interacts with different people in different situations.

Lamott (1972) uses the example of a married couple—John and Barbara having fun at a party. The transaction of having fun together involves the Child ego-state of both partners. When John suggests they have another drink and Barbara answers, "You always drink too much at parties," she has moved into her Parent state. John can respond by staying in his Child state and saying, 'Aw, come on, sweetie, let's have fun." Or, John may decide to respond by saying, "You know very well that I don't *always* drink too much at parties and furthermore you said you'd drive us home, and furthermore if I'm hung over tomorrow, it's my hangover and not yours, and anyway it's Sunday." He has shifted into his Adult—data-gathering, rational, problem-solving state; and his remarks are addressed to Barbara's Adult, although it is fair to guess that Barbara's Adult isn't listening (p. 132).†

In terms of P-A-C, the healthy personality is one in which the rational Adult is in control, but is indulgent toward the Child (who likes fun and sex), and resistant toward the Parent (who keeps trying to enforce ancient rules that tend to get in the way as the personality develops).

Gestalt Therapy

German for "whole," the term *gestalt* accurately describes this innovative therapy, which aims to put individuals in touch with their entire self. According to Fritz Perls (1969), who developed this form of therapy, individuals tend to block out awareness of aspects of themselves and their experience, looking at only part of who they are or what they are doing. The therapist's job is to make these individuals whole again by helping them recognize all the facets of their personalities and experiences. The individual is made aware of his or her feelings, thoughts, and actions as they occur together.

The individual is made aware of his or her feelings, thoughts, and actions as they occur together.

The goal of gestalt therapy is self-actualization and acceptance of responsibility for one's personality and one's life. Gestalt therapy frequently takes place in groups, although the emphasis is always on the individual. The therapist will point out all aspects of a person's behavior—tone of voice, eye movement, gestures—that the individual usually ignores. He challenges clients to control their feelings about certain situations and to recognize sensations from their body of which they are usually not aware. Because dreams are a part of personality, and therefore each person's responsibility, the therapist will often ask the client to determine the meaning of dreams by acting out the roles of objects and people in the dreams, rather than by introspection. In addition, clients are encouraged to take care of "unfinished business"—that is, to resolve problems from the past that affect current behavior. To do this, an individual may play the role of himself and his adversary and act out a dialogue concerning the conflict or tension he is experiencing.

Encounter Groups

The aim of encounter groups is to bring people together to increase trust, openness, and sensitivity. The idea is to make individuals aware of thoughts and feelings that they have not recognized before. A psychologist estimates that more than six million people have by now participated in some kind of encounter and they have been mostly middle-class Americans, including students, lawyers, policemen, clergymen, housewives, businessmen, teachers, and doctors. Encounter has become a revolution in interpersonal relations.

The seed was planted more than a quarter of a century ago by Kurt Lewin, the founder of Group Dynamics and creator of the first T-groups (training groups) in 1947 (Egan, 1970). About the same time Carl Rogers and his associates de-

†*From Kenneth Lamott, "Four Possible Life Positions,"* New York Times Magazine, *November 19, 1972, p. 21. © 1972 by The New York Times Company. Reprinted by permission.*

veloped a theory of intensive group interaction. A group of strangers could become close personal companions, if only briefly, provided they could be left to their own devices.

The encounter movement encompasses a range of variation. There are groups involved with sensory awareness, expressive movement, environmental awareness, social-emotional expression, problem solving, creativity, social sensitivity, social competence, and mystical experience (Mann, 1970). Cataloguing the incredibly explosive variations in helping people relate to one another is not possible here. We can choose just a few examples to give the flavor of group encounter, however.

Marathon Marathon groups sometimes seem to their participants to amount to endurance contests. The sheer elapse of time forces participants to put aside their social masks, hopefully to reveal the real self.

The rules of marathon are fairly simple (Lamott, 1969). Everyone stays until the end, and only the therapist is allowed to take naps. Physical assault is forbidden, but brutal frankness may be encouraged. No alcohol or drugs are allowed. Openness and intimacy are the watch words, and behavior in the group itself (not prestige and status in the outside world) is all that matters. Each marathon has different rules. In general, marathon regulations are designed to force intense personal contacts that are "real," rather than "polite" human interactions. Marathon groups are designed to help persons find an immediate breakthrough in a life crisis (Shepard and Lee, 1970).

. . . the human body and our feelings about it are vital dimensions of our view of the self and of the world.

Naked Encounter The naked encounter is a deliberate attempt to divest us of the disguise our clothing provides. Shedding your clothes reveals also the inner self to others. In a recent innovation, for example, videotapes are made of the naked participants during sessions. Each person is then given several opportunities to view his or her behavior and physical appearance through videotape playbacks. The tapes include facial close-ups, shots from the waist up, and full body profiles, as well as shots of walking, standing, turning, sitting, and talking.

Part of the purpose of this public encounter with the self was described by Blank (1969), who noted that the human body and our feelings about it are vital dimensions of our view of the self and of the world. Our body image is our idea of how our own bodies appear to others, and this image often does not agree with the images that others hold of us.

Effects of Encounter A study of encounter groups was recently conducted at Stanford University by Lieberman, Yalom, and Miles (1973). More than 200 students were randomly assigned to 17 groups representing ten major styles of encounter—National Training Laboratory (T-group), Gestalt therapy, transactional analysis, "Esalen eclectic," personal growth, Synanon, psychodrama, marathon, psychoanalytic, and leaderless encounter tapes. There were also control subjects who were not in any encounter group.

The participants were followed up six months and one year after the groups. In general, the results were not too encouraging: About one-third of the students showed positive effects, about one-third negative effects (including some who experienced psychological damage), and about one-third no effects. As in the case of psychotherapy in general, the individual characteristics of the group leader seemed more important in affecting group members than did the particular style or "school" of encounter used.

Summary

1. In recent years several new therapies have gained almost cult-like popularity. Among them is Arthur Janov's Primal therapy, in which clients try to reexperience childhood pain in order to find freedom in adult life.
2. Transactional Analysis (TA) examines the "games people play" in their interactions with one another. Transactional analysts help people to discover the "position" they developed in childhood and to put the Adult part of their personality in control.
3. Gestalt therapists use a variety of techniques to help clients get in touch with all aspects of themselves and integrate the self into a whole.
4. Numerous types of encounter groups are available in which people can meet with others for the purpose of increasing their openness and sensitivity toward one another.

PART 8

Relating to One Another

Psychology cannot confine itself to studying individuals as if they were isolated organisms, each in his or her private world. A fundamental aspect of being human is the way in which we affect—and, in turn, are affected by—our fellow human beings. We have emphasized this social aspect of being human throughout this book. In the final two chapters, however, we will focus most directly on the ways in which people related to one another, drawing from the field of *social psychology*.

Chapter 18 is concerned with the interrelated topics of *Attitudes and Influence.* We will discover that people's attitudes, whether they concern political candidates, consumer goods, or social values, are all formed in large measure through interactions with other people. We will also examine some of the techniques people use to influence the views and actions of others. The Psychological Issue following this chapter concerns *Prejudice,* that dangerous set of attitudes that directly influences our behavior toward entire groups of people.

Chapter 19 explores some of the central themes that run through our *Interpersonal Relationships*—needing others, perceiving others, liking others, loving others, and leaving others. Several of these themes relate closely to psychological processes that we discussed in previous chapters—"needing others" to social aspects of motivation, "perceiving others" to social aspects of perception, and "loving others" to social aspects of emotion. The Psychological Issue that follows Chapter 19 discusses some of the challenges and problems of interpersonal relationships in a sphere of tremendous importance both to individuals and to society as a whole, that of *Marriage and Divorce.*

Attitudes and Influence

CHAPTER 18

Attitudes and Influence

How good a job do you think the President is doing?

Do you approve or disapprove of sexual intercourse between unmarried people?

Are you in favor of capital punishment for certain crimes?

All in all, what is your opinion of the college you attend?

How do you feel about your psychology professor?

What brand of mouthwash, if any, do you prefer?

These questions seem to have little in common with one another. Their common characteristic, however, is that they all ask about your *attitudes*—the ways in which you evaluate people, objects, and issues. Attitudes are people's likes and dislikes, and as such they play a major role in determining social behavior, from trivial choices to crucial life decisions. Your attitudes are likely to play a major role in determining whom you vote for, what groups you join, what courses you take, and what products you buy.

No wonder, then, that attitudes have been the central focus of theory and research in social psychology. In fact, "attitude" is probably the most widely used single term in all the social sciences (Berkowitz, 1972). Attitudes have also been a central concern of people with an interest in shaping and changing other people's opinions and behavior, including pollsters and politicians, manufacturers and merchandisers, public relations consultants and propagandists. In this chapter we will focus on how attitudes are measured, where they come from, and how they can be changed. In the last section of the chapter, we will turn from attitude change to another sort of social influence—obedience to authority.

COMPONENTS OF ATTITUDES: THOUGHTS AND FEELINGS

Attitudes include both thoughts (or beliefs) and feelings about people, objects, or issues. Thoughts are generally referred to as the *cognitive* component of an attitude, and feelings as the *affective* component. For example, the cognitive component of Carl's attitude toward capital punishment might be the belief that capital punishment is immoral and that it does not effectively deter crime anyway. The affective component of this attitude might include the feeling of sadness and revulsion that Carl experiences whenever he hears about an execution.

In general, we expect the cognitive and affective aspects of an attitude to be consistent with each other. If, for example, you think highly of a particular candidate, you are also likely to feel good when that candidate gets elected. Or, if you have negative beliefs about a particular group of people, you may well feel uneasy when you come into contact with a member of that group.

In addition, we usually expect a person's attitude toward some object to be closely related to his or her behavior toward that object. If you have a positive attitude toward a candidate, you will probably act on this attitude by voting for her; if you have a negative attitude toward a particular actor, you will probably avoid his movies. As we will see later, however, although people are usually motivated to act in accord with their attitudes, in practice they don't always do so.

MEASURING ATTITUDES

Psychologists and other social scientists have devoted a great deal of attention to the problem of measuring attitudes. Many different measurement techniques have been developed, but most of them involve asking people direct questions about their views. One technique is to ask *open-ended questions,* which allow the respondents to make any response they wish. For example, a political pollster might ask, "When you think of Barbara Jordan, what are the first things that come to your mind?" Or a marketing researcher might ask a mother, "Now that you've had a chance to use our disposable diapers for a month, could you tell me how you feel about them?"

Answers to such open-ended questions can provide rich information about people's attitudes, but they may also be difficult to analyze quantitatively. Thus, most attitude measurement devices make use of *fixed-response questions,* in which the respondents are asked to select one of a given set of answers to a question. One common approach is to present people with a series of statements about some object or issue and to ask them to indicate how much they agree or disagree with each statement. For example, Figure 18.1 represents a series of questions that might be used to assess people's attitude toward capital punishment. The respondent's overall attitude score is determined by summing his or her answers on each of the individual questions. The more strongly a person agrees with items 1 and 4 and the more strongly he or she disagrees with items 2 and 3, the more favorable the person's attitude toward capital punishment might be said to be. In this case, as in many others, researchers are likely to assume that the attitude they are interested in is too complex to be adequately measured with a single question; therefore, they make use of a combination of questions, each of which gets at a slightly different aspect of the underlying attitude.

Another sort of fixed-response measure is called the *semantic differential,* developed by Charles Osgood and his coworkers (1957). In the semantic differential, a word or phrase is followed

Sample Items To Assess Attitudes Toward Capital Punishment

For each statement circle the number that expresses how much you agree or disagree.

1. Executing murderers is an effective way to deter other people from committing murder.

−3	−2	−1	+1	+2	+3
Strongly Disagree	Moderately Disagree	Slightly Disagree	Slightly Agree	Moderately Agree	Strongly Agree

2. Although capital punishment may have been appropriate in other times, today it can only be regarded as a "cruel and inhuman punishment."

−3	−2	−1	+1	+2	+3
Strongly Disagree	Moderately Disagree	Slightly Disagree	Slightly Agree	Moderately Agree	Strongly Agree

3. Capital punishment only serves to perpetuate violence in our society.

−3	−2	−1	+1	+2	+3
Strongly Disagree	Moderately Disagree	Slightly Disagree	Slightly Agree	Moderately Agree	Strongly Agree

4. There are times when a person has committed a crime so hideous that the only appropriate punishment is death.

−3	−2	−1	+1	+2	+3
Strongly Disagree	Moderately Disagree	Slightly Disagree	Slightly Agree	Moderately Agree	Strongly Agree

by a series of contrasting adjective pairs, as in Figure 18.2. The respondent is asked to rate the concept wherever it seems to belong on each scale. This method has frequently been used by political pollsters and marketing researchers, as well as by basic researchers, as a way of exploring in depth the beliefs and emotional connotations associated with particular candidates, products, or issues.

Of course, attitude measures are not infallible. They will produce accurate results only to the extent that the respondent has in fact an attitude about the object in question and is motivated to respond honestly. Attitude questionnaires and public opinion polls may sometimes *create* attitudes rather than simply measure them, since they often ask questions about matters that the respondent has never thought about before. Furthermore, people's expressed attitudes can sometimes be influenced by the specific situation in which the interview or questionnaire is exhibited. For example, Robert Shomer and Richard Centers (1970) had three groups of male students fill out a measure of attitudes about men's and women's roles. Those men who completed the scale in a classroom with other men proved to have the most "male chauvinist" attitudes; those who filled out the questionnaire in a room containing half men and half women expressed

Example Of The Semantic Differential Technique

Indicate how you would describe the following person by placing a check on the appropriate blank for each pair of adjectives.

Walter Cronkite

Unfriendly	___	___	___	___	___	Friendly
Fair	___	___	___	___	___	Unfair
Neat	___	___	___	___	___	Sloppy
Weak	___	___	___	___	___	Strong
Relaxed	___	___	___	___	___	Tense
Active	___	___	___	___	___	Passive
Good	___	___	___	___	___	Bad

FIG. 18 · 2 An illustration of the semantic differential technique for measuring attitudes.

in-between attitudes; and those who filled out the scale in a room containing 18 men and only one woman had the least male-chauvinist attitudes. The testing situation, ranging from the all-male "locker room atmosphere" to the perhaps consciousness-raising atmosphere of a lone woman in a group of men, apparently had an effect on the attitudes that the men chose to express. In spite of problems such as this, however, researchers are usually able to assess people's attitudes with a reasonable degree of accuracy.

WHERE DO ATTITUDES COME FROM?

We are not born with attitudes—they are learned, through our experience in the world and our interactions with other people. In this section we will examine three important ways in which we acquire attitudes. These three foundations of attitudes can be categorized, following the terminology of Daryl Bem (1970), as the *emotional*, the *cognitive*, and the *social*.

Emotional Foundations of Attitudes

Remember the last time you had a Coke? It probably seemed like a simple, uncomplicated event—you were thirsty and you got something to drink. Right? Wrong, according to the advertisers who spend millions shaping your attitudes toward their product. Knowing how much you enjoy music, for example, they taught you a song to sing. They suggested you would "like to

A TELEPHONE POLL THAT GOT HUNG UP

The trustworthiness of any opinion poll depends on how representative the sample of persons polled happens to be. A classic example of how sampling errors can distort results occurred in the case of a political poll conducted by *Literary Digest*. The magazine predicted that the Republican candidate, Alf Landon, would win the 1936 presidential election. The poll was conducted by selecting the names from lists of persons who had telephones. Today such a poll might work, but in 1936 only half the people in the United States had telephones, and these people tended to be richer and to vote Republican. The magazine's poll was thus biased and misread the results (Franklin D. Roosevelt was the winner). Nowadays, political pollsters are much more sophisticated, and although they sometimes make mistakes, political opinion polls tend to be remarkably accurate.

teach the world to sing in perfect harmony" and that you would "like to buy the world a Coke and keep it company." They not only sold you a Coke, they also sold you a sense of community to combat your anxiety over the modern, strife-torn world.

Or maybe you recently had a Pepsi—not so much because you were thirsty, but because you are "young in heart." You have "a lot of living to do" as a member of the Pepsi Generation (Nietzke, 1972). You may have had some trouble deciding between Coke and Pepsi, since the advertisers make you choose between "coming alive" and "getting the real thing." Who would want to miss either of those experiences? After all, you want the "real thing" to remind you how much better life was in the past when nothing was plastic, chemical, or imitation. This decision may be so tough that you don't make it at all—and choose 7-Up, "the un-cola," instead.

Commercial appeals like these are often remarkably successful, and they illustrate the way in which attitudes can be formed by linking particular objects to positive emotions. The basic technique involved is a variation of the classical conditioning that we examined in Chapter 5. By repeatedly pairing a product (for example, the Coke or Pepsi) with images and ideals that we are likely to feel good about, the advertisers attempt to make the good feeling spill over, or generalize to, the product itself. If the technique works, simply drinking a Coke or Pepsi can make you feel good, even when the commercial is not playing in the background.

Along similar lines, Arthur and Carolyn Staats (1958) attempted to show that attitudes toward national groups can be established by means of classical conditioning. They showed subjects the names of six different nationalities, followed by single words. Some of the nationalities, such as Dutch and Swedish, were followed by words that had either positive or negative emotional connotations. For some subjects, the word "Dutch" was always followed by a positive word, such as "happy" or "sweet," while the word "Swedish" was always followed by a negative word, such as "bitter" or "ugly." For other subjects, these pairings were reversed. Thus, the names of nationalities (which prior to the experiment had little emotional association for the subjects) served as conditioned stimuli, and the positive and negative words (which already had the power to produce emotional reactions) served as the unconditioned stimuli. The rest of the names of nationalities on the list (such as German and French) were always followed by neutral words, such as "chair" and "with." After looking at the lists, subjects were asked how they felt about each nationality name on semantic-differential scales, such as "pleasant-unpleasant."

Staats and Staats found that subjects rated the nationality that had been paired with positive words more positively than the nationality that had been paired with negative words. What's more, Staats and Staats claimed that this result was obtained even among subjects who were not aware of the fact that the experimenter was trying to condition them. This procedure, because it involves the use of words as unconditioned and conditioned stimuli, is called *semantic conditioning.* Page (1969) has criticized the Staats and Staats study on the grounds that it was easy for the subjects to discern what the experimenters had in mind and that they were simply trying to be "good subjects" and to please the experimenters. Nevertheless, the Staats and Staats study provides an analog of one way in which national and racial attitudes are in fact learned, especially in early life. If, for example, a white child hears the word "black" or "Negro" repeatedly paired with such unpleasant words as "bad" or "dirty," the child may gradually, through semantic conditioning, come to feel negatively toward blacks.

Classical conditioning helps explain the formation of attitudes that may seem quite irrational. When we take a look at our attitudes about certain people or groups, we are sometimes forced to say something like, "I don't know why I feel that way; I just do." This uncertainty may be due to the fact that the attitude does not have any logical or rational basis at all. Instead, it may be based on repeated pairings of emotional stimuli with the attitude object. Whether these pairings are accidental or calculated (as in the case of many advertising campaigns), they may bear little relation to the actual content of the attitude.

PEANUTS, MUSIC, AND THOUGHTS OF YOU

Different techniques can be used to make an audience feel good about a product or message. In one study, subjects who were given a snack of peanuts and Pepsi-Cola while they read were more persuaded by a written message than were subjects who went snackless (Janis, Kaye, and Kirschner, 1965). In another study, subjects were more influenced by messages that were accompanied by folk music than by those that were unaccompanied (Galizio and Hendrick, 1972). And journalist Joe McGinniss (1969) reported that the people in charge of "selling" Richard Nixon in 1968 made a point of including pleasant background music in all of his spot commercials.

Cognitive Foundations of Attitudes

Much of the time we *can* explain our own attitudes. And when we can do so, it is usually because of the way in which a particular attitude fits into a larger structure of beliefs and attitudes that we hold. For example, if you were to ask an American voter why she was supporting Jimmy Carter in the 1976 presidential election, she might give you an answer such as the following: "Well, he's a Democrat, he seems to have the support of the black community, and, anyway, I like his smile." Each element of this answer can be converted into a chain of reasoning, similar to the syllogisms we considered in Chapter 7. The implied syllogisms in this particular voter's cognitive structure are depicted in Figure 18.3. As the figure shows, each syllogism begins with two premises. One of these premises is a belief or attitude that corresponds to the voter's stated reason for prefering Carter (for example, "He's a Democrat"). The second premise is a belief or attitude that the voter has not stated, but that is implied in her reasoning (for example, "Democrats make better presidents than Republicans do"). When these two beliefs or attitudes are put together, they point to the conclusion ("Jimmy Carter would make a better President").

Many of our attitudes have cognitive foundations of this sort. The various arguments that are used to support a given attitude are called the *horizontal structure* of the attitude. Typically, the broader the horizontal attitude—that is, the more arguments we have for it—the more resistant that attitude is to change. In addition, attitudes have a *vertical structure,* which is the way the

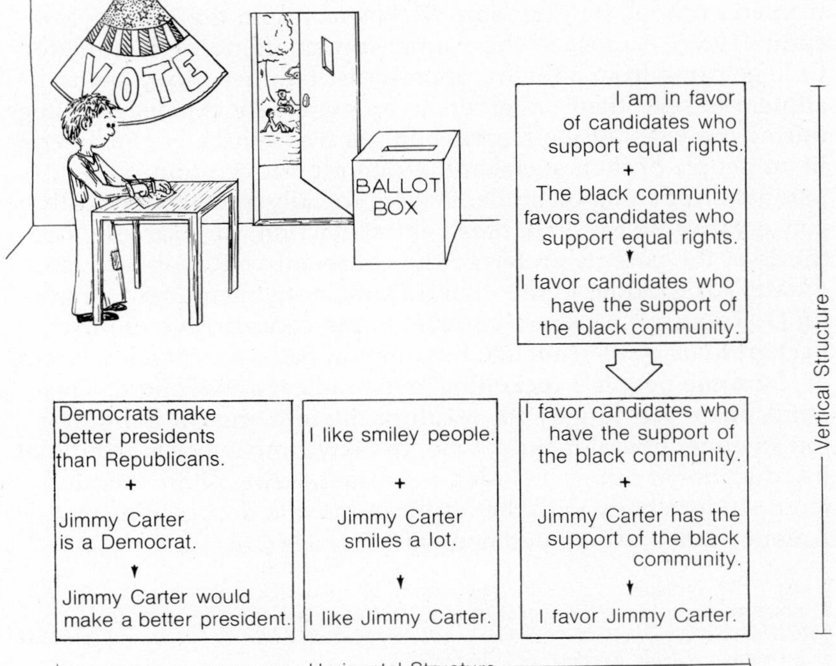

FIG. 18 · 3 An illustration of the horizontal and vertical structure of one hypothetical voter's attitude (adapted from Worchel and Cooper, 1976, p. 25). Other voters will begin with different premises and, as a result, will form different conclusions.

conclusion of one syllogism may serve as the starting point for another syllogism. (See Figure 18.3.)

A good deal of research supports the conclusion that people's beliefs and attitudes tend to be organized in coherent and consistent ways, as suggested by this illustration (see McGuire, 1960). But this is not to say that our attitudes are always consistent and logical. We have already seen that people's attitudes often have emotional bases that do not seem logical at all. In addition, people often achieve "consistency" in their attitude structure by engaging in cognitive contortions and rationalizations that are far from logical.

Social Foundations of Attitudes

Attitudes are social products, the result of our interactions with other people. As children we learn attitudes from our parents. When youngsters are rewarded for expressing the "right" attitudes and disapproved of for expressing the "wrong" ones, they learn that certain beliefs and views are preferable to others. In addition, children often use their parents as models for the attitudes they should hold. It is no accident that the larger majority of Americans adhere to their parents' choice of political party (Stone, 1974) or that children are more likely to smoke if their parents also smoke (Wohlford, 1970). As children reach adolescence, the influence of parents is often overshadowed by the influence of peers. Nevertheless, the influence of parents is likely to remain important, since the initial attitudes that parents instill are likely to provide a frame of reference from which later situations and issues are evaluated.

A classic study of the way in which parents and peers shape people's attitudes was conducted at Bennington College, an elite women's school, by Theodore M. Newcomb in the 1930s (Newcomb, 1965). Almost all the young women attending Bennington College came from affluent, upper-crust families—they *had* to be affluent to send their daughters to an extremely expensive college during the years of the Depression. As was generally characteristic of people of their social and economic background, the parents of Bennington students were socially and economically conservative. In the 1936 presidential election, for example, two-thirds of the parents preferred the conservative Republican candidate, Alf Landon, to the liberal Democratic incumbent, Franklin D. Roosevelt. In sharp contrast to the conservative family backgrounds of its students, Bennington had an extremely liberal or, by some people's reckoning, even radical atmosphere. This atmosphere was largely the result of the influence of Bennington's young, liberal faculty, who, in Newcomb's words, "felt that its educational duties included the familiarizing of an oversheltered student body with the implications of a depression-torn America and a war-threatened world" (page 216).†

†*From T. M. Newcomb, "Attitude Development, as a Function of Reference Groups: the Bennington Study," in H. Proshansky and B. Seidenberg (eds.), BASIC STUDIES IN SOCIAL PSYCHOLOGY, © copyright 1965 by Holt Rinehart & Winston. Reprinted by permission of Holt, Rinehart & Winston.*

One of Theodore Newcomb's psychology classes at Bennington College in the 1930's. Dr. Newcomb is at the far right.

These liberal lessons quickly penetrated the student body. A majority of the students abandoned the conservative attitudes of their parents and adopted the liberal views of the campus reference group. As Table 18.1 shows, for example, a majority of the freshmen women entering Bennington in 1936 shared their parents' preference for Landon, but a majority of the juniors and seniors, who had had a few years to soak up the prevailing political atmosphere, preferred either Roosevelt or, to their parent's undoubted chagrin, one of the more radical candidates. In addition, the juniors and seniors had more liberal views than the freshmen in the political and economic issues of the day, such as unemployment, public relief, and the rights of organized labor—issues that had been made prominent by President Roosevelt's New Deal.

These dramatic shifts in attitudes attest to the power of a social group to shape people's views. In Newcomb's terms, the

Table 18.1 Bennington College Students' Preferences in the 1936 Presidential Election

Candidate Favored	Freshmen	Juniors and Seniors
Alfred M. Landon (Republican)	62 percent	14 percent
Franklin D. Roosevelt (Democrat)	29 percent	54 percent
Socialist or Communist	9 percent	30 percent

Source: Adapted from Newcomb (1965).

college community became a *reference group* for many of the Bennington women—a group with which they identified and from which they derived many of their opinions. One of the reasons that people are likely to adopt group opinions is that having "popular" opinions often helps gain acceptance and prestige. Newcomb found, for example, that the Bennington women who were best liked and most respected among their classmates tended to be among those with the most liberal views. Some of the women whom Newcomb interviewed during their senior years explicitly acknowledged that they changed their opinions at least in part in order to gain acceptance and popularity. "All my life I've resented the protection of governesses and parents," one senior said. "What I most wanted here was the intellectual approval of teachers and the more advanced students. Then I found you can't be reactionary and be intellectually acceptable" (page 223).

As this woman's comment implies, identifying with the more liberal attitudes of the college community was also a way for many women to assert their independence from their parents. Another woman made this point explicit, saying, "I came to college to get away from my family, who never had any respect for my mind. Becoming a radical meant thinking for myself and, figuratively, thumbing my nose at my family. It also meant intellectual identification with the faculty and students that I most wanted to be like" (page 222).

The fact that many of the students adopted new attitudes in order to gain acceptance and assert their independence from their families does not mean that their attitude change was superficial or cosmetic. "I became a liberal at first because of its prestige value," one woman acknowledged, "[but] I remain so because the problems around which my liberalism centers are important" (page 222). Another woman emphasized that she was converted to new views because of their substance, not simply to adopt a radical image: "I simply got filled with new ideas here, and the only possible formulation of all of them was to adopt a radical approach. I can't see my own position in the world in any other terms" (page 223). Once people have adopted a new set of attitudes, for whatever reasons, these new attitudes become a central part of their self-definition. And when new issues arise, people tend to view them from the perspective of these attitudes.

Not all of the Bennington women adopted liberal or radical attitudes. A substantial minority of the students adhered to the conservative attitudes of their parents throughout their years at Bennington. Two of the women who remained conservative described their struggle with the prevailing campus attitudes in the following terms:

I wanted to disagree with all the noisy liberals, but I was afraid and I couldn't. So I built up a wall inside me against what they said. I found I couldn't compete, so I decided to stick to my father's ideas. For the last two years I've been insulated against all college influences. (page 218)

Family against family has been my struggle here. As soon as I felt really secure here I decided not to let the college atmosphere affect me too much. Every time I've tried to rebel against my family I've found out how terribly wrong I am, and so I've naturally kept to my parents' attitudes. (page 220)

It is important to note that the attitudes of the conservative minority also had a social foundation, just as those of the liberal majority did. Whereas the liberal women adopted the Bennington community as their primary reference group for political attitudes, the conservative women retained their home and family group as their primary reference group. And just as some of the liberal women made home and family a *negative* reference group, one that they did not want to identify with, the college community became a negative reference group for some of the staunchly conservative students. In both cases it is clear that attitudes were grounded in people's social groups.

In addition to providing us with most of our attitudes, our social groups and relationships also serve to support and reinforce the attitudes we already have. If you know that your friends share your opinions about politics, about religion, or about drugs, you are likely to hold these opinions more securely and confidently than if you feel you are alone in your views. To explore the role of social groups and relationships in supporting people's attitudes, Newcomb and his coworkers (1967) conducted a follow-up study of the Bennington women in the early 1960s, 25 years after his original study. One might have expected that the Bennington alumnae, now in their mid-forties, would have shifted back to relatively conservative attitudes, since they no longer were supported in their views by the liberal college community. Newcomb discovered, however, that the women retained highly liberal attitudes. In the 1960 presidential election, for example, Bennington women were much more likely than other women of Eastern upper-class backgrounds to prefer the liberal Democratic candidate, John F. Kennedy. The Bennington alumnae's more liberal attitudes extended to other issues of the early 1960s, such as favoring the admission of Communist China to the United Nations and approving of black student demonstrations. Newcomb emphasizes, however, that these liberal attitudes were not maintained in the absence of social support. To the contrary, the liberal Bennington women had gone on to marry liberal husbands, to make liberal friends, and to join liberal organizations, all of which tended to shore up their liberalness. In other words, the women succeeded in selecting new reference groups that provided support for their existing attitudes. As Daryl Bem (1970) notes, "We often select our reference groups because they share our attitudes, and then our reference groups in turn help develop and sustain our attitudes. The relationship is circular" (page 85).[†]

Although the original Bennington study was conducted 40 years ago, its lessons about the social bases of attitudes remain true for all of us today. Think about some of your own attitudes about various social issues. For example, consider your answers

PROPAGANDA

The word *propaganda* suggests that someone is attempting to fool people or manipulate them. But, ironically, the leaders we most admire and respect regularly use propaganda to convince people of the correctness of their policies. Propaganda has to be subtle to be effective. The textbooks you read may reinforce the basic principles of capitalism by utilizing math problems that deal with buying, selling, renting, investing, and compounding interest. You learn more than math when you must calculate the yearly profit a supermarket chain can make if it marks up its meat prices 1 percent to cover the cost of trading stamps. You would learn a different lesson if you had to figure out how many food stamps would be needed in one year to keep a child from suffering malnutrition. Propaganda is not always a deliberate intention of our educational system, but it is bound to reflect the society's value system and subtly reinforce it.

[†]*From D. J. Bem, BELIEFS, ATTITUDES, AND HUMAN AFFAIRS (Monterey, CA.: Brooks/Cole, 1970), reprinted by permission.*

to the list of questions that began this chapter. Now see whether you can identify the sources of these attitudes and the social support that may exist for them. You may discover that different attitudes have sources in different reference groups or relationships. For example, your attitudes about religion may be rooted in your family upbringing, while your views about politics may be based primarily on the views of your circle of friends in college. Chances are, though, that in almost every case you will discover that your attitude does have a social foundation. As Newcomb concluded, "Attitudes . . . are not acquired in a social vacuum" (1965, page 224).

It should be noted, finally, that the emotional, cognitive, and social foundations that we have considered are not independent of one another. In fact, social groups may make use of emotional techniques to instill attitudes in us. For example, liberal attitudes may have taken on positive emotional connotations for many of the Bennington students, because these attitudes were associated with people whom they liked and admired. And as we have already noted, these political attitudes were also embedded in interconnected cognitive structures. In general, the emotional, cognitive, and social factors work together to produce our attitudes.

Box 1

Conformity

To most of us, *conformity* is a dirty word evoking robotlike acceptance of the attitudes and actions of others. Buckling under to group pressure suggests that we are too weak to think for ourselves. Our heroes are likely to be the nonconformists of the world who march to the sound of a different drummer. At the same time, however, we recognize that conformity to the norms of our groups and culture are the price of living in social groups without anarchy and chaos. We conform to common standards of expression, behavior, and belief because they make our day-to-day interaction smoother and more predictable. In our culture, for example, a nod means "yes" and a shake of the head means "no"; in India, the expressions are reversed. Within either culture, a "nonconformist" who chose to ignore these conventions would not be much of a hero at all. And we conform to certain beliefs—from the notion that the Earth is round to the tenet that all people should have equal rights—because they provide a common basis for life in society. The issue, then, is not *whether* to conform or to remain independent, but *when* to conform and when to hold out for an unpopular position.

Solomon Asch (1951) conducted an experiment that dramatically illustrated the dilemma of whether or not to conform to group pressures. Asch assembled groups of eight subjects to participate in a study of visual judgment. The subjects sat around a table and judged the length of various lines. But only one member of each group was a

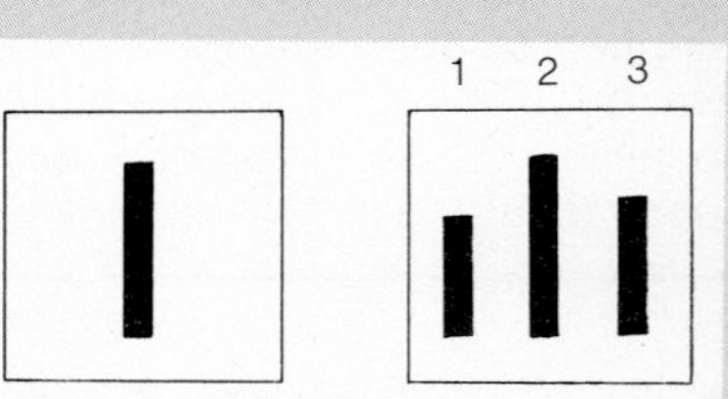

genuine subject. All the others were Asch's confederates, and on prearranged trials they reported ridiculously incorrect judgments. In a case such as that in the figure, the confederates each reported confidently that Line 1 was most similar in length to the comparison line on the left. These events put the real subject, who was one of the last to call out his decision, in a difficult situation. Should he report his real judgment, even though it would make him look silly in the eyes of other group members, or should he go along with the crowd? The situation was an extremely uncomfort-

CHANGING ATTITUDES

Once people's attitudes have been established, it is not easy to change them. People seem to cling stubbornly and sometimes irrationally to their beliefs and preferences and to reject even the most carefully designed and eloquent attempts at persuasion. Nevertheless, persuasion takes place every day, in forms ranging from a Washington lobbyist's success in convincing a Congressman to change his vote, to a doctor's success in convincing a patient to stop smoking. Beginning with an extensive program of research conducted by Carl Hovland and his colleagues in the late 1940s and 1950s (Hovland, Janis, and Kelley, 1953), social psychologists have made extensive attempts to discover just what sorts of persuasive appeals are most likely to work. These researchers have focused on the *source* of the communication, the content of the *message* itself, and the *audience* the communicator is trying to convince. The following is a brief sampling of some of their findings.

The Prestige Appeal

Who would be most effective in convincing you that you need only five or six hours of sleep at night—a Nobel Prize-winning physiologist or an unknown YMCA director? Which article

---

able one for many of Asch's subjects, and different subjects resolved the dilemma in different ways: some of the subjects never conformed, while others conformed almost all of the time. Overall, subjects conformed to the false group consensus on about 35 percent of the trials.

In some cases, subjects' confidence was genuinely shaken by the reports of the unanimous majority. One subject who went along with the group on almost every trial explained afterward, "If they had been doubtful I probably would have changed, but they answered with such confidence." Most of the subjects who went along with the majority admitted later that they really didn't believe that the majority was correct, but they were afraid of seeming foolish in the eyes of their fellow students. Similar effects can take place outside the laboratory. In jury deliberations, for example, a juror who finds himself to be a lone dissenter on the initial ballot will find it extremely difficult to hold out for his or her point of view. On the other hand, if there is at least one additional dissenter to provide support for one's minority opinion, conformity is drastically reduced. Asch found that when just one of the confederates in his groups was instructed to give the right answers instead of going along with the majority, the amount of conformity declined sharply from 32 percent to 5 percent.

Social psychologist Irving Janis (1972) has identified a particularly dangerous form of conformity that he calls *groupthink.* Groupthink refers to the tendency for members of a policy-making group to suppress all individual doubts and dissent, creating an illusion of unanimity. Both in President Kennedy's inner circle of advisers who gave the go-ahead to the ill-fated Bay of Pigs invasion and in the council who advised President Johnson to escalate the Vietnam war, critical judgment seems to have been suspended in favor of shared illusions. Especially in a group that has high morale and *esprit de corps,* no individual wants to be the one to bust the balloon by raising doubts or reservations. And the group as a whole acts to suppress such expression of doubts. Having suppressed all dissent, the group feels invulnerable, that nothing can go wrong—and, as a result, it is likely to make dangerous, ill-considered decisions.

about the effectiveness of antihistamine drugs would you be more likely to believe—one that appears in a prestigious medical journal or one that appears in a mass-circulation pictorial magazine? If you are like most of the subjects in experiments that used these materials, the messages of the famous physiologist (Bochner and Insko, 1966) and of the medical journal (Hovland and Weiss, 1953) would have a better chance of success. Within each of these experiments, subjects in different conditions were presented with precisely the same message, but the message was attributed to one or the other source. Not surprisingly, the same message was more effective when subjects thought it had been delivered by the more expert source. The *credibility* of a source is a factor that political propagandists and television advertisers are especially concerned with. That is why aspirin commercials are often delivered by a sincere dignified man in a "doctor's" white coat, and even orange juice commercials feature biology teachers or nutritionists.

It makes sense, of course, to take the opinion of an acknowledged expert more seriously than that of someone who knows little about the topic. In many cases, however, we are more easily persuaded by people whom we like and admire, even when we know that they have no special expertise in the area at hand. The football player who tells the world he uses a particular underarm deodorant may help the sales of that product even though the viewer knows that the athlete doesn't know any more about deodorant than the viewer does. Viewers who would like to define themselves as being similar to the sports star may well be influenced by his pitch. Even if these viewers can't equal the star in throwing touchdown passes or kicking field goals, they can at least have underarms that smell like his.

CLOTHES MAKE THE CAMPAIGNER

As good politicians have always known, the effectiveness of a campaigner can depend a great deal on his or her physical appearance. John Darley and Joel Cooper (1972) proved the point by confronting passersby at a shopping center with two groups of student campaigners. One group of students was well dressed and neatly groomed. The other group wore jeans and work shirts and had long hair. Without knowing anything more about the candidates that the two groups of students represented, most passersby indicated they were more likely to vote for the candidate suported by the neatly dressed workers. They also assumed that the neatly dressed campaigners' candidate was more conservative than the candidate of the hippie campaigners.

On Guard

Much of the time, we do not trust other people who we know are trying to influence us. As a result, we are often more likely to be convinced by a message if we overhear it than if it is directly addressed to us (Walster and Festinger, 1962). When we overhear a communication, we are less likely to reason that "he's just trying to persuade me." Consequently, we are less likely to discount the validity of the message. Advertisers are, of course, aware of this problem, and they try to get around it by presenting "candid" commercials in which we "overhear" housewives praising particular detergents in the privacy of their own homes. Although this technique may seem terribly transparent, it often seems to work.

Our aversion to being influenced reveals itself in another way. When people know in advance that someone is going to try to change their attitudes, they tend to resist. Jonathan Freedman and David Sears (1965) warned one group of teenagers, ten minutes beforehand, that they were going to hear a talk titled "Why Teenagers Should Not Be Allowed To Drive." Another group of teenagers were not told about the talk until just before the speaker started. Freedman and Sears found that those who were warned were less influenced by the talk than were the others. It may be that after the warning the subjects were able to marshal their defenses against the message, thinking up in advance all the reasons that teenagers *should* be allowed to drive. The implication for propagandists is clear: It is often best to sneak up on your audience and to deliver your message before people know what is about to happen.

Scare Tactics

Persuaders, whether with the best of intentions or the worst, often try to scare us into changing our attitudes. Scare tactics—or *fear appeals*—are often used for laudable reasons—by organizations that are trying to induce people to stop smoking or to drive more carefully, for example. Early research made it clear that if such fear appeals go too far, they are likely to backfire. Irving Janis and Seymour Feshbach (1953) exposed three groups of high school students to messages intended to get them to brush their teeth properly. The "strong fear" group heard a frightening lecture about how poor tooth brushing can result in gum infections that "can spread to your eyes, or your heart, or your joints and cause paralysis, kidney damage, or total blindness." The message was accompanied by slides that portrayed horribly decayed teeth and gory mouth infections. Janis and Feshbach found, though, that they had laid it on too thick. The students exposed to the high-fear communication were much less likely to improve their tooth-brushing practices in the week following the lecture than were students in the "moderate fear" and "low fear" conditions. The researchers concluded that scare appeals can be so scary that people defend themselves by dismissing the message completely.

For a long time after the appearance of the Janis and Fesbach study, advertisers generally refrained from using scare appeals. More recent research has suggested, however, that fear will motivate people to change their attitudes and behavior if it is kept within reasonable limits. James Dabbs and Howard Leventhal (1966) found, for example, that fear appeals were effective in motivating college students to get inoculations against tetanus. For fear appeals to be effective, two conditions must be met: first, the fear must be kept within limits; second, the audience must be given specific information about what they can do to reduce the threat. In recent years, advertisers seem to be following these recommendations—in fear-arousing appeals to motorists to use their seatbelts, for example (Worchel and Cooper, 1976).

SCARING YOURSELF OUT OF SMOKING

To help people stop smoking, Irving Janis and Leon Mann (1965) made use of a special sort of scare tactic—a procedure in which the smokers helped to scare themselves. Heavy smokers were asked to play the role of patients told by a physician (played by the experimenter) that they had developed lung cancer. Several scenes were carried out in the "doctor's office" to insure that the smokers would focus their attention on the threat of painful illness, hospitalization, and early death. Perhaps because the smokers themselves played an active role in the drama, the technique proved highly effective. Participants cut down on their smoking sharply, and their smoking was still down when the participants were recontacted 18 months later (Mann and Janis, 1968).

Group Support

As Newcomb's Bennington study demonstrated, people's attitudes are strongly rooted in their social groups and relationships. Thus, it is extremely difficult for a communicator to change a person's attitudes away from those held by that person's reference groups. Short of full-fledged brainwashing techniques (see Box 2), even the most skillful persuader will be stymied in his or her efforts to convince a labor union member that collective bargaining is an inefficient technique or to persuade a life-long Democrat to vote for a Republican candidate. Such attempts may have a better chance of success, however, if the persuader is able to show the person that other members of his or her reference group are also convinced of the argument. In one study (Kelley and Woodruff, 1956), students at a progressive teachers' college listened to a recorded message that argued for a return to more traditional teaching methods. The students heard the speech interrupted repeatedly by applause from the audience that attended the speech. Half of the students had been told that this enthusiastic audience consisted of members of their own college group; the other half had been told that the audience consisted of local townspeople. The researchers found that the subjects who believed that the applauding audience consisted of members of their own reference group (other students) were more likely to change their opinions in the direction advocated by the speaker than were the subjects who believed that the applause came from "outsiders."

In practice, of course, it is difficult to maintain the illusion that members of a particular group support a given viewpoint.

Instead, persuaders may attempt to convince entire groups of people at once. Although the persuaders may meet with a great deal of resistance along the way, any influence they do have will be more lasting if it has group support. Such group support also plays a prominent role in the techniques used by Alcoholics Anonymous to convince people to change their attitudes about drinking (see the Psychological Issue for Chapter 15).

ATTITUDES AND BEHAVIOR

It is generally assumed that if we can change people's *attitudes* about important issues the battle is half won. Once people's attitudes have been changed, the reasoning goes, they will change their behavior to match their new attitudes. If, for example, a man is convinced that Candidate Smith is preferable to Candidate Jones (the attitude), we expect him to act on his attitude by voting for Smith (the behavior). Similarly, if we convince a second man that Crunchies is a better breakfast cereal than Soggies (the attitude), he will ordinarily act on the attitude by buying Crunchies (the behavior). Of course, people don't *always* act on their attitudes. In a difficult situation, when people are faced with a variety of immediate pressures, they often end up behaving in ways that are quite contradictory to their attitudes or values. Nevertheless, the link from attitudes to behavior in a wide range of situations is well established (Brannon, 1976).

While we take this link between attitudes and behavior for granted, it is perhaps less obvious that the link goes in *both* directions—it can go from behavior to attitudes as well as vice versa. In fact, one of the most important ways in which people's attitudes are changed is by changing their behavior. Once a person has been induced to act in a particular way, his or her attitudes are likely to follow. Many studies have shown, for example, that favorable attitudes toward racial integration typically follow, rather than precede, actual desegregation (see the Psychological Issue at the end of this chapter).

Along similar lines, if a person makes a statement that does not initially agree with his or her real views, that person's views are likely to change to come into greater conformity with the statement he or she has made. Suppose, for example, that you were somewhat opposed to granting amnesty to Vietnam draft

FEELINGS ABOUT TRASH

Having attitudes about something does not necessarily mean that you will act in accordance with those attitudes. Leonard Bickman (1972) "planted" some litter in a public thoroughfare and then studied the people who passed by. He asked every fifth person whether he or she agreed that it is everyone's responsibility to pick up litter. Of those asked, 94 percent agreed with the statement. But only 2 percent of all the people actually stopped to pick up any of the litter.

Box 2

Brainwashing

The term "brainwashing" is a loaded one, with different meanings for different people. For some, it has come to mean almost any case of a person's being persuaded to do or think something that he or she later regrets having done or thought. For example, consumers complain that they are brainwashed into buying products they don't really want. For others, the term "brainwashing" has a sinister ring to it, with connotations of tortures, mind drugs, and brain stimulation. Most accurately, however, brainwashing refers to a set of techniques that are used in an attempt to change a captured person's basic attitudes and values. These techniques do not depend on physical tortures, drugs, or gadgets. Rather, they are based on a recognition of the social foundations of attitudes; they work (when they are successful) by tearing down the existing social foundations of a person's attitudes and erecting new ones in their place.

The word "brainwash" comes from the Chinese expression *hsi nao*, which literally means "wash brain." The Chinese Communists devoted a lot of effort to developing these techniques as part of the program of thought reform that followed their takeover of mainland China in 1949. Brainwashing techniques were used to convert Chinese young people and intellectuals, and similar techniques were also applied to Westerners in China and to American prisoners captured by the Chinese during the Korean War.

Brainwashing has two major phases. The first is to destroy the person's existing group ties and, in so doing, to break down his or her sense of identity. This may be done by isolating prisoners from other people, by restricting communication to them, and by making them feel guilty for their actions. For example, the Chinese would deliver American prisoners their mail only if it contained bad news. And they told the prisoners that their failure to receive mail proved that their loved ones at home had abandoned them (Schein, 1957).

The second phase of brainwashing is to give the prisoner a new set of relationships, tied to the new ideals that the brainwashers want the prisoners to adopt. Edgar Schein (1957) reports that Chinese "instructors" sometimes lived with American prisoners for long periods of time in order to establish close relationships with them. And they offered resisters, but were nevertheless induced by a friend to sign a petition supporting amnesty. It is quite likely that after signing the petition you would become more favorable to amnesty than you had been previously. Such an attitude shift can be explained in terms of Leon Festinger's (1957) theory of *cognitive dissonance,* which we discussed in Chapter 9. According to Festinger's theory, it is psychologically uncomfortable to entertain two clashing thoughts or cognitions—in this case, the cognitions that (a) I am opposed to amnesty, and (b) I've just signed a petition supporting amnesty. Therefore, you will be motivated to reduce the dissonance; and the best way to do so may be to conclude that amnesty is not so unreasonable after all.

The theory of cognitive dissonance also predicts that attitude change is most likely if you were not forced or bribed to sign the petition, but agreed to do so of your own free will. If you signed the petition only because someone "made you an offer you couldn't refuse" (like $20, or a threat to blackball you in a fraternity election), then your signing of the petition was not really inconsistent or "dissonant"—you did it for reasons that you were well aware of. And in such an event, there is no need to reduce dissonance by changing your attitudes. But if you signed the petition in the absence of such pressures, the dissonance is greater, and, hence, there is a stronger motive to change your

---

the prisoners special privileges if they would make public confessions or engage in other propaganda activities. By inducing the prisoners to engage in public behaviors that betrayed their old group and ideas, the brainwashers hoped that their private attitudes would change as well.

Brainwashing was back in the news recently when Patricia Hearst was placed on trial for taking part in a bank robbery while she was a captive of the militant radical group called the Symbionese Liberation Army (the SLA). One of the witnesses in Patty's defense was Robert Lifton, a psychiatrist who had done extensive research on Chinese brainwashing techniques. Lifton claimed that the SLA employed many techniques with Patty Hearst that came right out of the Communist Chinese's book. They toppled Patty's sense of self by locking her in a closet for weeks, and they created feelings of guilt and self-blame by branding her as "the daughter of a ruling class family, the Hearsts." When Patty emerged from the closet, they induced her to take steps to renounce her old identity, such as making a tape on which she publicly called her parents "the pig Hearsts." And the bank robbery itself (which, Lifton claimed, Patty was forced to take part in) further cut off her links to the past. Instead, Patty took on a new name ("Tania") and a new identity, as a member of the group that had captured her.

In spite of the power of these techniques, it is extremely difficult to brainwash someone successfully. Schein found that although the Chinese were successful in obtaining behavioral compliance and collaboration from many of their American prisoners, they produced very few ideological conversions. People's attitudes and ideals are rooted in decades of training in their original groups, and breaking down these strongly held attitudes is no easy matter. Nevertheless, there is no doubt that by systematically destroying and replacing people's group supports and self-images, lasting changes in beliefs and attitudes can be produced. During the Hearst trial, Robert Lifton was asked whether there is any system that would enable a prospective victim to avoid being brainwashed. His answer: "There is none. If one's captors are sufficiently determined, they can break down anyone" (reported by Turner, 1976).

attitude in such a way as to restore consistency. This line of reasoning was supported in a study by Festinger and J. Merrill Carlsmith (1959). In this study, students who had taken part in a boring experiment were offered either a token reward of $1 or a large bribe of $20 for telling other students that they really enjoyed the experiment. Later, Festinger and Carlsmith asked the subjects what they really thought about the experiment. The researchers found that subjects who had told the $1 lie now believed the experiment had been more fun than did subjects who had told the $20 lie. After all, Festinger and Carlsmith pointed out, it's not really "dissonant" or inconsistent to tell a white lie if you're being paid $20 to do so. But to tell a lie for only $1 does

Box 3

True Believers

Although people are motivated to maintain a consistency among their various beliefs, it often turns out to be consistency of a surprisingly illogical sort. In particular, we tend to be unwilling to admit that our strongly held convictions are wrong, even in the face of clear and undeniable evidence. This reluctance to give up our convictions is particularly strong when we have already taken actions based on our belief. In such a case, we are likely to search for another way to deal with the new evidence—a way to distort it and make it consistent with what we have always believed. As a result, Leon Festinger and his coworkers suggest, "The individual will frequently emerge, not only unshaken, but even more convinced of his beliefs than ever before. Indeed, he may even show new fervor for convincing and converting other people to his view" (Festinger, Riecken, and Schachter, 1956, page 3).

To find out what happens when a strong conviction is disconfirmed, Festinger, Henry Riecken, and Stanley

Schachter studied a religious sect that believed the end of the world was coming. The group members had announced that on a given day the world would be covered by a great flood and that only they, as true believers, would be saved—by a spaceship to be sent from outer space. When the fateful day came, the world did not end—but neither did the group's beliefs. To justify all the effort they had put into the plans and preparations for the cataclysm, the sect concluded that as a result of their faith, the end of the world had been put off temporarily. And to reassure themselves of the accuracy of this new conclusion, they stopped avoiding publicity and actively began to recruit converts to their cause. The more attention and support they received, the more reassured they were that their ideas made sense.

Jane Allyn Hardyck and Marcia Braden (1962) studied another group who had predicted the end of the world, in this case as a result of a nuclear attack. After living for 42 days and nights in a fallout shelter, awaiting the day of reckoning, they emerged unharmed and strengthened in their faith. They became convinced that God was using them to warn the world, and they continued to believe that an attack would come soon.

Such distortions of evidence in order to justify one's own actions is not limited to end-of-the-world cults. Indeed, at times we all seem to be rationalizing rather than rational creatures, ready to reinterpret the information that we receive in such a way as to avoid the need to admit that we have been in error. These tendencies can be explained in terms of Festinger's theory of cognitive dissonance which stresses the frequently irrational aspects of people's desire for cognitive consistency.

arouse dissonance—and that's the reason why the subjects were motivated to decide that they really believed what they had said.

Another way of explaining the tendency for people's behavior to affect their attitudes is Daryl Bem's (1972) *self-perception theory.* According to Bem, just as we may often infer *other people's* attitudes by observing their actions, we may also determine *our own* attitudes by observing our own actions. Bem writes:

> *Most people agree that the question, "Why do you eat brown bread?" can properly be answered with "Because I like it." I should like to convince you, however, that the question, "Why do you like brown bread?" frequently ought to be answered with "Because I eat it." (Bem, 1970, p. 54)*

Similarly, according to Bem's analysis a person may say to himself. "Well, I've just signed a petition favoring amnesty—and I wasn't even forced to do it. I guess I must be in favor of amnesty after all." Of course, there are limits on the applicability of Bem's theory. Sometimes we know full well what our attitudes about an issue are, and we don't need to spend time figuring them out. In many other cases, however, Bem's approach makes sense. Our attitudes about many issues *are* initially vague and confused, and they may finally take shape only after we have had a chance to reflect upon our own behavior. For example, Zick Rubin recently figured out (by reflecting on his own voting record), that he is in favor of banning handguns (by noting that he had just contributed to the National Coalition to Ban Handguns), and that he likes pretzels (by acknowledging that he keeps sneaking into the kitchen to find some). And even more recently, Rubin came to the conclusion that he endorses Bem's theory of self-perception (by reading the paragraph he has just written).

OBEDIENCE TO AUTHORITY

The most direct and time-honored form of social influence is *obedience*—doing something because an authority tells one to. Obedience is usually regarded as a positive quality—and, indeed, society would not be able to survive if people did not regularly follow the orders of their superiors. When obedience becomes blind and unquestioning, however, it may conflict with other important values, such as the value of the life and worth of our fellow human beings. It was obedience to orders that allowed so many Germans to participate in the massive human exterminations that took place during the Nazi era: "Gas chambers were built, death camps were guarded, daily quotas of corpses were produced with the same efficiency as the manufacture of appliances. These inhuman policies may have originated in the mind of a single person, but they could only be carried out on a massive scale if a very large number of people followed orders" (Milgram, 1963, page 373).

Stanley Milgram (1963; 1974) conceived of an experimental situation to investigate the conditions that lead people to obey an

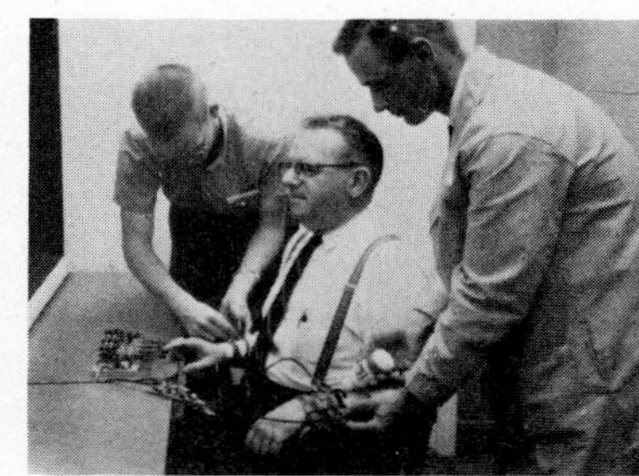

Milgram's Laboratory. Copyright © 1965 by Stanley Milgram. From the film *Obedience*, distributed by the New York University Film Library.

authority, even when it requires them to betray their own values and to harm innocent victims. Milgram's experiment began with an impressive-looking prop, a "shock generator" that had an instrument panel with 30 switches set in a horizontal line. Each switch had voltage designations ranging from 15 to 450 volts, with accompanying verbal labels ranging from "Slight Shock" to "Danger: Severe Shock." The last two switches were simply—and ominously—labeled "XXX." The machine was so carefully custom-built that no subject suspected that it was fake.

The subjects in Milgram's experiment were adults between 20 and 50 years of age from a wide variety of educational backgrounds and occupations. They were recruited by mail and through newspaper advertisements to take part in a study of the effects of punishment on learning. When a pair of subjects arrived at Milgram's laboratory at Yale University, one of them was assigned to the role of "teacher" and the other to the role of "learner." As the teacher looked on, the experimenter escorted the learner to an adjacent room, strapped him down to an "electric chair" apparatus, and attached an electrode to each wrist. The teacher was then seated in front of the shock generator in a different room from the learner. The teacher was to read a list of word pairs to the learner over an intercom; then he was to read the first word of each pair along with four possible responses. The learner was to indicate the correct response by pressing one of four switches in front of him, which lit up the corresponding number in a box at the top of the shock generator. Each time the learner got the answer wrong, the teacher was to administer a shock as "punishment." And after each error, the teacher was to increase the voltage by one level on the shock generator.

The learner was in fact a confederate of Milgram's, a mild-mannered 47-year-old accountant. He never actually received any shocks, although the teachers (who were the only real subjects) were thoroughly convinced that he did. To aid in the illusion, the teachers themselves were given a sample shock of 45 volts before the experiment began—and this shock was quite real. As the learning task progressed, the learner made frequent errors, according to a preprogrammed sequence. In one condition of the experiment (one of many that Milgram ran), no protests were heard from the learner until the 300-volt level was reached. At that point, the learner pounded loudly on the wall of the room where he sat strapped to the shock apparatus. After 315 volts, the learner pounded again, and his answers no longer appeared on the panel.

What was the subject to do now? When the pounding began, subjects usually turned to the experimenter for advice. The experimenter instructed them to treat the absence of an answer as a wrong answer and to continue to shock the learner as previously instructed. If at this point or thereafter subjects exhibited any reluctance to continue, the experimenter ordered them to continue, using one of a set of standard prods, such as "Please continue," "The experiment requires that you continue," and "You have no other choice; you must go on." If the subjects expressed concern that the learner might suffer serious injury, the experimenter politely, but firmly, replied, "Although the shocks may be painful, there is no permanent tissue damage, so please go on."

What would you have done in this situation? The vast majority of people who are asked this question confidently answer that once the learner stopped answering they would refuse to continue shocking him. But this is not what actually happened. Milgram's subjects found themselves in an extremely tense and uncomfortable situation. They were observed to sweat, tremble, bite their lip, and dig their fingernails into their flesh. Many of them repeatedly expressed concern about the learner's well-being. But in the face of the experimenter's stern orders, fully 65 percent of the subjects were obedient to the end, continuing to shock the learner until they reached the maximum level on the generator. In another condition of the experiment, the learner screamed, shouted, and begged to be released (the voice was actually a tape recording, but a very convincing one), but more than 60 percent of the subjects continued to shock him in spite of his protests.

When we have told students in our classes about these results, their first response is usually to focus on the personal and social characteristics of Milgram's sample of subjects. These men must have been sadists, some students suggested. Or if they were not sadists, they must have been weak-willed, or uneducated, or politically reactionary, or too stupid to know any better. What the students really seemed to be saying is, "Perhaps *they* acted in this way, but *I* never would." If this is your own feeling, the likelihood is that you are wrong. In fact, when Milgram conducted a similar experiment using students at Yale University as subjects, he obtained quite similar results. In another condition, he employed women as subjects and again found almost the identical pattern. If you had asked Milgram's subjects themselves how they thought they would behave in this situation, very few would have predicted that they would continue to shock the learner. But asking a hypothetical question about how you *would* behave is one thing, and actually placing you in a situation of this sort is quite another. The situation that Milgram's subjects found themselves in has a force that is much greater than most people realize.

Legitimate Authority

Just what was it about Milgram's experimental situation that compelled his subjects to keep following orders, even when they thought they might be seriously injuring another human being? There were no physical constraints in the situation. If they had wanted to, subjects could have simply gotten up and left the laboratory—and, indeed, a few subjects did. Moreover, the experimenter was not a physically imposing man, and he spoke in a soft and calm voice. But he was wearing a gray technician's coat, was doing "scientific research," and was obviously in full charge of his elegant laboratory. As a result, he was perceived by the subjects as being a *legitimate authority*—someone who had the right to dictate their behavior within the laboratory setting.

Obedience to legitimate authorities is deeply ingrained in all of us. If a person were to come up to you on the street and politely ask you to take your clothes off, you would regard that person as a weirdo and would certainly not comply. But if a doctor were to ask you the same question in his or her office, you would obey immediately. Similarly, if a young man were to approach you in the school cafeteria and ask you to clear the dishes off your table and take them to the kitchen, you would look at him unbelievingly. But if you were in the Army and the young man wore an officer's uniform, you would probably obey without even thinking about it. Milgram's results indicate that it is extremely difficult to defy such a legitimate authority, even when the authority's orders require one to injure an innocent human being.

When you stop to think about it, perhaps Milgram's results should not be so surprising after all. There have been several well-publicized events in our recent history in which apparently moral, well-meaning people followed the immoral orders of people perceived as legitimate authorities. The massacre of innocent civilians at My Lai, during the Vietnam war, was the most notable of these incidents. Defendants in the My Lai case tried to absolve themselves of guilt by pleading a familiar refrain: "I was just following orders." Both the killings at My Lai and, in its own way, the action of subordinates during the Watergate affair bring to our attention the dilemma of obedience to authority versus personal responsibility. At what point must obedience give way to individual conscience? Milgram's experiment dramatizes this dilemma by showing how powerful the forces eliciting obedience can be. As Milgram wrote: "If, in this study, an anonymous experimenter could successfully command adults to subdue a 50-year-old man and force on him painful electric shocks against his protests, one can only wonder what government, with its vastly greater authority and prestige, can command of its citizenry" (1965a, page 262).

WHAT WOULD YOU HAVE DONE AT MY LAI?

Many people believe that a person should not be held responsible for following the orders of a legitimate authority, even if these orders are immoral. A national sample of Americans was asked what they would have done if they had been soldiers in Vietnam and had been ordered to shoot innocent civilians. Half of the people questioned (51 percent) said they would follow orders and shoot. Many of these people were outraged by the trial of Lieutenant William Calley for his participation in killing civilians at My Lai, since they believed he was simply carrying out the policy set forth by his superiors. Given their view that one must obey orders, these people viewed the Army's case against Calley as a betrayal. For these people, "It is as if a subject in the Milgram experiment were brought to trial for administering shocks to another subject, and the chief of the laboratory came to testify against him" (Kelman and Lawrence, 1972, page 209). But other people in the sample took a different view, holding that each of us must accept ultimate responsibility for our own actions.

Reducing Obedience

As most elementary school teachers know, a disobedient child can set a bad example. Once one child begins to defy the teacher's authority, the other children may follow suit. In a variation of his experiment, Milgram found that a disobedient person can also set a *good* example. In this experimental condition, Milgram (1965b) assigned three-man teams of subjects to share the role of teacher. Once the learner began to protest, however, two members of the team (Milgram's confederates) announced that they would not continue to take part in the experiment, and they took seats on the sidelines. The experimenter continued to order the real subject, the only teacher left, to administer shocks. In this condition, however, the subjects were much more likely to defy the experimenter's orders. Only 10 percent of the subjects in this condition went up to the highest shock level. The other team members' act of defiance undermined the experimenter's authority and provided a concrete model of resistance that the subject could emulate. We need such principled models outside the laboratory as well, if we are to resist the dangers of blind obedience.

Although most of this chapter has been devoted to people's *attitudes*, Milgram's experiments help to demonstrate that people's actions are sometimes influenced more strongly by the pressures of specific situations than by their enduring attitudes. If you were to ask Milgram's subjects how they *felt* about shocking the learner, they would have told you almost to a man that they were strongly against it. But in the face of the pressures of the situation they were in, this attitude fell by the wayside. In recent years social psychologists have come increasingly to recognize that studying people's attitudes is not enough, just as personality psychologists have come to rely less on studying people's underlying traits (see Chapter 14). We must also pay closer attention to situational forces and how they work, for, as Milgram suggests, it is often not so much the kind of person one is as it is the kind of situation in which one is placed that determines one's actions.

SUMMARY

1. *Attitudes* are the ways in which we evaluate people, objects, and issues. Attitudes have both *cognitive* and *affective* components.
2. Among the devices used for measuring attitudes are *open-ended questions* and *fixed-response questions.* One type of fixed-response measure is the *semantic differential,* in which respondents are asked to rate concepts along several scales. Sometimes the questions themselves or the testing situation can influence an individual's responses.
3. Attitudes are acquired through emotional, cognitive, and social means. Emotionally, attitudes can be established by using classical conditioning to link positive emotions to a product or idea. When words are paired with certain emotions, *semantic conditioning* is said to have taken place.
4. Cognitively, attitudes can be acquired through a reasoning process that links the particular object or idea to one's already existing structure of beliefs and attitudes. The cognitive foundations of an attitude can have both a *horizontal structure* and a *vertical structure.* Not all of one's attitudes are logical or consistent, however.
5. The social acquisition of attitudes, as seen in the example of Bennington College students, involves identification with a *reference group* and adopting the attitudes of that group. Some people adopt attitudes the opposite of those of a group—the group has become a *negative* reference group. People tend to select reference groups that provide support for their existing attitudes.
6. Group pressure can give rise to *conformity,* even when the conforming individuals know that the group is wrong. Asch and others found that few people are willing to be a lone dissenter. When a group comes to a decision that members

are afraid to challenge (for the sake of keeping group solidarity), they are victims of *groupthink.*

7. The *credibility* of the source of a message will influence that source's ability to change our attitudes. A source has credibility if he or she is an expert or is liked and admired.
8. People are less likely to be persuaded by a message if they have been warned beforehand that someone is going to try to persuade them. People are more likely to be convinced by a message if they overhear it.
9. Scare tactics are sometimes highly effective, but at other times they can backfire—if a fear appeal goes too far, people tend to block out the message. A fear appeal is more successful if specific information is supplied for dealing with the fear-arousing situation.
10. It is extremely difficult to persuade someone to adopt an attitude at odds with the attitudes of his or her reference group. One method is to convince the person that other members of the reference group have this particular attitude.
11. *Brainwashing* refers to a set of techniques used to change a captured person's basic attitudes and values. Brainwashing has two major phases: (1) destroying the person's existing group ties and breaking down his or her sense of identity, and (2) providing a new set of relationships tied to new ideals. It is extremely difficult to brainwash someone successfully.
12. The link between attitudes and behaviors seems to go both ways—if one is somehow forced to behave as if he or she holds a particular attitude, that person's attitudes tend to change in alignment with this behavior—a phenomenon accounted for by the theory of *cognitive dissonance.* However, the force involved must be mild, so that the person feels a certain degree of choice in the matter.
13. The fact that behavior can lead to attitudes has also been accounted for by Bem's *self-perception theory.* According to Bem, people behave in certain ways, then reflect on their behavior, and finally arrive at attitudes that make sense in terms of the behavior.
14. Milgram's experiment showed that under certain conditions people will obey an authority even if it means betraying their values or harming another human being. Obedience is much more likely to occur in the presence of a *legitimate authority* and in the absence of dissenters. It seems, then, that the pressures of a specific situation can sometimes influence actions more strongly than do enduring attitudes.

psychological issue

Prejudice

***Prejudice* and *discrimination* are not synonymous.**

In our society, it often seems that "race" is only half a word—a word that is incomplete without adding "prejudice" or "discrimination." This is striking testimony to a simple fact of life in America: relations between races, as well as those between national groups, age groups, social classes, and sexes, are often characterized by prejudice. *Prejudice* and *discrimination* are not synonymous. The first refers to attitudes toward members of a particular group, and the second refers to actions. But, as we have seen in Chapter 18, attitudes and actions are usually closely intertwined. In America, both prejudice and discrimination, especially by whites toward blacks and other racial and ethnic minorities, has caused tremendous physical and psychological hardships for members of these minorities. And this prejudice and discrimination runs directly counter to our espoused values of equality for all people. It is important, therefore, that we look closely at what psychological research can tell us about the causes of prejudice and the possible ways of eliminating it.

Stereotypes

The literal meaning of prejudice is prejudgment. We prejudge members of other groups when we view them in terms of *stereotypes* that are seen as applying to entire groups of people. We introduced the notion of stereotypes in Chapter 7, when we discussed the central role of concepts or categories in human thought. If we were capable of responding to every person as an individual—in other words, if we didn't use categories at all—we would be free of prejudices about blacks, long-haired students, or old people. But freeing ourselves of categories completely is an unattainable ideal. We depend on categories in order to handle the tremendous quantity of information that constantly confronts us. What's more, stereotypes can sometimes be helpful, because people who have similar external attributes sometimes do behave similarly in other ways. Experienced cabdrivers are able to make fairly accurate predictions of how much individuals will tip by placing them in such categories as "Sport," "Stiff," or "Blowhard," based on their appearance and manner (Davis, 1959). But most of the racial and national stereotypes that we hold, whether of happy-go-lucky blacks, shrewd Jews, or inscrutable Orientals, have little if any basis in reality. And by relying on such stereotypes, we are blinded to the immense diversity among individuals. We expect people to behave like our stereotypes of those who happen to have the same skin color, speak with the same accent, or have the same background, rather than to behave like themselves.

If our stereotypes have little basis in reality, why do they persist as strongly as they do? A large part of the answer is the phenomenon of *selective perception* that we examined in Chapter 3. We tend to focus on information that is consistent with our stereotypes and to screen out or reinterpret information that is inconsistent with these preconceived notions.

Box I-1

The Black Self-Concept

Minority groups are not immune to the attitudes and norms of the majority. When the norms of American society state or imply that blacks are inferior to whites—and when, as a result, blacks are treated as inferior—it is hard for many blacks themselves to avoid getting the message, and believing it. For example, in a famous study conducted about 40 years ago, Kenneth and Mamie Clark (1947) found that black children as young as three years old rejected black dolls as inferior to white dolls. Many more recent studies have confirmed the Clarks' conclusions that black American children have often come away from experiences of discrimination with a sense of worthlessness and self-hatred (Pettigrew, 1964).

The Clarks' study and other evidence of the damaging psychological effects of discrimination were cited by the United States Supreme Court in its historic 1954 decision that public school segregation is unconstitutional. "To separate [black children] from others of similar age and qualification solely because of their race," wrote Chief Justice Earl Warren, "generates a feeling of inferiority as to their status in the community that may affect their hearts and minds in a way unlikely ever to be undone." Separate cannot be equal, the justices reasoned, as long as separateness goes along with norms suggesting that one group is superior to another.

In more recent years there are many signs of enhanced self-esteem among black children and of increased racial pride among black people more generally. This increased black pride seems attributable in large measure to the civil rights activities and black militancy of the 1960s. By demonstrating that they could in fact exert control over their environment, black activists were able to see themselves as effective, powerful people. As Daryl Bem (1970) writes, "Attitudes follow behavior, and there is no better way to make any man, black or white, become militant than to get him on a picket line or a sit-in" (page 67). And this period of militancy and increased pride has led in turn to more active and confident black participation in government and business in the 1970s.

> ...we all become skilled at perceiving only those events that are consistent with our prejudices.

For instance, once you have reached the conclusion that all Cubans are "lazy," you will be more likely to notice examples of "lazy Cubans." If you see a "lazy" Anglo, you will pay little attention, or else you will interpret it quite differently—"He must be resting after a long day's work." Without being fully aware of it, we all become skilled at perceiving only those events that are consistent with our prejudices. After a while, we amass a pile of evidence that assures us that our prejudices are justified. Movies and television often adopt popular stereotypes of members of various groups and, as a result, help to perpetuate them.

In addition, our prejudices may be sustained by the fact that we avoid informal contact with members of unfamiliar groups and, thus, never have a chance to subject our stereotypes to disconfirming evidence. This avoidance is sometimes fostered by tragic misunderstandings, in which members of each group indicate a willingness to get to know members of other groups better but assume that the others don't want to get to know *them.* Kaplan and Goldman (1973) found such a pattern in a study of white, black, and Mexican-American high school students. Members of each group said they favored more social mixing with members of the other groups, but they assumed that the other groups opposed such mixing. This phenomenon, in which hostility is maintained because of false assumptions that never get tested, has been called *autistic hostility.*

The Prejudiced Personality

There is evidence that some people tend to be generally prejudiced—not just toward blacks or toward Mexican-Americans or toward Jews, but toward practically *all* "outgroups." Eugene Hartley (1946) helped to make this point when he obtained measures of people's attitudes toward various minority groups, including three minorities that Hartley actually made up: Wallonians, Pirenians, and Danerieans. Hartley found that respondents who were prejudiced toward blacks and other outgroups expressed prejudice toward the made-up groups as well. "I don't know anything about them; therefore, I would exclude them from my country," one prejudiced respondent confessed.

> ...highly prejudiced people are likely to have *authoritarian personalities.*

In the 1940s a group of psychologists at the University of California at Berkeley, influenced by Freud's psychoanalytic theory of personality (see Chapter 14), looked intensively into the origins of a prejudiced personality. The researchers (Adorno, Frenkel-Brunswik,

A CASE OF AUTISTIC HOSTILITY

Person A	*Person B*
I'd like to meet her.	I'd like to get to know her.
But I don't suppose she'd like to meet me.	But she seems to be avoiding me.
So I guess she doesn't like me very much.	Maybe I'm not the sort of person she likes to spend time with.
Well, if she doesn't like me, then I don't like her either.	Well, in that case, she's not the sort of person I'd like to spend time with either.

Levinson, and Sanford, 1950) concluded that highly prejudiced people are likely to have *authoritarian personalities.* These people tend to see the world as divided sharply into two categories—the weak and the strong. They tend to be power oriented in their personal relationships. They are most comfortable when they are either taking orders from a superior or dishing it out to a subordinate. The Berkeley researchers believed that these were the sorts of people who would have been likely to be drawn to the Fascist ideology of Nazi Germany.

By means of detailed studies of such individuals, Adorno and his colleagues concluded that they tend to come from families that stress harsh discipline and obedience and in which there is anxiety about family status. People from such backgrounds may often find it difficult to accept personal weakness or to acknowledge their own sexual or aggressive motives. Instead, they are likely to make use of the Freudian defense mechanism of *projection,* seeing themselves and their own groups as being without weakness and, instead, seeing the undesirable traits that they are afraid of in members of outgroups. In this way the authoritarian personality arrives at his or her racial and religious prejudice.

Social Norms and Discrimination

Although research on the authoritarian personality has been valuable, it has become clear that individual bigotry can explain only a small proportion of the racial, religious, and ethnic prejudice and discrimination that are found in America. For example, even though overt discrimination against blacks has traditionally been greater in the South than in the North, white Southerners have not scored higher than white Northerners on measures of authoritarianism. Rather, the discrimination patterns against blacks in the South have been mainly a result of conformity to *social norms* that developed through the course of history.

The fact that social norms bear most of the responsibility for prejudice and discrimination helps to explain certain apparent inconsistencies in interracial behavior. Minard (1952) reported, for example, that black and white coal miners in McDowell, West Virginia followed a pattern of almost complete integration below the ground and almost complete segregation above the ground.

Box I-2

Realities of Racism

White hostility toward blacks goes back far and runs deep. James Jones (1972) pointed out that white English culture has for centuries included an animosity to the very idea of blackness. Prior to the sixteenth century, before Englishmen had had any contact with the black Africans, the English definition of the color black included the following:

Deeply stained with dirt; soiled, dirty, foul . . . Having dark or deadly purposes, malignant; pertaining to or involving death; deadly; baneful disastrous, sinister. . . . Foul, iniquitous, atrocious, horrible, wicked. (from the Oxford English Dictionary, *quoted by Jones, 1972, p. 151)*

It is perhaps not surprising, therefore, that when English voyagers to Africa first encountered black people they regarded them with distaste, as creatures less than human. And once black people were enslaved in Europe and America, their condition of servitude itself reinforced the white belief that blacks were by nature inferior.

The depth of racism in American culture can hardly be exaggerated. Thomas Jefferson believed in the innate inferiority of black people. And although he personally opposed slavery, he agreed to compromise with Southern slavery interests and to delete an antislavery statement from the Declaration of Independence. Abraham Lincoln was also convinced that black people were inferior to whites and felt that equality was not attainable as long as blacks and whites lived in the same society. He proposed that blacks set up a separate colony, either in this country or abroad, as the only solution to the race problem. And these are two of the Presidents who were *most* sympathetic to the plight of black people in America (Jones, 1972)!

In the early 1960s researchers showed white California teenagers questionnaires ostensibly filled out by either black or white students at another high school (Stein, Hardyck, and Smith, 1965). When the subjects were asked how "friendly" they thought they would feel toward the students whose questionnaire they were shown, race made little difference; the subjects said they would feel most friendly toward students who shared their own beliefs about various issues, regardless of their race. But when the subjects were asked how they would feel about inviting the student home for dinner, the pattern of results changed. Now the subjects paid more attention to the student's race, preferring to invite home a white than a black student, regardless of their similarity of beliefs.

No theory of prejudice that restricts itself to individual personality can explain these inconsistencies. But they make more sense when viewed in terms of people's conformity to changing norms of acceptable and unacceptable conduct (Pettigrew, 1971). We must recognize that prejudice, like our other attitudes, has a strong social foundation. We learn to be prejudiced not as a general way of life, but in the form of specific attitudes and behaviors illustrated to us by our parents, our peers, and the mass media. To reduce prejudice, therefore, massive psychotherapy is not the answer. Instead, we must develop ways of changing the social norms that perpetuate discriminatory behavior.

To reduce prejudice, massive psychotherapy is not the answer.

Reducing Prejudice

The best way to reduce prejudice is to take seriously the social-psychological principle (discussed in Chapter 18) that attitudes often follow behavior. Rather than preaching lofty ideals of equality, we need to *create* greater equality, by law or by individual action. Each of the long series of moves toward greater racial integration and equality in America has been met by resistance. Whites, and sometimes blacks as well, have argued that by integrating the buses, or the lunch counters, or the schools, we will only cause tension and discomfort, and as a result we will only make matters worse. And, of course, these critics have been right about the tension and discomfort. It is impossible to change long-standing and deeply ingrained behavior patterns without generating a great deal of tension. Nevertheless, the general experience has been that once such changes are instituted, people gradually come to accept them and even to like them. Surveys reveal, for example, that attitudes toward integration on the part of both black and white Americans are more favorable among those who have experienced it and least favorable among those who have had no interracial contacts (Pettigrew, 1971). As Bem (1970) concludes, "Legislation and court decisions *can*

Box I-3

Finding Out What It's Like To Be Green

One cure for prejudice may be to experience its effect yourself. Michael Weiner and Frances Wright (1973) demonstrated this in a study with two third-grade classes. One class was used as a control group and was given no special treatment. The other class was randomly divided into two subgroups: Orange children and Green children. Students in each subgroup were identified by colored armbands.

On the first day of the study, the Orange children were designated "superior." The teacher told the students that Orange children were smarter, cleaner, and better behaved than Green children. Orange children were granted special privileges, assigned to positions of power, and showered with praise. The children seemed to take the experiment very seriously, and tensions became evident between the two groups. On the second day of the study, roles were reversed, and the Green children became "superior."

On the third day of the study, Weiner and Wright asked students in both the experimental and control classrooms, all of whom were white, whether they would like to attend a picnic with some black children from another school. Ninety-six percent of the children in the experimental classroom—those who had experienced discrimination first-hand—said, "Yes," compared to only 60 percent of the control children. In addition, the researchers used an attitude scale to measure the extent of the children's prejudiced beliefs. Children in the experimental class showed less prejudice than children in the control class. And these differences remained just as strong when the two classes were retested two weeks later.

change the 'hearts and minds of men.' . . . They do so, in part, by effecting a change in behavior; then, when behavior has been changed, attitudes often follow" (p. 69).

We should not paint an overly rosy picture of the process of reducing prejudice. Attitudes of racism are deeply ingrained in our culture, and they cannot easily be erased. We must expect new efforts at integration to bring further resentment and conflict in their wake. But such conflict may be a necessary step toward the larger goal of achieving equality and justice. As Thomas Pettigrew (1971) puts it, "To prescribe more separation because of discomfort, racism, conflict, or the need for autonomy is like getting drunk again to cure a hangover. The nation's binge of *apartheid* must not be exacerbated but alleviated" (pp. 327-328).

Summary

1. *Prejudice* refers to attitudes toward members of a particular group; *discrimination* refers to actions toward a group of people based on one's prejudice.
2. People often respond to others in terms of *stereotypes*—notions of what people are like based on the racial, ethnic, or other groups to which they belong. Most stereotypes have little basis in reality, but they are perpetuated by processes such as selective perception, in which people notice only those aspects of people that coincide with their stereotypes. Stereotypes are also maintained by lack of informal contact with people from stereotyped groups; through phenomena such as autistic hostility, people assume that it is the members of the *other* group who oppose interaction between groups.
3. People who appear prejudiced toward all "outgroups" are characterized as having authoritarian personalities.
4. The responsibility for prejudice and discrimination in America goes to social norms that dictate appropriate and inappropriate conduct.
5. The best way to reduce prejudice is to bring people together—to desegregate schools, for example. Studies have shown that it takes contact with the "outgroup" people for "ingroup" people to break down their prejudices.

Interpersonal Relationships

CHAPTER 19

Interpersonal Relationships

Unless you've made a firm decision to spend the rest of your days sitting on top of a flagpole, your relationships with other people will undoubtedly remain among the most important parts of your life. From our earliest attachments to our parents to our later relationships with playmates, work associates, friends, and lovers, interpersonal relationships provide the most central satisfactions, as well as the most difficult tribulations, of being human. In this chapter, we will focus on several facets of the psychology of interpersonal relationships. First we will examine the human need to form relationships with others. Then we will explore the ways in which we form impressions of other people, and the factors that lead us to like or dislike others. After that, we will turn to the even more difficult topic of human love relationships, including the links between love and sex. And finally, we will consider why relationships end. As we pursue this examination, it will become clear that the psychology of interpersonal relationships is by no means an isolated topic. To understand our relationships with others we will find ourselves drawing upon many of the psychological concepts that were introduced in earlier chapters.

NEEDING OTHERS

According to the popular song, "People who need people are the luckiest people in the world."† If that's the case, then we can all consider ourselves to be lucky, because we all have a strong need for the companionship and support of other people.

The Need for Social Comparison

One of the main reasons that we seek the company of others is to be able to compare our own emotions and attitudes with those of other people. We saw in Chapter 18 that people's attitudes have a strong social foundation. In Theodore Newcomb's Bennington study, the students acquired their political attitudes either from their families or from the college community; no one acquired their attitudes in a social vacuum. More generally, Leon Festinger (1954) has pointed out that many of our life experiences would be thoroughly confusing and meaningless unless we had an opportunity to compare our own reactions with those of other people. Which situations should we fear and which should we feel comfortable in? When should we laugh, when should we cry, and when should we remain impassive? What are our own strengths and weaknesses? What standards of behavior should we teach our children? None of these questions can be answered by a person living in isolation. To answer them, we need to compare our own experiences and reactions with those of other people.

It is this need for *social comparison* that often leads us to seek the company of others when we are afraid or upset. This tendency was demonstrated by Stanley Schachter (1959) in an experiment with female college students. Half of the subjects (the high-fear group) were told that as part of an important scientific study, they would receive a series of extremely painful electric shocks. The other half of the subjects (the low-fear group) were told that they would experience mere "tingles" and that they would enjoy the experiment. Then the experimenter told the subjects that while he was setting up the equipment, they could choose to wait either in a room by themselves or in a room together with other subjects. Fully two-thirds of the high-fear subjects chose to wait with others, compared to only one-third of

the low-fear subjects. Thus, the fearful subjects tended to seek company, just as people are likely to huddle together during power failures or other potentially frightening events. In a followup study, Schachter demonstrated that fearful subjects did not want to wait with just anybody, but only with other subjects who were in the same situation that they were in. "Misery doesn't love just any kind of company," Schachter observed, "only miserable company." And the reasons subjects gave for this preference reflected the need for social comparison. In fact, the subjects were probably not sure just how they should react and behave in this strange set of circumstances. Should they feel fear for their safety? Anger at the diabolical experimenter? Gratitude for being allowed to suffer for the sake of science? Should they submit bravely to their fate or mount a protest? The subjects wanted to affiliate with others in order to find out.

Fearful or anxious people do not *always* seek others' company, however. Extremely fearful or intense feelings may sometimes lead to precisely the opposite reaction. Several days after President Kennedy's assassination, a nation-wide survey of Americans' reactions to the tragedy was conducted (Sheatsley and Feldman, 1964). A majority of those surveyed reported that immediately after hearing that the President had been shot, they had felt a desire to talk to others. But 40% of the sample said that they had wanted to be alone at this time. Significantly, the desire for privacy was greatest among those groups of people who admired President Kennedy the most. The feelings that these Americans experienced may have been so painful that they did not wish to expose them to others or to clarify them through social comparison.

The Provisions of Interpersonal Relationships

We are motivated not only to seek the company of others in general, but to form close and enduring relationships with specific other people. Social psychologist Robert Weiss (1974) believes that each of us needs to form two different kinds of interpersonal relationships—*emotional attachments* to one other person (usually a lover or spouse) and *social ties* to a network of friends. Each type of relationship provides its own special set of provisions. Emotional attachments provide a sense of comfort and security, and social ties provide a sense of group identity and integration. The adult need for an emotional attachment seems to develop from the infant's attachment to its parents. The infant feels secure and comfortable only when in the parent's presence, and terrified when the parent leaves (see Chapter 12). As adults, we no longer require the constant physical presence of an attachment figure, but we still retain a strong need for an emotional attachment in order to feel secure. Social ties, usually to a group of friends of one's own age, become important in childhood and even more so in adolescence. Adolescents achieve a sense of belonging and of identity by affiliating with and comparing themselves to other members of their peer group. And this need for a network of friends with whom we can share activities and concerns persists into adulthood.

Being Lonely

When people lack either an emotional attachment or a social network, the outcome is likely to be the condition called *loneliness*—an experience of longing and of emptiness that one noted psychiatrist, Harry Stack Sullivan, has described as "so terrible that it practically baffles clear recall" (Sullivan, 1953, p. 261). One does not have to be physically isolated in order to be lonely. Rather, loneliness stems from the lack of interpersonal relationships and of their provisions.

Robert Weiss (1973) has identified two kinds of loneliness. The loneliness of *emotional isolation* results from the loss or absence of an emotional attachment, and the loneliness of *social isolation* results from the loss or absence of social ties. Each of these conditions is likely to be extremely painful, including symptoms of restlessness and depression. Weiss has found, moreover, that one sort of relationship cannot readily substitute for another in alleviating loneliness. Thus a person suffering from the loss of a love relationship is likely to feel painfully lonely, even though he or she may have children at home or friends to spend time with. One divorced mother described her experience in the following terms:

> *Your house is so noisy all day long, phones, people, kids, all kinds of action going on and come eight o'clock everybody's in bed, and there's this dead silence. Like the whole world has just come to an end. All of a sudden you get this feeling that you're completely alone, that there is no one else in the world. You look out the window, you walk back and forth from room to room, you watch television, and you're dead. (Weiss, 1973, p. 136)*

And people who have close emotional attachments may still feel great loneliness if they lack a network of friends. Weiss recounts the case of one woman who had a close marriage, but who felt devastated when the couple moved to a new region where they had no friends: "Isolated in the new community, she listened hungrily to her husband's stories of meeting people during his work day and then was furious with envy. She was bored and miserable. Finally she and her husband moved into a suburb in which there were people they felt to be like themselves, where she could take a place for herself. Almost instantly her symptoms vanished" (Weiss, 1973, pp. 152-153).

Loneliness is a particularly difficult problem to bear because it is frequently regarded as a weakness or an indulgence. We are led to believe that we *should* be able to get along on our own, and that if we can't there must be something wrong with us. As a result, people are often unwilling to admit their loneliness to others, and even try to deny it to themselves. But, in fact, loneliness is an extremely common problem. In one national survey of Americans, 26% of those interviewed reported that they had felt

EVEN SNAILS CAN HELP

People who are physically isolated from others often become desperate in their need for companionship. Christopher Burney, who was held in solitary confinement by the Germans for 18 months during World War II, adopted as a pet a snail that he found in the exercise yard. "It was company of a sort," Burney (1952) later wrote, "as if it were an emissary from the world of real life." Isolation can also lead people to hallucinate about other people. Students at McGill University who took part in studies of complete isolation reported that "they felt as if another body were lying beside them in the cubicle; in one case the two bodies overlapped, partly occupying the same space" (Heron, 1957).

"very lonely or remote from other people" within the previous few weeks (Bradburn, 1969). Loneliness seems to be especially prevalent among unmarried, widowed, and divorced people, but none of us are entirely immune to it. Far from being a sign of weakness, loneliness is a manifestation of the basic need for interpersonal relationships that we all share. Although various activities can help us to cope with our loneliness, the only real cure seems to be the establishment of interpersonal relationships that will provide the resources that we so badly need (Weiss, 1973).

PERCEIVING OTHERS

You arrive in biology class on the first day of the term, and a bearded man wearing a rumpled suit stands up in front of the class and begins telling jokes about the sex life of planaria. On the cafeteria line at lunchtime you find yourself standing behind a petite woman with long dark hair who keeps looking around the room furtively as if she was a foreign spy. In the afternoon you go to the library and see someone whom you recognize from the newspaper as the star tackle on the football team, and are surprised to discover that he is immersed in a book of Emily Dickinson's poetry. In each of these cases, you inevitably begin to ask yourself questions: What sort of a person is this? Why is he or she behaving in these particular ways? Is this the sort of person I would like to get to know better? We are constantly forming impressions of other people, both out of sheer curiosity and because such impressions have a large impact on the way we relate to others. This process of forming inferences about other people is analogous to the way we come to perceive the physical environment (Chapter 3), and as a result it is called *person perception.*

'I DON'T LIKE THE WAY HE TALKS'

We form impressions about people not only from the way they look, but also from the way they talk. Former baseball pitcher Jim Bouton made the following observation in his diary of a major league season: "I'm not sure I'm going to like Don Mincher. It's prejudice, I know, but everytime I hear a Southern accent I think: Stupid. . . . It's like Lenny Bruce saying he could never associate a nuclear scientist with a Southern accent" (Bouton, 1971, p. 52). Each of us brings our own prejudices to our encounters with other people, but we're not always as ready as Bouton to admit them.

Physical Appearance

Even though we are warned not to judge a book by its cover, we can hardly avoid forming impressions of people on the basis of their physical appearance. A person's size, shape, color, and manner of dress are all likely to affect the inferences we make about the person's personality. These impressions often reflect the operation of physical stereotypes, similar to the group stereotypes that we discussed in the Psychological Issue in the preceding chapter. We mentally place a person in the category of those who have a particular physical characteristic, and we then infer that the person resembles other members of that category in other respects as well. Redheads may be assumed to be hot-tempered, people who wear glasses to be studious, men with short hair to be politically conservative. Whether or not these stereotypes have any basis to them, they often serve the function of organizing our initial impressions of a person.

Reputations

We often begin to form our impressions of people even before we meet them. This is because people are likely to be preceded by their reputations. Students learn what to expect from their professor by talking to students who took the same course the previous year. And before going out on a blind date, we are usually given a good deal of information about what he or she will be like. In each case, the person's reputation is likely to have an impact on the way a person is later perceived.

Harold Kelley (1950) conducted an experiment that demonstrated how a person's reputation can affect the way he is perceived. Kelley arranged to have students told that their class would be taken oven by a new instructor, whom they would be asked to evaluate at the end of the period. Before the instructor arrived, the students were given a brief description of him to read. Half of the students were told that the instructor was a

26-year-old graduate student who was considered to be "a rather warm person, industrious, critical, practical, and determined." The other half of the students received precisely the same information, except that the adjective "warm" was replaced with "cold." This difference of a single word proved to have a large impact on the students' reactions to the instructor. After the instructor had led the class in a 20-minute discussion, the students who had been told that he was "warm" rated him as more considerate, sociable, good-natured, and humorous than did the students who had been told that he was "cold." The instructor's reputation also affected students' willingness to interact with him: 56% of the "warm" subjects took part in the class discussion, compared to only 32% of the "cold" subjects.

It seems that people's reputations, just like stereotypes based on physical appearance or group membership, provide a context within which we then interpret their behavior. For example, "If a woman is told in advance that her blind date is extremely witty, she will be primed in advance to categorize his remarks as witty ones. If the same date were billed as solemn and humorless, the same 'witty' remarks might well fall flat. This is the secret of many comedians. Since they have the reputation of being uproariously funny, people are predisposed to laugh at practically everything they say." (Rubin, 1973, p. 93).†

Attribution Processes

In forming impressions of people, our primary goal is to make inferences about a person's underlying traits or dispositions on the basis of his or her observable actions. Such inferences are important because they allow us to predict how the person is likely to behave in the future. This inference process is not always an easy one, however. Suppose that you observe a person donating blood as part of the annual Red Cross drive. Do you infer that she is an unusually altruistic person, who decided to give blood because of her commitment to helping others? And, as a result, can we expect her to behave altruistically in the future? Perhaps. But what if you also knew that intense pressure had been put on all of the residents of her dormitory to give blood, and that the names of all those who refused to do so were to be posted publicly? In that case, it would be more difficult to infer anything about the woman's altruism from her behavior. Instead, her behavior might simply reflect conformity to group pressure. We are constantly confronted with dilemmas of this sort as we form impressions of people. In particular, we must try to determine whether a person's behavior reflects an underlying disposition of that person, or whether it is primarily a consequence of the situation in which the person was placed. The ways in which we try to sort the causes of people's behavior are called *attribution processes.*

In recent years, attribution processes have been the topic of a large outpouring of social-psychological research (Jones, et al., 1972). One of the central conclusions of this research is that people have a tendency to overestimate the degree to which other people's behavior is caused by their individual traits or dispositions, and to underestimate the extent to which it is caused by situational factors. For example, when students see a film of one of the subjects in Milgram's obedience experiment (Chapter 18) repeatedly administering shocks to the "learner," they often assume that the subject is an unusually sadistic person. In attributing this person's behavior to his distinctive personality trait (his "sadism"), the students underestimate the pressures that cause *most* people in this situation to behave in quite the same way. Even when we *know* that there are strong situational pressures affecting a person's behavior, we are still

TO ERR IS HUMAN

We usually like people who are intelligent, able, and competent. But most of us have misgivings about people who are *perfect.* In 1961, President John F. Kennedy made one of the worst blunders of his career, when he approved the ill-fated Bay of Pigs invasion in Cuba. But strangely enough, a Gallup Poll taken right after the fiasco showed that Kennedy's popularity had increased rather than decreased. As Elliot Aronson (1969) suggests, once we know that a person has high ability, evidence of that person's human fallibility is likely to make him seem more attractive. The failure of the Bay of Pigs invasion apparently proved to many Americans that their President wasn't perfect—and, as a result, they liked him more.

†*From Zick Rubin, LIKING AND LOVING (New York: Holt, Rinehart & Winston, 1973), pp. 64–65, 93, 154, 194.*

likely to overestimate the role of personal dispositions. In one study (Jones and Harris, 1967), students read statements that they were told had been written by a college debater who had to argue in favor of an assigned position. Even though the students knew that the debater had no choice in deciding which position to argue, they still tended to conclude that he privately supported the position that he was arguing for.

Edward Jones and Richard Nisbett (1972) note that whereas we tend to attribute other people's action to their distinctive traits or dispositions, we are more likely to attribute our *own* behavior to situational factors. For example, the public often attributes a political leader's actions to that leader's personal dispositions, be it his courage or his cowardice, his wits or his stupidity. When the political leader himself looks back at the same action, however, he is more likely to emphasize the situational constraints or pressures that made his decision inevitable. From the political leader's point of view, anyone in his right mind would have done the same thing. In actuality, of course, our actions are caused by individual dispositions *and* situational factors. The challenge of the attribution process is to sort out the relative contribution of each factor in any particular case.

ALPHABET AND ATTRACTION

As part of a study of the Maryland State Police force, researchers sent questionnaires to the 52 students in the force's Training Academy, and asked them to name their closest friends on the force. When social psychologist Mady Segal (1974) later examined the men's responses, she uncovered a startling result. Fully 44.6% of the friends that the men named were other men who were immediately adjacent to them in alphabetical order. If a man's name was Kroll, his best friends were likely to be named Krantz and Krupat; Adamses were friendly with Abbotts and Adlers, Wilsons with Weiners and Wizniaks. There turned out to be a simple explanation for the men's alphabetical attraction. Trainees in the academy were assigned dormitory rooms and classroom seats on the basis of alphabetical order. Thus, the closer any two men's last names were alphabetically, the more direct contact and exposure they were likely to have had.

LIKING OTHERS

Liking, perhaps even more than love, is what makes the world go round. On one series of surveys, the most common problem or wish listed by American high school students was "[I] want people to like me more" (Remmers & Radler, 1958). And our patterns of liking and disliking determine in large measure which people we will spend time with and which people we will avoid. Psychologists have explored many factors that lead us to like particular other people. In this section we will explore two such factors—proximity and similarity. In both cases, as we will see, liking can be explained by a basic economic principle: We like people who can provide us with the greatest possible rewards at the least possible cost. Of course, these rewards and costs are not usually financial ones. Rather, they are the social rewards that we gain from interacting with particular others and the social costs of interactions that are difficult or unpleasant.

The Nearness of You

If you live in California and I live in Michigan, it is not very likely that we will become fast friends, or even get to know each other. But even at much closer range, the physical *proximity* of any two people has a direct impact on their likelihood of becoming friends. One study in a college dormitory found a striking tendency for students to like the person next door more than the person two doors away, to like that person more than the person three doors away, and so on (Priest & Sawyer, 1967). Another study found that people assigned to be roommates become friends far more often than one would expect simply on the basis of their other characteristics (Newcomb, 1961).

As you may already be thinking, physical proximity doesn't *always* foster liking. It is certainly common enough for people who are assigned to be roommates to end the year, if they stick it out for that long, as mortal enemies. Close and frequent contact can breed hostility as well as attraction. Nevertheless, researchers have found that such contact more often leads to liking than to disliking. Contact with all sorts of people is likely to bring us certain social rewards, such as the opportunity to engage in joint activities or to compare our reactions and experiences. But with a roommate or someone else who lives close by, we can obtain these rewards without having to take the trouble of going far out of our way. Thus, physical proximity is likely to bring us rewards at low cost. And this interpersonal "profit" is translated into liking. It may sound crass, but that is the way liking often works—we like those who can bring us the biggest profit on the "interpersonal marketplace."

The same principle of proximity also applies to love and marriage. Studies by sociologists have documented that the closer a man and a woman live within a city, the more likely they are to marry one another (Katz & Hill, 1958). As Rubin (1973) writes, "The tendency to be attracted to people who are

Box 1
Beauty Is Best

Until very recently, most psychologists would not touch the topic of beauty with a ten-foot pole. Even while researchers busily investigated such bases of liking as proximity and similarity, they completely ignored the role of what would seem to be one of the most important bases of liking, physical attractiveness. Elliot Aronson (1969) suggested that psychologists may have refrained from studying the impact of physical attractiveness because they were afraid of what they might find. We are all taught that "Beauty is only skin deep," that a person's character and behavior are what really count. Perhaps psychologists feared that if they began to study the social impact of beauty they would discover that it is not skin deep after all—that it actually plays a major role in our relationships with others.

It may seem unfair or undemocratic for our physical appearance to have a large impact on our destinies. But democratic or not, it's better to tell it like it is than to pretend that beauty has little or no effect on interpersonal relationships. And once the taboo against studying beauty was broken, researchers found that its effects are great indeed. It will probably not shock you to learn that people's physical attractiveness has an immense impact on their appeal to the opposite sex (see Berscheid & Walster, 1974). But beautiful people—and we are using the term "beautiful" to refer to men as well as women—also tend to be perceived as better than people with average or below-average looks in many less obvious ways. Karen Dion, Ellen Berscheid, and Elaine Walster (1972) showed subjects photographs of male and female students of differing degrees of physical attractiveness. The subjects were asked to provide their impressions of these people and to make predictions about their future. The researchers found that the better-looking students were rated as more sensitive, kind, interesting, poised, and sociable than the less attractive students. The subjects also believed that the better-looking people had a greater chance of achieving success in their careers, becoming good husbands or wives, and finding happiness in their lives.

On the basis of results such as these, Dion and her colleagues concluded that we tend to have a stereotype of beautiful people that extends to positive characteristics that lie beneath the surface. This close at hand makes perfect sense in terms of the profit motive of the interpersonal marketplace. If a suitable mate lives next door, there is no need for a man in search of a partner to scour the entire block. If she lives in the neighborhood, there is no need for him to spend time and money on the cross-town bus. . . . 'When I'm not near the girl I love,' as the song goes, 'I love the girl I'm near.' " (p. 194).

Birds of a Feather

Once we have had an opportunity to meet another person, the single factor that plays the largest role in determining whether we will like each other is how *similar* we are. The principle that "Birds of a feather flock together" is not a new discovery of social psychologists. We were beaten to the punch by Aristotle many centuries ago:

And they are friends who have come to regard the same things as good and the same things as evil, they who are friends of the same people, and they who are enemies of the same people. . . . We like those who resemble us, and who are engaged in the same pursuits. . . .

As Aristotle's statement suggests, we tend to choose friends who are similar to us in many different respects, including age,

---

stereotype even affects our judgments of children. Margaret Clifford and Elaine Walster (1973) asked fifth-grade school teachers to provide their professional evaluations of a boy or girl, on the basis of information presented on that student's report card. In addition to extensive information about the student's grades and conduct, the report card had a small photograph of the student pasted in the corner. In half of the cases, the photograph was one of a physically attractive child, in the other half of the cases it was of an unattractive child. It turned out that the child's attractiveness had a large impact on the teachers' evaluations, even though all the other information presented was identical. The teachers assumed that the attractive children were more intelligent than the unattractive children, and they predicted that the attractive children would achieve a higher level of education. It is easy to see how such stereotypes can lead to self-fulfilling prophecies of the sort that we examined in the Psychological Issue on education (following Chapter 5). If good-looking children are *expected* to do better in school than less attractive childen, then teachers may relate to them in such a way as to confirm these expectations.

Beautiful people are favored in other ways as well. Physically attractive people are likely to be given an edge over less attractive people in many domains in which beauty is "supposed to be" irrelevant, such as getting jobs (Dipboye, Fromkin, & Wiback, 1975), getting lighter sentences in criminal trials (Efran, 1974), and winning national elections (Efran & Patterson, 1974). And in all of these respects, good looks seem to be just as much an advantage for men as they are for women.

Of course, beauty isn't always an advantage. Strikingly beautiful people may be seen as vain and egotistical (Dermer & Thiel, 1975), and they are sometimes more likely to be rejected (perhaps because of jealousy) by peers of their own sex (Krebs & Adinolfi, 1975). In addition, beauty remains to at least some extent "in the eye of the beholder," with different people varying somewhat in their physical preferences. Furthermore, it seems likely that the impact of physical attractiveness is greatest when we first meet someone. As a relationship progresses, physical attractiveness tends to recede in importance. And we often perceive people whom we love as being beautiful, regardless of what anyone else might think.

occupational status, educational level, and political preferences (Laumann, 1969). Similarities are important in our choice of husbands and wives as well. Hundreds of statistical studies have found husbands and wives to be much more similar to one another than one would expect by chance, on characteristics ranging from height to intelligence (Rubin, 1973).

The most critical similarities, however, are similarities of people's beliefs and attitudes. We already had a glimpse of the link between attitude similarity and liking in Chapter 18, when we discussed the social foundations of attitudes. In his study at Bennington, Theodore Newcomb found that many students

---

LIKING GOES ON TRIAL

How much someone is liked can have an effect on whether or not that person goes to jail. According to the famed lawyer Clarence Darrow, "Jurymen seldom convict a person they like, or acquit one they dislike. The main work of the trial lawyer is to make a jury like his client, or at least to feel sympathy for him; facts regarding the crime are relatively unimportant" (quoted in Sutherland, 1966, p. 442). Perhaps Darrow was overstating the case. But it remains clear that jurors' personal feelings toward defendants can have a large impact on their decisions.

---

adopted a liberal set of attitudes in order to gain the liking and acceptance of their classmates. In a later study, Newcomb provided a more direct demonstration of the influence of attitude similarity on liking. Newcomb (1961) rented a boarding house at the University of Michigan and provided free room and board for an entire term to students transferring to the university, in exchange for their participation in his study of friendship formation. He discovered that as the term progressed, friendship patterns among the students were determined primarily by similarities of attitudes and values. For example, one group of friends consisted of five men who were all enrolled in the liberal arts college and who had liberal political views and strong intellectual and artistic interests. Another clique consisted of three veterans, all in the college of engineering, politically conservative, and with interests that were more "practical" than "theoretical."

Our tendency to like other people with similar attitudes has also been demonstrated in a series of experiments in which subjects were shown a questionnaire that was supposedly filled out by another person. The other person's responses were fabricated in such a way as to indicate a specific degree of agreement with the subjects' own attitudes about a variety of topics. Subsequently the subjects were asked to indicate how much they thought they would like the person who filled out the questionnaire. The consistent result of such studies: The larger the proportion of items on which the "other person" agrees with the subject, the more the subject likes the other person (Byrne, 1971).

Why does similarity of attitudes have such a large impact on our likes and dislikes? Psychologists have suggested that it is rewarding to be agreed with for several reasons (Rubin, 1973):

> Agreement may provide a basis for engaging in joint activities, whether it be attending a prayer meeting or taking over a university hall.
>
> A person who agrees with you helps increase your confidence in your own opinion—and this, in turn, will bolster your self-esteem.
>
> Most people are vain enough to believe that anyone who shares their views must be a sensible and praiseworthy individual, while anyone who does not must have his head on backwards.
>
> People who agree about things that matter to them generally find it easier to communicate with each other.
>
> Finally, we often assume that people whose attitudes are similar to ours will like us—and, therefore, we tend to like them in turn.

There are, to be sure, exceptions to the "Birds of a feather" principle. We are sometimes attracted to people who are quite different from ourselves, especially if those people provide a fresh perspective that we would like to learn more about. Robert

JARGON

Newsman Edwin Newman, the author of a recent book called *Strictly Speaking* (1974), believes that the English language is going downhill. And he places part of the blame on the overblown terminology used by psychologists and other social scientists, which then becomes adopted by the general public. Newman has a point. Why, for example, do social psychologists persist in using such jargon as *interpersonal attraction* when they mean liking, or *residential propinquity* when they mean living next door? Perhaps they're afraid that if everyone understood what they were saying, it wouldn't sound quite so brilliant.

White (1976) provides an example of such a "friendship of opposites" between two teenage boys:

Ben, whose school experience had been so unstimulating that he never read a book beyond those assigned, discovered in Jamie a lively spirit of intellectual inquiry and an exciting knowledge of politics and history. Here was a whole world to which his friend opened the door and provided guidance. Jamie discovered in Ben a world previously closed to him, that of confident interaction with other people. Each admired the other, each copied the other, each used the other for practice. (White, 1976, p. 337)

On balance, however, the principle of similarity plays a much larger role in attracting people to one another than does the lure of diversity. After summarizing the psychological literature on similarity and liking, Rubin (1973) came to the following conclusion:

Diversity is valuable and enriching, and there is evidence that under certain conditions people actively seek it. But we also need to recognize without embarrassment that people with fundamentally different approaches to life are unlikely to become fast friends. For a human being to adapt to a rapidly changing world, he needs the companionship and support of others with whom he may sometimes disagree, but nevertheless feels a fundamental bond of likemindedness" (p. 154)

LOVING OTHERS

Although psychologists have been studying liking for some time now, they have been slower to grapple with the more delicate and complicated topic of love. In a presidential address to the American Psychological Association in 1956, Harry Harlow described the situation as he saw it:

Love is a wondrous state, deep, tender, and reassuring. Because of its intimate and personal nature it is regarded by some as an improper topic for experimental research. But, whatever our personal feelings may be, our assigned mission as psychologists is to analyze all facets of human and animal behavior into their component variables. So far as love or affection is concerned, psychologists have failed in their mission. The little we know about love does not transcend simple observation and the little we write about it has been written better by poets and novelists. (Harlow, 1958, p. 673)

In the two decades since Harlow made that statement, things have not changed drastically. Poets and novelists still describe love much more fully than psychologists do, and perhaps they always will. Nevertheless, progress has been made in the psychological study of love, especially within the past decade. One psychological approach is that taken by Dr. Harlow himself, who investigated mother-infant attachments (or "love") among infant monkeys (see Chapter 12). There is, of course, quite a jump from mother-infant love in monkeys to adult love relationships in human beings. But Harlow's research helped to demonstrate that one aspect of love is the need for close contact with another member of one's species, similar to what Robert Weiss calls the need for emotional attachment.

WHAT IS LOVE?

Love means different things to different people. Here are some ways in which students in a recent study of dating couples (Rubin, Peplau, & Hill, in preparation) described what love meant to them:

> "Love is really ambiguous. I have a feeling for her; I don't know what to call it; it's a warm feeling, an appreciation of her, an understanding of her, a consideration, a respect; if you want to call it love, sure."
>
> "Our love was pretty practical. It's just an overall very good feeling about a person, I think. I just wanted him to be there. Even if he was being really disgusting, I just liked being with him."
>
> "Love means that I'm not going to hide or hold things from her, that she is the person I'm going to be totally open with and I hope will be totally open with me. Obviously, that I care a lot, I'm laying myself bare—you are the one—you can accept me or reject me."

In Chapter 10 we discussed another approach to love, in the context of Stanley Schachter's labeling theory of emotion. From this perspective, love can be viewed as a label that people learn to place on their own physiological arousal. Most of the time, however, love does not involve intense physical symptoms. Instead, love can be viewed as a particular sort of attitude that one person has toward another person.

Measuring Love

Through the course of history love has been defined in countless ways, as everything from "a spirit all compact of fire" (by Shakespeare) to "a state of perceptual anesthesia" (by H.L. Mencken) to "not ever having to say you're sorry" (by Erich Segal). Not wishing to be outdone by these people of letters, Zick Rubin (1970; 1973) made an initial attempt to define and measure this attitude. On the basis of a questionnaire administered to several hundred dating couples at the University of Michigan, Rubin developed an attitude measure that he called a love scale. On this scale, respondents are asked to indicate how much they agree or disagree with a series of statements about their feelings toward another person, usually their boyfriend or girlfriend. As defined in Rubin's scale, love consists of three components, *attachment, caring,* and *intimacy.*

Sample Items From Rubin's Love Scale

Attachment
If I could never be with ______, I would be miserable.

Caring
If ______ were feeling badly, my first thought would be to cheer him or her up.

Intimacy
I feel that I can confide in ______ about practically everything.

Attachment refers to a person's need for the physical presence and emotional support of the other person. It corresponds to the sort of love studied by Harlow in infant monkeys, and the emotional attachment discussed by Weiss.

Caring refers to people's feelings of concern and responsibility for another person. Caring corresponds to Erich Fromm's definition of love as "the active concern for the life and growth of that which we love" (Fromm, 1956).

Intimacy refers to people's desire for close and confidential communication with the object of their love. When we are intimate with someone, we want to share certain of our thoughts and feelings with that person more fully than with anyone else.

Rubin views love as an attitude held by one person toward another that includes all three of these components. Skeptics may point out, of course, that a paper-and-pencil love scale does not really measure how much people love each other, but simply how much they *say* they love each other. But Rubin (1970) also obtained behavioral evidence for the love scale's validity. In one study, boyfriends' and girlfriends' scores on the love scale were checked out against the well-known folk wisdom that lovers spend a great deal of time staring into one another's eyes. Couples were observed through a one-way mirror in the psychological laboratory, while they were simply waiting for an experiment to begin. These surreptitious observations confirmed that "strong lovers" (couples whose members received above-average scores on the love scale) made significantly more eye contact than "weak lovers" (couples whose scores on the love scale were below average). Or, as the popular song has it, "I only have eyes for you."

LOVE MAGIC

People in many primitive societies believe in "love magic"—various charms, potions, or incantations that will cause one person to fall in love with another. Paul Rosenblatt (1971) sifted through anthropologists' reports of love magic in 23 societies, from the Chagga of East Africa to the Kwoma of New Guinea. He concluded that love magic often works, but it isn't really magic. Instead, such exotic practices of giving one's "victim" a charmed coconut, flashing a mirror at her, or blowing ashes in her face all serve to heighten the woman's love by indirectly communicating the man's interest in her. When love magic is practiced without the victim's knowledge, it isn't nearly so effective.

Love and Sex

Rubin's love scale did not include any items that specifically referred to sexual attraction or sexual behavior. Indeed, his conception of love could be applied to platonic friendships, as well as to romantic or sexual relationships. Rubin (1970) found that when people filled out his love scale in terms of their feelings toward their closest same-sex friends, women reported that they loved their friends more than men did. This result is hardly a surprising one, in the light of what we know about the roles of the two sexes. As we noted in Chapter 13, men in our society learn to "stay cool" and to suppress emotion especially when they are with other men. As a result, surveys have shown that women's friendships tend to be more intimate than men's, involving more spontaneous joint activities and more exchanging of confidences (e.g., Douvan & Adelson, 1966). Loving for men may often be channeled into a single opposite-sex relationship, while women may be more able to experience attachment, caring, and intimacy in other relationships as well.

Within opposite-sex, "romantic" relationships, what are the links between love and sex? This question is most often asked in reference to premarital relationships. Does sex serve to deepen a couple's love for one another, or is love more likely to flourish if sex is withheld? Does love add excitement to sex or fill it with anxiety? There are, to be sure, no simple answers to these questions. But some relevant information comes from a longitudinal study of 231 student dating couples recently conducted by Zick Rubin, Letitia Anne Peplau, and Charles Hill (in preparation). These researchers found that whether or not a couple had sexual intercourse had no systematic effect on the future of their relationship. Couples who had had intercourse were no more nor less likely to stay together over a two-year period than couples who had not had intercourse. While many men and women in this study felt that their sexual relationship helped to strengthen their love and commitment, others believed that their love would remain just as strong or stronger without sex.

Rubin and his coworkers also found that love and sex were more closely linked for women than for men in their sample (Peplau, Rubin, & Hill, 1977). Women tended to report greater love for their boyfriend if they had had sexual intercourse than if they had not. Love scores were particularly high among those women whose first sexual experience had been with their current boyfriend. No such links between love and sex were found among the men in the sample. Whether or not a man had had sexual intercourse with his girlfriend bore no relation to his reported love for her. This pattern of results can best be explained in terms of the persistence of a sexual "double standard" in contemporary America. Whereas it has often been considered appropriate for men to have sexual relations in casual relationships, women have traditionally been taught that sex is appropriate only if one is in love. As a result, women tend to be more reluctant than men to have sexual relations unless they believe they are in love. Furthermore, as the theory of cognitive dissonance discussed in Chapter 18 might predict, a woman who has sexual relations with her boyfriend may be especially likely to rationalize this action by deciding that she *must* be in love.

Although the sexual double standard still exists in America, there are signs that it is beginning to totter. In earlier decades, it was relatively common for men to have sexual relations with pickups or prostitutes, while women were expected to remain chaste until they were engaged or married. Surveys conducted in the 1970s suggest, however, that the norms for the two sexes are converging. The emerging norm seems to be that premarital sexual relations may be permissible for both men and women, but only in the context of close interpersonal relationships (e.g. Hunt, 1974).

LEAVING OTHERS

The "romantic ideal," celebrated in song and story, holds that love strikes at first sight, overcomes all obstacles, and lasts forever. The ending of most love stories, whether in fairy tales like "Sleeping Beauty" or comic books like *Young Romance,* is "and they lived happily ever after." But this ideal does not quite match up with reality. Love rarely strikes at first sight; it usually needs time to grow and develop. Love does not overcome all obstacles, such as those of race, religion, or social status; the large majority of love relationships and marriages are between people who come from highly similar social backgrounds (Rubin, 1973). And love does not necessarily last forever. Although love often leads to long-term relationships or to marriage, in many other cases true love runs its course and comes to an end.

Why Do Relationships End?

Relationships end for many different reasons, ranging from simple boredom to conflicts about life-styles. In their study of stu-

---

Box 2

Should We Study Love?

As psychologists begin to investigate love, shouts of criticism are being voiced by those who believe that love is not a proper object of study. Perhaps the most vocal of these critics has been United States Senator William Proxmire of Wisconsin. In his role as chairman of the Senate committee that oversees appropriations to the National Science Foundation, Proxmire habitually keeps a sharp eye out for federally-funded projects that seem impractical or frivolous. When he discovered in 1975 that the National Science Foundation had awarded a grant to social psychologist Ellen Berscheid to study aspects of romantic love, Proxmire was enraged. He fired off a press release in which he called the project "the biggest waste of the taxpayer's money for the month of March." He went on to say that "I believe that 200 million Americans want to leave some things in life a mystery, and right at the top of the things we don't want to know about is why a man falls in love with a woman and vice versa."

Soon afterward Proxmire expanded his attack to include other programs of research on interpersonal relationships. "I think it is time the National Science Foundation put a stop to the Federal version of 'The Love Machine,' " Proxmire declared, "and rearrange its research priorities to address our scientific, not our erotic curiosity."

Many psychologists and other scientists felt that Senator Proxmire's criticisms were cheap shots, phrased in such a way as to gain publicity rather than to really shed light on the underlying issues. Nevertheless, Proxmire's complaint did focus attention on serious issues about research on interpersonal relationships. Is the senator right when he claims that love is one of those phenomena that should be left shrouded in mystery, rather than poked at by inquisitive psychologists? And should taxpayers' money be invested in such efforts?

dent dating couples, Zick Rubin and his coworkers investigated some of the factors that lead people to leave one another (Hill, Rubin, & Peplau, 1976). Over a two-year period, about half of the couples in their sample stayed together and the other half broke up. The researchers found that the boyfriends and girlfriends in the couples who stayed together tended to be more similar to one another in age, intelligence, career plans, and physical attractiveness than were boyfriends and girlfriends in the couples who broke up. In addition, when people who had broken up were asked to explain why the relationship had ended, they frequently mentioned differences in interests, backgrounds, sexual attitudes, and ideas about marriage. It seems that similarities between people not only lead to attraction in the first place, but also encourage the continuation of relationships. Partners who have serious differences or disagreements are likely to end up going their separate ways.

Rubin and his coworkers also found that relationships were most likely to end if one of the partners was considerably more involved in the relationship than the other. Of the couples in which both members initially reported that they were equally involved in the relationship, only 23% broke up during the subsequent two-year period. But among those couples in which one partner was more involved than the other, 54% broke up. There seems to be an inherent lack of stability in relationships in which one partner is more invested than the other. In such a relationship, the more involved partner may become overly dependent and exploited, while the less involved partner may feel restless

---

Many people agree wholeheartedly with Senator Proxmire's indictment of research on love. There are even some psychologists who share his viewpoint. One psychologist went so far as to declare that "The scientist in even attempting to interject love into a laboratory situation is by the very nature of the proposition dehumanizing the state we call love" (Karmel, 1970). Many newspaper columnists and editorialists jumped on Proxmire's bandwagon, echoing his conclusion that trying to understand love is a ridiculous and money-wasting enterprise.

But many other people disagree vehemently with Proxmire's point of view, and the authors of this book are among them. Interpersonal relationships are extremely complicated phenomena, and psychologists have no illusions that they will ever unlock all of love's mysteries. But interpersonal relationships are also the source of great confusion and distress for many people. As we will see in the Psychological Issue that follows, for example, divorce rates in America have been skyrocketing, leaving a tremendous amount of human suffering in their wake. If further research of the sort that is reported in this chapter can make even a small contribution to people's understanding of their relationships with others, then the relatively small amount of money expended for such research will be more than justified.

Each of you will have to draw your own conclusion about this controversy. But speaking for ourselves, we agree wholeheartedly with a response to Senator Proxmire that was offered by New York *Times* columnist James Reston (1975): "If the sociologists and psychologists can get even a suggestion of the answer to our patterns of romantic love, marriage, disillusion, divorce—and the childen left behind—it could be the best investment of Federal money since Mr. Jefferson made the Louisiana Purchase."

and guilty. As a result, as sociologist Peter Blau writes, "Commitments must stay abreast for a love relationship to develop into a lasting mutual attachment. . . . Only when two lovers' affection for and commitment to one another expand at roughly the same pace do they tend mutually to support their love" (Blau, 1964, p. 84).

When Do Relationships End?

Hill, Rubin, and Peplau (1976) found that the breakups of the college student couples in their sample were most likely to take place at specific points during the school year—in the months of May-June, September, and December-January. At such times, when the school year is beginning or ending or during vacations, people may be more likely to be separated from one another or to meet new partners. In addition, if one has already been thinking about ending a relationship, such events as the end of the school year may make it easier to actually call the relationship off. For example, it is probably easier to say, "While we're apart we ought to date others" than it is to say "I've grown tired of you and would rather not date any more." By attributing the impending breakup to external circumstances, such as unavoidable physical separation, it may be possible to reduce some of the guilt and embarrassment that is otherwise likely to be associated with ending a close relationship.

The Aftermath of Breaking Up

The ending of a close relationship often leads to feelings of pain and distress, similar to the symptoms of loneliness that we discussed earlier. These feelings are likely to be most acute for the partner who was broken up with (assuming that the ending was not completely mutual), but they affect the partner who wanted to break up as well. But in spite of the pain involved, the ending of close relationships can teach us valuable lessons. By experiencing first-hand the difficulties of close relationships, we are likely to learn more about our own interpersonal needs, preferences, strengths, and weaknesses. These lessons can be of value to us as we enter new relationships. After the ending of her relationship with David, for example, Ruth told the researchers that "I don't regret having the experience at all. But after being in the supportive role, *I* want a little support now. That's the main thing I look for" (Hill, Rubin, & Peplau, 1976, p. 156). And after his breakup with Kathy, Joe indicated that he would exercise greater caution in future relationships. "If I fall in love again," he said, "it might be with the reservation that I'm going to keep awake this time" (p. 155). Breakups are most valuable if they take place before marriage. For, as we will see in the Psychological Issue that follows, marital breakups are likely to be considerably more painful and stressful than breakups that take place before marriage. As an anonymous wise man once said, "The best divorce is the one you get before you get married."

SUMMARY

1. People often seek out each other out of the need for *social comparison*—the need to compare one's experiences and reactions with those of other people. This is especially true when people are afraid or upset, although extremely intense feelings may also cause people to want to be alone.
2. According to Weiss, people have a need for two kinds of interpersonal relationships: *emotional attachments* to one other person, and *social ties* to a network of friends. When people lack either type of relationship they are likely to experience *loneliness.* Lack of emotional attachment brings *emotional isolation,* while lack of social ties produces *social isolation.*
3. The way we form inferences about people upon first seeing them is called *person perception.* Our perceptions of others are highly influenced by their physical appearance and by the stereotypes we hold for various physical characteristics.
4. A person's *reputation* often influences the way he or she is perceived. Furthermore, a person's actions often leads us to form ideas about his or her basic underlying traits—this method of trying to infer the causes of people's behavior is called *attribution processes.* Research has shown that most people's behavior is controlled more by situational factors than by underlying traits and that it is an error to attribute all of a person's actions to his her basic personality.
5. Studies have shown that physical attractiveness has a major impact on how we view people. Attractive people tend to be rated as more sensitive, kind, interesting, sociable, successful, and happy. "Beautiful" people are given the edge in school, in jobs, and in politics.
6. The physical *proximity* of any two people has a direct impact on their likelihood of becoming friends. Studies have shown that people who live next door to each other are more likely to become friends than people who leave two doors away, for example.
7. A major factor in whether two people will become friends is their *similarity* to each other. Friends and married couples tend to be similar in age, occupational status, educational level, and even height. However, the most important area of similarity is beliefs and attitudes—people who agree with us provide us with many kinds of rewards.
8. How does one measure love? Rubin developed a questionnaire that assumes love to be made up of three components: attachment, caring, and intimacy. A high score in all three areas is indicative of love for another person. Couples who scored high on the love scale were found to spend more time looking into each others' eyes than those who scored lower.
9. Whether or not a couple in love has sexual intercourse appears to have no systematic effect on the future of their

relationship. However, women tend to report greater love for their boyfriends if they have had intercourse.

10. Love does not necessarily last forever. Many factors can contribute to the ending of a relationship, including differences in interests, background, sexual attitudes, and ideas about marriage. Also, relationships are more likely to end if one partner is considerably more involved in the relationship than the other. Although the breakup of a relationship can be very painful, it can also help people to learn about themselves and about interpersonal relations.

psychological issue

Marriage and Divorce

Demographers—those energetic social scientists who chart social trends on the basis of census data and other nationwide characteristics—have been returning from their computers recently with puzzled looks on their faces. They have been charting trends in the frequency of marriage and divorce in America that, from a "rational" point of view, don't seem to make much sense. What demographers are finding is that the divorce rate in America has been climbing steadily and is now at an all-time high. In the period between 1972 and 1974 there was an average of 907,000 divorces each year in America, an annual rate *double* that of a decade earlier. It is reliably estimated that between 30 and 40 percent of marriages now taking place in America will end in divorce, a rate unprecedented in our nation's history (Norton and Glick, 1976).

These statistics might lead us to believe that Americans are becoming disillusioned with marriage—that they are deciding that the burdens of married life outweigh the benefits it might bring. But if that is the case, how do we account for another batch of statistics showing that 80 percent (about three-fourths of women and five-sixths of men) of those Americans who divorce eventually remarry? Even though these people decided that their marriages were not very satisfactory, they still insisted on coming back for more. And the news that about one in three marriages is destined to fail hasn't dissuaded young people from trying marriage out for themselves. Well over 90 percent of Americans marry at least once, and current mar-

Why are so many American couples deciding to get divorced?

riage rates show no signs of decline.

What can account for these contradictions? Even though the usual sequence is marriage followed by divorce, let's look at these two phenomena in reverse order, and perhaps we may gain some insights into the causes of the divorce boom and the undiminished popularity of marriage.

Divorce in America

Why are so many American couples deciding to get divorced? Many different culprits have been identified, from the fading of traditional religious values to the failure of couples to give sufficient consideration to their decision to marry. But of all the possible factors, two seem to have had the greatest impact: (1) there appears to have been a gradual shift in values from the notion that marriage is forever, "for better or for worse," to the notion that personal happiness and self-realization are the most important goals for individuals; and (2) this shift in values has been accompanied by changes in laws that make it much easier than it used to be to end a marriage. Most of the 50 states have adopted divorce reforms such as shortening the period a couple must be separated before getting a divorce and instituting "no-fault" divorce laws that declare that if a couple mutually agree to divorce it is essentially their own business.

Taken together, these ideological and legal changes have drastically changed the balance of forces acting on a couple with a troubled relationship. In the past, many couples would stay together even when their relationship was no longer very satisfying. In some cases, these couples' marital bonds seemed more like the walls of a prison (Levinger, 1976). Sociologist William Goode (1961) called marriages that stuck it out "empty shell" marriages†:

The atmosphere is without laughter or fun, and a sullen gloom pervades the household. Members do not discuss their problems or experiences with each other, and communication is kept to a minimum . . . Their rationalization for avoiding a divorce is, on the part of one or both, sacrifice for the children, neighborhood respectability, and a religious conviction that divorce is morally wrong. . . . The hostility in such a home is great, but arguments focus on the small issues, not the large ones. Facing the latter would, of course, lead directly to separation or divorce, but the couple has decided that staying together overrides other values, including each other's happiness and the psychological health of their children. 1961, (pages, 441–442)

There are still many such empty-shell marriages in America. But it is no longer as clear as it used to be that remaining in such marriages is the "right" thing to do. Today the "success" of a marriage is less likely to be judged by how long it lasts and more likely to be judged by the extent to which it brings happiness and personal fulfillment (Levinger, 1976).

Untying the Marital Knot

The divorce boom and the rising ethic of self-realization might suggest that ending a marriage is an easy matter. It might even suggest to some young people that there's no reason not to marry someone you're drawn to at the moment; after all, if it doesn't work, you can always get a divorce. This is an interesting theory, but nothing could be further from the truth. No matter how good or bad a marriage has been, terminating it is almost always an extremely painful, wrenching experience. Robert Weiss (1975) has conducted an extensive study of people in the process of separation or divorce. He concludes, "Most separations . . . come about only after a long and anguished process of mutual alienation from which both partners emerge bruised, their morale depleted, their self-esteem low, their ability to function damaged by the varied assaults of the failing marriage" (page 28).

†From W. J. Goode, "Family Disorganization," in R. K. Merton & R. A. Nisbet (eds.), CONTEMPORARY SOCIAL PROBLEMS (New York: Harcourt Brace Jovanovich, 1961), pp. 441–42. Reprinted by permission.

In addition, once a man and woman have divorced, their problems are by no means over. Instead, the experience of being on one's own after being married is often a terrifying one. One woman reported, "When the idea occurred to me that I could live without Dave and be happier, my next immediate feeling was just fear. It's really hard to explain. It was just terror" (Weiss, 1976, page 137).†

Many divorcing couples are surprised to discover that even though they found life with their partner to be intolerable, after the separation they remain strongly attached to the partner:

Here I was three days with someone of the opposite sex, trying to start rebuilding, and I just got overwhelmed with panic and being three thousand miles from Laura. And those waves built up until I was just white. It is an unbearable feeling. (Weiss, 1976, page 138)

Divorce is likely to be a traumatic experience not only for the separating couple, but also for their children. In 1973, six out of ten couples getting a divorce in America had children (Norton and Glick, 1976), and it is estimated that between 20 and 30 percent of children growing up in the 1970s will see their parents divorce (Bane, 1976). This experience is likely to cause shock, sadness, and insecurity for children of all ages. Most children of divorced parents recover from their initial distress within a year, but in a substantial number of cases children's self-esteem and social relations remain disturbed for much longer (Wallerstein and Kelly, cited by Weiss, 1975). On the other hand, studies of long-term psychological effects suggest that children from broken marriages may well experience *less* unhappiness in the long run than children in unbroken homes that are full of conflict and hostility. These studies argue against efforts to hold unhappy marriages together "for the sake of the children" (Bane, 1976).

Part of the new ideology is that divorce can be a liberating experience.

Part of the new ideology of divorce is that divorce can be a liberating experience. Some feminists look to divorce as a way in which a woman can extricate herself from the "wife/mother package" and regain her autonomy (Brown et al., 1976).† One divorced woman expressed her reactions in the following terms:

I had to put his needs before myself and I felt resentful, overburdened by the responsibility of keeping his life stable and positive when my own seemed negative and unstable. I resented being a mother. Now at last I have the opportunity to develop myself without the hostility of a husband. (Brown et al., 1976, page 122)

Carol Brown and coworkers at the Women's Research Center of Boston believe that for these trapped women divorce can be "the chance of a new lifetime." "Despite the

†*From Robert S. Weiss, "The Emotional Impact of Marital Separation,"* Journal of Social Issues, *Vol. 32, No. 1 (1976), p. 137, 138. Reprinted by permission.*

†*From Carol A. Brown, et. al., "Divorce: Chance of a New Lifetime,"* Journal of Social Issues, *Vol. 32, No. 1 (1976), p. 122. Reprinted by permission.*

problems," they write, "the experience of heading a family [without a husband] is often better for these women than marriage" (page 122). Nevertheless, the problems should not be underestimated. Even though divorce can be liberating for women, and in many cases for men as well, there are very few divorces that are not filled with tremendous pain and distress.

Coming Back for More

There are some people who have tried marriage, decided that they didn't like it, and resolved to remain single in the future. This was true of most of the sample of 30 divorced women interviewed by Brown and her coworkers (1976). But these women are in the minority. As we noted earlier, three-fourths of the women and five-sixths of the men who divorce eventually remarry. These people are not disillusioned with marriage as an institution. Their feeling seems to be that marriage is a good thing, and even though their first try did not succeed, they are willing to give it a second attempt. Robert Weiss (1975) stresses that the process of getting back into circulation and forming new attachments is a difficult one. Indeed, he finds that it usually takes a divorced person between two and four years to recover fully from the distress produced by the breakup. During this period, the divorced person may need to rely heavily on networks of friends, organizations like Parents Without Partners, or professional counselors for needed support and advice. But eventually most divorced people find satisfactory new attachments. Human beings learn from experience, and we are not doomed to make the same mistakes twice. One divorced woman whom Weiss interviewed summed it up as follows:

I have a friendship with this guy that has gone on for a long period of time. Every once in a while we will have a conversation and I will expect certain responses, because that is what I am conditioned to. And his reactions are entirely different from my husband's. He's a different person, that's all. So with one partner you can do everything and say everything wrong, but with another partner it's fine. So you shouldn't give up hope because you batted out once. (Weiss, 1975, page 308)

...in some colonies bachelors were assigned to live with "licensed" families and had to pay special taxes.

Why Marry?

The desire of the large majority of divorced people to try marriage again brings us back to one of the questions we started with: Why does such a large preponderance of people choose to marry at all? Part of the answer is that society has always put strong pressures on women and men to marry, as the only "appropriate" or "normal" thing to do. In colonial America, older single women were ridiculed as "old maids" and treated as failures in life. And bachelors were placed in practically the same category as criminals; in some colonies bachelors were assigned to live with "licensed" families and had to pay special taxes. This treatment of unmarried individuals provided an inducement for them to marry (Scanzoni and Scanzoni, 1976). Such negative attitudes, albeit in somewhat more subtle form, have persisted until the present day. Boys and girls learn from their parents and from the mass media that they are expected to marry and to "live happily ever after." And even if many marriages don't achieve the latter goal, the injunction to marry still comes through loud and clear.

At present the notion that marriage is the ideal life style for everyone is beginning to be questioned. For example, the women's movement has supported the idea that staying single can be more fulfilling than marriage for many women. And, as Letha and John Scanzoni (1976) note, "Enough examples of successful single women in business, education, government, the professions, and the arts serve to invalidate old notions about a woman's being a failure if she doesn't marry" (page 154). In fact, there is evidence that single women tend to have higher levels of intelligence, educational and occupational status than married women (Spreitzer and Riley, 1974). It is no longer a stigma to be over 30 and unmarried in America.

Nevertheless, the greater tolerance for remaining single has not diminished most Americans' desire to marry. In a recent national survey (the Roper Organization, 1974), 96 percent of the women and 92 percent of the men said they wanted to be married. And in a 1972 survey of 2,500 college students in the Boston area, 97.8 percent predicted that they would eventually marry—and all but 4 percent expected to do so within the next ten years (Rubin, Peplau, and Hill, in preparation).

Many reasons can be suggested for the continuing appeal of marriage—love, the desire for security, the desire for sex on a regular basis, the desire to have children, the desire to "make it legal," pressure from parents, and the force of tradition. One student in the Rubin, Peplau, and Hill study of dating couples listed three reasons for his decision to get married:

1. *I loved her and wanted to spend the rest of my life with her.*
2. *I felt lonesome when not seeing her for long periods.*
3. *I wanted to take her out of circulation.*

Another student explained her decision in the following terms:

Our parents never knew we were living together. One reason for marrying was to make a public statement that we were committed to each other. It would make things such as bank account, insurance and renting an apartment easier. We already felt married so there didn't seem to be any reason not to. Being married was a state I had always unquestionably known I would enter.

Perhaps most importantly, by committing men and women to one another marriage serves to keep people together even in the face of temporary fluctuations in their feelings of attraction for one another. Marriage makes it more likely that a relationship will withstand the ups and downs that are an inevitable part of any close relationship. As such, marriage can play a valuable stabilizing role in satisfying people's needs for close interpersonal relationships (Levinger, 1976). In addition, the fact that marriage has existed in every human society and in every era suggests that the institution of marriage is useful for society as a whole. As sociologist John Finley Scott (1966) writes, marriage "combines the functions of reproduction, child care, sexual gratification, and economic cooperation with an overall efficiency that no alternate arrangement has been able to match."

Summary

1. The American divorce rate is at an all-time high, and 30 to 40 percent of current marriages appear destined to end in divorce. However, 80 percent of people who divorce eventually remarry, and the popularity of marriage itself does not seem to have diminished.
2. The current high rate of divorce is the result of many factors, including a major change in attitudes toward marriage and in divorce laws making it easier to dissolve marriages.
3. Despite the "ease" of divorce today, it is still a highly traumatic experience, both for the couple and for their children. Still children are often better off if their unhappy parents do divorce rather than maintain an unhappy home.
4. Marriage is the norm in American society, and up until recently single men and women were treated negatively. Even though the single life is now no longer a stigma, the majority of men and women *do* want to marry. Apparently marriage fulfills both strong emotional needs and the needs of society.

Appendix
Glossary
Bibliography
Photographic Credits
Index

APPENDIX: Psychology and Numbers

You need to know something about statistics if you want to become a sophisticated consumer of the products of psychological research. More generally, a basic understanding of statistics has become increasingly essential to being a well-informed member of modern society. Your daily newspaper is filled with statistics about food prices, crime rates, income distributions, marriage and divorce rates, and other matters that directly relate to your personal well-being. Every time you turn on the television you are bombarded by statistical claims about calories, miles per gallon, or pain relief, attesting to the superiority of one product over another. In this day and age, there is no escape from numbers.

Statistics are simply numbers that are used to describe and interpret facts or observations. Social scientists often use such numbers to communicate, because words are too imprecise. Imagine doing research in which you had to report your findings using only such terms as "quite a lot," "not nearly as much," or "a whole bunch." It's hard to know whether "fast, fast, fast relief" is faster or slower than "immediate relief" or whether a huge crowd is bigger or smaller than a tremendous one. Such terms have no precise meaning. And, as the old saying goes, measures such as "a long time" depend on which end of the branding iron you're on.

But even though statistics are necessary tools for psychologists and other scientists, they have their pitfalls as well. Numbers can be used confusingly and misleadingly, especially by people who are trying to sell you something—whether a product, an idea, or a point of view. An advertiser's "Four out of five dentists recommend sugarless gum for their patients who chew gum" needs to be examined very carefully. It may also be the case that nine out of ten dentists would advise their patients not to chew gum at all. Similarly, a psychologist's statement that "There is a significant relationship between training in psychology and interpersonal sensitivity" (to use an example we introduced in Chapter 1) also needs to be closely scrutinized: What does it really mean for a relationship to be "significant"? How were each of the two variables measured? What group of subjects was used in computing this relationship? The importance of the psychologist's findings for you depends on the answer to questions like these.

In the next few pages we will take you on a brief tour of some of the statistical tools that are used by psychologists and other scientists to help describe and interpret their observations. First, we will discuss the basic statistics used to describe a single set of observations or scores. Then we will discuss the use of samples and the concept of statistical significance. Finally, we will discuss the use of correlation coefficients to describe the relationship between two sets of observations.

Descriptive Statistics

Both scientists and nonscientists are often confronted with sets of numbers that represent a set of observations or scores. For example, we may have a set of numbers representing the I.Q. scores of each student in a school, or the annual incomes of each of the employees of a company, or the number of pounds lifted by each of 50 weight-lifters. In order to make sense out of such sets of numbers, we must first be able to describe these "raw data" clearly and efficiently. For purposes of illustration, we can make up some numbers to use as our raw data. Just so our numbers represent something close to your heart and important to your survival, let's take examination scores.

Suppose your class is given a multiple-choice examination consisting of 25 questions, with 1 point for every correct answer and 0 points for each one you miss. The range of possible scores is 0 to 25. In practice, of course, it's quite likely that no one will get a score as low as 0 or as high as 25. Let's suppose that there are 23 students in the class, and the test-score data look like this:

Table 1: *Class Members' Scores on Examination*

Student	*Examination Score*
Leonard Ahern	20
Catherine Baskin	16
Patricia Breen	18
Michael Cavanaugh	18
Harold Costopoulos	19
Arlene DiNapoli	20
Paul Feinberg	22
Julia Hernandez	20
Mary Jameson	19
Joel King	13
Robert Liu	19
Fred Luna	18
Frances Mazurek	18
Denise Moeller	17
Elihu Noyes	21
William Piper	15
Louise Randolph	18
Kenneth Roderick	21
Delores Santos	24
Janet Slovin	21
Harmon Stewart	19
John Thibodeau	16
Helen Welsh	21

In summarizing such a set of scores, the first thing that an instructor is likely to do is to make a *frequency distribution* indicating how many students obtained each score, as in Table 2. Since no one in this class received a score of less than 13, the possible scores from 0 to 12 are lumped into a single category.

The information in this frequency distribution can also be displayed pictorially, by drawing a *histogram* (see Figure 1). In the histogram, each little box represents one test score. By showing how many boxes are piled on top of each other for each obtained score, the overall pattern of test results becomes easier to visualize.

Both the frequency distribution and the histogram provide a good overall description of

Table 2: *Frequency Distribution of Examination Scores in Table 1*

Examination Score	*Number of Students Receiving that Score*
0–12	0
13	1
14	0
15	1
16	2
17	1
18	5
19	4
20	3
21	4
22	1
23	0
24	1
25	0

the test scores in this class. In presenting results, it is often inefficient to provide the entire frequency distribution. Instead, we are likely to make use of statistics that *summarize* the overall distribution. There are two important types of summary statistics: measures of the *central tendency* of a distribution, to indicate the "average" or "typical" score, and measures of the *variability* of a distribution, to indicate how spread out the scores are.

The most frequently used measure of central tendency is the *mean*. The mean is another term for what we often call the *average* score. To compute the mean of a set of scores, first add up the individual scores (13, 15, 16, 16, 17, and so on) and then divide the sum by the number of cases (in this case 23). In our illustration, the mean score turns out to be $^{433}/_{23} = 18.8$. This number provides an index of how well the class as a whole did on the exam.

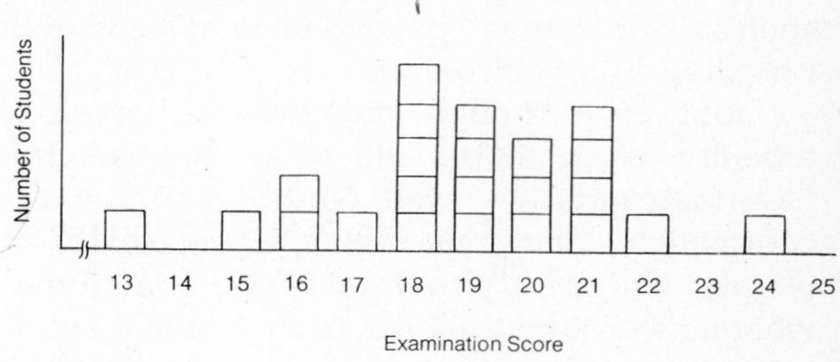

FIG. 1 Histogram, representing pictorially the distribution of examination scores given in Table 2. Each box represents one student's score on the exam.

The *median* is a slightly different sort of measure of central tendency. The median is simply the middlemost score in any set of scores. In our set of 23 scores for example, the median would be the twelfth highest (or twelfth lowest) score—that is, the score that falls right in the middle of the overall distribution. In our example, the median score turns out to be 19. Although the mean is the measure of central tendency that is most commonly used by psychologists, the median may sometimes provide a more useful summary of a distribution of scores than the mean. Let's say, for example, that we wanted to provide an indication of the "average" age of a group of five people, aged 18, 19, 20, 21, and 70. The mean age of these five people is 29.6. But the median age (20) would be more representative of the ages of most members of the group. Similarly, distributions of people's income are often summarized in terms of their median, rather then their means, to avoid giving too much weight to the small number of people with extremely high incomes.

The final measure of central tendency, the *mode* of a distribution, is simply the score that is more common than any other score. In our illustration, the mode is 18, since more students obtained that score than any other single score. Modes are most useful when we want to indicate which one of a small number of categories is most prevalent or "popular."

In addition to describing the central tendency of a set of scores, it is also useful to describe the variability of a set of scores—that is, how widely the scores are dispersed. The simplest way to summarize the variability of a distribution is to specify its *range*—that is, to indicate the lowest and highest scores actually obtained. In our illustration, the range of scores was from 13 to 24. In another class the range might have been narrower—say, from 17 to 21. The range is not a perfect summary of variability, however, because it can be radically changed as a result of one or two "oddball" scores. A fuller description of the variability of a set of scores is provided by its *standard deviation.* The standard deviation is computed by means of a formula that takes into account how far each individual score is from the mean of the distribution. The more closely packed the scores are around the mean, the lower the standard deviation of that distribution. The more widely dispersed the scores are, the higher the standard deviation. Consider, for example, the heights of two fifteen-member basketball teams, presented in the form of two histograms (Figure 2).

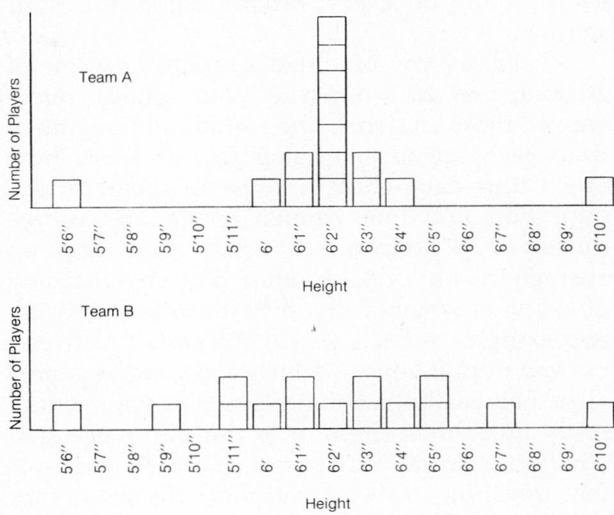

FIG. 2 These histograms represent the heights of the players on two basketball teams.

Although both teams include the same range of heights (from 5′6″ to 6′10″) and both teams have the same mean height (6′2″), on the whole there is more variety in the heights of members of Team A than of Team B. And, as a result, we would find that the standard deviation of the heights of Team A is greater than the standard deviation of the heights of Team B.

Sampling and Statistical Significance

Let's say that you wanted to know which sex spends more time studying at your school—women or men. (This example is adapted from Wing, 1969.) One way to find out would be to do a complete survey of the students at your school; ask each person how many hours per day he or she spends studying, and then compare the mean scores of the men and of the women. But such a complete survey would be difficult, if not impossible, to do. Instead, it may be possible to answer your question more conveniently by interviewing a *random sample* of female and male students. A random sample is one in which each member of the overall population being studied has an equal chance of ending up in the sample. If you stood in front of the gymnasium or in front of the library, you would be unlikely to obtain a random sample of students, since students are not equally likely to be found at these locations. A better sampling technique would be to begin with a complete list of students, and then choose every tenth or every fiftieth name for your sample.

Let's say you obtained a random sample of 20 men and 20 women at your school, interviewed these students, and found out how much time each spends studying (or, at least, how much time each student *claims* to spend studying). You find that women spend an average (mean) of 3.7 hours a day and the men spend an average (mean) of 3.3 hours a day. A remaining question is whether this difference between the two samples reflects a real difference between the two populations to which you want to generalize. Is it really true that women at your school study more than men, or is the difference that you found simply a matter of chance? To answer this question, tests of *statistical significance* are employed. There are three elements of any comparison between samples that are important in deciding whether the observed differences reflect real population differences. First, the greater the difference between the means of the two samples, the more likely it is that there will be a corresponding difference in the total population. Second, the larger the number of subjects in the samples, the more likely it is that the sample accurately reflects population data. And third, the smaller the variation of scores (or the standard deviation) within each sample, the more likely it is that the difference between samples reflects a real population difference. All of these factors are taken into account in tests that assess the statistical significance of differences between groups. The significance level of any obtained difference between groups is the probability that the difference was simply due to chance, rather than reflecting a true population difference. Thus, a significance level of .25 would indicate that there was a 25 % (or 1 in 4) chance that the difference in mean scores that we obtained was due to chance. A significance level of .05 indicates that there is only a 5% chance that the total populations are not really different. In general, psychologists accept a significance level of .05 as sufficiently small to make it reasonable to consider the difference to be a real one. The significance level of any difference is also called a *p* value, with "*p*" standing for "probability." Psychologists often compute *p* values when they conduct experiments, in order to determine whether any obtained differences in behavior between subjects in different experimental conditions are worth taking seriously.

Correlation Coefficients

The *correlation coefficient* is a statistic that describes the degree to which one set of scores is related to a second set of scores. For example, we can make use of correlations to tell us what the relationship is between how much students study and those students' grades, or to indicate the size of the relationship between husbands' and wives' scores on a measure of sex-role attitudes.

The best way to view the correlation coefficient is as a measure of the extent to which knowing one set of scores helps us to predict a second set of scores. Let's say that a class is given two examinations, one early in the term and one later in the term. We can represent the two sets of scores graphically by means of *scatterplots,* as in Figure 3. Each point on the scatterplot represents an individual student's score on both of the two tests. In Figure 3A, there is a good deal of consistency between students' scores on the two tests. As a result, it is possible to make a reasonably good prediction of how well the student will do on the second test on the basis of his or her performance on the first test. In Figure 3B, on the other hand, there is little consistency between scores on the two tests. In this case, knowing how well a student did on the first test is of little or no help in predicting his or her score on the second test. Although it is unlikely to be the case in this example, we may sometimes find *inverse* relationships between two sets of scores, so that a higher score on one measure is associated with a lower score on a second measure.

When such relationships between two sets of scores are converted into the form of a number, the obtained correlations can range from +1.00 (a perfect positive correlation) through .00 (no correlation at all) to −1.00 (perfect negative correlation). In practice, it is unusual to find "perfect" correlations of +1.00 or −1.00. Most of the correlations that psychologists encounter take the form of fractions, such as +.43 or −.37. The higher this fraction, whether in a positive or a negative direction, the stronger is the relationship between the two sets of scores.

In Figure 2A, the correlation between the two sets of test scores is quite high—approximately +.80. In Figure 2B, the correlation is close to .00.

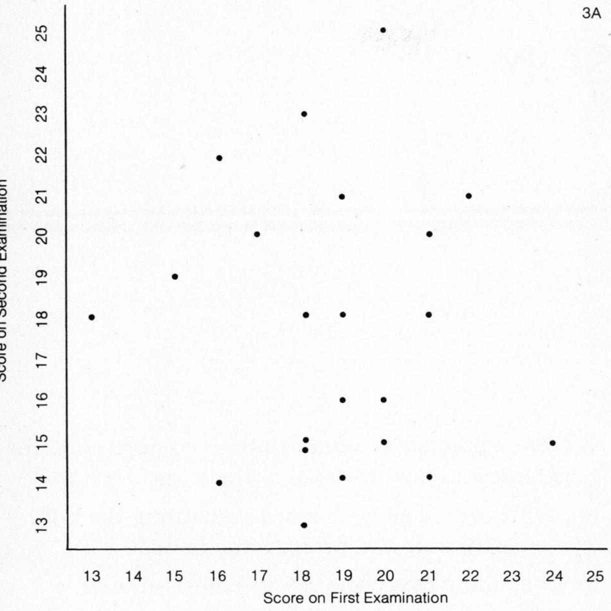

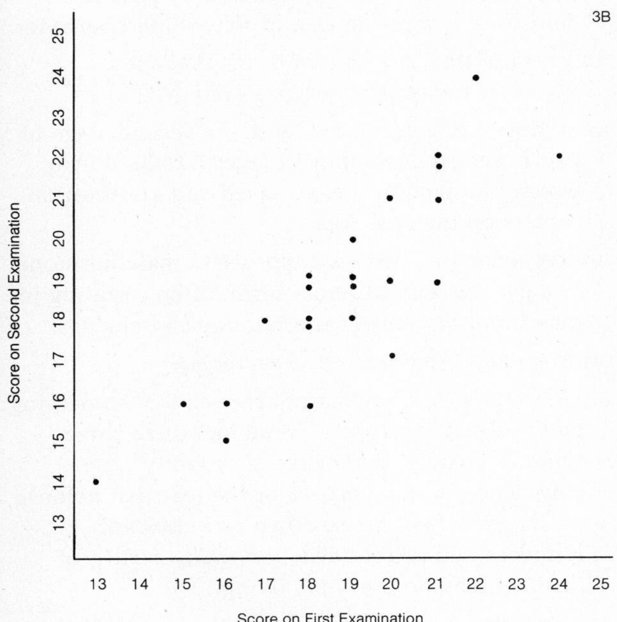

FIG. 3 Each of these scatterplots shows the relationship between students' scores on two examinations. In Figure 3A there is a high positive correlation between scores on the two examinations. In Figure 3B the correlation is near zero.

The correlation between two sets of scores provides an index of the extent to which two measures or events vary together. As we noted in Chapter 1, however, the fact that two measures are highly correlated with one another does not indicate that one event *caused* the other. If we found, for example, that there was a high positive correlation between students' hours of studying and their grades, it would not necessarily mean that studying led to higher grades. It is possible, for example, that the causal link actually went in the other direction, so that getting high grades encouraged students to study more. Or it may be that students who are interested in the course material are likely both to study a lot and to get high grades, but that neither of the latter variables exert a direct causal influence on the other. A significant correlation (that is, one that is unlikely to come about by chance) indicates only that a relationship is present. We must supplement our correlational analysis with other methods, such as experiments, if we want to *explain* that relationship.

GLOSSARY

abnormality See *adequacy approach; cultural model; medical model; statistical approach.*

achievement motive The striving to maintain or increase one's competence in activities in which a standard of excellence is thought to apply.

achromatic color blindness The inability to perceive color; vision in terms of black, white, and shades of gray. See also *dichromatic color blindness.*

acupuncture A medical practice, developed by the Chinese, in which the insertion of needles into various sites on the body surface relieves pain in either the surrounding area or distant body parts.

adequacy approach In abnormal psychology, defining normality in terms of the efficiency with which a person is able to carry out the tasks of everyday life.

afferent neurons The neurons that collect messages from inside and outside the body and transmit them to the central nervous system; sensory neurons. See also *efferent neurons.*

affiliation need The need of human beings to associate with one another.

alarm reaction According to Selye, the first stage in an animal's response to stress; it involves general physiological arousal. See also *exhaustion stage; resistance stage.*

all-or-none principle The idea that a stimulus must be of a minimum strength to stimulate an axon to fire and that once that threshold is reached the axon will fire completely.

alpha wave A rhythmic electrical impulse of the brain, occurring during wakefulness and relaxation.

amnesia A dissociative reaction characterized by loss of memory of one's identity.

amniocentesis Extracting and analyzing of cells from a pregnant woman's uterus to determine the genetic and health status of the fetus.

amniotic sac The membrane containing the fluid that surrounds and protects the fetus.

amphetamine psychosis A psychosis-like state produced by long-term or excessive use of amphetamines. It is characterized by paranoid delusions, compulsions, and stereotyped behavior.

amphetamines A group of drugs that act to stimulate the central nervous system.

anal stage According to Freud, the second stage of psychosexual development (ages 2 to 3), during which bowel control is achieved and gratification centers on the anal area.

androgenization Excess exposure to male hormone of a genetic female before birth, often resulting in masculinized genitals and tomboyish behavior.

androgyny See *psychological androgyny.*

anxiety A vague, unpleasant feeling that something bad is about to happen. Freud identified three types of anxiety: *moral anxiety,* or guilty conscience; *neurotic anxiety,* or the fear that defense mechanisms will break down and objectionable impulses will be released; and *reality anxiety,* or justified fears in everyday living.

anxiety attacks Overwhelming attacks of dread, uneasiness, and apprehension, accompanied by various physical symptoms.

aphasia Loss of language ability because of brain damage.

applied research Research designed to help solve a practical problem.

approach-approach conflict Having to choose between two equally attractive goals.

approach-avoidance conflict Having to choose between temptation and denial.

artificial insemination donation (A.I.D.) Implantation of an anonymous donor's sperm in the uterus.

association neurons Neurons found primarily in the central nervous system that make the connection between incoming and outgoing messages.

association theory The idea that the learning of concepts occurs primarily through mentally associating the attributes of an object with the label of the object. See also *verbal-mediation theory.*

attention The process of selecting and responding to certain stimuli while ignoring others.

attitudes The ways in which we think and feel about people, objects, and issues.

attribution processes People's methods of trying to infer the basic personality traits of others on the basis of observable behavior.

auditory nerve The nerve that carries messages from the ear to the hearing portion of the brain.

authoritarian child-rearing A child-rearing style in which the parent attempts to shape and control the behavior of the child according to specific standards of conduct. See also *permissive child-rearing.*

authority See *legitimate authority.*

autistic hostility The maintenance of hostility between people based on the false assumption that the "other" person or group is the hostile one.

autonomic nervous system The part of the peripheral nervous system that controls glands and involuntary muscles. See also *somatic nervous system.*

autonomous morality According to Piaget, moral independence—the ability to judge independently of the influence of others. See also *heteronomous morality.*

aversive control Punishment.

avoidance A defense mechanism characterized by refusal to put oneself in situations that will produce stress.

avoidance-avoidance conflict Having to choose between two undesirable goals.

axon A long fiber extending from a neuron and transmitting messages to other neurons, to muscles, or to glands.

axon terminal A knob at the end of each of the small fibers that branch off from the end of an axon.

axonal transmission The movement of electrical impulses along the surface of a neuron. See also *synaptic transmission.*

barbiturate A type of sedative drug which acts to depress the functioning of the central nervous system.

basic research Research conducted to advance knowledge, without any immediate concern for the practical uses of that knowledge.

behavior control See *behavior modification.*

behavior genetics The study of the hereditary factors affecting personality and behavior.

behavior modification Alteration or control of behavior through the systematic application of rewards and punishments; used primarily as a therapy technique.

behavior therapy Application of the principles of learning theory to abnormal behavior. Behavior therapy is based on the idea that the troubled individual is one who has been reinforced for inappropriate behaviors. See also *desensitization; operant therapy; role playing; token economy.*

behaviorism A school of psychology that emphasizes observable behavior as opposed to conscious processes.

binocular vision The cooperation of the two eyes in giving solidity and distance to viewed objects.

biofeedback A technique for monitoring bodily processes (such as brain waves or blood pressure) so that a person can identify fluctuations in these processes and try to control them.

biological engineering Scientific experimentation with human reproduction.

blind spot The area of the retina where the optic nerve leaves the eye.

brain stem The central core of the brain; its functions are connected to the fundamental processes of survival and the emotions.

brain waves Rhythmic electrical impulses given off by the neurons in the cerebral cortex.

brainstorming An approach to group problem solving in which everyone is encouraged to suggest whatever comes to mind without fear of ridicule or discouragement.

brainwashing A set of techniques used to destroy a person's existing group ties and sense of identity in order to provide a new set of relationships tied to new ideals.

brightness constancy The tendency for objects to appear to be the same brightness no matter what the lighting conditions.

CAI See *computer-assisted instruction.*

Cannon-Bard theory The idea that both the subjective experience and the physiological arousal associated with an emotion occur simultaneously, rather than one causing the other.

case study Research based on long-term examination of an individual subject.

catatonia A type of schizophrenia characterized by alternation between long periods of extreme immobility and bursts of aggressive or violent behavior.

catharsis The release of emotional tensions thought to occur when a person engages in or observes violent activity; in psychoanalysis, the release of pent-up emotions as the result of bringing buried thoughts to the surface of consciousness.

central nervous system The brain and spinal cord.

central sulcus A groove that passes through the top of the cerebral cortex. Along each side of the central sulcus are narrow strips of cortex controlling the motor and sensory responses of the body.

cerebellum A structure at the back of the brain concerned primarily with control of body position and movement.

cerebral cortex The largest area of the human brain, covering the rest of the brain parts; it is responsible for sensory and perceptual processes and is the site of thought, consciousness, and memory.

chaining Using conditioning methods to produce chains of learning, in which each act serves as a stimulus for the next act to be performed, resulting in a smooth sequence.

clairvoyance The ability to know about an object or event without employing the usual senses.

clang associations In schizophrenics, creation of sentences by associating words with similar sounds.

classical conditioning A type of learning in which a neutral stimulus, as the result of being paired with an unconditioned stimulus, comes to elicit the response originally elicited by the unconditioned stimulus. Also called Pavlovian conditioning or respondent conditioning.

client-centered therapy A humanistic approach to therapy, developed by Carl Rogers, in which the client is encouraged to express his/her true feelings and become his/her true self.

clinical psychology The subfield of psychology that focuses on diagnosing psychological problems and providing psychotherapy.

cloning Nonsexual reproduction of normally sexually reproducing animals, based on manipulation of single cells.

cochlea The spiral-shaped part of the inner ear that contains the receptor cells for hearing.

cognitive dissonance An internal state of unease produced when one perceives inconsistencies between one's attitudes and one's behavior.

cognitive labeling theory Schachter's idea that an emotion is the result of mental appraisal of physiological sensations that arise in a particular context.

cognitive motives Motives based in people's higher mental processes rather than in their physical needs.

collective unconscious According to Jung, a part of the human mind that is filled with archetypes of universal human experience and that is shared by all human beings.

color blindness See *achromatic color blindness; dichromatic color blindness.*

color constancy The tendency for objects to appear to be the same color despite changes in lighting conditions or proximity to other colors.

community psychology The subfield of psychology that focuses on preventing and treating psychological problems at a community level.

competence motive The need to confirm one's ability to interact effectively with one's environment.

compulsion An irrational desire to engage in ritualistic acts.

computer-assisted instruction (CAI) The use of computers to provide individualized educational instruction.

concept A word or idea that represents a category of things with related characteristics.

concrete operational period According to Piaget, the third stage of cognitive development (ages 7 to 12), during which the child learns to mentally manipulate objects and to understand concepts such as conservation.

conditioned response A response that has come to be elicited by a stimulus that does not naturally elicit that response.

conditioned stimulus A previously neutral stimulus that, through repeated pairing with an unconditioned stimulus, comes to elicit a response.

cones Light-sensitive cells in the retina that are responsible for color vision.

conformity Acceptance of the norms of a group or society.

consciousness A level of thought that integrates and regulates experience; it is sometimes necessary for normal activities, but often is not.

conservation The fact that a substance's weight, mass, or volume remains the same even when the substance changes shape.

consolidation phase The period after something is learned during which it is thought to be chemically consolidated in the neurons of the brain.

consumer psychology The subfield of psychology that is concerned with the application of psychological principles to the purchase and consumption of goods and services.

constancy The tendency to perceive objects in a constant way, despite changes of lighting or distance.

contact comfort The innate tendency to derive pleasure from contact with another body, especially that of one's mother.

continuous reinforcement Reinforcement of a response every time it is emitted.

control group In an experiment, a group of subjects against which the experimental group is compared.

cornea The transparent protective coating on the front part of the eye.

corpus callosum A mass of nerve fibers connecting the two hemispheres of the cerebral cortex.

correlation The degree to which two sets of measures are associated with one another.

correlation coefficient A statistic that describes the degree to which one set of scores is related to a second set of scores.

correlational studies Research in which psychologists try to discover a relationship (correlation) between two factors by measuring each separately and then comparing results.

counseling psychology The subfield of psychology that focuses on helping people with career decisions, marital problems, and readjustment to life after an illness or injury.

countertransference In psychoanalysis, the phenomenon that occurs when clients begin to react to the therapist on the basis of the therapist's problems rather than their own.

critical period A point early in an animal's life during which a relatively small amount of learning can produce a major and lasting effect; if the behavior is not learned at this time, it may never be learned at all.

cross-sectional study A research study based on subjects of different ages all measured at a single point in time. See also *longitudinal study.*

cross-situational consistency The assumption that people have the same personality at all times and in all situations.

cultural-familial retardation Mental retardation caused by growing up in a deprived environment rather than by any physiological disorder.

cultural model In abnormal psychology, defining normality in terms of what is approved by the greatest number of people in a culture.

cystic fibrosis A serious, often fatal, genetic disease producing malfunctions of certain glands.

decibel Unit for measuring the loudness of a sound.

deductive reasoning Drawing specific conclusions on the basis of a general body of information. See also *inductive reasoning.*

defense mechanism A method used by the ego to deny, change, or channel unacceptable impulses so that they need not be dealt with consciously.

delta sleep The stage of sleep in which the sleeper is hardest to waken; deep sleep.

delusions of grandeur The irrational belief that one is a famous person or religious figure.

delusions of persecution The irrational belief that other people are conspiring against one.

demoralization According to Jerome Frank, a feeling of unhappiness and powerlessness resulting from failure to meet the expectations of oneself or of others.

dendrites Short fibers projecting from a neuron that receive messages from other neurons.

dependent variable In an experiment, the behavior that is being measured—that may be affected by changes in the independent variable.

depolarization The process that occurs when a neural membrane temporarily loses its selective permeability, allowing positively charged ions to build up inside the cell.

depression Feelings of worthlessness, hopelessness, lethargy, and helplessness.
Depression may be triggered by external events (*exogenous* depression) or may appear as the result of forces within the individual (*endogenous* depression).

desensitization A method of behavior therapy in which the client is taught to relax in anxiety-producing situations.

developmental psychology The subfield of psychology concerned with human development throughout the life cycle.

dichromatic color blindness The inability to distinguish between red and green or between yellow and blue. See also *achromatic color blindness.*

discrimination In learning, the ability to distinguish between stimuli; responding to one stimulus while not responding to a similar stimulus. In social psychology, behaving differently toward members of a specific group on the basis of prejudice toward that group.

discriminative stimulus A stimulus that becomes associated with the delivery of reinforcement, because reinforcement occurs in its presence.

displacement Redirecting unconscious urges toward a more accessible or more socially acceptable object.

dissociative reactions Neurotic reactions characterized by a removal of some part of one's consciousness; dissociative reactions include amnesia, fugue states, sleepwalking, and multiple personality.

dominant gene A gene whose instructions always prevail. See also *recessive gene.*

double bind A situation in which an individual cannot win, because he or she is given contradictory directions.

downer Slang term for depressant drugs, especially barbiturates.

Down's syndrome A disorder caused by incorrect distribution of genetic material in the zygote; it is characterized by mental retardation and various physical abnormalities. Also called mongolism.

drive The psychological experiencing of a biological need.

drive reduction theory The idea that motivation involves a basic physiological need that is experienced as a psychological drive; this tense and unpleasant drive is reduced when the physiological need is satisfied.

ectomorph The slender physical type of person, long-boned, poorly muscled, and delicate. See also *endomorph; mesomorph.*

educable mentally retarded Those with an I.Q. in the 52 to 67 range, who are capable of achieving an education equal to sixth-grade level. See also *trainable mentally retarded.*

educational psychology The subfield of psychology involved with the design of educational settings and teaching techniques and with the training of teachers.

effectors Muscles and glands.

efferent neurons Neurons that carry messages from the central nervous system to the muscles and glands; motor neurons. See also *afferent neurons.*

ego According to Freud, that part of the personality that directs and controls basic biological urges by seeking to gratify them within socially acceptable bounds.

egocentrism The inability to see things from perspectives other than one's own.

eidetikers People who are able to retain sharp visual images of things no longer in their field of vision.

electrical stimulation of the brain (ESB) The application of an electrical current to specific areas of the brain in order to discover the functions of that area and to alter behavior.

electroencephalograph (EEG) A machine used to record brain waves. The printed-out record of the brain waves is called an electroencephalogram.

electroshock therapy Application of electric current to the brain in order to relieve symptoms of depression.

embryo In humans, the prenatal organism from the fourth day after conception through the eighth week.

emotion The experiencing, organizing, and interpreting of the bodily sensations accompanying a stimulus or event.

emotional isolation See *loneliness.*

encounter groups Therapy groups in which people can meet with others for the purpose of increasing their openness and sensitivity to one another.

endomorph The heavy, fat physical type of person. See also *ectomorph; mesomorph.*

energizers Antidepressant drugs used in the treatment of psychiatric patients.

engineering psychology The subfield of psychology that focuses on appropriate design of equipment to be used by human beings.

epilepsy A convulsive brain disorder characterized by mental blackouts and sometimes seizures.

epinephrine A hormone, secreted by the adrenal glands, that is involved in physiological arousal, especially that associated with fear. Also called adrenalin.

equilibrium The sense of balance.

erogenous zones Pleasure-giving areas of the body.

ESB See *electrical stimulation of the brain.*

ESP See *extrasensory perception.*

estrogen Female sex hormone.

exhaustion stage According to Selye, the final stage in an animal's physiological response to long-term stress. See also *alarm reaction; resistance stage.*

exorcism A ritual used to cast out evil spirits from the body.

experiment A study in which the researcher places subjects into different conditions and compares their effects.

experimental group In an experiment, the group of subjects being studied. See also *control group.*

experimental psychology The subfield of psychology that focuses on research on such fundamental psychological processes as perception, learning, memory, motivation, and emotion.

experimenter expectancy effects The fact that researchers can unintentionally affect the results of their research.

extinction The weakening of a learned response. In classical conditioning, it results from repeated presentation of the conditioned stimulus without the unconditioned stimulus; in operant conditioning, it results from withdrawal of reinforcement.

extrasensory perception (ESP) Perception of objects, events, or thoughts by other than normal sensory means.

extrinsic motivation Doing something for an external reward. See also *intrinsic motivation.*

farsightedness Poor visual acuity for close objects, caused by the image falling behind the retina. See also *nearsightedness.*

fear appeals Using scare tactics in an attempt to change people's attitudes.

fetus In humans, the prenatal organism from the ninth week following conception until birth.

fissure of Silvius A groove that runs from the bottom of the cerebral cortex toward the top of the brain at an oblique angle.

fissures Two grooves that divide the cerebral cortex into lobes.

fixed-interval schedule Administering reinforcement after a set period of time. See also *variable-interval schedule.*

fixed-ratio schedule Administering reinforcement after a fixed number of responses. See also *variable-ratio schedule.*

fixed-response questions In opinion polling, measuring devices in which respondents are asked to select one answer from a given set of answers to a question. See also *open-ended questions.*

formal operational period According to Piaget, the adolescent stage of cognitive development, during which the individual learns to deal with complex concepts and with such abstract notions as beliefs and values.

fovea A portion of the retina that contains only cones and that is particularly receptive to color.

fraternal twins Children conceived at the same time, but developed from separate eggs fertilized by separate sperm. See also *identical twins.*

free association A method used in psychoanalysis in which the client is asked to say whatever comes to mind.

frontal lobe The section of the cerebral cortex believed to be the site of personality and to be concerned with some aspects of speech.

frustration The blocking of one's efforts to attain a desired goal.

frustration-aggression hypothesis The idea that most aggressive behavior results from frustration.

fugue state A dissociative reaction in which the individual has amnesia and leaves his or her surroundings to start a new life in a new location with a new identity.

functional fixedness The inability to see a new use for a familiar object or to apply new problem-solving methods in novel situations.

functionalism An early school of psychology that emphasized practical applications of the study of conscious processes.

galvanic skin response (GSR) A change in the electrical conductivity of the skin caused by the activity of the sweat glands.

gene The unit of heredity. See also *dominant gene; recessive gene.*

generalization Making the same response to separate, but similar, stimuli.

genetic counseling Examining a couple's genetic background and advising them on the risks of their producing a defective child.

genetics The study of heredity.

genital stage According to Freud, the final period of psychosocial development; beginning with puberty, sexual energies are again focused on the genitals, and the individual seeks adult heterosexual relationships.

genotype The fundamental hereditary constitution of an organism. See also *phenotype.*

gestalt therapy A humanistic approach to therapy in which the client attempts to pull together all aspects of his or her personality into a unified whole.

glia Cells in the brain that surround, cushion, and nourish the nerve cells.

graphology Handwriting analysis.

gray matter Grayish tissue of the brain and spinal cord consisting mainly of nerve cell bodies and myelinated nerve fibers.

groupthink The tendency for members of a policy-making group to suppress all individual doubts and dissent, creating the illusion of unanimity.

GSR See *galvanic skin response.*

habituation Becoming used to a novel stimulus so that it no longer seems notable or upsetting.

hebephrenia A type of schizophrenia characterized by emotional disorganization, bizarre behavior, and rapid personality disintegration.

heritability The amount of variation of a genetic trait that is associated with differences in the genetic composition of the members of a particular group or population.

heteronomous morality According to Piaget, moral realism—morality based on acceptance of rules given by an authority; it is found in young children. See also *autonomous morality.*

higher-order conditioning The use of conditioning to produce further conditioning. In classical conditioning, it involves using a conditioned stimulus as an unconditioned stimulus in further conditioning. In operant conditioning, it involves secondary reinforcers.

humanistic psychology An approach to psychology that emphasizes the uniqueness, self-esteem, and dignity of the individual.

hyperphagic Pertaining to animals whose hypothalamus has been lesioned, resulting in compulsive overeating and enormous weight gain.

hypnosis A state of increased suggestibility, or willingness to comply with another person's directions, that is brought about through use of relaxation-producing techniques.

hypothalamus A structure in the brain stem that monitors body activities such as eating and sleeping and that plays a major role in controlling emotional behavior.

hypothesis An educated guess as to why something occurs as it does.

id According to Freud, the reservoir of basic biological urges that motivate the individual.

ideas of reference The belief that everything other people say and do somehow refers to onself.

identical twins Two individuals developed from the same fertilized egg. See also *fraternal twins.*

identity crisis According to Erikson, the adolescent's struggle to establish a stable sense of self.

ideology A system of beliefs to which people can have a strong commitment.

idiographic approach An approach to personality in which researchers focus on the detailed study of specific individuals. See also *nomothetic approach.*

imitative aggression Aggressive acts that duplicate those observed in another person. See also *nonimitative aggression.*

imprinting A form of learning in which certain stimuli very early in life produce behavior patterns that are not generally reversible.

incus One of the three small bones of the middle ear.

independent variable In an experiment, a factor manipulated by the experimenter in order to see what effect it has on the dependent variable.

individuation According to Jung, development of all parts of the personality to achieve an overall balance.

inductive reasoning The process of starting with observed facts and building a hypothesis that is consistent with them. See also *deductive reasoning.*

inferiority complex According to Adler, the real or imagined feelings of inferiority that motivate people to achieve goals.

insight A sudden understanding of a problem—seeing it in a new light, thereby finding a solution.

instincts Inborn, unlearned, biologically purposeful responses.

institutional violence Violence that is encouraged by people's roles in organizations or social institutions, such as prisons and armies.

intellectualization Reducing threats to the emotions by analyzing them intellectually, thereby detaching them from the self.

intelligence The capacity to acquire and apply knowledge.

intelligence quotient (I.Q.) A measure of mental ability obtained by dividing a person's mental age (as determined by a standardized test) by chronological age and multiplying by 100.

interpretation In psychoanalysis, pointing out aspects of the client's narrative that are important and explaining their significance.

interval schedule See *fixed-interval schedule; variable-interval schedule.*

intrinsic motivation Doing something for the pleasure of the activity itself. See also *extrinsic motivation.*

ion pump The chemical process by which potassium is brought into a neuron and sodium is pumped out.

I.Q. See *intelligence quotient.*

iris The colored portion of the eye which contains muscles that control the widening and narrowing of the pupil.

James-Lange theory The idea that an event or stimulus causes bodily changes and that these physiological effects in turn produce the subjectively experienced emotion.

kinesthesis The sensation of the body's position, movement, and tension.

Korsakoff's syndrome A memory disorder in which the patient is permanently unable to place new information in long-term storage in his/her brain.

Lamaze method Training for childbirth in which the expectant mother learns association relaxation of abdominal muscles with uterine contractions; the expected result is a relaxed and painless delivery.

language A system for communicating information, thoughts, or feelings.

latency period According to Freud, the period of psychosexual development (about ages 6 to 12) during which sexual urges are dormant.

latent dream content According to Freud, the hidden meaning of a dream.

learned helplessness Passivity; the feeling, as a result of experience, that one's actions are ineffective.

learning A relatively permanent change in behavior as the result of experience or practice.

learning by observation See *modeling.*

learning curve The fact that a person experiences the greatest memory loss immediately after learning and that the rate of loss declines as time passes.

legitimate authority Someone who appears to have the right to dictate one's behavior in a particular setting.

lens The portion of the eye that captures light and focuses it on the retina.

level of aspiration The goal that one hopes to achieve when undertaking a task.

locus of control The perceived site of factors that influence what happens to a person; persons with an *internal* locus of control believe their behaviors will generally be rewarded, whereas those with an *external* locus of control believe their own behaviors are ineffective and that external forces control their lives.

loneliness A feeling of longing and emptiness caused by a lack of emotional attachments *(emotional isolation)* or of social ties *(social isolation).*

longitudinal study A research study in which subjects are followed over a long period of time. See also *cross-sectional study.*

long-term memory Mental storage of information for an indefinite period of time.

LSD (lysergic acid diethylamide) A drug chemically derived from ergotic alkaloids and capable of inducing in human beings vivid imagery, hallucinations, and mental disorganization.

malleus One of the three small bones of the middle ear.

mania A state of intense excitement which may be so extreme that the individual becomes disoriented, incoherent, unresponsive to others, and potentially violent.

manic-depressive disorder A psychological disorder characterized by alteration between states of deep depression and extreme elation.

manifest dream content According to Freud, the surface meaning of a dream, hiding its latent content.

mantra A word or series of words on which to meditate.

marijuana A mild psychoactive drug made from the hemp plant, *Cannabis sativa.*

maturation The unfolding of inherited biological patterns that are preprogrammed into each individual.

mean A measure of central tendency that is determined by adding individual scores and dividing the total by the number of scores in order to arrive at an average. See also *median; mode.*

median A measure of central tendency represented by the score that falls in the exact middle of a distribution; half the scores fall above this number and half fall below. See also *mean; mode.*

medical model In abnormal psychology, defining normality in terms of health and disease and treating mental illness as a disease to be cured.

meditation A state of consciousness achieved by relaxing the body and focusing the mind on one thought or object.

medulla A structure in the brain stem that controls such basic rhythms as heartbeat and breathing and that contains reflex centers for vomiting, sneezing, coughing, and swallowing.

menarche The first menstrual period.

mental age A measure of intellectual ability obtained from tests that have been standardized using average scores of children at each age level.

mental retardation Low mental ability, as indicated by a score of 83 or lower on an I.Q. test. Mental retardation ranges from borderline (I.Q. 68 to 83), mild (52 to 67), and moderate (36 to 51) down through severe (20 to 35) and profound (below 20). See also *educable mentally retarded; trainable mentally retarded.*

mesomorph The muscular or athletic physical type. See also *ectomorph; endomorph.*

method of loci A memory system in which items to be learned are mentally placed in a set of familiar locations that follow some logical order.

microsleep Momentary loss of consciousness resulting from going for long periods of time without sleep.

midbrain A structure in the brain stem that acts as a relay center in complex reflexes involving hearing, vision, and the reception of pain.

mid-life crisis The sudden recognition, at around age 40, that one's life is half over, accompanied by a questioning of the meaning and accomplishments of one's life and a reassessment of one's goals.

Minnesota Multiphasic Personality Inventory (M.M.P.I.) A personality test, consisting of 550 items, originally designed to assess psychological disorders.

mnemonic devices Special techniques used to code and retrieve information stored in memory.

mode The score that occurs most frequently in a distribution—the most "popular" score. See also *mean; median.*

modeling Observing the behavior of others and emulating that behavior.

mongolism See *Down's syndrome.*

monocular cues Clues to an object's distance that can be perceived with only one eye.

morality See *automomous morality; heteronomous morality.*

motivated forgetting Forgetting things on purpose, because remembering them would be embarrassing or painful.

motivation A tendency to act to achieve a particular goal or state.

motives The internal factors that arouse and direct behavior.

motor neurons See *efferent neurons.*

Müller-Lyer illusion An optical illusion demonstrating that lines of equal length will appear unequal if arrow shapes pointing inward are placed on one line and arrow shapes pointing outward are placed on the other.

multiple personality A dissociative reaction characterized by the existence of two or more distinct personalities in one body.

myelin sheath A white, fatty substance encasing certain nerve fibers.

narcoanalysis The use of truth drugs to stimulate people to talk.

natural childbirth Childbirth without medication or instruments, usually involving relaxation training to reduce the pain of the delivery.

natural selection Darwin's principle that those organisms best able to adapt to their environment are the ones that will survive to produce offspring.

nearsightedness Poor visual acuity for distant objects, caused by the image falling in front of the retina. See also *farsightedness.*

Necker cube An ambiguous graphic presentation of a cube.

need A biological condition of deprivation that stimulates activity toward correcting the condition.

need to achieve See *achievement motive.*

negative reinforcement The strengthening of a response by removing an unpleasant stimulus.

neologisms Invented words that have meaning only to the inventor.

neurons The basic cells of the nervous system.

neuroses Relatively mild psychological disorders characterized by anxiety, inability to cope effectively with challenges, and difficulty in interpersonal relationships.

neurotransmitter See *transmitter substance.*

neutral stimulus A stimulus that does not produce a specific unconditioned response.

nominal realism Confusing names and symbols with the objects that they represent.

nomothetic approach An approach to personality in which researchers examine large numbers of people in order to discover similarities, differences, and general patterns of personality. See also *idiographic approach.*

nonimitative aggression Aggressive acts engaged in by children who have observed an aggressive model, but whose aggression does not duplicate that of the model.

nonreversal shift In experiments to determine people's use of concepts, a shift requiring subjects to notice that the relevant dimension of the concept being described has changed. See also *reversal shift.*

nonsense syllables Three-letter words (consonant-vowel-consonant) with no meaning; they are used in experiments on verbal learning and memory.

norepinephrine A hormone, secreted by the adrenal glands, involved in physiological arousal, especially that associated with anger. Also called noradrenalin.

norms See *social norms.*

NREM (nonREM) sleep That period of the night (about 75 percent) in which the person passes through four sleep stages, each characterized by specific EEG patterns, but does not dream. See also *REM sleep.*

object constancy The recognition that a physical object continues to exist even when it is out of sight or out of reach.

obsession A persistent unwanted thought.

obsessive-compulsive disorder A neurotic condition characterized by persistent unwanted thoughts and repeated, ritualistic behavior.

occipital lobe The section of the cerebral cortex primarily involved in seeing; it may also be involved in memory.

Oedipus conflict According to Freud, the young child's feeling of sexual attraction toward the opposite-sex parent and feeling of hostility toward the same-sex parent.

open-ended questions In opinion polling, measuring devices that allow respondents to give any answer they wish. See also *fixed-response questions.*

operant conditioning A type of learning in which behaviors increase or decrease in frequency as the result of application or withdrawal of rewards.

operant response A response that operates on the environment to produce some effect.

operant therapy A method of behavior therapy in which rewards are used to motivate a client to perform a desired behavior or to refrain from performing an undesired behavior.

optic nerve The nerve tract that carries messages from the eye to the visual portion of the brain.

oral stage According to Freud, the first stage in psychosexual development (from birth to age 2), during which the mouth area is the primary focus of pleasure.

organizational psychology The subfield of psychology that focuses on devising methods for businesses and other organizations to function more effectively.

overlearning Continuing to practice something after it is learned in order to retain more of it.

overregularization In language learning, a child's tendency to apply a grammatical rule in all instances—even in situations in which it is incorrect.

paranoid schizophrenia A type of psychosis characterized by intense delusions and hallucinations.

parapsychology The study of phenomena, such as ESP, that are beyond the usual bounds of psychology.

parascience The study of supernatural phenomena, such as ESP, UFOs, and the occult.

parasympathetic nervous system A subdivision of the autonomic nervous system; it acts to slow down bodily functions, especially after a stress reaction. See also *sympathetic nervous system.*

parietal lobe The section of the cerebral cortex concerned with the skin senses and the sense of bodily position.

partial reinforcement Rewarding a response on an intermittent schedule.

pegword method Storing information in memory by attaching items to be learned to already memorized words and images.

perception The active process of integrating and organizing sensations.

perceptual accentuation The tendency to see valued objects as larger or as more vivid than they actually are.

perceptual constancy See *constancy.*

perceptual selectivity The process of paying attention to only a small portion of the stimuli in one's environment.

perceptual set The tendency to perceive what one expects to.

peripheral nervous system Nerve fibers and tissues lying outside of the brain and spinal cord.

permissive child-rearing A child-rearing style in which the parent avoids punishing and controlling the child and encourages the child's initiative and self-reliance. See also *authoritarian child-rearing.*

person perception Forming inferences about other people on the basis of their physical appearance, reputation, or observable behavior.

personal unconscious According to Jung, repressed or forgotten material.

personality The distinctive patterns of behavior that characterize an individual's adaptation to his or her environment.

personality inventory A collection of statements or questions to be answered along such dimensions as agree-disagree and like-dislike; such tests are used to assess people's interests, attitudes, social relations, values, and adjustment.

personnel psychology The subfield of psychology concerned with selecting workers for particular jobs and with handling morale and job satisfaction.

peyote The Mexican name for the mescal cactus, from which mescaline is derived. Used as a drug, peyote produces intense sensory experiences and hallucinations.

phallic stage According to Freud, the stage of psychosexual development (ages 4 to 5) during which the sex organs become the focus of attention and the Oedipal conflict must be resolved.

phenothiazines Tranquilizers used in the treatment of psychiatric patients.

phenylketonuria (PKU) A genetic disease caused by impaired protein metabolism, and, if untreated, characterized by severe mental retardation, hyperactivity, and seizures.

phenotype The outward expression of an organism's genetic make-up—its observable characteristics. See also *genotype.*

phobia An intense irrational fear of a particular object or activity.

phoneme A class of closely related sounds all designated by a single symbol.

phrenology An approach to the study of

personality based on the idea that the bumps and hollows of the skull represent specific personality traits.

pitch The high or low quality of a sound.

PKU See *phenylketonuria.*

placebo effect The fact that many clients in therapy and patients under medical treatment improve simply because they *expect* to.

placenta A network of blood vessels and membranes connecting the fetus' umbilical cord to the uterus and serving as a passageway for nutrients and waste products.

Ponzo illusion An optical illusion in which horizontal lines placed over converging vertical lines appear to be unequal in length.

polarized axon The axon in its resting state, in which the inside of the neuron is negatively charged and the outside is positive.

polygraph An instrument that measures physiological changes that accompany heightened emotion; it is used as a lie detector.

pons A structure in the brain stem that houses a band of nerve fibers connecting the brain stem with the cerebellum.

positive reinforcement Rewarding a behavior in order to increase its frequency.

predisposition A readiness to behave or develop in a particular way.

prejudice An unfavorable attitude held about a particular group of people.

presbyopia A deterioration in vision for near objects, caused by the gradual brittling of the eye lens with age.

preoperational period According to Piaget, the second stage of cognitive development (ages 2 through 7), during which the child is egocentric and has not yet mastered such basic concepts as conservation.

primal therapy Arthur Janov's method of therapy, in which the client is asked to re-experience childhood pain and to release emotions built up over a lifetime.

primary reinforcers Stimuli that naturally increase a response, such as food, water, and affection. See also *secondary reinforcers.*

proactive interference Interference with a learning task that is caused by previously learned material. See also *retroactive interference.*

process schizophrenia Schizophrenia that develops gradually and slowly; it is more resistent to treatment than is reactive schizophrenia.

projection The unconscious attribution of one's own unacceptable thoughts and feelings to other people.

propaganda Dissemination of information designed to convince people of the value or rightness of a product or idea. The term often implies deception or distortion.

proximity The physical distance between people.

psilocybin A psychedelic drug derived from mushrooms.

psychedelic drugs Drugs that cause extreme alterations in perception and thought processes, often producing delusions, hallucinations, and intensified sensory awareness.

psychiatrist A medical doctor who specializes in the diagnosis and treatment of psychological disorders.

psychoactive drugs Drugs that have a noticeable impact on consciousness and behavior.

psychoanalysis The method of psychotherapy based on Freud's psychoanalytic theory of personality; its basic premise is that the unconscious mind contains buried impulses and desires that must be brought to the surface if neurotic symptoms are to disappear.

psychoanalytic theory Freud's theory that all human behavior is dominated by instinctual biological urges that must be controlled; it is the conflict between the urges and the efforts to control them that leads to emotional problems.

psychokinesis The ability to influence a physical object by sheer exercise of will.

psychological androgyny The ability to integrate both masculine and feminine traits into one's personality.

psychological reactance The tendency to do the opposite of whatever we feel others are trying to make us do; it serves as a way of reasserting our freedom.

psychology The science of human behavior.

psychoses Major psychological disorders characterized by a loss of contact with reality, loss of control over feelings and actions, and such symptoms as delusions and hallucinations.

psychosexual stages According to Freud, stages

that children go through in which their sexual energy is focused on different areas of the body. See also *anal stage; genital stage; latency period; oral stage; phallic stage.*

psychosomatic disease Physical disorder caused at least in part by stress or other psychological factors.

psychosurgery Brain surgery designed to relieve psychological symptoms.

psychotomimetic A drug that produces experiences similar to psychosis.

punishment An unpleasant event or outcome following a response.

pupil The opening in the eye that allows light rays to enter.

random sample In statistics, a sample in which each member of the population being studied has an equal chance of being chosen.

range The variability of a set of scores as indicated by the lowest and highest scores in the distribution.

ratio schedule See *fixed-ratio schedule; variable-ratio schedule.*

rationalization Justifying one's actions by substituting an acceptable explanation for the real, unacceptable reason.

reaction formation Developing behavior patterns the opposite of those that would create anxiety.

reactive schizophrenia Schizophrenia that strikes suddenly, in reaction to a stressful life event. See also *process schizophrenia.*

recall A measure of retention in which the individual must recount or reproduce something previously learned.

receptors Sensitive cells in the sense organs.

recessive gene A gene that is expressed only when a dominant gene for that trait is not present.

recognition A measure of retention in which the individual must identify something previously encountered.

reference group A group with which one identifies and from which one derives many of one's attitudes. A *negative* reference group is one that one does not want to identify with and therefore one adopts attitudes opposite to it.

reflex An automatic action involving sensory nerves, motor nerves, and the spinal cord, with no intervention from higher brain centers.

reinforcement Any event following a response that strengthens that response or that increases the probability of the response occurring again. See also *negative reinforcement; positive reinforcement; schedules of reinforcement.*

relearning A measure of retention in which an individual is asked to relearn material previously learned; the speed with which relearning takes place is an indication of how much information has been retained. Also called the savings method.

REM (rapid eye movement) sleep A period of sleep during which a specific EEG pattern occurs and the individual appears to be dreaming. See also *NREM sleep.*

repression The tendency to exclude unpleasant or painful memories or impulses from conscious awareness.

research See *applied research; basic research.*

resistance In psychoanalysis, the reluctance to bring important ideas into consciousness.

resistance stage According to Selye, the second stage in an animal's physiological response to stress; it involves mobilizing the body for fight or flight. See also *alarm reaction; exhaustion stage.*

respondent conditioning See *classical conditioning.*

reticular activating system Nerve tissue in the brain stem that serves to screen incoming messages and to alert higher brain centers to important information.

retina An inner lining at the back of the eye that contains the light-sensitive rods and cones.

retroactive interference Inability to recall previously learned material caused by interference of more recently learned material. See also *proactive interference.*

retrograde amnesia Loss of memory for events immediately preceding an accident or electroshock.

reversal shift In experiments to determine people's use of concepts, a shift requiring subjects to notice that the main attribute of the concept has been reversed. See also *nonreversal shift.*

rhodopsin (visual purple) A chemical in the rods of the retina that changes when exposed to light.

rods Light-sensitive cells in the retina that are essentially colorblind.

role playing In behavior therapy, practicing a set of desired behaviors in a protective setting in which clients need not worry about the consequences of their behavior.

rooting response The newborn baby's tendency to turn its head in the direction of a touch on its cheek.

Rorschach test A personality test in which individuals are asked to respond to a series of ambiguous inkblots.

sample A group of subjects representing a larger population.

savings See *relearning.*

schedules of reinforcement Administration of reinforcement according to a fixed or varying number of responses or time interval.

schizophrenia A type of psychosis characterized by serious alterations of perception, activity, emotion, thought, and personality. See also *catatonia; hebephrenia; paranoid schizophrenia; process schizophrenia; reactive schizophrenia; simple schizophrenia.*

secondary reinforcers Stimuli that become reinforcers as a result of association with primary reinforcers.

self-actualization According to Maslow, full realization of one's inherited potential as a human being.

self-esteem One's positive regard for oneself.

self-fulfilling prophecy The idea that one's expectations can influence or bring about that which one expects to happen.

self-perception theory Bem's idea that people arrive at attitudes after they behave in certain ways and reflect on that behavior.

self-reports People's own assessments of their thoughts and feelings, as reported to psychological researchers.

semantic conditioning Pairing of specific words with emotional stimuli in order to produce an emotional reaction to the words themselves.

semantic differential A type of fixed-response measure in which respondents are asked to rate concepts along several scales.

semicircular canals The sense organs for equilibrium; they are located in the inner ear.

sensation The direct reception and transmission of messages in the nervous system.

sensorimotor period According to Piaget, the first stage of cognitive development (from birth to age 2), during which the individual learns to coordinate sensory information and motor abilities.

sensory deprivation Placing a person in a specially designed environment devoid of sensory stimulation.

sensory neurons See *afferent neurons.*

sensory storage The momentary retention of sensory information after it has been received.

serial-position effect The tendency to remember the first and last items on a list better than the ones in the middle.

sex roles Social expectations about what men and women should do and should be like.

shaping Producing a desired behavior by rewarding responses that come closer and closer to the behavior until the desired response is finally achieved.

short-term memory Information that has just been learned and that may be retained for no more than 20 seconds before being forgotten or transferred to long-term memory. Short-term memory is limited to about seven pieces, or chunks, of information.

sickle-cell anemia A serious genetic disease affecting blood cells of persons descended from black Africans.

significance level A statistic indicating the extent to which an observed difference between samples reflects real differences and not chance.

simple schizophrenia A type of psychosis characterized by apathy, withdrawal, and antisocial activities.

size constancy The process by which one takes into account changing distances and other cues in order to perceive objects as staying the same size.

skin senses The receptors in the skin for pressure, temperature, and pain.

Skinner box An apparatus, developed by B. F. Skinner, used for studying operant conditioning of animals.

sleep apnea A disorder characterized by stoppage of breathing several times during a night's sleep.

social comparison The idea that people have a need to compare themselves with people in a similar situation in order to clarify their own feelings and experiences.

social isolation See *loneliness.*

social learning theory A behavioristic approach to personality that focuses on the roles of imitation and social rewards in the learning of patterns of behavior.

social norms Rules that dictate appropriate and inappropriate behavior in a society.

social psychology The subfield of psychology that focuses on the ways in which people's behavior is affected by other people and by the social environment.

somatic nervous system The part of the peripheral nervous system that controls voluntary muscles and hence most body movements. See also *autonomic nervous system.*

somatic therapy The use of drugs, electroshock, or surgery to treat the symptoms of psychological disorder.

specificity theory The idea that there are specific pain receptors that relay signals of pain directly to the brain.

spinal cord A cylindrical structure of nerve tissue stretching from the base of the spine down through the center of the backbone; it provides basic connections between motor and sensory neurons and serves as a pathway for messages traveling to and from the brain.

split-brain surgery Severing of the corpus callosum, thereby greatly reducing communication between the two cerebral hemispheres.

spontaneous recovery The sudden reappearance of an extinguished response.

standard deviation A statistic that indicates the amount of variability in a set of scores. It is computed on the basis of the distance of each score from the mean.

stapes One of the three small bones of the middle ear.

statistics Numbers used to describe and interpret data or observations.

statistical approach In abnormal psychology, defining abnormality in terms of what is true of the average person in a population.

standardization Adminstration of a test to a large sampling of subjects and using the results as a basis for determining the normal curve of scores for the test.

Stanford-Binet An intelligence test emphasizing the scholastic basics of reading, writing, and arithmetic.

stereotypes Notions of what people are like based on their race, sex, ethnic background, religion, occupation, or other such group membership.

stimulus control A situation in which a response occurs only in the presence of a specific discriminative stimulus.

stranger anxiety The tendency of an infant to panic and cry when approached by an unfamiliar person.

stress Pressures from one's environment that can lead to both physical and psychological disorder.

structuralism An early school of psychology that emphasized the structure of conscious processes.

superego According to Freud, the force within the self that acquires the values and ideals of the parents and society and imposes contraints on the id and ego; the conscience.

surrogate mother An artificial or substitute mother, such as those used by Harlow in his experiments with infant monkeys.

syllogism A logical statement comprising a major premise, a minor premise, and a conclusion.

sympathetic nervous system A subdivision of the autonomic nervous system; it acts to accelerate certain bodily processes in response to stress. See also *parasympathetic nervous system.*

synapse The microscopic gap that separates the end of each axon terminal from the dendrite or cell body of another neuron.

synaptic transmission The movement of nerve impulses from one neuron to another. See also *axonal transmission.*

synaptic vesicles Tiny sacs within an axon terminal that contain transmitter substance.

synesthesia The blending of senses, such as hearing color or seeing tastes.

TA See *transactional analysis.*

TAT See *Thematic Apperception Test.*

Tay-Sachs disease A fatal genetic disease striking infants descended from Eastern European Jews.

telepathy The awareness of another person's thoughts without benefit of normal sensory channels.

temporal lobe The section of the cerebral cortex that contains centers for hearing and speech and possibly sites for memory and learning.

testosterone Male hormone.

thalamus A structure in the brain stem that appears to control the sorting and relaying of messages to appropriate regions of the cerebral cortex.

Thematic Apperception Test (TAT) A personality test in which the person is asked to react to a series of drawings.

theory A set of ideas and principles that fit together to provide a perspective on some aspect of the world.

Theory X A set of assumptions about human nature, including the idea that people dislike work, tend to avoid responsibility, and need to be coerced into working.

Theory Y A set of assumptions about human nature, including the idea that people like to work, like responsibility, are creative, and can work well without external control.

thinking The mental activity of forming and using concepts.

timbre The richness or quality of a sound that comes from a particular sound source.

tip of the tongue (TOT) phenomenon The feeling of almost, but not quite, being able to recall a word or a name.

token economy A form of behavior therapy in which the individual is given a token for each task accomplished; the tokens can later be traded for whatever is rewarding to the particular individual.

TM See *transcendental meditation.*

trainable mentally retarded Those with an I.Q. in the 36 to 51 range who are not educable, but who can be taught to care for themselves and to carry out routine tasks.

trait theory The idea that numerous characteristics (traits) of personality can be used to describe a pattern for an individual. *Common* traits are found to some degree in all individuals, whereas *individual* traits are found only in specific persons.

transactional analysis (TA) A form of therapy, developed by Eric Berne, in which the interactions between people (the games people play) are probed.

transcendent function According to Jung, the ultimate stage of personality development, in which the parts of the personality are united into a fully realized self.

transcendental meditation (TM) A system of meditation developed by Maharishi Mahesh Yogi.

transference In psychoanalysis, the client's tendency to treat the analyst in the same way he or she would treat an important authority figure in his or her life.

transient global amnesia A disorder in which brain damage causes the patient to suffer attacks in which he or she is unable to hold onto information for more than a few seconds before forgetting it.

transmitter substance A chemical contained in the synaptic vesicles of an axon terminal; when the substance is released, it crosses the synapse and either stimulates or inhibits firing of the next neuron.

trial and error Trying as many solutions to a problem as possible, in hopes that one will finally work.

twins See *fraternal twins; identical twins.*

tympanic membrane The eardrum.

type theory The idea that people can be classified on the basis of an overall personality type, such as pessimist or phlegmatic.

unconditional positive regard In client-centered therapy, the idea that the therapist should not judge the behavior of the client and should accept anything the client has to say.

unconditioned response A response that normally occurs for a given stimulus.

unconditioned stimulus A stimulus that produces an unconditioned response.

unconscious See *collective unconscious; personal unconscious.*

variable See *dependent variable; independent variable.*

variable-interval schedule Administering reinforcement after a time interval has passed, with the interval varying around some average. See also *fixed-interval schedule.*

variable-ratio schedule Administering reinforcement after a number of responses, with the number varying around some average. See also *fixed-ratio schedule.*

verbal learning Retention in memory of words, letters, or other verbal material.

verbal-mediation theory The idea that, in concept learning, associations betwen attributes and labels occur only when a verbal response focuses attention on those attributes. See also *association theory.*

vibratese A system of signals used as a language for sending messages to the skin.

visual acuity The ability to discriminate details in the field of vision.

visual cliff An experimental apparatus designed to test depth perception in infants.

visual purple See *rhodopsin.*

visual threshold The smallest amount of stimulation the rods and cones will respond to.

wakefulness of choice Period of wakefulness interfering with the sleep cycle and controlled by the cerebral cortex.

wakefulness of necessity Normal wakefulness, controlled by portions of the brain stem.

Wechsler Adult Intelligence Scale (WAIS) A test of adult mental ability in which items are arranged in order of difficulty and in which scores on various subtests are weighted to contribute equally to an overall I.Q. score.

white matter Whitish nerve tissue of the brain and spinal cord consisting primarily of myelinated nerve fibers.

working through In psychoanalysis, the process of free association, interpretation, and overcoming resistance.

zygote The fertilized egg.

BIBLIOGRAPHY

Abse, D. W. *Hysteria and related mental disorders.* Baltimore: Williams and Wilkins, 1966.

Adams, R. L., and Fox, R. J. Mainlining Jesus: The new trip. *Society,* February 1972.

Adamson, B. E., and Taylor, O. W. Functional fixedness as related to elapsed time and set. *Journal of Experimental Psychology,* 1954, **47,** 122–126.

Adelson, J. What generation gap? *New York Times Magazine,* January 18, 1970.

Adolph, E. F. The internal environment and behavior: Water content. *American Journal of Psychiatry,* 1941, *97,* 1365–1372.

Adorno, T. W., Frenkel-Brunswik, E., Levinson, D. J., and Sanford, R. N. *The authoritarian personality.* New York: Harper & Row, 1950.

Agel, J. (Ed.). New ideas. *New York Times Magazine,* April 25, 1976.

Alexander, F. C., and Selesnick, S. T. *The history of psychiatry.* New York: Harper & Row, 1966.

Allport, G. W. The general and the unique in psychological science. *Journal of Personality,* 1962, **30,** 405–422.

Allport, G. W. *Personality: A psychological interpretation.* (2nd ed.) New York: Holt, Rinehart, and Winston, 1961.

Allport, G. W., and Vernon, P. E. *Studies in expressive movement.* New York: Macmillan, 1933.

Altus, W. D. Birth order and its sequelae. *Science,* 1966, **151,** 44–49.

Andelin, H. B. *Fascinating Womanhood.* New York: Bantam, 1963.

Andersson, B. The effect of injections and hypertonic solutions in parts of the hypothalamus of goats. *Acta Psychologica Scandinavica,* 1953, *28,* 188–201.

Angelino, H., Dollins, J., and Mech, E. Trends in the fears and worries of school children as related to socioeconomic status and age. *Journal of Genetic Psychology,* 1956, **89,** 263–276.

Anthony, D. S. Is graphology valid? *Psychology Today,* August 1967.

Aramoni, A. Machismo. *Psychology Today,* January 1972.

Arieti, S., and Meth, J. M. Rare, unclassifiable, collective, and exotic psychotic syndromes. In S. Arieti (Ed.), *American handbook of psychiatry,* vol. I. New York: Basic Books, 1959.

Aronson, E. Some antecedents of interpersonal attraction. In W. J. Arnold and D. Levine (Eds.), *Nebraska symposium on motivation, 1969.* Lincoln: University of Nebraska Press, 1969.

Asch, S. E. Effects of group pressure upon the modification and distortion of judgments. In H. Guetzkow (Ed.), *Groups, leadership, and men.* Pittsburgh: Carnegie Press, 1951.

Asher, J. John Ertl's neural efficiency analyzer: Bias-free test, or just a "neat gadget"? *APA Monitor,* March 1973.

Asimov, I. *Is anyone there?* Garden City, N. Y.: Doubleday, 1967.

Atallah, L. Report from a test-tube baby. *New York Times Magazine,* April 18, 1976.

Atkinson, K., MacWhinney, B., and Stoel, C. An experiment on recognition of babbling. *Papers and reports on child language development.* Stanford, Calif.: Stanford University Press, 1970.

Atkinson, R. C. Mnemotechnics in second-language learning. *American Psychologist,* 1975, **30,** 821–828.

Atkinson, R. C. Teaching children to read using a computer. *American Psychologist,* 1974, **29,** 169–178.

Atkinson, R. C., and Shiffrin, R. M. Human memory: A proposed system and its controlled processes. In K. W. Spence and J. T. Spence (Eds.), *The psychology of learning and motivation,* vol. 2. New York: Academic Press, 1968.

Atthowe, J. M., and Krasner, L. Preliminary report on the application of contingent reinforcement procedures (token economy) on a "chronic" psychiatric ward. *Journal of Abnormal Psychology,* 1968, **73,** 37–43.

Ausubel, F., Beckwith, J., and Janssen, K. The politics of genetic engineering: Who decides who's defective? *Psychology Today,* June 1974.

Ax, A. F. The physiological differentiation of emotional states. *Psychosomatic Medicine,* 1953, **15,** 433–442.

Ayllon, T., and Azrin, N. *The token economy: A motivational system for therapy and rehabilitation.* New York: Appleton-Century-Crofts, 1968.

Baer, D. M. Let's take another look at punishment. *Psychology Today,* October 1971.

Bahrick, H. P., Bahrick, P. O., and Wittlinger, R. P. Those unforgettable high-school days. *Psychology Today,* December 1974.

Baltes, P. B., and Schaie, K. W. Aging and IQ: The myth of the twilight years. *Psychology Today,* March 1974.

Bandura, A. *Aggression: A social learning analysis.* Englewood Cliffs, N.J.: Prentice-Hall, 1973.

Bandura, A. Behavioral psychotherapy. *Scientific American,* March 1967.

Bandura, A. Behavior theory and the models of man. *American Psychologist,* 1974, **12,** 859–869.

Bandura, A.: In A. E. Bergin and H. H. Strupp (Eds.), *Changing frontiers in the science of psychotherapy.* Chicago: Aldine-Atherton, 1972.

Bandura, A. *Social learning theory.* Morristown, N.J.: General Learning Press, 1971.

Bandura, A., Ross, D., and Ross, S. Imitation of film-mediated aggressive models. *Journal of Abnormal and Social Psychology,* 1963, **67,** 601–607.

Bane, M. J. Marital disruption and the lives of children. *Journal of Social Issues,* 1976, **32,** 103–117.

Barber, T. X. *LSD, marihuana, yoga, and hypnosis.* Chicago: Aldine, 1970.

Bardwick, J. *The psychology of women.* New York: Harper & Row, 1971.

Baron, R. A., Byrne, D., and Griffitt, W. *Social psychology.* Boston: Allyn & Bacon, 1974.

Barron, F. The creative personality: Akin to madness. *Psychology Today,* July 1972.

Barron, F., Jarvik, M., and Bunnell, S. The hallucinogenic drugs. *Scientific American,* April 1964.

Bartlett, F. C. *Remembering.* Cambridge, England: Cambridge University Press, 1932.

Bateson, G., Jackson, D. D., Haley, J., and Weakland, J. Toward a theory of schizophrenia. *Behavioral Science,* 1956, **1,** 251–264.

Batson, C. D. Latent aspects of "From Jerusalem to Jericho . . ." In M. P. Golden (Ed.), *The research experience.* Itasca, Ill.: Peacock, 1976.

Battle, E., and Rotter, J. B. Children's feelings of personal control as related to social class and ethnic groups. *Journal of Personality,* 1963, **31,** 482–490.

Baumrind, D. Current patterns of parental authority. *Developmental Psychology Monographs,* 1971, **4,** 1–103.

Belmont, L., and Marolla, F. A. Birth order, family size, and intelligence. *Science,* 1973, **182,** 1096–1101.

Bem, D. J. *Beliefs, attitudes, and human affairs.* Belmont, Calif.: Brooks/Cole, 1970.

Bem, D. J. Self-perception theory. In L. Berkowitz (Ed.), *Advances in experimental social psychology,* vol. 6. New York: Academic Press, 1972.

Bem, D. J., and Allen, A. On predicting some of the people some of the time: The search for cross-situational consistencies in behavior. *Psychological Review,* 1974, **81**, 506–520.

Bem, S. L. Androgyny vs. the tight little lives of fluffy women and chesty men. *Psychology Today,* September 1975.

Bem, S. L. Psychology looks at sex roles: Where have all the androgynous people gone? Paper presented at UCLA Symposium on Women, May 1972.

Bem, S. L., and Bem, D. J. Case study of a nonconscious ideology: Training the woman to know her place. In D. J. Bem, *Beliefs, attitudes, and human affairs.* Belmont, Calif.: Brooks/Cole, 1970.

Bem, S. L., and Bem, D. J. Does sex-biased job advertising "aid and abet" sex discrimination? *Journal of Applied Social Psychology,* 1973, **3**, 6–18.

Benda, C. E., Squires, N. D., Ogonik, J., and Wise, R. Personality factors in mild mental retardation: Family background and sociocultural patterns. *American Journal of Mental Deficiency,* 1963, **68**, 24–40.

Benedict, P. K., and Jacks, I. Mental illness in primitive societies. *Psychiatry,* 1954, **17**, 377–389.

Bengtson, V. L. *The social psychology of aging.* Indianapolis: Bobbs-Merrill, 1973.

Benson, H., Beary, J. F., and Carol, M. P. The relaxation response. *Psychiatry,* 1974, **37**, 37–46.

Benson, H., and Wallace, R. K. Decreased drug abuse with transcendental meditation—a study of 1,862 subjects. In C. J. Zafronetis (Ed.), *Drug abuse: Proceedings of the International Conference.* New York: Lea and Febiger, 1972.

Berger, R. J., Olley, P., and Oswald, I. The EEG, eye movements and dreams of the blind. *Quarterly Journal of Experimental Psychology,* 1962, **14**, 183–186.

Bergin, A. E., and Suinn, R. M. Individual psychotherapy and behavior therapy. In M. R. Rosenzweig and L. W. Porter (Eds.), *Annual Review of Psychology,* vol. 26. Palo Alto, Calif.: Annual Reviews, 1975.

Berkeley Men's Center Manifesto. In J. H. Pleck and J. Sawyer (Eds.), *Men and masculinity.* Englewood Cliffs, N.J.: Prentice-Hall, 1974.

Berkowitz, L. *Social psychology.* Glenview, Ill.: Scott, Foresman, 1972.

Berne, E. *Games people play.* New York: Grove Press, 1964.

Bernstein, A. C. How children learn about sex and birth. *Psychology Today,* January 1976.

Berscheid, E., and Walster, E. A little bit about love. In T. L. Huston (Ed.), *Foundations of interpersonal attraction.* New York: Academic Press, 1974.

Berkowitz, L. The case for bottling up rage. *Psychology Today,* July 1973.

Berscheid, E., and Walster, E. Physical attractiveness. In L. Berkowitz (Ed.), *Advances in experimental social Psychology,* vol. 7. New York: Academic Press, 1974.

Birren, J. E. The abuse of the urban aged. *Psychology Today,* March 1970.

Blank, L. Nudity as a quest for life the way it was before the apple, *Pychology Today,* June 1969.

Blatt, S. J., and Wild, C. M. *Schizophrenia: A developmental analysis.* New York: Academic Press, 1975.

Blau, P. M. *Exchange and power in social life.* New York: Wiley, 1964.

Block, J. H. Debatable conclusions about sex differences. *Contemporary Psychology,* 1976, **21**, 517–522.

Bloom, B. *Stability and change in human characteristics.* New York: Wiley, 1964.

Blum, R., et al. *Utopiates.* New York: Atherton, 1964.

Blum, S. Suicide. *Playboy,* November 1972.

Bochner, S., and Insko, C. A. Communicator discrepancy, source credibility, and opinion change. *Journal of Personality and Social Psychology,* 1966, **4**, 614–621.

Bolles, R. Species specific defense reactions in avoidance learning. *Psychological Review,* 1970, **71**, 32–48.

Bouton, J. *Ball four.* New York: Dell, 1971.

Bower, G. H. Memorizing with imaginary maps. In G. Lindzey, C. Hall, and R. F. Thompson, *Psychology.* New York: Worth, 1975.

Bower, G. H. Stimulus sampling theory of encoding variability. In A. W. Melton and E. Martin (Eds.), *Coding processes in human memory.* Washington, D. C.: Winston, 1972.

Bower, G. H., and Clark, M. C. Narrative stories as mediators for serial learning. *Psychonomic Science,* 1969, **14**, 181–182.

Bowers, K. Situationism in psychology: An analysis and a critique. *Psychological Review,* 1973, **80**, 307–336.

Bowlby, J. *Maternal care and mental health.* Geneva: World Health Organization, 1951.

Bradburn, N. *The structure of psychological well-being.* Chicago: Aldine, 1969.

Brady, J. V. Ulcers in "executive monkeys." *Scientific American,* October 1958.

Brannon, R. Attitudes and the prediction of behavior. In B. Seidenberg and A. Snadowsky (Eds.), *Social psychology: An introduction.* New York: Free Press, 1976.

Brehm, J. W. *A theory of psychological reactance.* New York: Academic Press, 1966.

Bridges, K. M. B. Emotional development in early infancy. *Child Development,* 1932, **3**, 324–341.

Bronfenbrenner, U. The split-level American family. *Saturday Review,* October 7, 1967.

Broverman, I. K., Broverman, D. M., Clarkson, F. E., Rosenkrantz, P. S., and Vogel, S. R. Sex-role stereotypes and clinical judgments of mental health. *Journal of Consulting and Clinical Psychology,* 1970, **34**, 1–7.

Broverman, I. K., Vogel, S. R., Broverman, D. M., Clarkson, F. E., and Rosenkrantz, P. S. Sex-role stereotypes: A current appraisal. *Journal of Social Issues,* 1972, **28**, 59–78.

Brown, C. A., Feldberg, R., Fox, E. M., and Kohen, J. Divorce: Chance of a new lifetime. *Journal of Social Issues,* 1976, **32**, 119–133.

Brown, R. *A first language: The early stages.* Cambridge, Mass.: Harvard University Press, 1973.

Brown, R. *Social psychology.* New York: Free Press, 1965.

Brown, R., and Herrnstein, R. J. *Psychology.* Boston: Little, Brown, 1975.

Brown, R., and Hildum, D. C. Expectancy and the identification of syllables. *Language,* 1956, **32**, 411–419.

Brown, R. W., and McNeil, D. The "tip of the tongue" phenomenon. *Journal of Verbal Learning and Verbal Behavior,* 1966, **5**, 325–327.

Bruner, J. S. On perceptual readiness. *Psychological Review,* 1957, **64**, 123–152.

Bruner, J. S., and Goodman, C. C. Value and need as organizing factors in perception. *Journal of Abnormal and Social Psychology,* 1947, **42**, 33–44.

Buckhout, R., Figueroa, D., and Hoff, E. Psychology and eyewitness identification. Center for Responsive Psychology, Report No. CR-1, November 1972.

Bucklew, J. The current status of theory in mental retardation. In N. H. Pronko (Ed.), *Panorama of psychology.* Belmont, Calif.: Brooks/Cole, 1969.

Buckner, H. T. Flying saucers are for people. *Trans-action,* May–June 1966.

Burgess, R. L., Clark, R. N., and Hendee, J. C. An experimental analysis of anti-litter procedures. *Journal of Applied Behavioral Analysis,* 1971, **4**, 71–75.

Burney, C. *Solitary confinement.* New York: Clerke and Cockeran, 1952.

Burton, A. *Interpersonal psychotherapy.* Englewood Cliffs, N.J.: Prentice-Hall, 1972.

Buss, A. H. *Psychology: Man in perspective.* New York: Wiley, 1973.

Buss, A. H. *Psychopathology.* New York: Wiley, 1966.

Butler, R. A. Curiosity in monkeys. *Scientific American,* February 1954.

Butler, R. N. Age: The life review. *Psychology Today,* December 1971.

Byrne, D. *The attraction paradigm.* New York: Academic Press, 1971.

Calder, N. *The mind of man.* New York: Viking, 1970.

Cameron, N. *Personality development and psychopathology.* Boston: Houghton Mifflin, 1963.

Candee, D. The moral psychology of Watergate. *Journal of Social Issues,* 1975, **31**, 183–192.

Cannon, W. B. *Bodily changes in pain, hunger, fear, and rage.* New York: Appleton, 1929.

Cannon, W. B. *The mechanical factors of digestion.* London: Arnold, 1911.

Carmichael, L., Hogan, H. P., and Walter, A. A. An experimental study of the effect of language on the reproduction of visually perceived form. *Journal of Experimental Psychology,* 1932, **15**, 73–86.

Carroll, J. B. *Language and thought.* Englewood Cliffs, N.J.: Prentice-Hall, 1964.

Carver, R. P. Speed readers don't read: They skim. *Psychology Today,* August 1972.

Cates, J. Psychology's manpower: Report on the 1968 National Register of Scientific and Technical Personnel. *American Psychologist,* 1970, **25**, 245–263.

Cates, J., and Dawson, W. Preliminary report of the 1970 National Register. *American Psychologist,* 1971, **26**, 390–392.

Ceraso, J. The interference theory of forgetting. *Scientific American,* April 1967.

Chafetz, M. E. Addictions: III. Alcoholism. In A. M. Freedman and H. I. Kaplan (Eds.), *Comprehensive textbook of psychiatry,* Baltimore: Williams & Wilkins, 1967.

Chesler, P. Men drive women crazy. *Psychology Today,* July 1971.

Chomsky, N. Language and the mind. *Psychology Today,* February 1968.

Chomsky, N., and Halle, M. *Sound patterns of English.* New York: Harper & Row, 1968.

Chorover, S. L. The pacification of the brain. *Psychology Today,* May 1974.

Christensen, A., and Arkowitz, H. Preliminary report on practice dating and feedback as treatment for college dating problems. *Journal of Counseling Psychology,* 1974, **21**, 92–95.

Christie, R., and Geis, F. L. (Eds.). *Studies in Machiavellianism.* New York: Academic Press, 1970.

Churchill, J. A. The relationship between intelligence and birth weight in twins. *Neurology,* 1965, **15**, 341–347.

Clark, K. B., and Clark, M. P. Racial identification and preference in Negro children. In T. M. Newcomb and E. L. Hartley (Eds.), *Readings in social psychology.* New York: Holt, 1947.

Clifford, M. M., and Walster, E. The effect of physical attractiveness on teacher expectation. *Sociology of Education,* 1973, **46**, 248–258.

Coleman, J. C. *Abnormal psychology and modern life.* (4th ed.) Glenview, Ill.: Scott, Foresman, 1972.

Coleman, J., Campbell, E., Hobson, C., McPartland, J., Mood, A., Weinfield, F., and York, R. *Equality of educational opportunity.* Washington, D.C.: U.S. Government Printing Office, 1966.

Colligan, D. The helpless feeling: The dangers of stress. *New York,* July 14, 1975.

Conklin, H. C. The relation of Hunanoo culture to the plant world. Doctoral dissertation, Yale University, 1954.

Coopersmith, S. *Antecedents of self-esteem.* San Francisco: W. H. Freeman, 1967.

Copp, J. D. Why hunters like to hunt. *Psychology Today,* December 1975.

Cox, A. Ends. *New York Times Magazine,* May 19, 1974.

Cox, C. M. *The early mental traits of three hundred geniuses.* (Vol. II of *Genetic studies of genius.*) Stanford, Calif.: Stanford University Press, 1926.

Cronbach, L. J. *Essentials of psychological testing.* (2nd ed.) New York: Harper & Row, 1960.

Cronbach, L. J. Five decades of public controversy over mental testing. *American Psychologist,* 1975, **30**, 1–14.

Crumbaugh, J. C. A scientific critique of parapsychology. In G. Schmeidler (Ed.), *Extrasensory perception.* New York: Atherton, 1969.

Curtis, H. *Biology,* 2nd ed. New York: Worth, 1975.

Cutler, N. Generation, maturation, and party affiliation: A cohort analysis. *Public Opinion Quarterly,* 1970, **33**, 583–588.

Dabbs, J. M., and Leventhal, H. Effects of varying the recommendations in a fear-arousing communication. *Journal of Personality and Social Psychology,* 1966, **4**, 525–531.

D'Andrade, R. G. Sex differences and cultural institutions. In E. E. Maccoby (Ed.), *The development of sex differences.* Stanford, Calif.: Stanford University Press, 1966.

Darley, J. M., and Batson, C. D. From Jerusalem to Jericho: A study of situational and dispositional variables in helping behavior. *Journal of Personality and Social Psychology,* 1973, **27**, 100–108.

Darley, J. M., and Cooper, J. The "clean for Gene" phenomenon: The effects of students' appearance on political campaigning. *Journal of Applied Social Psychology,* 1972, **2**, 24–33.

Davidson, P. O. Validity of the guilty knowledge technique. *Journal of Applied Psychology,* 1968, **52**, 62–65.

Davis, F. The cabdriver and his fare: Facets of a fleeting relationship. *American Journal of Sociology,* 1959, **65**, 158–165.

Davison, C., and Neale, J. M. *Abnormal psychology: An experimental clinical approach.* New York: Wiley, 1974.

Deaux, K., and Emswiler, T. Explanation of successful performance on sex-linked tasks: What is skill for the male is luck for the female. *Journal of Personality and Social Psychology,* 1974, **29**, 80–85.

Deci, E. Work: Who does not like it and why. *Psychology Today,* August 1972.

Deikman, A. J. Experimental meditation. *Journal of Nervous and Mental Disease,* 1963, **136**, 329–373.

Dember, W. N. Motivation and the cognitive revolution. *American Psychologist,* 1974, **29**, 161–168.

Dement, W. C. The effect of dream deprivation. *Science,* 1960, **131**, 1705–1707.

Dement, W. C. An essay on dreams: The role of physiology in understanding their nature. In *New directions in psychology,* Vol. II. New York: Holt, 1965.

Dempsey, D. Noise. *New York Times Magazine,* November 23, 1975.

Derlega, V. J., and Chaikin, A. L. *Sharing intimacy: What we reveal to others and why.* Englewood Cliffs, N.J.: Prentice-Hall, 1975.

Dermer, M., and Thiel, D. L. When beauty may fail. *Journal of Personality and Social Psychology,* 1975, **31**, 1168–1176.

Detterman, D. K., and Ellis, N. R. Determinants of induced amnesia in short-term memory. *Journal of Experimental Psychology,* 1972, **95**, 308–316.

Deutsch, J. A. Neural basis of memory. *Psychology Today,* May 1968.

Deutsch, M. and Collins, M. E. *Interracial housing.* Minneapolis: University of Minnesota Press, 1951.

Dichter, E. *Handbook of consumer motivations.* New York: McGraw-Hill, 1964.

Dick-Read, G. *Childbirth without fear.* New York: Harper & Row, 1944.

Dion, K. K., Berscheid, E., and Walster, E. What is beautiful is good. *Journal of Personality and Social Psychology,* 1972, **24**, 285–290.

Dipoye, R. L., Fromkin, H. L., and Wiback, H. Relative importance of applicant sex, attractiveness, and scholastic standing in evaluation of job applicant resumés. *Journal of Applied Psychology,* 1975, **60**, 39–43.

Dohrenwend, B. S. Social status and stressful life events. *Journal of Personality and Social Psychology,* 1973, **28**, 225–235.

Dollard, J., et al., *Frustration and aggression.* New Haven, Conn.: Yale University Press, 1939.

Douvan, E., and Adelson, J. *The adolescent experience.* New York: Wiley, 1966.

Doyle, A. C. "A Study in Scarlet," in *The Complete Sherlock Holmes.* Garden City, N.Y.: Doubleday, 1927.

Drabman, R. S., and Thomas, M. H. Does TV violence breed indifference? *Journal of Communication,* Autumn 1975.

Drucker, P. F. School around the bend. *Psychology Today,* June 1972.

Dutton, D. G., and Aron, A. P. Some evidence for heightened sexual attraction under conditions of high anxiety. *Journal of Personality and Social Psychology,* 1974, Vol. **30**, 510–517.

Dworkin, R. H., Burke, B. W., Maher, B. A., and Gottesman, I. I. A longitudinal study of the genetics of personality. *Journal of Personality and Social Psychology,* 1976, **34**, 510–518.

Edmiston, S. Out from under! A major report on women today. *Redbook,* May 1975.

Efran, M. G. The effect of physical appearance on the judgment of guilt, interpersonal attraction, and severity of recommended punishment in a simulated jury task. *Journal of Research on Personality,* 1974, **8**, 45–54.

Efran, M. G., and Patterson, E. W. J. Voters vote beautiful: The effect of physical appearance on a national election. *Canadian Journal of Behavioral Science,* 1974, **6**, 352–356.

Egan, G. *Encounter: Group processes for interpersonal Growth.* Belmont, Calif.: Brooks/Cole, 1970.

Ehrhardt, A. A., and Baker, S. W. Fetal androgens, human central nervous system differentiation, and behavior sex differences. In R. C. Friedman, R. M. Richart, and R. L. Vande Wiele (Eds.), *Sex differences in behavior.* New York: Wiley, 174.

Eibl-Eibsfeldt, I. *Ethology: The biology of behavior.* New York: Holt, Rinehart and Winston, 1970.

Ekman, P. The universal smile: Face muscles talk every language. *Psychology Today,* September 1975.

Ekman, P., Sorenson, E. R., and Friesen, W. V. Pan-cultural elements in facial displays of emotion. *Science,* 1969, **164**, 86–88.

Ekstrand, B. R. Effects of sleep on memory. *Journal of Experimental Psychology,* 1967, **75**, 64–72.

Elkind, D. *Cognitive development.* Homewood, Ill.: Learning Systems Company, 1975.

Elkind, D. Erik Erikson's eight stages of man. *New York Times Magazine,* April 5, 1970.

Elkind, D. Giant in the nursery: Jean Piaget. *New York Times Magazine,* May 26, 1969.

Ellis, H. *A study of British genius.* (New rev. ed.) Boston: Houghton Mifflin, 1926. (Originally published in 1904.)

Elton, C. F., and Shevel, L. R. *Who is talented? An analysis of achievement.* Iowa City: American College Testing Program, 1969.

Ember, C. R. Feminine task assignment and the social behavior of boys. *Ethos,* 1973, **1**, 424–439.

Emmons, W. H., and Simon, C. W. The non-recall of material presented during sleep. *American Journal of Psychology,* 1956, **69**, 76–81.

English, F. TA's Disney World. *Psychology Today,* April 1973.

Erikson, E. *Childhood and society.* New York: Norton, 1950.

Erikson, E. H. in *A healthy personality for every child. A fact finding report: A digest.* (Mid-century White House Conference on Children and Youth.) Raleigh, N.C.: Health Publications Institute, 1951.

Erlenmayer-Kimling, L., and Jarvik, L. F. Genetics and intelligence: A review. *Science,* 1963, **142,** 1477–1479.

Erlich, J. W. *The lost art of cross-examination.* Cited in Social Action and the Law Newsletter, February, 1974.

Evans, W. O. Mind-altering drugs and the future. *The Futurist,* June 1971.

Eysenck, H. J. The effects of psychotherapy: An evaluation. *Journal of Consulting Psychology,* 1952, **16**, 319–324.

Farberow, N. L. Self-destruction and identity. *Humanitas,* 1970, **6**, 45–68.

Farson, R. E. Emotional barriers to education. *Psychology Today,* October 1967.

Fein, R. A. Men and young children. In J. H. Pleck and J. Sawyer (Eds.), *Men and masculinity.* Englewood Cliffs, N.J.: Prentice-Hall, 1974.

Fenz, W. D., and Epstein, S. Gradients of physiological arousal in parachutists as a function of an approaching jump. *Psychosomatic Medicine,* 1967, **29**, 33–51.

Fernstrom, J. D., and Wurtmann, R. J. Nutrition and the brain. *Scientific American,* February 1974.

Festinger, L. Cognitive dissonance. *Scientific American,* October 1962.

Festinger, L. *A theory of cognitive dissonance.* Stanford, Calif.: Stanford University Press, 1957.

Festinger, L. A theory of social comparison processes. *Human Relations,* 1954, **7**, 117–140.

Festinger, L., and Carlsmith, J. M. Cognitive consequences of forced compliance. *Journal of Abnormal and Social Psychology,* 1959, **58**, 203–210.

Festinger, L., Riecken, H., and Schachter, S. *When prophecy fails.* Minneapolis: University of Minnesota Press, 1956.

Feuer, L. *The conflict of generations: The character and significance of student movements.* New York: Basic Books, 1969.

Fine, R. The psychology of blindfold chess: An introspective account. *Acta Psychologia,* 1965, **24**, 352–370.

Flanagan, J. C. The definition and measurement of ingenuity. In C. W. Taylor and F. Barron (Eds.), *Scientific creativity: Its recognition and development.* New York: Wiley, 1963.

Flapan, M. A paradigm for the analysis of childbearing motivations of married women prior to birth of the first child. *American Journal of Orthopsychiatry,* 1969, **39**, 402–417.

Fo, W. S. O., and O'Donnell, C. R. The buddy system: Relationship and contingency conditions in a community intervention program for youth with nonprofessionals as behavior change agents. *Journal of Consulting and Clinical Psychology,* 1974, **42,** 163–169.

Fort, J. The pleasure seekers. *Mind Over Matter,* 1970, **15**, (1), 65–83.

Foucault, M. *Madness and civilization: A history of insanity in the age of reason.* New York: Pantheon, 1965.

Francoeur, R. T. *Utopian motherhood.* Garden City, N.Y.: Doubleday, 1970.

Frank, G. *The Boston strangler.* New York: New American Library, 1966.

Frank, J. D. The bewildering world of psychotherapy. *Journal of Social Issues,* 1972, **28** (4), 27–40.

Frank, J. D. The demoralized mind. *Psychology Today,* April 1973. (a)

Frank, J. D. *Persuasion and healing: A comparative study of psychotherapy,* 2nd ed. Baltimore: Johns Hopkins University Press, 1973. (b)

Freedman, A. M., and Kaplan, H. I. (Eds.). *Psychiatry.* Baltimore: Williams & Wilkins, 1967.

Freedman, J. L., and Sears, D. Warning, distraction, and resistance to influence. *Journal of Personality and Social Psychology,* 1965, **1**, 262–265.

Freedman, L. Z. "Truth" drugs. *Scientific American,* March 1960.

Freeling, N. R., and Shemberg, K. M. The alleviation of test anxiety by systematic desensitization. *Behaviour Research and Therapy,* 1970, **8**, 293–299.

Freud, S. *Civilization and its discontents.* London: Hogarth, 1961. (First German ed., 1930.)

Freud, S. *The interpretation of dreams* (original 1900). In *The standard edition of the complete psychological works of Sigmund Freud,* Vols IV and V. London: Hogarth, 1953.

Freud, S. Mourning and melancholia, 1917. In *Collected Papers,* Vol. IV. London: Hogarth Press, 1950.

Freud, S. Analysis terminable and interminable. In J. Strachey (Ed. and tr.), *The Standard Edition of the Complete Psychological Works of Sigmund Freud,* Vol. 23. London: Hogarth Press, 1964.

Freud, S. 1913. Further recommendations on the technique of psychoanalysis. I: On beginning the treatment. In J. Strachey (Ed. and tr.), *The standard edition of the complete psychological works of Sigmund Freud,* vol. 12. London: Hogarth Press, 1958.

Freud, S. *The psychopathology of everyday life.* New York: Macmillan, 1915.

Freud, S. Recommendations for physicians on the psycho-analytic method. *Collected Papers,* Vol. 2. London: Hogarth Press, 1956.

Friedan, B. *The feminine mystique.* New York: Norton, 1963.

Friedberg, J. Electroshock therapy: Let's stop blasting the brain. *Psychology Today,* August 1975.

Friedenberg, E. Z. Current patterns of generational conflict. *Journal of Social Issues,* 1969, **25** (Figure 2), 21–38.

Friedman, M., and Rosenman, R. H. *Type A behavior and your heart.* New York: Knopf, 1974.

Fromm, E. *The art of loving.* New York: Harper & Row, 1956.

Funkenstein, D. The physiology of fear and anger. *Scientific American,* May 1955.

Galanter, E. Contemporary psychophysics. In R. Brown, et al., *New directions in psychology,* Vol. 1. New York: Holt, Rinehart and Winston, 1962.

Galizio, M., and Hendrick, C. Effect of musical accompaniment on attitude: The guitar as a prop for persuasion. *Journal of Applied Social Psychology,* 1972, **2**, 350–359.

Garcia, J. IQ: The conspiracy. *Psychology Today,* September 1972.

Garcia, J., and Koelling, R. A. Relation of cue to consequence in avoidance learning. *Psychonomic Science,* 1966, **4**, 123–124.

Gardner, H. Brain damage: A window on the mind. *Saturday Review,* August 9, 1975.

Gardner, H. *The shattered mind.* New York: Knopf, 1975.

Gardner, M. *Fads and fallacies in the name of science.* New York: Dover, 1952.

Gardner, R. A., and Gardner, B. T. Early signs of language in child and chimpanzee. *Science,* 1975, **187**, 752–753.

Gardner, R. A., and Gardner, B. T. Teaching sign language to a chimpanzee. *Science,* 1969, **165**, 664–672.

Gates, A. I. Recitation as a factor in memorizing. *Archives of Psychology,* 1917, No. 40.

Gazzaniga, M. S. The split brain in man. *Scientific American,* August 1967.

Geldard, F. A. Skin language: Body English. *Psychology Today,* December 1968.

Gergen, K. J., and Morse, S. J. Correlates of marijuana use among college students. *Journal of Applied Social Psychology,* 1972, **2**, 1–16.

Gersick, K. E. Fathers by choice: Characteristics of men who do and do not seek custody of their children following divorce. Doctoral dissertation, Harvard University, 1975.

Getzels, J. W., and Jackson, P. W. *Creativity and intelligence.* New York: Wiley, 1962.

Gibson, E. J., and Walk, R. D. The visual cliff. *Scientific American,* April 1960.

Gilder, G. *Sexual suicide.* New York: Quadrangle, 1973.

Girardeau, F. L., and Spradlin, J. E. Token rewards in a cottage program. *Mental Retardation,* 1964, **2**, 345–351.

Glass, D. C., Cohen, S., and Singer, J. E. Urban din fogs the brain. *Psychology Today,* May 1973.

Glass, D. C., and Singer, J. E. Experimental studies of uncontrollable and unpredictable noise. *Representative Research in Social Psychology,* 1973, **4**, 165–183.

Gleason, H. A. *An introduction to descriptive linguistics.* (Rev. ed.) New York: Holt, Rinehart and Winston, 1961.

Gmelch, G. Baseball magic. *Trans-action,* June 1971.

Goldberg, P. Are women prejudiced against women? *Trans-action,* April 1968.

Goldberg, S., and Lewis, M. Play behavior in the year-old infant: Early sex differences. *Child Development*, 1969, **40**, 21–31.

Goldfarb, W. Variations in adolescent adjustment of institutionally reared children. *American Journal of Orthopsychiatry*, 1947, **17**, 449–457.

Goodall, K. Shapers at work. *Psychology Today*, November 1972.

Goode, W. J. Family disorganization. In R. K. Merton and R. A. Nisbet (Eds.), *Contemporary social problems*. New York: Harcourt Brace Jovanovich, 1961.

Gore, P. M., and Rotter, J. B. A personality correlate of social action. *Journal of Personality*, 1963, **31**, 58–64.

Gottesman, I., and Shields, J. *Schizophrenia and genetics*. New York: Academic Press, 1972.

Gould, R. Adult life stages: Growth toward self-tolerance. *Psychology Today*, February 1975.

Gould R. The phases of adult life: A study in developmental psychology. *American Journal of Psychiatry*, 1972, **129**, 521–531.

Gray, C. R., and Gummerman, K. The enigmatic eidetic image: A critical examination of methods, data, and theories. *Psychological Bulletin*, 1975, **82**, 383–407.

Gray, F., Graubard, P. S., and Rosenberg, H. Little brother is changing you. *Psychology Today*, March 1974.

Greenblatt, M. Psychosurgery, in A. M. Freedman and H. I. Kaplan (Eds.), *Psychiatry*. Baltimore: Williams & Wilkins, 1967.

Greene, D., and Lepper, M. R. Intrinsic motivation: Turning play into work. *Psychology Today*, September 1974.

Greenspoon, J. The reinforcing effect of two spoken sounds on the frequency of two responses. *American Journal of Psychology*, 1955, **68**, 409–416.

Greer, C. *The great school legend: A revisionist interpretation of American public education*. New York: Basic Books, 1972.

Greer, G. *The female eunuch*. New York: McGraw-Hill, 1971.

Gregory, R. L. *Eye and brain: The psychology of seeing*. New York: McGraw-Hill, 1966.

Gregory, R. L. Visual illusions. *Scientific American*, May 1968.

Grinspoon, L. Marihuana. *Scientific American*, December 1969.

Grinspoon, L., and Hedblom, P. Amphetamines reconsidered. *Saturday Review*, July 8, 1972.

Groninger, L. D. Mnemonic imagery and forgetting. *Psychonomic Science*, 1971, **23**, 161–163.

Grossman, F. K. Brothers and sisters of retarded children. *Psychology Today*, April 1972.

Guilford, J. P. A factor analytic study across the domains of reasoning, creativity, and evaluation: Hypothesis and description of tests. *Reports from the psychology laboratory*. Los Angeles: University of Southern California, 1954.

Gustin, J. L. The revolt of youth. *Psychoanalysis and the Psychoanalytic Review*, 1961, **98**, 78–90.

Haber, R. N. Eidetic images. *Scientific American*, April 1969.

Haber, R. N. How we remember what we see. *Scientific American*, May 1970.

Haber, R. N., and Fried, A. H. *An introduction to psychology*. New York: Holt, Rinehart and Winston, 1975.

Halacy, D. S. *Man and memory*. New York: Harper & Row, 1970.

Hardyck, J. A., and Braden, M. Prophecy fails again: A report of a failure to replicate. *Journal of Abnormal and Social Psychology*, 1962, **65**, 136–141.

Harlow, H. F. Love in infant monkeys. *Scientific American*, March 1959.

Harlow, H. F. The nature of love. *American Psychologist*, 1958, **13**, 673–685.

Harlow, H. F., and Suomi, S. J. Generalization of behavior from monkey to man. In G. Lindzey, C. Hall, and R. Thompson (Eds.), *Psychology*. New York: Worth, 1975.

Harris, T. G. Jensen, genetics, and equalitarian diversity. *Psychology Today*, December 1973.

Harrower, M. Were Hitler's henchmen mad? *Psychology Today*, July 1976.

Hartley, E. L. *Problems in prejudice*. New York: Kings Crown, 1946.

Hartmann, E. L. *The functions of sleep*. New Haven, Conn.: Yale University Press, 1973.

Hartshorne, H., and May, M. A. *Studies in the nature of character*. Vols. I–III. New York: Macmillan, 1928–30.

Hastorf, A. H., Schneider, D. J., and Polefka, J. *Person perception*. Reading, Mass.: Addison-Wesley, 1970.

Hayes, K. J., and Hayes, C. The intellectual development of a home-raised chimpanzee. *Philosophical Society*, 1951, **95**, 105–109.

Hays, R. R. *The dangerous sex*. New York: Putnam's, 1964.

Hebb, D. O. The role of neurological ideas in psychology. *Journal of Personality*, 1951, **20**, 39–55.

Henley, N. M. The politics of touch. In P. Brown (Ed.), *Radical psychology*. New York: Harper & Row, 1973.

Henry, J. *Culture against man*. New York: Random House, 1963.

Heron, W. The pathology of boredom. *Scientific American*, January 1957.

Hertzberg, H., and McClelland, D. C. K. Paranoia. *Harper's*, June 1974.

Hess, E. H. Imprinting: An effect of early experience. *Science*, 1959, **130**, 133–141.

Hicks, R. F., and Kinsbourne, M. Human handedness: A partial cross-fostering study. *Science*, 1976, **192**, 908–910.

Hilgard, E. R. The domain of hypnosis, with some comments on alternative paradigms. *American Psychologist*, 1972, **28**, 972–982.

Hilgard, E. R. *Hypnotic susceptibility*. New York: Harcourt, 1965.

Hill, C. T., Rubin, Z., and Peplau, L. A. Breakups before marriage: The end of 103 affairs. *Journal of Social Issues*, 1976, **32** (Figure 1), 147–168.

Hochschild, A. R. Attending to, codifying, and managing feelings: Sex differences in love. Paper presented at American Sociological Association meeting, San Francisco, August 1975.

Hokanson, J. E. Psychophysiological evaluation of the catharsis hypothesis. In E. I. Megargee and J. E. Hokanson (Eds.), *The dynamics of aggression*. New York: Harper & Row, 1970.

Holland, J. L., and Richards, J. M., Jr. *Academic and nonacademic accomplishment: Correlated or uncorrelated?* Iowa City: American College Testing Program, 1965.

Holliday, A. R. A review of psychopharmacology. In B. B. Wolman (Ed.), *Handbook of clinical psychology*. New York: McGraw-Hill, 1965.

Holmes, D. S., and Jorgensen, B. W. Do personality and social psychologists study men more than women? *Representative Research in Social Psychology*, 1971, **2**, 71–76.

Holmes, T. H., and Masuda, M. Psychosomatic syndrome: When mothers-in-law or other disasters visit, a person can develop a bad, bad cold. Or worse. *Psychology Today*, April 1972.

Hoon, P. W., and Lindsley, O. R. A comparison of behavior and traditional therapy publication activity. *American Psychologist*, 1974, **29**, 694–697.

Hoover, E. L. Alpha: The first step to a new level of reality. *Human Behavior*, January-February 1972.

Hormuth, R. A proposed program to combat mental retardation. *Children*, 1963, **10**, 29–31.

Horner, M. Fail: Bright women. *Psychology Today*, November 1969.

Hovland, C. I., Janis, I. L., and Kelley, H. H. *Communication and persuasion*. New Haven, Conn.: Yale University Press, 1953.

Hovland, C. I., and Weiss, W. The influence of source credibility on communication effectiveness. *Public Opinion Quarterly*, 1952, **15**, 635–650.

Hunt, M. M. *Sexual behavior in the 1970s*. Chicago: Playboy Press, 1974.

Inhelder, B., Sinclair, M., and Bovet, M. *Apprentissage et structures de la connoissance*. Paris: Presses Universitaires de France, 1974.

Isen, A. M. Success, failure, and reaction to others: The warm glow of success. *Journal of Personality and Social Psychology*, 1970, **15**, 294–301.

Jackson, J. K. The adjustment of the family to alcoholism. *Journal of Marriage and Family Living*, 1956, **18**, 361–369.

James, W. *The principles of psychology*. New York: Holt, 1890.

James, W. What is an emotion? *Mind*, Vol. 9, 1884.

James, W. H., Woodruff, A. B., and Werner, W. Effects of internal and external control upon changes in smoking behavior. *Journal of Consulting Psychology*, 1965, **29**, 184–186.

Janis, I. L. *Victims of groupthink*. Boston: Houghton Mifflin, 1972.

Janis, I. L., and Feshbach, S. Effects of fear-arousing communications. *Journal of Abnormal and Social Psychology*, 1953, **48**, 78–92.

Janis, I. L., Kaye, D., and Kirschner, P. Facilitating effects of "eating-while-reading" on responsiveness to persuasive communications. *Journal of Personality and Social Psychology*, 1965, **1**, 181–186.

Janis, I. L., and Mann, L. Effectiveness of emotional role-playing in modifying smoking habits and attitudes. *Journal of Experimental Research in Personality*, 1965, **1**, 84–90.

Jenkins, J. G., and Dallenbach, K. M. Oblivisence during sleep and waking. *American Journal of Psychology,* 1924, **35,** 605–612.

Jensen, A. R. Counter response. *Journal of Social Issues,* 1969, **25** (Figure 4), 219–222. (a)

Jensen, A. R. How much can we boost IQ and scholastic achievement? *Harvard Educational Review,* 1969, **39,** 1–123. (b)

Jensen, A. R. Spelling errors and the serial position effect. *Journal of Educational Psychology,* 1962, **53,** 105–109.

Jersild, A. T., Markey, F. V., and Jersild, C. L. Children's fears, dreams, wishes, daydreams, likes, dislikes, pleasant and unpleasant memories. In A. T. Jersild, *Child psychology.* Englewood Cliffs, N.J.: Prentice-Hall, 1960 (originally published 1933).

Jones, E. E., et al. *Attribution: Perceiving the causes of behavior.* Morristown, N.J.: General Learning Press, 1972.

Jones, E. E., and Harris, V. A. The attribution of attitudes. *Journal of Experimental Social Psychology,* 1967, **3,** 1–24.

Jones, E. E., and Nisbett, R. E. The actor and the observer: Divergent perceptions of the causes of behavior. In Jones et al., *Attribution: Perceiving the causes of behavior.* Morristown, N.J.: General Learning Press, 1972.

Jones, J. M. *Prejudice and racism.* Reading, Mass.: Addison-Wesley, 1972.

Jones, M. C. The later careers of boys who were early or late maturing. *Child Development,* 1957, **28,** 113–128.

Jost, H., and Sontag, L. The genetic factor in autonomic nervous system function. *Psychosomatic Medicine,* 1944, **6,** 308–310.

Jourard, S. M., and Rubin, J. E. Self-disclosure and touching: A study of two modes of interpersonal encounter and their interreaction. *Journal of Humanistic Psychology,* 1968, **8,** 39–48.

Jung, C. *Man and his symbols.* Garden City, N.Y.: Doubleday, 1964.

Jung, C. G. *Psychologische typen.* Zurich: Rascher, 1921.

Kagan, J. The child: His struggle for identity. *Saturday Review,* December 7, 1968.

Kagan, J. Emergent themes in human development. *American Scientist,* 1976, **64,** 186–196.

Kagan, J., Kearsley, R. B., and Zelazo, P. R. Paper presented at the annual meeting of the American Association for the Advancement of Science, 1976.

Kahn, M., Baker, B. L., and Weiss, J. M. Treatment of insomnia by relaxation training. *Journal of Abnormal Psychology,* 1968, **73,** 556–558.

Kalish, R. A. *Late adulthood: Perspectives on human development.* Monterey, Calif.: Brooks/Cole, 1975.

Kalish, R. A. The old and new as generation gap allies. *Gerontologist,* 1969, **9,** 83–89.

Kamiya, J. Conscious control of brain waves. *Psychology Today,* April 1968.

Kaplan, R. M., and Goldman, R. D. Interracial perception among black, white, and Mexican-American high school students. *Journal of Personality and Social Psychology,* 1973, **28,** 383–389.

Karacan, I., and Williams, R. L. Insomnia: Old wine in a new bottle. *Psychiatric Quarterly,* 1971, **45,** 274–288.

Karmel, L. The case for love. Paper presented at the American Psychological Association convention, Miami Beach, 1970.

Kassarjian, H. H. Voting intentions and political perception. *Journal of Psychology,* 1963, **56,** 85–88.

Katchadourian, H. A., and Lunde, D. T. *Fundamentals of human sexuality.* (2nd ed.) New York: Holt, Rinehart, and Winston, 1975.

Katz, A. M., and Hill, R. Residential propinquity and marital selection: A review of theory, method, and fact. *Marriage and Family Living,* 1958, **20,** 27–34.

Katz, D. Why children attempt suicide. *Detroit Free Press,* February 3, 1974.

Kau, M. L., and Fischer, J. Self-modification of exercise behavior. *Journal of Behaviour Therapy and Experimental Psychiatry,* 1974, **5,** 213.

Kaufmann, H. *Introduction to the study of human behavior.* Philadelphia: Saunders, 1968.

Kausler, D. *The psychology of verbal learning and memory.* New York: Academic Press, 1974.

Keen, S. Janov and primal therapy: "The screaming cure." *Psychology Today,* February 1972.

Kelleher, R. T. Discrimination learning as a function of reversal and nonreversal shifts. *Journal of Experimental Psychology,* 1956, **51,** 379–384.

Kellogg, W. N. Communication and language in the home-raised chimpanzee. *Science,* 1968, **162,** 423–427.

Kelley, H. H. The warm-cold variable in first impressions of persons. *Journal of Personality,* 1950, **18,** 431–439.

Kelley, H. H., and Woodruff, C. L. Members' reactions to apparent group approval of a counternorm communication. *Journal of Abnormal and Social Psychology,* 1956, **52,** 67–74.

Kelly, G. A. *The psychology of personal constructs.* New York: Norton, 1955.

Kelman, H. C., and Lawrence, L. H. Assignment of responsibility in the case of Lt. Calley: Preliminary report on a national survey. *Journal of Social Issues,* 1972, **28** (Figure 1), 177–212.

Kendler, H. H., and D'Amato, M. F. A comparison of reversal shifts and nonreversal shifts in human concept formation and behavior. *Journal of Experimental Psychology,* 1955, **49,** 165–174.

Kendler, T. S., Kendler, H. H., and Wells, D. Reversal and nonreversal shifts in nursery school children. *Journal of Comparative and Physiological Psychology,* 1960, **53,** 83–88.

Keniston, K. The sources of student dissent. *Journal of Social Issues,* 1967, **23,** 108–132.

Kennedy, K. D. Letter to the editor. *Psychology Today,* January 1976.

Kerry, R. J. Phobia of outer space. *Journal of Mental Science,* 1960, **106,** 1383–1387.

Kessler, J. W. *Psychopathology of childhood.* Englewood Cliffs, N.J.: Prentice-Hall, 1966.

Kleitman, N. *Sleep and wakefulness.* Chicago: University of Chicago Press, 1939.

Kohlberg, L. A cognitive-developmental analysis of children's sex-role concepts and attitudes. In E. E. Maccoby (Ed.), *The development of sex differences.* Stanford, Calif.: Stanford University Press, 1966.

Kohlberg, L. The cognitive-developmental approach to socialization. In D. A. Goslin (Ed.), *Handbook of socialization theory and research.* Chicago: Rand McNally, 1969.

Kohlberg, L. The development of children's orientations toward a moral order: I. Sequence in the development of moral thought. *Vita Humana,* 1963, **6,** 11–33.

Kohler, I. Experiments with goggles. *Scientific American,* May 1962.

Köhler, W. *The mentality of apes.* New York: Harcourt, Brace, 1925.

Kotelchuck, M. The nature of the child's tie to his father. Doctoral dissertation, Harvard University, 1972.

Kozol, J. *Free schools.* Boston: Houghton Mifflin, 1972.

Krebs, D., and Adinolfi, A. A. Physical attractiveness, social relations, and personality style. *Journal of Personality and Social Psychology,* 1975, **31,** 245–253.

Krippner, S. An experimental study of hypnosis and telepathy. *The American Journal of Clinical Hypnosis,* 1968, **11,** 45–54.

Krippner, S., and Davidson, R. Parapsychology in the U.S.S.R. *Saturday Review,* August 26, 1972.

Krippner, S., and Hughes, W. Genius at work. *Psychology Today,* June 1970.

Krueger, W. C. F. The effect of overlearning on retention. *Journal of Experimental Psychology,* 1929, **12,** 71–78.

Kuhn, T. *The structure of scientific revolutions.* (2nd ed.) Chicago: University of Chicago Press, 1970.

Laing, R. D. *The politics of experience.* New York: Ballantine, 1967.

Lamott, K. The four possible life positions. *New York Times Magazine,* November 19, 1972.

Lamott, K. Marathon therapy is a psychological pressure cooker. *New York Times,* July 13, 1969.

Langer, E. J., and Abelson, R. P. A patient by any other name . . . : Clinician group difference in labeling bias. *Journal of Consulting and Clinical Psychology,* 1974, **42,** 4–9.

Langer, E. J., and Rodin, J. The effects of choice and enhanced personal responsibility for the aged: A field experiment in an institutional setting. *Journal of Personality and Social Psychology.* 1976, **34,** 191–198.

Laumann, E. O. Friends of urban men: An assessment of accuracy in reporting their socioeconomic attributes, mutual choice, and attitude agreement. *Sociometry,* 1969, **32,** 54–69.

Lehman, H. L. *Age and achievement.* Princeton, N.J.: Princeton University Press, 1953.

Lanzetta, J. T., Cartwright-Smith, J., and Kleck, R. E. Effects of nonverbal dissimulation on emotional experience and autonomic arousal. *Journal of Personality and Social Psychology,* 1976, **33,** 354–370.

Lashley, K. S. In search of the engram. In *Symposium of the Society for Experimental Biology,* vol. IV. New York: Cambridge University Press, 1950.

Layton, B. D. and Turnbull, B. Belief, evaluation, and

performance in an ESP task. *Journal of Experimental and Social Psychology,* 1975, **11,** 166–179.

Lazarus, A. A. *Behavior therapy and beyond.* New York: McGraw-Hill, 1971.

Lazarus, R. S. *The riddle of man.* Englewood Cliffs, N.J.: Prentice-Hall, 1974.

Leboyer, F. *Birth without violence.* New York: Knopf, 1975.

Leeper, R. The role of motivation in learning: A study of the phenomenon of differential motivation control on the utilization of habits. *Journal of Genetic Psychology,* 1935, **46,** 3–40.

LeMasters, E. E. Parenthood as crisis. *Marriage and Family Living,* 1957, **19,** 352–355.

Lenneberg, E. *The biological foundations of language.* New York: Wiley, 1967.

Lenneberg, E. H. The natural history of language. In F. Smith and G. A. Miller (Eds.), *The genesis of language: A psycholinguistic approach.* Cambridge, Mass.: MIT Press, 1966.

Lenneberg, E. H. On explaining language. *Science,* 1969, **164,** 635–643.

Lester, J. Women: The male fantasy. *Evergreen,* September 1970.

Levinger, G. A social psychological perspective on marital dissolution. *Journal of Social Issues,* 1976, **32,** (Figure 1), 21–47.

Levine, S. One man's experience. *Ms,* February 1973.

Levinson, D. J., et al. *The seasons of a man's life.* Scheduled to be published in 1977.

Lewin, R. Starved brains. *Psychology Today,* September, 1975.

Lewis, M. Culture and gender roles: There's no unisex in the nursery. *Psychology Today,* May 1972.

Lieberman, M. A., Yalom, I. D., and Miles, M. *Encounter groups: First facts.* New York: Basic Books, 1973.

Lindzey, G., Hall, C., and Thompson. R. *Psychology.* New York: Worth, 1975.

Lipinski, E., and Lipinski, B. G. Motivational factors in psychedelic drug use by male college students. In R. E. Hormon and A. M. Fox (Eds.), *Drug awareness.* New York: Avon, 1970.

Lipsey, M. W., and Brayfield, A. H. *The profession of psychology.* Howewood, Ill.: Learning Systems Company, 1975.

Lipsitt, L. P. Babies: They're a lot smarter than they look. *Psychology Today,* December 1971.

Lloyd, R. W., and Salzberg, H. C. Controlled social drinking: An alternative to abstinence as a treatment goal for some alcohol abusers. *Psychological Bulletin,* 1975, **82,** 815–842.

Loftus, E. F. Eyewitness testimony: Does the malleable human memory interfere with legal justice? *Social Action and the Law Newsletter,* April 1975.

Loftus, E. F. Reconstructing memory: The incredible eyewitness. *Psychology Today,* December 1974.

Lorayne, H., and Lucas, J. *The memory book.* New York: Ballantine, 1974.

Lorenz, K. The companion in the bird's world. *Auk,* 1937, **54,** 245–273.

Lorenz, K. *On aggression.* New York: Harcourt, Brace, and World, 1966.

Louria, D. *Nightmare drugs.* New York: Pocket Books, 1966.

Luborsky, L., Chandler, M., Auerbach, A. H., Cohen, J., and Bachrach, H. M. Factors influencing the outcome of psychotherapy: A review of quantitative research. *Psychological Bulletin,* 1971, **75,** 145–185.

Luce, G. G., and Peper, E. Mind over body, mind over mind. *New York Times Magazine,* September 12, 1971.

Luce, G. G., and Segal, J. What time is it? The body clock knows. *New York Times Magazine,* April 3, 1966.

Ludwig, A. M. Altered states of consciousness. *Archives of General Psychiatry,* 1966, **15,** 225–233.

Luria, A. R. *The mind of a mnemonist.* New York: Basic Books, 1968.

Maas, H., and Kuypers, J. *From thirty to seventy: A forty-year longitudinal study of adult life styles and personality.* San Francisco: Jossey-Bass, 1974.

Maccoby, E. E., and Jacklin, C. N. *The psychology of sex differences.* Stanford, Calif.: Stanford University Press, 1974.

Maher, B. A. *Principles of psychopathology.* New York: McGraw-Hill, 1966.

Mandell, A. J. Pro football fumbles the drug scandal. *Psychology Today,* June 1975.

Mandler, G. Emotion. In R. Brown, et al.,*New directions in psychology,* Vol. 1 New York: Holt, Rinehart and Winston, 1962.

Mann, L. Perceptual training: Misdirections and redirections. *American Journal of Orthopsychiatry,* 1970, **40,** 30–38.

Mann, L., and Janis, I. L. A follow-up study on the long-term effects of emotional role playing. *Journal of Personality and Social Psychology,* 1968, **8,** 339–342.

Mansson, H. H. The relation of dissonance reduction to cognitive, perceptual, consummatory, and learning measures of thirst. In P. G. Zimbardo (Ed.), *The cognitive control of motivation.* Glenview, Ill.: Scott, Foresman, 1968.

Maris, R. W. *Forces in urban suicide.* Homewood, Ill.: Dorsey, 1969.

Markle, G. E., and Nam, C. B. Sex predetermination: Its impact on fertility. *Social Biology,* 1971, **18,** 73–78.

Marks, L. E. Synesthesia: The lucky people with mixed-up senses. *Psychology Today.* June 1975.

Marler, P. Communication in monkeys and apes. In I. DeVore (Ed.), *Primate behavior: Field studies of monkeys and apes.* New York: Holt, Rinehart and Winston, 1965.

Marshall, D. S. Too much in Mangaia. *Psychology Today,* February 1971.

Marshall, J. The evidence: Do we see and hear what is? Or do our senses lie? *Psychology Today,* February 1969.

Maslow, A. H. A theory of human motivation. *Psychological Review,* 1943, **50,** 370–396.

Maslow, A. H. *Toward a psychology of being.* New York: Van Nostrand Reinhold, 1962.

Mastellone, M. Aversion therapy: Another use for the old rubber band. *Journal of Behaviour Therapy and Experimental Psychiatry,* 1974, **5,** 311.

Maugh, T. H. Marijuana: Does it damage the brain? *Science,* August 30, 1974.

Maupin, E. W. Individual differences in response to a Zen meditation exercise. *Journal of Consulting Psychology,* 1965, **29,** 139–145.

May, R. Contribution to: The therapeutic process in cross-cultural perspective: A symposium. *American Journal of Psychiatry,* 1968, **124,** 1179–1183.

Mayer, J., and Harris, T. G. Affluence: The fifth horseman of the apocalypse. *Psychology Today,* January 1970.

McBain, W. N., Fox, W., Kimura, S., Nakanishi, M., and Tirado, J. Quasi-sensory communication: An investigation using semantic matching and accentuated effect. *Journal of Personality and Social Psychology,* 1970, **14,** 281–291.

McCall, R. B. *Intelligence and heredity.* Homewood, Ill.: Learning Systems Company, 1975.

McClelland, D. C. Risk taking in children with high and low need for achievement. In J. W. Atkinson (Ed.), *Motives in fantasy, action, and society.* Princeton, N.J.: Van Nostrand, 1958.

McClelland, D. C. Testing for competence rather than for "intelligence." *American Psychologist,* 1973, **28,** 1–14.

McClelland, D. C. Toward a theory of motive acquisition. *American Psychologist,* 1965, **20,** 321–333.

McClelland, D. C., and Atkinson, J. W. The effect of different intensities of the hunger drive on perception. *Journal of Psychology,* 1948, **25,** 205–222.

McClelland, D. C., Atkinson, J. W., Clark, R. A., and Lowell, E. L. *The achievement motive.* New York: Appleton-Century-Crofts, 1953.

McConnell, J. V. Memory transfer through cannibalism in planarians. *Journal of Neuropsychiatry,* 1962, **3,** 542–548.

McDavid, J. W., and Harari, H. Stereotyping of names and popularity in grade-school children. *Child Development,* 1966, **37,** 453–460.

McGhie, A., and Chapman, J. S. Disorders of attention and perception in early schizophrenia. *British Journal of Medical Psychiatry,* 1961, **34,** 103–116.

McGinniss, J. *The selling of the president, 1968.* New York: Simon and Schuster, 1969.

McGregor, D. *The human side of enterprise.* New York: McGraw-Hill, 1960.

McGuire, W. J. A syllogistic analysis of cognitive relationships. In C. I. Hovland and M. J. Rosenberg (Eds.), *Attitude organization and change.* New Haven, Conn.: Yale University Press, 1960.

McKenna, W., and Kessler, S. J. Experimental design as a source of sex bias in social psychology. Paper presented at meeting of the American Psychological Association, New Orleans, September 1974.

McKinney, J. P., and Keele, T. Effects of increased mothering on the behavior of severely retarded boys. *American Journal of Mental Deficiency,* 1963, **67,** 556–562.

McMurray, G. A. Experimental study of a case of insensitivity to pain. *Archives of Neurological Psychiatry,* 1950, **64,** 650–667.

McNeil, E. B. *Neuroses and personality disorders.* Englewood Cliffs, N.J.: Prentice-Hall, 1970.

McNeil, E. B., and Blum, G. S. Handwriting and psychosexual dimensions of personality. *Journal of Projective Techniques,* 1952, **16,** 476–484.

Mead, M. *Culture and commitment: A study of the generation gap.* Garden City, N.Y.: Natural History Press, Doubleday, 1970.

Mead, M. *Male and female.* New York: Morrow, 1949.

Mednick, S. A. The associative basis of the creative process. *Psychological Review,* 1962, **69,** 220–232.

Meissner, W. W. Family dynamics and psychosomatic process. *Family Process,* 1966, **5,** 142–161.

Melzack, R. How acupuncture works. *Psychology Today,* June 1973.

Mendel, W. M., and Rapport, S. Determinants of the decision for psychiatric hospitalization. Paper presented at the annual meeting of the American Psychiatric Association, Boston, May 1968.

Messenger, J. C. The lack of the Irish. *Psychology Today,* February 1971.

Miale, F. R., and Selzer, M. *The Nuremberg mind: The psychology of the Nazi leaders.* New York: Quadrangle, 1976.

Milgram, S. Behavioral study of obedience. *Journal of Abnormal and Social Psychology,* 1963, **67,** 371–378.

Milgram, S. The experience of living in cities. *Science,* 1970, **167,** 1461–1468.

Milgram, S. Liberating effects of group pressure. *Journal of Personality and Social Psychology,* 1965, **1,** 127–134.

Milgram, S. *Obedience to authority: An experimental view.* New York: Harper & Row, 1974.

Miller, G. A. The magical number seven, plus or minus two: Some limits on our capacity for processing information. *Psychological Review,* 1956, **63,** 81–97.

Miller, G. A. On turning psychology over to the unwashed. *Psychology Today,* December 1969.

Miller, G. A. *Psychology: The science of mental life.* New York: Harper & Row, 1962.

Miller, G. A., Galanter, E., and Pribram, K. *Plans and the structure of behavior.* New York: Holt, Rinehart and Winston, 1960.

Miller, M. M., Guilleminault, C., Orem, J., Zarcone, V. P., and Dement, W. C. Sleeplessness, sleep attacks, and things that go wrong in the night. *Psychology Today,* December 1975.

Miller, N. E., and Banuazizi, A. Instrumental learning by curarized rats of a specific visceral response, intestinal or cardiac. *Journal of Comparative and Physiological Psychology,* 1968, **65,** 1–7.

Miller, P. R. The Chicago demonstrators: A study in identity. *Bulletin of the Atomic Scientists,* 1969, **25,** 3–6.

Milner, B. Amnesia following operation on the temporal lobes. In C. W. M. Whitty and O. L. Zangwill (Eds.), *Amnesia.* London: Butterworth, 1966.

Milner, P. M. *Physiological psychology.* New York: Holt, Rinehart and Winston, 1970.

Minard, R. D. Race relations in the Pocahontas coal field. *Journal of Social Issues,* 1952, **8,** 29–44.

Mischel, W. *Introduction to personality.* (2nd ed.) New York: Holt, Rinehart and Winston, 1976.

Mischel, W. *Personality and assessment.* New York: Holt, Rinehart and Winston, 1968.

Mischel, W. A social-learning view of sex differences in behavior. In E. E. Maccoby (Ed.), *The development of sex differences.* Stanford, Calif.: Stanford University Press, 1966.

Money, J., and Ehrhardt, A. A. *Man & woman, boy & girl.* Baltimore: Johns Hopkins University Press, 1972.

Montagu, A. *Touching: The human significance of the skin.* New York: Harper & Row, 1971.

Moore, B. S., Underwood, B., and Rosenhan, D. L. Affect and altruism. *Developmental Psychology,* 1973, **8,** 99–104.

Morgan, A. H. The heritability of hypnotic susceptibility in twins. *Journal of Abnormal Psychology,* 1973, **82,** 55–61.

Morishima, A. His spirit raises the ante for retardates. *Psychology Today,* June 1975.

Morris, D. *The naked ape.* New York: McGraw-Hill, 1967.

Morse, W., and Skinner, B. F. A second type of "superstition" in the pigeon. *American Journal of Psychology,* 1957, **70,** 308–311.

Morse, W. C., and Weiss, R. S. The function and meaning of work and the job. In D. G. Zytowski (Ed.), *Vocational behavior.* New York: Holt, Rinehart and Winston, 1968.

Moss, T., and Gengerelli, J. A. Telepathy and emotional stimuli: A controlled experiment. *Journal of Abnormal Psychology,* 1967, **72,** 341–348.

Mowrer, O. H. Hearing and speaking: An analysis of language learning. *Journal of Speech and Hearing Disorders,* 1958, **23,** 143–151.

Murphy, G. *Challenge of psychical research.* New York: Harper & Row, 1961.

Murray, H. A. *Explorations in personality.* New York: Oxford University Press, 1938.

Mussen, P., Conger, J. J., and Kagan, J. *Child development and personality.* (4th ed.) New York: Harper & Row, 1974.

Mussen, P. H., and Jones, M. C. Self-conceptions, motivations, and interpersonal attitudes of late and early maturing boys. *Child Development,* 1957, **28,** 243–256.

Nabokov, P. The peyote road. *New York Times Magazine,* March 9, 1969.

Naranjo, C., and Ornstein, R. E. *On the psychology of meditation.* New York: Viking, 1971.

Neaman, J. S. *Suggestion of the devil: The origins of madness.* Garden City, N.Y.: Doubleday, 1975.

Neill, A. S. *Summerhill: A radical approach to child rearing.* New York: Hart, 1960.

Newcomb, T. M. *The acquaintance process.* New York: Holt, Rinehart and Winston, 1961.

Newcomb, T. M. Attitude development as a function of reference groups: The Bennington study. In H. Proshansky and B. Seidenberg (Eds.), *Basic studies in social psychology.* New York: Holt, Rinehart and Winston, 1965.

Newcomb, T. M., Koenig, K. E., Flacks, R., and Warwick, D. P. *Persistence and change: Bennington College and its students after twenty-five years.* New York: Wiley, 1967.

Newman, E. *Strictly speaking.* Indianapolis: Bobbs-Merrill, 1974.

Newsweek. Coping with depression. *Newsweek,* January 8, 1973.

Newton, N. Childbirth and culture. *Psychology Today,* November 1970.

Nietzke, A. The American obsession with fun. *Saturday Review,* August 26, 1972.

Nisbett, R. E. Birth order and participation in dangerous sports. *Journal of Personality and Social Psychology,* 1968, **8,** 351–353.

Norton, A. J., and Glick, P. C. Marital instability: Past, present, and future. *Journal of Social Issues,* 1976, **32** (Figure 1), 5–20.

Olds, J. Self-stimulation of the brain. *Science,* 1958, **127,** 315–324.

Orlansky, H. Infant care and personality. *Psychological Bulletin,* 1949, **46,** 1–48.

Ornstein, R. E. *The psychology of consciousness.* San Francisco: W. H. Freeman, 1972.

Osgood, C. E., Suci, G. J., and Tannenbaum, P. H. *The measurement of meaning.* Urbana: University of Illinois Press, 1957.

Page, M. Social psychology of a classical conditioning of attitudes experiment. *Journal of Personality and Social Psychology,* 1969, **11,** 177–186.

Paivio, A. *Imagery and verbal processes.* New York: Holt, Rinehart and Winston, 1971.

Parke, R., and O'Leary, S. Father-mother-infant interaction in the newborn period: Some findings, some observations, some unresolved issues. In K. Riegel and J. Meacham (Eds.), *The developing individual in a changing world,* Vol. II, *Social and environmental issues.* The Hague: Mouton, 1975.

Parloff, M. B. Analytic group psychotherapy. In J. Marmor (Ed.), *Modern psychoanalysis.* New York: Basic Books, 1968.

Peck, E. *The baby trap.* New York: Pinnacle Books, 1972.

Penfield, W. The interpretive cortex. *Science,* 1959, **129,** 1719–1725.

Peplau, L. A., Rubin, Z., and Hill, C. T. Sexual intimacy in dating relationships, *Journal of Social Issues,* 1977, in press.

Perls, F. S. *Gestalt therapy verbatim.* Moab, Utah: Real People Press, 1969.

Peterson, L. R., and Peterson, M. J. Short-term retention of individual items. *Journal of Experimental Psychology,* 1959, **58,** 193–198.

Pettigrew, T. F. *A profile of the Negro American.* Princeton, N.J.: D. Van Nostrand, 1964.

Pettigrew, T. F. *Racially separate or together?* New York: McGraw-Hill, 1971.

Pettigrew, T. F. Regional differences in anti-Negro prejudice. *Journal of Abnormal and Social Psychology,* 1959, **59,** 28–36.

Piaget, J. *The construction of reality in the child.* New York: Basic Books, 1954.

Piaget, J. *The moral judgment of the child.* Glencoe, Ill.: Free Press, 1948. (Originally published in 1932.)

Piaget, J. *The origins of intelligence in children.* New York: International Universities Press, 1952.

Piaget, J. *The psychology of intelligence.* New York: Harcourt, 1950.

Pierrel, R., and Sherman, J. G. Train your pet the Barnabus way. *Brown Alumni Monthly,* February 1963.

Pines, M. *The brain changers: Scientists and the new mind control* New York: Harcourt Brace Jovanovich, 1973.

Pines, M. Head head start. *New York Times Magazine,* October 26, 1975.

Pines, M. Speak, memory: The riddle of recall and forgetfullness. *Saturday Review,* August 9, 1975.

Pleck, J. H. Men's roles in the family: A new look. Paper delivered at the World Family Sociology Conference, Merrill-Palmer Institute, Detroit, November 1975.

Pleck, J. H. My sex role—and ours. *Win,* April 11, 1974.

Pleck, J. H. The psychology of sex roles: Current data and some implications. Paper presented at Aspen Workshop on Women and Men, August 1975.

Pleck, J. H., and Sawyer, J. (Eds.). *Men and masculinity.* Englewood Cliffs, N.J.: Prentice-Hall, 1974.

Plumb, J. H. The great change in children. *Intellectual Digest,* April 1972.

Postman, N., and Weingartner, C. *Teaching as a subversive activity.* New York: Delacorte, 1969.

Premack, A. J., and Premack, D. Teaching language to an ape. *Scientific American,* November 1972.

Prescott, S., and Foster, K. Why researchers don't study women. Paper presented at meeting of the American Psychological Association, New Orleans, September 1974.

Pressey, S. L. Concerning the nature and nurture of genius. *Scientific Monthly,* September 1955.

Priest, R. F., and Sawyer, J. Proximity and peership: Bases of balance in interpersonal attraction. *American Journal of Sociology,* 1967, **72,** 633–649.

Radloff, L. Sex differences in depression: The effects of occupation and marital status. *Sex Roles,* 1975, **1,** 249–266.

Regestein, Q. R., and Howe, L. P. A psychotherapy group for skid-row alcoholics. *Massachusetts Journal of Mental Health,* 1972, **2,** 4–24.

Remmers, H. H., and Radler, D. H. Teenage attitudes. *Scientific American,* June 1958.

Restak, R. Genetic counseling for defective parents—the danger of knowing too much. *Psychology Today,* September 1975.

Restak, R. José Delgado: Exploring inner space. *Saturday Review,* August 9, 1975.

Reston, J. Proxmire on love. *New York Times,* March 14, 1975.

Revusky, S. The role of interference in association over a delay. In W. K. Honig and P. H. R. James (Eds.), *Animal memory.* New York: Academic Press, 1971.

Rheingold, H. L., Gewirtz, J. L., and Ross, H. W. Social conditioning of vocalizations in the infant. *Journal of Comparative and Physiological Psychology,* 1959, **52,** 68–73.

Rhine, J. B. Evidence of precognition in the covariance of salience ratios. *Journal of Parapsychology,* 1942, **6,** 111–143.

Richter, C. P. The self-selection of diets. In *Essays in Biology.* Berkeley: University of California Press, 1943.

Robinson, H. B., and Robinson, N. H. Mental retardation. In P. H. Mussen (Ed.), *Carmichael's manual of child psychology,* Vol. II. (3rd ed.) New York: Wiley, 1970.

Rock, I., and Kaufman, L. The moon illusion. *Science,* 1962, **136,** 1023–1031.

Rogers, C. R. *Client-centered therapy.* Boston: Houghton Mifflin, 1951.

Rogers, C. R., and Skinner, B. F. Some issues concerning the control of human behavior: A symposium. *Science,* 1956, **124,** 1057–1066.

Rogers, J. M. Drug abuse: Just what the doctor ordered. *Psychology Today,* September 1971.

The Roper Organization. *The Virginia Slims American opinion poll.* (Vol. 3) New York: The Roper Organization, 1974.

Rorschach, H. *Psychodiagnostics: A diagnostic test based on perception.* New York: Grune & Stratton, 1942.

Rorvik, D. M. The wave of the future: Brain waves. *Look,* October 6, 1970.

Rosenblatt, P. Communication in the practice of love magic. *Social Forces,* 1971, **49,** 482–487.

Rosenblatt, P. C., and Cunningham, M. R. Sex differences in cross-cultural perspective. In J. Archer and B. B. Lloyd (Eds.), *Explorations in sex differences.* Burgess Hill, Sussex: Harvester Press, in press.

Rosenfeld, A. If Oedipus' parents had only known. *Saturday Review,* September 7, 1974.

Rosenhan, D. L. On being sane in insane places. *Science,* 1973, **179,** 250–258.

Rosenthal, A. M. *Thirty-eight witnesses.* New York: McGraw-Hill, 1964.

Rosenthal, R. *Experimenter effects in behavioral research.* New York: Appleton-Century-Crofts, 1966.

Rosenthal, R., and Jacobson, L. *Pygmalion in the classroom: Teacher expectation and pupils' intellectual development.* New York: Holt, Rinehart and Winston, 1968.

Rosenzweig, M. R., Bennett, E. L., and Diamond, M. C. Brain changes in response to experience. *Scientific American,* February 1972.

Rosow, I. And then we were old. *Trans-action,* January-February, 1965.

Ross, H. M. Orthomolecular psychiatry: Vitamin pills for schizophrenics. *Psychology Today,* November 1974.

Ross, M. Suicide among physicians. *Psychiatry in Medicine,* 1971, **2,** 189–197.

Rotter, J. B. Generalized expectancies for internal and external control of reinforcements. *Psychological Monographs,* 1966, Vol. 80, No. 1, Whole No. 609.

Rowe, F. B., Brooks, S., and Watson, B. Communication through gestures. *American Annals of the Deaf,* 1960, **105,** 232–237.

Rubin, Z. The birth order of birth-order researchers. *Developmental Psychology,* 1970, **3,** 269–270.

Rubin, Z. *Liking and loving: An invitation to social psychology.* New York: Holt, Rinehart and Winston, 1973.

Rubin, Z. Measurement of romantic love. *Journal of Personality and Social Psychology,* 1970, **16,** 265–273.

Rubin, Z., Peplau, L. A., and Hill, C. T. *Becoming intimate: The development of male-female relationships.* In preparation.

Rudhyar, D. *The practice of astrology.* Baltimore: Penguin, 1968.

Russell, W., and Nathan, P. Traumatic amnesia. *Brain,* 1964, **69,** 280.

Sacerdote, P. Hypnosis in cancer patients. *American Journal of Clinical Hypnosis,* 1966, **9,** 100–108.

Sachs, B. D., and Marsan, E. Male rats prefer sex to food after 6 days of food deprivation. *Psychonomic Science,* 1972, **28,** 47–49.

Sage, W. ESP and the psychology establishment. *Human Behavior,* September-October 1972.

Sanford, F. H. *Psychology* (2nd ed.). Belmont, Calif.: Wadsworth, 1965.

Sarnoff, C. A. *Medical aspects of flying motivation.* Randolph Air Force Base, Texas: Air University School of Aviation Motivation, 1957.

Scanzoni, L., and Scanzoni, J. *Men, women, and change: A sociology of marriage and the family.* New York: McGraw-Hill, 1976.

Scarf, M. The anatomy of fear. *New York Times Magazine,* June 12, 1974.

Scarr-Salapatek, S., and Weinberg, R. A. The war over race and IQ: When black children grow up in white homes. *Psychology Today,* December 1975.

Schachter, S. Birth order, eminence, and higher education. *American Sociological Review,* 1963, **28,** 757–767.

Schachter, S. The interaction of cognitive and physiological determinants of emotional state. In L. Berkowitz (Ed.), *Advances in experimental social psychology,* Vol. 1. New York: Academic Press, 1964.

Schachter, S. *The psychology of affiliation.* Stanford, Calif.: Stanford University Press, 1959.

Schachter, S. Some extraordinary facts about obese humans and rats. *American Psychologist,* 1971, **26,** 129–144.

Schachter, S., Goldman, R., and Gordon, A. Effects of fear, food deprivation, and obesity on eating. *Journal of Personality and Social Psychology,* 1968, **10,** 91–97.

Schachter, S., and Singer, J. Cognitive, social, and physiological determinants of emotional state. *Psychological Review,* 1962, **69,** 379–399.

Scheerer, M. Problem-solving. *Scientific American,* April 1963.

Scheff, T. J. (Ed.). *Labeling madness.* Englewood Cliffs, N.J.: Prentice-Hall, 1975.

Schein, E. H. Reaction patterns to severe, chronic stress in American Army prisoners of war of the Chinese. *Journal of Social Issues,* 1957, **13,** 21–30.

Schmeck, H. M. Depression is called more common in women. *New York Times,* October 24, 1975.

Schmeidler, G. R. (Ed.). *Extrasensory perception.* New York: Atherton, 1969.

Schmeidler, G. R., and McConnell, R. A. *ESP and personality patterns.* New Haven, Conn.: Yale University Press, 1958.

Schneider, A. M., and Tarshis, B. *An introduction to physiological psychology.* New York: Random House, 1975.

Schultz, D. P. The human subject in psychological research. *Psychological Bulletin,* 1969, **72,** 214–228.

Schultz, J. H., and Luthe, W. *Autogenic training.* New York: Grune & Stratton, 1959.

Schuman, H. Personal origins of "Two sources of anti-war sentiment in America." In M. P. Golden (Ed.), *The research experience.* Itasca, Ill.: Peacock, 1976.

Schwartz, G. S., Davidson, R. J., and Maer, F. Right hemisphere lateralization and emotion in the human brain: Interactions with cognition. *Science,* 1975, **190,** 286–288.

Scott, J. F. Marriage is not a personal matter. *New York Times Magazine,* October 30, 1966.

Scott, J. P. A time to learn. *Psychology Today,* March 1969.

Seeman, M. Alienation, membership and political knowledge: A comparative study. *Public Opinion Quarterly,* 1966, **30,** 359–367.

Seeman, M., and Evans, J. W. Alienation and learning in a hospital setting. *American Sociological Review,* 1962, **27,** 772–783.

Segal, M. W. Alphabet and attraction: An unobtrusive measure of the effect of propinquity in a field setting. *Journal of Personality and Social Psychology,* 1974, **30,** 654–657.

Seiden, R. H. Campus tragedy: A study of student suicide. *Journal of Abnormal Psychology,* 1966, **71,** 389–399.

Seiden, R. H. We're driving young blacks to suicide. *Psychology Today,* August 1970.

Seidenberg, R. Drug advertising and perception of mental illness. *Mental Hygiene,* 1971, **55,** 21–31.

Seifert, K. Some problems of men in child care center work. *Child Welfare,* 1973, **102,** 167–171.

Seligman, M. E. P. *Helplessness: On depression, development, and death.* San Francisco: W. H. Freeman, 1975.

Seligman, M. E. P., and Hager, J. L. Biological boundaries of learning: The sauce-Béarnaise syndrome. *Psychology Today,* August 1972.

Selye, H. *The stress of life.* New York: McGraw-Hill, 1956.

Sheatsley, P. B., and Feldman, J. J. The assassination of President Kennedy: A preliminary report on public attitudes and behavior. *Public Opinion Quarterly,* 1964, **28,** 189–215.

Sheehy, G. *Passages: Predictable crises of adult life.* New York: Dutton, 1976.

Sheldon, W. H. *Atlas of man: A guide for somatotyping the adult male at all ages.* New York: Harper & Row, 1954.

Sheldon, W. H. *Varieties of human physique.* New York: Harper & Row, 1940.

Shelton, A. J. Igbo child-rearing, eldership, and dependence: A comparison of two cultures. In R. A. Kalish (Ed.), *Dependencies of old people.* In *Occasional papers in gerontology,* Vol. 6. Ann Arbor and Detroit: Institute of Gerontology, University of Michigan and Wayne State University, 1969.

Shepard, M., and Lee, M. *Marathon 16.* New York: Putnam's, 1970.

Shomer, R. W., and Centers, R. Differences in attitudinal responses under conditions of implicitly manipulated group salience. *Journal of Personality and Social Psychology,* 1970, **15,** 125–132.

Siegler, M., and Osmond, H. Mental illness is not romantic. *Psychology Today,* November 1974.

Sieveking, N. A., and Chappell, J. E. Reactions to the names "Counseling Center" and "Psychological Center." *Journal of Consulting and Clinical Psychology,* 1970, **34,** 124–127.

Sifneos, P. E. *Short-term psychotherapy and emotional crisis.* Cambridge, Mass.: Harvard University Press, 1972.

Siipola, E. M. A study of some effects of preparatory set. *Psychological Monographs,* 1935, **46** (210).

Silberman, C. E. *Crisis in the classroom.* New York: Random House, 1970.

Simonson, N. R., and Bahr, S. Self-disclosure by the professional and paraprofessional therapist. *Journal of Consulting and Clinical Psychology,* 1974, **42,** 359–363.

Simonton, D. K., Sociocultural context of individual creativity: A trans-historical time-series analysis. *Journal of Personality and Social Psychology,* in press.

Singer, J. L. The importance of daydreaming. *Psychology Today,* April 1968.

Sipes, R. G. War, sports, and aggression: An empirical test of two rival theories. *American Anthropologist,* 1973, **75,** 64–86.

Skeels, H. M. Adult status of children with contrasting early life experiences: A follow-up study. *Monographs of the Society for Research in Child Development,* 1966, **31** (3).

Skinner, B. F. *Science and human behavior.* New York: Macmillan, 1953.

Skinner, B. F. *Verbal behavior.* New York: Appleton-Century-Crofts, 1957.

Skinner, B. F. *Walden two.* New York: Macmillan, 1948.

Skipper, J. K., Jr., and McCaghy, C. H. Strip-teasers: The anatomy and career contingencies of a deviant occupation. *Social Problems,* 1970, **17,** 391–405.

Skodak, M., and Skeels, H. M. A final follow-up of one hundred adopted children. *Journal of Genetic Psychology,* 1949, **75,** 3–19.

Sloane, R. B., Staples, F. R., Cristol, A. H., Yorkston, N. J., and Whipple, K. *Psychotherapy versus behavior therapy.* Cambridge, Mass.: Harvard University Press, 1975.

Slobin, D. I. Children and language: They learn the same way all around the world. *Psychology Today,* July 1972.

Smart, R. G., and Fejer, D. Drug use among adolescents and their parents: Closing the generation gap in mood modification. *Journal of Abnormal Psychology,* 1972, **79,** 153–160.

Smith, A. The benefits of boredom. *Psychology Today,* April 1976.

Smith, B. M. The polygraph. *Scientific American,* January 1967.

Smith, J. C. Meditation as psychotherapy: A review of the literature. *Psychological Bulletin,* 1975, **82,** 558–564.

Snyder, S. H. The true speed trip: Schizophrenia. *Psychology Today,* January 1972.

Soal, S. G., and Bateman, F. *Modern experiments in telepathy.* New Haven, Conn.: Yale University Press, 1954.

Sobell, M. B., and Sobell, L. C. Alcoholics treated by individualized behavior therapy: One year treatment outcome. *Behaviour Research and Therapy,* 1973, **11,** 599–618.

Social Action and the Law Newsletter. Technical notes for lineup checklist. May 1975.

Solomon, F., and Fishman, J. R. Youth and peace: A psychosocial study of student peace demonstrators in Washington, D.C. *Journal of Social Issues,* 1964, **20** (Figure 4), 54–73.

Spearman, C. "General intelligence," objectively determined and measured. *American Journal of Psychology,* 1904, **15,** 201–293.

Spelt, D. K. The conditioning of the human fetus in utero. *Journal of Experimental Psychology,* 1948, **38,** 338–346.

Spitz, R. A. Anaclitic depression. *Psychoanalytic Study of the Child,* 1946, **1,** 313–342.

Spreitzer, E., and Riley, L. Factors associated with singlehood. *Journal of Marriage and the Family,* 1974, **36,** 533–542.

Srole, L., Langer, T. S., Michael, S. T., Opler, M. K., and Rennie, T. A. C. *Mental health in the metropolis: The Midtown Manhattan study.* New York: McGraw-Hill, 1962.

Staats, A. W., and Staats, C. K. Attitudes established by classical conditioning. *Journal of Abnormal and Social Psychology,* 1958, **57,** 37–40.

Stein, D. D., Hardyck, J. A., and Smith, M. B. Race and belief: An open and shut case. *Journal of Personality and Social Psychology,* 1965, **1,** 281–289.

Steinem, G. The myth of the masculine mystique. *International Education,* 1972, **1,** 30–35.

Stock, R. W. Will the baby be normal? *New York Times Magazine,* March 23, 1969.

Stone, C. P. Wildness and savageness in rats of different strains. In K. Lashley (Ed.), *Studies in the dynamics of behavior.* Chicago: University of Chicago Press, 1932.

Stone, S. Psychiatry through the ages. *Journal of Abnormal and Social Psychology,* 1937, **32,** 131–160.

Stone, W. F. *The psychology of politics.* New York: Free Press, 1974.

Stroebel, C. F. Psychophysiological pharmacology. In N. S. Greenfield and R. A. Sternbach (Eds.), *Handbook of Psychophysiology.* New York: Holt, Rinehart and Winston, 1972.

Stromeyer, C. F. Eidetikers. *Psychology Today,* November 1970.

Stuart, R. B. Prostitution as treatment of marital discord. Paper presented at meeting of American Psychological Association, San Francisco, 1968.

Stunkard, A., and Koch, C. The interpretation of gastric motility: Apparent bias in the reports of hunger by obese persons. *Archives of General Psychiatry,* 1964, **11,** 74–82.

Sudnow, D. Dead on arrival. *Trans-action,* November 1967.

Suedfeld, P. The benefits of boredom: Sensory deprivation reconsidered. *American Scientist,* January–February 1975.

Sullivan, H. S. *The interpersonal theory of psychiatry.* New York: Norton, 1953.

Suomi, S. J., Harlow, H. F., and McKinney, W. T. Monkey psychiatrists. *American Journal of Psychiatry,* 1972, **128,** 927–932.

Sutherland, E. *Principles of criminology.* Philadelphia: Lippincott, 1966.

Szasz, T. S. The ethics of addiction. *Harper's,* April 1972.

Szasz, T. S. *Ideology and insanity.* Garden City, N.Y.: Anchor Books, 1970.

Tanner, J. M. Sequence, tempo, and individual variation in growth and development of boys and girls aged twelve to sixteen. In J. Kagan and R. Coles (Ed.), *Twelve to sixteen: Early adolescence.* New York: Norton, 1972.

Taub, J. M. Dream recall and content following various durations of sleep. *Psychonomic Science,* 1970, **16,** 204–205.

Taub, J. M., and Burger, R. J. Extended sleep and performance: The Rip Van Winkle effect. *Psychonomic Science,* 1969, **16,** 204–205.

Taylor, D. W., Berry, P. C., and Block, C. H. Group participation, brainstorming, and creative thinking. *Administrative Science Quarterly,* 1958, **3,** 23–47.

Taylor, S. E., and Langer, E. J. Pregnancy: A social stigma? *Sex Roles,* in press.

Taylor, S. E., and Langer, E. J. Pregnancy as a social stimulus: Being pregnant in America. Unpublished paper, Department of Psychology and Social Relations, Harvard University, 1971.

Teitelbaum, P. Motivation and control of food intake. In C. F. Code (Ed.), *Handbook of physiology: Alimentary canal,* Vol. 1. Washington, D.C.: American Physiological Society, 1967.

Teitelbaum, P. Sensory control of hypothalamic hyperphagia. *Journal of Comparative and Physiological Psychology,* 1955, **48,** 156–163.

Terman, L. M. The discovery and encouragement of exceptional talent. *American Psychologist,* 1954, **9,** 221–230.

Terman, L. M., and Merrill, M. A. *Measuring intelligence: A guide to the administration of the new revised Stanford-Binet tests of intelligence.* Boston: Houghton-Mifflin, 1937.

Thigpen, C. H., and Cleckley, H. M. *The three faces of Eve.* New York: McGraw-Hill, 1957.

Thomas, A., Chess, S., and Birch, H. G. The origin of personality. *Scientific American,* August 1970.

Thorndike, E. L. Animal intelligence. *Psychological Monographs,* 1898, Vol. 1, No. 8.

Thurstone, L. L. Primary mental abilities. *Psychometric Monographs,* No. 1. Chicago: University of Chicago Press, 1938.

Time. Male and female: Differences between them. *Time,* March 20, 1972.

Time. The occult: A substitute faith. *Time,* June 19, 1972.

Time. Skinner's utopia: Panacea or path to hell? *Time,* September 20, 1971.

Toman, W. Birth order rules all. *Psychology Today,* December 1970.

Tresemer, D. Fear of success: Popular but unproven. *Psychology Today,* March 1974.

Trotter, R. J. Sybil: The case history of a woman divided among herself. *Science News,* May 26, 1973.

Tuber, D. S., Hothersall, D., and Voith, V. L. Animal clinical psychology: A modest proposal. *American Psychologist,* 1974, **29,** 762–766.

Turnbull, C. M. Some observations regarding the experiences and behavior of the Ba Mbuti pygmies. *American Journal of Psychology,* 1961, **74,** 304–308.

Turner, W. Hearst acts are likened to those of victims of Chinese. *New York Times,* February 28, 1976.

Ullmann, L. P., and Krasner, L. *A psychological approach to abnormal behavior,* 2nd ed. Englewood Cliffs, N.J.: Prentice-Hall, 1975.

Underwood, B. J. Interference and forgetting. *Psychological Review,* 1957, **64,** 49–60.

Ungerleider, J. T., and Fisher, D. The problems of LSD-25 and emotional disorder. In R. E. Hormon and A. M. Fox (Eds.), *Drug awareness.* New York: Avon, 1970.

Valenstein, E. S. Psychosurgery. In G. Lindzey, C. Hall, and R. F. Thompson, *Psychology.* New York: Worth, 1975.

Valins, S. Cognitive effects of false heart-rate feedback. *Journal of Personality and Social Psychology,* 1966, **4,** 400–408.

Vinokur, A., and Selzer, M. L. Desirable versus undesirable life events: Their relationship to stress and mental distress. *Journal of Personality and Social Psychology,* 1975, **32,** 329–337.

Viscott, D. S. *The making of a psychiatrist.* New York: Arbor House, 1972.

Vonnegut, M. *The Eden express: A personal account of schizophrenia.* New York: Praeger, 1975.

Wahler, R. O. Infant social development: Some experimental analyses of an infant-mother interaction during the first year of life. *Journal of Experimental Child Psychology,* 1969, **7,** 101–113.

Wallace, R. K., and Benson, H. The physiology of meditation. *Scientific American,* May 1972.

Wallach, M. A., and Kogan, N. Creativity and intelligence in children's thinking. *Trans-action,* January–February, 1967.

Wallechinsky, D., and Wallace, I. *The People's Almanac.* Garden City, N.Y.: Doubleday, 1975.

Walster, E., and Festinger, L. The effectiveness of "overheard" persuasive communications. *Journal of Abnormal and Social Psychology,* 1962, **65,** 395–402.

Warner, L. A second survey of psychological opinion on ESP. *Journal of Parapsychology,* 1952, **16,** 284–295.

Warren, J. R. Birth order and social behavior. *Psychological Bulletin,* 1966, **65,** 38–49.

The Watergate hearings. New York: Viking Press, 1973.

Watkins, J. G. Psychotherapeutic methods. In B. B. Wolman (Ed.), *Handbook of clinical psychology.* New York: McGraw-Hill, 1965.

Watson, J. B., and Rayner, R. Conditioned emotional reactions. *Journal of Experimental Psychology,* 1920, **3,** 1–14.

Weatherley, D. Self-perceived rate of physical maturation and personality in late adolescence. *Child Development,* 1964, **35,** 1197–1210.

Webb, E. J., Campbell, D. T., Schwartz, R. D., and Sechrest, L. *Unobtrusive measures: Nonreactive research in the social sciences.* Chicago: Rand McNally, 1966.

Wechsler, D. Intelligence defined and undefined: A relativistic appraisal. *American Psychologist,* 1975, **30,** 135–139.

Wecter, D. *The age of the Great Depression: 1929–1941.* New York: Macmillan, 1948.

Weil, A. Parapsychology: Andrew Weil's search for the true Geller, Parts I and II. *Psychology Today,* June 1974 and July 1974.

Weiner, M. J., and Wright, F. E. Effects of undergoing arbitrary discrimination upon subsequent attitudes toward a minority group. *Journal of Applied Social Psychology,* 1973, **3,** 94–102.

Weiss, J. M. Psychological factors in stress and disease. *Scientific American,* June 1972.

Weiss, M. Unlearning, In J. H. Pleck and J. Sawyer (Eds.), *Men and masculinity.* Englewood Cliffs, N.J.: Prentice-Hall, 1974.

Weiss, R. S. The emotional impact of marital separation. *Journal of Social Issues,* 1976, **32,** 135–145.

Weiss, R. S. *Loneliness: The experience of emotional and social isolation.* Cambridge: M.I.T. Press, 1973.

Weiss, R. S. *Marital separation.* New York: Basic Books, 1975.

Weiss, R. S. The provisions of social relationships. In Z. Rubin (Ed.), *Doing unto others: Joining, molding, conforming, helping, loving.* Englewood Cliffs, N.J.: Prentice-Hall, 1974.

Weissman, M. M., and Paykel, E. S. Moving and depression in women. *Society,* July–August 1972.

Weitzman, L. J., Eifler, D., Hokada, E., and Ross, C. Sex role socialization in picture books for preschool children. *American Journal of Sociology,* 1972, **77,** 1125–1150.

White, R. W. *The abnormal personality.* (3rd ed.) New York: Ronald Press, 1964.

White, R. W. *The enterprise of living: A view of personal growth.* (2nd ed.) New York: Holt, Rinehart, and Winston, 1976.

White, R. W. Motivation reconsidered: The concept of competence. *Psychological Review,* 1959, **66,** 297–333.

White, W. A. *Outlines of psychiatry.* (13th ed.) New York: Nervous and Mental Disease Publishing Company, 1932.

Whiting, B. and Edwards, C. P. A cross-cultural analysis of sex differences in the behavior of children aged three through 11. *Journal of Social Psychology,* 1973, **91,** 171–188.

Whiting, J. W. M. *Becoming a Kwoma.* New Haven, Conn.: Yale University Press, 1941.

Whitten, P., and Kagan, J. Jensen's dangerous half-truth. *Psychology Today,* August 1969.

Whorf, B. L. *Language, thought, and reality.* New York: MIT Press–Wiley, 1956.

Wickler, W. *The sexual code.* Garden City, N.Y.: Anchor, 1973.

Williams, R. L. Scientific racism and IQ: The silent mugging of the black community. *Psychology Today,* May 1974.

Wing, R. An introduction to statistics. Mimeographed handout, Department of Social Relations, Harvard University, 1969.

Winograd, T. Artificial intelligence: When will computers understand people? *Psychology Today,* May 1974.

Winterbottom, M. R. The relation of childhood training in independence to achievement motivation. Doctoral dissertation, University of Michigan, 1953.

Wohlford, P. Initiation of cigarette smoking: Is it related to parental smoking behavior? *Journal of Consulting and Clinical Psychology,* 1970, **34,** 148–151.

Wold, C. I. Characteristics of 26,000 suicide prevention center patients. *Bulletin of Suicidology,* 1970, **6,** 24–28.

Wolfe, J. B. Effectiveness of token rewards for chimpanzees. *Comparative Psychological Monographs,* 1936, **12,** 50.

Wolpe, J., and Lazarus, A. A. *Behavior therapy techniques: A guide to the treatment of neurosis.* Elmsford, N.Y.: Pergamon, 1966.

Wooldridge, D. E. *The machinery of the brain.* New York: McGraw-Hill, 1963.

Worchel, S., and Arnold, S. E. The effects of censorship and attractiveness of the censor in attitude change. *Journal of Experimental Social Psychology,* 1973, **9,** 365–377.

Worchel, S., and Cooper J. *Understanding social psychology.* Homewood, Ill.: Dorsey, 1976.

Yates, A. J. *Behavior therapy.* New York: Wiley, 1970.

Young, W. C., Goy, R. W., and Phoenix, C. H. Hormones and sexual behavior. *Science,* 1964, **143,** 212–218.

Zajonc, R. B. *Animal social behavior.* Morristown, N.J.: General Learning Press, 1972.

Zajonc, R. B. Family configurations and intelligence. *Science,* 1976, **192,** 227–236.

Zeigarnik. B. Uber das Behalten von erlededigten und unerledigten Handlungen. *Psychologische Forschung,* 1927, **9,** 1–85.

Zeigler, H. P., and Leibowitz, H. Apparent visual size as a function of distance for children and adults. *American Journal of Psychology,* 1957, **70,** 106–109.

Zigler, E. Familial mental retardation: A continuing dilemma. *Science,* 1967, **155,** 292–298.

Zigler, E., and Phillips, L. Psychiatric diagnosis and symptomatology. *Journal of Abnormal and Social Psychology,* 1961, **63,** 69–75.

Zimbardo, P. G. *The cognitive control of motivation.* Glenview, Ill.: Scott, Foresman, 1968.

Zimbardo, P. G., Haney, C., Banks, W. C., and Jaffe, D. The psychology of imprisonment: Privation, power, and pathology. In Z. Rubin (Ed.), *Doing unto others: Joining, molding, conforming, helping, loving.* Englewood Cliffs, N.J: Prentice-Hall, 1974.

Zimbardo, P. G., Weisenberg, M., Firestone, I., and Levy, B. Communicator effectiveness in producing public conformity and private attitude change. *Journal of Personality,* 1965, **33,** 233–256.

Zweigenhaft, R. L. Birth order, approval-seeking. and membership in Congress. *Journal of Individual Psychology,* 1975, **31,** 205–210.

Zung, W. W., and Wilson, W. P. Time estimation during sleep. *Biological Psychiatry,* 1971, **3,** 159–164.

PHOTOGRAPHIC CREDITS

Part I *xviii* Mary Ellen Mark, Magnum

Chapter 1 *2* Kent Reno, Jeroboam *5* Jan Lukas, Rapho/Photo Researchers *11* National Library of Medicine *17* Jim Amos, Photo Researchers *21* Ray Ellis, Rapho/Photo Researchers *27* Abigail Heyman, Magnum *32* The Bettmann Archive, Inc. *34* Bill Strode, Black Star *35* Dennis Stock, Magnum

Chapter 2 *36* H. Van Kooten, Zoologisch Laboratorium, Utrecht *41* Courtesy of Department of Physiology/Anatomy, University of California, Berkeley *42* Dr. Edwin R. Lewis, University of California, Berkeley *46* The American Museum of Natural History *47* Courtesy of Department of Physiology/Anatomy, University of California, Berkeley, Photo by Audrey Ross, Berkeley *48* Courtesy of Department of Physiology/Anatomy, University of California, Berkeley, Photo by Audrey Ross, Berkeley *53* Ray Ellis, Rapho/Photo Researchers *54* David Powers, Jeroboam *58* ©1972 Scientific American

Part II *68* Josephus Daniels, Rapho/Photo Researchers

Chapter 3 *70* Nacio Jan Brown, BBM Associates *74* Ralph N. Haber, University of Rochester *78* William Vandivert & Scientific American, April, 1970 *80* Bill Stanton, Magnum *82* Burk Uzzle, Magnum *86* Historical Pictures Service, Inc. *93* Audrey Ross, Berkeley *94* Audrey Ross, Berkeley *98* Wide World Photos, Inc.

Chapter 4 *102* Suzanne Arms, Jeroboam *105* Mitchell Payne, Jeroboam *106* The Bettmann Archive, Inc. *107* Karsh, Woodfin Camp & Associates *108* Ken Heyman *110* Ken Heyman *114* The Bettmann Archive, Inc. *116* Stern, Black Star *119* Dr. Peter M. Witt, North Carolina Department of Mental Health *121* Nacio Jan Brown, BBM Associates *126* Andy Mercado, Jeroboam *128* Raghubir Singh, Black Star

Part III *130* Peeter Vilms, Jeroboam

Chapter 5 *132* Elizabeth Crews, Jeroboam *135* Nina Leen, Time/Life Picture Agency *137* Library of Congress *142* Hugh Rogers, Monkmeyer Press Photo Service *143* Ken Heyman *145* Eileen Christelow, Jeroboam *149* Sybil Shelton, Monkmeyer Press Photo Service *150* Yerkes Regional Primate Research Center, Atlanta *156* Sybil Shelton, Monkmeyer Press Photo Service *158* Don Hogan Charles, New York Times

Chapter 6 *162* Joanne Leonard *165* Ken Heyman *169* Bill Owens, BBM Associates *170* Elizabeth Crews, Jeroboam *172* The Bettman Archive, Inc. *176* Courtesy of Bernard W. Agranoff, University of Michigan, Photo by Paul Klinger *180* Van Bucher, Photo Researchers *182* Baron Wolman, Woodfin Camp & Associates *188* N. Y. Times

Chapter 7 *192* Roger Malloch, Magnum *198* Charles Harbutt, Magnum *200* Burk Uzzle, Magnum *205* Burt Glinn, Magnum *209* Gary Freedman, Jeroboam *211* Suzanne Arms, Jeroboam *213* University of California, Santa Barbara *217* Ruth Silverman, BBM Associates *219* Ilke Hartmann, Jeroboam

Chapter 8 *222* William Rosenthal, Jeroboam *226* The Psychological Corporation *230* Van Bucher, Photo Researchers *232* Courtesy of Robert Williams, Washington University *235* Charles Harbutt, Magnum *240* Suzanne Arms, Jeroboam *242* Ken Heyman *245* Hank Lebo, Jeroboam *250* David Powers, Jeroboam *252* Joshua Popenoe, from INSIDE SUMMERHILL, copyright 1970 Hart Publishing Company, Inc., New York *253* Courtesy of Children's Television Workshop *254* Paolo Koch, Photo Researchers

Part IV *256* Constantine Manos, Magnum

Chapter 9 *258* David Powers, Jeroboam *260* Kent Reno, Jeroboam *262* Courtesy of Philip Teitelbaum, University of Pennsylvania *264* Elliot Erwitt, Magnum *268* Suzanne Arms, Jeroboam *271* Peeter Vilms, Jeroboam *272* Sepp Seitz, Magnum *279* David Powers, Jeroboam *280 Top* David Powers, Jeroboam *280 Bottom* Burt Glinn, Magnum *283* Peeter Vilms, Jeroboam

Chapter 10 *284* Nacio Jan Brown, BBM Associates *288 Top* Eileen Christelow, Jeroboam *288 Bottom* Courtesy of Merit Protective Service, Inc. of California, Photo by Audrey Ross, Berkeley *294* Charles Harbutt, Magnum *297* Mitchell Payne, Jeroboam *298* Paul Eckman *300* Peeter Vilms, Jeroboam *302* Leonard Freed, Magnum *304* U.S. Army, courtesy Walter Reed Army Institute of Research *307* Sepp Seitz, Magnum *311* Wide World Photos, Inc. *314* Courtesy of Albert Bandura, Stanford University *315* Courtesy of Albert Bandura, Stanford University *316* Wide World Photos, Inc.

Part V *318* Margaretta Mitchell

Chapter 11 *320* Hiroshi Hamaya, Magnum *329* Dr. Roberts Rugh, from FROM CONCEPTION TO BIRTH, copyright 1971 Harper & Row, Publishers, Inc., New York *330* Dr. Roberts Rugh, from FROM CONCEPTION TO BIRTH, copyright 1971 Harper & Row, Publishers, Inc., New York *331 Left* Dr. Roberts Rugh, from FROM CONCEPTION TO BIRTH, copyright 1971 Harper & Row, Publishers, Inc., New York *331 Center* Carnegie Institution of Washington, Department of Embryology, Davis Division *331 Right* Carnegie Institution of Washington, Department of Embryology, Davis Division *334* Lee Choplin, Black Star *336* Stern, Black Star *338* Peeter Vilms, Jeroboam *340* Erika, Photo Researchers *342* Suzanne Arms, Jeroboam *346* Suzanne Arms, Jeroboam *350* Kent Reno, Jeroboam *354* Ruth Silverman, BBM Associates

Chapter 12 *356* Burk Uzzle, Magnum *359* Ken Heyman *362* World Health Organization *363* Ken Heyman *364* Wisconsin Primate Laboratory, Madison *366* United Press International Photo *371* Margaretta Mitchell *373* David Power, Jeroboam *374* Charles Gatewood, Magnum *375* Bill Owens, Magnum *377* Hank Lebo, Jeroboam *378* Kent Reno, Jeroboam *383* Bill Stanton, Magnum *386* Ruth Silverman, BBM Associates

Part VI *388* David Powers, Jeroboam

Chapter 13 *390* Roger Lubin, Jeroboam *392* Hiroji Kubota, Magnum *395* Peeter Vilms, Jeroboam *398* Abigail Heyman, Magnum *401* David Powers, Jeroboam *403* Joanne Leonard *405* Leonard Freed, Magnum *408* Bruno Barbey, Magnum *410* Bob Adelman, Magnum *414* Hap Stewart, Jeroboam *417* Sherry Suris, Rapho/Photo Researchers

Chapter 14 *420* Elihu Blotnick, BBM Associates *422* Sigmund Freud Copyrights Ltd. *423* Sigmund Freud Copyrights Ltd. *427* Homer Sykes, Magnum *430* National Library of Medicine *435* Mitchell Payne, Jeroboam *436* Van Bucher, Photo Researchers *437* Van Bucher, Photo Researchers *438* Mitchell Payne, Jeroboam *440* Mitchell Payne, Jeroboam *445* National Library of Medicine *446* Courtesy of Bertha G. Maslow *452* Mark Godfrey, Magnum

Part VII *454* Hide Shibata

Chapter 15 *456* John Launois, Black Star *459* Museo del Prado *461* N. Bouvier, Geneva *462* Paul Almasy, World Health Organization *464* G. William Holland, Smith Kline Corporation *467* Mitchell Payne, Jeroboam *470* John Launois, Black Star *475* Bemis Company, Inc. *475* Leonard Freed, Magnum *477* Paul Almasy, World Health Organization

Chapter 16 *480* David Seymour, Magnum *482* Charles Harbutt, Magnum *487* Ken Heyman *492* Andy Mercado, Jeroboam, Inc. *493* Ellen Shumsky, Jeroboam *495* Hide Shibata *500* Adamson Collection, Netherne Hospital, London *503* Rosenwald Collection, National Gallery of Art, Washington, D.C. *506* Charles Gatewood, Magnum

Chapter 17 *508* Sepp Seitz, Magnum *510* Ken Heyman *512* Jan Lukas, Rapho/Photo Researchers *513* Paul Almasy, World Health Organization *518* Karen Preuss, Jeroboam *519* Sepp Seitz, Magnum *521* National Institute of Mental Health *526* David Powers, Jeroboam *529* Ken Heyman *532* David Glaubinger, Jeroboam

Part VII *534* William Rosenthal, Jeroboam

Chapter 18 *536* David Powers, Jeroboam *541* Thelma Shumsky, Jeroboam *545* Courtesy of Bennington College *550* Suzanne Arms, Jeroboam *553* Marc Riboud, Magnum *558* Copyright 1965 by Stanley Milgram, from the film "Obedience," distributed by the New York University Film Library *564* Leonard Freed, Magnum *565* Jan Lukas, Rapho/Photo Researchers *568* Marc & Evelyne Bernheim, Woodfin Camp & Associates

Chapter 19 *570* Ken Heyman *572* Mitchell Payne, Jeroboam *575* Roger Lubin, Jeroboam *577* Susan Ylvisaker, Jeroboam *582* Charles Harbutt, Magnum *585* Werner Hiebel, Alpha Press/Jeroboam *593* Ken Heyman *595* Constantine Manos, Magnum

INDEX

Tell Us What You Think...

We are committed to making *The Psychology of Being Human* a valuable tool for the teaching and learning of psychology. Because we want to be sure that *The Psychology of Being Human* continues to meet the needs and concerns of instructors and students, we would like your opinion of this edition. We invite you to tell us what you like about the text—as well as where you think improvements can be made. Your opinions will be taken into consideration in the preparation of future editions. Thank you for your help.

Please indicate whether you are ☐ an instructor ☐ a student

Your name ________________________________

School ________________________ City and State ________________________

Course Title ________________________________

How does this text compare with texts you are using in other courses?

☐ Excellent ☐ Good ☐ Fair ☐ Poor ☐ Very Poor

Please circle the chapters that were required in the course.

Part I.	Chapters 1 2		Part IV.	Chapters 9 10		Part VII.	Chapters 15 16 17
Part II.	Chapters 3 4		Part V.	Chapters 11 12		Part VIII.	Chapters 18 19
Part III.	Chapters 5 6 7 8		Part VI.	Chapters 13 14			

What chapters did you read that were not assigned by your instructor? (Give chapter numbers.) ________

Please tell us your overall impression of the text.	Excellent	Good	Adequate	Poor	Very Poor
1. Did you find the text to be logically organized?	____	____	____	____	____
2. Was it written in a clear and understandable style?	____	____	____	____	____
3. Did the graphics enhance readability and understanding of topics?	____	____	____	____	____
4. Did captions contribute to a further understanding of the material?	____	____	____	____	____
5. Were difficult concepts well explained?	____	____	____	____	____
6. Were the issues valuable to a further understanding of psychology?	____	____	____	____	____
7. Did the boxes contribute to the text?	____	____	____	____	____
8. Were the "teasers" interesting and fun to read?	____	____	____	____	____

Which chapters did you particularly like and why? (Give chapter numbers.) ________________________________

____

Which chapters did you dislike and why? ________________________________

____

After taking this course, are you now interested in taking more courses in this field? ☐ Yes ☐ No

Do you feel that this text had any influence on your decision? ☐ Yes ☐ No

How can this text be improved? ________________________________

____

What topics did the instructor discuss that were not covered in the text? ________________________________

Did you use the Study Guide? ☐ Yes ☐ No Comments ________________________________

____

____

Thank you very much

We need your advice

Because this book will be revised regularly, we would like to know what you think of it. Please fill in the brief questionnaire on the reverse of this card and mail it to us.

FIRST CLASS
Permit No. 17418
San Francisco, CA.

BUSINESS REPLY MAIL no postage stamp necessary if mailed in the United States

postage will be paid by

Ted Ricks

Canfield Press
850 Montgomery Street
San Francisco, CA. 94133

Just fold, tape and mail. No stamp necessary.